335 - 341

347 - 361

Swain

Hackney

Garner
ed. 13

Rogan, ed. 10

# Modern Rhetoric

WITH
READINGS

Cleanth Brooks YALE UNIVERSITY

Robert Penn Warren UNIVERSITY OF MINNESOTA

HARCOURT, BRACE AND COMPANY, NEW YORK

*TO DAVID M. CLAY*

# CONTENTS

# 3. EXPOSITION

# 4. ARGUMENT

# 5. DESCRIPTION                                   218

# 6. NARRATION                                     262

# A BOOK OF READINGS

## CONTENTS

# A Letter to the Instructor

THE AUTHORS of this book know that there is no short cut to the teaching of composition. Certainly this textbook embodies no special pedagogical gadgets guaranteed to enable the student to write well after a dozen easy lessons, or even after one hundred easy lessons. The authors are conscious of presenting a book that will seem in some respects quite conventional and even old-fashioned. The four kinds of discourse, for example, form an early and important part of the book. This textbook makes no pretension to being newfangled or modish.

Yet the study of linguistic behavior which has been carried on during the last twenty-five years—the discoveries and recoveries made in criticism, in semantics, and in related fields—ought to yield something of significance to the teaching of English composition. For, in a very real sense, these studies amount to a vigorous restudy of rhetoric, and constitute a re-emphasis upon this ancient and once pre-eminent art.

The revived interest in "rhetorical" problems has, in most minds, been associated with reading rather than with writing. There has been a great effort to enrich the reader's response to the texts of poetry, drama, and fiction. Yet one would expect this new interest in rhetorical problems to have some application, also, to the problem of writing.

*Modern Rhetoric* attempts to garner for composition some of the fruits of this revived interest in rhetorical techniques. This book *is a rhetoric,* though the authors have been content to omit most of the categories and terms dear to the rhetorics of the past. The book attempts to be modern in the best sense of that word. Yet the authors are perfectly willing for the book to appear thoroughly old-fashioned whenever a principle seems perennial and undated.

The basic practice of this book and the authors' best claim to possessing a method—though it is at once more and less than any "method"—is the constant analysis of specific passages. Indeed, this book may be described as a tissue of such analyzed passages. The passages, most of them from modern writers, present a number of examples of "how it is done," and, occasionally, of "how it is not done." The analyses, usually brief and invariably nontechnical, direct the student's attention to the relevant matter: How the author has connected one paragraph with another, or how he has managed to convey a sense of color and life, or how he has achieved an inflection of irony. There are a few, a very few, generalizations, and these are made as simple and practical as possible. There are, of course, a great many exercises that provide opportunities for the student to try his own muscles.

Example, then, rather than precept, and precept constantly related to example: Such is the "method" of this rhetoric. Why have the authors put so much weight upon this "method"?

In the first place, frankly because they saw no other way in which an effective rhetoric could be written. Style cannot be taught as an abstraction. Style exists only as an arrangement of concrete particulars. The student's resistance to abstractions here is thoroughly healthy: It is rooted in a sound instinct.

In the second place, there is, moreover, a great positive gain in making the book concrete and analytical. For most students, even poorly trained students, are intensely interested in the workings of language. They like to see how language works. They can even manage points of some subtlety *if the discussion has a context and if it is held to concrete particulars.*

In the third place, this method is justified by an appeal to experience. Most people who write well have learned to write by what is in essence this method; that is, by exposure to sound models, plus experiment with those models, plus practice. The gifted person, because he is gifted, instinctively makes his own analyses of his models, and in general works out his own salvation. In an important sense, every writer, including the humblest freshman, must work out his own salvation. But surely, if we are to have recourse to a book at all, that book can best occupy itself with collecting models and making them more readily available, more readily useful, to the writer, and particularly to the writer who is *not* especially gifted. Such a book may help the ordinary writer to follow, even at a distance, his more gifted brother.

But related to the method of this book are other features of organization that deserve some special comment. One of these (and one which may seem to require defense) is the relative amount of attention given to such topics as metaphor and tone.

If metaphor and tone were treated as ornaments and special graces, the space given them here would be excessive. But metaphor is actually one of the writer's basic tools; and tone has everything to do with fundamental meaning. One simply cannot treat the problem of slang and stereotyped expressions, or deal with the problem of jargon, without discussing metaphor and tone. In this text, as the instructor will find, discussion of these topics is intimately and constantly related to advertising, to propaganda, to the sportswriter's clichés, and to gobbledygook. Such phenomena are close to the student; he finds discussion of them interesting; and his own reading, even if it is limited to the newspaper and the popular magazines, makes the discussion of metaphor or tone practical and immediate for him.

It is on a practical basis that we have canvassed such topics in this book. Moreover, since the topics have most to do with the color and liveliness of prose, they must be dealt with as fundamental aspects of the problem of writing. Failure to do so in the past probably accounts for the flat and wooden quality of much modern prose—not to mention the downright confusion produced by the use of mixed metaphor, worn-out metaphor, and dead metaphor (see pp. 408 ff.). At any rate, we have decided that the choice lay between a rather thorough examination of such topics or no examination at all. The common practice of devoting a dozen paragraphs to figurative language, we are convinced, accomplishes nothing and is a sheer waste of time.

Another feature of this text is the recurrence of topics and the overlapping treatment of topics. The chapters which deal with the four kinds of discourse treat, in their analyses, topics which are given special attention in later chapters. Rhythm, for example, comes in for special discussion as part of Chapter 13, but the authors have never hesitated to comment on the rhythm of a particular passage whenever they have thought necessary at any point in this book.

This repetition and overlapping does not make for an obviously tidy, logical scheme. That has to be granted at once. But people do not learn to write by following the steps of a logical scheme. They learn by trying to take care of all the various elements at play, even though they must necessarily try to concentrate attention on some particular element. This book, in short, tries to make a practical solution to the problem of one-thing-at-a-time but also everything-at-once. The apparent untidiness and overlapping actually point to a necessary flexibility. So does the relegation to appendixes of certain more specialized discussions of logic. We dare say that for some classes the teacher will make little or no use of these appendixes. But these appendixes may prove of utmost importance to other teachers confronted with their own special problems.

What has just been said applies in full to the exercises. They range from fairly simple dictionary exercises to a few rather complex problems of analysis. They have to do with the student's reading, and they set problems for his own writing. They suggest explorations of the library and of the selections which comprise the READINGS part of this volume. Few instructors will probably wish to assign all of them, and there may well be instructors who will want to make up exercises even more specially tailored to the needs of particular classes or of particular students. In this connection, it may be pointed out that many of the exercises are suggestive rather than prescriptive, and that the READINGS at the end of this volume provide ample range for further exercises modeled upon, or suggested by, the variety of exercises actually printed in the text.

The READINGS section performs an important function within the whole project. Clearly the examples scattered throughout the text chapters, if they are to illustrate explicit points and if they are to be exhaustively analyzed, must be relatively brief. But in the READINGS there is room for whole items, and here we have placed thirty-eight essays, enough for a full semester's reading program. These essays should, however, be more than read: They constitute an integral part of the "method" of this book. They are tied to the text chapters by numerous, specific cross-references; they are used constantly in the text exercises; they fortify, and in a sense summarize, the text examples by presenting particulars *in whole contexts*.

Indeed, the authors of *Modern Rhetoric* were so convinced of the value of such integrated selections that, when faced with the need to omit something if the volume were to be kept less weighty than an unabridged dictionary, they elected to drop handbook material rather than Readings. For there are many standard handbooks available, any one of which the instructor may easily correlate with this text; but obviously there can be, except for this selection, no book of essays which exactly correlates with text chapters of this book.

The text is not designed to teach itself. But the authors hope that it is designed to offer substantial help to the instructor. In keeping with this view they have felt it proper to risk giving him more material than he needs rather than less; to allow *him* to make the decision as to what material should be stressed and what might be touched upon lightly or passed over. In general, they have sought to provide for the instructor's work chest as many tools as possible, leaving to the teacher himself, confronted with his varying special problems, the specific choice of the tools he needs.

One final point. This textbook, we have said, is a tissue of examples and analyses. As becomes a *Modern Rhetoric*, most of the passages are from modern prose writers. Many of the great stylists of our time are represented, but with them are many able craftsmen who can give models of the prose that does the honest daily work of the world. The examples thus indicate rather fully how modern prose at its best is written. The authors have been careful, however, to include a number of examples of how prose ought *not* to be written. This procedure, they feel, is important. In the hands of a resourceful instructor, particularly an instructor who has a sense of proportion and a sense of humor, these examples of "how it ought not to be done" can be used most effectively. Such examples, at the very least, can serve as constant reminders to the student that he is dealing, not with an abstraction, but with reality.

# Modern Rhetoric

# A Letter
# to the Student

YOU ENTER this course with the hope of becoming a better writer. To write well, however, is not merely a matter of learning a few tricks or skills. It is not a matter of memorizing rules. To write well you must think straight. And to learn to think straight is the aim of your education.

## THE MAIN CONSIDERATIONS

A writer, as Robert Louis Stevenson says in his "Essay on Style," is like a juggler who must keep several balls in the air at once. We can interpret his remark in this way. The writer has more than one consideration to keep in mind if he is to write well.

What are the considerations which a writer must keep in mind? This book is an attempt to answer that question; but even when this book is finished the answer will not be a complete one. For the present, however, we may try to reduce the considerations to three general types. We may define them in reference to various aspects of the act of writing:

1. The medium
2. The subject
3. The occasion

These terms, as we are using them, require some explanation.

### THE MEDIUM

A writer writes in a language, the substance, as it were, through which he exerts his force, the medium through which he communicates his ideas and feelings. This language operates in terms of certain principles and usages which a writer must observe if he is to exercise his full force or even, in some instances, to be understood at all. For example, grammar is an aspect of the medium itself. Rhythm is another aspect, and it may exercise a very powerful effect on the reader, even if he is not aware of it. Another aspect is diction—the qualities of the individual words even beyond their bare dictionary definitions.

These topics, and others related to them, will be discussed in the course of this book, but for the present it is important only that we understand them as representing aspects of the medium, of language itself.

## THE SUBJECT

A writer writes about something. The something may be his own feelings, his love or his hate, or again it may be the theory of aerodynamics. But in either instance he has a subject—and one that can be distinguished from all other possible subjects.

The nature of the subject will, in some respects, dictate the nature of the treatment. For instance, if a writer is interested in explaining a process of some kind, the running of an experiment in physics or the building of a log cabin, he will have to organize his material with some reference to the chronological order of the process. If he is trying to explain why he loves or hates someone, he will probably be concerned with the analysis of traits of character which have no necessary reference to chronology; therefore, his ordering of the material may well be in terms of degrees of importance and not in terms of time sequence.

Furthermore, the subject may dictate differences in diction. For instance, if the writer is trying to explain the process of an experiment in physics, his diction will be dry and technical, clear and factual; but if he is trying to define the grief experienced at the death of a friend, his diction may well be chosen to convey emotional effects.

Or the type of rhythm may vary according to the subject. The explanation of the experiment in physics will probably involve a rather flat rhythm, or at least an unobtrusive rhythm, but the attempt to define the grief at the death of the friend will probably depend to a considerable degree for its success on the rhythm employed, for the rhythm of language, even in prose, is of enormous importance in the communication of feelings.

## THE OCCASION

Third, a writer writes out of a special situation, the occasion. We may say that this situation involves three basic elements: the motivation of the writer; the nature of the reader; and the relationship between writer and reader.

## THE MOTIVATION OF THE WRITER

As for motivation, two general types may be distinguished: expression and communication. The writer may be primarily concerned to affirm his own feelings, to clarify his own mind, to define for himself his own sense of the world. When he writes from some such motivation, the urge to expression may be said to be dominant, and he has, on such an occasion, more in common with a man singing in the bath, with the child uttering the spontaneous cry of pain, or with the cat purring on the rug than he has with the judge handing down a decision from the bench, a teacher explaining a point of grammar from the platform, or a woman giving her daughter a recipe for pie. For the judge, the teacher, and the cook are not primarily concerned to express but to communicate something.

It may be said, however, that, in the ultimate sense, we never have a case of pure expression or pure communication. Even the cry of pain, which seems to be pure expression, may be said to presuppose a hearer; the hurt child redoubles its screams when it sees the mother approaching. And the poet who has written his poem without a conscious thought of the reader, who has been concerned with the effort of getting his own feelings and ideas into form, hurries to the post office to mail his finished poem to a magazine through which it can reach a number of readers.

Conversely, even the most objective presentation of an idea or analysis of a situation may involve an expressive element. To take an extreme instance, we may say that a man may take pleasure in the accuracy and tidiness of his working out of a mathematical demonstration and feel that those qualities "express" him.

If it is true that we can never find an example of pure expression or of pure communication, if we have to regard expression and

communication as, shall we say, the poles of the process of writing
or speaking, we can still see that a great deal of variation in the
relative proportions of communication and expression may exist.

## ACCENT ON EXPRESSION

When the writer is primarily concerned with expression, he does
not pay attention to his audience; if, under such circumstances, he
thinks of the audience, it is only to assume that there will be people
enough like himself to have an interest in his work. Yet even then,
even when the writer is primarily concerned with expression, his
private and individual intentions will have to be represented in a
medium that has public and general standards. When the writer
accepts language as his medium of expression, he also accepts the
standards of communication.

## ACCENT ON COMMUNICATION

When the writer is primarily concerned with communication
rather than expression, he must, however, give special attention to
the audience which he wishes to reach. He must consider the reader's interests and attitudes. Even if the writer wishes to give the
reader a new interest, he must work in terms of the interests that
already exist. When the writer does not, in some way, appeal to the
already existing interests, the reader will not even bother to finish
the book or article. Or if the writer wishes to make the reader change
his attitude on some issue, he must work in terms of already existing attitudes. Unless the writer can discover that he and the reader
have *some* attitudes in common, he can have no hope of convincing
the reader about the matter on which they disagree.

## THE NATURE OF THE READER

Just as the writer must concern himself with the reader's interests
and attitudes, so he must concern himself with the reader's training
and capacities. Every piece of writing is addressed to a more or
less limited audience. It is perfectly logical that a piece of writing
addressed to the specialist will not be understood by the layman.
Articles in professional medical journals or law journals employ
a language and a treatment largely incomprehensible to the ordinary reader. But the same thing holds true, though less obviously,

in regard to all differences of education or capacity. Because of differences in education, the housewife is not likely to understand the article on international finance that may be perfectly clear to the banker or businessman who is her husband. Or one housewife, because of innate intelligence and sensitivity, can understand and enjoy a certain novel, while another woman in the same block, who has been educated at the same school, is merely confused and annoyed by the book.

It is true that there are types of writing which have a relatively broad appeal—the novels of Dickens or the plays of Shakespeare—but we must remember that even their appeal is only relatively broad, and that there are a great number of people who infinitely prefer the sports page of the daily paper or the financial section or the comic strip to Dickens or Shakespeare. And remembering this, the writer must concern himself with the level of education and intelligence of the special group which he wishes to address.

## THE RELATIONSHIP BETWEEN READER AND WRITER

Just as the writer must consider his own motivation and the nature of his intended reader as components of the "occasion," so must he consider the relationship between himself and that reader. For instance, does he feel that he must speak down to his reader? If he does speak down, shall he take the tone of a man laying down the law from some position of authority—like a judge on a bench—or shall he take a tone of good-natured condescension? Or if he does not wish to speak down to his reader but regards the reader as on the same level with himself, shall he take a tone of friendly discussion or of serious, life-and-death argument?

The possible variations on this score are almost numberless, too, and the writer, if he is to be most effective, must take them into consideration. Is he, for instance, addressing a reader who is hostile and suspicious? If so, he must try to discover the approach which will mollify the hostility and allay the suspicions. Or if his reader is assumed to be friendly but unserious, how shall he adapt himself to that situation? Is he writing to a student who is anxious to learn or to a casual reader who must be lured into the subject under discussion? Obviously the writer must, if he wishes to succeed with his reader, study the relationship existing between himself and his intended reader and adapt his tone to that aspect of the occasion.

## TONE

The writer's relationship to his reader and to his subject may be summed up in the word *tone* (see Chapter 12). Just as the tone of voice indicates what the speaker's attitude is to his subject and his listener, so certain qualities of a piece of writing may indicate the attitude of the writer. Rhythms may be harsh and abrupt or lingering and subtle. Diction may be homely and direct or elaborate and suggestive. Sentence structure may be simple and downright or complicated by modifying and qualifying elements. Appeal may be made through logic or through persuasion. These and many other factors are related to the writer's conception of the relation between himself and the reader.

## KEEPING THE BALLS IN THE AIR

Under the headings of (1) medium, (2) subject, and (3) occasion, we have briefly discussed some of the basic considerations which the writer must keep in mind—the balls which the juggler of Stevenson's essay must keep simultaneously in the air. The word *simultaneously* is important here, for though we have necessarily had to discuss our topics in order, we are not to assume that the order is one of either importance or of time sequence. Can one say that a knowledge of the subject under discussion is more or less important than a knowledge of the principles and usages of the language in which the subject is to be discussed? Or that a knowledge of the principles and usages of the language is more or less important than the sense of the nature of the occasion?

In the process of writing there is no one consideration to which the writer must give his attention first. His mind, in so far as he is a conscious craftsman, will play among the various considerations in the attempt to produce a piece of writing which will fulfill at the same time the demands of the medium, the subject, and the occasion. In this book we shall take up various topics individually, and you may find it helpful when you are revising a theme to consider one question at a time. But the final piece of writing is always a fusion.

# YOUR BACKGROUND FOR SUCCESSFUL WRITING

The foregoing remarks, with their emphasis on the complicated demands that a good piece of writing must fulfill, have no doubt made the business of writing seem enormously difficult. And it is true that the simplest piece of writing, when well done, *is* the fruit of a great deal of effort. But you are not, with this book, starting your career as a writer from scratch. You already have behind you many years of effort which can be made to apply on the writing you now do. You are already the beneficiary of a long training.

This does not mean that this training has been wholly or even in large part training in writing—the study of grammar and rhetoric in school and the writing of weekly themes. Those things are part of your training, and a very important part, but it cannot be said that they are the most important part of the training on which you can now draw as you set about the present task.

## LANGUAGE AND EXPERIENCE

In the first place, your sense of your language was not acquired primarily from books. You began the process of learning that language when you were an infant, and the process has been a constant one ever since. Books have helped you, and they will help you even more, toward an effective use of your language. They will broaden your vocabulary, and will give you a sense of the subtleties and shadings of words. But already you—like any normal person of your age—are the master of enormous resources in your native tongue.

## A CAPACITY FOR STRAIGHT THINKING

In the second place, your experience has given you a great range of subjects, and a capacity for thinking logically about them. As for the subjects, almost any event of your day, any sport or craft which you understand, any skill or technique which you possess, any scene which you have witnessed, any book or article which you have read, any person whom you know—all these are potential subjects. And any one of them can become interesting in so far as it is actually important to you and in so far as you can think straight about it.

As for logical thinking, demands for the exercise of this faculty are made on you every day. You are constantly under the necessity of adjusting means to ends, of correcting errors in your calculations, of planning in terms of cause and effect, of estimating possibilities. To manage your simplest affairs you must have some capacity for straight thinking. When you come to the business of writing, you need merely to apply this capacity to the subject in hand—to see what is important about it for your interests and purposes, to stick to your point, to make one sentence follow from the previous sentence and lead to the next, to make one paragraph follow from the previous paragraph and lead to the next, to make one idea follow from another, to state the relations between things in terms of time, space, or causality, to emphasize the important item and subordinate the unimportant, to proportion your discourse so that it will have an introduction, a development, and a conclusion. All of these problems of analysis and organization are problems which you may have to confront when you start any piece of writing, but you confront them with the aid of all the straight thinking that you have ever done.

## A BROAD SOCIAL EXPERIENCE

In the third place, all of your experiences with other people in the past have provided a training that will help you adjust yourself to your intended reader. Your social experience, from your early childhood, has given you a training in tact, in grasping the truth about a human relationship, in adjusting your manner to the mood or prejudice of another person in order to convince, persuade, entertain, or instruct him. Every child is aware that, when he wants something from his mother or father, there is a right way to go about asking for it and a wrong way. And he knows that what is the right way for asking the mother may very well be the wrong way for asking the father. No doubt, the child never puts it to himself in these terms, but he acts on the truth behind these terms when he actually deals with mother or father. He develops early a sense of the occasion and a sensitivity to what we shall call problems of tone.

The discussion in this section comes to this: You already possess a great deal more of the equipment of the writer than you realize.

All of your experience in the past can be said, without too much wrenching of fact, to be a training for the writing which you will now do. Your problem is, in part, to learn to use the resources which you already possess. For unless you learn to use those resources, you will not be able to acquire new resources.

# chapter 7

# Some General Problems and the First Theme

WHERE should the study of writing begin? With considerations of the medium? Of the subject? Of the occasion? It is impossible to say that one of these is more important than the others, and it is impossible to say that one should logically precede the others.

It might be argued that, since the word is the smallest unit in composition, we should begin with the study of diction and move by easy stages through the study of the sentence and the paragraph to the study of the general problem of organization, with attention finally given to questions of the occasion.

But we could reply that when we choose words we choose them in relation to other words, in relation to some general subject and our general intention concerning that subject, and in relation to our attitude toward the reader. In the same way we could say that the study of the sentence, important as it is, should not necessarily precede the study of problems of more general organization. For it is the pattern of the sentences, not the individual sentence, which gives the thrust of our thought and defines the progression of our ideas. We are first, and finally, concerned with the nature of our complete utterance, our over-all idea, our main intention. And perhaps we should, therefore, be first concerned with general problems of organization.

## FINDING A TRUE SUBJECT

In the purely practical business of this and many other courses you will be called upon from the first to write compositions, essays, and reports. Your first problem will always be to define for yourself what your central idea is. Your second problem will always be to develop that idea clearly and forcefully. In other words, you must think before you write. And you must think as you write. For writing is both the expression of thought and an instrument of thought.

What constitutes a subject? As we have already observed, anything can be a subject—your autobiography, George Washington, a house, war, religion, boats, a picnic, chemical research. This answer is true as far as it goes. But if we put down the subject "George Washington" and then simply assemble various facts, ideas, and speculations about him, we find that we do not have a true subject. It is too vague, too inclusive; and the writer feels like a man trying to grab a handful of fog. The subject must be limited and fixed if it is to be manageable.

To limit and fix a subject we must think of it with reference to a basic interest—an interest dictated by an occasion assigned to us, or discovered for ourselves. The subject is not in and of itself a subject—George Washington, a house, war, religion, and so forth—but is so created by some mind. Even an idea as such is not a subject, say the idea of goodness or the idea of infinity. To become a true subject, a mind must work on that idea, define it, take some attitude toward it.

The true subject is a topic brought to focus. If we take, for instance, the topic "George Washington," we can think of various possible interests which might give us true subjects: "George Washington as the Type of the Colonial Planter," "The Development of Leadership in George Washington," "What the Frontier Taught George Washington," "George Washington as a Statesman," "The Influence of George Washington on American Political Thought," "Myths about George Washington," "The Courtships of George Washington," "George Washington as a Strategist." But this would be only the beginning of a list of true subjects. Whatever about George Washington might interest anybody would be a possible subject. So the true subject is something *about* a subject.

It may be objected that a large work on George Washington, say a biography, might contain many of the items listed above. That is true. But even in a large work there would be some fundamental line of interest and interpretation to which the other interests would be related and subordinated.

Before you undertake any piece of composition, you should try to frame the real subject, the central concern. You do not write about a house. You write about its appearance, the kind of life it suggests, its style of architecture, or your associations with it. You do not write about chemical research. You write about the method of chemical research, the achievements of chemical research, or the opportunities for chemical research. You do not write about goodness. You write about the different views of goodness which have been held by different societies or religions at different times, about the Christian idea of goodness, about goodness as exemplified by people you know or know about, or about the definition of goodness which you personally accept. You must search your own thoughts and feelings to find your true subject.

## APPLICATIONS

Below is a list of topics. No one of them is a true subject. They are all too general. Select five topics from the list and try to frame several true subjects for each.

| | |
|---|---|
| Divorce | The American Revolution |
| The United Nations | Communism |
| Alcoholic beverages | A church |
| Public education | The postal service |
| The jury system | The American Indian |
| Robert E. Lee | The revolver |
| The income tax | Patriotism |
| Amateurism in sport | Thrift |
| Military training | River traffic |
| Reading | Shakespeare's plays |

## UNITY

Once the writer has his true subject, he must not lose sight of it as he pursues various related ideas. A good piece of writing has UNITY. The fundamental interest, which is his subject, must permeate the whole composition. The composition must be *one* thing, and not a hodgepodge.

Unity is not arbitrary, something imposed from the outside. It is simply the indication that the writer's own mind can work systematically and can therefore arrive at a meaning. To put it another way, the unity of the composition is an indication that his mind has unity—that he is not scatterbrained.

Let us look at a theme which is not well unified.

## WHY I WISH TO BE AN ENGINEER

(1) I suppose that one reason I want to be an engineer and have made my college plans in that direction is that my father is an engineer. He was a student here at the State University back in 1909-1914. He began his college career with the intention of being a doctor, but he soon changed his mind. He finished his course in 1914, and worked as a draftsman for two years in Chicago in an engineering firm. But World War I got him into the army, and he wound up a major in the Engineering Corps. It was a valuable experience for him in more ways than one, for he says it taught him how to deal with men of all kinds and to get work done under pressure. Also it meant that he was to get a taste for action and adventure. After the war, he went to Mexico and worked on building a railroad in the mountains. He had many difficult construction problems to solve. I was born in Mexico, and I was raised in a family where they talked engineering all the time, for my mother was interested in my father's work.

(2) There is a great future for an engineer in this country. It makes me tired to hear people talk of the lack of opportunity in that line. It is true that during the Depression many engineers were out of work, but that applied to many occupations and professions. Besides, many of the engineers out of work were not well trained to begin with. If you are really well trained and are willing to put out your best efforts you can almost always get along. There is a great future for engineering here, for we are on the verge of a great technological revolution which will mean the rebuilding of much of the industrial plant and the development of new transport facilities. Besides, land reclamation and the expansion of public works are long-range programs. This country is an engineer's paradise, for we are the most mechanical-minded people in the world. They say that that is the great talent of America, and I see nothing to be ashamed of in that. Engineers make the world easier to live in for everybody. Think of things like the great bridges and dams, the highways and airports. What would we do without them?

(3) I like the life of action, and that is another reason I plan to be an engineer. My father had a very interesting life in Mexico. After five years there he went to Argentina. He had learned the language in Mexico, and had made a name for himself there. So he got a good offer in Argentina.

He sent my mother and me back to the U. S. until I grew up a little, but he came to see us at the end of the first year and took us back to Argentina with him. We lived there four years. Then he went to India, and supervised the building of some bridges there. But he did not take us to India with him. He understood that the climate was too bad. And he was right, because he almost died there of dysentery. He never left America again, but his talk about his adventures gave me a desire for an active life, and he has never discouraged me.

(4) I make my best marks in mathematics. Mathematics is the basis of engineering, and I think that a man should follow his best talent. I like other things, too, history for instance, and I read a good many novels and stories. But I cannot see myself making a profession of any of these things. Business would be too confining for me. I have an uncle who is a lawyer, and it seems to me that he never gets out of his office except to come home at night.

Taking everything together, I think that engineering is the right profession for me.

The writer here has a subject, which is expressed in the title. And if we examine the theme carefully we can dig out the reasons for his choice of a career: family background, the opportunity to make a good living, the appetite for action, and the aptitude for mathematics. These four reasons should give him the outline for his theme.

But he is constantly bringing in material which does not bear directly on the subject or which is developed without reference to the main line of interest. For instance, he is so much impressed with his father's life that he devotes far too much attention to it: most of the first and third paragraphs. For present purposes we only need to know the barest facts about the father's career. The last part of the second paragraph, too, is not relevant. The writer may have two points here—that an engineer feels himself characteristically American and that the engineer has the sense of being a useful member of society. But he does not state these points, and they are lost in his general remarks. If we get them at all, we get them by implication only. In the fourth paragraph, too, we find some irrelevant material—the reference to the writer's interest in history and fiction, and the remark about his uncle's occupation.

## COHERENCE

An effective discourse must have unity. And it must also have COHERENCE. That is, the elements of the discourse must stick together. This seems to be another way of saying that a discourse must have unity, and in one sense that is true. The distinction may be stated thus: When we speak of unity we are referring primarily to the nature of the materials as related to the subject, and when we speak of coherence we are referring primarily to the way the materials are organized to give a continuous development of the subject. A discourse which lacks coherence will, in the larger sense, seem to lack unity, for even if the materials individually relate to the subject, we will not be able to see how they relate to each other.

We can consider coherence in two respects: (1) as involving overall organization of the discourse, and (2) as involving local transitions within the discourse.

### COHERENCE THROUGH OVER-ALL ORGANIZATION

There is no one principle by which the materials of a discourse are to be organized. Obviously, a principle of organization good for describing a woman's face would not be good for telling the story of a baseball game or a battle, for explaining the causes of the Russian Revolution, or for arguing against the abolition of Greek letter fraternities. Different intentions involve different principles of organization. We shall study the basic intentions and some of their characteristic methods when we come to the chapters on description, narrative, exposition, and argument, but for the present we can content ourselves with the common-sense principle: One thing should lead to another.

The following student theme is coherent.

### THE PERSON I ADMIRE MOST

(1) I suppose that my uncle Conroy is the person I admire most in the world. This statement would probably seem strange to a person who happened to visit in our house and see the old man who sits at a corner of the hearth, hunched over, shabbily dressed, and not saying much. He looks like the complete failure, and by ordinary standards he is. He has

no money. He has no children. He is old and sick. But he has made his own kind of success, and I think he is happy.

(2) At one time in his life he was a success by ordinary standards. He was the son of a poor Methodist minister (my mother's father), but he ran away from home in Illinois to Oklahoma back in the days when things were beginning to boom out there. He had a fine house in Oklahoma City and a ranch. He was a hail-fellow-well-met, and men and women liked him. He was a sportsman, kept good horses, and took long hunting trips to Mexico and Canada. Then one day, on his own ranch, his horse stumbled in a gopher hole and threw him. He was badly hurt and was in the hospital for many months. While he was still in the hospital the Depression came on. If he had been well and able to take care of his affairs, he might have saved some of his money from the crash. But as it was he lost everything. So he came back to Illinois, and my mother and father took him in.

(3) It must have been an awful come-down for a man like that to be living on charity. But the worst was yet to happen, for he developed arthritis in a very painful form. I remember the first year or so, even though I was a very small child. He even tried to commit suicide with gas from the stove. But my mother saved him, and after that he began to change.

(4) The first thing was that he began to take an interest in us children. He would read to us and talk to us. He helped us with our lessons. That relieved mother a great deal and made her life easier. My father was an insurance man and had a lot of paper work to do. It got so that my uncle took an interest in that, and before long he was helping my father by doing reports and writing letters. He helped my father tide over the bad time of the Depression. Then when my mother was ill for a long time, he learned to do some of the housework, as much as his strength would permit, and even dressed the two smaller children.

(5) What he did was important, but more important was the way he did things. He was so natural about it. You never got the impression he was making any effort or sacrifice. We all got so we didn't notice what he did, and I am sure that that was what he wanted.

(6) As I look back now, or when I go home and see Uncle Conroy, the biggest achievement, however, seems to be the kind of example he gave us all. He was often in pain, but he was always cheerful. If he felt too bad he simply hid away from the family for a while in his room —what he called his "mope-room." He even made a joke out of that. And he didn't act like a man who had failed. He acted like a man who had found what he could do and was a success at it. And I think that he

is a success. We all admire success, and that is why I admire my uncle Conroy.

We can see how each section of this theme fits into the general pattern. The main business of the writer is to tell *why* he admires his uncle, but he does not immediately set up the reasons. First, by way of introduction, he gives a brief sketch of the man as he now appears—the man who is to be interpreted. The appearance of failure in contrast to the reality of success gives dramatic interest, and excites the reader's curiosity. In the second paragraph he tells of the uncle's days of outward success. This topic does not get into the theme merely because the uncle, as a matter of fact, had such success. Many things that happened to him are certainly omitted here. Instead, it gets in because the taste of worldly success makes the uncle's achievement and shift of values more impressive. The third paragraph presents the despair of the uncle—a normal response to bankruptcy and illness. This topic has a place in the general organization, for it states the thing that the uncle must fight against. The fourth, fifth, and sixth paragraphs define the nature of the uncle's achievement. The order here is one of ascending importance, toward a climax—the special practical things he did, the attitude he took toward the doing, the long-range effect of his example on others. (There is one small defect in the organization here. The reference to the uncle's cheerfulness in the sixth paragraph probably should go back into the fifth paragraph, for it really belongs under the heading of the uncle's attitude.) The sixth paragraph not only states the uncle's most important achievement, but serves as a kind of summary of the preceding material.

## COHERENCE THROUGH LOCAL TRANSITIONS

Thus far we have been talking about what is involved in the over-all organization of a piece of writing. But the question of local transitions within the discourse is also extremely important. How do we get from one section to another, one paragraph to another, one sentence to another?

Obviously there must be an intrinsic continuity: what one section, paragraph, or sentence presents must bear some relation to the whole subject and to what has just preceded. But even when there is this intrinsic continuity, we may have to help the reader by using certain devices of connection and transition, by giving him links or signposts.

We can begin a section, paragraph, or sentence with some reference to what has gone before. The repetition or rephrasing of something in the preceding unit will provide a link. For example, let us look at the link which ties together these two paragraphs:

. . . All of these factors result in a condition of *social unrest and economic uncertainty,* which seems to presage the end of our civilization.

*Social unrest and economic uncertainty,* however, are not always an unhealthy condition. Actually, that condition may be the prelude, not to ruin, but to great revolutionary gains. . . .

The repetition of the phrase "social unrest and economic uncertainty" at the beginning of the second paragraph provides the link between the two. But pronouns and other words of reference (like *such, similar,* and so forth) may serve the same purpose.

. . . All of these factors result in a condition of *social unrest and economic uncertainty,* which seems to presage the end of our civilization.

*This* situation, however, need not fill us with alarm. . . .

or:

*Such* a situation, however, is not unhealthy. . . .

Furthermore, there are words whose function is to indicate specific relations: conjunctions, conjunctive adverbs, and some adverbs. These words say what they mean. *And, or, nor* establish a coordinate connection. *But, however, nevertheless* establish a contrast. *So, therefore, consequently* establish a result. *Moreover* and *furthermore* indicate additions or elaborations. Notice how the word *however* is used in the example above.

Another way to establish continuity is found in a large group of more or less conventional phrases. Such phrases are self-explanatory: "in addition," "as has been said," "that is to say," "that is," "by consequence," "for example," "for instance," "as a result," "on the contrary."

None of these lists is complete. They are merely suggestive. But they may serve to indicate the function of such words and phrases so that the student can by his reading build up his own resources.

We must not use such transitional words and phrases unless they are necessary. They are not ornaments, and they impede the reader rather than help him if the sense is clear without them.

## EMPHASIS

A piece of writing may be unified and coherent and still not be effective if it does not observe the principle of EMPHASIS. When this principle is properly observed the intended scale of importance of elements in the discourse is clear to the reader. All cats are black in the dark, but all things should not look alike in the light of a reasonable writer's interest in his subject. To change our metaphor, there is a foreground and a background of interest, and the writer should be careful to place each item in its proper location. Like unity and coherence, emphasis is a principle of organization.

How do we emphasize an element in a piece of writing?

### EMPHASIS BY FLAT STATEMENT

The first and most obvious way is for the writer to state quite flatly his own view on the importance of a matter. If we turn back to the theme "The Person I Admire Most," we find that paragraphs 4, 5, and 6 represent a scale of importance.

(4) The first thing was that he began to take an interest in us children. . . .

(5) What he did was important, but *more important* was the way he did things. . . .

(6) As I look back now, or when I go home and see Uncle Conroy, the *biggest achievement*, however, seems to be the kind of example he gave us all. . . .

In depending on his own statement for emphasis the writer should remember that the actual content must justify the statement. Before he makes the statement, he must think through the subject and be sure that he really believes in his own statement.

### EMPHASIS BY POSITION

A second way is by position. "First or last" is a fairly sound rule for emphasis by position. This rule corresponds to two general methods for treating a subject. The main idea can be presented and then discussed or proved, or discussion or proof can lead up to the main idea. Ordinarily the second method is better, and the end is the most emphatic position, for the last impression on a reader is what counts most. But some rather conventionalized forms of writing, like news stories, put the most important material first. In any case, the middle is the least emphatic position.

## EMPHASIS BY PROPORTION

Proportion in itself is a means of emphasis. The most important topic in a discussion reasonably receives the fullest treatment. This principle, however, is more flexible than the preceding. In some writings the last and most important topic may have been so well prepared for by the foregoing discussion that it does not require elaborate treatment. The writer must decide each case on its own merits and be sure that he is not indulging in elaboration merely for the sake of elaboration.

## EMPHASIS BY STYLE

Even when there is no emphasis by proportion or position, the way of saying a thing may make it emphatic and memorable. So we have emphasis by style. Sharpness or vividness of phrasing, an illuminating comparison, an air of seriousness, a rhythm that sticks in the ear—any of these things or several of them in combination may give emphasis.

It is hard to say exactly what constitutes sharpness of phrasing, though we certainly recognize the dull phrase.

Suppose Patrick Henry had said: "Liberty is a very important thing for a man to have. It means that he can pursue his own designs and develop his own fortunes and seek his own happiness so long as he does not interfere with the rights of other people. Therefore liberty is a very important thing. I had rather have liberty than anything else, for it is the basis of everything else. I had rather die than lose liberty."

His audience would have yawned in his face. But what he actually said was, "I know not what course others may take; but as for me, give me liberty or give me death!" and the words have come a long way from the room in colonial Virginia where they were spoken. The dramatic quality of the statement, the swelling balance of the rhythm, the economy of language—these things make the statement memorable, when the mere idea, stated otherwise, would have been forgotten.

Or suppose that John Randolph had said about a fellow-politician: "Henry Clay seems to be a very brilliant man, but his apparent brilliance is really just superficial cleverness. He is vain and strutting. He is also very corrupt." Nobody would remember the remark. But he actually said, "So brilliant, yet so corrupt, which, like a rotten mackerel by moonlight, shines and stinks." The comparison sums up all he meant, vividly and unforgettably, and we have one of the most savage insults in the language.

Or suppose Lincoln had said at the end of his Second Inaugural Address: "We want to finish this war and have a fair peace. We do not want a vindictive peace but one that will restore the country to unity. We believe that we are right and are determined to win and have a fair peace. And after the war we must not forget to take care of the veterans and the dependents of those who were killed or wounded in the struggle." The sentiments would have done him credit, perhaps, but the sentiments would probably have vanished with the words spoken. What he actually said was:

With malice toward none, with charity for all, with firmness in the right as God gives us to see the right, let us strive on to finish the work we are in, to bind up the nation's wounds, to care for him who shall have borne the battle and for his widow and his orphan, to do all which may achieve and cherish a just and lasting peace among ourselves and with all nations.

Here again it is style which makes the difference—the precision and economy of statement, the concreteness and simplicity of expression, the full, sonorous, sustained rhythm.

Not many writers or speakers have the gift exhibited in these examples, but the principle exemplified here should apply to anything we write; the well-said thing is the memorable thing. No matter how important an idea is, it is lost if the words are blundering. And almost anyone can, by practice and attention, gain enough skill to write honestly and cleanly.

### MINOR DEVICES OF EMPHASIS

Flat statement, order of importance, proportion, and style are major means of emphasis, but there are certain minor ones. For instance, repetition of an idea can give it prominence. The danger here is that the repetition may become merely mechanical and therefore dull. To be effective, repetition must be combined with some variety and some progression in the treatment of the subject. Or there is the device of the short, isolated paragraph. The thing set off by itself strikes the eye. But not all short paragraphs are in themselves emphatic. The content and phrasing of the short paragraph must in itself appear worthy of the special presentation.

### FAULTY DEVICES OF EMPHASIS

There are certain devices of emphasis which often occur but which are frequently worse than useless. Irresponsible exaggeration always repels the reader. Catchwords and hackneyed phrases like "awfully," "terribly," "tremendously," "the most wonderful thing I ever saw," "you never saw anything like it," "I can't begin to tell you," make a claim on the reader's attention that he is rarely prepared to grant. Random underlining and italicizing, or the use of capitals and exclamation points usually defeat their own purpose. Writers use these devices when they aren't sure that what they have to say will stand on its own merits. To insist that what you have to say is important does not prove the point. And the writer's business is to prove that point.

In applying any of these means of emphasis the writer must first of all be sure that the thing emphasized is worth emphasizing. Common sense must help him here. Nothing else can.

## THE MAIN DIVISIONS OF A DISCOURSE

There are three main divisions into which any rounded discourse will fall: INTRODUCTION, BODY or DISCUSSION, and CONCLUSION. What should each accomplish, and what should be their relations to each other?

### THE INTRODUCTION

The introduction must really introduce. At some stage it must let the reader know the business in hand. Occasionally the title can be explicit enough to give the reader a good idea of that business, but usually the introduction must limit and fix the subject. It must state the precise question with which the discussion is to be concerned.

Sometimes the introduction can properly concern itself with the background of the subject. If the subject, for example, is a new process in industrial chemistry, and the audience is composed of general readers, it may be necessary to inform them about the function of such a process and about the nature of the old process before they can understand the significance of the new one. If you are explaining why a certain novel is good, you may properly introduce your remarks by saying what qualities you prize in fiction. Or if you are explaining the greatness of Galileo, you may not be able to make your point unless you describe the condition of science before he accomplished his work. But here, as when limiting and fixing the subject itself, you must have some idea of the audience. How much preparation is needed to make them get your point?

An introduction may tell the reader what method of investigation has provided the material for the discussion or what method of discussion you intend to pursue. This element in an introduction is ordinarily confined to more or less technical discussions. For instance, a physicist might describe the nature of his method of investigation before he analyzes his findings. Or an economist might tell what evidence he had assessed. As for the forecast of the method of discussion, this is only desirable when the method itself is of some importance. If, for instance, you are writing in defense of J. E. B. Stuart's cavalry operations at the time of the Battle of Gettysburg, your introduction might very well include a statement of your method. You might say that the points to be determined are: (1) Was Stuart acting under orders? (2) Was he acting against orders? (3) Was he acting at discretion? (4) If he was acting at discretion, what information was available to him? (5) On the grounds of information available to him, were his operations consistent with reason and military science? Then you might say that you propose to investigate these questions and rest your case upon the answers. Such an introduction is sometimes very useful when the material to be treated is complicated and the reader's interest might easily be distracted by some incidental matter. It serves as a blueprint or a signpost.

One other job may be performed by an introduction. It may be used to catch the reader's interest and lure him into the subject.

When an audience is already interested in the subject, this is super-fluous. But when you are writing for the general reader, this part of the work of the introduction may be very important. If you check through feature articles in newspapers or magazines, you will find that the introduction usually makes some bid for the reader's attention. It explains why the subject should interest the reader, how it touches his life, if only indirectly, or it presents some incident of dramatic interest, some suggestive anecdote, or some provocative question.

Of these four general functions of an introduction, the first is the only essential one: The introduction must always lead the reader to the subject and must show him clearly what it is. The other functions are to be performed only when the occasion demands.

## THE MAIN BODY OF THE WRITING

It is difficult to make any significant generalizations concern-ing the main body of a piece of writing. Different subjects and interests call for different methods, and several of our subsequent chapters will be devoted to such questions. But this much may be insisted on now: The body of the discussion should not betray the promise of the introduction. It should really develop the introduc-tion. If the body does betray the introduction but seems good in itself, then you must go back and rewrite the introduction. The two things must be geared together.

## THE CONCLUSION

The conclusion gives you your last chance at your reader. If you fail there, you have probably failed throughout your work.

Occasionally, a formal conclusion is not necessary, especially in short pieces where the reader can easily carry the whole business in his head. But when there is no conclusion, it is usually a good idea to make the last part of the main body of the theme the most important part, the climax, so that your strongest point will be freshest for the reader when he leaves you. As we have already said, the end is the most emphatic position.

In more elaborate pieces of writing some formal conclusion is necessary to give the reader a perspective on the whole discussion. It may involve a summary of things the body of the discussion has established, but it should do more than summarize. It must also show how those things fit together to support your position or the effect you desire. It may be that you want to explain something, to convince the reader of the truth of something, to persuade him to a course of action, to make him think for himself about something. Whatever your dominant purpose may be, the conclusion should bring it into clear focus. The worst effect of all is for the reader, as he puts down your pages, to have only a hazy notion of what you meant to say. He should, rather, have a clear idea.

## PROPORTIONING THE MAIN DIVISIONS

In talking about emphasis we mentioned the problem of proportion. But in that connection it was a matter of local concern. What of proportion in relation to the big main divisions?

Our answer cannot take the form of a mathematical ratio—the body five times longer than the introduction, or something of the sort, and six times longer than the conclusion. But we must remember that the introduction is just an introduction, a preparation for the main business, and that the main business is to be transacted in the body of the piece. If the introduction is long and cumbersome, and the body brief, then the reader gets the impression that the mountain has labored and brought forth a mouse. Likewise, if there is a formal conclusion, that conclusion should seem to be the blow that sinks the nail head in the wood. In short, it should "conclude" the theme—not start fresh considerations. If the conclusion is long and cumbersome, then the reader has another unfortunate impression. It is preposterous, too, for the mouse to labor and try to bring forth the mountain. Or to apply another saying, the tail should not wag the dog. As a kind of rule of thumb, we may venture that the body should be at least several times longer than the introduction or conclusion.

To think of the matter mechanically, however, is not the way to get at it. If the writer has a subject worthy of discussion, and if he understands the proper function of the introduction and conclusion, the problem of proportion is apt to take care of itself.

## THE OUTLINE

A person writing into a subject blind may come out, by luck or instinct, with a well-organized and well-proportioned composition.

But ordinarily the safe procedure is to think through the subject beforehand and set up a plan, an outline, of the projected discourse.

There are various types of outlines ranging from the formal sentence outline down to a scratch outline composed of jottings as they come to mind in the first survey of the subject. For the moment, however, we shall concern ourselves with a simple topic outline.

In our analysis of the student theme "The Person I Admire Most" (p. 16), we have already indicated what such a preliminary outline might be. Let us now set it up.

*Statement of the subject:* Why I admire my uncle Conroy

*Introduction:*
　I. My uncle as he now appears—apparent failure and real success

*Body:*
　II. The background of my uncle's achievement
　　A. His worldly success and ruin　(paragraph 2)
　　B. His illness and despair　(paragraph 3)
　III. The nature of my uncle's achievement
　　A. His practical achievements　(paragraph 4)
　　　1. Help with the children
　　　2. Help with my father's business
　　　3. Help with my mother's illness
　　B. His achievement in self-control　(paragraph 5)
　　　1. Naturalness of his actions
　　　2. Cheerfulness in the face of pain
　　　　(Now in paragraph 6; should be in paragraph 5)
　　C. His greatest achievement, an example to others—the summary of his other achievements　(paragraph 6)

*Conclusion:*
　IV. My uncle as a type of success and my admiration for him　(paragraph 6)

The writer of the theme probably should have made topic IV into a separate paragraph, a conclusion giving a statement of the author's definition of success and the application to his uncle's case. Nevertheless, he has written a theme which is fundamentally systematic, which builds continuously toward its point. The outline defines the stages in that progression.

A preliminary outline is a help in the actual writing of a theme, but it should not be followed slavishly. In the process of writing, new thoughts may come and new material may be suggested. The writer should always be ready to take advantage of these. He may have to stop the writing and go back to do a new outline, or he may be able to incorporate the new thoughts or new material in the actual body of the theme. In any event, it is a good idea to go back after the writing is completed and check against the original outline or, if necessary, make a new outline. When the bare bones are laid out, the writer can criticize the organization of his work.

It is always a question, too, how fully the outline can predict the scale of a piece of writing. If the author of "The Person I Admire Most" made an outline, he might not have been able to predict exactly how much space each topic would take. For instance, topic III-A might have developed into three paragraphs instead of one, or topics II-A and II-B might have been managed in one paragraph instead of two. Such problems usually have to be settled in the course of actual composition when the writer discovers the scale on which he is working. But the matter of scale and proportion in itself is something which we shall come to a little later.

The outline we have constructed for "The Person I Admire Most" is relatively simple. It should be adequate for the preliminary study of such a subject. But a student who has trouble in organizing his material may do well to consult the Appendix on the Outline in this book (p. 902). A little practice in making sentence outlines may increase his power to deal with a body of material. But there is no virtue in outlining for its own sake. It is a means to an end, a help to straight thinking and well-organized writing. It is not an end in itself.

## APPLICATIONS

I. Turn to the Readings and study two of the selections under Autobiography, "The Modern Gothic," by Vincent Sheean, and one other. What is the main line of interest in each, its true subject? Locate devices of linking and transition. What elements are emphasized? How do you know this? Do you find any examples of striking phrases, vivid comparisons, or memorable statements?

II. You will now write your first theme, an autobiography of 750 words or more. Remember that you have a particular audience, the instructor. That person is almost a stranger to you, but he is friendly and interested. He wants to know you better. For one thing, he wants to know the basic facts of your life. These facts are bound to be part of your story. But he wants to know a good deal more, something of the inside "you," your character, your training, your ambitions, your view of yourself.

But "yourself" is a big topic. Begin by thinking about it, by exploring it. Try to answer honestly, in your own mind, such questions as the following:

1. What kind of family do I have?
2. What kind of intellectual and moral training have I received?
3. What would I criticize about that training?
4. What people have had the greatest influence on me?
5. Has that influence been for good or bad?
6. What important experiences have I had? Why were they important to me?
7. What have I done that I am most proud of?
8. Have I made the most of my opportunities?
9. What is my own character like?
10. What are my strong points? Weak points?
11. What do I enjoy most?
12. What do I dislike most?
13. Did I get good training in high school?
14. Who were my good teachers? Why were they good for me?
15. Why did I come to college?
16. Did I drift here or do I have some reason?
17. What is my ambition?
18. What is my best talent? How does it relate to the career I plan?
19. What other questions should I answer to arrive at some estimate of myself?
20. Have I answered these questions thoughtfully and honestly?

You now have a large body of material laid out for your autobiography. You will not be able to use it all. In the first place, your theme will be too short for that. In the second place, if you tried to use it all, you might end with a lot of unorganized facts and remarks. But trying to answer these questions about yourself may have given you some perspective on yourself, the lead to some line of interest which will serve as the central idea of your theme and the spine for its organization. Or at least you may now see how various facts and ideas may be connected.

In trying to see how you can relate various facts and ideas to each other, you may find certain general questions helpful. For instance:

*a.* How far have circumstances (heredity, family situation, certain persons, and experience) made me what I am?
*b.* How far do I feel myself responsible for what I am?
*c.* How do I assess myself and my possibilities at this moment?

But do not feel bound by these questions. You may be able to frame others much more important for your own case.

After you have some notion of what you want to say about yourself, prepare an outline for the theme. As has been said earlier about out-lining, however, do not feel bound by the outline when you actually begin composition. Think over new ideas on their own merits even if this means a change of your plans. After you have finished a draft of the theme, check it by your outline. If the theme seems good but does not match the outline, revise the outline to conform with the theme. If the theme does not seem good, but the outline still seems satisfactory, revise the theme to make it conform to the outline. Attach the outline to the theme before you hand it in.

# The Kinds
# of Discourse

## THE MAIN INTENTION

WHEN a writer sets out to write he has some main intention, some central purpose. Let us look at this matter as an aspect of communication, and not as an aspect of expression. That is, let us suppose that the writer wishes to communicate something to a reader, to work some effect on him.

First, his main intention may be to explain something, to make clear to the reader some idea, to analyze a character or a situation, to define a term, to give directions. He may wish, in other words, to inform him.

Second, he may wish to make the reader change his mind, his attitude, his point of view, his feelings. He may appeal to the reader's powers of logic in a perfectly objective and impersonal fashion, or he may appeal to his emotions, but in either case the intention is to work a change in him.

Third, he may wish to make the reader see or hear something as vividly as the writer himself has seen or heard it, to make him get the feel of the thing, the quality of a direct experience. The thing in question may be a natural scene, a city street, a cat or a race horse, a person's face, the odor of a room, a piece of music.

Fourth, he may wish to tell the reader about an event—what happened and how it happened. The event may be grand or trivial, a battle or a ball game, a presidential campaign or a picnic, but whatever it is, the writer will be anxious to give the sequence in time and perhaps to give some notion of how one thing led to another. And above all his chief concern will be to give an immediate impression of the event, to give the sense of witnessing it.

## THE FOUR KINDS OF DISCOURSE

We can see, with only a moment of reflection, that these four types of intention correspond to the four basic kinds of discourse: EXPOSITION, ARGUMENT, DESCRIPTION, and NARRATION. Exposition embodies the wish to inform the reader, argument the wish to make the reader change his mind or attitude, description the wish to make the reader perceive something, narration the wish to make the reader grasp the movement of an event.

What is important here is to understand that these traditional kinds of discourse are not arbitrary divisions of the subject of writing, but that each corresponds to a main intention, a fundamental wish on the part of the writer. Each fulfills one of his needs. And it is important, too, to see that this main intention, this fundamental wish, relates both to the nature of the subject and the nature of the occasion. That is, one begins a piece of writing by asking himself what kind of treatment is natural to the subject and what kind of effect he wants to work on the reader.

## MIXTURE OF THE KINDS OF DISCOURSE

Thinking back over various articles and books you have read, you may remark that none of these kinds of discourse often appears in a pure form. For instance, a novel will describe as well as narrate, it will give sections of exposition, it may even present argument. A magazine article on international affairs may very well employ narrative, as in an illustrative anecdote, or description, as in presenting the statesmen on whose decisions the settlement of affairs depends. Both exposition and argument may be intertwined in a most complicated fashion: the writer must make clear to the reader the state of affairs, and that calls for exposition, and he will probably have in mind some convictions which he wants to see put into action by his reader, and that calls for argument. Even class reports, which tend to be almost pure exposition, may involve narrative. For instance, a report on a chemistry experiment may involve the presentation of an event—the setting up of the apparatus, the sequence of occurrences. In fact, the form of exposition which deals with such a process is sometimes called expository narration because it is necessarily bound to a sequence in time.

All of this does not mean that in a good and effective piece of writing the mixture of the kinds of discourse is irresponsible. There will always be a *main intention,* a fundamental wish. The class report will always be, by the nature of the case, an example of exposition. The novel, no matter how much exposition, description, and argument it contains, will always be an example of narration. Other instances may not be so clear-cut, but in any instance, a good writer knows for what purpose he is using a given type of discourse. He will use it to support his main intention.

Though most writing involves a mixture of the kinds of discourse, we can best study them in isolation, one by one. This study will mean the systematic analysis of relatively pure examples in order to observe the various types of organization appropriate to any one kind. It is only after one understands the kinds of discourse in a pure form that one can make them work together to give unity to a larger discourse.

## OBJECTIVE AND SUBJECTIVE DISCOURSE

Before we discuss at length the four kinds of discourse that we have distinguished, we may make some other distinctions that will be useful to us.

First, we shall distinguish the SUBJECTIVE and the OBJECTIVE use of language. Compare these two statements: "The girl had beautiful hair," and "The girl had black hair." The first statement is "subjective." It represents a perceiving *subject's* impression of, and interpretation of, a fact. The second statement is, by comparison, quite objective. It presents a fact objectively—that is, without personal interpretation and judgment. The fact presented is true, whether we think black hair is beautiful or not beautiful, or whether this head of black hair impresses us as beautiful or ugly. Subjective is inner and private; objective is outer and public. We tend to have quite different standards of beauty; we tend to have rather general standards of what is black.

But the statement that the girl has black hair is not wholly objective. The girl's hair may be a dark brown and the person who claims that it is black may not have as keen a discrimination of colors as another. By comparison the statement "The girl weighs 116 pounds" is more nearly objective. For unless the scales are wrong or the person who reads them has made an error, that statement depends upon a universal standard. The Bureau of Weights and Measures at Washington furnishes us with a very precise standard of what a pound is.

To sum up, the subjective represents the response of a subject who perceives, a response that reveals all the individuality of standard and bias and preconception and emotional coloring that attach to personal judgment. The objective represents an appeal to general standards with the elimination of personal bias and impression.

## SCIENTIFIC INTENTION

Here are some further examples of objective and subjective statements. We may write, "The water was 31 per cent saturated with filterable solids," or we may write, "The water was stained a muddy brown." We may write, "The man was 5 ft. 3½ in. tall," or we may write, "He was a runty little fellow." We may write, "The animal caught was a mature male of the species *Rattus norvegicus* weighing 1 lb. 3½ oz.," or we may write, "We caught a fat brown rat."

Now *all* these statements report facts, not merely the first members of each pair of statements. How then do the first members of each pair differ from the second members of the pair? They differ in making use of a defined and agreed-upon set of classifications and measurements. That is why we call them objective. The word *rat* may suggest something loathsome, furtive, and destructive. *Rattus norvegicus* does not. Muddy water may call up happy memories of the old swimming pool or unpleasant associations of dirt. The author interested in cold and scientific fact finds these associations, whether pleasant or unpleasant, quite irrelevant to his purpose; moreover, how muddy is muddy? On the other hand, 31 per cent saturation provides an accuracy with which he is very much concerned. What is a runt? What is a runty man? That will depend upon the point of view; moreover, it implies a judgment, a disparaging judgment. The measurement 5 ft. 3½ in. is an accurate statement and it gives us the fact quite apart from whether we think that it represents a satisfactory or an unsatisfactory height for a man.

Scientific statement, of course, represents our nearest approach to complete objectivity. Scientific statements make use of some agreed-upon scheme of reference: an accepted classification of mammals, or Mendelyeev's Periodic Table, or the metric system of weights and measures, and so on. A very important consequence follows from this fact: scientific statements make reference to *abstractions*. To illustrate, *Rattus norvegicus* is not any particular member of the brown rat family. It is the family itself: that compound of characteristics which defines the particular species called the brown rat. *Rattus norvegicus* is an *ideal* rat. The personal equation has been eliminated. Any competent biologist can say whether the specimen in question belongs to the family or not.

We can say, then, that when the writer's main purpose is scientific his language tends to be technical and objective. It is technical in that it consists of special terms used strictly with reference to an agreed-upon scheme. It is objective in that the emotional coloring of a particular observer has been eliminated. A strictly scientific purpose obviously demands an emotionally neutral vocabulary of this sort.

## ARTISTIC INTENTION

The strictly scientific intention, however, represents an extreme. Very little of our writing turns out to be purely scientific. Moreover, important as the scientific intention is, it is not the sole intention of the writer. Let us consider the other intention, and to make the contrast as sharp as possible, let us take this other intention in its most extreme form. We might call it an "artistic" intention, though in using the term "artistic" we do not mean to limit it to the higher and more serious forms of literature. As we shall use it here, "artistic intention" includes the purpose that directs the telling of a good joke or the description of an exciting boxing match, or the writing of a warm letter to an intimate friend, and many other kinds of discourse which we use in our everyday life. The writer with this intention insists that we "see" the object, feel the experience, respond imaginatively to the whole scene portrayed. He uses terms which are particular and concrete and which invite the reader's reaction. Moreover, such a writer tends to deal with objects in their immediacy and concreteness. He does not abstract certain qualities and characteristics as the scientist does; he tends to fuse and combine them. It is easy to see why.

A moment's reflection will show us that our actual experience of a thing comes to us with more fullness and richness than any single adjective, tied to the single sense, will indicate. We look at an apple and see the patch of red, and say, "The apple is red." But we are also prepared to say that it is, for example, "glossy" and "juicy-looking." Even though we have not touched this particular apple or tasted it, other senses than sight become involved in our experience of the apple. Our past experiences with apples are operating at the moment in our experience of the present apple. We see the apple and sense the special complex of qualities which mean "appleness"—the color, the texture of the skin, the fragrance, the juiciness. So when we come to describe something, in ordinary speech, we may not merely assemble adjectives with the intention of making them indicate the qualities to be perceived by a single sense. Our ordinary use of language indicates something of the complication of the perception. When, for example, we say "glossy" of the apple, we are, in a way, fusing two senses, sight and touch. Or when we look at the frozen lake and say, "The ice is glassy," we evoke, with the word *glassy*, a whole complex of qualities which are fused in the single word—slickness, hardness, transparency, and brightness.

The kind of richness and fullness about which we have been talking may involve also the element of interpretation. When we say, as above, "The ice is glassy," we attribute certain qualities to the ice, though, of course, our statement implies a person who perceives. But when we say, "The music is soothing," the reference to a person who perceives is much more positively and intimately involved in the statement. For here the music is described only in terms of its effect upon a hearer. The soothing effect may take place because the music is soft, or has a certain type of melody and rhythm, or for some other reason, but the statement as given does not even mention those qualities; it mentions only the effect on a hearer. In other words, here the subjective reference of the description is extremely important, for it is through the subjective reference, the effect on a hearer, that the person who reads the description becomes aware of the nature of the music in question.

Subjectivity, in the light of the artistic intention, becomes a virtue, not a vice. We want terms which suggest qualities, not bare technical terms which bar all but one meaning. The thing to be avoided is technical dryness, since the reader is to respond powerfully to the experience set forth.

What is the relation between the scientific-artistic distinction and the distinction of the four kinds of discourse?

In an offhand way we tend to think that exposition and argument employ language that is objective, logical, scientific, and that description and narration employ language that is subjective, emotional, artistic. Within limits, this is true, but only within limits. Exposition giving us information about an automobile motor would use objective, logical, scientific language, but exposition setting forth the motives of a human act might very well have to resort to the other kind of language. Or even if the main intention of argument is to convince by appealing to the logical faculties, we may have to resort to persuasion, to emotional appeals, to get a hearing for our argument, to present it with the right tone. Description may as well concern itself with the floor plan of a house as with a beautiful woman or the effect of a sonata. Narration may give us the stages of a laboratory experiment or the experience of a courtship or a prize fight.

We may regard the four kinds of discourse as representing different basic intentions, but any one of these intentions may use either or both of the two kinds of appeals (objective, logical, scientific or subjective, emotional, artistic).

In making the distinction between the two kinds of appeals we have deliberately used extreme examples. The extreme examples may make the difference come clear and sharp. In actual practice, however, our basic intention is not often purely scientific or purely artistic. And we must warn ourselves against a misleading oversimplification: we must not assume that all thinking can be conducted in a terminology that is technical and objective, and that all emotional language is vague and confused. To take extremes again, the poet may use language as precisely in his kind of discourse as the physicist in his.

Furthermore, though we have contrasted objective language with subjective language, and technical terms with suggestive and imaginative terms, we go badly astray if we assume that, since the scientific intention makes use of objective and technical language, the artistic intention makes use *merely* of suggestive and subjective language. Far from it. Even a novel may include description which is rather studiedly objective and a poem, on occasion, may make use of highly technical language.

Perhaps the best way to see the relation of these terms to the writer's intention is to return to our account of the nature of scientific language. It achieves its objectivity, as we have seen (p. 35), by using accepted terms and schemes of reference, and we have observed that these are arrived at by a process of abstraction. The individual's response is cut away from the term so as to leave it fixed and unchanging. But only abstractions (that is, generalized qualities and ideas) are fixed and unchanging. We get, not any individual rat, half-grown, mangy, dead in the trap, scuttling through the walls of a house, or the pet rat named "Jim," but rather *Rattus norvegicus,* that is, ratness—an abstract rat.

In other words, technical and objective terms represent a *reduced* language, core-meanings from which personal interpretation and implied meanings and suggestions have been removed. It is a specialized language which is developed by abstracting—cutting away —from the richer and more complex language of our ordinary experience all but the general qualities and characteristics.

Instead, therefore, of arranging our terms in neat oppositions thus:

|  SCIENTIFIC  |  ARTISTIC  |
|  objective  |  subjective  |
|  technical  |  suggestive  |

we must see them arranged in this way:

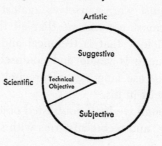

The segment of the circle represents a specialized intention with its appropriate devices. The circle as a whole represents our general intention of which the segment is a part. This may explain why in realizing the more general intention, we may use, not only a language which goes beyond the specialized techniques of the pure scientific intention, but also on occasion the specialized language as well.

Finally, we need to remind ourselves once more that in the discussion thus far we have dealt with extremes: that objective, for example, is not an absolute term but a relative term. *Beautiful* is more subjective than *white*, but *white* is more subjective than "the color without hue at one extreme end of the scale of grays, opposite to black." So with the other terms which we have used, such as subjective, technical, and so on. They are relative terms, not absolute. In actual practice we rarely make an appeal that is purely scientific or purely artistic, just as the four kinds of presentation rarely exist pure and unmixed. But it is necessary to make the distinction sharply, for in the chapters that follow we shall need to refer to the "objective" and "technical" as contrasted in direction with the "subjective" and the "suggestive."

# Exposition

EXPOSITION is the kind of discourse which explains or clarifies a subject. That is, as the word *exposition* quite literally means, it sets forth a subject. Its appeal is to the understanding. Description and narration may lead to understanding, but they lead to it by presenting the qualities and movement of their subject. Exposition, however, leads to understanding by explaining something about its subject. Argument involves understanding in that it aims to convince of the truth or desirability of something, but its aim is to convince, not merely to explain.

Exposition is the most common kind of writing, for it is applicable to anything which challenges the understanding—the definition of a word, the way to a street address, the structure of a plant, the mechanism of a watch, the meaning of a historical event, the motive of an act, the significance of a philosophical system.

## INTEREST

A piece of exposition may be regarded as the answer to a question about a subject. If the question has actually been asked us—"How do I get to the Court House?" or "What were the causes of the American Revolution?"—it is easy to frame an answer that does not waver from the point. But if we set out to write a piece of exposition without the benefit of a real, leading question, simply because we feel that a subject is interesting or important, we are very apt to give a confused account of the subject. We should always try to decide what INTEREST we want to appeal to.

An informal list may suggest the kind of interests to which exposition appeals:

> What is it?
> What does it mean?
> How is it put together?
> How does it work?
> Why is it the way it is?
> How did it come to be this way?
> When did it occur or exist?
> What is it worth?
> What is its importance?
> How well does it fulfill its intended function?

We can ask other questions, of course, about a thing, whatever that thing may be, but these are among the most usual.

Naturally, not all of these questions would be appropriate for the same subject. If we are trying to explain the nature of a triangle, we would scarcely ask when it occurred, for the nature of a triangle —what makes a figure a triangle and not something else—has no reference to time at all. Or if we are discussing the French Revolution, we would scarcely ask how well it fulfilled its intended function, for the Revolution was a complex event answering to no single intention. It would be appropriate, however, to ask about its causes or its importance.

Already, in an earlier chapter (p. 12), we have discussed the problem of locating the real subject in a general topic, the concern that will give unity to a composition. The problem here is the same, but narrowed to apply to the methods of exposition. The interest we wish to appeal to determines the line we will follow in our discussion and will give that discussion its proper unity. We may, for instance, want to define a word, either to instruct our reader or to clarify our own thinking. We may want to describe a subject—to tell what its qualities are and relate those qualities to those of another subject. We may want to account for a subject—tell how it came to exist. We may want to evaluate or criticize a subject. Any one of these endeavors would provide us with a unified discussion.

A writer, however, may appeal to more than one interest in the same composition, and in any extended discussion he is almost certain to appeal to more than one interest. But in doing so he must be careful to keep them distinct. He must not mix up the answer to one question with the answer to another. He must see the interests as representing different stages in his single over-all treatment. Furthermore, if he does appeal to more than one interest, he must be sure that some relation is established among them, and that there is a logical progression from one to another. In other words, there must be clear division among the parts, and significant relation among the parts.

Let us take an example. A student wishes to write a theme on Dickens's *Oliver Twist*. He knows that it is a novel, and he has a pretty good notion of what a novel is and can assume that his reader, too, has such a notion. But what kind of a novel is it? He decides that it is a novel of social protest. He is not so sure that his reader knows exactly what a novel of social protest is. So he sets out to define the term "novel of social protest," and decides that it is a novel in which the author's primary interest is to show the injustice in society. So far he has classified the novel and given a definition of the class into which it falls.

Next he may summarize the story, present the characters, and comment on Dickens's attitude expressed in them. Now he is answering the question, "How is it put together?" He is explaining the organization of the book.

Next, he may tell how Dickens drew on previous novels for suggestions in method, and on his own life and observation for material. Now he is answering the question, "Why is it the way it is?" He is giving an account of how the novel came to be.

He may conclude by saying that the novel is good because the plot keeps the reader in suspense and because the reader sympathizes with little Oliver. And he may add that the novel served a useful purpose by helping to bring about social reform. In the first statement he would be evaluating the novel purely as a novel—how well it fulfills certain requirements of fiction. In the second he would be evaluating the novel as a social force. In other words, he would be considering two different meanings of the question, "What is it worth?"

This would not be the only line of discussion possible for a theme on *Oliver Twist*, but it will illustrate how a writer may appeal to more than one interest and still be systematic.

## APPLICATIONS

I. In the section of Readings study "The Colors That Animals Can See," by H. Munro Fox, or "Learned Words and Popular Words," by James B. Greenough and George L. Kittredge. What interests are appealed to in the selection you choose?

II. Below is a list of general subjects. Select two or three that interest you, and for each state some interests that might be used as "real subjects." For instance, the general subject "Jet Propulsion" might provide several particular subjects: (1) the history of its development, (2) the engineering principles involved, (3) the comparison of jet propulsion with other methods of propulsion, (4) the effect on tactics in air warfare, (5) the effect on military strategy, (6) the effect on design of aircraft.

Baseball
The Eighteenth Amendment
Capital Punishment
Socialism
Laissez-faire Economics
The Potato
Marriage
The Horse
My Church
Photography
The Battle of Gettysburg
Military Discipline
Nationalism
Charity

Walt Whitman
Symphonic Music
Saint Paul
Nazism
Heroism
Blind Dates
Postal Service
Race Prejudice
The Diesel Engine
The Play *Hamlet*
Propaganda
The Kibitzer
Good Manners
Flower Gardening

III. Take one of the lists you have prepared of "real subjects" and try to see how several of the interests might be related to each other to give a pattern of discussion. Return to the section on outlining in Chapter 1 (and if your instructor suggests it, to the section on the Outline in Appendix 3, p. 902), and prepare a topic outline of the discussion.

## THE METHODS OF EXPOSITION

We shall now take up the study of the most usual methods of exposition—the ways we go about answering questions that demand exposition. This is not to say that there is a method to correspond to each question on our list. Some methods may be used in answering more than one question, and the answer to a single question may sometimes be made by more than one method or by a combination of methods. It is useful, however, to remember that the methods are ways of answering questions, of appealing to interests.

The same discourse—for example, an editorial, an essay, a theme, a chapter in a text book—may use more than one expository method. Often we do not find a method in its pure state. But here, where we are trying to understand the nature of each method, we shall be concerned with relatively pure examples.

## IDENTIFICATION

IDENTIFICATION is one of the simplest methods of exposition. It is one of the ways of answering the question, "What is it?" In one way, it is a kind of pointing by means of language. "Who is Mrs. Bertrand Smith?" somebody asks, and the answer is, "Oh, she is the blond woman in the black dress, sitting to the right of the white-haired old man." The reply has worked like pointing a finger. But perhaps Mrs. Smith is not there to be pointed at so easily. So the answer may be, "She is the woman who won the city golf tournament last year and then married the son of old Jason Smith, the banker." In either case the answer places the subject, Mrs. Smith, in such a context that she can be identified.

We constantly use such casual forms of identification. But we are using the same method if we begin an article on the Carmel Mission by writing: "The Carmel Mission stands just outside the village of Monterey, California. It was founded by Padre Junipero Serra who had come up from San Diego in the year 1770." We have tried to locate the subject.

The same principle may apply if the thing we are trying to identify, unlike Mrs. Smith or the Carmel Mission, has no concrete existence—if, for instance, it is Scholastic philosophy. To identify it we might begin: "Scholastic philosophy is that system of thought developed in the late Middle Ages in Western Europe by the Catholic Church. The most famous philosopher associated with this system is Saint Thomas Aquinas." Here, again, we are in the process of locating.

If identification becomes elaborate it tends to absorb other expository methods; it begins, for example, to use analysis, comparison, or contrast; and the simple intention of identification may be lost in other and perhaps more interesting intentions in the discussion. Even so, we can distinguish this intention, and see that it has a method appropriate to itself, the method of locating, or placing, of making recognition possible.

## EXPOSITORY DESCRIPTION: TECHNICAL DESCRIPTION

As identification may absorb other expository methods, so exposition itself may absorb other kinds of discourse and use them for its purpose. Description, for instance, is frequently used for an expository purpose. In fact, the kind of description usually associated with exposition is so different from ordinary description that it has a special name, EXPOSITORY DESCRIPTION or TECHNICAL DESCRIPTION.

We can distinguish between technical description and ordinary description by considering the different types of occasion from which they arise. First, there is the occasion that demands *information about* the thing described. Second, there is the occasion that demands an immediate impression of the thing described. The first kind is expository, or technical, in so far as it aims to enlarge the understanding. But the second type—the type we ordinarily think of when we use the word description—aims to suggest the qualities of the object as though it were immediately perceived. It aims to give an experience of the object through the imagination. We shall call this type SUGGESTIVE DESCRIPTION.

A full discussion of suggestive description will be reserved for a later chapter,[1] but for the present it is necessary to contrast it with technical description that we may better understand the use of description for exposition. Let us begin with some examples.

*TECHNICAL:*

### FOR QUICK SALE

*Wellington Boulevard*

Attractive Cape Cod cottage, lge. liv. rm., 13 x 25, knotty pine, stone fireplace; din. rm., sunny, 12 x 14; small den or libr., fireplace; kitchen, modern, elec. stove, lge. gas refrig., dishwasher, all practically new;

[1] See Chapter 5, pp. 219-23, below.

med.-size, concrete basement, gas furn., ht. watr.; 2 bedrms., 14 x 16, 15 x 18; 2 baths, lge. and small; roof white oak shingle. Lot well planted, landscaped, brook, 2 acres; heated garage, 2 cars; small greenhouse. Built by owner, 1936. Excellent condition. Take reasonable offer. Call: BE-1632.

*SUGGESTIVE:*

Dear Mother:

We have found a place at last, and we love it, Jack just as much as I. I must tell you about it, so you can have some notion before you come to see us here. Well, you don't see it from the highway, for there is a high hedge across the front of the property with just a little gap that lets you into the lane, a winding lane among a grove of white oaks, like a lane going down to a pasture on somebody's farm. That's the whole impression—just like a farm, a million miles away from town. When you pass the oaks you see a dip down to a brook, lined with willows, and a stone bridge, and just beyond the bridge the house on a slight rise that the brook curves around. The house is white and trim, two stories, but rather low, just seeming to crop out of the ground, with a couple of enormous oaks behind to give a background for it. You have the feeling that once you cross that bridge and enter that door you'll be safe and sound and the world will never come to bother you.

When you do enter, you know that your feeling is right. There is a long room with a big fireplace, and windows to the east for the morning sun. It is a perfect room for the furniture which Grandmother left me, just the sort of room she would have loved, peaceful and old-fashioned. The instant you come in, you think of a fire crackling on the hearth, and a kettle humming to heat water for tea, and you see the copper glinting on the andirons. . . .

The motives behind the two pieces of description are very different. The seller of the house wants to give information about the house. The buyer of the house, writing to her mother, wants to give the feel, the atmosphere, of the house.

The advertisement is an instance of technical description. Except in so far as we know the general type of Cape Cod cottage, we have no basis for visualizing the actual house. The writer of the advertisement has not been concerned that we should get an impression of his house; the only attempt in this direction is his use of the word *sunny* about the dining room. But if the writer has not been concerned to give us the picture and atmosphere of his house, he has been greatly concerned to give us a systematic and complete body of information about the house considered from a technical point of view as a shelter and a machine for living.

We should find the same motive behind a naturalist's description of a species of bird, a mechanic's description of the ignition system of an automobile, or a physiologist's description of the structure of the human brain. In none of these examples would there be any attempt to make us perceive the thing described except in so far as that attempt would enlarge our understanding.

In the excerpt from the letter above, however, the situation is reversed. The writer is concerned to make an appeal to her reader's senses, to establish the impression of the place, its quietness and isolation, its old-fashioned charm. The details she has selected for comment all contribute to this impression. The suggestive description does not, as does the technical, give a systematic and relatively complete body of information concerning the object. Instead, it simply presents the details that support the sensory and emotional effect the writer wishes to communicate. The technical description *tends* to be enumerative; the suggestive description *tends* to be selective and impressionistic.

There is another and very important distinction between the technical and the suggestive description. In the strictly technical description there is no place for interpretation by the writer. It is concerned only with the facts about the object, facts that can be observed by anyone. For example, when the writer of the advertisement of the Cape Cod cottage lists six rooms, or says that the living room is of knotty pine, he is stating a fact, something objective and beyond dispute. He is being strictly technical. But when he says that the cottage is "attractive" he is not being strictly technical. He is interpreting the situation according to his own idea of what constitutes attractiveness. Likewise when the buyer writes her letter and says that the house is peaceful and charming, she is interpreting. To another person with different tastes the place might not seem peaceful but depressing.

This is not to say that the suggestive description does not use facts. It must use facts if it is to give any sense of the reality of the thing described. But it uses its facts as related to some impression it wishes to communicate. The facts are interpreted.

Let us take another pair of examples, examples in which the difference is not so immediately obvious but is equally as important.

*TECHNICAL:*

The West Indies stand in a warm sea, and the trade winds, warmed and moistened by this sea, blow across all of them. These are the two great primary geographic facts about this group of islands whose area is but little larger than that of Great Britain.

These trade winds, always warm, but nevertheless refreshing sea breezes, blow mostly from the east or the northeast. Thus one side of every island is windward, and the other side is leeward. The third great geographical fact about these islands is that most of them are mountainous, giving to the windward sides much more rain than the leeward sides receive. This makes great differences in climate within short distances, a thing quite unknown in the eastern half of the United States, where our slowly whirling cyclonic winds blow in quick succession from all directions upon every spot of territory. Thus both sides of the Appalachian Mountains are nearly alike in their rainfall, forest growth, and productive possibilities. On the contrary, the West Indian mountains have different worlds on their different slopes. The eastern or windward side, cloud-bathed and eternally showered upon, is damp and dripping. There are jungles with velvety green ferns, and forests with huge trees. The rainbow is a prominent feature of the tropic landscape. On the windward side one receives a striking impression of lush vegetation. On the leeward side of the very same ridge and only a few miles distant there is another kind of world, the world of scanty rainfall, with all its devastating consequences to vegetation. A fourth great geographic fact is the division of these islands into two great arcs, an outer arc of limestone and an inner arc of volcanic islands. The limestone areas are low. The volcanic areas are from moderately high to very high. Some islands have both the limestone and the volcanic features.—J. RUSSELL SMITH and M. OGDEN PHILLIPS: *North America,* Chap. 40.[2]

*SUGGESTIVE:*

Take five-and-twenty heaps of cinders dumped here and there in an outside city lot; imagine some of them magnified into mountains, and the vacant lot the sea; and you will have a fit idea of the general aspect of the Encantadas, or Enchanted Isles. A group rather of extinct vol-

[2] From *North America* by J. Russell Smith and M. Ogden Phillips, copyright, 1940, by Harcourt, Brace and Company.

canoes than of isles; looking much as the world at large might, after a penal conflagration.

It is to be doubted whether any spot on earth can, in desolation, furnish a parallel to this group. Abandoned cemeteries of long ago, old cities by piecemeal tumbling to their ruin, these are melancholy enough; but like all else which has once been associated with humanity they still awaken in us some thoughts of sympathy, however sad. Hence, even the Dead Sea, along with whatever other emotions it may at times inspire, does not fail to touch in the pilgrim some of his less unpleasurable feelings. . . .

But the special curse, as one may call it, of the Encantadas, that which exalts them in desolation above Idumea and the Pole, is that to them change never comes; neither the change of seasons nor of sorrows. Cut by the Equator, they know not autumn and they know not spring; while already reduced to the lees of fire, ruin itself can work little more upon them. The showers refresh the deserts, but in these isles, rain never falls. Like split Syrian gourds, left withering in the sun, they are cracked by an everlasting drought beneath a torrid sky. "Have mercy upon me," the wailing spirit of the Encantadas seems to cry, "and send Lazarus that he may dip the tip of his finger in water and cool my tongue, for I am tormented in this flame." . . .

In many places the coast is rock-bound, or more properly, clinker-bound; tumbled masses of blackish or greenish stuff like the dross of an iron-furnace, forming dark clefts and caves here and there, into which a ceaseless sea pours a fury of foam; overhanging them with a swirl of grey, haggard mist, amidst which sail screaming flights of unearthly birds heightening the dismal din. However calm the sea without, there is no rest for these swells and those rocks, they lash and are lashed, even when the outer ocean is most at peace with itself. On the oppressive, clouded days such as are peculiar to this part of the watery Equator, the dark vitrified masses, many of which raise themselves among white whirlpools and breakers in detached and perilous places off the shore, present a most Plutonian sight. In no world but a fallen one could such lands exist.—HERMAN MELVILLE: "The Encantadas, or Enchanted Isles," *The Piazza Tales.*

The first of these passages is from a geography of North America. Though it is not as brutally synoptic as the advertisement for the sale of the Cape Cod cottage, it has essentially the same kind of organization; it is an enumeration of facts pertinent to the special technical interest involved. Four "great geographic" facts are listed, and the consequences in terms of climate, vegetation, and appearance are indicated. There are occasional, and feeble, attempts to make the reader see the islands, as for instance in the phrases "cloud-bathed," and "velvety-green ferns," but the tendency is toward generalized information, toward abstraction. For instance, instead of giving us the sight of the rainbow in terms of images which would stir our imaginations, the writers simply say, "The rainbow is a prominent feature of the tropic landscape." Or instead of picturing for us the arid slopes of the leeward side of the mountains, they simply offer the phrase, "all its devastating consequences to vegetation."

The second passage, like the first, is the description of a group of tropic islands. But Melville, the author, is not concerned to give us a list of the great geographic facts and their consequences. His description involves some of these facts, but the passage is not organized about an enumeration of them. It is organized in such a way as to return the reader continually to the sense of loneliness, ruin, and desolation which characterizes the islands.

The passage begins with the comparison to heaps of cinders in a dumping ground, with that association of the used-up, the finished, the valueless, the dreary. The first paragraph ends with the phrase "penal conflagration," which implies ideas not merely of ruin and waste but also of sin and punishment—sin and punishment on a universal scale. The next paragraph is based on the ideas of the unhuman desolation, the blankness. The third is based on the idea of changelessness, the terrible monotony; but this monotony is presented as a "special curse," and is finally defined by the cry of Dives in Hell. In other words, in both the curse and the Biblical reference, we find an echo of the notion of sin and punishment, a continuation of the idea in the first paragraph. In the last paragraph appears again the image of the wasteland of cinders in the phrases "clinker-bound" and "like the dross of an iron-furnace." And also in the constant tumult of the sea, in the phrase "lash and are lashed," appears the idea of punishment and suffering, which becomes explicit in the last sentence, "In no world but a fallen one could such lands exist."

In other words, the whole passage is based on two things, the image of the cinder heap and the idea of sin and punishment, which combine to give the notion of a world after the Judgment, the final desolation. And it is this notion that provides the organizing principle for the description. It is the key to the interpretation that Melville gives to his facts.

Since the purpose of technical description is to give information about its object, the kind of description called GENERALIZED DESCRIPTION is one form it sometimes assumes. Generalized description presents the characteristics of a type rather than of a particular individual. If we set out to write a theme about the collie as a type, giving the points and qualities of the breed, we are using generalized description. If, on the other hand, we set out to write a theme about Old Buck, our favorite dog, we are using suggestive description, for we want to make clear to the reader what qualities the particular dog has.

The following description of the North American Indian, from an old work on the subject, is obviously an example of generalized description.

The general appearance of a North American Indian can be given in few words. . . . They are about of the average height which man attains when his form is not cramped by premature or excessive labor, but their erect posture and slender figure give them the appearance of a tall race. Their limbs are well formed, but calculated rather for agility than strength, in which they rarely equal the more vigorous of European nations. They generally have small feet.

The most distinguishing peculiarities of the race are, the reddish or copper color of the skin; the prominence of the cheek-bone; and the color and quality of the hair. This is not absolutely straight, but somewhat wavy, and has not inaptly been compared to the mane of the horse —less from its coarseness than from its glossy hue and the manner in which it hangs. Their eyes are universally dark. The women are rather short, with broader faces, and a greater tendency to obesity than the men, but many of them possess a symmetrical figure, with an agreeable and attractive countenance.—CHARLES DE WOLF BROWNELL: *The Indian Races of North and South America*, Chap. 1.

The following description, however, is obviously particular and suggestive.

He had the spare, alert and jaunty figure that one often finds in army men, an almost professional military quality that somehow seemed to set his figure upon a horse as if he had grown there or had spent a lifetime in the cavalry. His face also had the same lean, bitter, professional military quality; his speech, although good-natured and very friendly, was clipped, incisive, jerky, and sporadic, his lean weather-beaten face was deeply, sharply scarred and sunken in the flanks, and he wore a small cropped mustache, and displayed long frontal teeth when he smiled—a spare, gaunt, toothy, yet attractive smile.

His left arm was withered, shrunken, almost useless; part of his hand and two fingers had been torn away by the blast or explosion which had destroyed his arm; but it was not this mutilation of the flesh that gave one the sense of a life that had been ruined, lost, and broken irretrievably. In fact, one quickly forgot his physical injury; his figure looked so spare, lean, jaunty, well-conditioned in its energetic fitness that one never thought of him as a cripple, nor pitied him for any disability. No: the ruin that one felt in him was never of the flesh, but of the spirit. Something seemed to have been exploded from his life—it was not the nerve-centers of his arms, but of his soul, that had been destroyed. There was in the man somewhere a terrible dead vacancy and emptiness, and that spare, lean figure that he carried so well seemed only to surround this vacancy like a kind of shell.—THOMAS WOLFE: *Of Time and the River,* Chap. 70.[3]

Let us summarize the distinction between technical description and suggestive description. The technical gives information about the object. The suggestive gives an immediate impression of the object. The technical *tells us something about* the object; the suggestive *gives* us the object in our imagination, almost as though it were before us. The technical tends to be abstract; the suggestive tends to be concrete. The technical tends to completeness in listing qualities of the object (with reference to the special interest that motivates the description); the suggestive tends to selectivity (with reference to the main impression desired). The technical employs a schematic organization defined by the special interest involved in the description (the listing of rooms, etc., in the first example, the listing of the four great geographical facts, etc., in the second). The suggestive employs an organization defined by the main impression and response desired (peacefulness and charm in the letter, burned-out desolation in the essay by Melville). In addition, technical description may be generalized and not particular.

[3] From *Of Time and the River* by Thomas Wolfe, copyright, 1935, by Charles Scribner's Sons.

We can list the distinctions:

| TECHNICAL | SUGGESTIVE |
|---|---|
| information | impression |
| about the object | the object |
| abstract | concrete |
| completeness | selectivity |
| schematic organization | impressionistic organization |
| no interpretation | interpretation |
| (general) | particular |

## OBJECTIVE AND SUBJECTIVE DESCRIPTION

Another distinction may be useful in our thinking about description, the distinction we have already made (p. 33) between OBJECTIVE and SUBJECTIVE.

When we say, "The apple is red," we point to a quality which the apple possesses. There is no reference here to any observer of the apple. This is a simple case of objective description. It is concerned only with the object being described.

But when we say, "The music is soothing," we refer to the effect of the music upon a listener. The soothing effect may occur because the music is soft, and has a certain kind of melody and rhythm, but our statement as given does not mention those qualities objectively. It only mentions the effect on the person who experiences the music, on the "subject" as he is called. The statement, then, is a simple example of subjective description.

Let us take some examples somewhat more complicated than our statements about the apple and the music.

(1) If anyone wants to exemplify the meaning of the word "fish," he cannot choose a better animal than a herring. The body, tapering to each end, is covered with thin, flexible scales, which are very easily rubbed off. The taper head, with its underhung jaw, is smooth and scaleless on the top; the large eye is partly covered by two folds of transparent skin, like eyelids—only immovable and with the slit between them vertical instead of horizontal; the cleft behind the gill-cover is very wide, and, when the cover is raised, the large red gills which lie underneath it are freely exposed. The rounded back bears the single moderately long dorsal fin about its middle.—THOMAS HENRY HUXLEY: "The Herring."

In this passage we find a clear instance of description without reference to any observer. Information is given about the object with no interpretation: the facts are the facts.

Let us turn to an example, however, in which an observer is specified, a passage in which Gulliver, a man of normal size who has been captured by the tiny Lilliputians, describes the house assigned to him.

(2) At the place where the carriage stopped, there stood an ancient temple, esteemed to be the largest in the whole kingdom, which having been polluted some years before by an unnatural murder, was, according to the zeal of those people, looked upon as profane, and therefore had been applied to common uses, and all the ornaments and furniture carried away. In this edifice it was determined I should lodge. The great gate fronting to the north was about four foot high, and almost two foot wide, through which I could easily creep. On each side of the gate was a small window not above six inches from the ground: into that on the left side, the King's smiths conveyed fourscore and eleven chains, like those that hang to a lady's watch in Europe, and almost as large, which were locked to my left leg with six and thirty padlocks. Over against this temple, on t'other side of the great highway, at twenty foot distance, there was a turret at least five foot high. Here the Emperor ascended with many principal lords of his court, to have an opportunity of viewing me, as I was told, for I could not see them.—JONATHAN SWIFT: *Gulliver's Travels*, Chap. 1.

An observer is introduced into this scene, but the observer is a mere observer, a kind of device for registering the facts, and no reference is made to the effect of the scene upon him. The facts are presented objectively in themselves and the items mentioned (such as measurement, shape, color) are items about which objective agreement would be relatively easy. So we see that the mere presence of an observer does not mean that a description may not be objective. The description is apparently subjective but is really objective.

Our next example also gives an observer:

(3) I know not how it was—but, with the first glimpse of the building, a sense of insufferable gloom pervaded my spirit. I say insufferable; for the feeling was unrelieved by any of that half-pleasurable, because poetic, sentiment, with which the mind usually receives even the sternest natural images of the desolate or terrible. I looked upon the scene before me—

upon the mere house, and the simple landscape features of the domain, upon the bleak walls, upon the vacant eye-like windows, upon a few rank sedges, and upon a few white trunks of decayed trees—with an utter depression of soul which I can compare to no earthly sensation more properly than to the after-dream of the reveler upon opium: the bitter lapse into every-day life, the hideous dropping off of the veil.— EDGAR ALLAN POE: "The Fall of the House of Usher."

The observer here, unlike Gulliver, is not a mere observer. What is important here is his reaction, his gloom, his depression. We get an impression of the scene, it is true, but the reaction is more important than the scene itself. We have only a small amount of factual information about the scene; there are the vacant windows in the building, there is the growth of sedge, there are the few decayed trees gone white. Everything else in the passage is devoted, directly or indirectly, to indicating a response to the scene. Not only is this true of the parts of the passage in which the narrator definitely states his personal reactions. It is also true of words like "bleak" and "eye-like" which pretend to describe the object but in reality indicate a response to the object. For example, the phrase "vacant eye-like windows" is really giving the morbid comparison of the house to a fleshless skull—is really implying that the house is a house of death.

What are we to make, however, of description in which no observer appears, but which indicates a very definite response for the reader? With this question in mind let us look at the following passage:

(4) The waters are out in Lincolnshire. An arch of the bridge in the park has been sapped and sopped away. The adjacent low-lying ground, for half a mile in breadth, is a stagnant river, with melancholy trees for islands in it, and a surface punctured all over, all day long, with falling rain. My Lady Dedlock's "place" has been extremely dreary. The weather, for many a day and night, has been so wet that the trees seem wet through, and the soft loppings and prunings of the woodsman's axe can make no crack or crackle as they fall. The deer, looking soaked, leave quagmires where they pass. The shot of a rifle loses its sharpness in the moist air, and its smoke moves in a tardy little cloud towards the green rise, coppice-topped, that makes a background for the falling rain. The view from my Lady Dedlock's own windows is alternately a lead-coloured view, and a view in Indian ink. The vases on the stone terrace

in the foreground catch the rain all day; and the heavy drops fall, drip, drip, drip, upon the broad flagged pavement, called, from old time, the Ghost's Walk, all night. On Sundays, the little church in the park is mouldy; the oaken pulpit breaks out into a cold sweat; and there is a general smell and taste as of the ancient Dedlocks in their graves.— CHARLES DICKENS: *Bleak House,* Vol. I, Chap. 2.

As we have said, no observer is officially introduced into this scene, but a certain response to it is strongly indicated, a certain mood is developed. All details are presented to reinforce the impression of dampness, depression, and gloom. The river is "stagnant," the blows of the ax make only "soft loppings," the report of the rifle "loses its sharpness in the moist air," the heavy drops "drip, drip, drip," the church is "mouldy," the pulpit "breaks out into a cold sweat," there is the general taste and smell of a tomb. Notice how the phrase "breaks out in a cold sweat," though applied to the damp wood of the pulpit actually serves to remind us of a situation that would make a human being do the same thing, and leads us up to the taste and smell of the Dedlocks in their graves. We can see that, though Dickens has apparently maintained an objective method (he has put no observer in the scene), the effect of the passage is actually much closer to that from Poe than to the objective passage by Huxley with which we started.

## APPLICATIONS

At the end of the chapter on Description (p. 256) there are a set of examples. Study these and find an example to fit each of the following requirements.

1. Without an observer and with no attempt to interpret, to create a mood.
2. With an observer but with no attempt to interpret the material— observer as a register.
3. With an observer whose responses interpret the material.
4. Without an observer but with an attempt to create a mood, to interpret the material.

## THE RELATION BETWEEN THE TECHNICAL-SUGGESTIVE DISTINCTION AND THE OBJECTIVE-SUBJECTIVE DISTINCTION

What is the relation between the technical-suggestive distinction and the objective-subjective distinction? We can best answer this question by remembering that technical description does not interpret its material and the suggestive description does. Then we can set up a scheme to answer our question:

| TECHNICAL | SUGGESTIVE |
|---|---|
| *Without an observer* | |
| (1) Without observer and with strictly objective method. (Huxley: "The Herring") | (4) Without observer, apparently objective in method, but with interpretation of material. (Dickens: *Bleak House*) |
| *With an observer* | |
| (2) With observer, apparently subjective in method, but with no reference to the observer's responses and with no interpretation. (Swift: *Gulliver's Travels*) | (3) With observer and with strictly subjective method. (Poe: "The Fall of the House of Usher") |

We cannot let this scheme stand, however, without some modifying comment.

First, technical description of the strictest kind, such as the description of a device in a handbook of mechanics ordinarily uses type 1.

Second, even when suggestive description puts the greatest emphasis on the interpretation of material, on the response of a specified observer or of the reader, it must still give an impression of the object itself. It is not a mere presentation of responses. In the description of the House of Usher, for instance, we do have a picture of the landscape. The point is that such physical items are used as will support the interpretation.

Third, even in a composition where the over-all intention is suggestive, elements of technical description may appear. For example, the writer may want to give some general information about an object or a class of objects. In his novel *Moby Dick*, Herman Melville is not primarily interested in writing a technical study of whaling and whaling ships, but we find in it such a description as the following, in which he is not trying to give us a vivid impression but to make us understand technically the characteristic structure of the tryworks of a whaler. So he uses a description which is objective and is essentially of type 1.

Besides her hoisted boats, an American whaler is outwardly distinguished by her try-works. She presents the curious anomaly of the most solid masonry joining with oak and hemp in constituting the completed ship. It is as if from the open field a brick-kiln were transported to her planks.

The try-works are planted between the foremast and mainmast, the most roomy part of the deck. The timbers beneath are of a peculiar strength, fitted to sustain the weight of an almost solid mass of brick and mortar, some ten feet by eight square, and five in height. The foundation does not penetrate the deck, but the masonry is firmly secured to the surface by ponderous knees of iron bracing it on all sides, and screwing it down to the timbers. On the flanks it is cased with wood, and at top completely covered by a large, sloping, battened hatchway. Removing this hatch we expose the great try-pots, two in number, and each of several barrels' capacity. When not in use, they are kept remarkably clean. Sometimes they are polished with soapstone and sand, till they shine within like silver punch-bowls.—HERMAN MELVILLE: *Moby Dick,* Chap. 46.

Another use of technical description in a composition where the over-all intention is suggestive may appear when the writer wants the reader to take a cool, detached, almost scientific attitude toward what is being presented. For example, *Gulliver's Travels* is a fantastic narrative, a set of absolutely impossible events, but the fact that Swift adopts an unemotional attitude, that he makes his description technical, tends to lead the reader to accept the fantasy. The reader, of course, knows that the events are not true, that no such creatures as the Lilliputians ever existed, but he is willing to accept the illusion.

With these reservations, our scheme of the relation of the technical-suggestive distinction to the objective-subjective distinction may be useful. What we must remember is that such distinctions and relations are not always mathematically clear-cut, that the mind may carry more than one interest at a time. And this idea may lead us to a more general consideration of the uses of technical and suggestive description.

## THE USES OF TECHNICAL AND SUGGESTIVE DESCRIPTION

We cannot say that either type of description is better than the other. Each has its uses, and at one time we find need for one and at another time the need for the other. In one department of our living we are concerned with information about the world; in another department, with the direct experience of the world; and the two types of description may be said to correspond to those two kinds of interest, to two kinds of motivation. The advertisement of the Cape Cod cottage is concerned with information about the object, the letter of the buyer, with her direct experience of the cottage and her feelings about it.

We have already referred to this distinction (p. 45), but we may return to it here in considering the distinction between the two kinds of description and remember that scientists appeal to our interest in information about the world and in explanation of the world, and that artists (of all kinds, painters, poets, novelists, musicians, and so forth) appeal to our interest in direct experience of the world. This means that we find technical description characteristically in scientific writing and suggestive description characteristically in the work of literary artists, poets or essayists or fiction writers. For instance, the geographers, describing the West Indies, are writing as scientists, and Melville, describing the Encantadas, is writing as an artist.

Most of us are neither scientists nor artists and never shall be, but we all have a little of the scientist and a little of the artist in us. We want to know about the world and we want to extend our experience of the world. At the same time, these two kinds of interest lead us, in so far as we become well-developed human beings, to the use of the two kinds of description. In so far as we are scientists we find a use for technical description, and in so far as we are artists we find a use for suggestive description.

All of this does not mean that we find technical description only in scientific works or suggestive description only in artistic works. Technical description may occur in a letter, an essay, a guidebook, a history, an advertisement—wherever and whenever the impulse appears to give information about the qualities of an object. By the same token, suggestive description may occur in any piece of writing which embodies the impulse for immediacy and vividness. Sometimes, as we have said, both types may appear in the same work, whether its prevailing temper is scientific or artistic.

## APPLICATIONS

**I.** Turn to the examples of description at the end of the chapter "Description" (pp. 256 ff.), and locate those which are technical. In each instance, explain your choice.

**II.** Write a technical description (about 300 words) on some particular subject with which you are acquainted, for example a farm, a building, a city block, a boat, a golf course, a business establishment, or a race track. In this theme you will indicate what serves to individualize your subject from other examples of the type to which it belongs. That is, you are not writing a piece of generalized description.

## EXPOSITORY NARRATION

As we can make a distinction between expository description and ordinary description we can make one between EXPOSITORY NARRATION and ordinary narration. Ordinary narration, as we shall see when we come to discuss it as a basic kind of discourse, is concerned with presenting an action. It aims to give the sense of the event as experienced, and it involves an appeal to the imagination. But narration may be employed merely to give information, to enlarge the understanding. If we give directions as to how to build a boat or make a cake, we are treating a sequence of events in time, and we are forced to use a form of narration. If we tell how radar works, we are again using a kind of narration. An instructor in military history lecturing on the First Battle of the Marne in World War I is concerned to make his class understand the stages of the event and the problems of tactics, but is not necessarily concerned to bring the event into the imagination of his audience. So he, too, is using expository narration.

Expository narration, like expository description, may take a generalized form. The lecturer on the First Battle of the Marne is not using generalized narration, for he is dealing with an individual event, but if he were to give instructions as to the proper method of executing a certain maneuver, he would be using generalized narration, for he would be concerned with a type of event, not with a particular event. So if we undertake to tell how a bill becomes a law or to give an account of fraternity rushing day, we should be using generalized narration. We would be concerned with a type of event.

## APPLICATIONS

Write a theme of approximately 300 words using the method of expository narration. The following list may suggest a subject.

| | |
|---|---|
| The Curing of Tobacco | A Chemical Experiment |
| Assault from the Sea | Cooking: A Science not an Art |
| The Production Line | Registration Day |
| Using a Library | A Charity Drive |
| Pigeon Raising | How the News Story Gets on |
| How Wheat is Marketed | the Front Page |

## ILLUSTRATION

Generalized description, as we have seen, is concerned with the qualities of a type, class, or group. ILLUSTRATION also aims to explain a type, class, or group, but it does so by presenting an example. It explains the general by presenting the particular.

Here is an example (and by our own phrase, "here is an example," we announce that we are here about to use the method of illustration) of the explanation of a class by presenting one member of it, a "Handsome Sailor":

In the time before steamships, or then more frequently than now, a stroller along the docks of any considerable seaport would occasionally have his attention arrested by a group of bronzed marines, man-of-war's men or merchant sailors in holiday attire ashore on liberty. In certain instances they would flank, or, like a bodyguard, quite surround some superior figure of their own class, moving along with them like Aldebaran among the lesser lights of his constellation. The signal object was the "Handsome Sailor," of the less prosaic time alike of the military and merchant navies. With no perceptible trace of the vainglorious about him, rather with the off-hand unaffectedness of natural regality, he seemed to accept the spontaneous homage of his shipmates. A somewhat remarkable instance recurs to me. In Liverpool, now half a century ago, I saw under the shadow of the great dingy street-wall of Prince's Dock (an obstruction long since removed) a common sailor, so intensely black that he must needs have been a native African of the unadulterate blood of Ham. A symmetric figure much above the average height. The two ends of a gay silk handkerchief thrown loose about the neck danced upon the displayed ebony of his chest; in his ears were big hoops of gold, and a Scotch Highland bonnet with a tartan band set off his shapely head.

It was a hot noon in July; and his face, lustrous with perspiration, beamed with barbaric good-humor. In jovial sallies right and left, his white teeth flashing into view, he rollicked along, the center of a company of his shipmates. . . . At each spontaneous tribute rendered by the wayfarers to this black pagod of a fellow—the tribute of a pause and stare, and less frequent an exclamation—the motley retinue showed that they took that sort of pride in the evoker of it which the Assyrian priests doubtless showed for their grand sculptured Bull when the faithful prostrated themselves.—HERMAN MELVILLE: *Billy Budd*, Chap. 1.

In the following parable told by Jesus we find a general idea illustrated by a particular instance:

And he began again to teach by the seaside: and there was gathered unto him a great multitude, so that he entered into a ship, and sat in the sea; and the whole multitude was by the sea on the land.

And he taught them many things by parables, and said unto them in his doctrine,

Hearken; Behold, there went out a sower to sow:

And it came to pass, as he sowed, some fell by the wayside, and the fowls of the air came and devoured it up.

And some fell on stony ground, where it had not much earth; and immediately it sprang up, because it had no depth of earth:

But when the sun was up, it was scorched; and because it had no root, it withered away.

And some fell among thorns, and the thorns grew up, and choked it, and it yielded no fruit.

And other fell on good ground, and did yield fruit that sprang up and increased; and brought forth, some thirty, some sixty, and some an hundred.

And he said unto them, He that hath ears to hear, let him hear.

And when he was alone, they that were about him with the twelve asked of him the parable.

And he said unto them, Unto you it is given to know the mystery of

ILLUSTRATION 63

the kingdom of God: but unto them that are without, all *these* things are done in parables:

That seeing they may see, and not perceive; and hearing they may hear, and not understand; lest at any time they should be converted, and *their* sins should be forgiven them.

And he said unto them, Know ye not this parable? and how then will ye know all parables?

The sower soweth the word.

And these are they by the wayside, where the word is sown; but when they have heard, Satan cometh immediately, and taketh away the word that was sown in their hearts.

And these are they likewise which are sown on stony ground; who, when they have heard the word, immediately receive it with gladness;

And have no root in themselves, and so endure for a time: afterward, when affliction or persecution ariseth for the word's sake, immediately they are offended.

And these are they which are sown among thorns; such as hear the word,

And the cares of this world, and the deceitfulness of riches, and the lusts of other things entering in, choke the word, and it becometh unfruitful.

And these are they which are sown on good ground; such as hear the word, and receive *it,* and bring forth fruit, some thirty-fold, some sixty, and some an hundred.—Mark 4:1-20.

The same method of giving the particular instance to explain the general idea appears here:

A good neighbor, as the term was understood in the days when as a little girl I lived on a farm in Southern Michigan, meant all that nowadays is combined in corner store, telephone, daily newspaper, and radio. But your neighbor was also your conscience. You had to behave yourself on account of what the neighbors would think.

A good neighbor knew everything there was to know about you—and liked you anyway. He never let you down—as long as you deserved his good opinion. Even when you failed in that, if you were in trouble he would come to your rescue. If one of the family was taken sick in the night, you ran over to the neighbors' to get someone to sit up until the doctor arrived. Only instead of sending for the doctor, you went for him. Or one of the neighbors did.

The Bouldrys were that kind of neighbors. Lem Bouldry was a good farmer and a good provider. Mis' Bouldry kept a hired girl and Lem had two men the year round. They even had a piano, while the most the other neighbors boasted was an organ or a melodeon. Mis' Bouldry changed her dress every afternoon (my mother did too; she said she thought more of herself when she did), and they kept the front yard mowed.

But the Covells were just the opposite—the most shiftless family the Lord ever let set foot on land. How they got along my father said he didn't know, unless it was by the grace of God. Covell himself was ten years younger than my father, yet everybody called him "Old Covell." His face and hands were like sole leather and if his hair had ever been washed, it was only when he got caught in a rainstorm. Father said Old Covell would borrow the shirt off your back, then bring it around to have it mended; Mother said, well, one thing certain, he wouldn't bring it around to be washed.

Yet the time Mis' Covell almost died with her last baby—and the baby did die—Mis' Bouldry took care of her; took care of the rest of the children too—four of them. She stayed right there in the Covell house, just going home to catch a little sleep now and then. She had to do that, for there wasn't so much as an extra sheet in the house, much less an extra bed. And Mis' Bouldry wasn't afraid to use her hands even if she did keep a hired girl—she did all the Covells' washing herself.

But even Old Covell, despite his shiftlessness, was a good neighbor in one way: he was a master hand at laying out the dead. Of course, he wasn't worth a cent to sit up with the sick, for if it was Summer he'd go outside to smoke his pipe and sleep; and if it was Winter he'd go into the kitchen and stick his feet in the oven to warm them and go to sleep there. But a dead man seemed to rouse some kind of pride and responsibility in him. There was no real undertaker nearer than ten miles, and often the roads were impassable. Folks sent for my mother when a child or woman died, but Old Covell handled all the men. Though he never wore a necktie himself, he kept on hand a supply of celluloid collars and little black bow ties for the dead. When he had a body to lay out, he'd call for the deceased's best pants and object strenuously if he found a hole in the socks. Next, he'd polish the boots and put on a white shirt, and fasten one of his black ties to the collar button. All in all, he would do a masterly job.

Of course, nobody paid Old Covell for this. Nobody ever thought of paying for just being neighborly. If anybody had ever offered to, they'd have been snubbed for fair. It was just the way everybody did in those half-forgotten times.—DELLA T. LUTES: "Are Neighbors Necessary?" [4]

[4] From "Are Neighbors Necessary?" by Della T. Lutes. Reprinted by permission of the *American Mercury* and Mrs. Cecily I. Dodd.

ILLUSTRATION 65

It is clear that in the excerpt from Melville description is used, in the parable narration is used, and in the essay on neighborliness both description and narration are used. But here we must observe that the description is not, strictly speaking, expository description. Taken in itself, it is suggestive description. It is used, however, for an expository purpose, to illustrate. The same situation prevails in regard to the narration. The parable, for instance, is an example of ordinary narration, and is not, in itself, expository narration. But it is used here for an expository purpose. In each of these instances, an expository intention dominates and gives unity to the composition.

## APPLICATIONS

Write a theme of some 300 words using the method of illustration. If none of the following topics interests you, take a subject of your own. You must remember, however, that your purpose is expository. Your primary intention is to indicate the relation between the particular instance you present and the class or idea of which it is an example. You must keep in mind the qualities which make the particular instance a good representative of its kind and must make those clear to the reader. You might even organize your theme by giving a generalized description of your subject, say a good officer, and then presenting an example. Or you might present your example, a certain individual officer, and indicate in the course of your presentation the general qualities of the type embodied in the individual.

What Makes a Good Officer?      Cowardice
True Courtesy                  A Typical Ranch
The Fraternity Man             Laziness Sometimes Pays
Family Happiness               Hope Springs Eternal
The Well-Rounded Man           Citizenship

## COMPARISON AND CONTRAST

In COMPARISON, as a method of exposition, we clarify a subject by indicating similarities between two or more things; in CONTRAST, by indicating differences. We constantly and instinctively use comparison and contrast, but they are not always used for expository purposes. For example, the poet making a comparison in a poem, or a painter making a contrast of two forms in planning the composition of a picture, may not be doing so for an expository purpose. The poet or the painter is acting with an appreciative or artistic motivation (see p. 35), as contrasted with an expository or scientific one, and all of us, even though we may not write poems or paint pictures, sometimes make comparisons and contrasts out of a similar motivation to gain vividness, to appeal to the imagination (see p. 401).

We also use comparison constantly and instinctively for expository purposes. A child asks, "What is a zebra?" And we are apt to reply, "Oh, a zebra—it's an animal sort of like a mule, but it's not as big as a mule. And it has stripes like a tiger, black and white stripes all over. But you remember that a tiger's stripes are black and orange." Here we have used both comparison and contrast. We have compared the shape of the zebra to that of the mule, but have contrasted the two animals in size. And we have compared the stripes of the zebra to the stripes of a tiger, but have contrasted them in color. If the child knows what mules and tigers are like, he now has a pretty good idea of a zebra. But our instinctive application of comparison and contrast can be made more useful if we are systematic.

To be systematic means, for one thing, to understand the purpose for which a comparison or contrast is made. We may distinguish three types of purpose. In the first place our purpose may be to inform the reader about one item, and we may do so by relating it to another item with which the reader is already familiar. Second, we may wish to inform the reader about both items involved, and do so by comparing or contrasting them in relation to some general principle with which the reader is already familiar and which would apply to both. For example, if we are reviewing two novels we may compare and contrast them by reference to what we assume our reader knows about the principles of fiction. Third, we may compare and contrast items with which the reader is already familiar for the purpose of informing him about some general principle or idea. For example, a student of political science, already well acquainted with the governmental systems of the United States and England, might undertake to compare and contrast those systems for the purpose of understanding, or of explaining to others, the nature of democratic government.

To be systematic means, also, to understand the area of interest involved in a comparison or contrast. Mere differences and mere similarities are not very instructive. To compare and contrast a hawk and a handsaw would not be very profitable. No common area of interest brings them together and makes them worth treating. A zoologist might, however, profitably compare a hawk and a wren, for his interest in them as living creatures would embrace both. Or a student of the laws of flight might compare a hawk and an airplane.

## WAYS OF ORGANIZING MATERIAL

When we come to apply comparison and contrast in extended form we find that there are two general ways of organizing the material. First, we can fully present one item and then fully present the other. Second, we can present a part of one item and then a part of the other, until we have touched on all the parts relevant to our comparison or contrast.

Each of these methods of organization has its utility. The first method is, generally speaking, appropriate when the two items treated are relatively uncomplicated, or when the points of comparison and contrast are fairly broad and obvious. It is clear that in a very extended and complicated presentation the reader could not carry enough detail in his mind to be properly aware of all the points of comparison and contrast. When a great many details are involved the second method is more apt to be useful. It is possible, of course, to work out a sort of compromise. One can present the first of the items in full, and then in presenting the second refer the reader, point by point, to the earlier treatment for comparison or contrast.

Here is an example of the first type of organization in a student's theme:

My father died when I was a small child, and I do not even remember him. I was raised by my mother and my maternal grandfather, in whose house we lived until I came to college. My mother loved her father and I have no reason to think he did not love her, but they were so different that I was aware from the first of a conflict between them. Or, if it was not a direct conflict between them, it was a conflict between what they stood for. And both of them exerted a strong influence over me. Therefore, as I grow up, I think more and more about their contrasting personalities and values and try to detect in myself the traces of each of them. I do this because I am trying to understand myself.

My grandfather, whose name was Carruthers McKenzie, was of Scotch-Irish blood, and belonged to the Presbyterian Church. He looked like those pictures of pre-Civil War statesmen who had long, bony faces, sunken cheeks, and straggly beards, like John C. Calhoun, for instance. He was a man with an iron will if I ever saw one, and all of his way of life was one long discipline for himself and everybody about him. But it was a discipline chiefly for himself. He never spent a day in bed in his life until his last illness, and yet he was probably ill a good part of his life. I used to see him spit blood when I was a child. After he died—and he died of a cancer of the stomach—the doctor told us that he could not understand how any man could keep on his feet so long without giving in to the pain which he must have suffered before his collapse. There was discipline enough left over for my mother and me and the two Negroes who worked about the place. We had morning prayers and evening prayers. I had to read the Bible an hour a day and learn long passages by heart. My grandfather was a prosperous man, but I never had a nickel to spend which I had not earned, and his rates of payment for my chores were not generous. I was never allowed to speak in the presence of my elders unless I could show some great practical reason for it. From the time I was eight on, I had to study three hours in the afternoon and at least two hours at night, except for week ends. My grandfather never uttered a word of praise to me except now and then the statement, "You have done your duty." As one could guess, my grandfather never told jokes, was scrupulous about all kinds of obligations, never touched an alcoholic beverage or even soft drinks, and wore sober black, winter and summer.

My mother must have taken after her own mother, who was of South German parentage, and a Catholic by training. Her people had come to this country just before her birth. My mother's mother had given up her religion to marry my grandfather, and had taken on his way of life, but she died very young. My mother looked like her pictures. My mother was rather short in stature and had a rather full but graceful figure, the kind they call "partridge-y." She had round, pink cheeks and a complexion like a child's. She had blue eyes, very large. They always seemed to be laughing. My mother loved to laugh and joke, and spent a great deal of time in the kitchen with Sally, the Negro cook. They laughed and talked together a great deal. My mother was a good mother, as the phrase goes; she loved me and she was careful of all my wants. But she also liked idleness. She would sit on the veranda half the afternoon and look across the yard, just rocking in her chair and enjoying the sunshine.

And she went to bridge parties and even took an occasional glass of wine or, as I imagine, a highball.

She was made for a good time and noise and people, and when my grandfather was out of the house, she used to romp and play with me or take me on long walks in the country back of our place. I am now sure that she would have got married very soon if she had not felt it best to keep me in my grandfather's house and with the advantages which his prosperity would give me. For after I grew up, when I was eighteen and went off to college, she got married.

She married the kind of man you would expect her to pick. He was big and strong-looking, with a heavy black mustache with a little gray in it. He smokes cigars and he likes fine whisky. He has a Packard agency in the city and he keeps a little plane out at the airport. He loves sports and a good time. My mother has married exactly the man for her, I think, and I am enough like my mother to think he is fine, too. But as I look back on my grandfather—he died three years ago when I was seventeen—I have a great admiration for him and a sneaking affection.

What follows is an example of the mixed type of organization. We can see how in the second paragraph the contrasting characteristics leads even to the use of balanced sentences treating a single point of contrast.

We have divided men into Red-bloods and Mollycoddles. "A Red-blood man" is a phrase which explains itself; "Mollycoddle" is its opposite. We have adopted it from a famous speech by Mr. Roosevelt,[5] and redeemed it—perverted it, if you will—to other uses. A few examples will make the notion clear. Shakespeare's Henry V is a typical Red-blood; so was Bismarck; so was Palmerston; so is almost any business man. On the other hand, typical Mollycoddles were Socrates, Voltaire, and Shelley. The terms, you will observe, are comprehensive and the types very broad. Generally speaking, men of action are Red-bloods. Not but what the Mollycoddles may act, and act efficiently. But, if so, he acts from principle, not from the instinct for action. The Red-blood, on the other hand, acts as the stone falls, and does indiscriminately anything that comes to hand. It is thus that he carries on the business of the world. He steps without reflection into the first place offered him and goes to work like a machine. The ideals and standards of his family, his class, his city, his country, his age, he swallows as naturally as he swallows food and drink. He is therefore always "in the swim"; and he

[5] Theodore Roosevelt.

is bound to "arrive," because he has set before him the attainable. You will find him everywhere in all the prominent positions. In a military age he is a soldier, in a commercial age a business man. He hates his enemies, and he may love his friends; but he does not require friends to love. A wife and children he does require, for the instinct to propagate the race is as strong in him as all other instincts. His domestic life, however, is not always happy; for he can seldom understand his wife. This is part of his general incapacity to understand any point of view but his own. He is incapable of an idea and contemptuous of a principle. He is the Samson, the blind force, dearest to Nature of her children. He neither looks back nor looks ahead. He lives in present action. And when he can no longer act, he loses his reasons for existence. The Red-blood is happiest if he dies in the prime of life; otherwise, he may easily end with suicide. For he has no inner life; and when the outer life fails, he can only fail with it. The instinct that animated him being dead, he dies too. Nature, who has blown through him, blows elsewhere. His stops are dumb; he is dead wood on the shore.

The Mollycoddle, on the other hand, is all inner life. He may indeed act, as I said, but he acts, so to speak, by accident; just as the Red-blood may reflect, but reflects by accident. The Mollycoddle in action is the Crank; it is he who accomplishes reforms; who abolished slavery, for example, and revolutionized prisons and lunatic asylums. Still, primarily, the Mollycoddle is a critic, not a man of action. He challenges all standards and all facts. If an institution is established, that is a reason why he will not accept it; if an idea is current, that is a reason why he should repudiate it. He questions everything, including life and the universe. And for that reason Nature hates him. On the Red-blood she heaps her favors; she gives him a good digestion, a clear complexion, and sound nerves. But to the Mollycoddle she apportions dyspepsia and black bile. In the universe and in society the Mollycoddle is "out of it" as inevitably as the Red-blood is "in it." At school, he is a "smug" or a "swat," while the Red-blood is captain of the Eleven. At college, he is an "intellectual," while the Red-blood is in the "best set." In the world, he courts failure while the Red-blood achieves success. The Red-blood sees nothing; but the Mollycoddle sees through everything. The Red-blood joins societies; the Mollycoddle is a non-joiner. Individualist of individualists, he can only stand alone, while the Red-blood requires the support of a crowd. The Mollycoddle engenders ideas, and the Red-blood exploits them. The Mollycoddle discovers and the Red-blood invents. The whole structure of civilization rests on foundations laid by Mollycoddles; but all the building is done by Red-bloods. The Red-blood despises the Mollycoddle, but, in the long run, he does what the Mollycoddle tells him. The Mollycoddle also despises the Red-blood, but he cannot do without him. Each thinks he is master of the other, and, in a sense, each is right. In his lifetime the Mollycoddle may be the slave of the Red-blood; but after his death, he is his master, though the Red-blood may know it not.

Nations, like men, may be classified roughly as Red-blood and Mollycoddle. To the latter class belong clearly the ancient Greeks, the Italians, the French and probably the Russians; to the former the Romans, the Germans, and the English. But the Red-blood nation *par excellence* is the American; so that in comparison with them, Europe as a whole might almost be called Mollycoddle. This characteristic of Americans is reflected in the predominant physical type—the great jaw and chin, the huge teeth, the predatory mouth; in their speech, where beauty and distinction are sacrificed to force; in their need to live and feel and act in masses. To be born a Mollycoddle in America is to be born to a hard fate. You must either emigrate or succumb. This, at least hitherto, has been the alternative practiced. Whether a Mollycoddle will ever be produced strong enough to breathe the American atmosphere and live, is a crucial question for the future. It is the question whether America will ever be civilized. For civilization, you will have perceived, depends on a just balance of Red-bloods and Mollycoddles. Without the Red-blood there would be no life at all, no stuff, so to speak, for the Mollycoddle to work upon; without the Mollycoddle, the stuff would remain shapeless and chaotic. The Red-blood is the matter, the Mollycoddle the form; the Red-blood the dough, the Mollycoddle the yeast. On these two poles turns the orb of human society. And if, at this point, you choose to say that the poles are points and have no dimensions, that strictly neither the Mollycoddle nor the Red-blood exist, and that real men contain elements of both mixed in different proportions, I have no quarrel with you except such as one has with the man who states the obvious. I am satisfied to have distinguished the ideal extremes between which the Actual vibrates. The detailed application of the conception I must leave to more patient researchers.—G. LOWES DICKINSON: "Red-bloods and Mollycoddles," *Appearances*.[6]

## APPLICATIONS

1. Work out in outline form the points of comparison or contrast for two or three of the following topics:
1. A country childhood and a city childhood
2. Military life and civilian life
3. Education in high school and education in college

[6] From: *Appearances* by G. Lowes Dickinson. Copyright 1914 by G. Lowes Dickinson. Reprinted by permission of Doubleday & Company, Inc.

4. George Washington and Abraham Lincoln
5. Catholicism and Protestantism
6. College football and professional football
7. The value of a liberal education and the value of a scientific education
8. Life on a farm and life on a ranch
9. Two novels
10. Two characters whom you know
11. The construction of land-based fighter planes and the construction of carrier-based fighter planes
12. Poor relations and rich relations
13. The American temperament and some other national temperament
14. General Eisenhower and General Montgomery

II. Write a theme of about 500 words on one of the above topics.

## CLASSIFICATION AND DIVISION

CLASSIFICATION and DIVISION are ways of thinking in terms of a system of classes.

By a class we mean a group whose members have significant characteristics in common. What constitutes a significant characteristic may vary according to the interest involved. For example, a maker of cosmetics may think of women in groups determined by complexion, and the secretary of a Y.W.C.A. may think in groups determined by religious affiliations. What is significant for the maker of cosmetics is not significant for the Y.W.C.A. secretary. Or, to take another example, the registrar of a college may group students according to grades, and the gymnasium instructor according to athletic ability. The registrar and the gymnasium instructor have different interests in classifying the same body of students.

By a system we mean a set of classes ranging from the most inclusive down through the less inclusive. Let us set up a simple example of such a system:

(I)

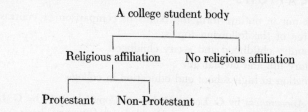

Here the group *student body* is the most inclusive class. Under it we find classes less and less inclusive.

What is the difference between classification and division? Our most useful way of thinking about this question is to regard them as opposite movements, one down and one up, within a system. In division we start with a class and divide it into subclasses by reference to whatever characteristic is dictated by the interest prompting the division. If, however, we start with the individuals, arrange them in groups and then relate those groups to a more inclusive group or a set of more inclusive groups, we have performed a classification.

Suppose we wish to classify the books we own. We may begin by sorting out the individual items into classes, let us say (1) short stories, (2) novels, (3) lyric poetry, (4) narrative poetry, (5) prose drama, (6) verse drama, (7) critical essays, (8) informal essays, (9) ethics, (10) logic, (11) political history, (12) economic history, (13) social history, (14) literary history, (15) geometry, (16) algebra. We see immediately that some of the classes are related to each other in terms of superior classes—more inclusive classes. For instance, we see that short stories and novels belong in a class together, the class of fiction, and we see that there are several kinds of history represented. Next, we observe that several classes, even more inclusive, are involved—literature, for example. So we can set up a scheme which covers this particular collection of books.

(II)

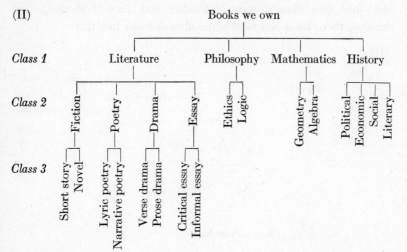

This scheme indicates the classification of the books in this particular collection. But we understand that we do not have examples of all kinds of books. For example, in class 1 we do not have science or theology. In class 2 under philosophy we have only ethics and logic, and under mathematics, only geometry and algebra. In class 3 under poetry, we have only lyric and narrative poetry, and under the essay, only critical and informal essays. So we find many classes blank in our particular scheme, classes which would not be blank in the scheme for the classification of books for a great library having copies of all kinds of books. The method of classification for our little collection and for the great library would be, however, the same.

The scheme which we have set up by classifying the books in our collection would indicate equally well a division, for the difference is not in the kind of scheme we arrive at but in the way we go about setting up the scheme.

In general, there are two kinds of schemes. Scheme I above is an example of the SIMPLE and scheme II an example of the COMPLEX.

In the simple scheme we recognize, at any stage, only two classes, which we can indicate by X and Non-X, for example, the class *Protestant* and the class *Non-Protestant*. No matter how far we carry such a scheme, we use this same method. For example, under the class *Protestant*, we would not put the various denominations, but only two classes, say *Methodist* and *Non-Methodist*. The dummy, then, for a simple scheme always looks like this:

(III)

$$X$$

$$X_1 \quad \text{Non-}X_1$$

$$X_2 \quad \text{Non-}X_2$$

$$X_3 \quad \text{Non-}X_3$$

$$X_4 \quad \text{Non-}X_4$$

In the complex scheme we recognize individually at each stage all the classes available. For example, in scheme II we indicate at the first stage four classes (*literature, philosophy, mathematics, history*) and would recognize other such general groups if they were represented in the collection with which we are dealing. At the second stage we indicate various groups under each head. For example, under the head of *literature* we indicate four classes (*fiction, poetry, drama, essay*). That is, we are prepared to indicate as many classes at any stage as we can distinguish on the basis of whatever interest is determining the process. The dummy for a complex scheme, then, varies from instance to instance, but is of this general type:

(IV)

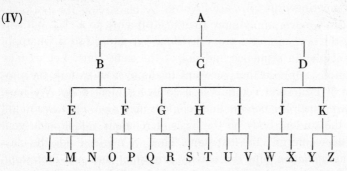

In dealing with such schemes it is customary to use the two terms GENUS (plural: GENERA) and SPECIES (plural: SPECIES) to indicate the superior and the inferior class in a system. The upper class is called the genus and each subclass immediately under it is called a species. For example, in the dummy above, D is a species of the genus A, and G is a species of the genus C. Or to return to scheme II the class *fiction* is a species of the genus *literature,* and the class *lyric poetry* is a species of the genus *poetry.* But we must remember that what is regarded as a species at one stage is regarded at the next stage below as a genus. The class *fiction,* for example, is regarded as a species of the genus *literature,* but as the genus including the species *short story* and the species *novel.* A class may be regarded as species or genus, according to whether we look above or below it.

To be useful a scheme must fulfill certain requirements:

I. There can be only one principle of division applied at each stage.

II. The subclass under any class must exhaust that class.

Rule I: We can best understand what is at stake here by looking at an extreme and ridiculous instance. Suppose we try to divide a student body into tall and short, men and women. Here two principles of division would be employed at the same time, namely, height and sex. But obviously these two principles cannot be applied at the same time, for they are at cross purposes with each other. They result in what is called a CROSS DIVISION. A member of the student body would necessarily be either a man or a woman, and at the same time would be classifiable with reference to height. Two competing principles are involved.

But can we ever apply more than one principle to a class without getting the nonsense of a cross division? We can do so if we apply the principles in sequence and not at the same time. Let us take an example. Suppose that we want to discover or exhibit the proportion of Protestant veterans in a college student body. We have here two principles, *veteran* and *religious affiliation*. First, we might divide the student body on the basis of religious affiliation in general. This would give the first stage. Then we might divide the class *religious affiliation* into the classes *Protestant* and *non-Protestant*. Thus, at the second stage, we have isolated the class *Protestant*, the particular religious affiliation we are concerned with. At this point we can introduce our second principle. So now we divide the class *Protestant* into the classes *veteran* and *nonveteran* for a third stage. So we get the following scheme:

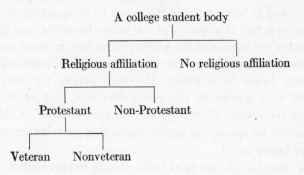

The thing to remember is to avoid applying the second principle until the first has been worked out to its conclusion. We do not apply the principle *veteran* until we have worked out the principle *religious affiliation* as far as our interest dictates. It may be said, of course, that when we apply the second principle *veteran* we are really beginning a new system. And in one sense this is true. But, in any case, the over-all scheme gives us exactly what we need.

Rule II: To restate this rule, the sum of the members of the sub-classes under a class must equal the sum of the members of the class. In other words, we must account in the subclasses for all members of the class. For example, dividing a student body into Methodists, Baptists, Jews, and Catholics does not account for all members of the student body if there are also in it some atheists and Presbyterians. This problem of accounting for all the members of a group does not arise in a simple system as indicated by scheme III. At any stage we have only X and Non-X as subgroups, and the formula necessarily takes all members into account. The problem does arise in a complex system. If in scheme II we had forgotten to include the class *philosophy* we would not have accounted for all the books in the collection being classified. And of course scheme II as it now stands would be shockingly defective in this regard if it were regarded as applying to the books of a large general library, which would have dozens of classes of books not accounted for here.

In an essay or some other type of discussion we may find a very elaborate system running through several stages, but ordinarily there are only one or two stages. The following selection is a classification of the kinds of thinking.

We do not think enough about thinking, and much of our confusion is the result of current illusions in regard to it. Let us forget for the moment any impressions we may have derived from the philosophers, and see what seems to happen in ourselves. The first thing that we notice is that our thought moves with such incredible rapidity that it is almost impossible to arrest any specimen of it long enough to have a look at it. When we are offered a penny for our thoughts we always find that we have recently had so many things in mind that we can easily make a selection which will not compromise us too nakedly. On inspection we shall find that even if we are not downright ashamed of a great part of our spontaneous thinking it is far too intimate, personal, ignoble, or trivial to permit us to reveal more than a small part of it. I believe this must be true of everyone. We do not, of course, know what goes on in other people's heads. They tell us very little and we tell them very little. The spigot of speech, rarely fully opened, could never emit more than driblets of the ever renewed hogshead of thought—*noch grösser wie's Heidelberger Fass* [even larger than the Heidelberg vat]. We find it hard to believe that other people's thoughts are as silly as our own, but they probably are.

We all appear to ourselves to be thinking all the time during our waking hours, and most of us are aware that we go on thinking while we are asleep, even more foolishly than when awake. When uninterrupted by some practical issue we are engaged in what is now known as a *reverie*. This is our spontaneous and favorite kind of thinking. We allow our ideas to take their own course and this course is determined by our hopes and fears, our spontaneous desires, their fulfillment or frustration; by our likes and dislikes, our loves and hates and resentments. There is nothing else anything like so interesting to ourselves as ourselves. All thought that is not more or less laboriously controlled and directed will inevitably circle about the beloved Ego. It is amusing and pathetic to observe this tendency in ourselves and in others. We learn politely and generously to overlook this truth, but if we dare to think of it, it blazes forth like the noontide sun.

The reverie or "free association of ideas" has of late become the subject of scientific research. While investigators are not yet agreed on the results, or at least on the proper interpretation to be given to them, there can be no doubt that our reveries form the chief index to our fundamental character. They are a reflection of our nature as modified by often hidden and forgotten experiences. We need not go into the matter further here, for it is only necessary to observe that the reverie is at all times a potent and in many cases an omnipotent rival to every other kind of thinking. It doubtless influences all our speculations in its persistent tendency to self-magnification and self-justification, which are its chief preoccupations, but it is the last thing to make directly or indirectly for honest increase of knowledge. Philosophers usually talk as if such thinking did not exist or were in some way negligible. This is what makes their speculations so unreal and often worthless.

The reverie, as any of us can see for himself, is frequently broken and interrupted by the necessity of a second kind of thinking. We have to made practical decisions. Shall we write a letter or no? Shall we take the subway or a bus? Shall we have dinner at seven or half-past? Shall we buy U. S. Rubber or a Liberty Bond? Decisions are easily distinguishable from the free flow of reverie. Sometimes they demand a good deal of careful pondering and the recollection of pertinent facts; often, however, they are made impulsively. They are a more difficult and laborious thing than the reverie, and we resent having to "make up our mind" when we are tired, or absorbed in a congenial reverie. Weighing a decision, it should be noted, does not necessarily add anything to our knowledge, although we may, of course, seek further information before making it.

A third kind of thinking is stimulated when anyone questions our belief and opinions. We sometimes find ourselves changing our minds without any resistance or heavy emotion, but if we are told that we are wrong we resent the imputation and harden our hearts. We are incredibly heedless in the formation of our beliefs, but find ourselves filled with an illicit passion for them when anyone proposes to rob us of their companionship. It is obviously not the ideas themselves that are dear to us, but our self-esteem, which is threatened. We are by nature stubbornly pledged to defend our own from attack, whether it be our person, our family, our property, or our opinion. A United States Senator once remarked to a friend of mine that God Almighty could not make him change his mind on our Latin-American policy. We may surrender, but rarely confess ourselves vanquished. In the intellectual world at least peace is without victory.

Few of us take the pains to study the origin of our cherished convictions; indeed, we have a natural repugnance to so doing. We like to continue to believe what we have been accustomed to accept as true, and the resentment aroused when doubt is cast upon any of our assumptions leads us to seek every manner of excuse for clinging to them. *The result is that most of our so-called reasoning consists in finding arguments for going on believing as we already do.*

I remember years ago attending a public dinner to which the Governor of the state was bidden. The chairman explained that His Excellency could not be present for certain "good" reasons; what the "real" reasons were the presiding officer said he would leave us to conjecture. This distinction between "good" and "real" reasons is one of the most clarifying and essential in the whole realm of thought. We can readily give what seem to us "good" reasons for being a Catholic or a Mason, a Republican or a Democrat, an adherent or opponent of the League of Nations. But the "real" reasons are usually on quite a different plane. Of course the importance of this distinction is popularly, if somewhat obscurely, recognized. The Baptist missionary is ready enough to see that the Buddhist is not such because his doctrines would bear careful inspection, but because he happened to be born in a Buddhist family in Tokio.

But it would be treason to his faith to acknowledge that his own partiality for certain doctrines is due to the fact that his mother was a member of the First Baptist Church of Oak Ridge. A savage can give all sorts of reasons for his belief that it is dangerous to step on a man's shadow, and a newspaper editor can advance plenty of arguments against the Bolsheviki. But neither of them may realize why he happens to be defending his particular opinion.

The "real" reasons for our beliefs are concealed from ourselves as well as from others. As we grow up we simply adopt the ideas presented to us in regard to such matters as religion, family relations, property, business, our country, and the state. We unconsciously absorb them from our environment. They are persistently whispered in our ear by the group in which we happen to live. Moreover, as Mr. Trotter has pointed out, these judgments, being the product of suggestion and not of reasoning, have the quality of perfect obviousness, so that to question them "is to the believer to carry skepticism to an insane degree, and will be met by contempt, disapproval, or condemnation, according to the nature of the belief in question. When, therefore, we find ourselves entertaining an opinion about the basis of which there is a quality of feeling which tells us that to inquire into it would be absurd, obviously unnecessary, unprofitable, undesirable, bad form, or wicked, we may know that that opinion is a non-rational one, and probably, therefore, founded upon inadequate evidence." [7]

Opinions, on the other hand, which are the result of experience or of honest reasoning do not have this quality of "primary certitude." I remember when as a youth I heard a group of businessmen discussing the question of the immortality of the soul, I was outraged by the sentiment of doubt expressed by one of the party. As I look back now I see that I had at the time no interest in the matter, and certainly no least argument to urge in favor of the belief in which I had been reared. But neither my personal indifference to the issue, nor the fact that I had previously given it no attention, served to prevent an angry resentment when I heard *my* ideas questioned.

This spontaneous and loyal support of our preconceptions—this process of finding "good" reasons to justify our routine beliefs—is known to modern psychologists as "rationalizing"—clearly only a new name for a very ancient thing. Our "good" reasons ordinarily have no value in promoting honest enlightenment, because, no matter how solemnly they may be marshaled, they are at bottom the result of personal preference or prejudice, and not of an honest desire to seek or accept new knowledge.

In our reveries we are frequently engaged in self-justification, for we

[7] *Instincts of the Herd*, p. 44.

cannot bear to think ourselves wrong, and yet have constant illustrations of our weaknesses and mistakes. So we spend much time finding fault with circumstances and the conduct of others, and shifting on to them with great ingenuity the onus of our own failures and disappointments. *Rationalizing is the self-exculpation which occurs when we feel ourselves, or our group, accused of misapprehension or error.*

The little word *my* is the most important one in all human affairs, and properly to reckon with it is the beginning of wisdom. It has the same force whether it is *my* dinner, *my* dog, and *my* house, or *my* faith, *my* country, and *my* God. We not only resent the imputation that our watch is wrong, or our car shabby, but that our conception of the canals of Mars, of the pronunciation of "Epictetus," of the medicinal value of salicine, or the date of Sargon I, are subject to revision.

Philosophers, scholars, and men of science exhibit a common sensitiveness in all decisions in which their *amour propre* is involved. Thousands of argumentative works have been written to vent a grudge. However stately their reasoning, it may be nothing but rationalizing, stimulated by the most commonplace of all motives. A history of philosophy and theology could be written in terms of grouches, wounded pride, and aversions, and it would be far more instructive than the usual treatments of these themes. Sometimes, under Providence, the lowly impulse of resentment leads to great achievements. Milton wrote his treatise on divorce as a result of his troubles with his seventeen-year-old wife, and when he was accused of being the leading spirit in a new sect, the Divorcers, he wrote his noble *Areopagitica* to prove his right to say what he thought fit, and incidentally to establish the advantage of a free press in the promotion of Truth.

All mankind, high and low, thinks in all the ways which have been described. The reverie goes on all the time not only in the mind of the mill hand and the Broadway flapper, but equally in weighty judges and godly bishops. It has gone on in all the philosophers, scientists, poets, and theologians that have ever lived. Aristotle's most abstruse speculations were doubtless tempered by highly irrelevant reflections. He is reported to have had very thin legs and small eyes, for which he doubtless had to find excuses, and he was wont to indulge in very conspicuous dress and rings and was accustomed to arrange his hair carefully.[8] Diogenes the Cynic exhibited the impudence of a touchy soul. His tub was his distinction. Tennyson in beginning his "Maud" could not forget his chagrin over losing his patrimony years before as the result of an unhappy investment in the Patent Decorative Carving Company. These facts are not recalled here as a gratuitous disparagement of the truly

[8] *Diogenes Laertius,* Book V.

great, but to insure a full realization of the tremendous competition which all really exacting thought has to face, even in the minds of the most highly endowed mortals.

And now the astonishing and perturbing suspicion emerges that perhaps almost all that had passed for social science, political economy, politics, and ethics in the past may be brushed aside by future generations as mainly rationalizing. John Dewey has already reached this conclusion in regard to philosophy.[9] Veblen [10] and other writers have revealed the various unperceived presuppositions of the traditional political economy, and now comes an Italian sociologist, Vilfredo Pareto, who, in his huge treatise on general sociology, devotes hundreds of pages to substantiating a similar thesis affecting all the social sciences.[11] This conclusion may be ranked by students of a hundred years hence as one of the several great discoveries of our age. It is by no means fully worked out, and it is so opposed to nature that it will be very slowly accepted by the great mass of those who consider themselves thoughtful. As a historical student I am personally fully reconciled to this newer view. Indeed, it seems to me inevitable that just as the various sciences of nature were, before the opening of the seventeenth century, largely masses of rationalizations to suit the religious sentiments of the period, so the social sciences have continued even to our own day to be rationalizations of uncritically accepted beliefs and customs.

*It will become apparent as we proceed that the fact that an idea is ancient and that it has been widely received is no argument in its favor, but should immediately suggest the necessity of carefully testing it as a probable instance of rationalization.*

This brings us to another kind of thought which can fairly easily be distinguished from the three kinds described above. It has not the usual qualities of the reverie, for it does not hover about our personal complacencies and humiliations. It is not made up of the homely decisions forced upon us by everyday needs, when we review our little stock of existing information, consult our conventional preferences and obligations, and make a choice of action. It is not the defense of our own cherished beliefs and prejudices just because they are our own—mere plausible

[9] *Reconstruction in Philosophy.*

[10] *The Place of Science in Modern Civilization.*

[11] *Traité de Sociologie Générale, passim.* The author's term *"derivations"* seems to be his precise way of expressing what we have called the "good" reasons, and his *"residus"* correspond to the "real" reasons. He well says, *"L'homme éprouve le besoin de raisonner, et en outre d'étendre une voile sur ses instincts et sur ses sentiments"*—hence, rationalization. (p. 788.) His aim is to reduce sociology to the "real" reasons. (p. 791.)

excuses for remaining of the same mind. On the contrary, it is that peculiar species of thought which leads us to *change* our mind.

It is this kind of thought that has raised man from his pristine, sub-savage ignorance and squalor to the degree of knowledge and comfort which he now possesses. On his capacity to continue and greatly extend this kind of thinking depends his chance of groping his way out of the plight in which the most highly civilized peoples of the world now find themselves. In the past this type of thinking has been called Reason. But so many misapprehensions have grown up around the word that some of us have become very suspicious of it. I suggest, therefore, that we substitute a recent name and speak of "creative thought" rather than of Reason. *For this kind of meditation begets knowledge, and knowledge is really creative inasmuch as it makes things look different from what they seemed before and may indeed work for their reconstruction.*

In certain moods some of us realize that we are observing things or making reflections with a seeming disregard of our personal preoccupations. We are not preening or defending ourselves; we are not faced by the necessity of any practical decision, nor are we apologizing for believing this or that. We are just wondering and looking and mayhap seeing what we never perceived before.

Curiosity is as clear and definite as any of our urges. We wonder what is in a sealed telegram or in a letter in which someone else is absorbed, or what is being said in the telephone booth or in low conversation. This inquisitiveness is vastly stimulated by jealousy, suspicion, or any hint that we ourselves are directly or indirectly involved. But there appears to be a fair amount of personal interest in other people's affairs even when they do not concern us except as a mystery to be unraveled or a tale to be told. The reports of a divorce suit will have "news value" for many weeks. They constitute a story, like a novel or play or moving picture. This is not an example of pure curiosity, however, since we readily identify ourselves with others, and their joys and despair then become our own.

We also take note of, or "observe," as Sherlock Holmes says, things which have nothing to do with our personal interests and make no personal appeal either direct or by way of sympathy. This is what Veblen so well calls "idle curiosity." And it is usually idle enough. Some of us when we face the line of people opposite us in a subway train impulsively consider them in detail and engage in rapid inferences and form theories in regard to them. On entering a room there are those who will perceive at a glance the degree of preciousness of the rugs, the character of the pictures, and the personality revealed by the books. But there are many, it would seem, who are so absorbed in their personal reverie or in some definite purpose that they have no bright-eyed energy for idle curiosity. The tendency to miscellaneous observation we come by honestly enough, for we note it in many of our animal relatives.

Veblen, however, uses the term "idle curiosity" somewhat ironically, as is his wont. It is idle only to those who fail to realize that it may be a very rare and indispensable thing from which almost all distinguished human achievement proceeds, since it may lead to systematic examination and seeking for things hitherto undiscovered. For research is but diligent search which enjoys the high flavor of primitive hunting. Occasionally and fitfully, idle curiosity thus leads to creative thought, which alters and broadens our own views and aspirations and may in turn, under highly favorable circumstances, affect the views and lives of others, even for generations to follow. An example or two will make this unique human process clear.

Galileo was a thoughtful youth and doubtless carried on a rich and varied reverie. He had artistic ability and might have turned out to be a musician or painter. When he had dwelt among the monks at Vallombrosa he had been tempted to lead the life of a religious. As a boy he busied himself with toy machines and he inherited a fondness for mathematics. All these facts are on record. We may safely assume also that, along with many other subjects of contemplation, the Pisan maidens found a vivid place in his thoughts.

One day when seventeen years old he wandered into the cathedral of his native town. In the midst of his reverie he looked up at the lamps hanging by long chains from the high ceiling of the church. Then something very difficult to explain occurred. He found himself no longer thinking of the building, worshipers, or the services; of his artistic or religious interests; of his reluctance to become a physician as his father wished. He forgot the question of a career and even the *graziosissime donne.* As he watched the swinging lamps he was suddenly wondering if mayhap their oscillations, whether long or short, did not occupy the same time. Then he tested this hypothesis by counting his pulse, for that was the only timepiece he had with him.

This observation, however remarkable in itself, was not enough to produce a really creative thought. Others may have noticed the same thing and yet nothing came of it. Most of our observations have no assignable results. Galileo may have seen that the warts on a peasant's face formed a perfect isosceles triangle, or he may have noticed with boyish glee that just as the officiating priest was uttering the solemn words, *Ecce agnus Dei,* a fly lit on the end of his nose. To be really creative, ideas have to be worked up and then "put over," so that they become a part of man's social heritage. The highly accurate pendulum clock was one of the later results of Galileo's discovery. He himself was led to reconsider and successfully to refute the old notions of falling bodies. It remained for Newton to prove that the moon was falling, and presumably all the heavenly bodies. This quite upset all the consecrated views of the heavens as managed by angelic engineers. The universality of the laws of gravitation stimulated the attempt to seek other and equally important natural laws and cast grave doubts on the miracles in which mankind had hitherto believed. In short, those who dared to include in their thought the discoveries of Galileo and his successors found themselves in a new earth surrounded by new heavens.

On the 28th of October, 1831, two hundred and fifty years after Galileo had noticed the isochronous vibrations of the lamps, creative thought and its currency had so far increased that Faraday was wondering what would happen if he mounted a disk of copper between the poles of a horseshoe magnet. As the disk revolved an electric current was produced. This would doubtless have seemed the idlest kind of experiment to the stanch businessmen of the time, who, it happened, were just then denouncing the child-labor bills in their anxiety to avail themselves to the full of the results of earlier idle curiosity. But should the dynamos and motors which have come into being as the outcome of Faraday's experiment be stopped this evening, the businessman of today, agitated over labor troubles, might, as he trudged home past lines of "dead" cars, through dark streets to an unlighted house, engage in a little creative thought of his own and perceive that he and his laborers would have no modern factories and mines to quarrel about if it had not been for the strange practical effects of the idle curiosity of scientists, inventors and engineers.

The examples of creative intelligence given above belong to the realm of modern scientific achievement, which furnishes the most striking instances of the effects of scrupulous, objective thinking. But there are, of course, other great realms in which the recording and embodiment of acute observation and insight have wrought themselves into the higher life of man. The great poets and dramatists and our modern story-tellers have found themselves engaged in productive reveries, noting and artistically presenting their discoveries for the delight and instruction of those who have the ability to appreciate them.

The process by which a fresh and original poem or drama comes into being is doubtless analogous to that which originates and elaborates so-called scientific discoveries; but there is clearly a temperamental difference. The genesis and advance of painting, sculpture, and music offer still other problems. We really as yet know shockingly little about these matters, and indeed very few people have the least curiosity about them.[12] Nevertheless, creative intelligence in its various forms is what makes man. Were it not for its slow, painful, and constantly discouraged operations through the ages man would be no more than a species of primate living on seeds, fruit, roots, and uncooked flesh, and wandering naked through the woods and over the plains like a chimpanzee.

The origin and progress and future promotion of civilization are ill understood and misconceived. These should be made the chief theme of education, but much hard work is necessary before we can construct our ideas of man and his capacities and free ourselves from innumerable persistent misapprehensions. There have been obstructionists in all times, not merely the lethargic masses, but the moralists, the rationalizing theologians, and most of the philosophers, all busily if unconsciously engaged in ratifying existing ignorance and mistakes and discouraging creative thought. Naturally, those who reassure us seem worthy of honor and respect. Equally naturally those who puzzle us with disturbing criticisms and invite us to change our ways are objects of suspicion and readily discredited. Our personal discontent does not ordinarily extend to any critical questioning of the general situation in which we find ourselves. In every age the prevailing conditions of civilization have appeared quite natural and inevitable to those who grew up in them. The cow asks no questions as to how it happens to have a dry stall and a supply of hay. The kitten laps its warm milk from a china saucer, without knowing anything about porcelain; the dog nestles in the corner of a divan with no sense of obligation to the inventors of upholstery and the manufacturers of down pillows. So we humans accept our breakfasts, our trains and telephones and orchestras and movies, our national Constitution, our moral code and standards of manners, with the simplicity and innocence of a pet rabbit. We have absolutely inexhaustible capacities for appropriating what others do for us with no thought of a "thank you." We do not feel called upon to make any least contribution to the merry game ourselves. Indeed, we are usually quite unaware that a game is being played at all.

We have now examined the various classes of thinking which we can readily observe in ourselves and which we have plenty of reasons to believe go on, and always have been going on, in our fellow men. We can sometimes get quite pure and sparkling examples of all four kinds,

[12] Recently a re-examination of creative thought has begun as a result of new knowledge which discredits many of the notions formerly held about "reason." See, for example, *Creative Intelligence*, by a group of American philosophic thinkers: John Dewey, *Essays in Experimental Logic* (both pretty hard books): and Veblen, *The Place of Science in Modern Civilization*. Easier than these and very stimulating are Dewey, *Reconstruction in Philosophy*, and Woodworth, *Dynamic Psychology*.

but commonly they are so confused and intermingled in our reverie as not to be readily distinguishable. The reverie is a reflection of our longings, exultations, and complacencies, our fears, suspicions, and disappointments. We are chiefly engaged in struggling to maintain our self-respect and in asserting that supremacy which we all crave and which seems to us our natural prerogative. It is not strange, but rather quite inevitable, that our beliefs about what is true and false, good and bad, right and wrong, should be mixed up with the reverie and be influenced by the same considerations which determine its character and course. We resent criticisms of our views exactly as we do of anything else connected with ourselves. Our notions of life and its ideals seem to us to be *our own* and as such necessarily true and right, to be defended at all costs.

*We very rarely consider, however, the process by which we gained our convictions.* If we did so, we could hardly fail to see that there was usually little ground for our confidence in them. Here and there, in this department of knowledge or that, some one of us might make a fair claim to have taken some trouble to get correct ideas of, let us say, the situation in Russia, the sources of our food supply, the origin of the Constitution, the revision of the tariff, the policy of the Holy Roman Apostolic Church, modern business organization, trade unions, birth control, socialism, the League of Nations, the excess-profits tax, preparedness, advertising in its social bearings; but only a very exceptional person would be entitled to opinions on all of even these few matters. And yet most of us have opinions on all these, and on many other questions of equal importance, of which we may know even less. We feel compelled, as self-respecting persons, to take sides when they come up for discussion. We even surprise ourselves by our omniscience. Without taking thought we see in a flash that it is most righteous and expedient to discourage birth control by legislative enactment, or that one who decries intervention in Mexico is clearly wrong, or that big advertising is essential to big business and that big business is the pride of the land. As godlike beings why should we not rejoice in our omniscience?

It is clear in any case, that our convictions on important matters are not the result of knowledge or critical thought, nor, it may be added, are they often dictated by supposed self-interest. Most of them are *pure prejudices* in the proper sense of that word. We do not form them ourselves. They are the whispering of "the voice of the herd." We have in the last analysis no responsibility for them and need assume none. They are not really our own ideas, but those of others no more well informed or inspired than ourselves, who have got them in the same humiliating manner as we. It should be our pride to revise our ideas and not to adhere to what passes for respectable opinion, for such opinion can frequently be shown to be not respectable at all. We should, in view of the considerations that have been mentioned, resent our supine credulity. As an English writer has remarked:

"If we feared the entertaining of an unverifiable opinion with the warmth with which we fear using the wrong implement at the dinner table, if the thought of holding a prejudice disgusted us as does a foul disease, then the dangers of man's susceptibility would be turned into advantages."—JAMES HARVEY ROBINSON: *The Mind in the Making*, Chap. 2.[13]

## APPLICATIONS

I. In the preceding excerpt from *The Mind in the Making* what species are put in the genus *thinking*? Is more than one stage involved in the classification here?

II. What expository methods previously studied are used here to develop the discussion? Give examples.

III. Write a theme of some 400 words based on a classification. The following list of topics may be useful, at least to suggest a subject:

| | |
|---|---|
| Liars I Have Known | The Air Arm |
| Mother Love | Types of Teachers |
| Breeds of Horses | Trout Flies |

## DEFINITION

In one sense we can say that DEFINITION answers the question, "What is it?" A small child asks, "What is a zebra?" and the grown-up replies, very unscientifically, that a zebra is a kind of horse, but not as big as a real horse, with black and white stripes. The grown-up has given a description of the animal.

In another and stricter sense, however, it can be said that a definition is not of a thing, but of the word referring to the thing. Its function is to tell how to use the word. It sets the bound or limit within which the word will apply—as the derivation of the word *definition* implies (it comes from two Latin words, *de* meaning *concerning*, and *finis* meaning *limit*). This idea of definition as the limiting of a word is illustrated in the demand frequently made during an argument: "Define your terms." And by TERM we mean

[13] From *The Mind in the Making* by James Harvey Robinson. Copyright, 1921, by Harper & Brothers. Copyright, 1949, by Bankers Trust Company.

any word or group of words that constitutes a unit of meaning—
that refers to one thing or idea.

We shall discuss definition as the definition of a term, but it is
clear that we cannot define a term without some knowledge of the
thing to which the term refers. So the process of making a definition
involves knowledge. It is not a mere game of words. Not only may
definition enlarge the understanding of the person who receives
a definition, but the process of definition may lead the maker of the
definition to clarify his own mind on the subject involved.

## PARTS OF A DEFINITION

A definition falls into two parts, the element to be defined and
the element which does the defining. The two elements form an
equation, that is, one can be substituted for the other in a statement
without changing the sense in any respect.

For example, we may define a *slave* as a human being who is the
legal property of another, and then set this up as an equation:

The *to-be-defined* = the *definer*
Slave       is   human being who is the legal property
                   of another.

Now if we make a statement using the word *slave*, we may substitute the *definer* ("human being who is the legal property of another") for that word without any change of sense. The statement,

1. To be a slave is worse than death.

has exactly the same meaning as the statement,

2. To be the legal property of another is worse than death.

We must remember that the adequacy of the original definition
is not the point here. We may have given an inadequate definition,
but in so far as we are willing to stand by our definition we are
willing to substitute the *definer* for the *to-be-defined* in any statement. Furthermore, the truth or falsity of any particular statement
is not relevant. What is relevant is that the two elements form an
equation, are CONVERTIBLE.

When the elements are not convertible, we do not have a real
definition.

## THE PROCESS OF DEFINITION

To get a notion of the process of definition let us take a very simple situation. A small child who has never seen a cat receives one as a pet. The father tells the child that the animal is a cat— a kitty. The proud parent now assumes that the child knows what the word *cat* means, but he may be surprised one day to find the child pointing at a Pekingese and calling, "Kitty, kitty." It is obvious that the child is using the word to mean any small, furry animal, and when the father takes him to the park the child is very apt to call a squirrel a kitty, too.

The father now undertakes to give the child a definition of *cat*. To do so he must instruct the child in the differences between a cat, a Pekingese, and a squirrel. In other words, he undertakes to break up the group the child has made (all small, furry animals) into certain subgroups (cats, Pekingese, squirrels) by focusing attention upon the differences, the DIFFERENTIA.

If the child understands his father, he now has the knowledge to give a definition of the word *cat*—a very inadequate definition but a kind of definition. If we question the child we may elicit a definition.

*Questioner:* What does *cat* mean?

*Child:* It's a little-bitty animal, and it's got fur.

*Questioner:* But dogs have fur, too, and dogs aren't cats.

*Child:* Yes, but dogs bark. Cats don't bark. Cats me-ow. And cats climb trees.

*Questioner:* But squirrels have fur, and they climb trees and are little-bitty.

*Child:* Yes, but squirrels don't just climb trees like cats. They live in trees. And they don't me-ow like cats.

The child has put *cat* into a group (small, furry animals) and then has distinguished the subgroup of cats from other subgroups of Pekingese and squirrels.

If we chart the child's reasoning we get something like this:

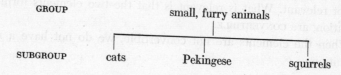

| GROUP | | small, furry animals | |
|---|---|---|---|
| SUBGROUP | cats | Pekingese | squirrels |

The pattern of the child's definition is the pattern of all definition. It involves, we see, the kind of scheme we have already studied
under classification and division. Here the class *small, furry animals*
is the genus, and the classes *cats, Pekingese,* and *squirrels* are the
species. Definition involves placing the relevant species under its
genus and then indicating the characteristics which distinguish it
from other species of the same genus. So we get the formula:

Definition of species = genus + differentia

The pattern of the child's definition of *cat* is the pattern of all
definition, but the particular definition will not serve in an adult
world. The classifications the child is using are not significant, since
smallness and furriness are not sufficiently particularized traits. A
zoologist would go about the business differently.

He might begin by saying: "A cat—*Felis domestica,* we call it—is
a digitigrade, carnivorous mammal, of the genus *Felis,* which includes the species tiger (*Felis tigris*), the species ocelot (*Felis par-
dalis*), the species lion (*Felis leo*), the species cougar (*Felis concolor*),
and several other species. All the species of the genus *Felis* have
lithe, graceful, long bodies, relatively short legs, with soft, padded
feet, strong claws which are retracted into sheaths when not in
use, powerful jaws with sharp teeth, and soft, beautifully marked
fur. The cat is the smallest species of the genus, usually measuring
so-and-so. It is the only species easily domesticated. . . ."

Like the child, the zoologist has set up a group (which he calls
a genus), and has given the characteristics of the group. Then he
has broken up the group into several subgroups (each of which he
calls a species). Last he has set about pointing out the differences
between the species *cat* and the other species of the same genus.
Set up as a scheme, his thinking has this form:

GENUS                         *Felis*

SPECIES    *Felis domestica*   *Felis tigris*   *Felis leo*   *Felis concolor*   etc.
             (cat)              (tiger)         (lion)        (cougar)

The form used by the zoologist is, we see, the same as that used
by the child. The difference is that the zoologist thinks in significant
classes. It is true that for him the words *genus* and *species* have a

somewhat different meaning from the meanings we use in referring to classification and division. For the zoologist the word *genus* means a group of species closely related structurally and by origin, and the word *species* means a group whose members possess numerous characteristics in common and do or may interbreed to preserve those characteristics. This difference comes from the fact that the zoologist is dealing with living forms. But despite these differences in the meaning of genus and species he uses them in his pattern of definition in the same way we have used them.

Though our thinking may follow the pattern of genus and species, we do not ordinarily use those terms in framing a definition. To define *bungalow* we may say that the species falls under the genus *house* and give the differentia distinguishing it from other species, other types of houses. Set up formally the scheme would be this:

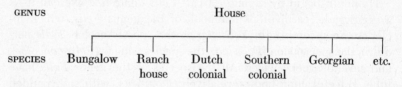

GENUS                            House

SPECIES   Bungalow    Ranch    Dutch    Southern    Georgian    etc.
                     house      colonial    colonial

Ordinarily, however, we would not use the technical terms. We might say: "A bungalow is a kind of house. It differs from some kinds, like the Dutch colonial, the Georgian, and the Southern colonial, in that it has only one story. But it differs from other one-story types, like the ranch house, in that its floor plan is so-and-so." The important thing is the pattern of thought.

### DEFINITION AND THE COMMON GROUND

If we are not content with a definition given us—for instance, the definition of *cat* given by the zoologist—we may push the giver back by asking more about the genus in which he has located the species under discussion. If we ask the zoologist about the genus *Felis,* he may say that it is a group under the family *Felidae,* which contains another genus, the genus *Lynx.* If, after he has established the differentia here between the genera *Felis* and *Lynx,* we are still not satisfied, he may patiently repeat the process, going up the scale to another group, for instance, mammals, and on above that to vertebrates, and on above that to animals. We would conclude with some very elaborate scheme, roughly as follows:

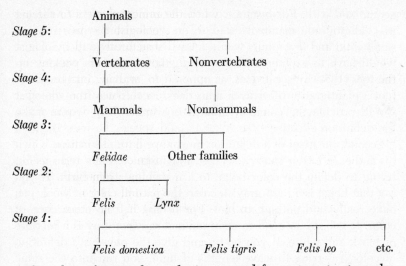

If we keep forcing the zoologist upward from stage to stage, he will in each instance give us a new definition by the same method. The only difference will be that what has been the main group in Stage 1, for example, becomes the subgroup in Stage 2, and so on up the scale. Here he is seeking a point where the questioner will feel at home, where he and the questioner will have common ground.

Common ground is necessary for an effective definition. Such common ground may be difficult to discover in a transaction between a scientist, for instance a zoologist, who employs a highly technical language and a highly technical scheme based on the structures of living creatures, and a layman who deals in language and in appearances in a rough-and-ready way. But if the scientist wishes to communicate with the layman he must find a common ground and a common language.

This principle of the common ground for a definition is very important, for it implies that a definition is not only *of some term* but is *for somebody*. The giver of the definition can only define by reference to what his particular audience already knows or is willing to learn.

This knowledge must be of two kinds.

First, since any definition must be in words, the giver of the definition must use words that his audience is, or can readily become, acquainted with. For instance, when the zoologist refers to the cat as a "digitigrade mammal," and so on, he is using words that no small child and few adults would know. In such cases, the zoologist would have to explain further that *digitigrade* means "walking on the toes" the way a cat does, as opposed to "walking on the whole foot" (plantigrade) the way a man does. In this way the zoologist would provide the common ground in words which would make the definition effective.

Second, the giver of a definition must appeal to information which his audience has or can readily get. For instance, there is no use in trying to define the color beige to a man blind from birth. If you say that beige is a light grayish color, the natural color of wool, you have really said nothing to him. For he has had no experience of color. It will do no good to continue and say that gray is a mixture of black and white. If you go on and give the physicist's definition of color, referring to wave lengths of light, you run into the same difficulty. He can grasp the notion of wave length, but he has no basis for knowing what light is. You run into a defect in his experience, in his knowledge.

### PRINCIPLES OF DEFINITION

Assuming, however, that the giver of the definition finds the common ground in regard to both words and knowledge, there are still certain principles to be observed if the *definer* is truly to enlarge the audience's understanding of the *to-be-defined*.

    I. The *to-be-defined* must be equivalent to the *definer*.

    II. The *to-be-defined* must not be part of the *definer*.

    III. The *definer* must not be negative unless the *to-be-defined* is negative.

    I. We see immediately that in principle I we are repeating the notion that a definition involves an equation, the possibility of substitution of one element of the definition for the other. But it may be useful to break this notion down:

    1. The *definer* must not be broader than the *to-be-defined*.

    2. The *definer* must not be narrower than the *to-be-defined*.

We have an example of the violation of principle 1 if we define *table* as a piece of furniture on which we put dishes, lamps, ashtrays, books, or knickknacks. The *definer* is here too broad because it would equally well apply to sideboards, chests of drawers, buffets, or what-nots—on which we put dishes, lamps, and so forth. The *definer* says some things that are true, but these true things apply too widely. To put it another way, we can say that the definition does not properly consider the differentia which would distinguish the various species under the genus furniture.

We have an example of the violation of principle 2 if we define *table* as the piece of furniture on which we serve our meals. Here the *definer* is too narrow, because it would not apply to some types of tables, such as end tables, study tables, bedside tables, or sewing tables. It really only applies to a subspecies of the species *table*, and not to the species. Yet the species *table* is what is involved in the definition.

II. The *to-be-defined* is part of the *definer* when it is defined in whole, or in part, in terms of itself. This occurs in two sorts of cases:

1. When a word or phrase of the *to-be-defined*, or a variation of a word or phrase, is significantly repeated in the *definer*.

2. When an idea of the *to-be-defined*, though in different words, is significantly repeated in the *definer*.

We get an example of the first when we define the word *statistician* by saying it means anyone who makes a profession of compiling and studying statistics. The trouble here is that *statistics* is a mere variation of *statistician*. The essential question, "What kind of thing does a statistician do?" is left unanswered because we have not yet defined statistics. Or if we define *man* as a human being, we commit the same error. In these cases the *definer* tells a truth, but it is not a new truth. It is a truth already implicit in the *to-be-defined*. There has been no real enlargement of understanding. To state the matter another way, there has been a circle in the definition: you come back to your starting point.

In the first type of circular definition, it is clear that when we repeat in the *definer* a word or words of the *to-be-defined* we repeat an idea already expressed. But it is possible to repeat an idea in different words, and this, too, gives a circle in the definition. For example, we have a circle in the definition when we say that *fast* means having a rapid rate of motion. The *definer* does not really enlarge our notion of the *to-be-defined* because the word *rapid*, the key word in the *definer*, really repeats the idea of *fast*, the word to be defined.

III. If we define a positive *to-be-defined* by a negative *definer* we may wind up with something like this: "Tiffin is what the English in India call a meal not eaten in the morning." Now it is perfectly true that tiffin is not eaten in the morning. It is eaten at noon. But the trouble with the negative statement is that it does not exclude other possibilities than morning. According to the definition given above, tiffin might just as well be eaten in the afternoon or the evening. The truth in the *definer* is not the whole truth, and the definition fails to establish the necessary equation between the elements of the definition.

When, however, the *to-be-defined* is negative—when its nature involves some deficiency—it is correct to use a negative *definer*. For example, it is correct to define the word *widow* as a woman who has lost her husband by death, for here the idea of loss, of deficiency, is the essential notion in the *to-be-defined*.

## APPLICATIONS

I. Some of the following statements are correct definitions and some are not. Locate those that are correct. State what principle of definition is violated by each that you find incorrect. If you lack the information necessary to judge some of the definitions, use a dictionary or some reference book like an encyclopedia. For example, statement 14 uses the word *anthropology*. If you do not know what anthropology is, try to find out. If anthropology studies more than morality, then the statement given in statement 14 is not a correct definition, because it violates principle I.

1. A soirée means a social function which does not take place in the afternoon.
2. The French word *cheval* means horse.
3. A collar is the thing a man wears around his neck.
4. A protuberance is a thing that protrudes.
5. A man is a featherless biped.
6. A collie is the Scotch shepherd dog.
7. A collie is a long-haired dog.
8. A hero is a man who is useful to society.
9. Interment is the act or ceremony of putting a dead body in the earth.
10. Molybdenum is a metallic element belonging to the chromium group, whitish in color, and resembling iron in malleability and difficult fusibility.

11. Patriotism is a holy sentiment.
12. Patriotism is the last refuge of the scoundrel.
13. Ethics means the science which studies moral values.
14. The science of anthropology is the science which studies morality.
15. Beauty is truth, truth beauty.
16. Faith is the substance of things hoped for, the evidence of things not seen.
17. A line is what is described by a moving point.
18. A straight line is the shortest distance between two points.
19. The word *poet* means a man interested in poetry.

II. Below is a list of words to be defined. In each definition indicate the genus and differentia. Let us take the word *river*. We might define it by saying that a river is a large, constantly flowing (differentia) stream (genus). By our statement we have indicated that the species *river* belongs to the genus *stream,* but is differentiated from other streams (brooks, rills, branches, runs, and creeks) by its size. Some of the problems will, however, be more complicated than this. If you do not have enough information to make a definition that satisfies you, use a dictionary or some reference work such as an encyclopedia. Do not hesitate to copy a definition from a dictionary. But if you do so, indicate the genus and differentia in the dictionary definition. Perhaps even the dictionary will not help you with a word like *democracy.* You may feel that the dictionary definition does not express what you think to be the really important thing. In that case, do not hesitate to risk your own judgment.

| | | |
|---|---|---|
| Pond | Noun | Democracy |
| House | Corporal | Capitalism |
| Lassitude | Color | Experiment |
| Anger | Depth | Yellow |
| Horse | Love | Charity |
| Psychiatrist | Liberty | Automobile |

## EXTENDED DEFINITION

Early in the discussion of definition we said that definition not only is useful to a person who receives it but may also be useful to the person who makes it. It is a way of thinking, a way of clarifying one's own views. This consideration is not very important in deal-ing with a word like *house.* With a little information we can make a workable definition. But sometimes a little information is not all we need. We may need to think through a very complicated set of relations. We may need a discussion and not a simple definition. Let us take for an example the following discussion of the meaning of the word *labor*.

It is easy to meet with definitions or at least descriptions of the term labour, especially among non-British economists. We need hardly notice the definition of Cicero, who says, *"Labor est functio quaedam vel animi vel corporis."* If we are thus to make labour include all action of mind or body, it includes all life. . . . Malthus expressly defines labour as follows: "The exertions of human beings employed with a view to remuneration. If the term be applied to other exertions, they must be particularly specified." In this proposition, however, the word remuneration is very uncertain in meaning. Does it mean only wages paid by other persons than the labourer, or does it include the benefit which a labourer may gain directly from his own labour? . . .

It is plain that labour must consist of some energy or action of the body or mind, but it does not follow that every kind of exertion is to be treated in economics. Lay has restricted the term by the following concise definition: *"Travail; action suivie, dirigée vers un but."* The action here contemplated excludes mere play and sport, which carries its whole purpose with it. There must be some extrinsic benefit to be purchased by the action, which moreover must be continued, consistent action, directed steadily to the same end. This correctly describes the great mass of economic labour which is directed simply to the earning of wages and the producing of the commodities which eventually constitute wages. But there is nothing in this definition to exclude the long-continued exertions of a boat's crew training for a race, the steady practice of a company of cricketers, or even the regular constitutional walk of the student who values his good health. Moreover, no considerable continuity of labour is requisite to bring it under economic laws. A poor man who gathers groundsell in the morning and sells it about the streets the same afternoon may complete the circle of economic action within twenty-four hours. . . .

Senior has given a definition of the term in question, saying, "Labour is the voluntary exertion of bodily or mental faculties for the purpose of production." Here the term production is made the scapegoat. Does production include the production of pleasure or prevention of pain in every way? Does it include the training of the cricketer? The word "voluntary," again, excludes the forced labour of slaves and prisoners, not to speak of draught animals. Yet many economic questions arise about the productiveness of the exertions of such agents. . . .

Some later economists consider pain or disagreeableness to be a necessary characteristic of labour, and probably with correctness. Thus Mill defines labour as "muscular or nervous action, including all feelings of a disagreeable kind, all bodily inconvenience or mental annoyance connected with the employment of one's thoughts or muscles, or both, in a particular occupation." He seems to intend that only what is disagreeable, inconvenient or annoying, shall be included. Professor Hearn also says that such effort as the term labour seems to imply is "more or less troublesome." It may be added that in all the dictionaries pain seems to be regarded as a necessary constituent of labour.

Nevertheless it cannot possibly be said that all economic labour is simple pain. Beyond doubt a workman in good health and spirits, and fresh from a good night's rest actually enjoys the customary exertion of his morning task. To a man brought up in the steady round of daily trade and labour, inactivity soon becomes tedious. Happiness has been defined as the reflex of unimpeded energy, and whatever exactly this may mean, there can be no doubt that any considerable degree of pleasure can be attained only by setting up some end to be worked for and then working. The real solution of the difficulty seems to be this—that, however agreeable labour may be when the muscles are recruited and the nerves unstrained, the hedonic condition is always changed as the labour proceeds. As we shall see, continued labour grows more and more painful, and when long-continued becomes almost intolerable. However pleasurable the beginning, the pleasure merges into pain. Now when we are engaged in mere sport, devoid of any conscious perception of future good or evil, exertion will not continue beyond the point when present pain and pleasure are balanced. No motive can exist for further action. But when we have any future utility in view the case is different. The mind of the labourer balances present pain against future good, so that the labour before it is terminated becomes purely painful. Now the problems and theorems of economics always turn upon the point where equality or equilibrium is attained; when labour is itself pleasurable no questions can arise about its continuance. There is the double gain—the pleasure of the labour itself and the pleasure of gaining its produce. No complicated calculus is needed where all is happy and certain. It is on this ground that we may probably dismiss from economic science all sports and other exertions to which may be applied the maxim—leave off as soon as you feel inclined. But it is far otherwise with that advanced point of economic labour when the question arises whether more labour will be repaid by the probability of future good.

I am by no means sure that it is possible to embody in a single definition the view here put forward. If obliged to attempt a definition, I should say that labour includes all exertion of body and/or mind eventually becoming painful if prolonged, and not wholly undertaken for the sake of immediate pleasure. This proposition plainly includes all painful exertion which we undergo in order to gain future pleasures or to ward off pains, in such a way as to leave a probable hedonic balance in our favor; but it does not exclude exertion which, even at the time of exertion, is producing such a balance.—WILLIAM STANLEY JEVONS: *The Principles of Economics*, Chap. 14.[14]

The author ends by putting labor in the general group of "exertion of body and/or mind," and by distinguishing it from other possible types of exertion. He has used the formula of definition. But he arrives at his own definition by a discussion of previous definitions. He criticizes them and indicates his reason for rejecting them. It is through this criticism that he sets up the differentia for his own definition.

Let us take another word, *liberty,* which is probably even more difficult to define than *labor.* Offhand, we think we have a very clear notion of its meaning, but when we try to define it we may become aware of our own ignorance or vagueness. We have some notion, no doubt, that *liberty* means being able to do what one likes. But reflection shows us that we cannot mean that if we hold that the word has any reference to the real world we live in. For no one is free to do what he likes. All sorts of things thwart us, our physical limitations, our intellectual limitations, our economic limitations, social pressures, laws. We can say, of course, that we choose to use the word *liberty* to refer to the state of being able to do what one likes; and that statement, if we are consistent in our use of the word, will constitute a kind of definition. But if we wish to use the word as having some reference to the actual situation of human beings, we must explore the concept more fully.

Such an exploration would undoubtedly lead us very far afield. We would find that we had gone far beyond the kind of vest-pocket definition which appears in a dictionary. We would write an essay or a book. And innumerable essays and books have been written in the attempt to define *liberty.*

How might we go about framing a definition of *liberty?*

The word *liberty* is used to refer to several different things. It

[14] From *The Principles of Economics* by William Stanley Jevons. Reprinted by permission of The Macmillan Company.

may refer to the theological question of the relation of the human will in relation to God's will and foreknowledge. It may refer to the psychological question of whether the human being makes choices or is a very complicated mechanism that responds but does not choose. It may refer to the question of the relation of the individual to society. Before we attempt a definition of the word we obviously must decide which reference here is our concern.

John Stuart Mill begins his famous essay "On Liberty" [15] by indicating the particular aspect of the subject which he intends to treat. "The subject of this Essay is not the so-called Liberty of the Will, so unfortunately opposed to the misnamed doctrine of Philosophical Necessity; but Civil or Social Liberty: The nature and limits of the power which can be legitimately exercised by society over the individual."

Having in this fashion confined his interest to social liberty, Mill then proceeds to distinguish the different conceptions of social liberty which have prevailed at different times and places: (1) immunities under a "governing One, or a governing tribe or caste" who did not govern "at the pleasure of the governed"; (2) constitutional checks under the same type of government as above; (3) the right to elect rulers; (4) the right to protection against the will of the majority as expressed through government; (5) the right to protection against social pressure. Set up as a scheme we have this:

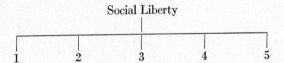

Social Liberty

1    2    3    4    5

Mill then goes on to point out that in the modern world conceptions 1, 2, and 3 are outmoded, for the historical situations accounting for them no longer prevail. Thus conceptions 4 and 5 are left as the special content of his subject—which may be called Social Liberty in its modern reference.

But Social Liberty in its modern reference has various areas of application, which must be distinguished from each other. These various areas of application are: (a) liberty of "consciousness"— liberty of conscience, of thought, and of opinion, and by extension, of expression; (b) liberty of "tastes and pursuits"—liberty

[15] Page 697 of Readings. Study the section from Mill's essay given there.

of framing the "plan of our life to suit our own character"; (c)
liberty of "combination"—liberty of individuals to unite, the individuals combining "being supposed to be of full age, and not forced
or deceived." So we can develop our scheme:

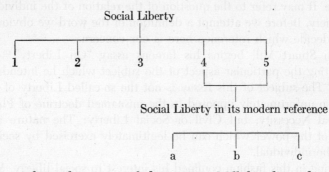

By making this series of distinctions Mill has limited and explained the area of his discussion. He can now proceed to frame
his definition with some assurance that his audience will see where
the definition can be applied and by what line of thought it was
developed.

All the way through his discussion Mill is conscious of the fact
that the liberty of one individual cannot be thought of apart from
the liberty of other individuals, for all are members of a society.
Therefore, if one individual, in pursuing what he takes to be his
liberty, infringes upon or limits the liberty of another individual,
he is not exercising his liberty but is doing something else. That is,
liberty must be understood as meaning the maximum liberty of all
individuals and not the mere opportunity of one individual to do
what he pleases.

Having developed that thought, Mill can now define Social Liberty in its modern reference as the pursuit of "our own good in
our own way, so long as we do not attempt to deprive others of
theirs, or impede their efforts to obtain it." It may be said, of course,
that Mill is really defining the term *justifiable liberty* and not the
term *liberty*. But this, he says, is the only liberty that "deserves the
name." That is, he would use the term *liberty* only to apply to the
situation just described, and his definition means something to us
because of the discussion that has preceded it.

Let us turn to another famous essay, "What is a University?" by

John Henry Newman,[16] as an example of extended definition. This is the first paragraph:

If I were asked to describe as briefly and popularly as I could, what a University was, I should draw my answer from its ancient designation of a *Studium Generale,* or "School of Universal Learning." This description implies the assemblage of strangers from all parts in one spot;—*from all parts;* else, how will you find professors and students for every department of knowledge? and *in one spot;* else, how can there be any school at all? Accordingly, in its simple and rudimental form, it is a school of knowledge of every kind, consisting of teachers and learners from every quarter. Many things are requisite to complete and satisfy the idea embodied in this description; but such as this a University seems to be in its essence, a place for the communication and circulation of thought, by means of personal intercourse, through a wide extent of country.

We remember that both Jevons and Mill move toward a definition through a discussion, but here we see that Newman starts with a definition. The definition is the basis for a discussion, the discussion being a development of the implications of the original definition.

## CHANGED USE OF A TERM

We can see another difference between the essay by Mill and that by Newman. Mill looks back over history to see what has been understood by liberty at different times in the past, but the definition he finally gives is for his own time and not for any past time. Newman, too, looks back to the past, and begins his first paragraph by referring to an earlier notion. But he does not contrast the earlier notion with a modern notion. Instead, he uses the old notion to help him define the word *university* in a modern reference. What he draws from the old term *Studium Generale* he applies to the new term *university.*

A study of the use of a term in the past may be useful, then, because of either continuity or contrast. For example, if we are asked to define the term *American democracy,* we may very profitably raise the historical question. Do we understand the same thing by it as the Founding Fathers did? What must we make of the fact

[16] Page 689 of Readings. Study the essay by Newman.

that the Founding Fathers did not believe in universal suffrage and that we may? Are there any elements of continuity?

## DERIVATION OF A TERM TO BE DEFINED

As it is sometimes useful to know the history of the use of a term, it is sometimes useful to know the derivation of a term. Every word has a history, and the history of the word itself may lead to a fuller notion of its meaning. For instance, it helps us to understand the meaning of the word *philosophy* to learn that it derives from a Greek word meaning the love of wisdom. The derivation may indicate or explain some basic meaning. For instance, an article on asceticism begins as follows:

ASCETICISM: the theory and practice of bodily abstinence and self-mortification, generally religious. The word is derived from a Greek word (ἀσκέω) meaning "to practice," or "to train," and it embodies a metaphor taken from the ancient wrestling place, where victory rewarded those who had best trained their bodies.—*Encyclopaedia Britannica*, 14th edition.

Here the derivation of the word really enlightens us about the significance of self-denial for the religious person: it is like the training of an athlete.

## METHODS OF EXTENDED DEFINITION

We begin to see some of the ways in which the simple definition may be extended. We may start by looking into the derivation of the term to be defined. We may follow Newman's method of defining a present term by reference to an old usage. We may look at the history of various meanings of a term as a background for a present meaning, as Mill looks at the history of *liberty*. We may extend the discussion through several stages as Mill does, to locate the precise area in which the definition will apply. We may develop a definition by a series of illustrations, comparisons, and contrasts, as Newman does in the body of his essay. We may do any or all of these things. We may, in fact, do anything that will really help to make our definition clear.

In writing an extended definition we may find, of course, that we are running away from the strict concern of definition into illustrations, for example, or comparisons and contrasts. Other intentions may become dominant over the intention to define. If we are setting out to write a definition, and *only* a definition, this wavering of intention may confuse us and our readers. But definition may be merely the beginning of a piece of exposition, and may be subordinate to other intentions. Then, what is important is to be able to use the method of definition as far as it is fruitful for understanding the subject. Definition is, in the end, a device for reaching understanding.

## *APPLICATIONS*

### I

Below are three examples of extended definition. What is the genus and what are the differentia involved in each? What methods has the author used in each instance to extend the definition?

**A.** Chemistry is that branch of science which has the task of investigating the materials out of which the universe is made. It is not concerned with the forms into which they may be fashioned. Such objects as chairs, tables, vases, bottles, or wires are of no significance in chemistry; but such substances as glass, wool, iron, sulfur, and clay, as the materials out of which they are made, are what it studies. Chemistry is concerned not only with the composition of such substances, but also with their inner structure. Further, these materials are constantly undergoing change in nature: iron rusts, wood decays, sugar ferments, coal burns, limestone rock is eaten away by water, and living organisms digest their foods and build up their structures. Chemistry investigates such changes—the conditions under which they occur, the mechanism by which they take place, the new substances that are formed as their result, and the energy that is liberated or absorbed by them. Chemistry also studies the way in which these and similar changes can be carried out in the laboratory or on a larger scale in the chemical plant. As a result of investigations along these lines, chemistry has found how metals can be extracted from their ores; how impoverished fields can be made fertile again; and how the materials that are found in nature can be converted into thousands of new substances to help feed the race, to cure the sick, and to provide such comfort and even luxury for the common man as was not enjoyed by the wealthy of an earlier generation.
—JOHN ARREND TIMM: *General Chemistry*, Chap. 1.[17]

[17] By permission from *General Chemistry* by John Arend Timm, copyrighted 1944. McGraw-Hill Book Company.

**B.** At first, then, instead of asking what religion is, I should prefer to ask what characterizes the aspirations of a person who gives me the impression of being religious: a person who is religiously enlightened appears to me to be one who has, to the best of his ability, liberated himself from the fetters of his selfish desires and is preoccupied with thoughts, feelings, and aspirations to which he clings because of their super-personal value.

It seems to me that what is important is the force of this super-personal content and the depth of the conviction concerning its overpowering meaningfulness, regardless of whether any attempt is made to unite this content with a Divine Being, for otherwise it would not be possible to count Buddha and Spinoza as religious personalities.

Accordingly, a religious person is devout in the sense that he has no doubt of the significance and loftiness of those super-personal objects and goals which neither require nor are capable of rational foundation. They exist with the same necessity and matter-of-factness as he himself. In this sense religion is the age-old endeavor of mankind to become clearly and completely conscious of these values and goals and constantly to strengthen and extend their effects.—ALBERT EINSTEIN: "Science and Religion." [18]

**C.** No words are oftener on our lips than thinking and thought. So profuse and varied, indeed, is our use of these words that it is not easy to define just what we mean by them. The aim of this chapter is to find a single consistent meaning. Assistance may be had by considering some typical ways in which the terms are employed. In the first place *thought* is used broadly, not to say loosely. Everything that comes to mind, that "goes through our heads," is called a thought. To think of a thing is just to be conscious of it in any way whatsoever. Second, the term is restricted by excluding whatever is directly presented; we think (or think of) only such things as we do not directly see, hear, smell, or taste. Then, third, the meaning is further limited to beliefs that rest upon some kind of evidence or testimony. Of this third types, two kinds—or, rather, two degrees—must be discriminated. In some cases, a belief is accepted with slight or almost no attempt to state the grounds that support it. In other cases, the ground or basis for a belief is deliberately sought and its adequacy to support the belief examined. This process is called reflective thought; it alone is truly educative in value. . . . We shall now briefly describe each of the four senses.

1. In its loosest sense, thinking signifies every thing that, as we say,

[18] From *Science News Letter*, September 21, 1940. Reprinted by permission of Science Service.

is "in our heads" or that "goes through our minds." He who offers "a penny for your thoughts" does not expect to drive any great bargain. In calling the object of his demand *thoughts,* he does not intend to ascribe to them dignity, consecutiveness, or truth. Any idle fancy, trivial recollection, or flitting impression will satisfy his demand. Daydreaming, building of castles in the air, that loose flux of casual and disconnected material that floats through our minds in relaxed moments are, in this random sense, *thinking.* More of our waking life than we should care to admit, even to ourselves, is likely to be whiled away in this inconsequential trifling with idle fancy and unsubstantial hope.

In this sense, silly folk and dullards *think.* The story is told of a man in slight repute for intelligence, who, desiring to be chosen selectman in his New England town, addressed a knot of neighbors in this wise: "I hear you don't believe I know enough to hold office. I wish you to understand that I am thinking about something or other most the time." Now reflective thought is like this random coursing of things through the mind in that it consists of a succession of things thought of; but it is unlike, in that the mere chance occurrence of any chance "something or other" in an irregular sequence does not suffice. Reflection involves not simply a sequence of ideas, but a *con*sequence—a consecutive ordering in such a way that each determines the next as its proper outcome, while each in turn leans back on its predecessors. The successive portions of the reflective thought grow out of one another and support one another; they do not come and go in a medley. Each phase is a step from something to something—technically speaking, it is a term of thought. Each term leaves a deposit which is utilized in the next term. The stream or flow becomes a train, chain, or thread.

2. Even when thinking is used in a broad sense, it is usually restricted to matters not directly perceived: to what we do not see, smell, hear, or touch. We ask the man telling a story if he saw a certain incident happen, and his reply may be, "No, I only thought of it." A note of invention, as distinct from faithful record of observation, is present. Most important in this class are successions of imaginative incidents and episodes which, having a certain coherence, hanging together on a continuous thread, lie between kaleidoscopic flights of fancy and considerations deliberately employed to establish a conclusion. The imaginative stories poured forth by children possess all degrees of internal congruity; some are disjointed, some are articulated. When connected, they stimulate reflective thought; indeed, they usually occur in minds of logical capacity. These imaginative enterprises often precede thinking of the close-knit type and prepare the way for it. But *they do not aim at knowledge, at belief about facts or in truths;* and thereby they are

marked off from reflective thought even when they most resemble it. Those who express such thoughts do not expect credence, but rather credit for a well-constructed plot or a well-arranged climax. They produce good stories, not—unless by chance—knowledge. Such thoughts are an efflorescence of feeling; the enhancement of a mood or sentiment is their aim; congruity of emotion, their binding tie.

3. In its next sense, thought denotes belief resting upon some basis: that is, real or supposed knowledge going beyond what is directly present. It is marked by *acceptance or rejection of something as reasonably probable or improbable*. This phase of thought, however, includes two such distinct types of belief that, even though their difference is strictly one of degree, not of kind, it becomes practically important to consider them separately. Some beliefs are accepted when their grounds have not themselves been considered, others are accepted because their grounds have been examined.

When we say, "Men used to think the world was flat," or "I thought you went to the house," we express belief: something is accepted, held to, acquiesced in, or affirmed. But such thoughts may mean a supposition accepted without reference to its real grounds. These may be adequate, they may not; but their value with reference to the support they afford the belief has not been considered.

Such thoughts grow up unconsciously and without reference to the attainment of correct belief. They are picked up—we know not how. From obscure sources and by unnoticed channels they insinuate themselves into acceptance and become unconsciously a part of our mental furniture. Tradition, instruction, imitation—all of which depend upon authority in some form, or appeal to our own advantage, or fall in with a strong passion—are responsible for them. Such thoughts are prejudices, that is, prejudgments, not judgments proper that rest upon a survey of evidence.

4. Thoughts that result in belief have an importance attached to them which leads to reflective thought, to conscious inquiry into the nature, conditions, and hearing of the belief. To *think* of whales and camels in the clouds is to entertain ourselves with fancies, terminable at our pleasure, which do not lead to any belief in particular. But to think of the world as flat is to ascribe a quality to a real thing as its real property. This conclusion denotes a connection among things and hence is not, like imaginative thought, plastic to our mood. Belief in the world's flatness commits him who holds it to thinking in certain specific ways of other objects such as the heavenly bodies, antipodes, the possibility of navigation. It prescribes to him actions in accordance with his conception of these objects.

The consequences of a belief upon other beliefs and upon behaviour may be so important, then, that men are forced to consider the grounds or reasons of their belief and its logical consequences. This means reflective thought—thought in its eulogistic and emphatic sense.

Men *thought* the world was flat until Columbus thought it to be round. The earlier thought was a belief held because men had not the energy or the courage to question what those about them accepted and taught, especially as it was suggested and seemingly confirmed by obvious and sensible facts. The thought of Columbus was a *reasoned conclusion*. It marked the close of study into facts, of scrutiny and revision of evidence, of working out the implications of various hypotheses, and of comparing these theoretical results with one another and with known facts. Because Columbus did not accept unhesitatingly the current traditional theory, because he doubted and inquired, he arrived at his thought. Skeptical of what, from long habit, seemed most certain, and credulous of what seemed impossible, he went on thinking until he could produce evidence for both his confidence and his disbelief. Even if his conclusion had finally turned out wrong, it would have been a different sort of belief from those it antagonized, because it was reached by a different method. *Active, persistent, and careful consideration of any belief or supposed form of knowledge in the light of the grounds that support it, and the further conclusions to which it tends,* constitutes reflective thought. Any one of the first three kinds of thought may elicit this type; but once begun, it is a conscious and voluntary effort to establish belief upon a firm basis of reasons.—JOHN DEWEY: *How We Think,* Chap. 1.[19]

## II

Here are some statements about religion. Which are definitions? In any which does not have the form of definition, can you see what definition may lie behind the statement? What genus and differentia are involved in each definition?

1. "Religion, after trying to see as best I could what various religions and religious people had in common, I felt impelled to define as the reaction of the personality as a whole to its experience of the Universe as a whole."—J. S. HUXLEY.

2. Religion is "morality tinged with emotion."—MATTHEW ARNOLD.

3. Religion is the "belief in spiritual beings."—E. B. TYLOR.

4. Religion is "that voice of the deepest human experience."—MATTHEW ARNOLD.

[19] From *How We Think* by John Dewey. Reprinted by special permission of D. C. Heath and Company, Boston, Mass.

5. Religion is the "opium of the people."—KARL MARX.

6. Religion is "a propitiation or conciliation of powers superior to man which are believed to direct or control the course of nature and of human life."—SIR JAMES FRAZER.

7. "Pure religion and undefiled before God is this, to visit the fatherless and widows in their affliction, and to keep himself unspotted from the world."—ST. JAMES.

### III

Write an extended definition (600 words or more) of one of the words listed below, using the following pattern of discussion in so far as it will apply in the particular case:

a. Derivation of the word—does the origin enlighten us?
b. History of the application of the word—do earlier applications differ from the present application?
c. Genus and differentia in present application—how can the species be distinguished from other significant species?
d. Analysis of species—does it have any "subspecies," and if so, how are they to be distinguished from each other?
e. Application of the definition to individual instances—does the definition really meet this test, and does it enlighten us about the individual instances?

| | | |
|---|---|---|
| Republic | Empire | Contemplate |
| Cynicism | Pecuniary | Vaccination |
| Fascism | Imagination | Radical |
| Culture | Theology | Democracy |
| | Cathedral | |

(NOTE: For the derivation of a word any large dictionary can be consulted. For the history of its applications the *Oxford English Dictionary* provides the best source of information. For other sources of special information required in extending the definition, the instructor can provide suggestions. Most of the work for this theme will be in the reading and thinking before you begin to write. Study your subject. Be sure that you have something to say. Then prepare an outline before you actually begin to write.)

## ANALYSIS: THE TWO KINDS

ANALYSIS is the method of dividing into component parts. The word means loosening into parts. The method can be applied to anything that can be thought of as having parts. We can analyze an object such as a dog, a house, a tree, a picture. We can analyze an idea such as nationalism, religion, or treachery. We can analyze an organization such as a church, a corporation, a university, or a government.

We must make a distinction between PHYSICAL ANALYSIS and CONCEPTUAL ANALYSIS.

In physical analysis some object is spatially separated into its components. If a clockmaker takes a clock apart, he performs a physical analysis. If a student of zoology dissects a pickled dogfish, he performs a physical analysis. If a chemist makes a chemical analysis of a sample of butter, he performs a physical analysis.

Obviously an idea cannot be separated into parts like cogs and springs or chemical elements. An idea can be analyzed only into other ideas. For instance, the idea of nationalism can be analyzed only in terms of human motives, attitudes, and interests. Nor can an organization be analyzed by spatial separation. For example, a corporation cannot be analyzed by physically grouping the individual chairs, desks, typewriters, and filing cabinets which appear in various departments. These objects do not constitute the departments, nor do the physical persons employed in the respective departments. We can analyze a corporation only by understanding what constitutes the function of a department.

In dealing with nationalism or a corporation, then, we must perform the analysis in our minds, by the use of our reason. This is conceptual analysis. It must be remembered, however, that conceptual analysis may be used to report on subjects which have physical existence. For instance, when the chemist, instead of performing a chemical analysis before his class, describes the composition of a substance, he is giving a conceptual analysis. The fact that he has earlier made a chemical analysis of the substance in his laboratory does not mean that the present analysis is physical.

Conceptual analysis is the kind which concerns us here, the kind which we can perform in our minds and report in words, in a discourse.

## ANALYSIS AND STRUCTURE

Analysis, as we have said, is a method of dividing into parts. In this statement we should emphasize the word *method*. An analysis does not take place by accident, but by design, in the light of some principle. A baby tearing up the morning paper can scarcely be said to perform an analysis.

We can propose an analysis only if we regard the thing analyzed as constituting a determinate structure. A thing constitutes a structure when its components may be regarded not as assembled at random but as being organized, as having necessary relations to each other. For example, we do not regard a pile of bricks as a structure, but we do so regard a brick wall. We regard an automobile as a structure, a human body, a corporation, a textbook, a tree. In each of these things some principle determines the relation among the parts.

According to our different interests, we may regard the same object as having various kinds of structure. For example, the botanist would regard an apple as one kind of structure, and therefore would analyze it into, shall we say, stem, skin, flesh, seeds, and so forth, whereas a chemist would regard it as another kind and would analyze it into certain chemical elements, or a painter would regard it as still another kind and would analyze it into a pattern of color. Each man would perform his analysis in terms of a particular interest, and the interest prompting his analysis would decide the kind of structure which he took the object to be, and the kind of structure which he took it to be would determine what might be regarded as a part of the structure.

In illustrating the fact that the same thing may be regarded as having different kinds of structure, we have used an example having physical existence, an apple. But the same thing may hold good of something with no physical existence, say a short story. We may regard it as a grammatical structure, for it is made up of words. Or we may regard it as a fictional structure, that is, as being composed of plot, of characters, of theme—things which we can think of and discuss as separate elements. Or an institution may be regarded as having different kinds of structure. For instance, we may regard the family as an educational structure, an economic structure, or a moral structure. Each of these structures implies different relationships among the members of a family.

## ANALYSIS: RELATION AMONG PARTS

We have said that a thing may be regarded as a structure when its parts may be regarded not as assembled at random but as being organized, as having necessary relations to each other. So a complete analysis does not merely specify the parts of the thing analyzed but indicates the relation among parts. It tells how the parts fulfill their individual functions in composing the structure in which they participate. It tells what principle binds them together. For instance, a lecturer in political science analyzing the structure of our government would not only name the three main divisions—legislative, judicial, and executive—but would indicate the significance of each in the government. Otherwise, his audience would learn little from him. Or if we analyze a theme into its parts—introduction, discussion, and conclusion—we make our analysis intelligible by telling what constitutes an introduction, what it is supposed to accomplish.

We have said that in making an analysis it is useful to indicate the relation among the parts distinguished. In fact, we may go even further and say that a part is to be distinguished as an element which has some significant relation to the whole. In analyzing the ignition system of an automobile we are not concerned with the color of the insulation on the wires. The color has no significant relation. Or in analyzing a corporation we can scarcely be concerned with the age of the second vice-president or his taste in cigars. We are concerned only with his relation to the corporation as a corporation, not with his individual qualities in so far as they have no bearing on his job.

## ANALYSIS AND EXPOSITORY DESCRIPTION

Such analysis as we have been discussing—analysis which divides a thing into its parts—can be regarded as a form of expository description (p. 45). It is a way of explaining the thing analyzed. It is technical in its method, and aims, not at giving a vivid immediate impression, but at leading to an understanding of the thing analyzed. When the analysis is concerned with a type, we have generalized description. In the example below we see that the analysis is of a type of mechanism, not of a particular set of radar equipment. It is concerned with the parts which must be present in any radar set if that set is to fulfill its proper function. We notice that, though the primary intention is to distinguish the parts, there is also a clear indication of the use of each part in the structure.

Practically every radar set is made up of the following major parts or components:

1, A modulator; 2, A radio-frequency oscillator; 3, An antenna with suitable scanning mechanism; 4, A receiver; and 5, An indicator.

While the physical form for each of these components may vary widely from one kind of radar set to another, each radar must have this complement of parts in order to function.

1. The *modulator* is a device for taking power from the primary source (which may be the commercial power line, a special engine or motor-driven generator, or storage batteries) and forming suitable voltage pulses to drive the r-f oscillator in its bursts of radio-frequency oscillations. In other words, it is the modulator which turns on the radio-frequency oscillator to oscillate violently for a millionth of a second or so, turns it off sharply and keeps it in repose until time for the next burst.

2. The *radio-frequency oscillator* is a vacuum tube of suitable design, or a group of such tubes, which will oscillate at the desired radio frequency and give the desired bursts of radio-frequency power when connected to the modulator. The development of suitable oscillator tubes has been one of the major achievements of the radar art. It is a relatively simple job to produce a radio-frequency oscillator which will give oscillations of any desired frequency provided one is satisfied with a power of only a few thousandths of a watt. In the receiving part of a radar circuit this amount of power is adequate. A practical radar transmitter, however, must generate during its momentary bursts of oscillation a power which may run into hundreds of kilowatts. Since the oscillator is turned on a small fraction of the time, the average power is usually hundreds of times less than the peak power, but even the average power may run up to the order of one kilowatt. Thus, practical radar equipment requires extremely high frequency oscillators running at powers thousands of times greater than was thought possible a few years ago.

3. The problem of *antenna* design is also one of the major problems in radar, incomprehensible as this may seem to the operator of a home radio receiver, who finds a few yards of wire strung up on his roof ade-

quate for his purpose. A suitable radar antenna must have the following characteristics:

    a. It must be directional; that is, it must concentrate the radio energy into a definitely defined beam, since this is the method by which the direction to the objects detected is determined.

    b. It must be highly efficient. All of the generated power must go into the beam and none must leak off into "side lobes" in other directions, since such side lobes may often be fatally confusing; and,

    c. The radar antenna must be capable of being directed or scanned from one point in space to another, and on shipboard and in aircraft it must frequently be stabilized to take out the motions of the ship or airplane itself.

An antenna may be made directional either by building it up of an array of small antennas or dipoles, suitably spaced and phased to concentrate the energy in one direction, or it may be built on the searchlight principle of spraying the energy into a large parabolic "mirror," which focuses the energy into a beam. In either case, the larger the antenna, the sharper the beam for any given wave length. Sometimes antennas may be longer in one direction than the other, giving a beam which is sharper in the first direction and thus fan shaped.

The *scanning* of the portion of space which the radar set is intended to cover must usually be done by mechanical movement of the antenna structure itself. This means that the structure, whatever its size, must swing around or up and down to direct the beam in the necessary direction. In certain cases where one needs to scan only a small sector, techniques have been worked out for rapid electrical scanning not requiring the motion of the whole antenna structure itself. So far, however, there has been no method for extending this rapid electrical scanning to cover more than a relatively small sector. Radars for directing guns which need accurate and fast data in a small sector are making use, however, of this valuable technique.

To carry the radio-frequency energy from the oscillator to the antenna, and the echo from the antenna to the receiver, wires and coaxial cables are used at ordinary wave lengths. For microwaves, however, it is more efficient to use wave guides, which essentially are carefully proportioned hollow pipes—and the transmission system hence is often called "plumbing."

4. The problem of the *receiver* for radar is also a complex one. In practically all radars the superheterodyne principle is employed, which involves generating at low power a radio frequency fairly close to that received, and "beating" this against the received signals, forming an intermediate frequency, which is then amplified many times. Curiously

enough the crystal, used as a detector and mixer, has again come into its own in microwave receivers. The peculiar characteristics of pulse signals require that receivers be built with extremely fast response, much faster even than that required in television. The final stages must prepare the signals for suitable presentation in the indicator. The receiver normally occupies a relatively small box in the complete radar set, and yet this box represents a marvel of engineering ingenuity. A particularly difficult piece of development is concerned with a part closely connected with the receiver. This is a method of disconnecting the receiver from the antenna during intervals when the transmitter is operating so that the receiver will not be paralyzed or burned out by the stupendous bursts of radio-frequency energy generated by the transmitter. Within a millionth of a second after the transmitter has completed its pulse, however, the receiver must be open to receive the relatively weak echo signals; but now the transmitter part of the circuit must be closed off so it will not absorb any of this energy.

5. It is the *indicator* of a radar that presents the information collected in a form best adapted to efficient use of the set. Nearly (but not quite) all radar indicators consist of one or more cathode-ray tubes. In the simplest or "A" type of presentation the electron beam is given a deflection proportional to time in one direction—say, horizontally—and proportional to the strength of the echo pulse in the other—say, vertically. If no signals are visible, then one sees a bright horizontal line (the "time base") across the tube face, the distance along this line representing time elapsed after the outgoing pulse. A returning echo then gives a V-shaped break in the line at the point corresponding to the time it took the echo to come back. The position of the "pip" along this line measures the distance to the reflecting object. There are many variations of this type of indicator for special purposes, but most radars have an A-scope, even when other types are also provided.

Many types of radar whose antennas "scan" various directions employ the PPI tube. Here the time base starts from the center of the tube and moves radially outward in a direction corresponding to that in which the antenna is pointing. This time base rotates in synchronism with the antenna. The returning signal, instead of causing a break in the time base, simply intensifies its brilliance for an instant. Hence each signal appears as a bright spot of light at a position corresponding to the range and bearing of the target. Thus a maplike picture of all reflecting objects appears in the cathode-ray tube face.

Since the antenna can usually be rotated only slowly (e.g., from 1 to 20 r.p.m.) and since the light from an ordinary cathode-ray tube fades away almost instantly, one might expect not to see a "map" at all, but only bright flashes at various spots as the antenna revolves. Some way had to be found to make the brightness of these flashes persist for many seconds after they were produced. Special screens were developed which continue to glow for some time after being lighted by a signal. Thus the whole map is displayed at once.—OFFICE OF WAR INFORMATION: *Radar: A Report on Science at War.*[20]

## APPLICATIONS

You are now to write a theme of 500 words analyzing a mechanism, institution, or idea. In doing so, you should consider the following points:

a. Identify or define the thing to be analyzed.
b. Specify what principle of structure is to be considered.
c. Indicate the parts.
d. State what relations exist among the parts in reference to the principle of the whole structure.

The list of topics below may suggest a subject for your theme:

A regiment of infantry
A university
Nationalism
Morality
The internal combustion engine
A newspaper
A political party
A television set

A church
A business organization
A football team
American Sectionalism
A poem
A picture
True charity
A hospital

## FUNCTIONAL ANALYSIS

The kind of analysis which we have been discussing provides the answer to such a question as, "How is it put together?" But when we undertake to answer the question, "How does it work?" we give what is called FUNCTIONAL ANALYSIS. We have to say how the parts of a thing, whatever that thing is, relate to each other in action so that that thing fulfills its characteristic function. We are, furthermore, concerned with the stages of a process. We have to explain how something comes about, and this means that our analysis will be in a time sequence.

[20] From *Radar: A Report on Science at War,* issued by the Office of War Information, sponsored by the Office of Scientific Research and Development, the War Department and the Navy Department, obtainable from the Superintendent of Documents, U. S. Government Printing Office.

Since it is in time sequence, this kind of analysis is a form of expository narration. It may be of a particular event, say the stages by which an inventor arrived at the solution of a problem, or it may be of an event which is characteristically repeated, say the manufacture of hydrochloric acid or the training of a football squad. In the latter instance, the analysis of the stages of an event characteristically repeated, we get generalized narration.

It is easiest to understand functional analysis if we think of it as applied to some mechanism. If we take an alarm clock, for instance, we can see how the spring provides power, how this power is controlled by a system of reducing gears and a checking device so that it does not expend itself in one spurt, how the pace of expenditure is evenly controlled so that the movement of the hands serves as a register of time, and how at a certain fixed point the alarm is released. We are concerned with the parts here, but only in so far as they relate to the special function of the mechanism. In so far as we undertake to explain the process by which the special function is fulfilled, we are giving a functional analysis. In other words, our primary concern is with stages in a process, and the parts are interesting to us only in so far as they are associated with stages. To take another example, it is not functional analysis to list the components of apple pie and describe their relation to each other, but it is functional analysis to tell how to make a pie. When we give these directions, we are dealing with stages in a process.

The same general principle, the concern with stages, applies when we are dealing, not with a mechanism or with directions for making or doing something, but with an organization or institution. It is one thing, for instance, to describe the organization of our government, and it is quite another to tell how a bill becomes law, how legality may be tested in the Supreme Court, and how the law may be enforced. In telling how the bill becomes law, and so on, we are giving a functional analysis.

Functional analysis, then, is the method by which we distinguish the stages in a process which may be regarded as having a characteristic function or purpose. Though we use the word *functional* to describe the particular kind of analysis, we may distinguish between the characteristic function and the characteristic purpose of whatever is analyzed. An example may enlighten us. If we are discussing a university, we can treat the subject in terms of purpose, for it is an institution created by men to gain certain ends. But if we are discussing the circulation of the blood, we can treat the subject only in terms of a characteristic function. We cannot say that purpose is involved. Or to take another contrasted pair of examples, if we give directions for making an apple pie, we are treating our subject in terms of purpose, but if we discuss the stages of development of an apple, we are treating the subject in terms of function. In both instances we can, of course, observe a regular pattern, but in one case we interpret the pattern as representing purpose and in the other as representing function.

Sometimes we can fruitfully distinguish both function and purpose in a thing which we wish to analyze. For instance, it might be said that we give an analysis of a radar set in terms of function: it operates because of certain natural laws which cannot be said to represent purpose. But at the same time the equipment is constructed to use those natural laws for a purpose. Man has a purpose in constructing the equipment. To construct the set man has manipulated certain materials in terms of natural laws (the only way he could manipulate the materials) to achieve a certain purpose. He cannot manipulate his circulatory system. So we may take the fact of manipulation as the point of distinction.

What is the significance of this distinction for purposes of exposition? It is a way of defining our subject, of knowing exactly what sort of structure we are dealing with. And that in itself is a step toward understanding.

Below is an example of functional analysis applied to a mechanism, something created by man to fulfill a certain purpose, a radar set. Contrast the method used here with the previous analysis of the set into its parts.

In radar, unlike communications, the transmitter and the receiver are located at the same place, and more often than not have a common antenna. The transmitter is actually sending out energy only a very small part of the time; it sends out this energy in very intense bursts of small duration, called pulses. These pulses may be only a millionth of a second long. After each pulse, the transmitter waits a relatively long time—a few thousandths of a second—before sending out the next pulse. During the interval between pulses, the receiver is working and the signals it receives are the echoes of the powerful transmitted pulse from nearby objects. The nearest objects will give echoes coming very soon after the transmitter pulse is finished; those farther away give later returns. The elapsed time between the transmission of the pulse and the reception of its echo measures the distance of the object giving that echo—ship, airplane, mountain, or building—from the place where the radar set is located. This is possible because the elapsed time is just that required for the pulse, which travels with the speed of light, to get there and back. Light travels very fast, as everybody knows, hence these intervals are very small. Their exact measurement is one of the technical triumphs of modern radar. Since light goes 186,000 miles a second, or 328 yards each millionth of a second, and since it must travel twice—out and back—the distance from radar to target, an object 1,000 yards from the radar will give an echo only six-millionths of a second later than the transmitted pulse. This is a rather short time, by prewar standards, but we have learned how to measure time like this with an accuracy which corresponds to only 5 or 10 yards range, or about one-thirtieth of a millionth of a second.

The use of pulses, as we have seen, gives a simple means of measuring the range. How, then, is the direction in which a target lies determined? This is done by providing the radar with a directional antenna, which sends out the pulses in a narrow beam, like a searchlight. This antenna may be rotated as the pulses are sent out, and we get back a "pip" (radar slang for a target indication) when the antenna is pointed toward its target. We get the strongest pip when the beam of energy sent out by the radar is pointed directly at the target. The bearing of the antenna —which is also the bearing of the target—may then be read off and used to point a warship's guns, or set the course of a bomber, or direct a fighter to intercept an enemy plane, or for other use the particular purpose of the equipment dictates.

An even more spectacular indication of the direction and range of the target is obtained with the use of the PPI—Plan Position Indicator. In this case, the radar echoes are caused to draw a map on the face of a cathode-ray tube. The radar operator could imagine himself suspended high above the set, whether on a ship or plane or on the ground, looking down on the scene spread out below. No matter how many targets surround the radar set, each is indicated by a blob of light on the tube face—the direction of the blob from the center indicating the target's range. The whole picture is there. It is not like television; the blobs do not actually look like ships or planes, but are interpretable to a trained operator.

Still other ways of displaying radar echoes are used. On a battleship, for example, where exact range is desired to lay the 16-inch guns, the radar echoes are so displayed that the operator can read a range scale down to a few yards. In the case of Army antiaircraft fire, the radar antenna actually moves automatically so that it always points at the plane without help from an operator, and the guns follow automatically by remote control. Other types of radar use other types of displays, designed to perform one or another special purpose.

What we may call the sharpness of vision of a radar set—its ability to distinguish separately the echoes from two targets close together and at the same distance from the radar—depends on the sharpness of the radar beam. With an antenna of given size, the beam will become sharper and sharper as the wave length decreases. In fact, for a given antenna size, the beam width is just proportional to the wave length. The earliest radar worked on wave lengths of several meters, with correspondingly broad beams, unless large antennas were used. Then there was a great flowering of equipment working near a meter and a half, which was, at the beginning of the war, about the shortest wave length at which radio techniques had been worked out. The wartime period of development has witnessed an intensive exploitation of shorter and shorter wave lengths.
—OFFICE OF WAR INFORMATION: *Radar: A Report on Science at War.*

Here is an example of functional analysis applied to an organization, our financial system. This is not a very orderly piece of exposition as compared with the analysis of radar. But we can reduce it to order by extracting the answers to several questions: (1) What would be the four functions of a financial system in our society? (2) How were these functions related to each other to produce the present system? (3) How would these functions be related in what Brandeis calls a beneficent system?

How the masters of credit-financing gradually, through processes of interlocking directorates, achieved their complete overlordship of finance, industry, insurance, communication, and transportation is a long story—too long to be told here. The interested reader can get it most vividly in Louis (now Justice) Brandeis' *Other People's Money.* In that book he declares:

"The dominant element in our financial oligarchy is the investment banker. Associated banks, trust companies and life insurance companies are his tools. Controlled railroads, public service and industrial corporations are his subjects. Though properly but middlemen, these bankers bestride as masters America's business world, so that practically no large enterprise can be undertaken successfully without their participation or approval."

It is well to ponder these words: "practically no large enterprise can be undertaken successfully without their participation or approval." They are an ironic commentary upon the statement so often made by the defenders of the economic *status quo* that the present system is one which encourages the utmost freedom of initiative. "These bankers bestride as masters America's business world."

"The key to their power," Brandeis continues, "is combination." In the first place, there was the legal consolidation of banks and trust companies; then there were affiliations brought about by stockholders, voting trusts, and interlocking directorates in banking institutions which were not legally connected; and finally, there were the gentlemen's agreements, joint transactions, and "banking ethics," which unofficially eliminated competition among the investment bankers.

In the second place, the organization of railroads into huge systems, the large consolidations of public service corporations, and the creation of industrial trusts directly played into the hands of the associated New York bankers, for these businesses were so vast that no local, independent bank could supply the necessary funds.

These factors alone, however, "could not have produced the Money Trust . . . another and more potent factor of combination was added." It is this third factor that is most astounding.

Investment bankers were dealers in stocks, bonds, and notes. As such, they performed one necessary function in our kind of society. In order that they should possess the public's confidence, they had to be able, with complete objectivity, to estimate the soundness of what they sold. Hence they could not themselves, properly, have an interest in the investments. They had to be middlemen pure and simple.

But not so. Through the purchases of voting stock they became the directing power in the very enterprises—railroads, public service and industrial corporations—that were the *issuers* of the securities they sold.

But more than this. They purchased voting stock in the great enterprises, like life insurance companies and other corporate reservoirs of the people's savings, that were the buyers of securities. So they made for themselves a ready market for the securities which they themselves issued.

And finally, they became the governing power in banks and trust companies. These were the depositories of the savings of the people. As holders of these savings they were able to make loans to (their own) corporations; these in turn could issue securities that the investment bankers could readily sell to their own corporations as well as buy at figures acceptable to themselves and sell at conveniently higher prices to their own depositors and the public.

"Thus four distinct functions, each essential to business, and each exercised, originally, by a distinct set of men became united in the investment banker. It is to this union of business functions that the existence of the Money Trust is mainly due."

And Brandeis concludes his analysis with this ominous observation:

"The development of our financial oligarchy followed, in this respect, lines with which the history of political despotism has familiarized us: usurpation, proceeding by gradual encroachment rather than by violent acts; subtle and often long-concealed concentration of distinct functions, which are beneficent when separately administered, and dangerous only when combined in the same persons. It was by such processes as these that Caesar Augustus became master of Rome."—H. A. OVERSTREET: *A Declaration of Interdependence,* Chap. 3.[21]

## APPLICATIONS

Write a functional analysis of some mechanism, process, or organization. In preparing your material keep the following points in mind:

*a.* Indicate the nature of the purpose or function involved.

*b.* Distinguish the stages in the fulfillment of that function or purpose.

*c.* State the relation of each stage to a part of the thing involved. (For instance, in dealing with a mechanism we think of a part as performing some function; in dealing with an organization we think of the business of some person or department; in dealing with directions for making something, we think of the parts of the thing to be made.)

*d.* State the relation of each stage to the one following.

The list of topics below may be useful for suggestions:

1. How funds are collected for the Community Chest
2. The nomination of a Presidential Candidate
3. The Rag Rug
4. The Rotary Press
5. A Voting Machine
6. An operation for appendicitis
7. Hotel dining room
8. Staging a play
9. Organizing a drive against juvenile delinquency

[21] Reprinted from *A Declaration of Interdependence* by H. A. Overstreet, by permission of W. W. Norton & Company, Inc. Copyright 1937 by the publishers. The late Justice Brandeis is quoted by permission of Susan Brandeis.

## CHRONOLOGICAL ANALYSIS

Sometimes we are called upon to deal with a subject which we cannot easily treat with reference to function or purpose. For instance, a historical event.

It is true that a historical event may involve human purposes, many human purposes, but the event itself cannot be understood merely by reference to those purposes. The individual purposes may be too numerous, too various, and too confused. By the same token we cannot find a characteristic function. Or different people may find different functions, as it were, according to their interpretation of history. For example, it is hardly precise to say that the French Revolution had a function in our sense of the word, in the sense that the human heart has a function in the circulation of the blood.

If we cannot discuss an event, however, with reference to a purpose or function, we may, at least, try to distinguish the stages in the process. We can sort out the steps. Our concern is to establish the facts in their chronological order and to arrange them so that they can be grasped as some sort of pattern. We may want to do this as a preliminary to further study, but if we can do no more we can at least try to see the pattern of sequence in time. This kind of analysis we may call CHRONOLOGICAL ANALYSIS.

For example, in an article on the last days of General Rommel, who was in command of the German forces supposed to defend France against the British and American landings on D-Day, June 6, 1944, the author analyzes the complex event into its stages:

There were to be five acts in the swift concluding drama of Rommel's career—and of his world. Roughly stated, their themes in sequence were: initial stupefaction, improvisation, frustration, desperation, and final liquidation.—WILLIAM HARLAN HALE: "The End of Marshal Rommel."

Then the author proceeds to discuss each stage. The chronological analysis gives him the frame for his treatment, for his interpretation.

## CAUSAL ANALYSIS

We often want to go beyond a mere sequence in time. One way to do this is to consider cause and effect. CAUSAL ANALYSIS is concerned with two questions: "What caused this?" and "Given this set of circumstances, what effect will follow?" In answering the first we must reason from effect back to cause, and in answering the second, from cause forward to effect. Again, as with chronological analysis, this kind of analysis usually takes the form of expository narration. We are accustomed to think of cause and effect in a time sequence, a chain of happenings.

## CAUSE

What do we understand by cause? We all have a rough-and-ready notion. We have to have a notion of it in order to manage our daily lives. The burnt child shuns the fire only after he has learned that a certain act, putting his finger in the flame, is followed by a certain unpleasant effect, a burn. He has made a connection between events.

Cause is a certain kind of connection between events. It is the kind of connection that enables us to say that without event A, event B would not have come about, and whenever you have A you will have B.[22]

## IMMEDIATE CONNECTION

The connection between cause and effect, between our A and our B, is relatively immediate. Sometimes we encounter an idea of cause that ignores the immediate connection—that regards as a cause of B whatever goes to provide, however remotely, the conditions that have resulted in the existence of B. In the poem "Flower in the Crannied Wall," by Tennyson, we see that idea:

> Flower in the crannied wall,
> I pluck you out of the crannies,
> I hold you here, root and all, in my hand,
> Little flower—but *if* I could understand
> What you are, root and all, and all in all,
> I should know what God and man is.

[22] The use of the word *event* here may be objected to. It may be said, for instance, that the word *thing* might be substituted, at least on some occasions, for the word *event*. We may say that a nail is the cause of the fact that the picture hangs on the wall, and that a nail is a thing. But it is not the nail as a thing that sustains the picture. It is its state of being in the wall that causes the picture to be sustained, and its state of being in the wall is an

The poet says that if he could explain the flower he could explain God and man. He is here thinking of a tissue of relationships binding the whole universe so that to know the "cause" of the flower would be to know the entire universe.

To take another example, one might say, by this wide use of the word *cause*, that the birth of the grandfather (A) is the "cause" of the death of the grandson (B)—for had the grandfather not existed, the grandson would not have existed, and had the grandson not existed, he could not have died.

In our discussion, however, we are concerned with a more immediate idea of cause: the death of the grandson is in our ordinary view caused by, shall we say, a fall from a stepladder and not by the birth of the grandfather. By and large, the more immediate the relation between A and B the more certainly it can be discussed as cause.

### CAUSE AND INTEREST

What we take to be the cause of an event is, in one way, dictated by our special interest in the event. When the little grandson falls from the stepladder and is killed, a neighbor, commenting on the event, would be satisfied by the fact of the fall from the ladder as the cause. But the mother might take her own carelessness as the cause: she left the stepladder standing on the edge of the back porch instead of putting it away in the closet where it belonged. Or a physiologist might take a more scientific view of the cause and say that death was the result of a fracture of the skull of such and such a nature.

In its own perspective, in relation to the special interest brought to bear on the event, each of these statements may be true. What is important is to know what we are doing when we take a particular line of interest to explain an event.

### A CONDITION

An event does not take place in complete isolation. It takes place in the world, and many factors constitute its setting. To study the

---

event. There must be things, of course, for there to be events, but the event is what we are concerned with. The state of a thing is an event, in the meaning of the word in our discussion.

cause of something we must give some attention to the setting, the situation in which it occurs.

Let us take a simple instance, one that could be set up as an experiment. To a clockwork device which will sway back and forth when hung on a string, we attach a little bell. The bell will ring as the device oscillates on its string. The whole thing is hung inside a large glass jar. When the mechanism swings, we can hear the bell ring. But let us pump the air out of the jar. The bell will continue to swing back and forth and the clapper will strike the sides of the bell, but now we can hear no sound. The bell does not ring.[23]

We know why. For there to be a sound, there must be a medium in which the sound waves can travel to our ears. When there was air in the jar there was a sound because the air was the medium for the waves. But when there is no air, there is no sound.

In this situation we may call the air a CONDITION. And a condition, as we use the word, is whatever factor existing in a situation will permit the effect to appear. It is a factor that we regard as a kind of background to the event being considered. Yet it must be a significant background. Some background factors are not significant. For instance, in our experiment the color of the glass of the jar is not significant. It has no relation to the event. A change in the color of the glass will not alter the event.[24]

[23] This account of the experiment is paraphrased from L. S. Stebbing, *A Modern Introduction to Logic*, 2nd ed., London, 1933, pp. 270-71.

[24] How do we distinguish a condition from a cause? If, in our jar experiment, we are thinking of cause in its most immediate connection, we may take the stroke of the clapper against the side of the bell to be the cause of the sound. In that case, we regard the motion generated by the clockwork mechanism to be, like the presence of the air, a condition. But we might take the motion of the mechanism to be the cause, and regard the free-swinging clapper as a condition, a factor that permits the event to take place.

So we cannot make an absolute distinction between condition and cause. We must return to our notion that the interest we bring to bear on a situation is significant in our taking one factor rather than another to be the cause. We focus our interest on one factor, and assume the presence of the others. For instance, Tennyson, looking at his flower in the crannied wall, might have said that the cause was the fact that a bird had dropped a seed there. But without the conditions of nutrition, moisture, heat, and light, he would not have had the flower. When he selected one factor as the cause of the event, he was assuming the presence of the others. In a fuller sense, then, *the* cause

## SUFFICIENT CONDITION AND NECESSARY CONDITION

There are two kinds of condition, SUFFICIENT CONDITION and NECESSARY CONDITION.

Let us take a situation in which the event B occurs. In this situation X is a factor, a condition. The condition X is a sufficient condition if, other things being the same, B occurs whenever X is present. But suppose that B occurs on some occasions when X is not present. For example, the bell of our experiment might be heard when some other gas than air was present in the jar. In that case the air is a sufficient condition, but it is not necessary: some other gas will do. Or to take another example, we may say that whenever we do not bank the furnace at night, the fire goes out. Not banking the furnace is, then, a sufficient condition. But it is not a necessary condition. The furnace may also go out if the damper is closed or if there is not enough fuel.

To illustrate a necessary condition, we may take a situation in which B never occurs when the condition Y is absent. It is necessary for Y to be present for B to occur. Thus we may say that nutrition is a necessary condition of human life, or that fuel is a necessary condition for the functioning of the furnace.

But we can have a condition that is necessary and not sufficient. To have the spark plugs in order is a necessary condition for the running of our automobile. But this is not a sufficient condition. Among other things, we must have the battery connected. Nor is nutrition a sufficient condition of human life. Many other conditions must prevail at the same time for life to exist.

## THE PRINCIPLE OF UNIFORMITY

When we say that A is the cause of B, we are not merely referring to the particular case of a particular A and a particular B. We are also implying that a general principle exists, that under the

---

of the flower is the complex of factors, of conditions. And so it may be said of any event.

What is important in thinking about cause is to know what we are doing if we take some single factor to be the cause of an event. We must try to know how the factor we have selected is related to other factors. Or if we take a group of factors to be the cause, we must try to know what relation they bear to each other and to the event. And this leads us to the distinction, discussed above, between two kinds of condition.

same circumstances any A would cause a B. We imply a principle of uniformity behind the particular case. Let us take a simple instance:

Tom asks, "Why did Jane behave so strangely last night at dinner?"

Jack replies, "Because she was mad at her husband."

Tom asks, "How do you know?"

Jack replies, "That's the way she always behaves when she gets mad at him."

Tom asks, "You must have been around the family a lot?"

Jack replies, "Sure, I lived in the house for a year."

When Jack says that the cause of Jane's conduct was her anger at her husband he is not merely commenting on the particular instance. And Tom's further question elicits the fact that a principle of uniformity is involved: Jane behaves this way *every* time she gets angry with her husband. The principle here may not be one on which we can depend with any great degree of certainty. On some future occasion she may not merely be short with her husband at dinner but may kick the cat, get a divorce, or shoot her husband in the shoulder with a Smith and Wesson .38. But past observation gives us some degree of probability that when Jane is angry with her husband she merely behaves in a certain way at dinner, that a principle of uniformity is involved.

The same principle is involved in what we call a law of nature. A chemist says that when we ignite hydrogen in the presence of oxygen we will get water, $H_2O$. The element hydrogen and the element oxygen will always behave the same way under specified conditions. At least we believe that to be true because the two elements have always behaved that way in the past. We must appeal to experience and to a number of instances.

Furthermore, the principle of uniformity refers only to the essential characteristics of the situation. For instance, it doesn't matter whether the laboratory worker igniting hydrogen in the presence of oxygen is a Catholic or a Jew, a Republican or a Democrat, a Chinese or a Greek. Or to take Charles Lamb's story of the boy who accidentally discovered how to roast a pig by burning down a house, the boy had not isolated the essential characteristic of the situation: he had not learned that he didn't have to burn down a house every time he wanted roast pig but could make a small fire in the yard. He had not isolated the essential characteristic of fire that would do the roasting.

Or let us examine the treatment of the sick in a certain primitive tribe. The medicine man undertakes to cure the patient by a draught of a brew, the sacrifice of three cocks, and a dance around the pallet. In a fair number of instances the patient recovers. A modern physician examining the situation regards the sacrifice and dancing as irrelevant to a cure. But he analyzes the brew and discovers that one of the plants always present has a purgative effect. He has located the essential characteristic, and now only has to persuade the tribe that a dose of castor oil is cheaper, quicker, and better for stomach-ache than the medicine man's ritual. The principle of uniformity applies to the essential characteristic, the effect of castor oil on the human body.

## APPLICATIONS

1. Analyze the following situation to determine the conditions, the factors relevant to the event. Can you think of any that must be involved but are not specified here? Identify the different factors which different "interests" might select as *the* cause of Mr. Mead's death—for instance, the interest of a political reformer, a child welfare agency, a physiologist. Can you think of other interests?

Mr. Alford owns an old apartment building which does not conform to the safety regulations of the city. Because of Mr. Alford's political connections the fire inspection of his building is superficial.

In one of the apartments of the building lives a family by the name of Gordon, composed of Mr. and Mrs. Gordon, their son Jimmy, and Mrs. Gordon's mother. Mr. Gordon has managed to get the apartment by means of business pressure put upon Mr. Alford.

Mrs. Gordon is a rather careless housekeeper and allows trash to accumulate in closets and pantries. Mrs. Gordon's mother, an impatient and irritable woman, one day locks young Jimmy in the pantry because of some piece of misbehavior. In his bad temper Jimmy kicks the brooms and mops about. A metal mop head falls against a piece of exposed electric wiring and the short circuit ignites some old papers and rags which Mrs. Gordon has left in the pantry.

Jimmy's screams warn the family, which escapes from the burning building, but Mr. Mead, asleep in an apartment above, is burned to death.

**II.** Read "The Hickman Story" in the Readings (p. 600). Apply to it the same questions you have just applied to the account of the death of Mr. Mead.

**III.** Each of the following statements has been given at one time or another as *the* cause of the victory of the Federal Government over the Confederacy in the American Civil War. In the light of common sense and what historical information you possess, would you accept any of these statements as a statement of *the* cause? If not, why not?

1. The North had well-established industries.
2. The grand strategy of the North was better than that of the South.
3. The North had a constantly replenished reservoir of military replacements from European immigration.
4. The Southern railroads were inferior to those of the North.
5. The principle of States Rights weakened the central government of the Confederacy and prevented concerted action.
6. Bad intelligence work by Lee's cavalry before Gettysburg lost the battle.
7. England did not recognize the Confederacy.
8. The North was fighting for a great ideal.

**IV.** Discuss the question of the essential characteristic in relation to each of the following statements.

1. By a Sunday School superintendent: "Jimmie Clark has just won the debating prize in the university. It just goes to show what a boy from our church can do."
2. By a mother: "As soon as Thomas caught that cold I gave him a good scolding for not drying his hair after swimming, and put him to bed in my room—you know he is not more than a baby yet and likes to be there—and gave him some cough drops and some quinine, and turned the light down so it wouldn't shine in his eyes, and read to him till he went to sleep—and you know, I cured him in no time. He was well the next morning."
3. By an old man being congratulated on his hundredth birthday: "I attribute my long life to the fact I never smoked or chewed or drank and lived at peace with my neighbors."
4. By a despondent student: "The reason I don't make good grades in math is that I don't have a good memory."

## REASONING ABOUT CAUSE

How do we reason about the cause-and-effect relation in a situation?

To begin with we must keep in mind two primary notions:

1. A cannot be the cause of B if A is ever absent when B is present.

2. A cannot be the cause of B if B is ever absent when A is present.

This is but another way of saying that, under a given set of circumstances, A and B are uniformly related.

Let us notice the phrase, "under a given set of circumstances." It is relatively easy in a laboratory to control the circumstances of an experiment, and to repeat the experiment any number of times in the same circumstances. This gives the experimenter the chance to try different combinations of factors until he has isolated the one factor or the group of factors which he can regard as a cause. If, for example, his situation has factors A, X, Y, and Z as possible causes for the effect B, he can show by a process of elimination that A will cause B, and that X, Y, and Z will not.

But it is hard to control the circumstances outside of the laboratory. And many events in the outside world that we want to explain cannot be repeated at will. We must examine the cases we have and try to make sense of them. Furthermore, many events are enormously complicated. More than one factor contributes to the effect, and we have a complex and not a simple cause. Situations involving human behavior are difficult to treat in terms of cause and effect, but we are constantly making the effort despite the complexity of factors involved. The advertising man, the politician, the teacher, the mother of a family, the sociologist, the historian—they are all trying to reason about human behavior. We must make the effort, even if we know that we can scarcely hope for a full measure of success.

Even if we cannot hope for full success in dealing with complicated situations we can at least reduce our margin of error by remembering certain things. First, we can examine the situation to try to see what is essential in it. In every event there are certain factors that are not relevant to the event, things that are merely associated with it. We must rule those factors out of our consideration.

For an example, we can take the following passage:

Whenever I see the movement of a locomotive I hear the whistle and see the valves opening and wheels turning; but I have no right to conclude that the whistling and the turning of wheels are the cause of the movement of the engine.

The peasants say that a cold wind blows in late spring because the oaks are budding, and really every spring cold winds do blow when the oak is budding. But I do not know what causes the cold winds to blow when the oak buds unfold, I cannot agree with the peasants that the unfolding of the oak buds is the cause of the cold wind, for the force of the wind is beyond the influence of the buds. I see only a coincidence of occurrences such as happens with all the phenomena of life, and I see that however much and however carefully I observe the hands of the watch, and the valves and wheels of the engine, and the oak, I shall not discover the cause of the bells ringing, the engine moving, or of the winds of spring. To do that I must entirely change my point of view and study the laws of the movement of steam, of the bells, and of the wind.
—LEO TOLSTOY: *War and Peace*, Book XI, Chap. 1.

The fact that something is merely associated with something else in time does not mean that it is to be regarded as either cause or effect of the thing. In fact, one of the commonest failures in reasoning about cause and effect is to assume that if something comes after something else it is to be regarded as the effect. The Russian peasant in Tolstoy's novel thinks the cold wind is the effect of the budding of the oak because it comes after it. To avoid such an error, we must try to find the essential characteristic in the situation we are studying.

We must remember, too, that we are concerned with a principle of uniformity. That means that we must consider more than one case. We must check other situations which seem similar to our situation in order to find what is constant from one to the other. For example, if a historian should wish to find what situations provoke revolutions, he would study as many revolutions as possible to locate the common factors. Then he might venture a conclusion. But studying one revolution would scarcely give him grounds for a conclusion. When we try to find the cause of a given effect, we appeal to what we know about uniformities beyond the particular situation.

We must remember that we are dealing with a complex of factors. Therefore we must not be too ready to seize on one factor as *the* cause. We must analyze as fully as possible the factors involved and try to see what group of factors must be present for our effect to take place. In situations involving human behavior, for example, a historical event, we may have difficulty distinguishing between factors that are relevant to the event and factors that are present as mere background. If we can accomplish this much, we have done a great deal. Then if we discuss some single factor or group of factors as cause, we must remember the relation of that factor or group of factors to the other factors present.

One last caution: in studying a situation we must try to be systematic. In the foregoing discussion of cause many of the ideas have probably struck the student as something he already knew. He *has* known them. He has been making judgments of cause and effect all his life—in fishing and hunting, in games, in gardening, in laboratory work, in crossing the street. Being acquainted with the ideas is not, however, quite enough. One must make a practice of applying them systematically to a situation. If the student can think straight about a problem of cause and effect, then it will be easy for him to write well about it. And to think straight, he must be systematic in applying ideas (see Appendix on Causal Analysis, p. 89).

## APPLICATIONS

I. We have said that in dealing with human affairs strict reasoning about cause and effect is scarcely possible. In the Readings (p. 573) we find a discussion of the causes of war by Will Durant. We must notice that the author is discussing war in general and not a particular war, though he makes reference to particular wars. How strictly is he using the word *cause?* How would you argue your view on this?

II. Study "The Method of Scientific Investigation" by ·T. H. Huxley (p. 559). Does it give you a fuller understanding of the idea of cause? Of natural law? Frame a definition of natural law.

III. Write a theme which undertakes to give a causal analysis of some situation. The following list is intended merely to suggest the sort of topic which might be chosen.
1. Why we lost (or won) the last game
2. Why Japan lost the war
3. Why volcanoes erupt
4. Why Mr. Blank made a success of his business
5. Why my father bought his particular make of car
6. Why I chose this college

7. The causes of juvenile delinquency
8. What we must know about alcoholism
9. The tornado

## EXPOSITORY METHODS AND THEIR USES

In this chapter we have considered various expository methods in relatively pure form, for example, definition by itself, or illustration by itself. But in actual practice the methods are often mixed. We move from one to another as the occasion demands. This is only natural, for the methods are methods of thought and in treating the same subject we may be compelled to use different kinds of thinking to reach a full understanding. Or in appealing to a single interest we may have to use different methods. Suppose we are dealing with the question, "What is it worth?" We have to make an evaluation of whatever the "it" happens to be. But to make an evaluation we may have to classify the thing, then analyze it, then think of its effects, then compare it with a standard we set up for the kind of thing it is.

We must not be bound by the methods. We must see them as tools which we use. And at any moment we should be able to use whatever will accomplish the purpose at hand.

## SUMMARY

EXPOSITION is the kind of discourse which explains or clarifies a subject. It appeals to the understanding, and can be applied to anything which challenges the understanding.

A piece of exposition may be regarded as the answer to a question, whether or not the question has in reality been asked. In giving a piece of exposition one should know what question, or questions, he wishes to answer, what INTEREST he wishes to appeal to. For example, "What is it?" "What does it mean?" "How is it put together?" "How does it work?" "When did it exist or occur?" "What is it worth?" If a writer wishes to appeal to more than one interest, he should keep these various interests distinct and should establish the relationship among them.

IDENTIFICATION and ILLUSTRATION are simple ways of answering the question, "What is it?"

Identification is a kind of pointing by language, a way of locating the subject in time and place, or in relation to some system. When it becomes elaborate it tends to move over into other types of exposition, such as comparison or classification.

Illustration is the method employed when some class or group is identified by giving a particular instance of the class or group. The particular instance may be an object, an event, a person, an idea—anything which may be conceived of as belonging to a certain class or group.

EXPOSITORY DESCRIPTION or TECHNICAL DESCRIPTION is the kind of description which does not aim at presenting a vivid impression of its subject, as does ordinary or SUGGESTIVE DESCRIPTION, but aims at giving information about its subject. It is scientific rather than artistic in its nature. GENERALIZED DESCRIPTION is expository description applied to a class.

EXPOSITORY NARRATION corresponds to ordinary narration as expository description corresponds to ordinary description. It is narration used to give information, and may be applied to a class to give GENERALIZED NARRATION.

In COMPARISON we clarify a subject by indicating similarities between two or more things, in CONTRAST by indicating differences. Comparison and contrast as methods of exposition are most effective when used systematically. This means that they should represent some purpose and should be undertaken in some area of interest. Comparison and contrast may be organized in either of two ways. We may fully present one item, and then fully present another. Or we may present one part of one item and then a part of the other, until we have touched on all the parts relevant to our comparison or contrast. The methods, of course, may sometimes be mixed.

CLASSIFICATION and DIVISION are ways of thinking in terms of a system of classes. A class is a group whose members have significant characteristics in common. What constitutes a significant characteristic, however, may vary according to the interest involved. For instance, a cosmetic-maker may classify women by complexion and the secretary of a Y.W.C.A. by religious affiliation. A system is a set of classes ranging from a most inclusive class down through less and less inclusive classes. Division represents a downward movement of subdivision by classes from a most inclusive class through less and less inclusive classes. Classification, however, starts with individuals, arranges them in groups, and then relates those groups to more inclusive groups above. To be useful a scheme of classes must conform to the following rules of division:

I. There can be only one principle of division applied at each stage.

II. The subgroups under any group must exhaust that group.

III. The same principle of division that is applied in the first stage must be continued through successive stages if such exist.

DEFINITION is one way to answer the question, "What is it?" But strictly speaking, definition is of a word, or phrase, and not of the thing indicated by the word or phrase. It is a way of telling how properly to use the word or phrase. It sets the limit of meaning. But a definition cannot be made without knowledge of the thing behind the word. So the process of definition may lead to an enlargement of understanding not only of the word but of the thing referred to.

A definition has two parts, the element to be defined and the element that defines. The elements are parts of an equation. That is, one may be used for the other in a discourse without changing the meaning.

The process of definition is the placing of the *to-be-defined* in a group (called the GENUS) and the differentiating of it from other members of the same group (SPECIES) by pointing out the qualities which distinguish it (DIFFERENTIA).

Definition is not only of some term but is for somebody. The audience must be considered, and the definition must refer to what the audience knows or is willing to learn. The language and the experience of the audience must be regarded. There must be a common ground for the definition.

Once the common ground is established, there are certain principles to be regarded:

I. The *to-be-defined* must be equivalent to the *definer*.

II. The *to-be-defined* must not be part of the *definer*.

III. The *definer* must not be negative unless the *to-be-defined* is negative.

For a complicated *to-be-defined* the simple definition may not be satisfactory. It is sometimes impossible to appeal to a generally accepted notion, and the writer must develop his own definition in detail. For example, a word like *democracy* or *liberty* cannot be defined simply. It requires an EXTENDED DEFINITION, a discussion.

The DERIVATION of a word is sometimes helpful in setting up a definition, even when the application of the word has changed during its history.

ANALYSIS is the method of dividing into component parts. It can be applied to anything that can be thought of as having parts. There are two kinds of analysis, PHYSICAL ANALYSIS and CONCEPTUAL ANALYSIS. In physical analysis some object is spatially separated into its components, as when a clockmaker takes a clock apart. But things like ideas and institutions cannot be dealt with except in the mind, by the use of reason, as when we analyze the organization of a government. Conceptual analysis, the kind which is performed in the mind and can be reported in words, is what concerns us here.

We can propose an analysis only if we regard the thing to be analyzed as having a structure. A thing has a structure when its components may be regarded not as assembled at random but as being organized, as having necessary relations to each other. The same thing may be regarded as being different kinds of structures. The botanist regards the apple as one kind of structure, and the chemist, as another. The same principle may apply to things which cannot be physically analyzed, such as ideas or organizations.

Analysis when fully realized not only divides into parts but indicates the relation among parts, their place in the structure. In fact, we may regard a part as whatever can be described as having a necessary place in a structure.

FUNCTIONAL ANALYSIS answers the question, "How does it work?" It is concerned not primarily with the parts of a thing analyzed but with the stages of some sequence. This means that functional analysis is a kind of expository narration.

Functional analysis can be applied to anything which involves a process: to the working of a mechanism or the working of an institution, to natural processes, such as the growth of a seed, or to human processes, such as making or doing something.

CHRONOLOGICAL ANALYSIS is concerned with determining the stages of an event when the event is one which cannot be treated as having a function, for example, a historical event. It is a preliminary step toward fuller understanding and interpretation.

CAUSAL ANALYSIS deals with the relation of cause and effect.

CAUSE is the kind of connection between events that enables us to say that without event A, event B would not have come about, and whenever you have A, you will have B.

The connection must be considered as relatively IMMEDIATE. In one sense, the whole universe is a tissue of relationships and anything, however remote, may be taken to be a "cause" of something else. But only immediate connections tell us very much.

What we take to be the cause of an event may be dictated by our INTEREST. A coroner investigating the death of a child would state the cause as a fall from a stepladder, whereas the mother might take her negligence to be the cause.

An event does not take place in complete isolation. Various factors constitute a setting for the event. A factor which, existing in the situation, will permit the effect to appear is called a CONDITION.

There are two kinds of condition, SUFFICIENT CONDITION and NECESSARY CONDITION.

For example, take a situation in which the event B occurs and in which the factor X is present as a condition. The condition X is sufficient if, whenever X is present, B occurs. But in such an example, if B still occurs with X absent and some other factor taking its place, then X is not a necessary condition. A necessary condition is one which must be present for the effect to take place.

When we speak of a cause we refer to some PRINCIPLE OF UNIFORMITY. Under the same circumstances the A would always cause the B. This is the principle involved in what is called a law of nature. Hydrogen ignited in the presence of oxygen *always* gives us water.

To reason about cause, we must keep in mind two principles:

1. A cannot be the cause of B if A is ever absent when B is present.

2. A cannot be the cause of B if B is ever absent when A is present. That is, A and B are uniformly related.

## APPLICATIONS

1. Return to "What Is a University?" by Newman (p. 689) and "On Liberty" by Mill (p. 697), with which you are already acquainted as examples of extended definition. What expository methods other than definition do you find?

II. What methods do you find in "The Marxian View of History," by Carl Becker (p. 634), or in "The Threat of Science," by Christian Gauss (p. 659)?

III. Select a subject for an expository theme. You are expected to use several methods of exposition in this theme, but do not begin by trying to decide which ones. Begin by collecting information. Then think through your subject, remembering that you are trying to explain it very fully to someone who is relatively ignorant of it. To keep track of your own thinking you may find it useful to jot down your ideas just as they come. Then you can try to put the notes into order—into a kind of scratch outline.

For instance, if you are writing on the importance of the internal combustion engine, you might want to tell (1) what that type of engine is, (2) how it is similar to, or differs from, other types of engine, (3) how it was invented and developed, and (4) how it has affected transportation, industry, agriculture, the economic system, and social habits.

Upon examining your scratch outline, you would find, in this instance, that in topic 1 you were using definition and perhaps functional analysis, in topic 2 comparison and contrast, in topic 3 chronological and perhaps causal analysis, and in topic 4 causal analysis. But you might also find that classification and division would be helpful, for internal combustion engines are of various kinds having different structures and uses. So your theme would use several expository methods. But if the subject is "The Importance of the Internal Combustion Engine," topic 4 will provide the main body; topics 1, 2, and 3 will be useful only in so far as they lead to a fuller understanding of topic 4.

At this point, prepare a formal outline of your theme, indicating for each stage in the outline, as a marginal note, what kind of exposition will be used at that point. But do not feel obliged to use every kind of exposition discussed in this chapter. Use what is useful.

Write a theme of approximately 1,000 words. On the margin indicate at each stage what expository method you are using.

# CHAPTER
# 4

# Argument

ARGUMENT is the kind of discourse used to make the audience (reader or listener) think or act as the arguer desires. It is sometimes said that the purpose of argument is not double, as just stated, but single—in other words, that its purpose is to lead the audience to act. In the final analysis there is justification for this view, for a way of thinking means by implication a way of acting, and acting is the fulfillment of a way of thinking. As Justice Holmes says, "Every idea is an incitement." But in practice we can distinguish between the two purposes.

## THE APPEAL OF ARGUMENT

It is sometimes said that argument may make either or both of two appeals, the appeal to understanding and the appeal to emotions, and that in appealing to the understanding, argument aims to CONVINCE, and in appealing to the emotions, aims to PERSUADE. Here we shall take a stricter view, and treat argument as an appeal to the understanding. How, then, does it differ from other forms of discourse, which also involve, in various ways, an appeal to the understanding?

## ARGUMENT AND CONFLICT

Argument differs from the other kinds of discourse because of the basic situation in which it originates. Argument implies conflict or the possibility of conflict. We do not argue with a person who already agrees with us, but with a person who is opposed to us or who is undecided. Furthermore, argument implies a conflict between positions. We do not argue about a subject if only one position can possibly be taken in regard to it. The arguer presumably believes that his position is the only reasonable position, but by the fact of arguing at all he recognizes that another position, no matter how mistakenly, is held or may be held. The purpose of argument is to resolve the conflict in which the argument originates. The arguer argues to convince, to win.

The situation of conflict distinguishes argument from the other kinds of discourse, but in the course of achieving his purpose of resolving the conflict the arguer may resort to the other kinds of discourse, especially to exposition. In fact, if a dispute is really based on the misunderstanding of a set of facts, mere exposition may be enough to win the argument. Argument, like the other kinds of discourse, rarely appears in an absolutely pure form. Here, as in the other kinds of discourse, we define a particular piece of speaking or writing in terms of its dominant intention. The dominant intention of a piece of argument, no matter how much description, narration, or exposition it may use, is to make the audience change its mind or conduct.

Argument, either as the dominant intention or a subsidiary intention, may appear in many forms. It appears in conversation, in public addresses, in the lawyer's presentation of his case, in feature articles, in editorials, in textbooks on any subject, in essays, in poetry, in history, in drama, in fiction. It properly appears wherever the possibility of conflict between positions appears. The salesman trying to sell a car uses argument. The historian trying to prove that a certain event took place at a certain time uses argument. The congressman speaking on behalf of a bill uses argument. The dramatist setting two characters into conflict may use argument. But no matter what form argument takes, the general principles involved remain the same. In this chapter we shall try to examine some of the principles. With many of them we are already acquainted, for in so far as we have been able to argue reasonably we have always been thinking in accordance with them.

## ARGUMENT AND THE UNDERSTANDING

Argument gains its ends by an appeal to the understanding, to man's reasoning nature. We ordinarily recognize this fact when we say of a speaker, "He didn't really have an argument; he merely carried the audience by appealing to their emotions." Such a speaker has persuaded but he has not convinced. The advertiser who puts the picture of a sweet-faced, gray-haired grandmother beside the picture of his ice box is not appealing to reason but to emotion. He may have a good sales argument in favor of his ice box on grounds of economy, efficiency, or convenience, but he is not presenting it. The political speaker who screams, "Every red-blooded American will vote for John Jones, the friend of the people!" is not offering an argument any more than the defense lawyer who points to the accused murderer and, with tears in his voice, demands of the jury, "This man before you, this simple man who loves his children, who prays for them every night—would you send him to the gallows? You fathers and mothers, would you make those poor babes fatherless?" The advertiser may sell the ice box, the politician may get the votes, the lawyer may get an acquittal for the accused by the appeal to the emotions, but in no case has an argument been offered.

The objection may be raised: "What does it matter if the advertiser or politician or lawyer didn't offer an argument? The ice box *was* good—or the politician *was* honest and able—or the accused *was* innocent." If the ice box was good, etc., then the question is merely a practical one: Is the simple appeal to the emotions the best and safest way of achieving the good purpose? Perhaps not, for if an audience becomes aware that no real argument is being offered, that there is only an attempt to play on its emotions, it may feel that it is being treated like a child, that proper respect is not being paid to its powers of reason, that it is being duped and betrayed. So the appeal to the emotions may backfire, and regardless of the merits of the case there may be blind resentment instead of blind agreement.

But another objection may be raised: "Suppose the advertiser or politician or lawyer did gain his purpose, no matter what the merit of the case. He won, didn't he? And isn't the object to win?"

If the ice box was not good, the question now becomes a moral one: Is a man entitled to practice a fraud merely because he has the ability to do so—in this instance to sway people by the appeal to the emotions? But the same question would apply if the man did not appeal to the emotions of his audience but offered them misleading arguments.

If the appeal to the understanding is the appeal of argument, then what becomes of the appeal to the emotions? Nothing becomes of it. It is still a very important consideration. It remains important even in relation to argument. If we have a good case on logical grounds, we may still lose it because we present it untactfully, because we do not know how to make the most of the temperament and attitude of the audience. Frequently the problem may be to "persuade" the audience to give our logical case an examination. Persuasion begins in the attempt to find common ground in attitudes, feelings, sentiments. And only if we find such common ground as a starting point can we ordinarily hope, in the end, to win an agreement about the matter of argument. Persuasion is very important in the strategy of argument, and at the end of this chapter we shall discuss it. But for the present we shall consider questions arising from the consideration of argument as an appeal to the understanding.

## WHAT ARGUMENT IS ABOUT

What is argument about? People argue about anything, we may answer. But that is not a specific answer.

To illustrate:

John comes upon a group obviously engaged in a heated argument. "What are you arguing about?"

Jack answers: "Football."

John asks: "What about football?"

Jack answers: "About who won the Army-Navy game in 1936."

John laughs and says: "For the Lord's sake, what are you wasting your breath for? Why don't you telephone the information bureau at the newspaper and find out?"

John is right. When a fact can be established by investigation, there is no need to establish it by argument. Why argue about the length of a piece of string if there is a ruler handy?

Or again suppose John asks his first question, and Jack replies, "Football."

John asks: "What about football?"

Jack answers: "Which is the better game, football or basketball?"

John laughs again, and says: "For the Lord's sake, what are you wasting your breath for? You can't settle that. A guy just likes the game he likes. Take me, I like tennis better than either of them."

John is right again. An argument about a matter of mere taste is useless, and in so far as the word "better" [1] in the above conversation merely means what one happens to like, there is no proper matter for argument.

Anyone sees immediately the absurdity of an argument between two children about whether candy is better than pie. Such a disagreement permits of no conclusion. No process of reason can lead to an agreement between the taste buds of Sally's mouth and the taste buds of Susie's mouth, for both sets of taste buds give "truth" for the person to whom they belong. But a doctor could argue that spinach is better than either candy or pie for the child. He can do so because he has a definite objective standard, the child's health, to which he can appeal.

In other words, a matter of absolute taste is not a matter for argument. Only a matter of judgment is a matter for argument. We must remember, however, that there is no single sharp and fast line

[1] Expressions like "better," "more desirable," "to be preferred," "greater," "good," "acceptable," and so forth, may indicate mere preference, an unarguable question of taste, and in ordinary usage this is frequently so. When dealing with such an expression, one should ask questions which will determine whether or not the word has an objective content. Take the simple statement: "That is a good horse." We immediately have to ask, "Good for what?" For draying, for racing, for the bridle path, for the show ring, for the range? Or does the speaker merely mean that the horse is gentle, responsive, and affectionate, a sort of pet? By forcing the question we may discover the real meaning behind the original statement. But sometimes there is no meaning beyond the question of taste. Somebody says: "Jake is a good guy." If you force the question here and get the reply, "Oh, he's just regular, I like to be around him," you discover that the statement has no objective content. It tells you nothing about Jake. As the philosopher Spinoza puts it, Paul's opinion about Peter tells more about Paul than about Peter.

Useful forcing questions to apply to such expressions are: What is *it* good, desirable, etc. for? What is *it* good in relation to? Is the standard invoked objective and therefore worth discussing?

between matters of taste and matters of judgment. In between obvious extremes, there is a vast body of matters about which it is difficult to be sure, and each question must be examined on its own merits.

Let us take, for example, an argument about whether Wordsworth or Longfellow is the finer poet. Are we dealing with a matter of taste or a matter of judgment?

If one person says, "I don't care what other people think, I just like Longfellow better," he is treating the whole business as a matter of taste. He is making no appeal to reason. But if another person tries to set up a standard for poetic excellence in general and tests the poets by that standard, he is making an appeal to judgment. He might say, for instance, that Wordsworth has greater originality in subject matter, has more serious ideas, has had more influence on later poets, and uses fresher and more suggestive metaphors. He might not win agreement, but he is at least using the method of argument, is trying to appeal to reason in terms of an objective standard.

But let us come back to our original illustration. We notice that in both instances when Jack says that he and his friends are arguing about football, John asks: "What about football?"

John is bound to ask this question if he has any real curiosity about the argument. For football, in itself, is no matter for argument. It may provide the material for an argument, but that is all. There must be something "about" football which is the matter for argument. So John asks the question.

Jack answers: "Oh, about the Michigan-Purdue game last Saturday."

John says: "Gosh, but you are thick-headed. What *about* the game?"

Jack answers: "About Randall and Bolewiensky."

John says: "Well, I give up! What *about* Randall and Bolewiensky?"

Jack answers: "About who is the more useful player."

John says: "Well, it is sure time you were telling me."

John's thick-headed friend has finally managed to state what the argument is about. If there is an argument here, somebody holds that Randall is a more useful player than Bolewiensky and somebody denies it. In other words, the argument is about a PROPOSITION.

A proposition is what an argument is about, and is the only thing an argument can be about. The argument develops when somebody affirms a proposition and somebody else denies it.

## THE PROPOSITION: TWO KINDS

A proposition is the declaration of a judgment. It is a statement that can be believed, doubted, or disbelieved. A proposition states something as a fact or states that some line of action should or should not be followed. So we have PROPOSITIONS OF FACT and PROPOSITIONS OF POLICY. A lawyer arguing that his client has an alibi for a certain time is dealing with a proposition of fact. A bond salesman trying to sell a bond to an investor is dealing with a proposition of policy. The typical statement of a proposition of fact is *is* or *does*. The typical statement of a proposition of policy is *should*.

The mere presence in a statement, however, of *is* or *does* cannot be taken to indicate a proposition of fact. For instance, the following statement uses *is:*

It is desirable to abolish the poll tax.

But the statement means that the poll tax *should* be abolished. It indicates a line of action. Therefore, it is a proposition of policy.

Likewise, the mere presence of *should* does not necessarily indicate a proposition of policy. For instance:

Any experienced reader of poetry should regard Wordsworth as a better poet than Longfellow.

This statement really means that any experienced reader of poetry *does* regard Wordsworth as a better poet than Longfellow. It is a statement of fact that may be believed, doubted, or disbelieved.

So the typical form of a proposition can be disguised, and one must look to the fundamental intention of a statement and not to its accidental phrasing.

## THE STATEMENT OF THE PROPOSITION

In formal debate the proposition is ordinarily given as a resolution: *Resolved,* That the United States should adopt free trade.

Or: *Resolved,* That the language requirements for the B.A. degree should be abolished.

Formal debates, however, make up only a fraction of all argument. We find argument in a hundred other places—wherever anyone is trying to lead us to accept something as a fact or to accept a line of action. Ordinarily the proposition underlying an argument is not formally stated, and sometimes may not be stated at all. For instance, the arguer may refrain from giving the proposition because he is sure the audience already grasps it, or because he wishes to lead the audience by degrees to discover it for themselves. In certain kinds of propaganda, for example, the arguer deliberately conceals the proposition in order to deceive the audience.

If an arguer wishes to think straight he ought to be able to state his proposition. If he is to be effective he must know exactly what is at stake in the argument, and the best way to be sure that he knows what is at stake is to frame the proposition, at least for himself. And the proposition should be single, clear, and unprejudiced.

### THE SINGLE PROPOSITION

A proposition should be single. It should not express more than one idea for argument. We must fix here on the phrase, "one idea for argument." Even the proposition, "This rose is red," expresses more than one idea. It says that the "this" is a rose, and it says that the "this" is red. But obviously it intends to present only one point for argument—the redness. Presumably the idea that the "this" is a rose is expected to pass without question.

It is always possible, of course, that someone may challenge an idea which is not put forward for argument but is implied in the proposition. In such a case the argument then turns on a new proposition. For instance, suppose I say, "The whale is the most intelligent fish." Obviously, I intend the argument to turn on the question of the intelligence of the whale. But a zoologist may challenge another idea of my proposition by saying that a whale is not a fish. This may start another argument based on the idea in my original proposition that a whale is a fish. Or I may take the zoologist's word that the whale is a mammal, and restate my original proposition: "A whale is the most intelligent creature living in water."

To say that a proposition should be single does not mean that a total argument may not involve more than one arguable idea.

THE STATEMENT OF THE PROPOSITION

Many arguable ideas may appear in the course of an argument. But each idea should be treated separately to avoid confusion. The discussion of this question will be postponed, however, until we treat the organization of argument.

## THE CLEAR PROPOSITION

A clear proposition says what we mean. But it is not easy to say what we mean. Most words as we ordinarily use them do not have very precise limits. Even words which refer to an objective physical situation may be vague. How "tall" is a tall man? Five feet, eleven? Six feet? Six feet, three? Any of these men would be well above average height, but there is a great range here. So we may say "tallish," "tall," or "very tall" to indicate the scale; but even then we might hesitate about the choice of a word. Or take the word "bald." How much hair must be lacking before we can say that a man is bald? The word does not fix an objective standard although it does refer to an objective situation.

The problem is even more complicated when we come to words like "good," "cute," or "progressive" which do not refer to objective physical situations. What is really said in the proposition, "Mary is the cutest girl in town"? The word "cute" indicates some laudatory or appreciative attitude on the part of the speaker, but it does not tell us very much about Mary. Or if we hear, "Mr. Black is a progressive citizen," what are we to understand? That Black works hard, pays his taxes, treats his family decently, saves money, and stays out of jail? Or that he is interested in improving the local school, bringing new factories to town, and planting flowers in the park? Or that he has a certain political philosophy? Such a word tells us very little about Mr. Black. It seems to indicate some general approval on the part of the speaker, but we don't know exactly what, and the odds are that he does not know either. The word is vague.

Let us take another example of vagueness, the proposition, "Soviet Russia is more democratic than England."

A person defending the above proposition might argue that Russia is more democratic than England because in its system there are no hereditary titles, because great fortunes cannot be accumulated, and because the worker is glorified. A person attacking the proposition might argue that England is more democratic because actual political power is in the hands of leaders chosen by the majority of voters in free elections, because there is freedom of speech, and because a man can choose his occupation. The word "democratic" is vague, and the two disputants are using it in different senses. They can have no argument on the original proposition until they have agreed on a definition of democracy. And this, of course, may mean that the argument shifts to a new proposition: "Democracy is so-and-so."

Many words, like "democracy," have no generally accepted meaning to which we can refer. Even the dictionary does not help us much with such a word. It can give us authority for a word like "horse," for to zoology a horse is a horse wherever we find it. As for "democracy," the dictionary may give us some idea of several more or less well-accepted senses and may start us on the way to a clear statement, but the dictionary definition can rarely be full enough to cover the meaning of such a word as it will appear in an argument. In framing a proposition we should try to fix the definition (pp. 88-96) of any significant word, to determine exactly what we mean by it, and then we should stick to that definition. Until both parties to an argument agree about terms, there can be no fruitful meeting, indeed, no meeting.

### THE UNPREJUDICED PROPOSITION

A proposition should not only be single and clear. It should also be unprejudiced. That is, it should not smuggle into the proposition anything which implies a foregone conclusion to the argument. The following is not an unprejudiced proposition: "The unsanitary condition of the slaughter pens at Morgansville is detrimental to the public health." It is prejudiced, for the adjective *unsanitary* really means "detrimental to the public health." If we accept that word into the proposition, there is nothing arguable: the point of the argument has been already settled. The question has been begged, to use the phrase ordinarily applied to such a situation.

### APPLICATIONS

I. Study the following propositions with these considerations in mind:

a. Distinguish propositions of fact and propositions of policy.

b. Do any violate the principle of the single idea?

c. Indicate vague propositions and discuss the nature of the difficulty.

d. If any are question-begging, restate them in proper form.

e. Are any non-arguable? If so, why?

1. A good book is the best friend a man can have.

2. "When at the height of efficiency you will do better work."—An advertisement

3. No good Democrat will vote for a Republican.

4. Mussolini was a great man.

5. A true American is a man who typifies the best qualities of his country.

6. Square dancing is more interesting than ballroom dancing.

7. Edison was a greater man than Napoleon.

8. The horse has made more contribution to human happiness than the cow.

9. Amateur athletics are more desirable than professional athletics.

10. This so-called insurance collector is really an impostor.

11. Capital punishment is no deterrent to crime.

12. Immorality and frivolity should be discouraged by teachers.

13. Drinking and card playing should be discouraged by teachers.

14. Drinking, card playing, and other immorality should be discouraged by teachers.

15. The atomic bomb is the most important invention since the steam engine.

16. The atomic bomb is the most useful invention since the steam engine.

17. War is necessary to maintain the manhood of the race.

18. In our present situation high wages do not mean higher prices.

19. The Washington Monument is 490 feet high.

20. Man is a rational animal.

21. This unreasonable request should not be granted.

22. Installment selling has bad economic consequences.

23. Mary Pickford is the most attractive actress the screen has ever presented.

24. "There is a good deal of human nature in man."—SAMUEL CLEMENS

**II.** Frame (1) a set of improperly stated propositions and (2) a set of properly stated propositions involving five of the following topics:

| | |
|---|---|
| United Nations | Intoxicants |
| Hobbies | Tennis |
| Religion | Reading habits |
| Motherhood | Profession of medicine |
| War | Foreign missions |

| Fraternities | College marriages |
| Student government | State socialism |
| Honor system | Compulsory savings |
| Commercial aviation | Movie going |
| Stamp collecting | Farming |

## HISTORY OF THE QUESTION

We have to understand our proposition before we can argue about it. Some propositions can be understood immediately, but some can only be understood if we go into the HISTORY OF THE QUESTION—that is, if we inform ourselves about the circumstances which brought the argument into being. For instance, in a debate about tariffs some knowledge of how they have worked in this country and elsewhere would be almost essential to a full understanding of what is really at stake at the present moment. Even a matter of definition of words in a proposition may depend on our knowledge of the history of the question. For similar reasons it is important to understand the OCCASION OF THE DISCUSSION—that is, what makes the argument significant at the present moment.

## ISSUES

But once we understand our proposition we are still not ready to argue it. Common sense tells us that there may be many arguments for and against a given proposition. Though the proposition properly stated is single, reasons for and against it may be plural. The single idea of the proposition may raise various questions for controversy. When a question is ESSENTIAL to the proposition, we call it an ISSUE. And any question is essential if its defeat means the defeat of the proposition. An issue, then, is a point of fundamental importance in the argument, and the affirmative side, the side supporting the proposition, must win on all issues in order to win on the proposition.

Let us take a simple example. The constitution of a certain college honor society, which we shall call the Corinthians, specifies that a student to be eligible for membership must (1) have a scholastic average of B or above, (2) have won a letter in at least one college sport, (3) have made some substantial contributions.to the general good of the college community, and (4) have conducted himself as a gentleman during the period of his college career. William Smith is proposed for election. His sponsor argues that Smith has made an A-average, has won the state junior championship in swimming, has brought about a reform of the student council system by his editorials in the college paper, and is a person of high character and good manners. Smith seems certain of election until one Corinthian refers to the constitution and regretfully points out that Smith cannot fulfill requirement 2. "But he is an excellent athlete," the sponsor retorts; "he can out-swim anybody in this school."

"That's not the point," the other Corinthian replies. "The constitution explicitly states that to be eligible a student must have won a letter in at least one sport. And Rutherford College has no swimming team, and therefore does not give a letter for swimming."

If the constitution is taken seriously, Smith's eligibility must be denied. The proposition is that Smith is eligible for membership in the Corinthians, and the constitution is the source of authority for the requirements for eligibility. Each of those requirements is *essential*, and in the argument about Smith's eligibility would therefore properly be an issue.

## ADMITTED ISSUES AND CRUCIAL ISSUES

It is important to notice here that the opposition does not contest Smith's eligibility on every point. It admits that Smith has made a scholastic average of B or above, has made some substantial contribution to the general good of the college community, and has conducted himself as a gentleman. The proposition really depends on the college letter in athletics. Now in most arguments, some issues are uncontested. These are called ADMITTED ISSUES. The remaining issues (or issue) are called CRUCIAL ISSUES. They are the points on which the real argument takes place.

## LOCATING THE ISSUES: ANALYSIS OF THE PROPOSITION

Let us return for a moment to the case of Smith's eligibility. Suppose someone says: "Well, Smith ought to be elected, and if a man like Smith can't get in under the present constitution, then the constitution ought to be changed." That may be true, but that is another problem, and would have to be considered on its own merits. This situation is similar to certain cases at law in which one may feel that the letter of the law defeats justice. For example, a defending lawyer in a first-degree murder case may argue that his client had suffered intolerable provocation, that the victim had grievously slandered the defendant's wife, and that the defendant, a simple man raised in rather primitive surroundings, had thought killing the slanderer to be the only course of honor and decency. The prosecution argues that this is no issue in the case, because the legal definition of murder is such and such, and makes no recognition of the provocation of slander, or of the personal background of the accused. The prosecutor is, of course, right. The law defines the issues by which the proposition, that so-and-so is guilty of murder in the first degree, must stand or fall. If the jury does acquit the defendant, it does so out of sentiment, prejudice, or some notion of justice which is inconsistent with the law.

The case of William Smith or of the murderer is very simple, for the issues are defined beforehand by a document—eligibility for membership by the constitution of the Corinthians, or murder by the law. In many arguments, however, we must locate the issues for ourselves. We do this by making an ANALYSIS of the proposition.

In making the analysis of a proposition we do not arbitrarily decide that certain questions are issues. They are implied in the proposition, and we must locate them, or discover them. In a rough-and-tumble argument, undertaken without preparation, two reasonably intelligent opponents will eventually isolate at least some of the issues; but in the clash of argument, issues develop more or less hit-or-miss. If there is time for preparation, as there usually is in writing a theme or an article, we should try to determine the issues beforehand.

The first step in this process is to set up all the possible arguments on each side of the proposition. In first draft such a list may be a very crude affair, with important and unimportant items jumbled together, but it will give a kind of preview of the problem. Even in this form, however, we can see that arguments tend to go in pairs, a negative as opposed to an affirmative. Not all arguments may, however, be paired. The negative may admit certain points, and naturally does not offer arguments in regard to them.

Let us set up such a preliminary list for the proposition of policy that the United States should adopt universal military training.

| AFFIRMATIVE (A) | NEGATIVE (N) |
|---|---|
| 1. There is a dangerous international situation and the United States has no clearly defined policy to meet it. | |
| 2. The present army of the United States will be inadequate for a major conflict as soon as the atomic bomb is possessed by other nations. | |
| 3. Within a few years our trained reserves will be over-age. | |
| 4. The next war will probably move rapidly to a decision and will give no time to train and equip an army. | |
| 5. The tensions in international relations at present are serious and a war may come within a few years. | No nation can now afford to undertake a war, least of all the nations which might be arrayed against us. Further, there are no insuperable difficulties to peace. |
| 6. Our possible enemies are maintaining large armies. | If other nations are assured of our good faith by our relative disarmament, they will reduce their own forces. |
| 7. Military training gives young men a sense of responsibility and discipline which is valuable in any occupation of later life. | The time spent in military training seriously impairs the education of young men, and reduces their efficiency in later life. |
| 8. The United Nations does not guarantee our safety. | The United Nations has not been given a fair trial; we must show our good faith in it. |
| 9. No cost is too great to pay for our national safety. | The country is burdened with a great national debt and needs to practice economy if our system is to survive. |

AFFIRMATIVE (A)                     NEGATIVE (N)

10. Military training does not fos-   Military life fosters immorality.
ter immorality.

11. Military training will produce    The next war will be a war of
specialists and even if the next      specialists, and a large body of
war is a war fought with              ordinary troops would be useless.
atomic bombs, robot planes,
etc., trained men are required
to operate such mechanisms
and ground troops will always
be required to occupy and
hold territory.

12. Universal military training does   Universal military training would
not aggravate the international        signify to the world that we had
situation. Instead our pre-            no faith in the possibility of peace
paredness would tend to pre-           and would precipitate an arma-
vent a conflict.                       ment race.

13. Victory would be possible in       The next war, if it comes, will be
a future war, for there is             a war of total destruction; there-
reason to believe that defenses        fore the only hope of survival for
can be developed against the           civilization is to bend every effort
new methods of attack.                 for peace by developing a world
federation or a world government.

This list is not systematic. The items are jotted down as they occur in a first survey of the subject. So in revising the list we must try to put things together that are closely related in meaning. For instance, if we finally keep 7 and 10, we must put them in some relation to each other, for they both bear on the effect of military training on the education and the morality of young men.

Order, however, is not the only thing we must consider. There are four other considerations which we can introduce at this stage.

I. Are the arguments all significant?
II. Do they cover the subject?
III. Do they overlap each other?
IV. Does any really include more than one idea?

With these considerations in mind we can see that 7, 9, and 10 do not bear on the proposition. They raise questions concerning the effects on education (7) and morality (10) of military training, and of the cost (9) of the military training. Obviously, if the national survival is at stake (and that is what is implied in the word *should* of the proposition), these questions are not significant.

Upon inspection we may discover that the issues do not cover the subject. First, we may notice that, though 2, 3, and 4 imply the need for military policy, no such argument is stated. And certainly such an important point should be stated. Second, we discover that the question of pacifism is nowhere mentioned. Pacifism is a sweeping and important argument, either when grounded on the notion that all war is sinful and is never justifiable or when grounded on the idea that nonviolence eventually defeats violence. A person arguing the negative side might not believe in pacifism and therefore would not wish to raise the objection, but anyone intending to support the affirmative side would have to include the argument for the sake of completeness. He cannot be sure what arguments may appear.

As for overlapping among arguments, we find several instances. Items 1A and 5A overlap, for they both affirm the danger in the existing situation. Furthermore, 2A, 3A, and 4A might be fused, for they are closely related as arguments for the notion that a military policy is needed. And if items 7 and 10 had not already been excluded as not significant, they should be fused.

Last we find that item 1A really includes two ideas, one concerning the danger in the international situation and the other concerning the lack of any policy, either political or military, to combat the danger. The same is true of 13N, which states two ideas, one that another war would destroy all civilization, the other that the hope for survival lies in a world federation or a world government.

If now we try to systematize what we have, we get something like the following:

AFFIRMATIVE                              NEGATIVE

1. There is a dangerous international situation.

2. The United States has no policy to meet the danger, either political or military. (1, 8) [2]

---

[2] Numbers in parentheses refer to numbers in first draft of possible issues.

| AFFIRMATIVE | NEGATIVE |
|---|---|
| 3. There is need for a military policy, for (a) as soon as the secret of the atomic bomb is in the hands of other nations, our present force will be inadequate for a major conflict, (b) within a few years our trained reserves will be over-age, and (c) the speed with which the next war would move to a decision would give no time to train and equip an army. (2, 3, 4) | The need is for a political policy. |
| 4. Our possible enemies are maintaining large armies. (6) | If other nations are assured of our good faith, they will reduce their armaments. (6) |
| 5. Military training would help to prepare specialists, and even if the next war is fought with atomic bombs, robot planes, etc., large numbers of men are required to operate such mechanisms and ground troops will always be required to occupy and hold territory. (11) | The next war will be a war of specialists, and military training would not produce them. Furthermore, in such a war, large bodies of troops would be useless. |
| 6. Our preparedness would tend to prevent a conflict. | Universal military training would signify that we had no faith in peace and would precipitate an armament race. (12) |
| 7. Victory would be possible in a future war, for there is reason to believe that defenses can be developed against the new methods of attack. (13) | The next war, if it comes, will be a war of total destruction for all involved. (13) |
| 8. We can hope for the development of international safeguards, but we cannot be sure of them at this date. (8) | The only hope for survival lies in world federation or world government. (13) |
| 9. There are theoretical arguments against pacifism even on re- | War is morally wrong and should not be resorted to for any reason. |

ligious grounds. (For instance, most churches do not preach pacifism as such.) If we take the argument that nonviolence always conquers violence in the end, we find no evidence for this in history. In any case the argument for pacifism is irrelevant on practical grounds because in neither this country nor any other are there many pacifists.

But even if war were not wrong on moral grounds, pacifism would still be a good policy, for nonviolence always conquers violence in the end.

We see here that some new material has been introduced. Since a statement has emerged that there is need for a military policy (3), the negative counters by stating the need for a political policy instead. And the arguments for and against pacifism now appear in the list. We also see that there are no negative arguments for items 1 and 2. The negative admits these points.

## STOCK QUESTIONS

The second draft is more systematic and complete than the first. But we can further simplify the treatment and more definitely locate the issues. We need to carry on our analysis and find the big, main issues under which merely particular arguments can be organized. We are here dealing with what is called a proposition of policy, which means that the argument is about the best way of accomplishing some end; and in arguments of this sort there are certain STOCK QUESTIONS which can be applied to the material as a kind of guide for locating issues. These stock questions help us, first, to simplify our material, and second, to establish the essentiality of our issues.[3]

   I. Is there a need for some change?
  II. Will the policy suggested by the proposition be effective?
 III. Are the possible benefits of this policy greater than any new disadvantage which it may create?
  IV. Is the proposed policy better than any alternative policy?

[3] See essential issues, p. 152.

Upon reflection we may see that I includes 1, 2, 3, and 4; that
II includes 5 and 7; that III includes 6; [4] and that IV includes 8
and 9.

We should now be prepared to set up the issues. When formally
stated, issues appear as questions so phrased that the affirmative
must answer *yes* to them if the proposition is to stand.

| STOCK   QUESTION | ISSUE |
|---|---|
| I. _____ | 1. Is there a dangerous international situation? (1) [5] |
| | 2. Is there need for a military policy? (2, 3, 4) |
| II. _____ | 3. Would the universal military training be an effective military policy? (5, 6, 7) |
| III. _____ | 4. Would the advantages of universal military training outweigh the dangers that it might create or aggravate? (6) |
| IV. _____ | 5. Is universal military training better than any alternative policy? (8, 9) |

To summarize what we have done thus far: First, we have set
up, more or less at random, opposed particular arguments. Whenever we have found a pairing of an affirmative and a negative argu-

---

[4] It might be said that 6 really belongs under II, and that there is no III to
be considered in the present argument. There is some ground for this view,
for if, as 6A states, preparedness would help prevent a conflict, then that
policy would be effective in maintaining national safety. But if, as in 6N,
emphasis is on the new, or increased danger, which preparedness would create
by precipitating an armament race, then we can consider this as a definite
disadvantage—it *increases* the danger already existing. It will be found that
in practice II and III often overlap to a degree, but the difference in emphasis
between them is important. We can find, however, perfectly clear-cut cases of
difference between II and III. For example, a farmer might decide that a dam
on a creek would stop erosion on his land—would be an effective policy for
that purpose (II). But he then might discover that the dam would flood some
of his best pasture land further up the creek. This would be a new disadvantage, and would raise a new question (III).

It might also be said that 5 belongs under IV, for the negative, by implication at least, suggests an alternative policy, the creation of an army of specialists. But this really raises the question of the effectiveness of the policy suggested by the proposition. So II and IV overlap on this point.

[5] Numbers in parentheses refer to numbers in the second draft of possible
issues.

ment, we have located a point of collision, a possible issue. Second, we have analyzed these possible issues to see that they (1) are relevant and essential, (2) cover the subject, and (3) do not overlap each other or do not individually include more than one possible issue. Third, after the analysis we have drawn a revised list of affirmative and negative arguments. Fourth, to the revised list we have applied the four stock questions as a guide: (1) Is there a need for change? (2) Will the policy suggested by the proposition be effective? (3) Are the possible benefits of this policy greater than any new disadvantages which it might create? (4) Is the proposed policy better than any alternative policy? We have given each issue thus defined the form of a question which demands an affirmative answer if the proposition is to be supported. These questions are the issues.

We may note that the first issue, since it is not contested by the negative on our list, is an admitted issue. We may note also that under each issue we have indicated the particular arguments from the revised list which should be discussed under the general head provided by that issue. For instance, under issue 2, we have placed arguments 2, 3, and 4 from the revised list.

If we have done our work well, we now have the material organized for our argument. This does not mean that the arguments need follow this order. We might, for example, want to dispose of the question of pacifism and to point out reasons for pessimism concerning a system of international arrangements (topic 5 in our final list of issues) before arguing the specific merits of universal training. Or the strategy of persuasion for a particular audience might make us take a very indirect approach to the whole subject. We might, for instance, want to paint a vivid picture of the destruction our cities would suffer if we were caught unprepared. But the arrangement of issues as set up provides a reasonable scheme for treating the subject. A student, in the theme given below, has followed this scheme in arguing on the affirmative side. (The numbers in parentheses refer to the steps in the revised draft.)

## SHOULD THE UNITED STATES ADOPT UNIVERSAL MILITARY TRAINING?

(1) No thinking person can deny that the world at this date is in terrible confusion. While World War II was going on, many of us thought

that victory over the evil forces of Nazism and Fascism would bring in a new day and give us a happier world than man had ever known. Those of us who were really in the show had to feel that way to keep on going. We had to feel that or we had to be sure we didn't feel anything at all. But in May, 1947, now that we are back home and in school or holding jobs, we find that what we expected has not come true. Any newspaper we pick up tells us that much.

There are several things making for this terrible confusion. The conquered countries are in a desperate condition and some of those on the winning side are not much better. France, Greece, and China are suffering from many shortages and actual hunger, at times to the point of starvation. In the conquered countries there are many people who are just waiting for a chance to avenge their defeat, and they are ready to sign on with anybody who may help them. Behind this confusion there is the struggle between two very different notions of how the world ought to be run. Soviet Russia stands for one notion, and the United States stands for the other. In other countries, France, Germany, Italy, China, and even England, those two notions divide the people into parties and even into armed camps. The two notions are communism and democracy. There is the making here of a war which would make previous war look like a Boy Scout jamboree.

(2) The United States has no clear policy in international affairs to meet this crisis. The loan to Greece and Turkey is something, but nobody could say that it is a long-range policy and answers all our questions. We do not even know what we want to do about the United Nations.

(3) It is certainly important to get a foreign policy and work for peace, but it is also important to get a military policy. When the war was over everybody wanted to get home, and this was only human. Also the atomic bomb made us feel safe. But the result is that right now we are a disarmed nation, and (3a) soon the atomic bomb will be in the hands of other nations. (3b) Within a few years, too, most of our trained reserves will be a little too old to make the best soldiers. (3c) And if another war comes, it will move so fast there will not be time to train and equip forces. (4) Our possible enemies are not making this mistake, for they are maintaining large armies and are training new men. As soon as they get the secret of the bomb, our edge will be gone.

Universal military training is something that we need to safeguard our future. I know that there are arguments against this, but I do not believe that they will stand up against the facts.

(5) The first argument which you often hear is that universal military training would not be desirable because the new type of war will be a

war of specialists which universal military training would not produce. But this depends on the kind of training which is given. The training can be adapted to changing military needs. But in any case, there is good reason to believe that there will always be a place for the guy in the mud. I was one of them myself, and I know that they always had to send us in sooner or later. Large bodies of troops will be required to occupy and hold territory.

(6) The second argument [6] is that universal military training would provoke an armament race. The answer is that the race is already on, but at the present is merely a one-sided race. The other countries are racing to get what we have got—the A-bomb. But they are also building up big armies. If we showed that we mean to be strong, it might discourage other countries and make them want to come to an understanding.

(7) The third argument is that the next war, if it comes, will be a war of general suicide. It is said that nobody will survive except a few starved and diseased people among the ruins. This picture is too pessimistic. I do not want to deny what horrors of war can be, for I have seen some of them in West Germany when we went in. But the history of war shows that for every weapon of offense a weapon of defense develops sooner or later. Our scientists and military men should develop defenses just as they should develop weapons of offense. We have to do all we can to be sure that we are prepared if the war comes. And one of the things necessary is to adopt universal military training.

(8) Even people who admit that a strong military policy might be effective in itself sometimes argue that a better plan is to try to set up a world system of some kind. Any sensible person wants to avoid war, and one way to do that is to work for international understanding. But we are a long way from a system which we can depend on, and there is no reason why we should commit suicide as a nation in trying to get one. If we are strong we can enter into any international arrangements with a good bargaining position.

(9) There is one other argument which sometimes crops up in discussions about military training. That is the pacifist argument. People say that war is sinful and that you should never fight. Now I respect some of the people who argue that way. One of my best high school buddies was a pacifist, and when war came he went to a C.O. camp. I respect him, but I think that he was a crackpot. It is against human

[6] This argument is not placed according to the scheme. It really concerns a disadvantage which might be created by the proposed policy (stock question III), but here it is placed between two arguments for the effectiveness of universal military training (stock question II).

nature to take everything lying down, and that is really what pacifism amounts to. The man who lies down gets stepped on. History shows that. But there really aren't enough pacifists in this country or any other to make the subject worth arguing about.

To sum up, I say, "Work for peace, but prepare for war." Teddy Roosevelt's idea of walking softly and carrying a big stick still makes sense, for the world has not changed much since his day. And one big stick that the United States can carry is universal military training.

## PROPOSITIONS OF FACT

The proposition argued above is, of course, a proposition of policy. But how do we go about establishing the issue, or issues, in a proposition of fact? In the case of the eligibility of William Smith for membership in the Corinthians, the issues were defined before-hand by a document—the constitution of the society. But there are propositions of fact in which the issues are not established before-hand by any such definition.

Let us take a very simple instance, one in which there can be only a single issue. If two men in the wilderness wish to cross a stream, one of them may propose that they drop a tree across it. The other objects that the available tree is too short. They can establish the height of the tree by geometric calculation, but they cannot establish the width of the stream. Therefore the proposition (the tree is long enough) is a matter of judgment, and is subject to argument. Several arguments, good or bad, may be offered on either side, but there is only one issue: Is the tree long enough? In such cases of simple fact, the proposition itself establishes the issue. But in other cases the fact may not be simple, and there may be no prior definition of the issues (as in the case of William Smith and the Corinthians).

Let us take such an example: John did right in leaving his fortune to the Ashford Medical Foundation.

First, are we sure that this is a proposition of fact? At first glance it may look like a proposition of policy, for it contains the phrase "did right"—which seems to imply policy. Certainly, we would have a proposition of policy if it were stated: John will do right to. . . . Or: John should leave. . . . But in its original form, the proposition concerns an event that has already taken place, and concerns the nature of the event, not a course of action to be pursued. This becomes clear if we translate the proposition into the standard form: John's conduct in leaving his fortune to the Ashford Medical Foundation *is* (or *was*) right. So we have an *is* proposition, not a *should* proposition.

Second, how can we establish the issues? To do so, we must decide what we mean by the word "right"—the predicate of the proposition. Suppose the opponents agree that a deed is morally right *only* if it fulfills *all* of the following requirements: (1) the doer is responsible, (2) the doer undertakes the deed for a laudable motive, and (3) the consequences of the deed are beneficial. The issues then become:

1. Was John of sound mind when he made his will?
2. Was his motive laudable?
3. Will the money be used for a beneficial activity?

The affirmative must establish all of these points in order to win the argument. Suppose that there is no doubt of John's sanity, and no doubt that the money will be used for a good purpose. Suppose that these facts are admitted. Yet if the negative establishes that John, in a fit of fury at his daughter for making a marriage without his consent, changed his will, then the motive is a bad one, for the deed comes out of spite and offended vanity. Therefore the proposition would be lost.

In such propositions of fact, where the fact is complex, the locating of the issues becomes a matter of analyzing the fact. In practice this may mean defining the key word (or words) in the proposition, as *right* in the example that we have just discussed.

## APPLICATIONS

I. Analyze two or three of the following propositions to develop the issues. Distinguish between the admitted and crucial issues. Write a theme of 500 words defending or attacking one of the propositions.

1. Fraternities should be abolished.
2. The manufacture and sale of spiritous liquors should be prohibited by law.
3. Democracy means the worship of the mediocre.
4. Religion is the opium of the people.
5. The elective system should be replaced by fixed curricula.
6. A law prohibiting jurisdictional strikes is needed.

7. Religion should be encouraged even by the unbeliever.

8. All veterans' organizations should be disbanded.

9. We must have government ownership of the coal mines.

10. All children should be taught some manual skill.

11. Only intramural athletics should be permitted in this college.

12. The profit motive is an important condition of our economic and social distress.

II. Study "The Marxian View of History," by Carl Becker, in Readings (p. 634). What issues has the author selected as crucial in this debate?

## EVIDENCE

When you get into an argument, you may be pretty sure that your opponent will be from Missouri. He will say, "Seeing is believing," and what he wants is the EVIDENCE. Without evidence you can only offer your own unsupported views, which you already know the opponent will not accept—for if he did accept them there would have been no argument in the first place.

Evidence is whatever can be offered as support for a proposition.

## KINDS OF EVIDENCE: FACT AND OPINION

What constitutes evidence? People constantly appeal to facts, or try to appeal to facts, to support argument. "The facts of the case" are important as evidence, but they are not the only thing which can be used as evidence. People also appeal to opinions of other people who are supposed to have authority. "Expert testimony" is offered in the courtroom as evidence to support a case. The murder trial may bring out the alienist, the ballistics expert, the medical examiner, and any number of other experts whose opinions are to be considered by the jury. Presumably they base their testimony on facts, but what the jury is asked to accept is their *opinion*, their judgment of the facts.

The expert may be wrong, and experts frequently disagree among themselves; and what they disagree about is ordinarily not the facts but their interpretation of the facts. Opinion, therefore, appears as evidence. But not only the so-called expert opinion may appear as evidence. Even before the law we find what is called the character witness, and what the character witness finally offers is his opinion. In ordinary argument people constantly invoke opinion of all sort— "Mr. Allen says so, and I should think he would know," or "The New York *Times* says so." The author of the student theme on universal military training invokes the opinion of Teddy Roosevelt: Roosevelt's opinion about carrying the big stick is used as evidence.

Fact or opinion may constitute evidence. What tests can we apply to them to satisfy ourselves that they are worth admitting into an argument?

### FACTS AS EVIDENCE

A fact must be made to stick. That is, the fact must be a fact. What is offered as a fact may turn out to be merely a mistaken opinion. We know this pattern well from detective stories. A "fact" points to the guilt of a certain character. He is arrested by the stupid police sergeant. The clever detective proves that the "fact" was not a fact at all. The true criminal had worn the hooded raincoat which everybody at the house party associated with Miss Perkins, and he had been mistaken for her in the mist on the beach. The "fact"—that Miss Perkins was observed near the scene of the crime at a certain hour—turns out to be not a fact at all, and justice is done.

To stick, a fact must be (1) verifiable or (2) attested by a reliable source.

### VERIFICATION

Certain facts can be established by referring to some regularity in nature—that a certain type of cord would not support a certain weight, that potassium permanganate will explode under certain conditions, that the robin's egg is a certain shade of blue with brown markings, that a certain night of the year did not have a full moon, that *rigor mortis* sets in at a certain time after death. Such facts belong to a pattern in nature which is observable, and to test a particular fact we refer it to the pattern. We have an example in a story about one of Abraham Lincoln's law cases. A witness testified that he had observed a certain event. Lincoln asked him how, and he replied that he had seen it by moonlight. By producing an almanac, Lincoln showed that there had been no moon on the night in question. Lincoln tested the fact by referring it to a natural pattern. We shall here use the word *verifiable* in this sense.

### FACT ESTABLISHED BY TESTIMONY

Suppose, however, Lincoln had not been able to check the witness by an almanac. What questions could he have asked to determine the reliability of the evidence offered by the witness? Four questions are relevant in such cases:

1. Was there opportunity for the witness to observe the event?
2. Was the witness physically capable of observing the event?
3. Was the witness intellectually capable of understanding the event and reporting accurately?
4. Was the witness honest?

The first question is clear enough, but the others are a little more complicated. For instance, if a blind newsman attests that Bill Sims was present in a railway station at such a time, how good is his evidence? Was he capable of observing the event? If it can be demonstrated that the blind man is capable of recognizing a step and was acquainted with the step of Bill Sims, who stopped at his newsstand every day to buy cigarettes, then it can be assumed that the newsman is capable of recognizing Bill Sims' presence at a certain time. If, furthermore, it can be accepted that the newsman has common sense, is not given to delusions, flights of fancy, or exaggerations, and has a good memory, then it can be assumed that he is intellectually capable of understanding and reporting the event. What remains is the question of honesty. If the newsman has no connection with the case, if no malice, profit, or other special interest is involved, then it can be readily assumed that his report is an honest one. But if some motive which might make him color or falsify the report can be established, then this fact must be assessed in relation to what is known about the newsman's general character. Generally speaking, an interested witness is a poor witness. Even if he is honest, his report does not carry prompt conviction, especially to a hostile or indifferent audience.

The case we have given for reliability here—the blind newsman's testimony—is a relatively simple one. But it illustrates the kind of questions that must be raised in all situations involving testimony. A historian trying to determine the truth about an event long past, a

Congressional committee conducting a hearing on an economic situation, a farmer shopping for a new tractor are all engaged in assessing the reliability of testimony, and must ask the same questions.

To sum up: only facts that are verifiable or reliably attested should be admitted into the argument.

## OPINION AS EVIDENCE

We can set up a parallel set of tests for the admission of opinion into the argument. Corresponding to the first requirement for the admission of a fact, we find the authority of an opinion. There is no use in introducing an opinion to support our argument if the opinion will carry little or no weight. For instance, no lawyer would want to introduce as expert a witness who had no reputation for competence in his particular field. The manufacturer of athletic supplies wants a champion, not a dud, to endorse his tennis racquet, and the manufacturer of cosmetics wants a lady of fashion or a famous actress to give a testimonial for the facial cream. We should be as sure as possible that any authority which we invoke in an argument is a real authority: a second-rate navy is no navy, and a second-rate authority is no authority, when the moment of combat comes.

## TESTS OF AUTHORITY

How do we find out if an authority is real authority? "Ask the man who owns one," a famous advertising slogan suggests; and the maker of a washing machine shows the picture of a happy housewife standing by her prized contraption. The advertisers here appeal to authority on the principle that the proof of the pudding is in the eating: ask the eater, for he is an authority. This is a kind of rough-and-ready authority based on experience, useful but very limited in the degree of conviction which it can carry. Very probably the automobile buyer has not used many different makes of cars and the housewife has not used many different kinds of washing machines. The opinion of an impartial technical expert who had tested many makes of car or washing machine for efficiency, durability, and so forth, would carry much more authority. Here we appeal to experience too, but to the experience of the expert.

Authority is very often based on an appeal to success. The rich man is supposed to know how to make money, the famous painter how to paint pictures, the heavyweight champion how to fight. Success carries prestige and predisposes us to accept the pronouncement of the successful man. But we should still scrutinize each case. Perhaps the rich man got rich by luck—he *happened* to get into business at a time of expansion and rising markets. No doubt he himself attributes his success to his own sterling character, shrewdness, and indefatigable industry, but we may be more inclined to trust the evidence of the economic situation of his time. Or the famous painter may have struck a prejudice and a fashion of his time, and history is littered with the carcasses of artists of all kinds whose success was the accident of the moment. The heavyweight gives us a better case, for it is a simpler case—he merely had to square off with one man at one moment and slug it out. But perhaps a granite jaw, a fighting heart, and an explosive punch gave him the championship, and all that he has to say about training, footwork, and strategy may be wrong. He didn't succeed by luck, like the businessman or the painter—he really did flatten the opponent by his own force—but he may give the wrong reasons for his success. The fact of success doesn't mean that the successful man really knows the conditions of his success. And he can speak with authority only if at that point he knows. Many successful people are like the man who lived to be a hundred and revealed his secret for long life: "I never read less than one chapter of the Holy Writ a day or drink more than three slugs of likker a night."

Not infrequently we encounter an appeal to what, for lack of a better phrase, we may call authority by transference. Because a man is considered an authority in one field, it is assumed that he is an authority on anything. The famous musician is used as an authority on statesmanship, the great mathematician is appealed to as an authority on morality, and the great physicist on religion; the All-America fullback endorses a certain breakfast food, and a debutante prefers such-and-such a cigarette. This sort of reasoning is obviously nonsensical and pernicious, for it is simply a means of imposing on the gullibility of the audience. And because it is a means of imposing on gullibility, it is very common.

Authority, too, has some relation to time. What was acceptable as authority at one time may not be acceptable at another. In any field where the body of knowledge is constantly being enlarged and revised, timeliness is very important. A book on chemistry or physics written ten years ago may now lack authority in certain respects, or a history of the American Civil War written in 1875 may now be considered very misleading. Or should George Washington's views on foreign policy influence our own? We want the best authority of *our* time.

What tests, in the end, can we apply? There are no ready-made tests. We must, in the end, use our own judgment to select the authority by which we wish to support our argument. This seems to leave us where we started; but that is not quite true. Finding the man who might know is, after all, different from finding out for ourselves what he knows. If we are dealing with authority presumably based on experience, we can ask about the nature of the experience (one washing machine or ten washing machines?) and the intelligence and training of the person who has had the experience. If we are dealing with authority based on success, we can inquire into the nature of the success (how much was luck?) and into the capacity of the successful person for analyzing the means to success. And we should not forget to ask if the authority of the successful man is being used as authority by transference. Furthermore, we have to ask if our authority is timely.

Let us suppose that we wish to find an authority on some point of American history. It will not do to go to the library and take down the first book on the subject. The mere fact of print bestows no authority, for every error is somewhere embalmed between boards. We have to find out something about the author. Is he of recent date? (That is, would he have available the latest research on the subject?) Does he have any special bias or prejudice which must be discounted? Does he occupy a responsible position or has he had other professional recognition? (That is, is he on the faculty of some important university, have his works been favorably reviewed, and so forth?) How do his views compare with the views of some other historians of recognized importance? And all this means that we have to find out something about the field of American history, even if we are not capable of settling the particular point in question by our own investigation.

## AUTHORITY AND THE AUDIENCE

One more thing must be considered. The authority is going to be used for a particular audience, and is intended to be effective for that audience—if not the opponent, at least some listener. Effective authority is authority which is acceptable to the particular audience. The Mohammedan *Koran* carries no authority to a Catholic, the Pope carries no authority to a Methodist, and the first chapter of Genesis carries no authority to a geologist. If we can use an authority our audience already knows and respects, we have an initial advantage. If this is not possible, then we must establish the prestige of the authority. We can sometimes do this merely by informing the audience, but sometimes we must resort to persuasion. And, as we have said, the discussion of persuasion will be postponed.

## *APPLICATIONS*

**I.** Analyze the evidence offered in the following selections in the Readings:

1. "The Colors That Animals Can See" by H. Munro Fox (p. 547)
2. "Have Nations Any Morals?" by W. T. Stace (p. 624), or "The Scientist Fights for Peace" by Louis N. Ridenour (p. 651)

**II.** Analyze and criticize the evidence offered in some advertisements of common commodities, for instance, a tooth paste, a breakfast food, an automobile or truck, a cigarette, a face powder, a laundry soap.

**III.** Analyze and criticize the evidence offered in several political editorials or articles.

**IV.** Study the three items on Mary Queen of Scots under Biography in the Readings (pp. 803-30). In comparing the different views expressed there, what problems of evidence come to your mind?

**V.** Analyze the evidence you have offered in the theme done on one of the propositions which were suggested in the Applications on page 165 of this chapter. Would you now care to revise your theme?

## REASONING

Once we have our evidence we must know how to reason about it if it is to support our position. So reasoning is essential to argument.

The whole process of living, from first to last, is a long education in the use of reason. Fire burns, cats scratch, pulling things off tables brings a frown or a spanking—we learn these great truths early. Later on we learn other truths—a stitch in time saves nine, honesty is the best policy, to be good is to be happy. We say we learn from experience (or from somebody else's experience), but that is not quite true. Experience would teach nothing if we could not reason about experience.

Reasoning, therefore, is not something which we learn from books. The race learned it the hard way over a long time: if your powers of reason failed you too often you were liquidated by the falling tree, a saber-toothed tiger, or a neighbor who had *reasoned* out that a sharp stone tied to the end of a stout stick gave him certain advantages in a dispute. But we can train our powers of reason by learning something about the reasoning process.

### SUBJECT AND ATTRIBUTE

Reasoning is the process by which the mind moves from certain data (the evidence) to a conclusion which was not given. We can make this progress from data to conclusion because we recognize some regularity in the world we are dealing with. We recognize a regularity of cause and effect, and a regularity of subject and attribute.

The cause-and-effect relationship has already been discussed at some length in the chapter on Exposition.[7] We continually use the cause-and-effect relationship in our ordinary reasoning. But we also continually use the subject-attribute relationship. For instance, we know that green apples are sour. Therefore we do not eat the green apple we find on the bough. Here green apples (subject) are affirmed to have a certain attribute (sour), and when we encounter the subject we conclude that the attribute is present. Or we believe that a sales tax is unfair. So we vote against such-and-such a tax because it is a sales tax.

## INDUCTION: GENERALIZATION

Let us examine two examples of reasoning, examples of the kind of reasoning called INDUCTION. A businessman has hired five boys

[7] Pages 124-34. A further discussion appears in the Appendix on Cause (pp. 891 ff.).

at different times from the Hawkins School and has found them all
honest, well mannered, and well educated. Therefore, when the
sixth boy comes along for a job the man will be inclined to hire him.
In other words, the man has generalized from the five instances
to the conclusion that all boys from Hawkins School are honest,
well mannered, and well educated. The man has made a GENERAL-
IZATION, moving from a number of particular instances to the
general conclusion that all instances of the type investigated will
be of this same sort.

To take a second example of generalization, after long observation men have concluded that water always freezes at a certain
temperature, 32 degrees. Behind this conclusion, as behind the conclusion about the boys of Hawkins School, lies the assumption that
a certain regularity exists. In regard to the water, we assume that
the same kind of thing in nature always behaves the same way
under the same conditions—metal expands when heated; in a
vacuum falling bodies, no matter what their mass, move at the
same rate. Without this assumption of regularity we could not
accept the conclusion we arrive at from examining the individual
instances, and in fact, all science is based upon this assumption.

The principle of regularity also applies in the reasoning about
the boys from Hawkins School. We assume that certain intellectual
standards are maintained, that certain manners are insisted upon,
that honesty is inculcated, and that the stupid, idle, boorish, or dishonest boy is not graduated. It does not matter that the conclusions
we reach in these two instances compel different degrees of assent.
We scarcely doubt that the next pail of water we leave out will
freeze at a certain temperature, but we do doubt that absolutely
all graduates of Hawkins School are models of education, manners,
and honesty. We recognize here that the principle of regularity
(Hawkins' standards) in human nature is scarcely as dependable
as the principle of regularity in nature. The school has tried to
weed out the incompetent, the boorish, and the dishonest, but
human nature is very complicated and human organizations are
very fallible.

### THE INDUCTIVE LEAP

We recognize that the conclusion we reach about the boys from
Hawkins School is only a probability, but students of logic tell us

that from the strictly logical standpoint the conclusion that water always freezes at 32 degrees is also a probability. This is true because no argument which moves from *some* to *all* can give more than a probability. Undoubtedly millions of instances of water freezing at 32 degrees have been observed, but *all* instances—past, present, and future—have not been observed. After examining a certain number of instances we take the leap from the some to the all, the INDUCTIVE LEAP. We cannot be sure about the all. It does no good to appeal to the principle of regularity in nature by saying that water is water and will always behave the same way, for that principle is itself simply derived from the inspection of a number of instances and itself represents a leap from some to all.

What tests can we apply to reduce the risk of error in making the inductive leap?

## TESTS FOR GENERALIZATION

First, a fair number of instances must be investigated. An instance or two proves nothing. Somebody says: "All Chinese are short and slender. Why, I used to know one out in Wyoming, and he wasn't more than five feet tall and I bet he didn't weigh more than a hundred pounds." Or: "All boys from St. Joseph's College are snobs. There was a fellow from home. . . ." We all know this type of reasoning, and can see that it proves nothing. A fair number of instances have not been examined. But there is no way to determine certainly what is a fair number of instances. We simply have to use the evidence possible to us under the given circumstances and remember that only the untrained mind is rash enough to leap without looking.

Second, the instances investigated must be typical. In a laboratory the scientist may be able to test a substance to be sure it is typical of its kind. He could detect alcohol in a sample of water and would, therefore, not use that sample in an experiment to demonstrate the freezing point of water.

But sometimes we have to assume, without testing the fact, that the instances available are typical. For example, the businessman who has hired five boys from Hawkins School assumes that they are typical—that other boys from the school will be like them. At other times, however, when we are making out a case, we can choose from among a number of instances for our investigation; in such a situation we should be sure that the instances chosen are representative. Let us consider the problem of a sociologist who, for some purpose, wishes to give a description of the life in the southern Appalachians. The sociologist picks three settlements, investigates the pattern of life there, and concludes that life (in general) in the southern Appalachians is such-and-such. But an opponent may point out that the settlements chosen are not typical, that the people are of Swiss descent and maintain a good many Swiss customs. The sociologist's generalization, then, may be worthless because his instances are not typical.

Third, if negative instances occur they must be explained. Obviously, any negative instance occurring among those which we are using as a basis for a generalization will reduce the validity of the generalization unless we can demonstrate that the negative instance is *not* typical, and therefore need not be considered. For example, if the businessman who has hired five Hawkins boys and found them all honest, hires a sixth and finds that he is pilfering in the stock room, the businessman may decide that he must give up the generalization that the Hawkins graduates are desirable employees. But he discovers that the boy who did the pilfering is a very special case, that he is really unbalanced, is a kleptomaniac, and consequently cannot be taken as typical. Therefore, the businessman returns to his generalization that Hawkins graduates are desirable employees.

To summarize, the tests for making a generalization are:
1. A fair number of instances must be investigated.
2. The instances investigated must be typical.
3. All negative instances must be explained.

### INDUCTION: ANALOGY

Another type of induction is by ANALOGY. This type of reasoning is based on the idea that if two instances are alike in a number of important points they will be alike in the point in question. For example, a board of directors might argue that Jim Brown would make a good corporation executive because he has been a colonel in the army. The analogy here is between the requirements for a good army officer and a good business executive. The points of similarity might be taken as the ability to deal with men, the ability to make and execute policy, the willingness to take responsibility.

Then if Brown has been successful as a colonel it may be assumed that he will be successful as a business executive.

We can arrive at certain tests for analogy similar to those for generalization:

1. The two instances compared must be similar in important respects.

2. Differences between the two instances must be accounted for as being unimportant.

In addition to these tests, we must remember that increasing the number of similar instances tends to strengthen our argument. For example, if Brown, the man being considered for an executive position in the corporation, has been a successful division chief in a government bureau as well as a successful colonel, his case is strengthened in the eyes of the board. But in the case of analogy, as of generalization, we can arrive only at probability.

## DEDUCTION

On this point of probability we can distinguish the two types of induction (generalization and analogy) from the type of reasoning known as DEDUCTION. Deduction does not give probability; it gives certitude.

The most familiar example of deduction is found in ordinary geometry, the geometry we studied in high school. The system starts with certain axioms. For instance: "Things that are equal to the same thing are equal to each other." Or: "If equals be added to equals the wholes are equal."

There is no attempt in the system of geometry to prove these axioms. They are the starting point we accept. (They are LOGICALLY PRIMITIVE in the deductive system of geometry.) Once we accept them, the whole system *necessarily* follows. Accepting the axioms we can deduce our first theorem. Then, having thus obtained the first theorem, we can prove the second, and so on throughout the system generated by the axioms. Once we have the axioms the system must necessarily follow. It cannot be otherwise.

### THE SYLLOGISM

Deductive reasoning appears, however, in other forms than geometry. Let us take an example of the type of reasoning called the SYLLOGISM:

All men are mortal.
Socrates was a man.
∴ Socrates was mortal.

We are reasoning here about a relation among three classes, mortal creatures, men, and Socrates. It may help us to think of the matter as a series of concentric circles, one small (Socrates), one medium-size (men), and one large (mortal creatures). We put the medium-size circle in the large one, and then the small circle in the medium-size circle. Then, obviously, the small circle is included in the large circle. We see this from a chart:

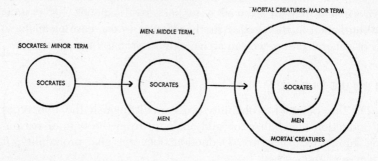

Each class is indicated by a TERM in the syllogism, the small class by the MINOR TERM, the medium-size class by the MIDDLE TERM, and the large class by the MAJOR TERM. The syllogism itself is composed of three propositions, the first two called PREMISES, and the third called the CONCLUSION. The proposition containing the major term is called the MAJOR PREMISE, and that containing the minor term the MINOR PREMISE.

All men are mortal.  (major premise)
Socrates was a man.  (minor premise)
∴ Socrates was mortal.  (conclusion)

The minor term is, we see, the subject of the conclusion, the major term the predicate of the conclusion, and the middle term the term that has made their relation in the conclusion possible.

Let us take another piece of reasoning that seems to have the same form:

Some soldiers are corporals.
All sergeants are soldiers.
∴. All sergeants are corporals.

We sense immediately that there has been a slip in the reasoning.
And we can see why if we chart the relations among the classes in
the syllogism:

The major premise (Some soldiers are corporals) says that the
class *corporals* falls within the class *soldiers,* but the word *some*
tells us that part of the class *soldiers* falls outside the class *corporals.*
So for this premise we get Fig. 1.

The minor premise (All sergeants are soldiers) says that the class
*sergeants* falls within the class *soldiers,* but this means that some
of the class *soldiers* falls outside the class *sergeants.* So we get Fig. 2.

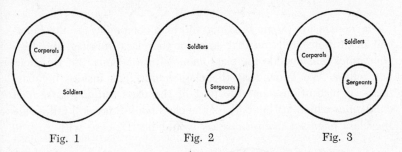

Fig. 1                    Fig. 2                    Fig. 3

The conclusion (All sergeants are corporals) says that the class
*sergeants* falls within the class *corporals.* It pretends to make the
same kind of figure we had for Socrates in the end, but it cannot do
so. For it is clear that the premises have given us no ground for any
relation between the class *sergeants* and the class *corporals.* The
premises have merely put the two classes within the third class
*soldiers.* So the only figure we could reasonably get would be Fig. 3.

The argument is not VALID. There has been a slip in the reasoning.

This is not the only kind of slip in reasoning that we may make
in dealing with classes. Let us take another example:

All banks are financial institutions.
Some building and loan companies are not banks.
∴. Some building and loan companies are not financial institu-
    tions.

The major premise (All banks are financial institutions) says that the class *banks* falls within the class *financial institutions.* So we get Fig. 4.

The minor premise (Some building and loan companies are not banks) says that part of the class *building and loan companies* falls outside the class *banks.* This gives Fig. 5.

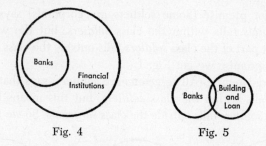

Fig. 4                              Fig. 5

The conclusion (Some building and loan companies are not financial institutions) tells us that some of the class *building and loan companies* falls outside the class *financial institutions.* But this does not follow. We know that the class *banks* falls inside the class financial institutions, and the part of the class *building and loan companies* which falls outside of the class *banks* may still fall inside the class *financial institutions,* as would be the case with Fig. 6.

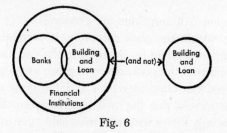

Fig. 6

In either one of the faulty arguments given above we know at a glance that the conclusion is wrong, because we know the facts of the case. We know that sergeants are not corporals and that all building and loan companies are financial institutions. But sometimes we may not know the facts; then we have to depend on the correctness of the reasoning. For instance, are we impressed by the following argument of a political candidate?

"Every Congressman who voted for the Jones-Higgins Bill betrayed this state. But I did not vote for it. Therefore, I am no traitor
to your interests, but will fight to the death for them. . . ."

We are not impressed, for the candidate has not offered any
finally convincing argument that he is not a traitor to the public
interest. Voting for the Jones-Higgins Bill is not the only way a
Congressman can betray the public interest.

What he wants his conclusion to look like is represented in Fig. 7.
But all we are sure of is that the candidate belongs outside the class

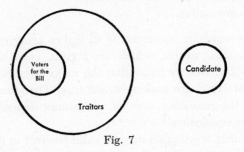

Fig. 7

of those who voted for the Jones-Higgins Bill. For all he has proved,
he may still be inside the class of traitors to the public interest, and
we may have Fig. 8.

In any reasoning about relations among classes, it is necessary
for us to look behind the words and see what and how much is said
to be included within what. And it is some-
times helpful to use charts such as we have
made above, at least until one is experienced in dealing with this type of reasoning. And when we make a chart if, in
diagramming the second premise, we automatically diagram the conclusion, then the
argument is valid. This is the case, we
recall, with the chart about Socrates. We
diagram the major premise by putting the
class *men* into the class mortal *creatures*.

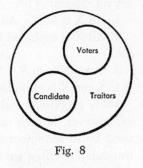

Fig. 8

Then when we diagram the minor premise by putting the class
*Socrates* into the class *men* we find that we have automatically

diagrammed the conclusion: Socrates was mortal. Socrates is put into the class of mortal creatures.[8]

## VALID SYLLOGISM AND TRUE CONCLUSION

We have spoken of valid syllogisms, those in which the process of reasoning is correct. But we may reason correctly and still not have a true conclusion if we start with a mistaken assumption, a premise which is not true. For instance, let us look at this syllogism:

All legless creatures that crawl are snakes.
Worms are legless creatures that crawl.
∴ Worms are snakes.

In this the reasoning is correct: *If* all legless creatures that crawl were snakes, then worms, which are legless, crawling creatures, would be snakes. But we know that the major premise (All legless creatures that crawl are snakes) is not true. Therefore, no matter how correct the reasoning may be, we cannot depend upon it to give us a true conclusion.

In other words, a syllogism may be valid (correct in its reasoning) and its conclusion may be untrue. But we always want true conclusions. Therefore, we must be careful to inspect our premises. Truth of the premises is as necessary as correct reasoning.

## KINDS OF PROPOSITIONS

We can make four basic kinds of propositions about relations among classes:

1. All X is in Y.    *All men are mortal.*
2. All X is excluded from Y. (Or: No X is in Y.)    *No whales are fish.*
3. Some X is in Y.    *Some women are cruel.*
4. Some X is excluded from Y.    *Some heroes are not recognized*

Many propositions about relations among classes do not come to us, however, in such simple forms. When that is true, our first step must be to see into which of these basic kinds the proposition is translatable. Often we can do this almost instinctively. There is no difficulty, for instance, in seeing that the proposition, "Warm gases

[8] For a more detailed discussion see the Appendix on the Syllogism, p. 897.

ascend," can be translated into the form, "All warm gases are in the class of things that ascend." But some instances are more difficult and require careful analysis. Propositions containing restrictive and exclusive terms such as *all but, only,* and *all except* are especially apt to give trouble.

For example, the proposition, "None but the brave deserve the fair," seems at first glance to mean, "All the brave deserve the fair." But a little reflection shows us that such is not the case, and that it really means, "All who deserve the fair are some of the brave," and is an example of type 1. Or to take another proposition, to say, "Only students willing to work will pass this course," does not mean, "All students willing to work will pass this course." Rather, it means, "All who pass this course will be in the class of those who are willing to work." Students who are badly prepared or are stupid may not pass even if they are willing to work.

## APPLICATIONS

I. Restate the following propositions according to the appropriate basic type:

1. None but a fool fails to learn by experience.
2. All's well that ends well.
3. Only women bear children.
4. Democracies alone can afford mistakes.
5. If a man is not responsible for his acts, he deserves no praise for them.
6. No success gives happiness in the end if attained by fraud.
7. The only success worth having comes through effort.
8. If you do not respect your fellowman, you will not have his respect.
9. All but the foolish seek to know God's will.
10. Many men are generous only because they hope for praise.

II. In three of the following indicate the major term, the minor term, and the middle term. Explain your choice in each instance.

1. All whales are mammals.
   All men are mammals.
   ∴ Men are whales.
2. No member of this fraternity chapter has ever gone to jail.
   Men who go to jail are disgraced.
   ∴ No member of this chapter has ever been disgraced.

3. You certainly want to cut expenses in your office.
The Blitz typewriter will cut expenses.
∴ You should buy the Blitz.

4. All governments deceive their citizens.
This official communiqué is published by the government.
∴ The communiqué is not true.

5. All members of the Jackson family are distinguished.
Jason is a member of the family.
∴ Jason Jackson is distinguished.

6. The Jackson family has been distinguished in our history.
Joseph is a member of the family.
∴ Joseph Jackson is distinguished.

III. Some of the arguments given above are valid and some are invalid. Distinguish the valid from the invalid, using a chart in each case to illustrate the reasoning.

### REASONING BY *EITHER–OR*

In addition to the ordinary syllogism, there are two kinds of syllogism which we shall look at briefly. The first we shall call reasoning by *either–or,* though it has a technical name, the DISJUNCTIVE SYLLOGISM.

Let us set up an example. Upon going into the kitchen and finding the steak off the table and on the floor under the sink, we think that either the cat or the dog has pulled it down. Then we discover that the cat is locked in the barn to catch rats. Therefore the dog must have committed the crime. The formula is simple. We decide on two possibilities. We exclude one. Naturally the other becomes our conclusion.

To get a true conclusion, we must be sure, as with the ordinary syllogism, that our starting point is dependable.

First, the *either–or* premise must really cover the case. The alternatives must be exhaustive. In the example of the cat and dog, if the cat was locked in the barn and the dog was out chasing rabbits, the premise simply does not cover the case. We have to investigate further to cover the possibilities. We find that, after all, it was curly-headed little Willie who pulled the steak off the table and deserves the licking.

Second, we must really mean the *either–or.* The possibilities must be distinct with no overlap between them. They must be exclusive.

Let us examine a piece of reasoning which may be faulty because there is an overlap between the possibilities set up.

> To maintain peace we must have either the United Nations or a
> system of international police.
> But a system of international police is undesirable.
> ∴ We must have the United Nations.

If we take it in fact that the United Nations does *not* involve a basic system of international police, then the conclusion is valid. But if we take it that the United Nations does involve a system of international police, then the conclusion is not acceptable. It is not because the two items of the *either–or* are not distinct: international police occurs in both of them, stated in one and implied in the other. The result is that in one premise we say that international police is undesirable, and then say it is desirable (under another name) in the conclusion. But this makes nonsense.

To be sure that our starting point for reasoning by *either–or* is satisfactory we have to know what we are talking about. We must examine the facts and use our common sense to be sure that the *either–or* covers the case and that there is no overlap between the items.

## APPLICATIONS

Discuss the following instances of reasoning by *either-or:*

1. What is not animal must be vegetable or mineral.
   This is not animal.
   ∴ This must be vegetable or mineral.

2. Bankruptcies are caused either by dishonesty or by idleness.
   John Sutter's bankruptcy was not caused by idleness.
   ∴ John Sutter must be dishonest.

3. Williams is either a coward or a traitor if he told our plans.
   We know he is a coward.
   ∴ He is no traitor.

## REASONING BY *IF–THEN*

Reasoning by *if–then* deals with a condition and a result. The condition being fulfilled, the result follows. The technical name of this kind of reasoning is the HYPOTHETICAL SYLLOGISM.

We constantly use reasoning of this kind, as in the statement, "If you had banked the furnace, we would have had heat this morning." Fully stated, the argument would go like this:

If you do not bank the furnace, the fire will die.
But you did not bank the furnace.
∴. The fire died.

The reasoning above is correct. We have affirmed the *if*, the condition, and therefore the result necessarily follows. But the reasoning is also correct if we deny the *then*, as in the following instance:

If you do not bank the furnace, the fire will die.
But the fire has not died.
∴. You did bank the furnace.

The following example does not, however, give us correct reasoning:

If you do not bank the furnace, the fire will die.
The fire died.
∴. You did not bank the furnace.

The conclusion here is not *necessarily* acceptable. The fire may have died because the furnace was not banked, but it also may have died from other causes. For instance, there may not have been enough fuel. That is, not banking the furnace is a sufficient but not a necessary condition of the fire's going out. (See the discussion of sufficient and necessary conditions, p. 128.) For the reasoning in this last example to be valid, the *if* would have to mean *only if*. Most errors in reasoning of the type of *if–then* come about because we interpret an *if* as an *only if*. Of course, there are instances where the *if* is legitimately to be interpreted as *only if*. But this is a matter of the truth of the premise with which we start, and if we mean *only if* we should say so in the premise.

## APPLICATIONS

Examine the pieces of reasoning below. Which are acceptable as they stand? Which could be accepted if the *if* were to be taken as *only if*?

1. If there is smoke, there must be fire.
   But there is no smoke.
   ∴ There is no fire.

2. If you leave bounds you will be expelled from school.
You have not been expelled from school.
∴ You did not leave bounds.

3. If you leave bounds you will be expelled from school.
But you have not left bounds.
∴ You will not be expelled from school.

4. If you leave bounds you will be expelled from school.
But you have been expelled from school.
∴ You did leave bounds.

5. If you do not catch this car, you will be late.
But you did not catch the car.
∴ You will be late.

6. If you do not catch this car, you will be late.
But you are late.
∴ You did not catch the car.

## FALLACIES

In discussing each type of reasoning, inductive or deductive, we have tried to indicate the characteristic errors into which we may fall. An argument that does not follow the course of reason—an argument that involves such an error—is called a FALLACY. In induction a generalization based on too few instances is a fallacy (p. 175). Or an analogy based on instances different in important respects is a fallacy (pp. 175-76). And again, in deduction when the major and the minor terms are not properly related in the syllogism we have a fallacy (pp. 178-81).

There are fallacies which we have not touched on, at least not directly, which are all too common in argument. They are EQUIVOCATION, BEGGING THE QUESTION, IGNORING THE QUESTION, and NON SEQUITUR (Latin for "it does not follow").

### EQUIVOCATION

Equivocation is the fallacy of using the same term in different meanings in the same argument. Here is a well-known example:

Even scientists recognize a power beyond nature, for they speak of "natural law"; and if there is law, there must be a power to make the law; such a power beyond nature is called God; therefore scientists believe in God.

Here the word *law* is used equivocally, in two meanings. In the sense in which scientists use it when they speak of "natural law" it means the recognition of regularity in natural process—the law of gravity, for example. Here the sense is descriptive. But in the second sense it means what is ordinarily meant in government, a command given by a superior authority. Here the sense is prescriptive. Since the whole argument is based on the word *law*, it does not make sense *as an argument* if the word shifts its meaning. It may be true that a number of scientists do believe in God, but that does not make this a good argument.

## BEGGING THE QUESTION

Begging the question occurs when the arguer assumes something to be true which really needs proof. We have already seen (p. 150) how this occurs in prejudiced propositions, such as "This unjust tax should be repealed." To say that the tax is unjust is equivalent to saying that it should be repealed. Yet the repeal is what the argument is supposed to be about. The word *unjust* smuggles into the proposition as already accepted what is supposed to be at stake and under debate.

The same principle appears on a larger scale whenever we argue in a circle. For example:

A: I admire Rembrandt's painting "The Night Watch."
B: Why?
A: Because it is a great painting.
B: How do you know?
A: All the best critics say it is.
B: How do you know who are the best critics?
A: Why, the best critics are those who recognize great painting.

Here speaker A gives a circle in the proof. He sets out to prove that the painting is great by appealing to the best critics, and then identifies the best critics as those who recognize great painting. This instance is very simple, but sometimes the begging may be concealed in a very elaborate argument. We must always be on the watch for it, for such question-begging is an attempt to establish a thing *by itself*.

## IGNORING THE QUESTION

An arguer ignores the question when he introduces any consideration that will distract from what is really at stake. There are numberless ways of doing this. A competing question may be set up so that argument is shifted to new ground. Or an appeal may be made to some emotional attitude having nothing to do with the logic of the case. For instance, if a man arguing for a Republican candidate shifts the issue from the candidate's qualifications to the praise of Lincoln, the great hero of the party, he is ignoring the question. Or if a Democrat leaves a present question and begins to discuss the glorious achievements of Thomas Jefferson, he is ignoring the question. Or if a lawyer defending a man accused of murder does not deal with the question of guilt, but argues that the victim was a wicked man or that the family of the accused is worthy of pity, we have the same situation.

One of the commonest forms of ignoring the question is to shift from the question to the character or personality of the opponent. We get an instance when the husband criticizes his wife and she replies, "Well, you aren't so perfect yourself!" She has ignored the rights and wrongs of the question, her own burnt bread or bad arithmetic or overbid at bridge, and has begun to discuss his shortcomings. Or we get an instance when we argue that we cannot endorse a certain political measure because the Congressman who proposes it is divorced or drinks. We have shifted from the measure to the man.

## NON SEQUITUR

*Non sequitur,* as we have said, means, "It does not follow." In one sense, of course, any fallacy is a *non sequitur,* because by the very nature of the case the conclusion does not follow from fallacious reasoning. But here we shall use the term to cover certain more special kinds of argument.

For instance, it may be argued: "William Brown doesn't drink or smoke, and so he ought to make a good husband." But it is obvious that a man who does not drink or smoke may still make a bad husband. He may gamble, or loaf, or beat his wife. Or it may be argued: "Harry Thompson would make a good governor, because he belongs to the upper classes." We know, however, that belonging to a certain social class proves nothing about a man's ability or integrity. So the conclusion that Thompson would make a good governor does not follow. A connection has been asserted which does not exist.

A somewhat more complicated form of *non sequitur* appears in a piece of parental reasoning like this: "As soon as I increased Billie's allowance, his grades at school began to fall. Therefore we ought to reduce his allowance since having extra money makes him idle." But Billie may have been suffering from eye strain, or may have fallen in love, or may now be taking up a subject for which he is badly prepared. Or let us take another example: "Just after Herbert Hoover was elected President we had the greatest depression in history. How can you respect a man like that?"

In the argument about Billie and the argument about Hoover the same thing has happened. It is argued that because A (an increase in Billie's allowance or the election of Hoover) precedes B (Billie's bad grades or the depression), A must necessarily be the cause of B. This occurs when the arguer does not understand the nature of a cause (pp. 131-34) or does not take the trouble to analyze the situation. He simply assumes that if one thing precedes another, it is the cause of that other.

## FALLACIES AND REFUTATION

Some understanding of fallacies is useful to help us reason straight, but it is also useful to help us locate defects in an opposing argument. If we can point out a fallacy in an opposing argument, we can REFUTE that argument, and REFUTATION is a powerful secondary weapon for maintaining our own position. Even if we are not engaged in a debate but are simply writing a piece of argument, we often find that we have to refute certain arguments—arguments which we can anticipate. Or we may want to refute certain arguments already made in order to clear the ground for our own views.

It is not necessary to memorize a list of fallacies to discover defects in reasoning or to reason straight. Many people who have never heard the word *fallacy* can reason straight or locate defects in the reasoning of another person. When we meet the example of a fallacy in cold type on the page of a textbook, we are inclined to say, "Nobody with common sense would commit such an error."

That is true. But common sense is not so common, after all, and sometimes we have to work for it.

## APPLICATIONS

I. The selection "How to Detect Propaganda," in Readings (p. 566), is really an analysis of certain fallacies, but fallacies used quite deliberately to deceive the public. Which of the false appeals analyzed there correspond to fallacies which we have studied here under other names, and which are new?

II. Identify the invalid arguments among the following instances, and explain the fallacy, or fallacies, involved in each.

1. The holder of one hand in this poker game is bound to win. Jack holds one hand, and therefore is bound to win.

2. On the sea coast a dying man usually breathes his last just as the tide begins to ebb because the going out of the water takes his strength with it.

3. You should not read the poetry of Byron because his private life was immoral.

4. Telegrams bring bad luck.

5. No man can live without faith. Faith is the mark of a good Christian. Therefore all men are Christians.

6. I am strongly opposed to our participation in any European war, because Washington, the Father of our beloved country, warned us against foreign entanglements.

7. The Irish love whisky, and so I am not going to hire Pat McGoon.

8. After taking several bottles of Lightfoot's Liver Syrup, Mrs. Jones felt much better. So Mrs. Smith immediately bought a bottle.

9. Nothing is better than peace of mind. But half a loaf is better than nothing. Therefore half a loaf is better than peace of mind.

## THE IMPLIED SYLLOGISM

When we first study the syllogism we are inclined to feel that to do so is a waste of time because in actual practice we rarely use or encounter it. It seems so remote from the texture of living argument and reasoning that we think it impractical, nothing but a schoolbook exercise.

Now it is true that we rarely encounter the syllogism in the form which we have treated here. But that does not mean that it may not lie behind many arguments which we make or attend to. As a

matter of fact, syllogistic reasoning is often embedded in the body
of a discourse like the bones in the flesh—and it may serve the same
purpose as the bones. This may be so even when part of the syllogism is never stated at all, when it is assumed that the audience
will supply the unstated part. We may say that such a piece of
reasoning is an implied syllogism. But it has a technical name,
ENTHYMEME ("in the mind").

A hunter says: "This setter has not been well trained. It is gun-
shy." Behind his remark lies a syllogism, which we can formally
set up:

A gun-shy setter is not well trained.  (major premise)
This setter is gun-shy.  (minor premise)
∴ This setter is not well trained.

We see immediately that in the hunter's remark the major premise
does not appear. It is assumed that his audience has it in mind. So
in his statement we have an implied, and not a developed, syllogism.

Similarly, a minor premise or a conclusion may be suppressed.
In the following example the conclusion is suppressed: "A girl who
is selfish with her mother and father probably won't make a good
wife, and Susie certainly imposes on her parents. Now that ought
to give you something to think about if you continue to go around
with her." Set up formally, the syllogism appears:

A girl who is selfish, etc., probably won't make a good wife.
Susie is selfish (imposes on her parents).
∴ Susie will not make a good wife (what you had better think
about).

These examples are very simple, and we seize on their meaning
in a flash without the necessity of framing the argument in full.
But sometimes the basic argument is more deeply embedded in the
midst of evidence, examples, and other material. Here is a paragraph from an editorial:

Nobody denies that our economic situation is desperate and that we
are facing a crisis, and nobody denies that there is great need for wise
legislation in all matters affecting the business of the nation. We must
scrutinize with redoubled attention every bill which comes before
Congress and try to see what its effect will be in this sphere of activity.
This is undoubtedly necessary with the present bill to lower taxes. If it
is passed it will have an inflationary effect. What attitude shall we take
toward the present bill?

The main point here concerns the tax reduction bill. It is assumed that the present situation is desperate and that good legislation is needed. All of that is background. The argument to follow can really be divided into two syllogisms linked together:

Tax reduction promotes inflation.
The present bill would reduce taxes.
∴ The present bill would promote inflation.

The conclusion of this syllogism provides a premise for the next one, the link in the argument.

Whatever produces inflation is bad.
The present bill would promote inflation.
∴ The present bill is bad.

Neither the major premise nor the conclusion of this syllogism is stated in the editorial. The editorial writer feels that his reader knows that inflation is bad, and he feels that the conclusion about this particular bill will strike the reader more powerfully if the reader is forced to come to it himself. The reader will himself answer the question: "What attitude shall we take toward the present bill?"

An extended argument may be a tissue or chain of implied syllogisms, the conclusion of one becoming a premise in the next. The writer trusts his reader to grasp the line of reasoning without the full statement. But a chain is no stronger than its weakest link, and if we are making an argument we must be careful not to insert a link that will not bear the strain of the argument. A good way to avoid this danger is to go back over an argument to inspect each implied syllogism and to make sure that in its developed form it would be valid.

## APPLICATIONS

**I.** State in developed form the implied syllogisms in the following examples:

1. You should not be surprised that Governor Terry speaks something less than the strict truth, for after all he is a successful politician.

2. "I am an aristocrat. I love justice and hate equality."—JOHN RANDOLPH

3. "Fools say they learn from their own experience. I have always contrived to get my experience at the expense of others."—BISMARCK

4. I know that Homer Wilson is the thief, for he was the only man present who could not look me in the eye.

5. We can depend upon her. She has never failed us yet.

6. Science requires freedom for its full development, and therefore our country should see its great flowering.

7. "In the foregoing, we have discussed three reasons why the profit-economy would seem to be in its decline. In the first place, we noted that its motivation is too low. Whatever the system be into which we pass, we shall ask that it substitute socialized for unsocialized motivation. Or, perhaps more accurately, we shall demand that it at least give greater opportunity for such socialized motivation. The present system practically compels all of us to be self-seekers. The individual with wide social sympathies has only a precarious place in the system. In all probability, in the relentless competition of self-interest, he fails. The profit economy, in short, compels us all to live on a lower level than that on which most of us would wish to live; and since, in any event, we must live we are forced to make our compromise with the system."— HARRY A. OVERSTREET: *We Move in New Directions.*[9]

**II.** Compose an argument of 200 words illustrating the process of reasoning by the linking of enthymemes. Then set up the enthymemes in developed form (as syllogisms) and indicate the relationship among them.

## EXTENDED ARGUMENT: THE BRIEF

The composition of an extended argument calls for very careful planning. One point must lead to another, effect must be traced to cause, premise must give conclusion. Random thoughts, no matter how important in themselves, will not carry conviction. Therefore it is a good idea to think through an argument before beginning the actual writing. To prepare a systematic outline of the argument is the best way to be sure that the subject is covered and the relationship among the parts is clear.

When a lawyer prepares the BRIEF of a case, he does just this. The brief is not a set of jottings and suggestions. It is the full outline of an argument. *The brief is the arrangement in logical sequence and in logical relationship of the evidence and the argument on one side of the dispute. The brief makes complete sense in itself, even to a reader who is not previously familiar with the dispute.*

[9] Reprinted from *We Move in New Directions* by H. A. Overstreet, by permission of W. W. Norton & Co., Inc. Copyright 1933 by the publishers.

The process of drawing a brief in the law or for a formal debate of any sort is a very complicated one. But for ordinary purposes we can dispense with some of the subtleties and refinements useful to the lawyer or debater. We cannot, however, dispense with the requirements listed above: logical sequence, logical relationship, completeness.

## PARTS OF THE BRIEF

The brief is divided into three general sections: INTRODUCTION, ARGUMENT or DISCUSSION, and CONCLUSION.

The introduction should give whatever information is necessary for an understanding of the situation: proposition, definition of terms, history of the question, immediate occasion of the dispute, statement of admissions and issues. Not all of these items are necessary in all briefs, but the proposition and the statement of issues are always demanded. In any event, *nothing not acceptable to both sides* should appear in the introduction. The argument presents all the evidence and the inferences drawn from that evidence step by step to lead to the single conclusion desired. When such are demanded it also presents refutations of opposing views and answers possible objections to its own. The conclusion summarizes the fundamental points of the argument and when necessary shows how they relate to the question at stake.

## ORGANIZATION OF THE BRIEF

It is important so to arrange the items of the brief on the page that the relationship among them is immediately clear. Each of the three main sections should be treated independently, with a system of numbering complete under that section. Main headings under a section should be given Roman numerals, the subdivisions scaling down in importance marked *A, 1, a.* A dummy form will make the system clear.

I. _____
   A. _____
      1. _____
         a. _____
         b. _____
      2. _____
         a. _____

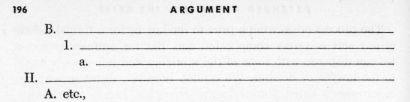

B. _____

1. _____

a. _____

II. _____

A. etc.,

It is important to keep the indentations on the left margin consistent in each class and to be sure that a class of lower importance is more deeply indented than the class just above it. If more subdivisions are needed than are indicated here, the system can be begun over again with the key numerals and letters in parentheses. For instance, if subdivisions are needed under *a*, we can use (*I*), (*A*), (*I*), and so forth. But for ordinary purposes such an extension is rarely necessary.

In the second section of the brief (the argument), a new element is introduced that is not shown in the dummy above. Here we have to indicate the relation of evidence to the inferences drawn from the evidence. That is, *I* is true *because* of *A*, and *A* is true *because* of *1* and *2*, and *1* is true *because* of *a* and *b*. We give the conclusion (as *I*) and work back through a chain of reasons.

So for the argument we can fill out the dummy thus:

I. _____ *because* (or *for*) [10]

A. _____ *because*

1. _____ *because*

a. _____ *and*

b. _____

[10] We may make a distinction for this purpose of a brief between *because* and *for*, using *because* to mean the *cause of*, and *for* to mean the *reason for believing the truth of*. Let us take a simple example:

*Because:*

I. Three people died in Morgansville in traffic accidents this week, *because*

A. The driver, in one instance, was intoxicated, *and*

B. The streets, in the other instances, were slick with ice.

*For:*

I. Three people died in Morgansville in traffic accidents this week, *for*

A. I saw one person die, *and*

B. The Morgansville *Herald* reported the deaths of two other persons in the issue of May 21.

The point here is to indicate clearly what is being asserted, the cause of an event or the reason for believing the event to have occurred.

Thus all the relationships are indicated as a chain of proof. If we need to interrupt the chain of proof to refute an opposing view or to answer an objection, we can do it as follows:

> c  (following *b* above). The view that 'so-and-so) is true
>      can be refuted because
>      (I) _____ *and*
>      (II) _____

*or:*

> c. The objection that (so-and-so) is not valid because
>      (I) _____
>      (II) _____

Such a form can be used at any necessary level, and not merely at the level of *a, b,* and so on.

## EXAMPLE OF THE BRIEF

Let us see how we would go about using a brief in preparing a theme. Suppose we have been given the proposition: "Scientists should refuse to participate in research which may lead to the production of military weapons."

We may have an immediate, almost instinctive reaction to the proposition, either for or against it, or we may not be able to reach a conclusion without further consideration. In either case, we feel it worth while to get some acquaintance with the literature on the subject. If we have not made up our own mind, the arguments by others may help us. If we have made up our own mind, we may find arguments in support of our view, and we shall certainly encounter arguments against our view which we should be prepared to refute.

If we went to the library to investigate the question we might find a body of material such as that reprinted in the Readings: *Dawn over Zero,* by William Laurence (p. 592), "A Scientist Rebels," by Norbert Wiener (p. 648), "The Scientist Fights for Peace," by Louis N. Ridenour (p. 651), and "The Threat of Science," by Christian Gauss (p. 659). After reading such material we might have reached an opinion of our own. Let us suppose that we wish to attack the proposition, to take the negative side.

Sometimes the history of a question is important, and that is true

here. The events of the past war make the question very important.
So we may begin our brief with the "History of the Question."
Then we may move on to a statement of the "Occasion for Discussion." That is, the immediate discussion is provoked by a general
debate going on over the country. Then we want to be sure that
we know exactly what the real issues are. So we set up a section
on "Issues." Then we are ready to give the body of the argument.
We might make a brief like the following:

*Introduction:*

   I. Proposition: Scientists should refuse to participate in research which
      may lead to the production of military weapons.
  II. History of the Question
      A. The atomic bomb made clear the destructive power of modern
         science.
         1. Scientists realize this power.
            a. Dr. Kistiakowsky, who witnessed the Alamogordo ex-
               plosion called it "the nearest thing to doomsday."
               (William L. Laurence, *Dawn over Zero: The Story of
               the Atomic Bomb,* New York, Alfred A. Knopf, 1946,
               p. 11)
            b. Albert Einstein says that atomic war might destroy two-
               thirds of mankind. ("Einstein on the Atomic Bomb," as
               told to Raymond Swing, *Atlantic Monthly,* CLXXVI,
               November 1945, 43)
         2. Laymen realize this power.
            a. The press has been full of information on this point, and
               there have been numerous articles and books, like John
               Hersey's *Hiroshima* (New York, Alfred A. Knopf, 1946),
               and Norman Cousins's *Modern Man is Obsolete* (New
               York, Macmillan, 1946).
      B. Efforts have been made to curb the use of atomic energy for war.
         1. The Atomic Commission has been set up in this country.
         2. The United Nations are trying to reach an agreement to
            bar the bomb.
 III. Occasion for Discussion
      A. There has been debate among scientists about their responsi-
         bility.
         1. Norbert Wiener refused to give information about research
            having military significance. ("A Scientist Rebels," *Atlantic
            Monthly,* CLXXIX, January 1947, 46)

2. Louis N. Ridenour attacked Dr. Wiener's position. ("The Scientist Fights for Peace," *Atlantic Monthly*, CLXXIX, May 1947, 80-83)

3. *The American Scholar* published a forum on the relation of scientists to war (XVI, Spring 1947, 213-225) and a set of letters in reply ("Should the Scientists Resist Military Intrusion?" XVI, Summer 1947, 353-360).

IV. Issues
   A. Does the scientist behave morally by refusing to participate?
   B. Does the refusal to participate practically serve the cause of peace?

*Argument:*

I. To refuse is not moral, *for*
   A. In so far as the scale of war is a determining factor, the refusal is morally meaningless, *for*
      1. The fact of killing constitutes the moral question without reference to the number of victims. (Louis N. Ridenour, *op. cit.*, p. 82)
   B. The scientist who refuses neglects some of the broader moral issues, *for*
      1. If he believes that this system of government has moral value, it is worth defending in war, *and*
      2. If in case of such a war he had not assisted in preparation or refused to participate in research, after the commencement of war, he would want victory at somebody else's expense.

II. To refuse is not practical, *for*
   A. No distinction can now be drawn between research which may have a military value and research which may not, *for*
      1. Scientific advance depends on a number of individual discoveries and ideas, the importance of no one of which by itself can be predicted, *for*
         a. No one scientist or discovery made the atomic bomb possible. (William L. Laurence, *op. cit.*)
      2. A scientific discovery may lead to both a peaceful and a warlike purpose, *for*
         a. An airplane may drop a bomb or carry serum.
   B. In total war the "whole range of industrial and technical know-how in the world becomes a military factor." (William Yandell Elliott, "Facts and Values," *American Scholar*, XVI, Summer 1947, 358)

C. The idea that the scientist is a special case to be distinguished from the farmer, factory worker or manager, mother, and so forth, can be refuted, *for*

 1. Food, manufactured goods, and manpower are all necessary in war.

D. If scientists did refuse to participate, the cause of peace would not necessarily be advanced, *for*

 1. If the scientists in this country should refuse, the policy in other countries would not be affected, *and*
 2. If scientists everywhere refused to work, war could still be carried on with the weapons which can now be manufactured.

E. The problem of maintaining peace is not a scientific one, *for*

 1. Science does not define values (Christian Gauss, "The Threat of Science," *Scribner's*, LXXXVII, May 1930, 467-478), *and*
 2. Peace must be maintained at the practical level of applied values, *for*

    a. World-wide economic adjustments would promote peace, *and*
    b. Political arrangements are necessary to set up the machinery of peace.

*Conclusion:*

I. It follows that the scientist would serve no moral or practical purpose by refusing to continue his research.

We notice that in such a brief every item is a complete sentence making its own point, and that if we read the argument through the relationship of each item to the chain of proof is clear. Furthermore, whenever a reference is given for some printed piece of evidence, the reference is given full bibliographical form.[11]

When such a brief has been completed, most of the work for an argument has been done. All that remains is to develop the material so that it will be attractive reading. Here is a student theme developed from the preceding brief.

## SHOULD THE SCIENTISTS STRIKE?

INTRODUCTION     The scientists of the world are in a peculiar position. For a long time, almost ever since the beginning of modern science, people have been looking to the scien-

[11] See Appendix 3, pp. 902-28 for information about bibliographical forms.

¹ I

² II, A

³ II, A, 1

⁴ II, A, 1, a

⁵ II, A, 1, b

⁶ II, A, 2

⁷ II, A, 2, a

⁸ II, B

⁹ II, B, 1

¹⁰ II, B, 2

¹¹ III, A

¹² III, A, 1

tists for a better world for them to live in. And in our time we were all taught from childhood that the scientists would not only bring plenty to the world but would also bring peace. Many of the scientists themselves must have believed this too. But now science has just shown everybody how powerful it is to destroy as well as to create, and some of the scientists are afraid of what they have done. ¹ Some of them have gone so far as to say that they will refuse to engage in any research leading to the invention of military weapons.

² The day the atomic bomb fell on Hiroshima science became the central fact for warfare. Science has always been used to improve weapons, but this time it provided *the* weapon which in a single instant destroyed a city and conquered an empire.

³ The scientists were the first to realize that this was a new period in history. William L. Laurence in his book *Dawn over Zero: The Story of the Atomic Bomb* * tells how ⁴ Dr. Kistiakowsky, one of the scientists watching the trial explosion at Alamogordo, New Mexico, said it was "the nearest thing to doomsday that one could possibly imagine." And ⁵ Albert Einstein, the great scientist whose work made the bomb possible, has said that the bomb may destroy two-thirds of mankind. †

⁶ Ordinary people, too, are aware of the danger as we can tell by picking up any newspaper or magazine. Almost everybody has read ⁷ John Hersey's story of Hiroshima ‡ and the horrible effects of the bomb, and many people have read the book by Cousins called *Modern Man is Obsolete*. §

⁸ Some things have been done to curb the use of atomic energy for war. For example, ⁹ the Atomic Commission has been set up in this country, and the ¹⁰ United Nations are trying to control the use of atomic energy.

¹¹ It is only natural that scientists, who made the bomb, should try to do something about the use of science for war. When ¹² Norbert Wiener, who is a

* New York, Alfred A. Knopf, 1946, p. 11.

† "Einstein on the Atomic Bomb," as told to Raymond Swing, *Atlantic Monthly*, CLXXVI, November 1945, 43.

‡ New York, Alfred A. Knopf, 1946.

§ New York, Macmillan, 1946.

prominent mathematician and who did research for World War II, was asked for some information about his work, he wrote a letter refusing to have anything more to do with creating armaments. His letter was published under the title "A Scientist Rebels." * This letter caused a long debate among scientists which is still going on. The scientists cannot agree about Dr. Wiener's course of action. For instance, [13] Louis N. Ridenour † attacked Dr. Wiener's position, and the [14] *American Scholar* ‡ published a forum on the relation of scientists to war with letters in reply in a later issue.

[15] Since this is a problem that concerns everybody, we should all think about it. I am not a scientist or a politician, but I do have my views on the subject for what they are worth. It seems to me that Dr. Wiener is wrong. I shall try to argue my views on two main points. [16] First, is the refusal of a scientist to participate in any research that may be used for military purposes morally good? [17] Second, if he refuses, does he really serve the cause of peace? I do not mean to say that these two questions can be completely separated, but for the sake of this discussion I shall try to keep them separate.

There are several objections to the idea that a refusal to participate in such research is morally good. [18] First, it seems clear to me that on moral grounds there is no difference between an old-fashioned war and a new-fashioned one. [19] The number of people killed, and whether they are soldiers in the field or civilians in cities, does not change the moral question. That has been there all the time. I shall quote from the article by Louis N. Ridenour, who has written an answer to Dr. Wiener. On this point he says: "God told Moses, 'Thou shalt not kill'—not 'Thou shalt not kill with atomic energy, for that is so effective as to be sinful.' " §

[20] Second, the scientist who refuses research on Dr. Wiener's grounds does not see some of the broader moral

The marginal annotations, left column:

[13] III, A, 2
[14] III, A, 3

[15] IV

[16] IV, A

[17] IV, B

ARGUMENT
[18] I, A

[19] I, A, 1

[20] I, B

* *Atlantic Monthly*, CLXXIX, January 1947, 46.
 † "The Scientist Fights for Peace," *Atlantic Monthly*, CLXXIX, May 1947, 80-83.
 ‡ XVI, Spring 1947, 213-225, Summer 1947, 353-360.
 § Ridenour, *op. cit.*, p. 82.

<sup>21</sup> I, B, 1

issues. <sup>21</sup> If he believes that this country gives a moral way of life, with more liberty than some other, he might have to admit that war would be necessary under some circumstances to defend it. But this would contradict his

<sup>22</sup> I, B, 2

other opinion. <sup>22</sup> And if he still held to his refusal to participate in research, he would still want to share in the benefits of victory in such a war. This means that he would want somebody else to do the scientific work and the fighting so that he could keep his own hands clean and his conscience clear. But that does not seem moral to me, to make somebody else do the dirty work for you.

<sup>23</sup> II

<sup>23</sup> I shall turn now to the question, does the scientist's refusal do any practical good? Does it serve the cause of peace? I believe that Dr. Wiener has made this matter appear too simple just as he has made the matter of morality appear too simple. There are several objections that occur to me.

<sup>24</sup> II, A

<sup>24</sup> First, how can the scientist tell which piece of research may serve a military purpose and which will not?

<sup>25</sup> II, A, 1

<sup>25</sup> Scientific advance depends on a number of individual discoveries and ideas. Anybody who reads *Dawn over*

<sup>26</sup> II, A, 1, a

*Zero,* which I have already mentioned, <sup>26</sup> will see how many single pieces of research lay behind the atomic bomb. And nobody could have guessed that many of

<sup>27</sup> II, A, 2

them would ever be used to kill human beings. <sup>27</sup> Furthermore, when the scientific discovery does lead to a machine or a process, that machine or process may be used

<sup>28</sup> II, A, 2, a

for either a peaceful or a warlike purpose. <sup>28</sup> An airplane dropped the bomb on Hiroshima and an airplane may be used to carry serum to a baby dying of diphtheria.

<sup>29</sup> II, B

<sup>29</sup> When we think about what is required to carry on a modern war, we see another objection. Food, all sorts of manufactured goods, and man power are necessary, as well as weapons. The farm, the factory and the nursery are just as important from one point of view as the laboratory. William Yandell Elliott, Professor of Government at Harvard University, has made this point in writing about science and war: * "The whole range of industrial and technical know-how in the world be-

<sup>30</sup> II, C

comes a military factor." <sup>30</sup> Would Dr. Wiener want

* "Facts and Values," *American Scholar,* XVI, Summer 1947, 358.

every farmer to quit raising corn, every worker to quit
making automobiles or playing cards, and every woman
31 II, C, 1        to stop having children? 31 To be consistent he would
have to demand that, for food, manufactured goods, and
man power are all necessary in war.

32 II, D           32 For a third objection, I can suggest that even if Dr.
Wiener's view were adopted by all the scientists in this
33 II, D, 1        country peace would not be guaranteed. 33 There is no
reason to believe that all other nations would stop re-
34 II, D, 2        search. 34 Furthermore, even if all scientists everywhere
refused to work, war could still be carried on with the
weapons which people already know how to make.

35 II, E           35 This leads to my last objection, that the problem of
maintaining peace is not a scientific one at all. Science
gives us the technical know-how, as Dr. Elliott calls it,
but it does not tell us what to do with that know-how.
36 II, E, 1        36 We have to figure out the good and the bad for ourselves. I can refer to an essay by Christian Gauss on this
point. He says: "Quite evidently there are certain questions which the scientist can answer and certain others
which he cannot. Among these latter are questions as
important as the following: Is this holy or is this obscene?
Is this beautiful or is this ugly? Is this good or is this
evil?" *

37 II, E, 2        37 When we get around to figuring out the good and
bad for ourselves, we find that we are involved in things
38 II, E, 2, a     like economics and politics and not in science. 38 If
scientific methods were applied to producing food and
goods all over the world, many of the causes for war
would be removed. But that is an economic problem.
39 II, E, 2, b     39 And it is by political arrangements at home and
abroad that we can set up the actual machinery for
peace.

CONCLUSION         If my line of argument is sound, then the refusal of a
scientist to participate in any research which might have
military value is not admirable morally and does no
practical good. And if that is true, the scientist should
continue to follow his chosen occupation. He can work
for peace in other ways which we hope will be more
effective than his laboratory strike.

* "The Threat of Science," *Scribner's,* LXXXVII, May
1930, 470.

# ORDER OF THE BRIEF AND ORDER OF THE ARGUMENT

We notice that the author of the theme has very closely followed the brief, step by step. This is not always necessary. Sometimes the author may want to plunge into the very middle of his argument, at what he considers the crucial point, and then later set up the background of the question. Or he may move to the question by anecdote or illustration and thus catch the interest of his audience. Or he may state his conclusion first, and then give his reasons. We rarely find an article or essay which sticks slavishly to the line of the brief.

But the ability to draw up a brief remains important. It is a very good way for the author to clear his own mind. After he has cleared his own mind, he can then more readily adapt his method to his audience. And in any event, it is advisable for the inexperienced writer to follow very closely the line of the brief when he comes to the actual composition of his argument.

The theme given above is rather elaborate and runs to nearly 2,000 words. It is really a "readings" theme in the form of an argument. But the same method can be used on a theme of any scale. Even in a very short theme involving an argument, it is well to brief the material before beginning the actual writing.

## APPLICATIONS

I. Prepare the brief that might lie behind the argument of either of the speakers in "The Marxian View of History," by Carl Becker (Readings, p. 634).

II. Study "Have Nations Any Morals?" by W. T. Stace (Readings, p. 624) with the following questions in mind:

a. What is the basic proposition for which the author is arguing? Does the title indicate it? If not, state it in your own words as a formal proposition.

b. What issue or issues has the author selected as crucial?

c. Has the author followed in the essay the order of what a brief would have been? If not, how (and why) has he departed from that order?

d. What kinds of discourse has the author used in the essay?

**III.** Prepare a brief to defend or attack one of the following propositions, or one in which you have some special interest:

1. The honor system should be abandoned (or adopted) by this institution.

2. Religion should be encouraged even by the unbeliever.

3. Hitler was justified in his attack on Russia in June of 1941.

4. Great Britain should have made peace with Hitler after the Battle of Britain to maintain Western solidarity against Russia.

5. The elective system should be replaced by fixed curricula.

6. The third term for the President should be abolished.

7. A Republican victory in the next national election would be for the best interest of the country.

8. A federal equalization fund should be established to improve the educational system in poor states.

9. Fraternities have no place in a democratic society.

10. All veterans' organizations should be abolished by law.

11. The federal government should adopt such policies as are necessary to distribute industry more evenly over the country.

12. A federal anti-lynching law is desirable.

13. The President should be elected by direct vote.

14. The coal mines should be nationalized.

15. The United States would benefit from a greatly increased immigration.

16. Socialized medicine is desirable.

17. Thomas Wolfe is a better novelist than Ernest Hemingway (or substitute two other names).

**IV.** Write a theme of 1,000 words based on your brief, indicating by reference in the theme each division and subdivision of the brief. (It is possible, of course, that in the process of composing the theme itself new and better ideas will occur to you. If so, revise the brief to make it consistent with the theme.)

**V.** Locate and give formal developments to five enthymemes in the essay from Readings which you have briefed, and to several in your own theme.

## PERSUASION

In the beginning of this chapter we said that, though argument makes the appeal to reason and aims at conviction, the appeal to the emotions, persuasion, may be very important as the strategy of presenting an argument. The appeal to reason and the appeal to emotion can be distinguished, but both may appear in the same discourse.

The human being is a unit, after all, and his reason and his emotions are but different aspects of that unity. Even the most rigorously impersonal and logical mathematician is driven to his work by some *desire*—he feels that knowledge is good in itself, that using his faculties is good, that to satisfy his curiosity is good. He is not thinking what his work is good *for*, merely that it is good.

Though all our reasoning is undertaken in the broad context of our emotional life and in the end we want it to lead to satisfactions of the emotional life, the emotions may locally, at a given moment, get in the way of the exercise of reason. Then we get a kind of short circuit, and the short-range satisfaction of the emotions will defeat the long-range satisfaction. So Tom Smith votes Republican (or Democratic) against his long-range interests, just because his grandfather fought under General Sherman (or General Lee). So Jack Brown hits the bottle to avoid a problem instead of facing the problem and trying to solve it. So Susie Perkins makes a joke at the expense of a friend just to please her own vanity in her wit, and loses a friend.

Reason should serve to show us the way to long-run satisfaction; but sometimes, human nature being what it is, we have to appeal to short-range satisfactions in order to lead someone to see the long-range satisfaction. We have to make a person feel that the immediate effort is worth while. Our problem is to find the way to establish fruitful contact with him. That is the problem of persuasion in argument.

We cannot expect our ideas, no matter how good they are, to make their way readily if we do not know how to present them. Even the scientist is irritated and put off if he does not find clarity in the discussion he is attending to—no matter how valuable the ideas may be in that discussion; and mathematicians talk about "elegance" in a proof just as a woman might speak of style in a dress or a painter about the execution of a picture. And when we get away from the cold, accurate language of mathematics and science into the warm and confused language of the ordinary world, the way of presenting an idea becomes even more important. The right way may predispose our audience to hear us out, to listen with sympathy, to give us the benefit of the doubt.

## THE OCCASION AND THE "RIGHT WAY"

What is the "right way"? There is no single right way, for what is right for one subject and one audience is wrong for another. But the right way always accomplishes one basic thing: it catches the attention of the audience, and it defines a common ground for speaker or writer and audience.

The good writer or speaker is aware of his occasion (p. 3), and the occasion involves (1) the speaker, (2) the subject, and (3) the audience. All three are interrelated, and we have to ask several questions about them:

1. What is the attitude of the audience toward the subject?
2. What is the speaker's attitude toward the subject?
3. What kinds of treatment will the subject permit?
4. What is the audience's attitude toward the speaker?
5. What is the speaker's attitude toward his audience?

The right way to catch and hold the attention of the audience and to find common ground with them depends on the answers to these five questions.

If we are addressing an audience already specially interested in our subject, half our battle is won. The writer of an article in a scientific journal can assume that his reader is interested; he is addressing the specialist. The speaker addressing a mass meeting to protest a particular tax bill can depend on his audience. But the writer of an article on a scientific subject or on some theory of taxation in a popular magazine like the *Atlantic Monthly* or *Collier's* has to capture his audience, and capture it quickly.

What catches the eye? The moving object or the bright object, not the fixed or the dull. And what catches the eye catches the mind. So drama and vividness are important. The sharp anecdote, the interesting or shocking scene, the memorable phrase, the disturbing question—all of these devices may be used to catch the attention. We know them all from the pages of magazines, the platform, and the pulpit. When they are really relevant to the topic under discussion—when the anecdote makes a point or the question truly leads into the discussion—such devices are effective. When they are not relevant, the audience may feel that it is being patronized and imposed upon.

Sometimes, however, the writer can dispense with devices like scenes or anecdotes, and catch the attention of the audience by showing immediately that the topic which the audience had felt was very remote from its concerns is really of great importance. For instance, Tibet is fairly remote from the concerns of the ordinary citizen, but if the writer can show that Tibet may become very significant in the general political picture of the Orient and that world stability depends on stability in the Orient, then the ordinary citizen realizes that he has some interest in Tibet. The problem, then, is to move fast enough; you have to prove to the reader immediately that what you are talking about really concerns him and may affect his life.

Once the audience's attention has been caught, the game is merely begun. Vividness remains important, even though the vividness may no longer concern scenes or anecdotes but phrasing or apt similes and metaphors, and the drama may not involve people but the clash of ideas and opinions. The audience must be constantly aware of what is going on, what issues are at stake, how the argument moves from one point to another, and that ground has been gained. It must catch the sense of impending climax, the sense of an objective. Without clarity of language and organization this is not possible: we cannot then hold the attention of the audience.

These considerations are relative to a particular situation—to the answers we would have to give to our first three questions in the particular situation. We might, for instance, catch the attention of an audience which had a neutral attitude toward our subject, but then find that in doing so we had falsified our own attitude toward the subject. The anecdote that might be right for a political article might be wrong for the pulpit simply because in the pulpit it would falsify the basic attitude of the speaker toward the subject. If the speaker is urgent and serious about his subject and wants to impress that fact upon his audience, he cannot use devices which contradict his own basic attitude, or if he does so he must use great skill in making the transition back to the effect he fundamentally desires. And for some subjects certain methods of treatment are inapplicable. Even clarity is a relative matter, for what is clear to some people is not clear to others, and some subjects cannot be simplified beyond a certain point. The question is always, "Clear for whom and clear about what?"

## THE COMMON GROUND

So far we have been concerned with the problem of catching and holding the attention of the audience. But there is the problem of finding the common ground. This is the final problem, for if we do not find this common ground, everything else is meaningless. We have already touched on this question in speaking of the possibility of catching the interest of the audience by showing that a subject—like Tibet—which had seemed to be of no concern is really of great concern. In such attempts we try to find the common ground between the audience and the subject.

But there remains the problem of finding the common ground between audience and speaker or writer. Without finding this, it is impossible to convince the audience. As we have said earlier, in the most impersonal and technical piece of argument, it is assumed that there is the common ground of definition and reason. This common ground must always be found, but most often this is not enough. We have to overcome prejudices, personal hostilities, habits of feeling and thinking, inherited attitudes. And to do this we must find a starting point acceptable to the audience. Let us take an example.

Suppose Mr. Brown has a strong anti-Semitic attitude and Mr. Smith is arguing against that view.

SMITH: Look here, I know how you feel, but I'm just curious to know how it squares with your other views. It just doesn't seem consistent with what I know about you.

BROWN: What do you mean?

SMITH: Well, just the way you manage your affairs, the way you treat people.

BROWN: What's that got to do with it?

SMITH: Well, nobody ever said you aren't a straight shooter, or didn't believe in justice, or any of these things. Like that time when you—

BROWN: That hasn't got anything to do with it.

SMITH: You don't deny that you believe in people getting justice.

BROWN: Sure, I don't deny that, but—

Smith has tried to locate the common ground. He has made Brown admit that he has a notion of justice. Now he has the job of making Brown see what justice would mean in a particular situation. That may be a hard job, but at least there is a starting point in the common agreement that justice is desirable. But suppose that Brown denies that he is interested in justice.

BROWN: Look here, I know justice is all right, by and large. But, buddy, this is a tough world and a man's got to look out for himself. He's got to watch his interests.

SMITH: OK, let's forget that justice stuff. A man's got to watch his own interests. That's right. It's a good practical point of view.

BROWN: I'm a practical man.

SMITH: Well, the question just boils down to what a man's interests are, doesn't it?

BROWN: Sure.

SMITH: Now on the Jewish question, maybe our interests aren't as simple as they sometimes seem—

Smith has here accepted the common ground of practical self-interest. Now his job is to show that in the light of self-interest anti-Semitism may be a short-sighted policy in any society. Again, he may not convince his friend, but at least he has a starting point.

We have to find the starting point. If there is no starting point possible, argument is not possible. There remains only the resort to force if a question is to be resolved.

To find the common ground we must know our audience and know ourselves. And when we are sure about what we do agree on we must say to the audience: "We disagree about the question before us, but we really agree on something more important than the question before us, something that lies deeper than the question. And since we do agree on that deeper question, I can show you that we ought to agree on the present question." We do not say that in so many words, but that is what we mean to convey.

We must convey this if we are to overcome the hostile attitude of the audience. By and large, we must convince the audience that our own attitude toward it is friendly. There are times when a brutal shock may bring an audience to its senses and may startle it into thought, but even then the audience, in the end, must come to feel that the motive behind giving the shock is a responsible one. Hard words mean nothing to a man unless he respects or likes the speaker of the hard words. So tact, fair-mindedness, patience, and respect for the audience are essential. They are not only essential for persuasion in argument. They are important for many kinds of writing. And all of this comes down to a matter of TONE. The chapter on Tone will discuss this subject at length.

## APPLICATIONS

I. Try to locate some of the devices for catching and holding attention in the following essays:

"Have Nations Any Morals?" by W. T. Stace (p. 624)
"The Marxian View of History," by Carl Becker (p. 634)
"It Was a Stable World," by Robert Graves (p. 798)
"Wordsworth in the Tropics," by Aldous Huxley (p. 762)

II. Try to locate in the first two of the above essays some indications of fair-mindedness, tact, and respect for the audience.

III. What is the common ground established between speaker and audience in each of these essays?

IV. Return to the theme written from your brief (p. 200). Imagine an audience hostile to your line of thought, and analyze the attitudes that might account for the situation. Then write an introduction intended to persuade such an audience to give you a hearing.

## SUMMARY

Argument is the kind of discourse used to make the audience (reader or listener) think or act as the arguer desires. It appeals to the understanding, and aims to CONVINCE. It differs from the other forms of discourse in that it arises, directly or indirectly, from a situation of conflict in ideas or attitudes.

An argument cannot be about a subject considered as a vague generality, or about a question of mere taste. An argument must be about a PROPOSITION, a statement that can be believed, doubted, or denied. A proposition represents a judgment.

There are two kinds of propositions, Propositions of FACT and propositions of POLICY. The proposition of fact asserts that something is true. The proposition of policy asserts that a certain line of action is desirable.

A proposition should be SINGLE. It should not express more than one idea for argument. Even though an extended argument involves several propositions, each one must still be single, and must be argued individually.

A proposition should be CLEAR. That is, it should not contain terms which are not understood, and the accepted terms should be understood in a single sense for the purpose of that argument. An argument cannot proceed unless all concerned accept the definition of the terms involved.

A proposition should be UNPREJUDICED. The wording should not smuggle in anything which would imply a foregone conclusion to the argument, anything that "begs the question."

Some propositions can be understood immediately, but for some we must know the HISTORY OF THE QUESTION in order to know exactly what is at stake. And for similar reasons it is sometimes necessary to know the OCCASION OF THE DISCUSSION. The particular circumstances may modify the meaning.

The single idea of the proposition may raise several reasons for and against it. We should study the proposition to determine what are the points on which controversy may focus. An essential point is called an ISSUE.

A point is essential if its defeat means the defeat of the proposition. The supporter of a proposition must win on all the issues to win on the proposition. A whole argument can hinge on one point, or issue.

There are two kinds of issues, ADMITTED and CRUCIAL. An issue on which both parties to an argument are in agreement is admitted. The issue (or issues) on which they are not in agreement is crucial.

We arrive at the issues by making an ANALYSIS of the proposition. To analyze a proposition, all possible arguments on both sides are listed, the affirmative facing its negative, when such pairing is possible. There is no pair for an admitted issue. That is, there is nothing on the opposing side against it. The next step is to reduce the points of argument to the fundamental ones.

When the proposition is one of policy certain STOCK QUESTIONS may help to reduce the arguments to order. These stock questions, which can be applied to the individual points, are:

1. Is there a need for change?
2. Will the policy suggested be effective?
3. Are the possible benefits of the suggested policy greater than any new disadvantages?
4. Is there any alternative policy better than the proposed one?

In a proposition of fact the location of the issues becomes a

problem of defining the fact, or facts, by which the proposition
stands or falls.

The actual process of argument involves EVIDENCE, whatever can
be offered as support for an argument. Evidence is of two kinds,
FACT and OPINION.

To be accepted as fact a piece of evidence must be VERIFIABLE
or ATTESTED by a reliable source.

Verifiable evidence, as we use the phrase here, is the kind
that can be established by referring to some regularity in nature.
For instance, it can be verified by a test that a certain cord will
support a certain weight or that water will freeze at a certain temperature. Or it can be verified that the moon was full on a certain
night.

Evidence by testimony can be subjected to the following tests:

1. Was there opportunity for the witness to observe the event?

2. Was the witness physically capable of observing the event?

3. Was the witness intellectually capable of understanding and
reporting?

4. Was the witness honest?

But neither verifiable evidence nor attested evidence is valuable
if it is not truly relevant to the issue in question.

The reliability of evidence of opinion depends on the AUTHORITY
of the person giving the opinion. Experience and success are generally taken to signify authority, but neither is reliable unless the
person who is experienced or successful is capable of analyzing his
experience or the means of his success. Authority, too, must be
considered in relation to time. What is acceptable as authority at
one time may not be accepted at another. The authority of a physicist of 1850 would not necessarily be accepted today. Furthermore,
what is acceptable as authority for one audience may not be acceptable for another.

In evidence of opinion, as in evidence of fact, the question of
relevance must be considered.

Once evidence is available it must be reasoned about in an argument. Reasoning is the process by which the mind moves from
certain given data (evidence) to a conclusion that was not given.

There are two types of reasoning, INDUCTION and DEDUCTION.

There are two types of induction, GENERALIZATION and ANALOGY.

Generalization is the process of moving from a number of particular instances to a general conclusion that all instances of the type being investigated will be the same. For example, if five boys from the Hawkins School prove honest we generalize that all boys from that school will prove honest. But there is always a risk in generalization. At the best it can only give probability. There is an INDUCTIVE LEAP.

To reduce the risk of error, the following rules can be applied:

1. A fair number of instances must be investigated. One or two instances indicate nothing.

2. The instances investigated must be typical of the class being investigated.

3. If negative instances occur they must be explained.

Analogy is the type of reasoning based on the idea that if two instances are alike in a number of particulars they will be alike in the point in question. For example, it may be reasoned that a man who has made a success as a high officer in the army will make a success as a business executive, for both things involve the ability to organize and to command.

As in generalization, there is always a risk in analogy. To reduce the risk, the following rules can be applied:

1. The two instances compared must be alike in important respects.

2. Differences between the two instances must be accounted for.

Whereas induction can give only probability, deduction can give certitude. A deduction starts from certain assumptions, like the axioms in geometry, which if accepted *necessarily* generate the system that follows.

Deductive reasoning appears in the SYLLOGISM. The syllogism consists of two propositions, called premises, and a conclusion, as follows:

All men are mortal.   (major premise)
Socrates was a man.   (minor premise)
∴ Socrates was mortal.   (conclusion)

The premises involve three terms, the MAJOR TERM, the MINOR TERM, and the MIDDLE TERM. The major term is the term that constitutes the predicate of the conclusion (*mortal*), the minor term the subject of the conclusion (*Socrates*), the middle term the link between the major and minor terms (*man, men*). The process establishes relations among classes. We can chart the syllogism above by thinking of a nest of boxes: a small box (Socrates) placed in a medium-size box (men), and that placed in a large box (mortal creatures).

When the process of reasoning is correct in a syllogism, the syllogism is said to be VALID. But a valid syllogism may not give a true conclusion if the premises are not true. Therefore, to be sure of getting a true conclusion the premises must be inspected.

In addition to the ordinary syllogism there are two other types, the EITHER–OR (called the DISJUNCTIVE) syllogism, and the IF–THEN (called the HYPOTHETICAL) syllogism.

In reasoning by *either–or,* two possibilities are set up, one is ruled out, and therefore the second must be accepted. The two items of the *either–or* must really cover the case—cover all possibilities. And the two items must not have any overlap.

Reasoning by *if–then* deals with a condition and a result. If the condition is fulfilled, the result follows. Most errors in this form of reasoning come from misinterpreting the *if* of the condition to mean *only if.*

An argument, either inductive or deductive, that does not follow the course of reason is called a FALLACY. There are numerous fallacies, but four of common occurrence are EQUIVOCATION, BEGGING THE QUESTION, IGNORING THE QUESTION, and NON SEQUITUR (Latin for "it does not follow").

Equivocation occurs when a significant word in an argument is used in two senses.

Begging the question occurs when the arguer assumes something to be true which really needs proof, as in a prejudiced proposition or in arguing in a circle.

An arguer ignores the question when he introduces any consideration which will distract from what is really at stake, as when he shifts the interest of the argument or makes an appeal to the emotions and prejudices of the audience.

*Non sequitur* occurs when an arguer asserts a connection between two items which does not exist; for example, when a thing is taken to be the cause of another simply because it comes before it in time or is associated with it.

Some understanding of fallacies is useful to straight thinking, but it is also useful for REFUTATION, the attack on an opposing argument.

Syllogisms in developed form rarely appear in extended argument, but the implied syllogism, called ENTHYMEME, is common. A syllogism is implied when one of the three elements, major premise, minor premise, or conclusion, is suppressed, and it is assumed that the audience can supply it. Often an extended argument is a chain of enthymemes.

The composition of an extended argument calls for careful planning. The systematic outline for an extended argument is called a BRIEF. It is the arrangement in logical sequence and in logical relationship of the evidence and the argument on one side of a dispute. The brief makes complete sense in itself, even to a reader who is not previously acquainted with the dispute.

The brief is divided into three parts, INTRODUCTION, ARGUMENT or DISCUSSION, and CONCLUSION. The introduction gives whatever is necessary for an understanding of the situation, certainly the proposition and the statement of admissions and issues, and sometimes the definition of terms, the history of the question, and the immediate occasion of the dispute. Each of the three main sections of the brief is to be treated independently. Within the section, main headings are indicated by Roman numerals, with subdivisions indicated in descending importance by *A, 1, a.* In the section of argument the relation between evidence and inference is indicated. For example, *I* is true *because* of *A,* and *A* is true *because* of *1* and *2,* and *1* is true *because* of *a* and *b.* The brief moves down from statement through a chain of proof.

After the brief is made, the arguer may not necessarily follow its order. He may, for instance, begin his actual presentation at what he considers a crucial point. But the brief does provide him with the skeleton of the argument.

It has been said that argument, strictly considered, appeals to the reason. But PERSUASION, the appeal to the emotions, is very useful in leading the audience to the content of the argument.

Persuasion depends to a large extent upon VIVIDNESS of presentation and upon discovering the COMMON GROUND between the arguer and his audience. The quality of vividness catches interest, and the discovery of a common ground overcomes hostility or indifference. For persuasion, it is necessary to exhibit tact, fair-mindedness, patience, and respect for the audience.

# Description

DESCRIPTION, as we shall understand the word in this discussion, is the kind of discourse concerned with the appearance of the world. It tells what qualities a thing has, what impression it makes on our senses. It aims to suggest to the imagination the thing as it appears immediately before an observer. We call this kind of description SUGGESTIVE to distinguish it from another kind, expository description, or technical description, which is really a form of exposition, and has already been discussed.[1]

## RELATION OF SUGGESTIVE DESCRIPTION TO OTHER KINDS OF DISCOURSE

Even suggestive description may appear in close association with other kinds of discourse. It may be used in connection with exposition [2] or with argument,[3] but more often, in fact quite commonly, it appears in connection with narration. When we are telling a story, we must, if we wish our audience to grasp it as real, give some impression of the scene and of the persons involved. In neither conversation nor writing do we ordinarily set up the necessary description as a long, separate, preliminary part of the whole composition; instead, we tend to weave it into the body of the narrative as the occasion demands. The vivid stroke of description, small in itself

[1] Page 45. Review the section on the distinction between suggestive description and technical description.
[2] See Chap. 3, p. 65.
[3] See Chap. 4, p. 208.

and apparently unimportant, may lend the touch of reality and may stir the imagination so that the reader is ready to accept and respond to the whole composition.

Here is a piece of narrative which has been stripped of all its descriptive elements:

The other waved the cigar, the other hand in Horace's face. Horace shook it, and freed his hand. "I thought I recognized you when you got on at Oxford," Snopes said, "but I— May I set down?" he said, already shoving at Horace's knee with his leg. He flung the overcoat on the seat and sat down as the train stopped. "Yes, sir, I'm always glad to see any of the boys, any time . . ." He leaned across Horace and peered out the window at a station. " 'Course you ain't in my county no longer, but what I say a man's friends is his friends, whichever way they vote. Because a friend is a friend, and whether he can do anything for me or not . . ." He leaned back, the cigar in his fingers.

Here is the passage in its original form, with the descriptive elements italicized. Notice how they give the sense of reality, or the immediately observable world, to what otherwise would be a bare synopsis of events.

The other waved the cigar, the other hand, *palm-up, the third finger discolored faintly at the base of a huge ring,* in Horace's face. Horace shook it and freed his hand. "I thought I recognized you when you got on at Oxford," Snopes said, "but I— May I set down?" he said, already shoving at Horace's knee with his leg. He flung the overcoat—*a shoddy blue garment with a greasy velvet collar*—on the seat and sat down as the train stopped. "Yes, sir, I'm always glad to see any of the boys, any time . . ." He leaned across Horace and peered out the window at a *small dingy station with its cryptic bulletin board chalked over, an express truck bearing a wire chicken coop containing two forlorn fowls, at three or four men in overalls gone restfully against the wall, chewing.* " 'Course you ain't in my county no longer, but what I say a man's friends is his friends, whichever way they vote. Because a friend is a friend, and whether he can do anything for me or not . . ." He leaned back, the *unlighted* cigar in his fingers.—WILLIAM FAULKNER: *Sanctuary,* Chap. 19.[4]

It is clear that in the passage above description is subordinate to narrative. As a matter of fact, description is usually subordinate

[4] From *Sanctuary* by William Faulkner, copyright, 1931, by Random House, Inc.

when it appears mixed with some other kind of discourse, and it rarely appears alone in any very extended form. This is only to be expected, for description, which has to do with the appearance of the world, cannot satisfy us very long. We are constantly straining beyond the appearance of things; we want to see what they do and know what they mean, or we are interested in our own responses to and ideas about them. Therefore, though description can present us with the vivid appearance of things, it is constantly moving over, in ordinary use, into narrative and exposition and, even, argument, the kinds of discourse which express our fuller interests.

This is not to say, however, that a capacity for description is not important for any writer. Without the resources of description most kinds of composition would be very bare and unconvincing—fiction, poetry, letters, feature articles, reporting, history, essays, biography, speeches, and even certain kinds of philosophical writing. Description is far more important than its mere proportion in what we read would seem to indicate. And furthermore, any attempt to understand its principles will sharpen our own perceptions and increase our pleasure in both literature and the real world we live in.

## SUGGESTIVE DESCRIPTION AND THE SENSES

Description, and particularly suggestive description, is the kind of discourse that has primarily to do with the appearance of the world, with the way things present themselves to our sense. We say, "The apple is red," and we refer to what the sense of sight tells us about the apple. But we also say, "The tweed is rough," or "The music is loud," or "The milk is sweet," or "The lilies are fragrant," and in so doing appeal to other senses, touch, hearing, taste, smell. We are also aware of the world in terms of heat and cold, and weight, pressure, and strain, and we have a language to describe that awareness, too.

The descriptive sentences just given are crude and general. They do not make us vividly aware of the thing described. A good writer is not satisfied with such crude and general descriptions. He is interested in making close discriminations and in indicating slight differences. Therefore, he must be a good observer. Even if he is writing a description of an imagined object rather than one really before his eyes, he can be successful only if his mind is stored with impressions drawn from actual experience.

Therefore, a person who wants to become a good writer should make some effort to train his powers of observation and to expand his vocabulary, especially in words that indicate differences in perception. He must tie his perceptions and his words together. The loud noise must cease to be loud noise for him, and must become the crash, the bang, the thud, the clatter, the clash, the boom, the bong, the clang, the howl, the wail, the scream, or whatever most vividly presents the thing he has heard. And the same for the other senses, for all the senses are important to the writer who wants to give a clear picture of the world.

Here are three bits of description, each one primarily concerned with impressions of a single sense. Note the discriminations made in each passage and the language used to record the close observation.

To tell when the scythe is sharp enough this is the rule. First the stone clangs and grinds against the iron harshly; then it rings musically to one note; then, at last, it purrs as though the iron and stone were exactly suited. When you hear this, your scythe is sharp enough; and I, when I heard it that June dawn, with everything quite silent except the birds, let down the scythe and bent myself to mow.—HILAIRE BELLOC: "The Mowing of a Field," *Hills and the Sea*.[5]

He knew the inchoate sharp excitement of hot dandelions in young Spring grass at noon; the smell of cellars, cobwebs, and built-on secret earth; in July, of watermelons bedded in sweet hay, inside a farmer's covered wagon; of cantaloupe and crated peaches; and the scent of orange rind, bitter-sweet, before a fire of coals.—THOMAS WOLFE: *Look Homeward, Angel*, Chap. 8.

When I think of hills, I think of the upward strength I tread upon. When water is the object of my thought, I feel the cool shock of the plunge and the quick yielding of the waves that crisp and curl and ripple about my body. The pleasing changes of rough and smooth, pliant and rigid, curved and straight in the bark and branches of a tree give the truth to my hand. The immovable rock, with its juts and warped surfaces, bends beneath my fingers into all manner of grooves and hollows. The bulge of a watermelon and the puffed-up rotundities of squashes that sprout, bud, and ripen in that strange garden planted some-

[5] From *Hills and the Sea* by Hilaire Belloc, copyright, 1935, by Charles Scribner's Sons.

where behind my finger-tips are the ludicrous in my tactual memory and imagination.—HELEN KELLER: *The World I Live In,* Chap. 1.[6]

In the first of these selections the sense of hearing is dominant, in the second the sense of smell, and in the third, the sense of touch. But in the third selection, which comes from a remarkable book written by a woman blind and deaf almost from birth, we also find temperature and pressure and strain: the coolness of the water and the "upward strength" of the hill.

As we can see from the quotations above, especially from the first two, a single sense may be dominant in a piece of description. But generally speaking, we may limit ourselves far too much if we insist on making the impression of a single sense dominant. This is certainly true if we think of description as a business of tying the single adjective to the single sense impression, as we do when we say, "The apple is red." When we observe the apple we observe much more than the color, and if we describe only the color, even if we find the exact word or phrase—such as "tawny-freckled" instead of the general word *red*—we still leave out, as we have said earlier, a great deal that we have observed.[7]

We have observed not only color. We are prepared to say that the apple is, for example, "slick-looking," or "juicy-looking," and many other things besides. Other senses than sight are involved in our experience of the apple. Our past experiences with apples are operating in our experience of the present apple. We are not touching the present apple, but we are prepared to say that it is slick-looking. And so on. We see the apple and sense the complex of qualities which mean "appleness"—the color, the texture, the fragrance, the juiciness. That is to say, our experience of the apple is more massive than the response of one sense. A good writer often tries to indicate something of the massiveness of perception.

Our ordinary use of language illustrates this massiveness. When we say "slick-looking" of the apple, we are, in a way, fusing two senses, sight and touch. Or when we look at a frozen lake and say, "The ice is glassy," we evoke with the word *glassy* a whole complex of qualities which are fused in the single word—slickness, hard-

[6] From *The World I Live In* by Helen Keller, copyright, 1908, by the Century Company. Reprinted by permission of Appleton-Century-Crofts, Inc.

[7] See p. 36 above.

ness, transparency, brightness. Though description may sometimes confine itself to the report of a single sense, it frequently tries to fuse the report of several senses to give impression of the fullness of the experience, the unity of perception.

## APPLICATIONS

In the description of the Dedlock estate (p. 55) Dickens gives an impression of the unity of the perception. To what senses has he appealed? What words or phrases strike you as particularly vivid?

## THE DOMINANT IMPRESSION

We have already seen how the facts selected by Melville in his description of the volcanic islands (p. 48), by Poe in his description of the House of Usher (p. 54), and by Dickens in his description of the Dedlock estate (p. 55) are all related to the single effect the writer desires to create. Each writer wishes to leave his reader with a single DOMINANT IMPRESSION, a single attitude, a single feeling.

A writer should try to select and organize his material so that such a single impression is dominant. Vividness of detail is important, for without that the reader does not really grasp the object in his imagination, but vividness alone is not enough to insure a good description. There must be the basic line of feeling, the unifying idea, to make it memorable for him. Contradictory and irrelevant items in a description disturb the reader and leave him at a loss. In such a case he may not even understand why the description is given in the first place.

For example, if Dickens had presented in some detail the roaring fires on the hearths in the Dedlock mansion and the steaming roasts and puddings on the table, he would have distracted from the interpretation he wishes the scene to bear. Undoubtedly the Dedlock family had roaring fires and steaming roasts, but that is not the point. The point is what the writer wants a description to work on the reader.

## APPLICATIONS

I. In the set of examples at the end of the chapter, select two that seem successful in creating a particular mood. Then underscore the details which contribute to the dominant impression. Do you find any contradictory items?

II. Take some scene that you are well acquainted with and that impresses you as having a very definite mood. Make an informal list of the items of the scene that are relevant to this dominant impression. Make another list of items that are irrelevant or contradictory.

## PATTERN AND TEXTURE IN DESCRIPTION

Even if a writer knows what dominant impression he wishes to give and knows what items will contribute to his effect, he still has to settle certain questions of method. No one can lay down formulas that will assure the writer of success, but the understanding of certain principles will help him avoid confusion and will sharpen his effects.

We can consider the problem under two general heads: PATTERN and TEXTURE. The first, pattern, has to do with the general organization; the second, texture, has to do with the nature of the details, and their interrelation.

### PATTERN

Under pattern we are here concerned with the various principles by which a piece of description may be organized. If one observes a person, an object, or a scene, it has its proper unity—in a flash we recognize a friend, a tree, a familiar room, a meadow with woods beyond. But if, when we set out to describe one of these things, we give a mere catalogue of unrelated details, a mere enumeration of this, that, and the other, the sense of vital unity is gone.

The reason is not far to seek. In fact, when we look at something, even though our attention is focused on some one aspect, we are constantly aware of the totality; it is all there before us at one time. In description, however, the details are presented to us one after another; instead of the simultaneous presentation which we find in fact, we now have presentation in sequence. Since simultaneous presentation is impossible in description, the writer must provide some pattern into which the reader can fit the details if he is to give them a proper unity.

## 1. PATTERN FROM FIXED POINT OF VIEW

The most obvious method of ordering details is dictated by the arrangement of the details in the object; we describe from left to right, or from top to bottom, giving each item as it comes. But as it comes to whom? There must be an observer, specified or implied. And that observer occupies, as it were, a certain fixed point of view, specified or implied, from which he can read off the details. Study the following description of an English cathedral:

Let us go together up the more retired street, at the end of which we can see the pinnacles of one of the towers, and then through the low, grey gateway with its battlemented top and small latticed window in the center, into the inner private-looking road or close, where nothing goes in but the carts of the tradesmen who supply the bishop and the chapter, and here there are little shaven grassplots, fenced in by neat rails, before old-fashioned groups of somewhat diminutive and excessively trim houses, with little oriel and bay windows jutting out here and there, and deep wooden cornices and eaves painted cream colour and white, and small porches to their doors in the shape of cockleshells, or little, crooked, thick, indescribable, wooden gables warped a little on one side; and so forward till we come to the larger houses, also old-fashioned, but of red brick, and with gardens behind them, and fruit walls, which show here and there, among the nectarines, the vestiges of an old cloister arch or shaft; and looking in front on the cathedral square itself, laid out in rigid divisions of smooth grass and gravel walk, yet not uncheerful, especially on the sunny side, where the canons' children are walking with their nurserymaids. And so, taking care not to tread on the grass, we will go along the straight walk to the west front, and there stand for a time, looking up at its deep-pointed porches and the dark places between their pillars where there were statues once, and where the fragments, here and there, of a stately figure are still left, which has in it the likeness of a king, perhaps indeed a king on earth, perhaps a saintly king long ago in heaven; and so higher and higher up to the great mouldering wall of rugged sculpture and confused arcades, shattered, and grey, and grisly with heads of dragons and mocking fiends, worn by the rain and swirling winds into yet unseemlier shape, and coloured on their stony scales by the deep russet-orange lichen, melancholy gold; and so, higher still, to the bleak towers, so far above that the eye loses itself among the bosses of their traceries, though they are rude and strong, and only sees, like a drift of eddying black points, now closing, now scattering, and now settling suddenly into invisible places among the bosses and flowers, the crowd of restless birds that fill the whole square with that strange clangour of theirs, so harsh and yet so soothing, like the cries of birds on a solitary coast between the cliffs and sea.—JOHN RUSKIN: *The Stones of Venice,* Vol. I, Chap. 4.

In this passage, the author has very carefully specified the observer, in this case the reader, who is invited to go with him. And he specifies even more carefully the point in space from which the cathedral is to be viewed; he even conducts the reader to that point on the west side. The order of the details in the description then follows the order in which the observer would meet those details as he raised his eyes slowly upward. The items given us in the earlier part of the passage belong to the ground level; the last item is the birds above the tower.

## 2. PATTERN FROM MOVING POINT

Sometimes, however, the observer, specified or implied, does not occupy a fixed point in space, but moves from one point to another. Then another principle of sequence comes into play, a principle well illustrated by the following passage:

Our path took us between the Sakhara and the Sukhur by a narrow gorge with sandy floor and steep bare walls. Its head was rough. We had to scramble up shelves of coarse-faced stone, and along a great fault in the hill-side between two tilted red reefs of hard rock. The summit of the pass was a knife-edge, and from it we went down an encumbered gap, half-blocked by one fallen boulder which had been hammered over with the tribal marks of all the generations of men who had used this road. Afterwards there opened tree-grown spaces, collecting grounds in winter for the sheets of rain which poured off the glazed sides of the Sukhur. There were granite outcrops here and there, and a fine silver sand underfoot in the still damp water-channels. The drainage was towards Heiran.—T. E. LAWRENCE: *Seven Pillars of Wisdom,* Chap. 31.[8]

## 3. PATTERN OF FRAME IMAGE

Sometimes, however, the object of a description is too large or unwieldy for unity of impression to be achieved by either of the methods involving, as specified or implied, a "real" point of view. In such a case, the writer may give unity by means of what we

---

[8] From: *Seven Pillars of Wisdom* by T. E. Lawrence. Copyright 1926, 1935 by Doubleday & Company, Inc.

may call a FRAME IMAGE; he can compare the whole object to some smaller object which can be visualized, and which will serve as a frame into which the reader's imagination can fit the necessary details of the object being described. For instance, let us take the following example:

The nether sky opens and Europe is disclosed as a prone and emaciated figure, the Alps shaping like a backbone, and the branching mountain-chains like ribs, the peninsular plateau of Spain forming a head. Broad and lengthy lowlands stretch from the north of France across Russia like a grey-green garment hemmed by the Ural mountains and the glistening Arctic Ocean.—THOMAS HARDY: *The Dynasts*, Part I.[9]

In this example, the writer has begun by providing the frame image and then giving the details which are to be set in the frame. But sometimes the writer will reverse the process; that is, he will first give the details, perhaps a swarm of them which stimulate and baffle the reader's imagination, and then give the frame image which will suddenly reduce all to order. Here is a very simple example of the method:

I studied M. de Charlus. The tuft of his grey hair, the eye, the brow of which was raised by his monocle to emit a smile, the red flowers in his buttonhole formed, so to speak, the three mobile apices of a convulsive and striking triangle.—MARCEL PROUST: *The Guermantes Way*, Part I, Chap. 1.

## 4. PATTERN BY MOOD

In the types of pattern thus far discussed, the position of an observer, specified or implied, determines the organization of the details, but his reactions and interests are irrelevant. We shall now turn, however, to examples in which the emphasis is subjective, in which the reactions and interests of the observer, specified or implied, provide the basic principle for ordering and unifying the details.

The first of these patterns based on the observer we may call pattern by mood. We have already had examples of this. The passage from Poe's "The Fall of the House of Usher" (p. 54) gives us an example with the observer specified, and the passage from

[9] From Thomas Hardy: *The Dynasts*. Copyright, 1904 by The Macmillan Company and used with their permission.

Dickens's *Bleak House* (p. 55) gives us an example with the observer implied. In neither of these descriptions does the writer follow a mechanical order. Instead, he arranges the items of the scene to build toward the subjective effect desired. At the end Poe describes the effect of his scene as the horrible dropping off of a veil, and Dickens concludes with the general taste and smell of the Dedlocks in their graves. In each of these passages the mood is established very early and pervades the whole, though with mounting intensity.

In some instances of effective description, however, the mood does not so definitely pervade the whole passage. Rather, it may appear early as a kind of lead and then be dropped or be presented only by implication. Or the description may begin with an accumulation of details which seem to be collected almost at random but are brought to focus in the end by the emergence of a dominant mood.

The following passage is an example of the last type of pattern:

Except for the Marabar Caves—and they are twenty miles off—the city of Chandrapore presents nothing extraordinary. Edged rather than washed by the river Ganges, it trails for a couple of miles along the bank, scarcely distinguishable from the rubbish it deposits so freely. There are no bathing-steps on the river front, as the Ganges happens not to be holy here; indeed there is no river front, and bazaars shut out the wide and shifting panorama of the stream. The streets are mean, the temples ineffective, and though a few fine houses exist they are hidden away in gardens or down alleys whose filth deters all but the invited guest. Chandrapore was never large or beautiful, but two hundred years ago it lay on the road between Upper India, then imperial, and the sea, and the fine houses date from that period. The zest for decoration stopped in the eighteenth century, nor was it ever democratic. There is no painting and scarcely any carving in the bazaars. The very wood seems made of mud, the inhabitants of mud moving. So abased, so monotonous is everything that meets the eye, that when the Ganges comes down it might be expected to wash the excrescence back into the soil. Houses do fall, people are drowned and left rotting, but the general outline of the town persists, swelling here, shrinking there, like some low but indestructible form of life.—E. M. FORSTER: *A Passage to India,* Chap. 1.[10]

[10] From *A Passage to India* by E. M. Forster, copyright, 1924, by Harcourt, Brace and Company, Inc.

## 5. PATTERN BY INTEREST

Just as mood may give the principle of unity, so a special interest may provide it. If a man out to shoot quail and a man out to paint a landscape look at the same field, their different interests mean different kinds of observation. The hunter focuses attention on the clump of brush as possible cover for a covey; the painter looks at it merely as one form in his total composition and as a patch of color in relation to other colors, the tawny of the dry sage and the blackness of the tree trunks beyond.

In the following passage there are many details which would be vivid in any description, but we notice that what holds the whole passage together is the special interest with which the scene is regarded. Here a soldier is inspecting a bridge which he intends to dynamite. The structure of the bridge and the location of the enemy defenses are what finally concern him.

The late afternoon sun that still came over the brown shoulder of the mountain showed the bridge dark against the steep emptiness of the gorge. It was a steel bridge of a single span and there was a sentry box at each end. It was wide enough for two motor cars to pass and it spanned, in solid-flung metal grace, a deep gorge at the bottom of which, far below, a brook leaped in white water through rocks and boulders down to the main stream of the pass.

The sun was in Robert Jordan's eyes and the bridge showed only in outline. Then the sun lessened and was gone and looking up through the trees at the brown, rounded height that it had gone behind, he saw, now, that he no longer looked into the glare, that the mountain slope was a delicate new green and that there were patches of old snow under the crest.

Then he was looking at the bridge again in the sudden short trueness of the little light that would be left, and studying its construction. The problem of its demolition was not difficult. As he watched he took out a notebook from his breast pocket and made several quick line sketches. As he made the drawings he did not figure the charges. He would do that later. Now he was noting the points where the explosive should be placed in order to cut the support of the span and drop a section of it back into the gorge. It could be done unhurriedly, scientifically and correctly with a half dozen charges laid and braced to explode simultaneously; or it could be done roughly with two big ones. They would need to be very big ones, on opposite sides and should go at the same time.—ERNEST HEMINGWAY: *For Whom the Bell Tolls*, Chap. 3.[11]

It does not greatly matter what the nature of the interest is. The dynamiter's interest in the bridge holds this passage together, and makes the bridge serve as a focus for the scene. But in the following passage the comparison which Huckleberry Finn draws between houses in town and the house of the Grangerford plantation provides the unifying interest:

It was a mighty nice family, and a mighty nice house, too. I hadn't seen no house out in the country before that was so nice and had so much style. It didn't have an iron latch on the front door, nor a wooden one with a buckskin string, but a brass knob to turn, the same as houses in a town. There warn't no bed in the parlor, nor a sign of a bed; but heaps of parlors in town has beds in them. There was a big fireplace that was bricked on the bottom, and the bricks was kept clean and red by pouring water on them and scrubbing them with another brick; sometimes they wash them over with red water-paint that they call Spanish-brown, same as they do in town. They had big brass dog-irons that could hold up a saw-log. There was a clock on the middle of the mantelpiece, with a picture of a town painted on the bottom half of the glass front, and a round place in the middle of it for the sun, and you could see the pendulum swinging behind it.—SAMUEL CLEMENS: *The Adventures of Huckleberry Finn*, Chap. 17.

### 6. IMPRESSIONISTIC PATTERN

In the examples of pattern by mood and pattern by interest given above, we find more than a mere listing of things or the qualities of things. Something is said about the things; we find fully formed sentences, one leading to another to give a unified paragraph. But it is possible to list things or qualities with relation to a dominant mood or interest and successfully give an impression of unity by enumeration without formal organization. This method is called impressionistic. Here is an example of it, the description of the main street in a small Middlewestern town.

From a second-story window the sign, "W. P. Kennicott, Phys. & Surgeon," gilt on black sand.

[11] From *For Whom the Bell Tolls* by Ernest Hemingway, copyright, 1940, by Charles Scribner's Sons.

A small wooden motion-picture theater called "The Rosebud Movie Palace." Lithographs announcing a film called, "Fatty in Love."

Howland & Gould's Grocery. In the display window, black, overripe bananas and lettuce on which a cat was sleeping. Shelves lined with red crepe paper which was now faded and torn and concentrically spotted. Flat against the wall of the second story the signs of the lodges—the Knights of Pythias, the Maccabees, the Woodmen, the Masons.

Dahl & Oleson's Meat Market—a reek of blood.—SINCLAIR LEWIS: *Main Street*, Chap. 4.[12]

## 7. PATTERN OF ABSORBED DESCRIPTION

As has already been pointed out, description is frequently used in conjunction, almost in fusion, with other modes. It is difficult sometimes to say of a passage whether it is primarily descriptive or narrative or expository or argumentative in its emphasis. But sometimes we observe passages which, we feel, are primarily descriptive in emphasis but which are organized in terms of, for instance, a narrative element. In such passages the descriptive details, if given in isolation, would be merely an enumeration of items with only a slight degree of unity of impression. But the line of action or explanation or argument holds them together, gives them their focus, so that the reader gets an effect of unity. It is difficult to find an appropriate name for this method, but perhaps the phrase "absorbed description" will serve.

Here is an example of absorbed description:

They called a special meeting of the Board of Aldermen. A deputation waited upon her, knocked at the door through which no visitor had passed since she ceased giving china-painting lessons eight or ten years earlier. They were admitted by the old Negro into a dim hall from which a stairway mounted into still more shadow. It smelled of dust and disuse—a close, dank smell. The Negro led them into the parlor. It was furnished in heavy, leather-covered furniture. When the Negro opened the blinds of one window, they could see that the leather was cracked; and when they sat down, a faint dust rose sluggishly about their thighs, spinning with slow motes in the single sun-ray. On a tarnished gilt easel before the fireplace stood a crayon portrait of Miss Emily's father.

They rose when she entered—a small, fat woman in black, with a thin gold chain descending to her waist and vanishing into her belt, leaning

[12] From *Main Street* by Sinclair Lewis, copyright, 1920, by Harcourt, Brace and Company, Inc.

on an ebony cane with a tarnished gold head. Her skeleton was small and spare; perhaps that was why what would have been merely plumpness in another was obesity in her. She looked bloated, like a body long submerged in motionless water, and of that pallid hue. Her eyes, lost in the fatty ridges of her face, looked like two small pieces of coal pressed into a lump of dough as they moved from one face to another while the visitors stated their errand.

She did not ask them to sit. She just stood in the door and listened quietly until the spokesman came to a stumbling halt. Then they could hear the invisible watch ticking at the end of the gold chain.—WILLIAM FAULKNER: "A Rose for Emily." [13]

In the passage above we can readily isolate the parts which are purely descriptive. For instance, in the second paragraph, except for the first part of the first sentence and the last part of the last sentence, there is nothing but description. But in the following passage the description is much more completely absorbed; it is a matter of words and phrases, and not of sentences and sections of paragraphs, and yet the scene is very fully suggested.

In the square bedroom with the big window Mama and Papa were lolling back on their pillows handing each other things from the wide black tray on the small table with the crossed legs. They were smiling and they smiled even more when the little boy, with the feeling of sleep still in his skin and hair, came in and walked up to the bed. Leaning against it, his bare toes wriggling in the white fur rug, he went on eating peanuts which he took from his pajama pocket. He was four years old.

"Here's my baby," said Mama. "Lift him up, will you?"

He went limp as a rag for Papa to take him under the arms and swing him up over a broad, tough chest. He sank between his parents like a bear cub in a warm litter, and lay there comfortably. He took another peanut between his teeth, cracked the shell, picked out the nut whole and ate it.—KATHERINE ANNE PORTER: "The Downward Path to Wisdom." [14]

### 8. MIXED PATTERNS

We have tried to distinguish several typical methods for unifying description, but in actual practice these methods may often be

[13] From "A Rose for Emily," *These Thirteen* by William Faulkner, copyright, 1931, by Random House, Inc.

[14] From *The Leaning Tower and Other Stories* by Katherine Anne Porter, copyright, 1944, by Katherine Anne Porter. Reprinted by permission of Harcourt, Brace and Company, Inc.

combined. Sometimes the most vivid effects can be obtained by the mixed method. Here is an example:

About four in the morning, as the captain and Herrick sat together on the rail, there arose from the midst of the night, in front of them, the voice of the breakers. Each sprang to his feet and stared and listened. The sound was continuous, like the passing of a train; no rise or fall could be distinguished; minute by minute the ocean heaved with an equal potency against the invisible isle; and as time passed, and Herrick waited in vain for any vicissitude in the volume of that roaring, a sense of the eternal weighed upon his mind. To the expert eye, the isle itself was to be inferred from a certain string of blots along the starry heaven. And the schooner was laid to and anxiously observed till daylight.

There was little or no morning bank. A brightening came in the east; then a wash of some ineffable, faint, nameless hue between crimson and silver; and then coals of fire. These glimmered awhile on the sealine, and seemed to brighten and darken and spread out; and still the night and the stars reigned undisturbed. It was as though a spark should catch and glow and creep along the foot of some heavy and almost incombustible wall-hanging, and the room itself be scarcely menaced. Yet a little after, and the whole east glowed with gold and scarlet, and the hollow of heaven was filled with the daylight.

The isle—the undiscovered, the scarce believed in—now lay before them and close aboard; and Herrick thought that never in his dreams had he beheld anything more strange and delicate. The beach was excellently white, the continuous barrier of trees inimitably green; the land perhaps ten feet high, the trees thirty more. Every here and there, as the schooner coasted northward, the wood was intermitted; and he could see clear over the inconsiderable strip of land (as a man looks over a wall) to the lagoon within; and clear over that, again, to where the far side of the atoll prolonged its pencilling of trees against the morning sky. He tortured himself to find analogies. The isle was like the rim of a great vessel sunken in the waters; it was like the embankment of an annular railway grown upon with wood. So slender it seemed amidst the outrageous breakers, so frail and pretty, he would scarce have wondered to see it sink and disappear without a sound, and the waves close smoothly over its descent.—ROBERT LOUIS STEVENSON: *The Ebb Tide*, Chap. 7.[15]

In the passage by Stevenson we notice that we have a location and an observer specified. At one time in the course of the descrip-

[15] From *The Ebb Tide* by Robert Louis Stevenson, copyright, 1905, by Charles Scribner's Sons.

tion (the view across the atoll) we find the method of simple spatial ordering used. At another time, the principle of sequence comes into play. In fact, it comes into play in two different ways. First, we have the principle of sequence in time (in the coming of dawn) and then we have it in space, with the moving point of view, as the schooner coasts northward along the island. But we also find the frame image used to give us a clearer notion of the island: Herrick, the observer, "tortured himself to find analogies," and to describe the atoll we find the frame image of the "rim of a great vessel sunken in the waters," or of the "embankment of an annular railway grown upon with wood." We may notice, furthermore, that a certain mood, the response to a fragile and dreamlike beauty, dominates the whole description—Herrick's response to the scene, and we may notice that there is an organization in terms of climax, for only at the end of the passage as given here do we get the full statement of the frame image and of the basic mood.

If the passage were read in its full context, we should be able to observe that the method of unity in terms of interest is employed throughout, for the schooner is seeking an entrance to the harbor inside the atoll, and the final concern, in reference to the narrative, is to find anchorage.

The use of a mixed method, certainly of a mixed method which employs as many individual methods as the above passage, offers certain difficulties to the inexperienced writer. By and large, it is better for the inexperienced writer to try the simpler approaches to his material, at least until he is confident that he understands the principles involved in the various methods and has acquired some skill in adapting them.

### APPLICATIONS

In the rest of this chapter and in the section of selections (p. 256 ff.) there are a number of descriptive passages. List the different types of pattern you find illustrated among them.

### TEXTURE: SELECTION IN DESCRIPTION

Pattern, as we have seen, is concerned with the ordering of the details of description. Texture, which we shall now discuss, is concerned with the nature of the details presented.

How are the details actually presented in a description selected from among all the details which might have been presented? Already, in discussing the difference between technical and suggestive description and in explaining what is meant by a dominant impression, we have touched on the problem of SELECTION (pp. 45-56, 223), but we have not explored it.

It is clear that no one can hope to render all of the details of an object to be described, and it is also clear that if one could render all of the details we should have a mere enumeration, tedious and mechanical, without giving the unified impression the object actually makes upon an observer. But what the writer wants to do is to give his reader such a unified impression. To do this he must select the details which will suggest the whole object and set the reader's imagination to work.

But what are the grounds on which selection is to be made? We may break this question down into two other questions:

1. What details are vivid in the object?
2. What details are significant for the impression the writer considers dominant?

Vividness and significance—these are the two considerations which should govern selection of details. It is possible that the same detail may be both vivid and significant, but for the purpose of discussion we can consider these qualities independently.

## VIVIDNESS

A descriptive detail is vivid if it is striking, if it can set the imagination to work so that the reader calls up the object in his mind's eye. In the following description the most obvious quality of the scene, the contrast between brilliant light and black shadow, is emphasized. The writer does not give a detailed description of the town. Instead, he gives what would be the most obvious and striking characteristic, the light effect which would blur out other aspects of the Arab town when the observer first encountered it.

But when at last we anchored in the outer harbor, off the white town hung between the blazing sky and its reflection in the mirage which swept and rolled over the wide lagoon, then the heat of Arabia came out like a drawn sword and struck us speechless. It was midday; and the noon sun in the East, like moonlight, put to sleep the colors. There were only lights and shadows, the white houses and black gaps of streets; in front, the pallid lustre of the haze shimmering upon the inner harbors; behind, the dazzle of league after league of featureless sand, running up to an edge of low hills, faintly suggested in the far away mist of heat.— T. E. LAWRENCE: *Seven Pillars of Wisdom*, Chap. 8.[16]

This seizing on the most striking and obvious characteristic is a very natural method. Time after time we encounter a bit of description introduced by some such statement as, "The most impressive feature of his face was his wide, innocent, childlike blue eyes which seemed to offer trust to all the world," or, "The first thing you noticed as you topped the hill was a pond lying in the cup of the valley, reflecting the brilliance of the sky." The writer indicates what feature in the object would first catch attention.

Vividness, however, may be gained by indicating some detail which might escape ordinary observation. In such a case, it is the precision and subtlety of the description which makes the object come alive for us. John Burroughs, the naturalist, in a passage on the art of observation, gives a list of vivid details which would escape most observers but which present a vivid sense of a series of scenes and moments:

His senses are so delicate that in his evening walk he feels the warm and cool streaks in the air, his nose detects the most fugitive odors, his ears the most furtive sounds. As he stands musing in the April twilight, he hears that fine, elusive stir and rustle made by the angleworms reaching out from their holes for leaves and grasses; he hears the whistling wings of the wood-cock as it goes swiftly by him in the dusk; he hears the call of the killdee come down out of the March sky; he hears far above him in the early morning the squeaking cackle of the arriving blackbirds pushing north; he hears the soft, prolonged, lulling call of the little owl in the cedars in the early spring twilight; he hears at night the roar of the distant waterfall, and the rumble of the train miles across country when the air is "hollow"; before a storm he notes how distant objects stand out and are brought near on those brilliant days that we call "weather-breeders." When the mercury is at zero or lower, he notes how the passing trains hiss and simmer as if the rails or wheels were red-hot.—JOHN BURROUGHS: *Leaf and Tendril*, Chap. 1.[17]

[16] From: *Seven Pillars of Wisdom* by T. E. Lawrence. Copyright 1926, 1935 by Doubleday & Company, Inc.

[17] From *Leaf and Tendril* by John Burroughs, through the courtesy of Houghton Mifflin Company.

The rustling of the angleworms gives a vivid and immediate sense of the stillness; more vivid and immediate than any number of more usual and easily observable details. Or take the squeaking cackle of the blackbirds; it is the absolutely right phrase to describe the sound, and because of the accuracy of the observation, our imagination fills the sky with the flock of birds passing over.

Were it not for the detail of the dyed hand, we would have only a vague sense of the presence of the handsome young sailor in the following description:

Cast in a mould peculiar to the finest physical examples of those Englishmen in whom the Saxon strain would seem not at all to partake of any Norman or other admixture, he showed in face that humane look of reposeful good nature which the Greek sculptor in some instances gave to his heroic strong man, Hercules. But this again was subtly modified by another and pervasive quality. The ear, small and shapely, the arch of the foot, the curve in the mouth and nostril, even the indurated hand dyed to the orange-tawny of the toucan's bill, a hand telling of the halyards and tar-buckets; but above all, something in the mobile expression, and every chance attitude and movement, something suggestive of a mother eminently favored by Love and the Graces; all this strangely indicated a lineage in direct contradiction to his lot.— HERMAN MELVILLE: *Billy Budd,* Chap. 2.

And in the following portrait it is the detail of the pimples that makes the person come alive to the reader's imagination:

Complicated, but light, transparent, and innocently immodest was the dress of his daughter, tall and slender, with magnificent hair gracefully combed; her breath was sweet with violet-scented tablets, and she had a number of tiny and most delicate pink pimples near her lips and between her slightly powdered shoulder blades.—IVAN BUNIN: "The Gentleman from San Francisco." [18]

The process of seizing on either the striking characteristic or the small, sharply perceived detail may lead to exaggeration and caricature. The detail, as it were, becomes the whole object. In the first of the following passages, Dickens takes the obvious oiliness of Mr. Chadband as the key to the description of his appearance and, finally, of his character:

[18] Reprinted from *The Gentleman from San Francisco* by Ivan Bunin, by permission of Alfred A. Knopf, Inc. Copyright 1923 by Alfred A. Knopf, Inc.

Mr. Chadband is a large yellow man, with a fat smile, and a general appearance of having a good deal of train oil in his system. Mrs. Chadband is a stern, severe-looking, silent woman. Mr. Chadband moves softly and cumbrously, not unlike a bear who has been taught to walk upright. He is very much embarrassed about the arms, as if they were inconvenient to him, and he wanted to grovel; is very much in a perspiration about the head; and never speaks without first putting up his great hand, as delivering a token to his hearers that he is going to edify them. —CHARLES DICKENS: *Bleak House*, Chap. 19.

Dickens uses a striking detail and exaggerates it into the whole person, but in the following passage the writer uses the trivial detail of Miss Plimsoll's nose, and the little drop of moisture at its tip, as the main feature of the comic portrait of the poor old maid.

Miss Plimsoll's nose was sharp and pointed like that of Voltaire. It was also extremely sensitive to cold. When the thermometer fell below 60° it turned scarlet; below 50° it seemed a blue tinge with a little white morbid circle at the end; and at 40° it became sniffly and bore a permanent though precarious drop below its pointed tip. I remember with what interest I watched that drop as we drove from the station at Sofia. My parents went in front in the first carriage and Miss Plimsoll and I followed in the brougham. The night was cold and we drove along an endless wind-swept boulevard punctuated by street lamps. With the approach of each successive lamp Miss Plimsoll's pinched little face beside me would first be illuminated frontways, and then as we came opposite the lamp, spring into a sharp little silhouette, at the point of which the drop flashed and trembled like a diamond.—HAROLD NICOLSON: "Miss Plimsoll," *Some People*.[19]

## APPLICATIONS

I. In examples of description already studied in this chapter and in the group of examples at the end (p. 256 ff.), indicate some details which are used because they are striking, and some that are used because they are suggestive and provoke the imagination of the reader.

II. Locate an example, in the selections at the end of the chapter, of the method of caricature or exaggeration.

III. Write a brief description, say 250 to 300 words, of some scene or person of your acquaintance, making an honest attempt to use vivid and suggestive details.

[19] From *Some People* by Harold Nicolson. Reprinted by permission of the author and Constable and Company.

**SIGNIFICANCE**

By significance in the selection of detail we mean the quality which contributes to the dominant impression of a description. And by the dominant impression we mean the mood the writer intends to communicate, the attitude he intends to create in the reader, or idea about the object he wishes to suggest.

We have already touched on this topic in our discussion of the dominant impression (p. 223) and in our remarks on the passage from Poe's "The Fall of the House of Usher" (p. 54), the description of the Dedlock estate from Dickens's *Bleak House* (p. 55), and the passage from Melville's "The Encantadas" (p. 48). In each of these examples, as we have seen, the selection is made to build up a certain mood or to indicate a certain idea. In each example, the writer refrains from introducing any item which might distract from the dominant impression.

In the following description of the Arab town, Jidda, we can see how the writer uses details that contribute to the effect of stealth and sinister, brooding quiet:

The style of architecture was like crazy Elizabethan half-timber work, in the elaborate Cheshire fashion, but gone gimcrack to an incredible degree. House-fronts were fretted, pierced and pargetted till they looked as though cut out of cardboard for a romantic stage-setting. Every storey jutted, every window leaned one way or other; often the very walls sloped. It was like a dead city, so clean underfoot, and so quiet. Its winding, even streets were floored with damp sand solidified by time and as silent as the tread of any carpet. The lattices and wall-returns deadened all reverberation of voice. There were no carts, nor any street wide enough for carts, no shod animals, no bustle anywhere. Everything was hushed, strained, even furtive. The doors of houses shut softly as we passed. There were no loud dogs, no crying children; indeed, except in the bazaar, still half asleep, there were few wayfarers of any kind; and the people we did meet, all thin, and as it were wasted by disease, with scarred, hairless faces and screwed up eyes, slipped past us quickly and cautiously, not looking at us. Their skimp, white robes, shaven polls with little skull-caps, red cotton shoulder shawls, and bare feet were so same as to be almost a uniform.—T. E. LAWRENCE: *Seven Pillars of Wisdom*, Chap. 9.[20]

[20] From: *Seven Pillars of Wisdom* by T. W. Lawrence. Copyright 1926, 1935 by Doubleday & Company, Inc.

The same method can be used in description to give an impression of the character of a person. The following portrait of Eustacia Vye, the heroine of Thomas Hardy's novel *The Return of the Native*, deals ostensibly with appearance of the young woman, but all the details of her appearance are really chosen, as Hardy himself indicates rather explicitly now and then, to give us an impression of her inner nature.

She was in person full-limbed and somewhat heavy; without ruddiness, as without pallor; and soft to the touch as a cloud. To see her hair was to fancy that a whole winter did not contain darkness enough to form its shadow: it closed over her forehead like nightfall extinguishing the western glow.

Her nerves extended into those tresses, and her temper could always be softened by stroking them down. When her hair was brushed she would instantly sink into stillness and look like the Sphinx. If, in passing under one of the Egdon banks, any of its thick skeins were caught, as they sometimes were, by a prickly tuft of the large *Ulex Europaeus*—which will act as a sort of hairbrush—she would go back a few steps, and pass against it a second time.

She had Pagan eyes, full of nocturnal mysteries, and their light, as it came and went, and came again, was partially hampered by their oppressive lids and lashes; and of these the under lid was much fuller than it usually is with English women. This enabled her to indulge in reverie without seeming to do so: she might have been believed capable of sleeping without closing them up. Assuming that the souls of men and women were visible essences, you could fancy the color of Eustacia's soul to be flame-like. The sparks from it that rose into her dark pupils gave the same impression. . . .

Her presence brought memories of such things as Bourbon roses, rubies, and tropical midnights; her moods recalled lotus-eaters and the march in "Athalie"; her motions, the ebb and flow of the sea; her voice, the viola. In a dim light, and with a slight rearrangement of her hair, her general figure might have stood for that of either of the higher female deities. The new moon behind her head, an old helmet upon it, a diadem of accidental dew-drops round her brow, would have been adjuncts sufficient to strike the note of Artemis, Athene, or Hera respectively, with as close an approximation to the antique as that which passes muster on many respected canvases.—THOMAS HARDY: *Return of the Native*, Chap. 7.

In the following description of a Mexican revolutionist who is both sentimental and cruel, energetic and self-indulgent, lazy and sinister, the explicit definition of the character does not appear, but is suggested by the details selected:

Braggioni catches her glance solidly as if he had been waiting for it, leans forward, balancing his paunch between his spread knees, and sings with tremendous emphasis, weighing his words. He had, the song relates, no father and no mother, nor even a friend to console him; lonely as a wave of the sea he comes and goes, lonely as a wave. His mouth opens round and yearns sideways, his balloon cheeks grow oily with the labor of song. He bulges marvellously in his expensive garments. Over his lavender collar, crushed upon a purple necktie, held by a diamond hoop; over his ammunition belt of tooled leather worked in silver, buckled cruelly around his gaping middle: over the tops of his glossy yellow shoes Braggioni swells with ominous ripeness, his mauve silk hose stretched taut, his ankles bound with the stout leather thongs of his shoes.

When he stretches his eyelids at Laura she notes again that his eyes are the true tawny yellow cat's eyes.—KATHERINE ANNE PORTER: "Flowering Judas." [21]

As the details of description may be used to suggest the character of a person described, so they may be used to indicate the attitude the writer wishes the reader to take toward a scene or event. The following passage gives a battle scene, but the writer uses certain descriptive touches to play down ironically the violence or the event. We know that horror and excitement and suffering are involved here, and the writer knows it too. But he takes a certain actual and emotional distance from the scene—the flags "laugh," the cannon merely "denounce," the "jaunty" brigade marches "airily," there is a calm white house beyond. The impression of distance, of unreality, and of triviality actually works to suggest to us, by contract, the real violence.

In another direction he saw a magnificent brigade going with the evident intention of driving the enemy from a wood. They passed in out of sight, and presently there was a most awe-inspiring racket in the wood. The noise was unspeakable. Having stirred this prodigious uproar and, apparently, finding it too prodigious, the brigade, after a little time, came marching airily out again with its fine formation in

[21] From *Flowering Judas and Other Stories* by Katherine Anne Porter, copyright, 1935, by Katherine Anne Porter. Reprinted by permission of Harcourt, Brace and Company, Inc.

nowise disturbed. There were no traces of speed in its movements. The brigade was jaunty and seemed to point a proud thumb at the yelling wood.

On a slope to the left there was a long row of guns, gruff and maddened, denouncing the enemy, who, down through the woods, were forming for another attack in the pitiless monotony of conflicts. The round red discharges from the guns made a crimson flare and a high, thick smoke. Occasionally glimpses could be caught of groups of the toiling artillerymen. In the rear of this row of guns stood a house, calm and white, amid bursting shells. A congregation of horses, tied to a long railing, were tugging frenziedly at their bridles. Men were running hither and thither.

The detached battle between the four regiments lasted for some time. There chanced to be no interference, and they settled their dispute by themselves. They struck savagely and powerfully at each other for a period of minutes, and then the lighter-hued regiments faltered and drew back, leaving the dark-blue lines shouting. The youth could see the two flags shaking with laughter amid the smoke remnants.—STEPHEN CRANE: *The Red Badge of Courage,* Chap. 22.[22]

## ATMOSPHERE

In each of the above passages the author has, as we say, created a certain atmosphere. By atmosphere we mean the mood, the general feeling associated in the description with the scene, person, or event described. We have commented, for instance, on the atmosphere of gloom and dampness and decay in the descriptions by Poe and Dickens, or that of furtiveness and stealth and exhaustion in the description of Jidda by T. E. Lawrence, or that of ironical jauntiness and impersonal distance in the description by Stephen Crane.

We know, however, even as we use these words to define the atmosphere of this or that piece of description, that the labels we put on the passages are too vague and loose to define really the effect given. Our defining words do not really define the atmosphere; they merely give a kind of crude indication, a not very dependable clue, to the effect we find in the actual description.

Our inability to define the atmosphere in general terms indicates the importance of the way the author himself goes about present-

[22] From *The Red Badge of Courage,* by Stephen Crane, copyright, 1925, by D. Appleton and Company. Reprinted by permission of Appleton-Century-Crofts, Inc.

ing it to us. The atmosphere is the general feeling he wants his work to convey, the prevailing attitude of mind which he wishes us to adopt toward his subject, but he knows that he cannot create it simply by using the loose, general words which we have used above in trying to define the effect of the passages. Therefore, he undertakes to give us such concrete details, such aspects of his object, as will stir our imaginations not only to grasp the appearance of the object (or the sound, the color, and so forth, if he is appealing to other senses than that of sight), but to adopt a certain feeling and attitude toward the object and toward the general context of the object in his work.[23]

We have said earlier that suggestive description aims not to tell us about its object but to give us the object; but it also can be said that it aims not to tell us what feelings to have about the object and what attitudes to take toward it, but to create those feelings and attitudes within us. Vividness and immediacy, not only in regard to the physical qualities of the object, but in regard to the feelings and attitudes involved, are what the writer desires.

## APPLICATIONS

I. Locate, in the examples at the end of the chapter, two instances in which description leads the reader to an understanding of the character of the person described. Try to define in general terms the character of the person presented. What evidence among the details of the portrait can you find for your interpretation?

II. Write a description of a person, real or imaginary, with the intention of indicating the person's character. If you have difficulty in

[23] Perhaps this should be explained a little more fully. By the context of the object we mean what is around it in the piece of writing. For instance, in a story the context of a piece of description would be the events narrated, the analyses of character, and so forth, before and after the piece of description. A good author, no matter what he is writing, a story, an essay, a letter, intends some connection between the effect of a piece of description and the rest of his composition. The atmosphere of the description implies, as it were, the attitudes the author wishes the reader to take toward the whole piece of work. If we read the description of Egdon Heath at the beginning of Thomas Hardy's *Return of the Native,* the somber, brooding atmosphere of the scene implies the attitude the author wished the reader to take toward the violent, tragic human story, just as the atmosphere of the description of Eustacia Vye, the heroine of the novel, which is quoted above, implies the qualities of character and action we are to find in her.

doing this, it may be useful to try the following method: Choose some person whom you know very well and of whose character you think you have a very clear conception. Make a list of the person's characteristics. From that list select those which seem most important. Then make a list of the details of the person's appearance and of his little habits or mannerisms. Decide which of these items seem to indicate something about the person's character. By correlating your two lists you may find the material for your portrait. But do not feel bound by the facts of the case. If you start with a real person and find that you can make a more vivid and convincing portrait by adding details from your imagination, go ahead and do just that.

## DESCRIPTION OF FEELINGS AND STATES OF MIND

In our previous discussion we have seen how a description may evoke in the reader a certain mood or attitude which the writer wishes to communicate. There is some relation, then, between the physical details of the object described and human feelings. This leads us to another kind of description, not of objects or persons, but of feelings or states of mind. How can such an intangible, without physical existence and with no possible appeal to our senses, be described?

Strictly speaking, the literal feeling or state of mind cannot be described because it cannot be perceived through the senses. But we have seen how a character, which is also intangible, can be indicated through description. For instance, Hardy's description of Eustacia Vye's physical appearance indicates her inner nature. By a kind of parallel process we can indicate a state of mind, that of the writer himself or of some person about whom he is writing.

Our common speech recognizes the principle behind this process. For instance, if a man has an evil nature, we may say that he has a "black heart," or if a man is cheerful and optimistic we may say that he has a "sunny disposition." The abstract, general words *evil* and *cheerful* are replaced by the concrete words *black* and *sunny*, which properly belong to the physical world. Hardy is simply applying this principle in a more elaborate form when he writes of Eustacia:

Her presence brought memories of such things as Bourbon roses, rubies, and tropical midnights; her moods recalled the lotus-eaters and the march in "Athalie"; her motions, the ebb and flow of the sea; her voice, the viola.

This is a way of saying that Eustacia has a brooding, passionate, willful nature; but Hardy's words say much more than we can convey by our generalizing words. If we begin to try to elaborate in our own way, we find ourselves using such words as *sumptuous, rich, deep, stormy,*—the adjectives implied in Hardy's description; and then we realize that these words, too, are carrying us toward physical description, for words like *stormy* and *deep* have come to apply to such a thing as a personality by a kind of transference from their basic meanings (see Chapter 11).

Here is an example of the description, not of a personality, but of a state of feeling, the feeling at the moment of passing from sleep to waking:

"I was not asleep," I answered as I awoke.

I said this in good faith. The great modification which the act of awakening effects in us is not so much that of introducing us to the clear life of consciousness, as that of making us lose all memory of that other, rather more diffused light in which our mind has been resting, as in the opaline depths of the sea. The tide of thought, half veiled from our perception, over which we were drifting still a moment ago, kept us in a state of motion perfectly sufficient to enable us to refer to it by the name of wakefulness. But then our actual awakenings produce an interruption of memory. A little later we describe these states as sleep because we no longer remember them. And when shines that bright star which at the moment of waking illuminates behind the sleeper the whole expense of his sleep, it makes him imagine for a few moments that this was not a sleeping but a waking state; a shooting star, it must be added, which blots out with the fading of its light not only the false existence but the very appearance of our dream, and merely enables him who has awoken to say to himself: "I was asleep."—MARCEL PROUST: *The Guermantes Way*, Part II, Chap. 1.[24]

The same use of physical description to indicate a mental state appears in the following passage:

Sterne's discovery was made. It was repugnant to his imagination, shocking to his ideas of honesty, shocking to his conception of mankind. This enormity affected one's outlook on what was possible in this world:

[24] From *The Guermantes Way* by Marcel Proust, tr. by C. K. Scott Moncrieff. Reprinted by permission of Random House, Inc.

it was as if for instance the sun had turned blue, throwing a new and sinister light on men and nature. Really in the first moment he had felt sickish, as though he had got a blow below the belt: for a second the very color of the sea seemed changed—appeared queer to his wandering eye; and he had a passing, unsteady sensation in all his limbs as though the earth had started turning the other way.—JOSEPH CONRAD: "The End of the Tether." [25]

We notice in the above quotation how the author begins by making a general statement: the discovery is repugnant, is shocking, changes Sterne's outlook. But we notice how quickly these generalities shade over into concrete presentations which are intended to evoke in us a direct sense of Sterne's sensation: the blue sun, a blow below the belt, the sudden reversal of the earth's motion.

In the following passage we find a slightly different application of the same principle. Above we have been dealing with the description of a momentary feeling; here we shall be dealing with the description of a protracted situation, a state of being. A wife has discovered that her husband's conception of life, his "mansion," is oppressive and deadening for her:

But when, as the months had elapsed, she had followed him further and he had led her into the mansion of his own habitation, then, *then* she had seen where she really was.

She could live it over again, the incredulous terror with which she had taken the measure of her dwelling. Between those four walls she had lived ever since; they were to surround her for the rest of her life. It was the house of darkness, the house of dumbness, the house of suffocation. Osmond's beautiful mind gave it neither light nor air; Osmond's beautiful mind indeed seemed to peep down from a small high window and mock at her. Of course it had not been physical suffering; for physical suffering there might have been a remedy. She could come and go; she had her liberty; her husband was perfectly polite. He took himself so seriously; it was perfectly appalling. Under all his culture, his cleverness, his amenity, under his good-nature, his facility, his knowledge of life, his egotism lay hidden like a serpent in a bank of flowers.—HENRY JAMES: *The Portrait of a Lady*, Chap. 42.

The descriptions of states of feeling just considered are direct in treatment. That is, we are introduced as fully as may be into the

[25] From *Youth: A Narrative* by Joseph Conrad. Reprinted by permission of J. M. Dent and Sons, Ltd., through the courtesy of the Conrad estate.

consciousness of the person who has the feeling or experiences the state of mind, the seaman Sterne or the disappointed wife. But there is an indirect way of using description to portray feeling or state of mind, a way which presents the symptoms but does not endeavor to describe the feeling or the state of mind itself. This way is analogous, of course, to the use of description of a person's physical appearance to indicate his character, without giving any general statements about the character.

If we describe a person as having shifty eyes and a flabby mouth, the reader is very apt to draw certain conclusions about that person's character. And by the same token, if we describe a person at the moments when his lips whiten, the blood flushes his cheeks, his eyes flash, and his respiration is rapid, the reader is apt to conclude that the person is laboring under great rage or other excitement. Such descriptions of the symptoms, as it were, of a state of feeling can, when well done, be very effective in giving the reader a sense of the reality of the situation being presented. We shall draw another example from the work of Marcel Proust, who is a master in the art of presenting states of feeling by either direct or indirect methods.

I made the invalid sit at the foot of the staircase in the hall, and went up to warn my mother. I told her that my grandmother had come home feeling slightly unwell, after an attack of giddiness. As soon as I began to speak, my mother's face was convulsed by the paroxysm of a despair which was yet already so resigned that I realized that for many years she had been holding herself quietly in readiness for an uncalendared but final day. She asked me no question; it seemed that, just as malevolence likes to exaggerate the sufferings of other people, so in her devotion she would not admit that her mother was seriously ill, especially with a disease which might affect the brain. Mamma shuddered, her eyes wept without tears, she ran to give orders for the doctor to be fetched at once; but when Françoise asked who was ill she could not reply, her voice stuck in her throat. She came running downstairs with me, struggling to banish from her face the sob that contracted it.—MARCEL PROUST: *The Guermantes Way*, Part II, Chap. 1.[26]

[26] From *The Guermantes Way* by Marcel Proust, tr. by C. K. Scott Moncrieff Reprinted by permission of Random House, Inc.

## APPLICATIONS

I. Make a list of physical symptoms which you might use to indicate the following states: (1) fear, (2) rage, (3) disgust, (4) drowsiness, and (5) despair.

II. Describe briefly, say in 250 words, a person experiencing one of these states.

## FIGURATIVE LANGUAGE IN THE DESCRIPTION OF FEELINGS AND STATES OF MIND

It should be obvious from the examples given above that when a writer comes to describe a feeling or a state of mind he is often forced to use figurative language. For instance, when Henry James (p. 246) wishes to describe the feeling of the wife who discovers that her husband is unsympathetic and egotistical, he resorts to figurative language: the wife feels she has been imprisoned in the "house of dumbness," the "house of suffocation," and most of the passage is an elaboration of this comparison of her condition to an imprisonment. The whole question of figurative language will be discussed at some length elsewhere in this book (p. 403), but the question is of so much importance for description that we must at least touch upon it here.

We may say, for the sake of convenience, that such comparisons have two functions in description, in enriching the texture. First, they may make for vividness and immediacy. Second, they may serve to interpret the object described or an attitude toward it.

If we write of a girl's hair that it is very black and glossy, we do little to stir the imagination of the reader to a full sense of the quality of the hair. But if we write that her hair is like a raven's wing, then we have done something to set the imagination of the reader to work. The comparison just used is, unfortunately, a rather trite one; it has been used so often that its power to stir the imagination is almost gone. But when Hardy writes of Eustacia Vye's hair that "a whole winter did not contain darkness enough to form its shadow," or that it "closed over her forehead like nightfall," the imagination is stirred, and the image of Eustacia is evoked. But more than mere vividness has been gained by Hardy's comparisons. These particular comparisons also contribute to our impression of Eustacia's character—the brooding, the mystery, the sense of violence—the "nocturnal" quality, to use the word which Hardy himself uses of her later on. That is, the comparisons not only increase the vividness, but interpret the object of the comparison.

But we do often find that the function of a comparison is merely to increase vividness, to help the reader to grasp the object, or that the interpretative value of the comparison is very slight. For instance, when Ruskin describes the street leading up to the cathedral (p. 225), he writes that the house had "small porches to their doors in the shape of cockleshells." The chief function here, no doubt, is to make the impression more vivid, though we are aware of some interpretative force in *cockleshell*—an implication of quaintness, of cuteness, of childlike diminutiveness. Or when Faulkner describes Miss Emily (p. 232): "Her eyes, lost in the fatty ridges of her face, looked like two small pieces of coal pressed into a lump of dough," the chief effect is to startle us, by this caricature of a face, to visualize Miss Emily. But if we are acquainted with the story in which the sentence appears we realize that some interpretation may also be involved—the pallor, the pasty quality of the flesh, the unhuman quality of the comparison, are appropriate for this house of decay and death.

When we come, however, to Stevenson's comparison of the atoll to a basin almost submerged in water (p. 233), we have almost as pure an example as it would be possible to find of a comparison which works to aid in vividness without any interpretative force.

On the other hand, we can find many passages in which the interpretative value of the comparisons is more important than the value of vividness. For instance, when Poe refers to the "eye-like windows" of the House of Usher (p. 55) there is undoubtedly some value of vividness—that is, the comparison does help the imagination to create the house; but at the same time the chief importance of the comparison is to create an atmosphere, to interpret the scene. Or when Melville compares the vast volcanic islands to "split Syrian gourds" (p. 49), the function is primarily interpretative. By that time in the passage we already have a very strong visual impression of the islands, and in any case, split, withering gourds do not strongly suggest the picture of islands. But the gourds do strongly suggest the idea of waste and desolation—the interpretative aspect. In the last sentence of the passage from E. M. Forster (p. 228) we have an excellent case of the interpretative emphasis in a comparison: the Indian city is like "some low but indestructible form of life."

It must always be remembered, however, that the comparison which is primarily interpretative in intent must involve some basic connection between the things compared. The split gourds do bear some resemblance to the desolate islands: the cracked, parched islands, and the cracked, parched gourds.

A good comparison cannot be purely arbitrary. When T. E. Lawrence writes of the arrival at an Arabian port, "the heat of Arabia came out like a drawn sword and struck us speechless" (p. 235), we have nothing which corresponds as far as shape is concerned with the sword, but we do have the metallic glitter of sea and sand, the suddenness and violence of the heat after days at sea; and then, at the level of interpretation, we have the notion of ferocity and deadliness—the pitiless heat and the drawn blade. Or when Proust uses the comparison of various depths of the sea and of various kinds of light to describe the process of waking, there is no object which corresponds to those things; but the vague shadings and confusions of dawning consciousness provide the basis for the comparison.

It does not matter on what basis the comparison is established—by what senses or feelings—but there must be some primary connection if interpretation is to be established. A comparison, even if it does carry an appropriate interpretation, must not be so farfetched that the reader cannot accept it. At the same time the comparison which is too trite or too obvious does not stir the imagination. There is no rule for establishing these limits. The writer must simply depend on observation of the practice of others and on his own experience.

## APPLICATIONS

**I.** From the examples of description already studied and from the group at the end of the chapter select twenty comparisons which are effective. Try to state in your own words what each comparison implies. Try to determine what the basis of the comparison is, that is, what is common between the two things involved in the comparison.

**II.** Write a brief description of some feeling you have experienced, a sudden grief, shock at betrayal by a friend, the distress of a sleepless night, joy at unexpected good fortune.

# CHOICE OF WORDS IN THE TEXTURE
## OF DESCRIPTION

As the selection of details and the use of figurative language helps to determine the texture of a description, so does the choice of words. The problem of diction, the choice of words, is naturally important for all writing and is discussed elsewhere in this book, but it must be touched on here in connection with description.

Inexperienced writers tend to make adjectives bear the burden in description. They do this because the adjective is the part of speech which refers to the qualities of things, and description is the kind of discourse which is chiefly concerned with the appearance of things. An inexperienced writer, therefore, tends to overload his description with adjectives, with the idea of specifying all the qualities of the thing being presented. Such a writer forgets that suggestion is often better than enumeration, and that the mere listing of qualities is not the best way to evoke an image in the reader's mind.

Let us look at the following portrait:

The woman's face was fat and shapeless, so fat that it looked soft, unresilient, grayish, and unhealthy. The features were blurred because her face was fat. But her small, black glistening eyes had a quick inquisitive motion as they moved from one face to another while the visitors stated their errand.

In that description the writer has piled up the adjectives, trying to specify each of the qualities of the woman's face and eyes. The result is a rather confused impression. Let us now take the passage as William Faulkner originally wrote it (p. 232) before we tampered with it:

Her eyes, lost in the fatty ridges of her face, looked like two small pieces of coal pressed into a lump of dough as they moved from one face to another while the visitors stated their errand.

Here the writer has managed to dispense with most of the adjectives, for the dough implies *soft, unresilient, grayish, shapeless, blurred,* and (when associated with flesh) *unhealthy,* and the coal implies *black* and *glistening.* The use of a comparison of this kind will frequently enable the writer to dispense with adjectives. But if the writer must use adjectives he should be sure that each adjective really adds something essential to the description. Rather than give the list of adjectives above, one could simply say that the face was "fat and doughy."

The discussion above really returns us to the question of selection. But it does not touch on the use of parts of speech other than adjectives. One can frequently get greater vividness by using nouns, adverbs, and verbs. For instance, notice the descriptive force of the italicized nouns in the following examples:

The very smoke coming out of their chimneys was poverty-stricken. Little *rags* and *shreds* of smoke, so unlike the great silvery *plumes* that uncurled from the Sheridans' chimneys.—KATHERINE MANSFIELD: "The Garden Party."

They crept up the hill in the twilight and entered the cottage. It was built of *mud-walls*, the surface of which had been washed by many rains into *channels* and *depressions* that left none of the original flat *face* visible; while here and there in the thatch above a rafter showed like a *bone* protruding through the *skin*.—THOMAS HARDY: "The Withered Arm."

And a wind blew there, tossing the withered tops of last year's grasses, and *mists* ran with the wind, and ragged *shadows* with the *mists*, and *mare's-tails* of clear *moonlight* among the *shadows*, so that now the boles of birches on the forest's edge beyond the fences were but opal *blurs* and now cut *alabaster*.—WILBUR DANIEL STEELE: "How Beautiful with Shoes."

We can see that in these passages, the nouns are of two kinds. First, there are those which simply point to some items in the thing described, such as *channels, depressions, mists, shadows, moonlight*. Second, there are those which involve comparisons, such as *rags, shreds, alabaster, bone*, and *skin*.

When we turn to the use of adverbs, we find that this part of speech sometimes enables a writer to get an effect with great economy by fusing the quality of a thing with its action. When Dickens writes in describing Chadband that he "moves softly and cumbrously, not unlike a bear who has been taught to walk upright" (p. 238), the adverbs *softly* and *cumbrously* give a much more vivid and immediate effect than would be possible if we broke the description up in the following fashion: Mr. Chadband is soft, heavy, and awkward-looking. When he walks his motion is not unlike that of a bear which has been taught to walk upright.

Let us take two sentences from Stephen Crane's description of a battle (pp. 241-42) and see how the italicized adverbs used focus the main effect in each sentence:

Having stirred this prodigious uproar and, apparently, finding it too prodigious, the brigade, after a little time, came marching *airily* out again with its fine formation in nowise disturbed. . . . A congregation of horses, tied to a long railing, were tugging *frenziedly* at their bridles.

In both of these sentences the adverb is the key word. In the first, *airily,* with its implications of lightness, casualness, slight disdainfulness, and girlishness, is the key to the irony of the passage. In the second, *frenziedly* focuses the attention on the quality of the action—the important thing about the scene by the railing.

Or look at the effect of the italicized adverbs in the following passage from Katherine Anne Porter's description of Braggioni (p. 241):

His mouth opens round and yearns *sideways,* his balloon cheeks grow oily with the labor of song. He bulges *marvellously* in his expensive garments.

In the use of verbs, the same concentration of effect is possible, for frequently the right verb can imply something about the nature of the thing or person performing an action as well as about the nature of the action. In the sentence by Katherine Anne Porter just quoted, the verbs *yearns* and *bulges* are extremely important. *Yearns* implies the sentimental expression on the fat revolutionist's face, and *bulges* implies the brute heft of the man, in contrast to the sentimental song he sings. So the two verbs here really indicate the contrast in his nature, as well as in his appearance.

In the following passage, which describes a herd of wild horses corraled in a barn-lot, notice how the variety and accuracy of the italicized forms [27] give the impression of furious, aimless motion, and define the atmosphere of violence of the scene:

"Come on, grab a holt," the Texan said. Eck grasped the wire also. The horses *laid* back against it, the pink faces *tossing* above the *back-surging* mass. "Pull him up, pull him up," the Texan said sharply. "They couldn't get up here in the wagon even if they wanted to." The wagon moved gradually backward until the head of the first horse was *snubbed*

[27] Some of the verbs, we notice, appear in the form of participles.

up to the tail-gate. The Texan took a turn of wire quickly about one of the wagon stakes. "Keep the slack out of it," he said. He *vanished* and *reappeared,* almost in the same second, with a pair of heavy wire-cutters. "Hold them like that," he said, and *leaped.* He *vanished,* broad hat, *flapping* vest, wire-cutters and all, into a kaleidoscopic maelstrom of long teeth and wild eyes and *slashing* feet, from which presently the horses began to *burst,* one by one like partridges *flushing,* each wearing a neck-lace of barbed wire. The first one crossed the lot at top speed, on a straight line. It *galloped* into the fence without any diminution whatever. The wire *gave, recovered,* and *slammed* the horse to earth where it lay for a moment, *glaring,* its legs still *galloping* in air. It scrambled up without having ceased to gallop and crossed the lot and *galloped* into the opposite fence and was *slammed* again to earth. The others were now freed. They *whipped* and *whirled* about the lot like dizzy fish in a bowl. It had seemed like a big lot until now, but now the very idea that all that fury and motion should be transpiring inside any one fence was something to be repudiated with contempt, like a mirror trick.—WILLIAM FAULKNER: *The Hamlet,* Book IV, Chap. 1.[28]

Verbs like *tossing, vanished, reappeared, leaped, slashing, slammed, whipped, whirled,* give a constant sense of seething, vio-lent motion, and as the passage continues in the part not quoted here we find such additional verbs as *feinting, dodging, weaving, ripped, shook,* and *streaked.*

A good writer can make adjectives, nouns, adverbs, and verbs all serve his purpose. He can blend them to give his effect.

## APPLICATIONS

In the examples at the end of this chapter, locate some adjectives, nouns, adverbs, and verbs which you think are used with strong de-scriptive effect. In each instance, try to explain what makes the word effective.

## SUMMARY

Description is the kind of discourse that tells what something is like, what qualities it has, what impression it makes. It deals pri-marily with the appearance of the world.

[28] From *The Hamlet* by William Faulkner. Reprinted by permission of Random House, Inc.

We can distinguish two kinds of description, TECHNICAL and SUGGESTIVE.

Technical description may really be considered as one type of exposition, the kind of discourse concerned with explanation, with analysis and classification. But suggestive description also is related to the other forms of discourse. It frequently appears in connection with narrative of all types, and sometimes with exposition and argument.

Description, and especially suggestive description, has to do with the appearance of the world, and hence with the way the world presents itself to our senses. Any one of the senses, and the perceptions of heat and cold, of pressure and strain, may be involved in description, or any combination of them. Hence, a capacity for close observation is important for good description.

In suggestive description the writer should be concerned to give a DOMINANT IMPRESSION, the unified effect to which the details contribute, the basic mood or idea of the description.

Even if a writer knows what dominant impression he wishes to give, he must still solve certain problems of method. These may be considered under two heads, PATTERN and TEXTURE. Pattern has to do with general organization, and texture with the nature of the details and their relation to each other.

In description with an objective emphasis any one of three types of POINT OF VIEW may dictate the organization:

1. Order in the object as observed from a fixed position
2. Order in the object as observed from a shifting position
3. Order in an imaginary FRAME IMAGE

In description with a subjective emphasis either of two methods may be used to organize the details:

4. In reference to the mood or attitude
5. In reference to an interest

In addition to these types of pattern, three others may be distinguished:

6. By a listing of details with relation to a dominant mood or interest but without formal organization—IMPRESSIONISTIC PATTERN
7. In reference to a frame of narrative, argument, or exposition in which the descriptive material is absorbed—ABSORBED DESCRIPTION
8. By mixed patterns

As pattern is concerned with the organization of details, so texture is concerned with the nature of the details presented. This problem is, first, a problem of SELECTION. Selection may be considered in two aspects, VIVIDNESS and SIGNIFICANCE, but it must be remembered that the same detail may be both vivid and significant.

A detail may be vivid because it is obvious and striking, or because, though not obvious, it stimulates the reader's imagination to re-create the object described. A detail may be significant if it contributes to the dominant impression, that is, the mood, the attitude, or the idea the writer wishes to communicate.

The dominant impression may be not only of some physical object, say a scene or a person, but of the character of a person. The physical details may indicate the inner nature of the person described. By the same process, that of indicating the intangible by the tangible, feelings and states of mind may be described. This may involve the use of the physical symptoms of the feeling or state of mind and the use of figurative language. But figurative language is often important in description to indicate or to heighten the dominant impression.

The choice of words is also important in determining the texture of description. Inexperienced writers tend to rely on adjectives, but other parts of speech, nouns, adverbs, and verbs, can be used with effect. A good writer tries to use the full resources of his language and to combine its elements into a unified whole.


## EXAMPLES

On the following pages are a number of examples of description. These have already been discussed in this chapter with regard to the study of special topics, and the instructor may frame new problems for investigation. For review, however, the following suggestions may be helpful.

1. Locate instances of appeals to different senses. What words, phrases, and comparisons make such appeals?

2. Find instances of several types of pattern.

3. Are there any instances of caricature?

4. In instances where description is used to suggest a character, an atmosphere, or a state of feeling, try to state in your own words what the character, atmosphere, or state of feeling is. What details contribute to your impression?

5. Locate a number of comparisons. Which are used for vividness?

Which are used for interpretation? Are there any that seem too strained to be effective? Are there any that seem stale?

**A.** A knot of country boys, gabbling at one another like starlings, shrilled a cheer as we came rattling over a stone bridge beneath which a stream shallowly washed its bank of osiers.—WALTER DE LA MARE: *Memoirs of a Midget,* Chap. 2.

**B.** Charmian is a hatchet faced, terra cotta colored little goblin, swift in her movements, and neatly finished at the hands and feet.—GEORGE BERNARD SHAW: *Caesar and Cleopatra,* Act IV.

**C.** Without being robust, her health was perfect, her needlework exquisite, her temper equable and calm; she loved and was loved by her girl-friends; she read romantic verses and select novels; above all, she danced. That was the greatest pleasure in life for her; not for the sake of her partners—those were surely only round dances, and the partners didn't count; what counted was the joy of motion, the sense of treading lightly, in perfect time, a sylph in spotless muslin, enriched with a ribbon or a flower, playing discreetly with her fan, and sailing through the air with feet that seemed scarcely to touch the ground.— GEORGE SANTAYANA: *Persons and Places,* Chap. 1.[29]

**D.** Leaning over the parapet he enjoyed, once more, the strangely intimate companionship of the sea. He glanced down into the water whose uneven floor was diapered with long weedy patches, fragments of fallen rock, and brighter patches of sand; he inhaled the pungent odor of sea-wrack and listened to the breathings of the waves. They lapped softly against the rounded boulders which strewed the shore like a flock of nodding Behemoths. He remembered his visits at daybreak to the beach—those unspoken confidences with the sunlit element to whose friendly caresses he had abandoned his body. How calm it was, too, in this evening light. Near at hand, somewhere, lay a sounding cave; it sang a melody of moist content. Shadows lengthened; fishing boats, moving outward for the night-work, steered darkly across the luminous river at his feet. Those jewel-like morning tints of blue and green had faded from the water; the southern cliff-scenery, projections of it, caught a fiery glare. Bastions of flame. . . .

The air seemed to have become unusually cool and bracing.—NORMAN DOUGLAS: *South Wind,* Chap. 49.[30]

[29] From *Persons and Places* by George Santayana, copyright, 1944, 1945, by Charles Scribner's Sons.

[30] From *South Wind* by Norman Douglas. Reprinted by permission of Dodd, Mead & Company, Inc.

**E.** So the day has taken place, all the visionary business of the day. The young cattle stand in the straw of the stack yard, the sun gleams on their white fleece, the eyes of Io, and the man with the side-whiskers carries more yellow straw into the compound. The sun comes in all down one side, and above, in the sky, all the gables and grey stone chimney-stacks are floating in pure dreams.

There is threshed wheat smouldering in the great barn, the fire of life: and the sound of the threshing machine, running, drumming.

The threshing machine, running, drumming, waving its steam in a corner of a great field, the rapid nucleus of darkness beside the yellow ricks: and the rich plough-land comes up, ripples up in endless grape-colored ripples, like a tide of procreant desire: the machine sighs and drums, wind blows the chaff in little eddies, blows the clothes of the men on the ricks close against their limbs: the men on the stacks in the wind against a bare blue heaven, their limbs blown clean in contour naked shapely animated fragments of earth active in heaven.

Coming home, by the purple and crimson hedges, red with berries, up hill over the heavy ground to the stone, old three-pointed house with its raised chimney-stacks, the old manor lifting its fair, pure stone amid trees and foliage, rising from the lawn, we pass the pond where white ducks hastily launch upon the lustrous dark grey waters.

So up the steps to the porch, through the doorway, and into the interior, fragrant with all the memories of old age, and of bygone, remembered lustiness.—D. H. LAWRENCE: *Letters.*[31]

**F.** When I say they [the gondoliers of Venice] are associated with its [the city's] silence, I should immediately add that they are associated also with its sound. Among themselves they are extraordinarily talkative company. They chatter at the *traghetti* [landings], where they always have some sharp point under discussion; they bawl across the canals; they bespeak your commands as you approach; they defy each other from afar. If you happen to have a *traghetto* under your window, you are well aware that they are a vocal race. I should go even farther than I went just now, and say that the voice of the gondolier is, in fact, the voice of Venice. There is scarcely any other, and that, indeed, is part of the interest of the place. There is no noise there save distinctly human noise; no rumbling, no vague uproar, no rattle of wheels and hoofs. It is all articulate, personal sound. One may say, indeed, that Venice is, emphatically, the city of conversation; people talk all over the place, because there is nothing to interfere with their being heard. Among the

[31] From *The Letters of D. H. Lawrence* by D. H. Lawrence, copyright, 1932, by The Viking Press, Inc.

populace it is a kind of family party. The still water carries the voice, and good Venetians exchange confidences at a distance of a half a mile. It saves a world of trouble, and they don't like trouble. Their delightful garrulous language helps them to make Venetian life a long *conversazione*. This language, with its soft elisions, its odd transpositions, its kindly contempt for consonants and other disagreeables, has in it something peculiarly human and accommodating.—HENRY JAMES: "Venice," *Portraits of Places*.

**G.** The dress of the rider and the accouterments of his horse, were peculiarly unfit for the traveller in such a country. A coat of linked mail, with long sleeves, plated gauntlets, and a steel breastplate, had not been esteemed sufficient weight of armor; there was also his triangular shield suspended round his neck, and his barred helmet of steel, over which he had a hood and collar of mail, which was drawn around the warrior's shoulders and throat, and filled up the vacancy between the hauberk and the head-piece. His lower limbs were sheathed, like his body, in flexible mail, securing the legs and thighs, while the feet rested in plated shoes, which corresponded with the gauntlets. A long, broad, straight-shaped, double-edged falchion, with a handle formed like a cross, corresponded with a stout poniard on the other side. The Knight also bore, secured to his saddle, with one end resting on his stirrup, the long steel-headed lance, his own proper weapon, which, as he rode, projected backwards, and displayed its little pennoncelle, to dally with the faint breeze, or drop in the dead calm.—WALTER SCOTT: *The Talisman*, Bk. I, Chap. 1.

**H.** Say that I had walked and wandered by unknown roads, and suddenly, after climbing a gentle hill, had seen before me for the first time the valley of Usk, just above Newbridge. I think it was on one of those strange days in summer when the sky is at once so grey and luminous that I achieved this adventure. There are no clouds in the upper air, the sky is simply covered with a veil which is, as I say, both grey and luminous, and there is no breath of wind, and every leaf is still.

But now and again as the day goes on the veil will brighten, and the sun almost appear; and then here and there in the woods it is as if white moons were descending. On such a day, then, I saw that wonderful and most lovely valley; the Usk, here purged of its muddy tidal waters, now like the sky, grey and silvery and luminous, winding in mystic esses, and the dense forest bending down to it, and the grey stone bridge crossing it. Down the valley in the distance was Caerleon-on-Usk; over the hill, somewhere in the lower slopes of the forest, Caerwent, also a Roman

city, was buried in the earth, and gave up now and again strange relics—
fragments of the temple of "Nodens, god of the depths." I saw the lonely
house between the dark forest and the silver river, and years after I
wrote "The Great God Pan," an endeavor to pass on the vague, inde-
finable sense of awe and mystery and terror that I had received.—ARTHUR
MACHEN: *Far Off Things*, Chap. 1.[32]

I. Ratmiroff gazed gloomily after his wife—even then he could not
fail to observe the enchanting grace of her figure, or her movements—
and crushing his cigarette with a heavy blow against the marble slab
of the chimney-piece, he flung it far from him. His cheeks suddenly
paled, a convulsive quiver flitted across his chin, and his eyes wandered
dully and fiercely over the floor, as though in search of something. . . .
Every trace of elegance had vanished from his face. That must have
been the sort of expression it had assumed when he flogged the white
Russian peasants.—IVAN TURGENEV: *Smoke*, Chap. 15.

J. He was a Mr. Cornelius Vanslyperken, a tall, meagre-looking per-
sonage, with very narrow shoulders and very small head. Perfectly straight
up and down, protruding in no part, he reminded you of some tall parish
pump, with a great knob at its top. His face was gaunt, cheeks hollow,
nose and chin showing an effection for each other, and evidently lament-
ing the gulf between them which prevented their meeting. Both appear
to have fretted themselves to the utmost degree of tenuity from disappointment in love; as for the nose, it had a pearly round tear hanging at
its tip, as if it wept.—FREDERICK MARRYAT: *The Dog Fiend*, Chap. 1.

K. Her heart seemed so full, that it spilt its new gush of happiness, as
it were, like rich and sunny wine out of an overbrimming goblet.—
NATHANIEL HAWTHORNE: *The Marble Faun*, Chap. 15.

L. But I eat. I gradually lose all knowledge of particulars as I eat.
I am becoming weighed down with food. These delicious mouthfuls of
roast duck, fitly piled with vegetables, following each other in exquisite
rotation of warmth, weight, sweet and bitter, past my palate, down my
gullet, into my stomach, have established my body. I feel quiet, gravity,
control. All is solid now. Instinctively my palate now requires and
anticipates sweetness and lightness, something sugared and evanescent;
and cool wine, fitting glove-like over those finer nerves that seem to
tremble from the roof of my mouth and make it spread (as I drink) into
a domed cavern, green with vine leaves, musk-scented, purple with
grapes. Now I can look steadily into the mill-race that foams beneath.

[32] Reprinted from *Far Off Things* by Arthur Machen, by permission of
Alfred A. Knopf, Inc. Copyright 1923 by Alfred A. Knopf, Inc.

By what particular name are we to call it? Let Rhoda speak, whose face
I see reflected mistily in the looking-glass opposite; Rhoda whom I interrupted when she rocked her petals in a brown basin, asking for the
pocket-knife that Bernard had stolen. Love is not a whirl-pool to her.
She is not giddy when she looks down. She looks far away over our
heads, beyond India.—VIRGINIA WOOLF: *The Waves*, Section 4.[33]

**M.** Cape Cod is the bared and bended arm of Massachusetts; the
shoulder is at Buzzard's Bay; the elbow, or crazy-bone, at Cape Malle-
barre; the wrist at Truro; and the sandy fist at Provincetown,—behind
which the state stands on her guard, with her back to the Green Mountains, and her feet planted on the floor of the ocean, like an athlete protecting her Bay,—boxing with northeast storms, and, ever and anon,
heaving up her Atlantic adversary from the lap of earth,—ready to thrust
forward her other fist, which keeps guard while upon her breast at
Cape Ann.—HENRY DAVID THOREAU: *Cape Cod*, Chap. 1.

**N.** In search of a place proper for this, I found a little plain on the
side of a rising hill, whose front towards this little plain was steep as a
house-side, so that nothing could come down upon me from the top;
on the side of this rock there was a hollow place, worn a little way in,
like the entrance or door of a cave; but there was not really any cave,
or way into the rock at all.

On the flat of the green, just before this hollow place, I resolved to
pitch my tent. This plain was not above an hundred yards broad,
and about twice as long, and lay like a green before my door, and at
the end of it descended irregularly every way down into the low grounds
by the seaside. It was on the NNW. side of the hill, so that I was sheltered
from the heat every day, till it came to a W. and by S. sun, or thereabouts,
which in those countries is near the setting.—DANIEL DEFOE: *Robinson
Crusoe*.

[33] From *The Waves* by Virginia Woolf, copyright, 1931, by Harcourt, Brace
and Company, Inc.

**CHAPTER**

**6**

# Narration

NARRATION is the kind of discourse concerned with action, with life in motion. It answers the question: "What happened?" It tells a story.

We ordinarily think of story-telling as being the special province of the writer of fiction, of short stories and novels, but fiction is only one type of narration, and here we shall be concerned with narration as a kind of discourse—with narration in general. Fiction involves many special problems which will not be touched on here.

Let us examine what we mean by the word *action* as used in the statement that narration is the kind of discourse concerned with action. We may discuss action under three heads, *movement, time,* and *meaning.*

## MOVEMENT

Description gives us the picture of the world as fixed at a given moment, of its objects as existing at that moment. It is a portrait, a snapshot, a still life. Narration gives us a moving picture, its objects in operation, life in motion. Its emphasis is not on the thing in motion, but on the nature of the motion itself. It is concerned with a transformation from one stage to another stage. It not only answers the question, "What happened?" it also answers the question, "How did it happen?"—that is, what was the process of passing from the first stage to the last stage?

This special emphasis on movement itself means that narration does not explain a process (though it may do so) but *presents* a process. It places the event before our eyes. Narration does not *tell about* the story. It *tells* the story. Like description, narration gives the quality of immediacy.

## TIME

The movement of a process, an event, is through time, from one point to another. But narration does not give us a mere segment of time, but a *unit* of time, and a unit is a thing which is complete in itself. It may be part of a larger thing, and it may contain smaller parts, but in itself it is complete. The unit of time, therefore, is the time in which a process fulfills itself. We now emphasize, not the fact of movement, but the movement from a beginning to an end. We begin a story at the moment when something is ripe to happen, when one condition prevails but is unstable, and end it when the something has finished happening, when a new condition prevails and is stable. And in between those two moments are all the moments which mark the stages of change.

But you may recall narratives which did not begin with that first moment when something was ripe to happen. For instance, a narrative may begin with a man in the very midst of his difficulties and problems, say on the battlefield or at the moment of a marital crisis or when he hears that he has lost his fortune, and then cut back to his previous experiences to explain how he came to be in such a situation. Such a narrative does not move in an orderly fashion from A to Z. It begins, instead, with G, H, I and then cuts back to A, B, and C. But we must distinguish here between two things: how the narrator treated the sequence in time and how the sequence existed in time. The narrator may have given us G, H, and I first in order to catch our interest. He may have thought that A, B, and C, would not be interesting to us until we knew what they were to lead to. But when he does finally cut back to A, B, and C, we become aware of the full sequence in time and set it up in our imaginations A, B, C . . . G, H, I. . . . In other words, we must distinguish between the *way* (G, H, I–A, B, C . . .) the narrator tells us something and the *thing* (A, B, C, D, E, F, G . . .) which he tells. The *thing* told always represents a unit of time, no matter how much the narrator may violate its natural order.

## MEANING

An action, as we are using the word, is not merely a series of events but is a meaningful series. We have already implied this in saying that narration gives us a unit of time, with a beginning and an end. In other words, the events must be stages in a process and not merely a random collection held together in time. They must have a unity of meaning. Suppose we should read:

President Wilson presented his war message to Congress on April 6, 1917. War was declared. Thus the United States embarked on its first great adventure in world affairs. On April 8, 1917, just two days later, Albert Mayfield was born in Marysville, Illinois. He was a healthy baby, and grew rapidly. By the time of the Armistice he weighed 25 pounds. On December 12, 1918, the troopship *Mason*, returning to New York from Cherbourg, struck a floating mine off Ireland and sank. Two hundred and sixteen men were lost.

Several events are recounted in this passage, but as it is presented to us, nothing holds those events together. They have no significant relation to each other. They do not constitute an action, merely a sequence in time. But suppose we rewrite the passage:

President Wilson presented his war message to Congress on April 6, 1917. War was declared. Thus the United States embarked on its first great adventure in world affairs. On April 8, 1917, just two days later, Albert Mayfield was born in Marysville, Illinois. Scarcely before the ink had dried on the headlines of the extra of the Marysville *Courier* announcing the declaration of war, Albert embarked on his own great adventure in world affairs. He was a healthy baby, and grew rapidly. By the time of the Armistice he weighed 25 pounds. On December 12, 1918, the troopship *Mason*, returning to New York from Cherbourg, struck a floating mine off Ireland and sank. Two hundred and sixteen men were lost. Among those men was Sidney Mayfield, a captain of artillery, a quiet, unobtrusive, middle-aged insurance salesman, who left a widow and an infant son. That son was Albert Mayfield. So Albert grew up into a world which the war—a war he could not remember—had defined. It had defined the little world of his home, the silent, bitter woman who was his mother, the poverty and the cheerless discipline, and it had defined the big world outside.

Now we are moving toward an action. The random events are given some relationship to each other. We have unity and meaning.

We may want to go on and find out more about Albert and about the long-range effects of the war on his life, but what we have is, as far as it goes, an action in itself as well as the part of a bigger action, the story of Albert's life.

We have said that an action must have unity of meaning. This implies that one thing leads to another, or if one thing does not lead to the other, that they both belong to a body of related events all bearing on the point of the action. For instance, in the paragraph about Albert Mayfield, the declaration of war by the United States did not directly cause the floating mine to be in a particular spot off Ireland, but both events belong in the body of events contributing to the formation of Albert's character.

In seeking the unity of an action, we must often think of the persons involved. Events do not merely happen to people, but people also cause events. People have desires and impulses, and these desires and impulses are translated into deeds. Therefore, the human motives involved may contribute to the unity of an action. This human element, MOTIVATION, may provide the line which runs through the individual events and binds them together. And when motivation does not provide us with the line, we must think of the events as leading to some human response. For example, no motivation in the sense just used binds the little story of Albert Mayfield together, but the effect of the events on Albert Mayfield, his response to them, provides the unity and the meaning.

If we summarize what we mean by an action, we arrive at something like this. It is a connected sequence of events. It involves a change from one condition to another. It must have a beginning and an end. It must have unity and meaning. It must stimulate and satisfy an interest.

## NARRATIVE AND NARRATION

Before we leave this preliminary discussion of narration, it may be well, as a kind of caution, to make a distinction between narration and narrative. Strictly considered, narration is a certain way of speaking or writing, a kind of discourse, and a narrative is the thing produced by its application, a discourse, either spoken or written, which presents an action. We must remember, however, that the method of narration may be used without giving us a satisfactory narrative. Suppose a woman should say:

Why, my dear, I had the pleasantest afternoon yesterday. I went down to lunch with Ethel—at the Green Room of the Millet Hotel—and we had delicious shrimp. You know, the kind they serve there. Then I went to get a facial. And guess who was there! Milly Seaver. I hadn't seen her in ages. Really, not for ages. She was looking awful well, even if she is beginning—I oughtn't say this, but it's true—to show her age just a little. You know how blondes are. She said she was getting a permanent and was in a hurry because her husband was taking her to Chicago that night on a business trip. Then I left the beauty shop and went to a movie. It wasn't very good, but I enjoyed being there in the cool, after such a hot day. But I had to come home early, before the show was over. You see, Mike, that's my biggest child, had to go to a Scout meeting. And besides, I like an early dinner for the children. Also, my new shoes weren't very comfortable, and I was glad to get home. But Milly Seaver —you really ought to see her— she's getting . . .

This rattletrap of a woman has used the method of narration, but she has used it without the distinguishing interest of narration, the presentation of an action. She has given us a sequence of events in time, but that sequence of events does not constitute an action in the real sense. The unity is a unity in time—she went down town early in the afternoon and came home late—but there is no unity of meaning in the events themselves. One may say, of course, that we get some notion of her character from the way she spends her time, and that this constitutes a meaning. But ordinarily we insist on a little more than that when we say that a sequence of events constitutes an action.

It is not profitable, however, to demand a single line of demarcation between what is narration and non-narration, between what is narrative and what is non-narrative. If we understand the extremes—the random and unrelated accumulation events at the one extreme, and the fully realized action at the other—we can use common sense to discriminate among the examples of the shadowland in between. And in our ordinary speaking and writing we shall frequently have reason to move into that shadowland where definitions are not as clear as day.

# NARRATION AND THE OTHER KINDS OF DISCOURSE

We have been discussing narration (and narrative) as a thing in itself. But it bears certain relations to the other kinds of discourse—description, exposition, and argument. What are these relations?

We can break this general question down into two other questions:

1. How does narration use other kinds of discourse?
2. How do other kinds of discourse use narration?

## HOW NARRATION USES OTHER KINDS OF DISCOURSE

Let us take up the first question. A narrative may have within it descriptive, argumentative, or expository elements. In fact, any rather full narrative will almost certainly have them, but they will be, if the prevailing motive of the piece of writing is narrative, absorbed into the narrative intention.

A narrative presents us with an action. But an action implies things or persons which act and are acted upon. And the word *presents* implies that we are not told about those things or persons but are given some sense of their actual presence, their appearance, their nature. And this means that, in a greater or lesser degree, they are described. So description comes in to give us that impression of immediacy which is important for all narrative except the most bare and synoptic kind.

The same line of reasoning leads us to an awareness of the importance of exposition in narrative. A narrative involves an action, and we have defined an action as a sequence of events related to create a meaning. One thing leads to another. There is a connection of cause and effect, or at least the events are connected with each other by means of some idea. For instance, in the little example given above about Albert Mayfield and World War I, the war is the cause of the particular situation in which the boy grows up. We must understand this in order to get the point.

Exposition is the kind of discourse concerned with explanation, with making us understand something, and in so far as a narrative employs explanation to bring us to an understanding of its point, it involves exposition. Some narratives, it is true, may simply arrange their materials so that the reader is aware of the point without having to depend on any explanation, but in any rather fully developed narrative some element of exposition, even though a very slight one, is apt to appear.

Let us turn to the writing of a little narrative. Suppose we start with the following passage:

George Barton, a poor boy about twelve years old of nondescript appearance, was forced to sell the mastiff, which he had reared from a puppy and which he loved very much, for two reasons. First, having lost his job, he could no longer buy proper food for a dog of such size. Second, after it had frightened a child in the neighborhood, he was afraid that someone would poison it.

But this is not a narrative. It is concerned with an action, the fact that the boy sells his dog, but its primary concern is with the causes of the action and with what the action illustrates rather than with the immediate presentation of the action in time. Let us rewrite the passage.

George Barton owned a mastiff which he had reared from a puppy. He loved it very much. But he lost his job and could no longer buy proper food for it. Then the dog frightened a little child of the neighborhood who was eating a piece of bread. George was now afraid that someone would poison it. So he sold it.

This is a narrative. The causes of the action are given here, as before, but now they are absorbed into the movement of the action itself and appear to us in their natural sequence. When we wrote in the first example that George sold the dog for two reasons, we violated the whole nature of narrative—the movement in time—because we made, not the action itself, but the causes of the action, the thing of primary interest. The first piece of writing is expository: it explains why the boy sold the dog. The second piece of writing is narrative: it tells us what happened.

This second piece of writing is, however, a very poor, dull, and incomplete piece of narrative. It can scarcely be said, for one thing, to *present* the event at all. It gives us little sense of the immediate quality of the event. It is so bare of detail that the imagination of the reader can find little to work on. We have the basic facts given in a bare synopsis. But if we fill in the synopsis a little we can make it satisfy us somewhat better.

George Barton was a nondescript little boy, scarcely to be distinguished from the other boys living in Duck Alley. He had a pasty face, not remarkable in any way, eyes not blue and not brown but some nondescript hazel color, and a tangle of neutral colored hair. His clothes were the anonymous, drab, cast-off items worn by all the children of Duck Alley, that grimy street, scarcely a street at all but a dirt track, which ran between the sluggish, algae-crusted bayou and a scattering of shanties. His life there was unremarkable and cheerless enough, with a feeble, querulous, stooped, defeated father, a mother who had long since resigned herself to her misery, and a sullen older brother, with a mean laugh and a hard set of knuckles, who tormented George for amusement when he was not off prowling with his cronies. But this home did not distinguish George from the other children of Duck Alley. It was like many of the others. What distinguished George was his dog.

One day two years back—it was the summer when he was ten— George had found the dog. It was a puppy then, a scrawny, starving creature with absurd big paws, sniffling feebly in the garbage dump at the end of Duck Alley. No one could have guessed then that it would grow into a sleek, powerful animal, as big as a pony.

George brought it home, and defended it against the protests and jeers and random kicks of the family. "I'll feed him," he asserted. "He won't never eat a bite I don't make the money to pay for." And he was as good as his word. There was no job too hard for him, for he could look forward to evening when he would squat by the old goods box which served as a kennel and watch Jibby gnaw at the hunk of meat he had bought.

Suppose we begin the narrative in that way. We have added several elements to the bare synopsis given before. We know now why the dog is so important to the boy. There is no direct statement on this point, but we see that he lives an isolated and loveless life, and that the dog satisfies a craving of his nature for companionship and affection. We also see that now he has a reason for his own efforts, a center for his life. In other words we can imaginatively grasp his own state of mind. As we have just stated the matter, it is given as explanation, as exposition, but in the narrative itself this expository element is absorbed into situation and action. But in addition to this element, we have added little bits of description which are woven into the narrative to help us visualize the scene and George himself. The description which is absorbed into the narrative helps put the whole thing before us, helps to present it rather than tell about it.

The thing to emphasize here is that the narrative is concerned to make us sense the fullness of the process—to make us see, hear, feel, and understand the event as a single thing. Description alone might make us see or hear some aspect of the event. Exposition might make us understand its meaning, its causes or results. But narrative, when it is fully effective, makes us aware directly of the event as happening.

To return to our little narrative. Suppose we should carry on our suggested revision to the moment when George sells his dog. Would there be anything still lacking to make the narrative fully satisfying? Perhaps there would be. Perhaps the meaning of the action would not be very clear. Let us continue it at a point after George has lost his job and the dog has frightened the child.

George sold the dog to John Simpson, a boy who lived in one of the big brick houses on the hill back of town. John Simpson's father was rich. John could feed Jibby. John could take care of him. Nobody would poison Jibby up at John Simpson's house, behind the high iron fence. George comforted himself with these thoughts.

Sometimes, however, they did not comfort him enough, and he felt the old loneliness and emptiness which he had felt before Jibby came. But he was getting to be a big boy now, big and tough, and he put those feelings out of his mind as well as he could. He did not work regularly now, but hung around with the Duck Alley gang in the railroad yards. He almost forgot Jibby.

One day on the main street of town he met John Simpson and the dog, such a big, powerful, sleek dog now that he scarcely recognized him. He went up to the dog. "Hi, Jibby, hi, boy!" he said, and began to pull the dog's ears and scratch his head as he had done three years before, in the evenings, back by the goods box, after Jibby had bolted his supper. The dog nuzzled him and licked his hands. George looked up at the other boy and exclaimed, "Jeez, look at him. Look at him, will ya. Ain't he smart? He remembers me!"

John Simpson stood there and for a moment did not utter a word. Then he said, "Take your hands off that dog. He belongs to me."

George stepped back.

"Come here, Blaze," John Simpson ordered, and the dog went to him. He fondled the dog's head, and the dog licked his hands.

George turned around and walked off.

This is somewhat more complete than the previous version. If we stop with the sale of the dog, we do have an example of narration, but the reader no doubt is somewhat confused about the exact meaning of the event presented. Perhaps the reader feels sorry for the boy. Perhaps he is aware that poverty is the cause of the boy's loss of the dog. Those things may be taken as meanings of the piece of narration given. But they are not brought to focus. The reader may not be sure exactly what is intended. He is certain to feel that the narrative is rather fragmentary.

But with the addition of the next section dealing with the meeting of George and John Simpson, the reader is more certain of the direction of the narrative, of the significance. The contrast between John Simpson, who owns the dog, and George, who merely loves it, gives us a point which is clear even without any comment. And many narratives, even some examples of that highly elaborated form of narration called fiction, deliver their point without any comment.

In the new section, we may notice, however, that more is involved than the mere contrast between the two boys. The dog licks John Simpson's hands, too. How does this tie in with what we have just said? This is, as it were, a kind of betrayal of George's affection for the dog. Another question: What is George's attitude as he turns and walks off? Perhaps the reader senses the boy's resentment at the betrayal. But the writer might want more. He might want a more positive conclusion. For example, he might want to make this event a kind of turning point in George's growing up, a seemingly trivial event which had a far-reaching effect on his life. He might continue.

The next day George hunted a job. He found one at the lumberyard where he had worked before when Jibby was a puppy. He worked as steadily now as he had worked in the old days when he looked forward to getting home to feed the dog and squat by him in the dusk, or if it was winter, in the dark. But he did not love the dog now. He was through with that.

But he worked because he had learned one thing. It was a thing which he was never to forget. He had learned that even love was one of the things you cannot get unless you have the money to pay for it.

This would give us a conclusion. It would give the effect of the event on George, not merely the first reaction of resentment or hurt feelings, but the effect which would prevail over a long period of time. Neither the reader nor the writer may agree that what George learns is the truth—that money is the basis of everything, even of those things like love and loyalty and kindness—but what George learns is the "truth" for him, the thing by which he will conduct his life for a time to come.

The important thing to understand here is, however, that a point is made, whether or not the reader accepts the point as true. The narrative is complete. It is not complete merely because a summarizing statement has been made by the writer. Certainly, the summarizing statement would not make the narrative complete if the thing it says were not something which could grow reasonably out of the event for a person in George's situation. And many narratives imply rather than state their meaning. But a full narrative does involve significance, a meaning, a point, as something which grows out of the sequence of events.

We have just said that the narrative is complete. This does not necessarily mean that George will never change his mind about what is the meaning of the experience he has had. The narrative might well be part of a long story or a novel which showed how for thirty years to come George conducted his life by the hard, materialistic "truth" he had learned and then found, even in the moment of his practical success, when he had grown rich and powerful, that his "truth" was really a profound mistake and that he had to learn a new truth.

This revision might not make a good story. The event concerning the dog might be too trivial or sentimental to serve as the basis for a good piece of fiction. But it will illustrate our own statement that the significance of a narrative stems from what the narrative immediately involves. George's later experiences, including elements not involved in the little narrative given here, might make him (or the reader) revise the notion of the truth of its point. But the point, *in so far as it is already implicit in the particular narrative,* would be there, and the narrative would be complete, in terms of George's interpretation of it.

The idea of completeness as applied to narrative always involves the idea of an interpretation, stated or implied, of the events narrated. The interpretation may be made by a character in the narrative, as by George in this case, or it may be made by the reader on the basis of the presentation of the material, or it may be stated by the writer. But in all cases of fully developed narrative, an interpretation is involved. And this means that our understanding is appealed to. And a narrative may use exposition to make this appeal to our understanding, as the last paragraph of our narrative about George does.

## APPLICATIONS

**I.** In the section of Readings study "Mary Queen of Scots," by James A. Froude, and "The Last Days," by Richard Wingfield. What is the difference of interpretation here between the two accounts of the same event? What details can you fix on in each which supports its special interpretation?

**II.** What is the interpretation, or point, of "I Get a Colt to Break In," by Lincoln Steffens?

**III.** Write a short narrative, around 250 words, about some experience of your own which has taught you something.

### HOW OTHER KINDS OF DISCOURSE USE NARRATION

Strictly speaking, description can scarcely be said to use narration as an aid. It is, of course, possible to find cases in which description involves movement—a man's habitual acts, for instance, in a description of a character. But we must keep in mind the distinction between an act and an action in the sense in which we have been using the word *action*. A character description might even involve an action, but our interest in action is so much more vital than our interest in mere appearance that we should probably feel that the description was incidental to the narration rather than the narration incidental to the description. An object in motion catches the eye.

The situation, however, is different in regard to exposition and argument. Frequently in extended discourses which are primarily intended to explain something to us or to convince us of something we find bits of narrative used to dramatize an attitude, to illustrate a point, to bring an idea home to us. Sermons and speeches are often full of anecdotes. The preacher tells his congregation the story of a deathbed confession. The politician tells his audience how such and such a law, which he is pledged to help repeal if elected, has ruined the life of John Doe over in Murray County. The after-dinner speaker tells the club members a joke. But the story of the deathbed confession or of the ruin of John Doe over in Murray County or the story about the two Irishmen must have a point related to the main business in hand. If it does not have such a relation, the listeners feel that the speaker has dragged it in by the tail, merely to catch their attention, that somehow he has not played fair.

What is true of the sermon or political address or after-dinner speech is true of informal essays, informational articles, character sketches, travel books, philosophical essays, essays of opinion, memoirs, historical studies, and many other types of writing. And here, too, the narrative may be used to bring directly home to the reader what argument or exposition can only give in general terms. For instance, observe how the general statement with which the following paragraph begins takes on significance in narrative:

Undergraduate life at Cambridge [Massachusetts] has not lacked for bitter passages, which compel notice from any anatomist of society. On the one hand there has long been a snobbery moulded of New England pride and juvenile cruelty which is probably more savage than any known to Fifth Avenue and Newport. Its favorite illustration is the time-worn tale of the lonely lad who to feign that he had *one* friend used to go out as dusk fell over the yard and call beneath his own windows, "Oh, Reinhardt!" And on the other it has moments of mad, terrible loyalty —exampled by the episode which is still recalled, awesomely without names, over the coffee and liqueurs when Harvard men meet in Beacon Street or the South Seas. It is the true story of a Harvard senior at a party in Brookline, who suddenly enraged by a jocular remark made concerning the girl whom he later married, publicly slapped the face of his best friend—and then in an access of remorse walked to an open fire and held his offending hand in the flame until it shrivelled away to the wrist.—DIXON WECTER: *The Saga of American Society,* Chap. 7.[1]

Or let us take the following passage, which has the same basic pattern, the movement from a general proposition to an illustration in narrative:

There are men of all nations who feel the fascination of a life unequally divided between months of hardship and short days of riot and spending; but in the end it is the hardship that holds them. The Chinese, taking them as they come, are not like this. They frankly detest hard work. A large belly among them is an honorable thing, because it means that the owner of it does not swink for his living. I never met a Chinese

[1] From *The Saga of American Society* by Dixon Wecter, copyright, 1937, by Charles Scribner's Sons.

outside of the caravans who was what we should call sentimental about his work. Camel pullers alone have a different spirit, a queer spirit. Time and again when the men were talking around the fire and cursing the weather, the bad taste of the water, or the dust blown into their food, I have heard one ask, rhetorically, "What is a camel puller?" . . .

Then another would say, "Yes, but this is the good life—do we not all come back to it?" and be approved in a chorus of grunts and oaths. Once a veteran said the last word: "I put all my money into land in the newly opened country Behind the Hills, and my nephew farms it for me. My old woman is there, so two years ago when they had the troubles on the Great Road and my legs hurt I thought I would finish with it all—defile its mother! I thought I would sleep on a warm *k'ang* and gossip with the neighbors and maybe smoke a little opium, and not work hard any more. But I am not far from the road, in my place, and after a while in the day and the night when I hear the bells of the *lien-tze* go by, *ting-lang, ting-lang,* there was a pain in my heart—*hsin-li nan-kuo.* So I said, "Dogs defile it! I will go back on the Gobi one more time and pull camels."—OWEN LATTIMORE: *The Desert Road to Turkestan,* Chap. 8.[2]

### EXPOSITORY NARRATION

In the examples just given we have seen how a narrative may be used to illustrate an idea. But in addition to this ordinary use of narration in exposition or argument, there is a special type called EXPOSITORY NARRATION. This is the type found, for instance, in the account of a laboratory experiment or in the directions for making or doing something. The method of narration is used here—stage by stage a process is outlined—but the intention is not the intention of true narration. The intention here is not to present an action so that it can be grasped imaginatively but merely to explain a process. The appeal is strictly to the understanding, and therefore this type is best considered as a form of exposition. A discussion of it has already appeared in the chapter on exposition (pp. 60-61).

## PATTERN IN NARRATION

In the course of time one hears and reads many different narratives—jokes, novels, short stories, anecdotes, newspaper reports—

[2] From *The Desert Road to Turkestan* by Owen Lattimore. Reprinted by permission of Little, Brown and Company and the Atlantic Monthly Press.

and they seem to have many different kinds of organization. But is there some fundamental principle of pattern which underlies all the particular kinds of pattern we find in narratives? If we can find such a principle, then we have taken an important step toward being able to write good narrative.

We must return at this point to a distinction we have already made in discussing time as an aspect of an action (p. 263), the distinction between events existing in time in their natural order, and the events as a narrator may re-order them by means of cutbacks and shifts when he composes his narrative. That is, the natural order A-Z may be shifted, to heighten interest or for other reasons, into an artificial order such as *G, H, I—A, B, C—J, K, L,* and so forth.

We should remember in making this distinction that it applies as well to narratives using imaginary events as to narratives using actual material. Imaginary events, as well as real events, have a natural order, their order in time. In discussing here the pattern of an action we shall be referring to the natural order and not to an artificial order which a narrator might adopt for special purposes.

We have defined an action as a meaningful sequence of events. Such a sequence may be real, that is, observed, but observed events constitute an action only in so far as we detect their meaning. Or such a sequence of events may be imaginary, made up to embody a meaning. The principle of pattern will apply equally well to either kind of action, and in seeking examples to illustrate our principle we shall sometimes draw on factual material and sometimes on imaginary material. In both kinds of examples we shall be asking what is the shape events must take in order to constitute an action.

We can begin to answer our question by saying that an action has a beginning, a middle, and an end. Let us try to analyze what is really at stake in this answer.

### BEGINNING

An action does not spring from nothing. It arises from a situation. The situation, however, must be an unstable one, ready to lead to change, and containing in it the seeds of the future developments.

A situation may be very simple or very complicated. In the joke we begin, "Two Irishmen met on a bridge at midnight in a strange city. The first Irishman said . . ." We have a minimum of information here, but all we may need for the joke. The situation could not be simpler. But the principle is the same as in an enormously complicated situation, for instance, the situation from which German Nazism developed. That situation contains more elements than we can hope to enumerate. There is the conflict between capital and labor, the insecurity of the lower middle class, the fear of Bolshevism, the economic collapse and the inflation of currency, the tradition of German militarism, the demand for revenge after the defeat in World War I, the example of Italian Fascism, the personality of Hitler, his bitterness and frustration. An interaction of all these factors and many more gives us the unstable situation in which are latent the subsequent developments.

Given this material, the writer of an account of Nazism must first present the situation clearly enough for the reader to see how the rest will follow. In dealing with matters of fact, as such a writer of history would be doing, his first task would be to analyze the body of material to be sure he knew what was really significant for future developments, and his second task would be to present the material so that the reader would see the relation among the various elements. It is true that the reader may not understand the significance of the situation when it is first presented to him, but he must be given enough to go on, to rouse and sustain his interest, to show that there is a line of possible development. And he must be given enough for him to feel, when he looks back over the whole narrative, that the action is really a logical development from the situation.

The problem is essentially the same for a writer who is dealing with imaginary events. The only difference is that he does not have to analyze factual materials already given him but has to create or adapt his materials. If we glance at Act I of Shakespeare's *Romeo and Juliet,* we find a good example of a beginning. We learn that there is a feud between the houses of Capulet and Montague, that bloodshed and violence are imminent, that Romeo is an idealistic young man anxious to fall in love. Very early we have enough to account for the future events. Or if we go back to our own improvised narrative of George and the dog, the situation presenting the misery and lovelessness of the boy's life gives us enough to account for the later importance of the dog to the boy.

The beginning, the presentation of the situation, enables us to understand the narrative. Therefore, that part of the narrative is often given the name of EXPOSITION. But we must keep the word in this special sense distinct from the more general sense in which it signifies one of the kinds of discourse.

It is not to be understood, however, that the exposition of a narrative is merely a kind of necessary evil, a body of dull information which the reader must absorb before he can settle down to the real story. It need not be explanatory or descriptive material in isolation, or a colorless summary of the situation from which the action stems. Instead, the exposition may appear as an episode, a fragment of action, interesting in itself. If we think back on the opening scene of *Romeo and Juliet,* we remember that we see a street fight. We are not *told about* the feud between the rival houses of Capulet and Montague, but actually see it in operation. Not all kinds of exposition can take a direct form, but in general it can be said that all exposition which can be directly presented should have the direct form.

## MIDDLE

The middle is the main body of the action. It is a series of stages in the process. It involves the points of mounting tension, or increasing complication, developing from the original situation. This mounting tension, this suspense, leads us to the point of greatest intensity or greatest suspense, called technically the CLIMAX. The climax is the focal point, the turning point of the narrative.

To return to our historical example of the rise of Nazism, we would find such points of mounting tension as the beer hall *putsch* in Munich, Hitler's imprisonment and the writing of *Mein Kampf,* the street fights against the German communists, the election of Hitler as chancellor, the Reichstag fire, the purge of the party, the claims on Sudetenland. Looking back on the events of the past twenty-five years, we can see the points of crisis, the stages at which new tensions emerged. If a historian were writing an account of those years, he might center his attention on those stages. They might provide him with natural chapter divisions.

The same principle applies in any narrative, the simple joke or the elaborate novel. If one is telling or writing about real events, one tries to focus attention on those which mark real stages of development. And if one is making up a narrative, he arranges his imaginary material in the same way. He wants to create suspense, to hold the interest of his audience. If his narrative seems to be a mere drift of events, he cannot hold their interest. He can do so only in so far as the narrative emerges in well-defined stages of increasing complication.

We can see this very clearly in the main body of *Romeo and Juliet:* Romeo meets Juliet; the marriage takes place; Romeo kills Juliet's kinsman Tybalt while trying to stop a duel; Romeo is banished, and so on. Or we can see it in the little account of the boy and the dog: George gets a job to feed the dog; the dog becomes the center of his life; he loses the job; the dog frightens the child; George sells the dog, and so on.

Just as we have a technical name for the beginning of a narrative (*exposition*), so we have one for the middle: COMPLICATION.

### END

As for the end of an action, it is not simply the point where the action stops. It is, rather, the point at which the forces implicit in the situation have worked themselves out. Whether it is the gag line of the joke or Berlin shattered under British and American bombs and Russian shells, the principle is the same. The end of an action, however, is not necessarily the physical victory of one set of forces over another. It may be in the reconciliation of forces, or it may be in the fusion of previously opposing forces to create a new force. Take, for instance, the conclusion of the Constitutional Convention that defined the United States: we may regard this end as a fusion of conflicting forces. As a matter of fact, the end of an action may simply be a new awareness on the part of a person involved, directly or indirectly, in the action. We know how we can look back on an experience of our own and recognize the point at which some attitude of our own had been changed by it.

When we come to writing a narrative, we regard the end as the point where the action achieves its full meaning. It is the point where the reader is willing to say, "Oh, yes, I see what it is all about." If we look back on our narrative of the boy and the dog we see that if we had stopped with the sale of the dog, the meaning would have been very blurred. A reader would not have been quite sure what was at stake. He might have felt sorry for the boy in a vague sort of way. But the meeting with John Simpson and the dog gives us in direct terms, as a contrast, a much more sharply defined meaning. This could be an end. We, as readers, see that there is an issue, a question, raised by the narrative—the question of legal ownership of the dog opposed to the demands of affection. The narrative now has a point. If we go on to write the last paragraph we simply indicate the fact of George's awareness and the effect on him. By means of George's awareness we have made the point more explicit, but it *was* implicit at the moment when the two boys had their little encounter. The technical term for the end of a narrative is DENOUEMENT.

## EXAMPLES OF NARRATIVE PATTERN

Let us look at a few examples of narrative with the idea of indicating the structure, or pattern, of each. The first is the account of how Robinson Crusoe, who fancied himself absolutely alone on his desert island, found a footprint:

It happened one day about noon, going towards my boat, I was exceedingly surprised with the print of a man's naked foot on the shore, which was very plain to be seen in the sand. I stood like one thunderstruck, or as if I had seen an apparition: I listened, I looked round me, but I could hear nothing, nor see anything. I went up to a rising ground, to look farther; I went up the shore and down the shore, but it was all one; I could see no other impression but that one. I went to it again to see if there were any more, and to observe if it might not be my fancy; but there was no room for that, for there was exactly the print of a foot, toes, heel, and every part of a foot: how it came thither I knew not, nor could I in the least imagine; but, after innumerable fluttering thoughts, like a man perfectly confused and out of myself, I came home to my fortification, not feeling, as we say, the ground I went on, but terrified to the last degree; looking behind me at every two or three steps, mistaking every bush and tree, and fancying every stump at a distance to be a man. Nor is it possible to describe how many various shapes my affrighted imagination represented things to me in, how many wild ideas were found every moment in my fancy, and what strange unaccountable whimsies came into my thoughts by the way.—DANIEL DEFOE: *Robinson Crusoe.*

A piece of narrative could scarcely be simpler than this, but we see that it follows the basic pattern. The situation is given, the time and place. The complication follows on the discovery of the print—

the first reaction, the looking about and listening, the going to higher ground for a wider view, the return to verify the existence of the print. Then follows the flight and the terror consequent upon the discovery. And it is this terror, changing the whole aspect of the familiar landscape, which constitutes the denouement. Crusoe's life cannot be the same again. This fact is not specified, but it is strongly implied.

Our next example makes its point more explicitly:

And also Mohammet loved well a good Hermit that dwelled in the Deserts a Mile from Mount Sinai, in the Way that Men go from Arabia toward Chaldea and toward Ind, one Day's journey from the Sea, where the Merchants of Venice come often for Merchandise. And so often went Mohammet to this Hermit, that all his Men were wroth; for he would gladly hear this Hermit preach and make his Men wake all Night. And therefore his Men thought to put the Hermit to Death. And so it befell upon a Night, that Mohammet was drunken of good Wine, and he fell asleep. And his Men took Mohammet's Sword out of his Sheath, whiles he slept, and therewith they slew this Hermit, and put his Sword all bloody in his Sheath again. And at the Morrow, when he found the Hermit dead, he was fully sorry and wroth, and would have done his Men to Death. But they all, with one accord, said that he himself had slain him, when he was drunk, and showed him his Sword all bloody. And he trowed that they had said Truth. And then he cursed the Wine and them that drink it. And therefore Saracens that be devout drink never any Wine.—SIR JOHN MANDEVILLE: *Travels*, Chap. 16.

This, too, falls into the pattern. The exposition is a little less simple here than in our earlier example, for now we are concerned not only with the physical facts but with human motives leading up to the action—Mohammet's love of the hermit, his custom of listening to the sermons, the irritation of the men. The complication falls into three divisions—the killing of the hermit, the discovery of the deed and Mohammet's anger, the lie and the bloody sword in his own scabbard. The denouement has two divisions—Mohammet's curse on wine and the result among devout followers in later times.

Our next example is an anecdote told about an argument between the Duke of Windsor and Winston Churchill. We have here merely a clash of opinion:

The Windsors' dinner was very grand, and the guests consisted of assorted notables from up and down the coast, mostly English people of high rank who were holidaying in the South. My Lords Rothermere and Beaverbrook had been prevented from attending by colds. (Lord Beaverbrook's cold did not prevent his attendance at the Casino, where we saw him afterward.) When some of the more overpowering guests had departed, after the long and stately meal in the white-and-gold dining room, the Duke of Windsor and Mr. Churchill settled down to a prolonged argument with the rest of the party listening in silence. The Duke had read with amazement Mr. Churchill's recent articles on Spain and his newest one (out that day, I believe) in which he appealed for an alliance with Soviet Russia. "You of all people, Winston," was the gist of his argument, "you cannot wish to make friends of these murderers and thieves." At one point Mr. Churchill, who was defending his point of view stubbornly and with undiplomatic vigor, said: "Sir, I would make a friend of the devil himself, if it would save England." It resulted plainly from the statements on the two sides that the self-willed, pleasure-loving little Prince, filled to the fingertips with royal prejudice, had no conception of the deadly danger to England involved in his dalliance with Hitler, while Mr. Churchill, disliking the Bolshevik theory and practice as much as ever, was so thoroughly aware of England's peril that he would seek the alliance of Stalin at once. We sat by the fireplace, Mr. Churchill frowning with intentness at the floor in front of him, mincing no words, reminding H.R.H. of the British constitution, on occasion—"when our kings are in conflict with our constitution we change our kings," he said—and declaring flatly that the nation stood in the gravest danger of its long history. The kilted Duke in his Stuart tartan sat on the edge of the sofa, eagerly interrupting whenever he could, contesting every point, but receiving—in terms of the utmost politeness so far as the words went—an object lesson in political wisdom and public spirit. The rest of us sat fixed in silence; there was something dramatically final, irrevocable about this dispute.—VINCENT SHEEAN: *Between the Thunder and the Sun*, Chap. 1.[3]

This is scarcely a narrative at all, simply a little incident almost buried in the comment with which the author has surrounded the event. But the author has hinted at the action, and has given enough for us to grasp its natural structure and order (as contrasted with the way the author has told it, for the author has not stuck to the chronological order of event).

[3] From *Between the Thunder and the Sun* by Vincent Sheean. Reprinted by permission of Random House, Inc.

*Situation:*

Dinner with Windsors. Nature of gathering. World of pleasure and privilege. Churchill and his articles on Spain.

*Complication:*

Prolonged argument. The Duke's amazement at Churchill's articles, especially his demand for an alliance with Russia. The Duke's stubbornness. He eagerly leans forward from sofa, contesting every point. Churchill's remarks on relation of kingship to English constitution, the danger to England, and so forth. The Duke's statement: "You of all people, Winston, cannot wish to make friends of these murderers and thieves."

*Denouement:*

Churchill's reply: "Sir, I would make a friend of the devil himself, if it would save England."

We do not know all that occurred at that conversation. We do not need to know it to have a notion of the action, in our sense of the word. For, in this connection, action is the word we apply to a meaningful event, and the things which merely happened and have no bearing on the meaning of the event are not, properly speaking, a part of the action. The writer has omitted them from his account.

Here is a more fully developed narrative, the story of Andrew Jackson's most famous duel, the duel with Charles Dickinson, who had made some remarks reflecting on the character of Rachel Jackson, Andrew Jackson's wife.

[*Exposition*]

On Thursday, May 29, 1806, Andrew Jackson rose at five o'clock, and after breakfast told Rachel that he would be gone for a couple of days and meanwhile he might have some trouble with Mr. Dickinson. Rachel probably knew what the trouble would be and she did not ask. Rachel had had her private channels of information concerning the Sevier affray. At six-thirty Jackson joined Overton at Nashville. Overton had the pistols. With three others they departed for the Kentucky line.

Mr. Dickinson and eight companions were already on the road. "Goodby, darling," he told his young wife. "I shall be sure to be home tomorrow evening." This confidence was not altogether assumed. He was a snap shot. At the word of command and firing apparently without aim,

he could put four balls in a mark twenty-four feet away, each ball touching another. The persistent tradition on the countryside, that to worry
Jackson he left several such examples of his marksmanship along the
road, is unconfirmed by any member of the Dickinson or Jackson parties.
But the story that he had offered on the streets of Nashville to wager
he could kill Jackson at the first fire was vouchsafed by John Overton,
the brother of Jackson's second, a few days after the duel.

Jackson said he was glad that "the other side" had started so early.
It was a guarantee against further delay. Jackson had chafed over the
seven days that had elapsed since the acceptance of the challenge. At
their first interview, Overton and Dr. Hanson Catlett, Mr. Dickinson's
second, had agreed that the meeting should be on Friday, May thirtieth,
near Harrison's Mills on Red River just beyond the Kentucky boundary.
Jackson protested at once. He did not wish to ride forty miles to preserve
the fiction of a delicate regard for Tennessee's unenforceable statute
against dueling. He did not wish to wait a week for something that could
be done in a few hours. Dickinson's excuse was that he desired to borrow
a pair of pistols. Overton offered the choice of Jackson's pistols, pledging
Jackson to the use of the other. These were the weapons that had been
employed by Coffee and McNairy.

As they rode Jackson talked a great deal, scrupulously avoiding the
subject that burdened every mind. Really, however, there was nothing
more to be profitably said on that head. General Overton was a Revolutionary soldier of long acquaintance with the Code. With his principal
he had canvassed every possible aspect of the issue forthcoming. "Distance . . . twenty-four feet; the parties to stand facing each other, with
their pistols down perpendicularly. When they are READY, the single
word FIRE! to be given; at which they are to fire as soon as they please.
Should either fire before the word is given we [the seconds] pledge ourselves to shoot him down instantly." Jackson was neither a quick shot,
nor an especially good one for the western country. He had decided not
to compete with Dickinson for the first fire. He expected to be hit, perhaps
badly. But he counted on the resources of his will to sustain him until
he could aim deliberately and shoot to kill, if it were the last act of his
life.

*[Complication]*

On the first leg of the ride they traversed the old Kentucky road, the
route by which, fifteen years before, Andrew Jackson had carried Rachel
Robards from her husband's home, the present journey being a part of
the long sequel to the other. Jackson rambled on in a shrill voice. Thomas
Jefferson was "the best Republican in theory and the worst in practice"

he had ever seen. And he lacked courage. How long were we to support the affronts of England—impressment of seamen, cuffing about of our ocean commerce? Perhaps as long as Mr. Jefferson stayed in office. Well, that would be two years, and certainly his successor should be a stouter man. "We must fight England again. In the last war I was not old enough to be any account." He prayed that the next might come "before I get too old to fight."

General Overton asked how old Jackson reckoned he would have to be for that. In England's case about a hundred, Jackson said.

He spoke of Burr. A year ago, this day, Jackson had borne him from the banquet in Nashville to the Hermitage. He recalled their first meeting in 1797 when both were in Congress. Jackson also met General Hamilton that winter. "Personally, no gentleman could help liking Hamilton. But his political views were all English." At heart a monarchist. "Why, did he not urge Washington to take a crown!"

Burr also had his failings. He had made a mistake, observed Jackson, with admirable detachment, a political mistake, when he fought Hamilton. And about his Western projects the General was none too sanguine. Burr relied overmuch on what others told him. Besides, there was Jefferson to be reckoned with. "Burr is as far from a fool as I ever saw, and yet he is as easily fooled as any man I ever knew."

The day was warm, and a little after ten o'clock the party stopped for refreshment. Jackson took a mint julep, ate lightly and rested until mid-afternoon. The party reached Miller's Tavern in Kentucky about eight o'clock. After a supper of fried chicken, waffles, sweet potatoes and coffee, Jackson repaired to the porch to chat with the inn's company. No one guessed his errand. At ten o'clock he knocked the ashes from his pipe and went to bed. Asleep in ten minutes, he had to be roused at five in the morning.

The parties met on the bank of the Red River at a break in a poplar woods. Doctor Catlett won the toss for choice of position, but as the sun had not come through the trees this signified nothing. The giving of the word fell to Overton. Jackson's pistols were to be used after all, Dickinson taking his pick. The nine-inch barrels were charged with ounce balls of seventy caliber. The ground was paced off, the principals took their places. Jackson wore a dark-blue frock coat and trousers of the same material; Mr. Dickinson a shorter coat of blue, and gray trousers.

"Gentlemen, are you ready?" called General Overton.

"Ready," said Dickinson quickly.

"Yes, sir," said Jackson.

"*Fere!*" cried Overton in the Old-Country accent.

[*Denouement*]

Dickinson fired almost instantly. A fleck of dust rose from Jackson's coat and his left hand clutched his chest. For an instant he thought himself dying, but, fighting for self-command, slowly he raised his pistol.

Dickinson recoiled a step horror-stricken. "My God! Have I missed him?"

Overton presented his pistol. "Back to the mark, sir!"

Dickinson folded his arms. Jackson's spare form straightened. He aimed. There was a hollow "clock" as the hammer stopped at half-cock. He drew it back, sighted again and fired. Dickinson swayed to the ground.

As they reached the horses Overton noticed that his friend's left boot was filled with blood. "Oh, I believe that he pinked me," said Jackson quickly, "but I don't want those people to know," indicating the group that bent over Dickinson. Jackson's surgeon found that Dickinson's aim had been perfectly true, but he had judged the position of Jackson's heart by the set of his coat, and Jackson wore his coats loosely on account of the excessive slenderness of his figure. "But I should have hit him," he exclaimed, "if he had shot me through the brain."—MARQUIS JAMES: *The Life of Andrew Jackson*, Chap. 8.[4]

The event narrated above is historically true. It had causes running back before the episode of the duel (Dickinson had insulted Jackson's wife), and was to have consequences long after the duel. But the writer is not immediately concerned with causes or effects. He is concerned with rendering the episode itself, the duel. We can see that in doing so he naturally gives his account in three sections, the exposition, the complication, and the denouement, as we have indicated.

The exposition describes the attitudes of the two duelists as they make ready and gives the terms of the duel. The complication seems to have a good deal of material off the point—Jackson's long conversation about politics—but we shall see that even this apparent digression is related to the point the author wishes to make in his narrative. Then the complication gives the details as the opponents face each other and Dickinson fires. The denouement falls into two related parts, Jackson's self-command when hit and his shooting of Dickinson, and his remark after the event.

Both Vincent Sheean and Marquis James are using narrative to

[4] From *The Life of Andrew Jackson*. By Marquis James, copyright 1938. Used by special permission of the Publishers, the Bobbs-Merrill Company, Inc.

attitude toward her. In the episode itself we are concerned with the single, significant flash which exhibits Jackson's will. What preceded or followed the duel is not relevant to that consideration, taken in itself. Even though this little narrative is part of a much larger narrative, the account of Jackson's entire life, we are justified in interpreting it as a unit in so far as it is dominated by one basic intention.

One word of caution should be given before we leave the topic of proportion. In many cases of narrative, one cannot draw a single hard and fast line between, say, the exposition and the complication. Instead, there may be some overlapping or an intermingling of the two elements. A certain amount of exposition is always necessary early in a narrative, but we can recall instances, especially of extended narratives, in which the complication is interrupted by the insertion of bits of exposition. A biographer, for instance, may interrupt his narrative to explain a political situation, or a novelist may give what is called a CUTBACK to an earlier scene or situation needed to explain a present action (p. 263).

## APPLICATIONS

**I.** In the section on Readings study "The Siege of the Alamo," by Marquis James, and "I Get a Colt to Break In," by Lincoln Steffens. Indicate the general divisions of the action. In the middle, the complication, how many stages do you distinguish? Does the denouement have more than one element?

**II.** Select some subject, real or imaginary, which you think would make an interesting narrative. Make a set of informal notes dividing up the material and indicating the basic pattern which a narrative would take. What would be necessary in the exposition? In the complication? In the denouement? You might set these details and topics down under the proper heads in the order you feel they should appear in a finished narrative. When you have finished the notes, write a statement in a sentence or two giving what you consider to be the idea or point of the narrative to be written. Looking back over your notes, ask yourself if the material indicated would really make that point.

## TEXTURE AND SELECTION

When we turn from questions of organization to questions of detail we turn from pattern to texture. SELECTION is as important for narration as it is for description. Skillful selection permits a large action to be narrated in a relatively brief space without seeming to be stinted, as in the following account of the voyage of St. Paul to Rome:

Now when much time was spent, and when sailing was now dangerous, because the fast was now already past, Paul admonished them,

And said unto them, Sirs, I perceive that this voyage will be with hurt and much damage, not only of the lading and ship, but also of our lives.

Nevertheless the centurion believed the master and the owner of the ship, more than those things which were spoken by Paul.

And because the haven was not commodious to winter in, the more part advised to depart thence also, if by any means they might attain to Phenice, and there to winter; which is an haven of Crete, and lieth toward the southwest and northwest.

And when the south wind blew softly, supposing that they had obtained their purpose, loosing thence, they sailed close by Crete.

But not long after there arose against it a tempestuous wind called Euroclydon.

And when the ship was caught, and could not bear up into the wind, we let her drive.

And running under a certain island which is called Clauda, we had much work to come by the boat:

Which when they had taken up, they used helps, undergirding the ship; and, fearing lest they should fall into the quicksands, struck sail, and so were driven.

And we being exceedingly tossed with a tempest, the next day they lightened the ship;

And the third day we cast out with our own hands the tackling of the ship.

And when neither sun nor stars in many days appeared, and no small tempest lay on us, all hope that we should be saved was then taken away.

But after long abstinence Paul stood forth in the midst of them, and said, Sirs, ye should have hearkened unto me, and not have loosed from Crete, and to have gained this harm and loss.

And now I exhort you to be of good cheer: for there shall be no loss of any man's life among you, but of the ship.

For there stood by me this night the angel of God, whose I am, and whom I serve,

Saying, Fear not, Paul; thou must be brought before Caesar: and, lo, God hath given thee all them that sail with thee.

Wherefore, sirs, be of good cheer: for I believe God, that it shall be even as it was told me.

Howbeit we must be cast upon a certain island.

But when the fourteenth night was come, as we were driven up and down in Adria, about midnight the shipmen deemed that they drew near to some country;

And sounded, and found it twenty fathoms; and when they had gone a little further, they sounded again, and found it fifteen fathoms.

Then fearing lest we should have fallen upon rocks, they cast four anchors out of the stern, and wished for the day.

And as the shipmen were about to flee out of the ship, when they had let down the boat into the sea, under color as though they would have cast anchors out of the foreship,

Paul said to the centurion and to the soldiers, Except these abide in the ship, ye cannot be saved.

Then the soldiers cut off the ropes of the boat, and let her fall off.

And while the day was coming on, Paul besought them all to take meat, saying, This day is the fourteenth day that ye have tarried and continued fasting, having taken nothing.

Wherefore I pray you to take some meat: for this is for your health: for there shall not be an hair fallen from the head of any of you.

And when he had thus spoken, he took bread, and gave thanks to God in the presence of them all: and when he had broken it, he began to eat.

Then were they all of good cheer, and they also took some meat.

And we were in all in the ship two hundred threescore and sixteen souls.

And when they had eaten enough, they lightened the ship, and cast out the wheat into the sea.

And when it was day, they knew not the land: but they discovered a certain creek with a shore, into the which they were minded, if it were possible, to thrust in the ship.

And when they had taken up the anchors, they committed themselves unto the sea, and loosed the rudder bands, and hoisted up the mainsail to the wind, and made toward shore.

And falling into a place where two seas met, they ran the ship aground; and the forepart stuck fast, and remained unmoveable, but the hinder part was broken with the violence of the waves.

And the soldiers' counsel was to kill the prisoners, lest any of them should swim out, and escape.

But the centurion, willing to save Paul, kept them from their purpose; and commanded that they which could swim should cast themselves first into the sea, and get to land:

And the rest, some on boards, and some on broken pieces of the ship. And so it came to pass, that they escaped all safely to land.—Acts 27:9-44.

A writer does not want to present all the details of an event, either real or imaginary. He wants to present those which clarify the line of action and contribute to his point. No stage of the action should be omitted, yet no details should be included which distract from the real concern of the narrative. There is no arbitrary rule in such a matter. A writer must keep firmly in mind what his real concern is and judge for himself. For example, in the episode of Jackson's duel, it might seem at first glance that the section about Jackson's conversation on the road is unnecessary and distracts from the real concern of the narrative. But this would be so only if the duel itself were taken to be the real concern. Actually, the real intent of the author is the revelation of Jackson's character, and, therefore, the conversation on the way, illustrating his calmness and confidence, is relevant to the effect intended.

Even in a narrative dealing with fact the author may heighten the interest by leaving out merely casual material. In treating the episode of Jackson's duel Marquis James may know that, after his opponent was hit, Jackson actually said more than is given here. The author, however, presents just those remarks which contribute to our awareness of Jackson's character. In dealing with matters of fact, a writer does not want to distort the truth by omissions, but the mere fact can scarcely justify itself. The narrator should be concerned with the significant fact. When he is dealing with imaginary events, the writer has a freer hand and a greater responsibility; for now he cannot rely on the interest which mere fact as fact can sometimes evoke in the reader. With the imaginary narrative a detail can never pay its way because it is interesting in itself. It must contribute to the main business or to the vividness of the impression.

A narrative is a more or less immediate presentation of events. Therefore vividness is important, the detail which can stir the imagination. The small gesture, the trivial word, may be important here. And here the details which, strictly speaking, are descriptive may be absorbed into the narrative effect. For instance, the cut and color of Jackson's and Dickinson's clothes, the kind of woods by which the meeting took place, and the Irish accent of General Overton when he gave the command to fire contribute to the impression of reality. Marquis James is much concerned to give an immediate presentation, but if we turn back to Vincent Sheean's anecdote of the Duke of Windsor and Churchill, we find that immediacy is not very important to the author. He is chiefly concerned to present a clash of opinions. Even here, however, we get the details of the Stuart tartan which the kilted Duke wears, his posture on the sofa, and Churchill's position staring at the floor.

## APPLICATIONS

**I.** In the section of Readings study "The Hickman Story" by John Bartlow Martin or "Mary Queen of Scots" by James Froude to locate details which are especially vivid or contribute to the main concern of the narrative chosen.

**II.** Take the outline of a narrative which you have prepared in the last exercise and from it write a narrative of some 500 or 600 words. Then criticize your selection of details on the basis of significance and vividness. If you are not satisfied, revise your composition.

## POINT OF VIEW

The term POINT OF VIEW implies some of the most important considerations of narration. In ordinary speech this phrase has a meaning different from the meaning of the technical term to be discussed here. In ordinary speech we say, "From my point of view, I think James was perfectly right," or, "I understand Sarah's point of view, but I don't agree with it." What we understand by point of view in these two statements is an attitude, a set of values, a body of ideas, or something of that order. We could rewrite the sentences above in these terms and not change the meaning: "According to my set of values (or my ideas, or my attitude), I think James was perfectly right." Or: "I understand Sarah's ideas (or set of values, or attitude), but I don't agree with them." But in discussing narration we shall use the term to mean the point from which the action of a narrative is viewed.

In discussing point of view in description we mean a physical point from which the specified or implied observer looks at the thing described (pp. 225-27). In discussing narration we do not mean a physical point; we mean, rather, a person who bears some relation to the action, either as observer or participant, and whose intelligence serves as the index of the action for the reader. Point of view, then, involves two questions: Who tells the story? What is his relation to the action?

In broad terms, there are two possible points of view, the first person and the third person. When we read, "That summer when we were staying at Bayport, I had the most astonishing experience of my life," we know that we are dealing with the first-person point of view. When we read, "When Jake Millen, at the age of sixty, surveyed the wreck of his career, he knew that only one course was left open to him," we know that we are dealing with a third-person point of view. That is, in the first example, an "I," real or fictitious, is telling us about an experience in which he himself was involved; in the second example, an author, writing impersonally, is telling us about an experience in which another person was involved.

There are, however, certain shadings and variations possible within these two broad general divisions of point of view.

What are the variations possible within the first person? The distinctions here are to be made on the basis of the relation of the first-person narrator to the action which he narrates. There are two extreme positions possible here. First, the narrator may tell of an action in which he is the main, or at least an important, participant. That is, he tells his "own story." We are all familiar with this type of treatment. Most autobiographies, for example, are of this kind; for example, the life of Lincoln Steffens (see Readings, p. 85). Occasionally we encounter a piece of informal history using this method, for example, T. E. Lawrence's *Seven Pillars of Wisdom*. Many short stories and novels create an imaginary "I" who is the main character of the story and who tells the story. For instance, Defoe's *Robinson Crusoe*, or Hemingway's *A Farewell to Arms*.

At the other extreme, the narrator, either real or imaginary, recounts an action of which he is merely an observer. This, also, is a familiar type of treatment. Memoirs tend to take this form, for frequently the writer of memoirs has not himself played a conspicuous role in affairs but has been in a position to observe important events. The account of General Eisenhower by his aide, Captain Butcher, is a good example of this type. The same type of treatment appears, of course, in fiction. Poe's "The Fall of the House of Usher" is a notable instance, and Ring Lardner's story "Haircut" is another.

Thus we may have the two types of the first-person point of view: *narrator—main character*, and *narrator—mere observer*. But in between these two extremes many variations are possible, cases in which the narrator participates directly in the action and has something at stake in its outcome but in which he is not the main character.

But what of the variations possible within the third-person point of view?

In this point of view the narrative is given by an author writing impersonally, that is, as a kind of disembodied intelligence before whom the events are played out. What is the relation of this impersonal author, this disembodied intelligence, to the action? In the first place, he does not participate in the action; he is merely an observer. The question then becomes this: How much of the action does the author observe? And here, as in dealing with the first-person point of view, we can define the two extreme positions.

One extreme we may call the PANORAMIC point of view. In this method the author may report any aspect or all aspects of an action, and may go into the head of any or all of the characters involved in the action. His eye, as it were, sweeps the entire field and he reports whatever is interesting or relevant. In an imaginary narrative there is no limit to what may be seen or reported according to this method, the most private acts and the most secret thoughts or sensations of any or all of the characters may be reported, for the author is the creator of the whole thing. But when a writer is using this method in presenting a nonimaginative narrative, say a piece of history, he is, of course, limited by what facts or plausible deductions are available to him. He cannot be as thoroughgoing in applying the method as the writer of an imaginary narrative, though within the limits of the facts available to him he may do so. Many pieces of historical and biographical writing use this method, and, of course, it is not uncommon in fiction. For instance, it appears in the following scene from Thackeray's novel *Vanity Fair,* presenting the city of Brussels when the false news comes that Napoleon has won the Battle of Quatre Bras, an engagement just before Waterloo.

We of peaceful London city have never beheld—and please God shall never witness—such a scene of hurry and alarm as that which Brussels presented. Crowds rushed to the Namur gate, from which direction the noise proceeded, and many rode along the level *chaussée*, to be in advance of any intelligence from the army. Each man asked his neighbor for news; and even great English lords and ladies condescended to speak to persons whom they did not know. The friends of the French went abroad, wild with excitement, and prophesying the triumph of their Emperor. The merchants closed their shops, and came out to swell the general chorus of alarm and clamor. Women rushed to the churches, and crowded the chapels, and knelt and prayed on the flags and steps. The dull sound of cannon went on rolling, rolling. Presently carriages with travellers began to leave the town, galloping away by the Ghent barrier. The prophecies of the French partisans began to pass for facts. "He has cut the army in two," it was said. "He is marching straight on Brussels. He will overpower the English, and be here tonight." "He will overpower the English," shrieked Isidor to his master, "and will be here tonight." The man bounded in and out from the lodgings to the street, always returning with some fresh particulars of disaster. Jos's face grew paler and paler. Alarm began to take entire possession of the stout civilian. All the champagne he drank brought no courage to him. Before sunset he was worked up to such a pitch of nervousness as gratified his friend Isidor to behold, who now counted upon the spoils of the owner of the laced coat.

The women were away all this time. After hearing the firing for a moment, the stout Major's wife bethought her of her friend in the next chamber, and ran in to watch, and if possible to console, Amelia. The idea that she had that helpless and gentle creature to protect, gave additional strength to the natural courage of the honest Irishwoman. She passed five hours by her friend's side, sometimes in remonstrance, sometimes talking cheerfully, oftener in silence, and terrified mental supplication.—WILLIAM MAKEPEACE THACKERAY: *Vanity Fair*, Chap. 32.

At the other extreme from the panoramic point of view we find what we may call the point of view of SHARP FOCUS. The author does not sweep the entire field of the action, but keeps his, and his reader's, attention focused on one character and on that character's relation to the action. Accordingly, the parts of the action not directly participated in by the selected character are not reported by the author. To use a figure of speech, the character may be regarded as a kind of prism through which the action is refracted. Here is an example of the method:

He was hungry, for, except some biscuits which he had asked two grudging curates to bring him, he had eaten nothing since breakfast-

time. He sat down at an uncovered wooden table opposite two work-girls
and a mechanic. A slatternly girl waited on him.

"How much is a plate of peas?" he asked.

"Three halfpence, sir," said the girl.

"Bring me a plate of peas," he said, "and a bottle of ginger beer."

He spoke roughly in order to belie his air of gentility for his entry
had been followed by a pause of talk. His face was heated. To appear
natural he pushed his cap back on his head and planted his elbows on
the table. The mechanic and the two work-girls examined him point by
point before resuming their conversation in a subdued voice. The girl
brought him a plate of grocer's hot peas, seasoned with pepper and
vinegar, a fork and his ginger beer. He ate his food greedily and found
it so good that he made a note of the shop mentally. When he had eaten
all the peas he sipped his ginger beer and sat for some time thinking of
Corley's adventure. In his imagination he beheld the pair of lovers walking along some dark road; he heard Corley's voice in deep energetic
gallantries, and saw again the leer of the young woman's mouth. This
vision made him feel keenly his own poverty of purse and spirit. He was
tired of knocking about, of pulling the devil by the tail, of shifts and
intrigues. He would be thirty-one in November. Would he never get a
good job? Would he never have a home of his own? He thought how
pleasant it would be to have a warm fire to sit by and a good dinner to
sit down to. He had walked the streets long enough with friends and
with girls. He knew what those friends were worth: he knew the girls
too. Experience had embittered his heart against the world. But all
hope had not left him. He felt better after having eaten than he had
felt before, less weary of his life, less vanquished in spirit. He might yet
be able to settle down in some snug corner and live happily if he could
only come across some good simple-minded girl with a little of the
ready.—JAMES JOYCE: "Two Gallants," *Dubliners*.[5]

In between the extremes of the panoramic point of view and the
point of view of sharp focus there are, of course, all sorts of gradations and mixtures of the two methods. The choice of one of the
methods or the mixing of the two is not a matter to be settled
arbitrarily, for the method should reflect a special interest involved in the narrative. For instance, the panoramic point of view
is well suited to the rendering of some large and complicated action,
a battle, a mob scene, the burning of a city, where the interest lies

---

[5] From *Dubliners* by James Joyce, copyright, 1925, by The Viking Press,
Inc., and now included in *The Portable James Joyce*, published by The Viking
Press, Inc., New York.

in the sweep of events. Or the point of view of sharp focus is suited to a narrative in which the interest is primarily in the psychological analysis of the experience of some single character. A narrative may well involve both such interests, and then the writer may mix his methods according to the need of the particular moment.

But use of the panoramic point of view is not restricted to action which covers a physically broad field, like a battle. Take, for instance, this example:

One night toward the end of March Gertrude did not appear for dinner. She had never been absent at the evening meal before, though it was a common enough occurrence in the house.

"One of our sheep has strayed," the red-haired woman said. Now that spring was coming she had returned to the brown silk dress she had worn in the fall. A smile of calculated indifference was on her face. "Perhaps she is wandering by the docks and sighing for her homeland."

"What do you mean?" Marian said.

The woman pulled her salad plate closer to the edge of the table and poised her fork over it thoughtfully. "Nothing is so good as Europe, you know," she said, looking up from her plate and glancing at the entire table with the easy innocence and half-surprise of the guilty.

"You know that isn't true," Marian said sharply. "For Gertrude America appears more beautiful than any country can be in reality."

"They are very tricky," the woman said flatly.

The others at the table were listening, alternately seeming to agree with both Marian and the woman, and then suddenly and cautiously retreating into themselves, admitting to nothing except the existence of all possibilities. Florence was sitting at the end of the table and had not heard the first part of the conversation. "Where is Gertrude?" she said abruptly.

"Flown the coop," a timid young girl said.

"Have you seen her all day?" Marian asked. "I haven't."

Florence said that she had not. The meal went on.

A woman, close to seventy, with hair dyed jet black, brushed past the table and hobbled over to her own group. One of her feet was slightly malformed and it made her walk strangely, as if she were constantly trotting. She seldom ever spoke to anyone and seemed deeply engrossed in work of enormous importance.—ELIZABETH HARDWICK: *The Ghostly Lover,* Chap. 25.[6]

[6] From *The Ghostly Lover* by Elizabeth Hardwick, copyright, 1945, by Elizabeth Hardwick. Reprinted by permission of Harcourt, Brace and Company, Inc.

Here we find the event rendered as it would appear to the mere observer, in its externals only. The scene is restricted but the use of the panoramic method gives a kind of psychological distance, an impersonality, which corresponds in effect to the physical distance and impersonality one finds in the panoramic rendering of a scene which is physically large.

## SCALE

The foregoing discussion leads us logically into a consideration of what may be called SCALE in narrative. As the dominant interest in a narrative or a part of a narrative may define the point of view, so it may define the scale on which it is treated. Here, too, we can think in terms of extremes of method, SUMMARY RENDERING and FULL RENDERING. The tendency in narration is to reduce the scale to that of summary in parts which are necessary only for continuity or, as it were, scaffolding, and to expand the scale in those parts which present the more significant moments. The following selection, which concludes Guy de Maupassant's story "The Diamond Necklace" illustrates the principle clearly. The main character, Mathilde Loisel, has been a vain, frivolous woman, who lived in day dreams of rich and fashionable life. When she is finally invited to a ball she borrows what she understands to be a diamond necklace from a friend, Madame Forestier. The necklace is lost at the ball, and Mathilde and her husband buy one to replace it, getting the money from usurers. At this point the selection picks up the story:

She learned the heavy cares of a household, the odious work of a kitchen. She washed the dishes, using her rosy nails upon the greasy pots and the bottoms of the stewpans. She washed the soiled linen, the chemises and dishcloths, which she hung on the line to dry; she took down the refuse to the street each morning and brought up the water, stopping at each landing to breathe. And, clothed like a woman of the people, she went to the grocer's, the butcher's, and the fruiterer's, with her basket on her arm, shopping, haggling to the last sou her miserable money.

Every month it was necessary to renew some notes, thus obtaining time, and to pay others.

The husband worked evenings, putting the accounts of some merchant in order, and at night he often copied manuscript at five sou a page.

And this life lasted ten years.

At the end of ten years, they had restored all, all, with interest of the usurers, and the compound interest besides.

Mme. Loisel looked old now. She had become a strong, hard woman, the rough woman of the poor household. Her hair tangled, her skirts awry, her hands red, she talked in loud tones, and washed the floors with a great swishing of water. But sometimes, when her husband was at the office, she would sit by the window and remember that evening of the ball, where she had been so beautiful and so happy.

What would have happened if she had not lost the necklace? Who knows? Who knows? How life is strange and changeful! How little is needed to ruin one or to save one!

One Sunday, as she was walking in the Champs Elysées, to restore herself after the work of the week, she suddenly saw a woman with a child. It was Madame Forestier, still young, still beautiful, still charming. Madame Loisel was moved. Should she speak to her? Yes, certainly. Now that she had paid, she would tell her all. Why not?

She approached her. "Good morning, Jeanne."

Her friend did not recognize her, and was surprised to be addressed by this woman of the people. She stammered: "But, Madame—I do not know—you must be mistaken—"

"No, I am Mathilde Loisel."

Her friend uttered a cry of surprise: "Oh, my poor Mathilde! How you are changed—"

"Yes, I have seen some hard days since I saw you—some miserable ones —and all because of you—"

"Because of me? How?"

"You remember the diamond necklace you loaned me to wear to the Minister's ball?"

"Yes, very well."

"Well, I lost it."

"How is that, since you returned it to me?"

"I returned one like it. And it has taken us ten years to pay for it. You can understand that it was not easy for us who have nothing. But it is finished, and I am very glad."

Madame Forestier stopped. She said: "You say that you bought a diamond necklace to replace mine?"

"Yes. You did not know it then? They were very like."

And she smiled with a joy that was proud and naive.

Madame Forestier was touched, and seized both her hands as she said: "Oh, my poor Mathilde! My necklace was false. It was not worth over five hundred francs!"—GUY DE MAUPASSANT: "The Diamond Neck-lace."

We notice here that the first half of the passage covers a time of ten years, the second half a time of three or four minutes. The ten years are summarized. The meeting in the park is rendered fully, word for word, instant by instant. We can readily see the reason why the writer summarized the ten years: they are all alike, a dreary grind of misery, and what is important is their result, Mathilde's new energy and fortitude, not the single events within them. As for the last scene, we can see that it is important in itself: it is dramatic, it is the moment when Mathilde realizes her situation, it is the result of all her past experience.

In the half of the selection rendered by summary we observe, however, that certain details do give us the impression of the qual-ity and movement of life—Mathilde's bargaining, her voice now coarse and rough, the way she scrubs the floor with great swishing sweeps of the wet mop. Narrative summary differs from the mere summary of ideas; when successful it still gives some hint of the quality and movement of life.

## APPLICATIONS

I. In the Readings what point of view is used in "Dawn over Zero," by William Laurence, "Reveries over Childhood," by W. B. Yeats, and "Siege of the Alamo," by Marquis James?

II. Write a brief narrative, about 250 words, in the third person, with a sharp focus, presenting a character's feelings and thoughts, as well as his actions.

## DIALOGUE

Narration often involves the use of dialogue—not only fiction but historical writing, biography, and other types. Dialogue sometimes seems to be an easy way to get a story told. The writer—especially an inexperienced writer—thinks that he knows how people talk and that to set down talk will be easier than to present material in the straight narrative form which he himself will have to compose. But the problem is not so simple as that. First, to compose effective dialogue is not easy, and second, the continual use of dialogue tends to give an impression of monotony.

On the first point it can be said that dialogue which is effective on the page is rarely a direct transcript of what people would say in conversation. Conversation is often stumbling, wandering, diffuse. The real point at issue in an actual conversation frequently becomes lost in mere wordiness or in the distractions of side issues and matters of incidental interest. The writer of dialogue cannot afford to duplicate such a conversation; if he does so, the reader will not be readily able to follow the line of significance. So the writer must organize the material to permit the reader to follow the development of the issue at stake. There must be an impression of give-and-take and a forward thrust of idea.

Let us examine a piece of unsatisfactory dialogue:

Gertrude collapsed into her chair, helpless with amusement; giving herself up to her laughter, she made him feel suddenly ashamed of that remembered delight.

"Oh—oh—oh—oh!" she cried. "That is the most ridiculous thing I ever heard of. You call that girl a shy arbutus. And at your age, too. You certainly are silly."

"Well! I don't think it is so funny. You don't know the girl the way I do, and furthermore she is very modest and appealing. All sorts of people think so. For example, I have heard Mrs. Buckley say—"

"The shy arbutus! As I said, it is perfectly ridiculous. I don't want to be impolite, but she isn't exactly an arbutus, and as for Mrs. Buckley's opinion, you know what a sentimental old biddy she is, and how she gushes over everything. A shy arbutus. Forgive me, Harry, but that's too funny. How old *are* you?"

He flung his cigarette at the back-log and grinned.

"I knew it was no use," he grumbled amiably. "I can't make you see her, and it's no use trying. I know Mrs. Buckley is sentimental and does gush, but I don't think I am gushy, and I have also heard Tom Barker comment on the girl. Very favorably, too. And he is a hard-headed sort of fellow. Why, you remember, don't you, how he always brings a conversation right down to common sense. There was that time we were talking about performance of that pianist—you know, the one who played at the Murdocks' house—last November—and everybody said how good she was, but Tom just said, 'Nuts, all she's got is ten quite ordinary fingers and a very extraordinary figure—but it is the fingers that have to play the piano!' That's just like old Tom. But to come back to the subject, Tom may understand the girl, but I can't make you see her, and it's no use trying."

"I heard that pianist, and she was rather good, I thought. Whatever Tom Barker thought. But the trouble with you is, you're in love with this girl. It is a well known fact that a man in love is not able to exercise his best judgment. But it's precisely when you're in love that you need to keep your wits about you. Or the wits of your friends. Now I've come to the conclusion that you *mustn't* marry her, Harry. There are very good reasons."

"Well—I don't know. I don't think that being in love has done anything to my judgment."

"*No!* It is certainly my considered opinion that to marry that girl would be ruinous for you. You must think about your career. And more important, about your happiness. Won't she bore you to death in three years. She is quite dull. Now the kind of girl you want is somebody with some spirit and mischief. A girl who has got some smartness, and who could amuse your friends. Think of the dull parties with this girl in the saddle."

The trouble here is that the dialogue is loaded with irrelevant material. People do load their conversations with irrelevant material, but dialogue in narrative cannot afford that weight. It kills the forward thrust.

Let us now look at the same piece of dialogue as it actually occurs in a story, stripped to the essentials:

"Oh—oh—oh—oh!" she cried.

"Well!"

"The shy arbutus! . . . Forgive me, Harry, but that's too funny. How old *are* you?"

He flung his cigarette at the back-log and grinned.

"I knew it was no use," he grunted amiably. "I can't make you see her, and it's no use trying."

"Well—I can see this much. You *are* in love with her. Or you couldn't possibly be such a fool. But it's precisely when you're in love that you need to keep your wits about you. Or the wits of your friends. . . . You *mustn't* marry her, Harry."

"Well—I don't know."

"*No!* . . . It would be ruinous."—CONRAD AIKEN: "Spider, Spider." [7]

[7] From "Spider, Spider" in *Costumes by Eros,* published by Charles Scribner's Sons. Copyright, 1928, by Conrad Aiken.

In the passage above the line of interest is clear, and the collision between Gertrude and Harry is quite definite. In the expanded version there is a blurring of the effect. This blurred effect may actually be given by the conversation of a Gertrude and Harry in real life, but that has no final bearing on the case here. The problem of the writer of dialogue is a problem of selection and logical organization.

There is also, however, the problem of giving the dialogue a realistic surface. There must be, in addition to the logical organization, an impression of real life, a sense of the pauses, the changes, the waverings of conversation. But this must be an *impression* and not a word-for-word recording. There is no rule for giving this impression, but there are certain considerations which may help a writer to give it.

First, we can notice, as in the example above, that the breaks and the italicized words are of some use in this respect. We get the impression of the sudden shift of idea or the hesitancy of a speaker. And from the italicized words we get the impression of Gertrude's voice, with the slight satirical emphasis. But these are devices that would not always apply, and in any case should be used sparingly.

Second, and more important, the writer can try to indicate the fact that each speaker has his own way of phrasing things and his own rhythm of voice. Expertness in giving such an impression can only come from close observation—an awareness of the little catch phrases a person tends to repeat, of the type of sentence structure he tends to use, of the mannerisms of speech.

Third, in addition to the individual qualities of speech, there are the qualities dependent on cultural background, race, geographical origin, and so forth, qualities which are shared by members of a group. The commonest way to indicate such qualities is by mere dialectal peculiarities, when that will apply at all. But mere peculiarity of spelling is a crude device, and in the end usually becomes monotonous. It is better for the writer to use such a device sparingly, and to focus his attention on the vocabulary, idiom, and rhythm of the class to which his speaking character belongs.

Here are some examples in which the language used by a speaker gives some impression of his social group and of his individuality:

A boy who is the son of a jockey:

I guess looking at it, now, my old man was cut out for a fat guy, one of those regular little roly fat guys you see around, but he sure never got that way, except a little toward the last, and then it wasn't his fault, he was riding over the jumps only and he could afford to carry plenty of weight then. I remember the way he'd pull on a rubber shirt over a couple of jerseys and a big sweat shirt over that, and got me to run with him in the forenoon in the hot sun.—ERNEST HEMINGWAY: "My Old Man." [8]

## A Southern Negro:

"What makes you want to talk like that before these chillen?" Nancy said. "Whyn't you go on to work. You done et. You want Mr. Jason to catch you hanging around his kitchen, talking that way before these chillen?"

"Talking what way?" Caddy said.

"I cant hang around white man's kitchen," Jesus said. "But white man can hang around mine. White man can come in my house, but I cant stop him. When white man wants to come in my house, I aint got no house. I cant stop him, but he cant kick me outen it. He cant do that."
—WILLIAM FAULKNER: "That Evening Sun." [9]

## A pretentious, servile woman:

"Well now, that is so like you," returned Miss Knag. "Ha! ha! ha! Of club feet! Oh very good. As I often remark to the young ladies, 'Well I must say, and I do not care who knows it, of all the ready humor—hem—I ever heard anywhere'—and I have heard a good deal; for when my dear brother was alive (I kept house for him, Miss Nickleby), we had to supper once a week two or three young men, highly celebrated in those days for their humor, Madame Mantalini—'Of all the ready humor,' I say to the young ladies, 'I ever heard, Madame Mantalini's is the most remarkable—hem. It is so gentle, so sarcastic, and yet so good-natured (as I was observing to Miss Simmonds only this morning), that how, or when, or by what means she acquired it, is to me a mystery indeed.'"

Here Miss Knag paused to take breath, and while she pauses it may be observed—not that she was marvellously loquacious and marvellously deferential to Madame Mantalini, since these are facts which require no comment; but that every now and then, she was accustomed, in the

[8] From *Three Stories and Ten Poems* by Ernest Hemingway, copyright, 1923, by Charles Scribner's Sons.

[9] From "That Evening Sun," *These Thirteen* by William Faulkner, copyright, 1931, by Random House, Inc.

torrent of her discourse, to introduce a loud, shrill, clear, "hem!" the import and meaning of which was variously interpreted by her acquaintance . . .—CHARLES DICKENS: *Nicholas Nickleby,* Chap. 17.

A fatherly professor:

"You may be right, and then you may have a one-sided view. When I say that your prejudice is literary, I mean that you have read what universities are like and applied that reading here. You have condemned without participating. You know, there may be good things, even in this town. Why, I sometimes think you even like me a bit." Dr. Whitlock smiled. "You see, there is indifference, intellectual servility, a vague attempt at education. But to know these things is not enough. You have to go deeper, you must understand; your conviction must be intellectual as well as emotional. There are more than economic reasons at stake, and there may be greater social injustice in this small university town than in the smashing of a miner's strike by hired bullies."—MICHAEL DE CAPITE: *No Bright Banner,* Chap. 7.[10]

We have said earlier that logical organization, the development of the point at issue in a dialogue, is extremely important. But occasionally there is little or no point at issue, and then the intended significance of a passage may be the exhibition of the speaker's character, as in the speech by Miss Knag from *Nicholas Nickleby,* quoted above. There the wandering sentences, the interpolations, and the characteristic "hem!" indicate the quality of her mind, just as some of the remarks themselves indicate her mixture of vanity, pretentiousness, and servility.

In some instances, of course, a piece of dialogue may develop a point and at the same time contain elements which are irrelevant to that point but indicate the character of the speaker. Here is the famous passage between Falstaff and Mistress Quickly, who is trying to remind Falstaff that he had promised to marry her. Her talkativeness and fuzzy-mindedness appear here in the very way she presents the argument, the point, to Falstaff:

Marry, if thou wert an honest man, thyself and the money too. Thou didst swear to me upon a parcel-gilt goblet, sitting in my Dolphin-chamber, at the round table, by a seacoal fire, upon Wednesday in Wheeson-week, when the prince broke thy head for liking his father to

[10] Reprinted from *No Bright Banner* by Michael de Capite, by permission of The John Day Company, Inc.

a singing-man of Windsor, thou didst swear to me then, as I was washing thy wound, to marry me and make me my lady thy wife. Canst thou deny it? Did not goodwife Keech, the butcher's wife, come in then and call me gossip Quickly? coming in to borrow a mess of vinegar; telling us she had a good dish of prawns; whereby thou didst desire to eat some, whereby I told thee they were ill for a green wound? And didst thou not, when she was gone down stairs, desire me to be no more so familiarity with such poor people; saying that ere long they would call me madam? And didst thou not kiss me and bid me fetch thee thirty shillings?—WILLIAM SHAKESPEARE: *Henry IV, Part II,* Act II.

## CHARACTERIZATION

Early in this discussion we pointed out the relation between persons and action. Most narratives, from news stories to novels, are about people. Things happen to people and people make things happen. To understand an action we must understand the people involved, their natures, their motives, their responses, and to present an action so that it is satisfying we must present the people. This process is called CHARACTERIZATION.

A news story gives a minimum of characterization. It merely identifies the persons involved—"Adam Perkins, age thirty-three, of 1217 Sunset Drive"—and then proceeds to give the bare facts of the event. If it deals with motive it does so in the barest possible way. If Adam Perkins has committed suicide, the news story may report that he had been in ill health and had, according to his wife, been worrying about financial reverses, but it will give no detail. On the other hand, a novel or biography usually gives very full characterization. It seeks to make us understand very fully the relation between the character and the events and the effect of events on character. In between the news story and the novel or biography, there are all sorts of narratives which present more or less fully the relationship between character and event and which try to answer the fundamental questions: Why does the character do what he does to cause the event? Why does he respond as he does to the event?

To answer these questions, the writer of a narrative must characterize the person. This is as important for narratives dealing with matters of fact, such as biography or history, as it is for narratives dealing with imaginary persons, such as novels or short stories. The difference between the two types is simply this: The biographer must interpret the facts in order to understand the character and present him, and the writer of fiction must create the details in order to present the character.

Whether the details of a character are drawn from fact or from imagination, it is important to remember that a character cannot be effectively presented as a mere accumulation of details. The details must be related to each other to build up a unified impression, the sense of an individual personality. As this impression of an individual personality relates to an action, we are concerned with motive or response. What is the main motive of a character, or what is his main response? We must be sure that we have an answer to this question before we can give an effective characterization. Then we must be sure that we have given a clear indication of this main fact of the character.

Once the main fact of the character is established in the writer's mind, he must relate other details of the character to it. That is, the character must be consistent. We know that real people are often very complicated and do things which seem inconsistent. The same person does good things and bad things, generous things and selfish things, wise things and stupid things, but even so, we usually feel that there is an explanation for such inconsistency, that the very inconsistencies can be understood in relation to a deeper consistency of character. And the object of the writer should be to contribute to this deeper understanding of character. He may present the inconsistent details, but at the same time he wants to present them as part of a comprehensible whole. There is no formula for accomplishing this, and the only way we can learn to do it is by studying human nature as we can observe it in life and in books.

Once the conception of a character is clear, we can, however, think systematically about methods of presenting it. Generally speaking, there are five methods: by appearance and mannerisms, by analysis, by speech, by reaction of other persons, by action.

Appearance and mannerisms really involve description, considered independently or as absorbed into narration, but description as an indication of the inner nature of persons. We have already seen how in Dickens's description of Chadband (p. 238) the physical oiliness of the man is taken as a lead to his "oily" personality, and how his mannerism of lifting a hand before speaking gives the suggestion of false piety and vanity, of a hypocritical preacher.

As the method of description suggests the character, that of analysis states it and explains it. This is really a kind of exposition drawn into the service of narration. It may be very obvious and systematic, as when we write:

Jack Staple's character is marked by what seems, at first inspection, to be a fundamental inconsistency: on some occasions he is kind and generous even to a fault, and at the same time he is capable of extreme cruelty. But the inconsistency disappears into a frightening consistency once we realize that the spring of his every action is a profound egotism, an egotism which can express itself as well through good as through evil. Both gratitude and fear can flatter his ego.

But in the following example, the analysis is absorbed into the account of a meeting between T. E. Lawrence, the British agent sent to Arabia in World War I to stir a revolt against Turkey, and a chieftain whom he was considering as a possible leader of the revolt:

Abdulla, on a white mare, came to us softly with a bevy of richly armed slaves on foot about him, through the silent respectful salutes of the town. He was flushed with his success at Taif, and happy. I was seeing him for the first time, while Storrs was an old friend, and on the best of terms; yet, before long, as they spoke together, I began to suspect him of a constant cheerfulness. His eyes had a confirmed twinkle; and though only thirty-five, he was putting on flesh. It might be due to too much laughter. Life seemed very merry for Abdulla. He was short, strong, fair-skinned, with a carefully trimmed brown beard, masking his round smooth face and short lips. In manner he was open, or affected openness, and was charming on acquaintance. He stood not on ceremony, but jested with all comers in most easy fashion; yet, when we fell into serious talk, the veil of humour seemed to fade away. He then chose his words, and argued shrewdly. Of course, he was in discussion with Storrs, who demanded a high standard from his opponent.

The Arabs thought Abdulla a far-seeing statesman and an astute politician. Astute he certainly was, but not greatly enough to convince us always of his sincerity. His ambition was patent. Rumour made him the brain of his father and of the Arab revolt; but he seemed too easy for that. His object was, of course, the winning of Arab independence and the building up of Arab nations, but he meant to keep the direction of the new states in the family. So he watched us, and played through us to the British gallery.

On our part, I was playing for effect, watching, criticizing him. The Sherif's rebellion had been unsatisfactory for the last few months (standing still, which, with an irregular war, was the prelude to disaster): and my suspicion was that its lack was leadership: not intellect, nor judgment, nor political wisdom, but the flame of enthusiasm, that would set the desert on fire. My visit was mainly to find the yet unknown master-spirit of the affair, and measure his capacity to carry the revolt to the goal I had conceived for it. As our conversation continued, I became more and more sure that Abdulla was too balanced, too cool, too humorous to be a prophet: especially the armed prophet who, if history be true, succeeded in revolutions. His value would come perhaps in the peace after success. During the physical struggle, when singleness of eye and magnetism, devotion and self-sacrifice were needed, Abdulla would be a tool too complex for a simple purpose, though he could not be ignored, even now.—T. E. LAWRENCE: *Seven Pillars of Wisdom*, Chap. 8.[11]

Under the topic of dialogue we have already discussed some of the ways by which speech indicates character: Miss Knag's habit of saying "hem," or the professor's special, somewhat stilted vocabulary and turn of phrase. But further, we must distinguish between what is said and the way of saying it. The ideas or attitudes expressed should spring from the character and exhibit it, and the vocabulary, rhythm, and mannerisms (if there are mannerisms) should be significant.

It is difficult to find a brief example of the method of indicating character by the reactions of other people, for usually a fully developed scene is required to make such a point. But the principle is simple and we can observe it constantly in real life: the feelings and behavior of those around a person act as a mirror of that person's character. And we often encounter it in narratives, sometimes with some such obvious signal as, "When I first met Mr. Dobbs, I felt an uneasiness which I was at a loss to explain, for he was so civil, so fatherly . . ."; but the method may be used without the signal. The reactions may form part of the narrative itself.

The method which most concerns the writer of narrative is, of course, the exhibiting of character through action. Again it is diffi-

[11] From: *Seven Pillars of Wisdom* by T. E. Lawrence. Copyright 1926, 1935 by Doubleday & Company, Inc.

cult to illustrate this method by a brief extract, for we can be sure
that a single act is properly expressive of character only if we test
that act against the other acts in the narrative. Any good short story
or novel or biography will illustrate the matter. But in general terms,
we must ask if the particular incident is vivid, significant in itself,
and consistent with other incidents. Our final test here is human
nature, and thorough observation is the best teacher.

## APPLICATIONS

I. In the section of Readings study "The Webb School," by J. A. Rice,
"Mary Queen of Scots," by James A. Froude, "The Last Days," by
Richard Wingfield, and "Mrs. Battle's Opinions on Whist," by Charles
Lamb. Do you find any effective examples of rendering character by
description, by analysis, by speech, by reactions of others, or by action?

II. Write a piece of characteristic dialogue on any subject illustrating
the speech of some member of a special group such as college students,
lawyers, Irish laborers, Southern Negroes, ranch hands, or clergymen.

III. Take a person, real or imaginary, and write an analysis of his
character, in some 150 or 200 words. Then compose a narrative of 500
words in which this person exhibits his character in action and speech.

## SUMMARY

Narration is the kind of discourse concerned with action, with
life in motion. It tells a story. An action, as we use the word here,
may be discussed with reference to *movement, time,* and *meaning.*

The essence of narration is to give a sense of movement—the passing from one stage to another stage. Narration does not explain a
process but places the events before our eyes to give a quality of
immediacy. The movement of an action is through time, but narration gives not a mere segment of time, but rather a unit of time, and
this unity is determined by the fact that the process presented in
narration extends from the moment when one condition prevails but
is unstable, to the moment when the process is completed by the
establishment of another and stable condition. As for meaning,
action does not merely involve change, but significant change. The
stages of the process are related to each other in such a way that
they are comprehensible and make a point. In so far as the action

presented concerns human beings the comprehensibility involves MOTIVATION of events and human reaction to events.

Narration is a kind of discourse, and a NARRATIVE is the particular thing produced by the application of the method of narration. But the method of narration may be used without producing a satisfactory narrative. Events may be narrated which do not constitute an action—which are held together simply by the fact that they form a sequence in time.

The relation of narration to the other kinds of discourse may be discussed under two heads:

1. How does narration use the other kinds of discourse?
2. How do the other kinds of discourse use narration?

A narrative may, and usually does, employ the other kinds: exposition of issues involved or argument concerning them, description of characters or setting.

As for the second question, description rarely appears by itself in an extended form, and though it may use the acts, say, of a person described, it can scarcely be thought to present fully rendered actions. But both exposition and argument frequently use narration —more or less fully rendered actions—for illustrative purposes.

Is there a basic PATTERN which a narrative tends to take? This question may be approached by considering, not methods of narration, but the way in which an action appears in fact. An action arises in a situation. It moves through stages of tension to some sort of breaking point. At the breaking point a change definitely takes place to create a new situation different in meaning from the original situation in that the old tensions are relieved and a point of rest is reached. The stages of narration correspond to these divisions in an action. The beginning, the original situation, is technically called EXPOSITION. The middle, comprising the stages of mounting tension, is called COMPLICATION. The end, the definition of the new situation, is called the DENOUEMENT. The breaking point, the crisis of the action, is called the CLIMAX. These aspects of an action, even when they are not always fully presented in a narrative, as, for example, in a brief anecdote, are nevertheless always implied.

The relation of the stages of a narrative to each other raises the question of PROPORTION. But there is no mathematical ratio which can be depended upon to settle the question of proportion. Each case must be considered in terms of the material involved and the intention of the writer. The writer may, however, ask himself these guiding questions:

1. Does the exposition give all the information really necessary to establish the situation for the reader?

2. Is it burdened with information which is really unnecessary and distracting?

3. Does the complication clearly define for the reader the essential stages of the development of the action?

4. Does it confuse the reader by presenting material which does not bear on the development of the action?

5. Does the denouement give the reader enough to make the point of the narrative clear?

6. Does it blur the point by putting in irrelevant material or by so extending relevant material that a sharp focus is lost?

As the ordering of the parts of a narrative is a problem of pattern, so the rendering of the surface details is a problem of TEXTURE. Even in a narrative which deals with matters of fact, the writer cannot hope to render all details, and if he could he would simply blur the effect. He must use a principle of SELECTION. He should try to sharpen the interest of the reader by presenting only those details which have some bearing on the central concern, or which suggest the immediate quality of the event.

POINT OF VIEW, in reference to narration, means a person who bears some relation to the action, either as observer or participant, and whose intelligence serves as the index of the action for the reader. Point of view, then, involves two questions:

1. Who tells the story?

2. What is his relation to the action?

Broadly speaking, there are two possible points of view, the first person and the third person. In the first, for instance, an "I," real or fictitious, relates an event in which he himself is involved. In the second, an author, writing impersonally, relates an event in which another person is involved.

There are, however, certain shadings and variations possible within these two broad general divisions.

In the first-person point of view, two extreme positions may be distinguished.

1. The narrator may tell of an action in which he is the main, or a main, participant.

2. The narrator may tell of an action in which he has not participated, and which he has merely observed.

These two extreme positions may be called (1) NARRATOR—MAIN CHARACTER and (2) NARRATOR—MERE OBSERVER. But between them are many possible variations, corresponding to the degree in which the narrator is involved in the action.

In the third-person point of view, two extreme positions may likewise be distinguished.

1. In the PANORAMIC point of view, the writer may report any or all the aspects of an action, and may go into the head of any or all the characters involved. (In nonimaginative writing, history, for instance, the writer who employs this method is limited, of course, by what facts or plausible references are available to him.)

2. In the point of view of SHARP FOCUS, the writer keeps his attention focused on one character and on that character's relation to the action. The parts of the action not directly participated in by the selected character are not reported by the writer.

Between these two extreme positions there are all sorts of gradations and mixtures possible.

In all cases the dominant interest defines the point of view.

As the dominant interest defines the point of view, so it defines the SCALE in a piece of narration. There are two extremes of scale:

1. SUMMARY RENDERING, which is used primarily in those parts necessary for continuity or scaffolding.

2. FULL RENDERING, which is used primarily in those parts of greatest interest and importance—the main scenes of a narrative.

Narration often involves the use of DIALOGUE. Dialogue sometimes appears to be an easy method of presenting an event, but in fact it is one of the most difficult. It is difficult because it is not a mere transcript of what people say; it must be carefully planned and organized to develop a point or issue. Therefore it presents a problem in selection and logical ordering. At the same time good dialogue must give an impression of naturalness, of the pauses and waverings of conversation.

Another problem in dialogue is that of giving the impression of the speech of the individual. People have different mannerisms, different idioms, different vocabularies, different rhythms, depending on personal peculiarities, educational background, geographical origin, social class, and so forth. Close observation of people and of methods used by competent writers is the only guide here.

Most narratives involve people, and to understand such a narrative we must understand the people involved, their natures, their motives, and their responses. The process of presenting this information is called CHARACTERIZATION.

Characterization does not mean the mere accumulation of details about the persons being characterized. The details must be related to each other to build up a unified impression. To do this the writer should concern himself with the main motive of a character in relation to the events, or by the main effect of the events on him. Generally speaking, there are five methods for presenting character: by description of appearance or mannerisms, by analysis of character, by speech, by reaction of other persons, and by action. The last is the most important method, for it is most closely connected with the main concern of narrative, the rendering of action.

| CHAPTER |
|---|
| **7** |

# The Paragraph

## THE PARAGRAPH AS A CONVENIENCE
## TO THE READER

A PARAGRAPH, mechanically considered, is a division of the composition, a division set off by an indentation of its first sentence. (It may be marked in manuscript by the sign ¶.) Paragraph divisions signal to the reader that the division so set off constitutes a unit of thought.

For the reader this marking off of the whole composition into segments is a convenience, though not a strict necessity. A truly well-organized, well-written piece of prose would presumably be no worse as a piece of prose if we decided to print it with no paragraph divisions whatsoever. Printed thus, it would say precisely what it said before. The reader, however, would probably be irritated at failing to find these pointers to its organization. His reading might be made more difficult. Yet, with perhaps a little more studied attention, he could doubtless find the organization, if it were actually there. There is good reason, however, for the convention of paragraphing. Since communication of one's thoughts is at best a difficult business, it is the part of common sense, not to mention good manners, to mark for the reader the divisions of our thought, and thus make the thought structure visible upon the page.

Where should these divisions occur? How long should a paragraph be? In answering these questions, let us again begin by adopting the position of the reader. For him, a composition composed of paragraphs no longer than one or two sentences each might as well be printed without paragraph divisions at all. Segmentation on this scale would tell the reader little more about organization than the segmentation already given by the division into sentences. The opposite extreme would, of course, be quite as bad. For paragraphs of six or seven hundred words each would tell the reader little or nothing about the thought structure.

Common sense dictates that the length of the normal paragraph will lie between these extremes. But this is not to say that an *occasional* very short paragraph—even a paragraph of only one sentence—may not tell the reader a great deal. By its very shortness the importance of the paragraph would be emphasized. Similarly, an occasional long paragraph would do no damage and might serve to emphasize the unity of a long passage—always provided, of course, that the long passage actually constitutes a unit. We may sum up, then, by saying that there is no formula for ascertaining the length of paragraphs. Only common sense and the requirements of the particular occasion can determine how long any paragraph ought to be.

## THE PARAGRAPH AS A UNIT OF THOUGHT

Thus far we have looked at the paragraph from the perspective of the reader's convenience. We have said that paragraphing can make visible to him the divisions of the writer's thought. But paragraphing, obviously, can be of help to the reader only if the indicated paragraphs are genuine units of thought—not faked units—not mere random bits of writing arbitrarily marked off as units. *For a paragraph undertakes to discuss one topic or one aspect of a topic.*

The preceding sentence defines the paragraph but defines it in such fashion that the student may well question the usefulness of the definition. What, after all, is a topic? It is not easy to define; and we have probably made matters more difficult by adding "or one aspect of a topic." A discussion of "one aspect of a topic" might be thought to cover almost anything.

It ought to be admitted immediately that paragraphing is to some extent a matter of taste, not a matter of logic. Accordingly, any realistic definition must be rather loose and general. Fortunately, we do not construct paragraphs by applying definitions. In the practical problem of composition the student will find his best approach is to remind himself that the paragraph is a *part* of the composition. Earlier in this text (p. 112) we discussed the difference between a part and a mere lump or fragment. We saw that a true part has its characteristic organization which is related to the larger organization of the whole. A paragraph thus has its "part" to play —its own particular job to do—in the larger structure of meaning.

## THE STRUCTURE OF THE PARAGRAPH

The paragraph, however, has its own structure, and there are various ways of indicating that structure. One of these ways is to build the paragraph around one sentence (the TOPIC SENTENCE) which states the central thought of the whole paragraph. We may think of the topic sentence as a kind of backbone, or spine, which supports the body of the paragraph and around which the rest of the structure is formed. Here is an example.

The reader of a novel—by which I mean the critical reader—is himself a novelist; he is the maker of a book which may or may not please his taste when it is finished, but of a book for which he must take his own share of the responsibility. The author does his part, but he cannot transfer his book like a bubble into the brain of the critic; he cannot make sure that the critic will possess his work. The reader must therefore become, for his part, a novelist, never permitting himself to suppose that the creation of the book is solely the affair of the author. The difference between them is immense, of course, and so much so that a critic is always inclined to extend and intensify it. The opposition that he conceives between the creative and the critical task is a very real one; but in modestly belittling his own side of the business he is apt to forget an essential portion of it. The writer of the novel works in a manner that would be utterly impossible to the critic, no doubt, and with a liberty and with a range that would disconcert him entirely. But in one quarter their work coincides; both of them make the novel.— PERCY LUBBOCK: *The Craft of Fiction*, Chap. 2.[1]

In this paragraph the first sentence is the topic sentence. It states the thesis which the paragraph as a whole develops. It is frequently said that every paragraph contains a topic sentence,

[1] From *The Craft of Fiction*, by Percy Lubbock, through the permission of Peter Smith.

stated or implied. It might be more sensible, however, to say that some paragraphs have topic sentences and that others do not; for an implied topic sentence is one which the reader is able to construct for himself as a way of summarizing the paragraph in question. It is obvious that any composition possessing the very minimum of unity may always be summed up in some kind of sentence. The "implied" topic sentence, therefore, is an abstraction—a not very useful kind of ghost sentence. In this book, therefore, we shall mean by "topic sentence" only an actual sentence; and though insisting that every paragraph have unity, we shall admit the existence of paragraphs that do not embody a topic sentence.

The topic sentence may begin the paragraph (see the paragraph quoted above). But a topic sentence may occur elsewhere. Here, for example, is a paragraph in which the topic sentence brings the paragraph to a close.

The artistic temperament is a disease that afflicts amateurs. It is a disease which arises from men not having sufficient power of expression to utter and get rid of the element of art in their being. It is healthful to every sane man to utter the art within him; it is essential to every sane man to get rid of the art within him at all costs. Artists of a large and wholesome vitality get rid of their art easily, as they breathe easily, or perspire easily. But in artists of less force, the thing becomes a pressure, and produces a definite pain, which is called the artistic temperament. Thus, very great artists are able to be ordinary men—men like Shakespeare or Browning. There are many real tragedies of the artistic temperament, tragedies of vanity or violence or fear. But the great tragedy of the artistic temperament is that it cannot produce any art.—G. K. CHESTERTON: "On the Wit of Whistler," *Heretics.*[2]

The last sentence of this paragraph makes a generalized statement of the point developed in the preceding sentences. The topic sentence serves, in this instance, as a kind of summary. The beginning and the end of a paragraph constitute emphatic positions for the topic sentence. But topic sentences may occur at any place in the paragraph.

[2] Reprinted by permission of Dodd, Mead & Company from *Heretics* by G. K. Chesterton. Copyright, 1905, 1932, by G. K. Chesterton.

## APPLICATIONS

I

Do the following paragraphs contain topic sentences? What are these topic sentences?

**A.** Popular amusements had more generally evolved from diversions that were originally available only to the wealthy. The theatre in America had at first been primarily class entertainment, the democratic audiences in the large playhouses of the mid-nineteenth century, as we have seen, offering a marked contrast to the more exclusive theatre patronage of the colonial period. And from this gradually democratized theatre had developed the even more popular minstrel shows, burlesques, and vaudeville. But the first appeal of moving pictures was to the masses rather than the classes. They were cheap and popular from the very beginning. The support which in time enabled them to raise their standard of entertainment came entirely from their nickel-paying customers.—FOSTER DULLES: *America Learns to Play*, Chap. 17.[3]

**B.** Such was the man who, at the age of thirty-three, became headmaster of Rugby. His outward appearance was the index of his inward character: everything about him denoted energy, earnestness, and the best intentions. His legs, perhaps, were shorter than they should have been; but the sturdy athletic frame, especially when it was swathed (as it usually was) in the flowing robes of a Doctor of Divinity, was full of an imposing vigour; and his head, set decisively upon the collar, stock and bands of ecclesiastical tradition, clearly belonged to a person of eminence. The thick, dark clusters of his hair, his bushy eyebrows and curling whiskers, his straight nose and bulky chin, his firm and upward-curving lower lip—all these revealed a temperament of ardor and determination. His eyes were bright and large; they were also obviously honest. And yet—why was it?—was it in the lines of the mouth or the frown on the forehead?—it was hard to say, but it was unmistakable—there was a slightly puzzled look upon the face of Dr. Arnold.—LYTTON STRACHEY: "Dr. Arnold," *Eminent Victorians*.[4]

**C.** It is odd that American men are so frequently presented in European caricatures of the type, in fiction, plays, and films, as being extremely ill-mannered, loud, rough customers. Such Americans exist, of course, just as sneering Englishmen, bullying Teutons, insolent Latins

---

[3] From *America Learns to Play*, by Foster R. Dulles, copyright, 1940, by D. Appleton-Century Company, Inc. Reprinted by permission of Appleton-Century-Crofts, Inc.

[4] From *Eminent Victorians* by Lytton Strachey. Reprinted by permission of Harcourt, Brace and Company, Inc.

also exist. But it has always seemed to me that American manners in general tend to err on the side of formality and solemnity. They are rather like those of elderly English dons and clergymen. The ordinary English are much more casual. We do not take enough trouble, for example, with our introductions. Terrified of appearing pompous, we hastily mumble names or hastily accept a mumble of names, so that our introductions do not serve their purpose, and often, not knowing to whom we are talking, we saunter into the most dreadful traps. The deliberate ceremony that most Americans make of introductions protects them from these dangers and errors.—J. B. PRIESTLEY: *Midnight on the Desert,* Chap. 6.[5]

## II

Construct paragraphs which will incorporate these sentences as topic sentences.

1. A period of apprenticeship is an excellent thing for any artist.
2. Baseball still remains our national sport.
3. If we are to have a democracy, we must have an educated electorate.

## SOME TYPICAL STRUCTURAL PRINCIPLES

We do not undertake in this chapter to give an exhaustive classification of the principles of organization that govern paragraph structure. There is value, however, in mentioning and illustrating some of the typical principles. In this connection the student will find it useful to turn back to the earlier chapters of this book which treat exposition, argument, description, and narration. A paragraph, as we have seen, is a part of the whole composition. Since this is true, one would expect to find that the principles which govern the whole organization ought to apply, in some measure, to the organization of the parts (that is, to the paragraphs).

What are some of the methods by which we organize a piece of exposition? The chapter on Exposition mentions such methods as classification and division, comparison and contrast, illustration, definition, chronological analysis, causal analysis, and many more. But if we attempt to apply these principles of organization to the paragraph—even to the paragraphs of an expository essay—we find that they have varying degrees of applicability.

[5] From *Midnight on the Desert* by J. B. Priestley, copyright, 1937, by Harper and Brothers.

Illustration, for example, applies rather directly to paragraph construction. (See the paragraphs quoted from Melville on p. 58, or the sixth paragraph quoted from Della Lutes on p. 63 f.) Comparison and contrast are also methods quite applicable to paragraph structure. Consider, for example, G. Lowes Dickinson's "Red-bloods and Mollycoddles" (several paragraphs of which are quoted on pp. 69 ff.). The essay as a whole makes a classification, but it is organized in terms of comparison and contrast. The individual paragraphs of this essay are developed on the same principle. The first paragraph begins with a suggested definition and proceeds to elaborate and particularize that definition by comparison and contrast. The next paragraph emphasizes the traits of the Mollycoddle (as opposed to the Red-blood), but in illustrating the nature of the Mollycoddle it further emphasizes his traits by means of a series of contrasts with his opposite. The third paragraph extends the classification from individuals to nations. Its first sentence, which we may take as the topic sentence, reads: "Nations, like men, may be classified roughly as Red-blood and Mollycoddle." The rest of the paragraph illustrates this generalization through a series of contrasts of national characteristics.

There are other expository methods, however, which have less direct applicability to paragraph construction. Take, for example, the method of definition (discussed at length on pp. 88-105). As one illustration of definition (p. 103) we offered an excerpt from Newman's essay "What Is a University?" It so happens that the illustration consists of exactly one paragraph, the first paragraph of the essay.

If I were asked to describe as briefly and popularly as I could, what a University was, I should draw my answer from its ancient designation of a *Studium Generale,* or "School of Universal Learning." This description implies the assemblage of strangers from all parts in one spot;—*from all parts;* else, how will you find professors and students for every department of knowledge? and *in one spot;* else, how can there be any school at all? Accordingly, in its simple and rudimental form, it is a school of knowledge of every kind, consisting of teachers and learners from every quarter. Many things are requisite to complete and satisfy the idea embodied in this description; but such as this a University seems to be in its essence, a place for the communication and circulation of thought, by means of personal intercourse, through a wide extent of country.

It is not this paragraph, however, but Newman's whole essay that gives us his full definition of the term *university:* his first paragraph is a rather special case. What is the structure of the other paragraphs of his essay? They play their part in developing the definition of a university which the whole essay undertakes to make. But they are not themselves organized as definitions. Some provide illustrations, others make comparisons and furnish contrasts, and all take the structure of their specialized functions. Even the structure of the first paragraph might be more practically described thus: the paragraph begins by defining a university as a *Studium Generale,* and then proceeds to develop two or three basic implications of this term; that is, the structure is a generalization plus several particularizations.

We can say in general that the more complex methods of exposition and argument, such as functional analysis, chronological analysis, causal analysis, and syllogistic reasoning, rarely determine the structure of a single paragraph. Their very complexity prevents their doing so. For the paragraph as one of the smaller parts in extended composition usually has a simpler structure. It states a point and elaborates it, or it contrasts two points, or it illustrates an argument, or it makes a particular application.

Some paragraphs, however, do have a rather explicit logical structure in which the topic sentence states a conclusion which follows from premises stated in the body of the paragraph. Here is a paragraph so constructed.

A really great pitcher must have control. Charles Ramsey had wonderful speed and a curve that broke as sharply as any that I have ever seen. He dazzled opposing batters with his fireball or made them break their backs reaching for pitches that broke sharply away from the plate. Charles had nearly everything—he even fielded his position brilliantly—but he lacked control. Even on his best days his control was less than certain. Shrewd batters learned this, and waited him out, frequently successfully, for a base on balls. On his worst days he simply couldn't find the plate. A pitcher without control cannot win close games. This is why I have to scratch Ramsey from my list of great pitchers.

This is a rather simple paragraph, and on a simple enough subject; yet it is characterized by a logical structure. We can see this plainly by putting this argument in the form of a syllogism.

A great pitcher must not be lacking in control.   (major premise)
Charles Ramsey is lacking in control.   (minor premise)
∴. Charles Ramsey is not a great pitcher.   (conclusion)

Few paragraphs, however, are shaped to conform so neatly to the logical skeleton of a syllogism. We might remember that few arguments are expressed in fully developed syllogisms. They are rather a series of enthymemes, or, as we put it on page 193, a "chain of implied syllogisms, the conclusion of one becoming a premise of the next." Such a chain of reasoning is often exhibited in the characteristic paragraph organization in essays which present an argument. Norbert Wiener's "A Scientist Rebels" (p. 688) will provide an illustration.

The student attempting to present a chain of reasoning will find that preliminary outlines are very helpful—indeed may be indispensable. The student should turn back to Chapter 1 (pp. 26-28) and reread what has been said about outlines. (Outlining is also discussed and summarized in the Appendix on the Outline, p. 902.) A brief (p. 194) is of special utility in fashioning a close-knit fabric of argument. Such a brief as that given on page 195 states a point as a main heading, and proceeds to marshal the supporting proofs in proper degrees of subordination.

This sort of brief goes far toward suggesting paragraph structure. The divisions and the more important subdivisions become paragraphs: and the sentences that constitute the headings become topic sentences.

But outlining—unless we have made specifically a paragraph outline (see Appendix on the Outline, p. 902)—does not determine paragraph structure. Outlining will not settle, for example, the problem of scale. (Are topics *a* and *b* to constitute one paragraph or four? Should A be developed as a short paragraph, and 1, *a*, and *b* made to constitute a long paragraph which follows it?) It will be interesting in this connection to see how the student theme printed on page 16 develops the brief printed on page 27. The student theme presents *one* way to develop the brief, not the *only* way to develop it. See also the comments on the partial outline of Gauss's "The Threat of Science" (Appendix on the Outline, p. 902).

Thus far we have examined paragraph structure primarily in the light of the methods of organization discussed in the chapters on Exposition and Argument. But the chapters on Description and Narration and the section on Expository Description (pp. 45-56) will suggest other ways in which paragraphs may be organized, and, on the whole, some of the simpler kinds of organization: simple time sequence, for example, or simple sequence of objects arranged in space.

Consider first a paragraph from Conrad's "The Secret Sharer." [6]

On my right hand there were lines of fishing-stakes resembling a mysterious system of half-submerged bamboo fences, incomprehensible in its division of the domain of tropical fishes, and crazy of aspect as if abandoned for ever by some nomad tribe of fishermen now gone to the other end of the ocean; for there was no sign of human habitation as far as the eye could reach. To the left a group of barren islets, suggesting ruins of stone walls, towers, and blockhouses, had its foundations set in a blue sea that itself looked solid, so still and stable did it lie below my feet; even the track of light from the westering sun shone smoothly, without that animated glitter which tells of an imperceptible ripple. And when I turned my head to take a parting glance at the tug which had just left us anchored outside the bar, I saw the straight line of the flat shore joined to the stable sea, edge to edge, with a perfect and unusual closeness, in one levelled floor half brown, half blue under the enormous dome of the sky.

Here we have a fixed observer. He tells us what he sees on his right hand, then on his left, and finally, turning his head, what he sees behind him. (There is even an implied look upward: "the . . . dome of the sky.") The order of composition is simple and even mechanical, though the writing itself is not mechanical. Notice, for example, the sense of finality and completeness given by the last sentence. The observer's survey comes to rest in "the straight line" of shore and sea "under the enormous dome of the sky." The paragraph thus rounds out and completes its chosen topic. It is thoroughly unified, though it does *not* contain a topic sentence.

[6] From *'Twixt Land and Sea* by Joseph Conrad. Reprinted by permission of J. M. Dent and Sons, Ltd., through the courtesy of the Conrad estate.

But we may also have a scene described through the eyes of an observer who is shifting his position. The paragraph from Lawrence's *Seven Pillars of Wisdom* (p. 226) furnishes an illustration. Moreover, a scene may be described in terms of an image which provides a frame of reference for it. Thomas Hardy describes the continent of Europe under the figure of a human being (see p. 227).

The various ways in which description (and descriptive paragraphs) may be organized have been summarized on page 255 (which the student should reread). Now these methods of description all apply to descriptive paragraphs as well as to description as a kind of discourse. In fact, the examples printed in Chapter 5 to illustrate these methods are, almost without exception, distinct paragraphs. The student can learn from them, therefore, a great deal about paragraph development.

Some of the more subjective modes of paragraph development, however, call for a bit of further discussion. It is in these that the principle of organization is least clear; the structure of the paragraph will seem most nearly subjective—a mere matter of caprice. It will be these paragraphs, then, which will seem to the student to stretch the very concept of the paragraph to a dangerous limit. Consider, for example, the paragraph quoted from E. M. Forster's *A Passage to India* on page 228. Why did not Forster begin a new paragraph with sentence five, "Chandrapore was never . . ."? Or consider the passage quoted from Sinclair Lewis's *Main Street* (p. 230). The passage is printed as four paragraphs. Two are composed of one sentence; one, of two sentences. Only the third paragraph has more than two sentences. Would anything be lost if all four paragraphs were lumped together in one medium-length paragraph?

A defense can be offered in both instances. Forster presumably felt his description of Chandrapore was a unit—that for him at least it had a "felt unity." Lewis presumably used the ultrashort paragraphs for a special effect: to suggest someone walking down "Main Street," observing the buildings as he walks. We get a paragraph for each store. But much more is at stake than the defense of these two examples. The defense may or may not be adequate, and if the student feels it to be inadequate, he is quite possibly right. At any rate, he is right to raise the question. For the question goes to the heart of the problem of paragraph structure. To repeat: there is no precise formula by which the length or structure of a paragraph may be determined. As we have said earlier (p. 317), the student must use his best judgment: he must use his common sense and his taste. Unless he is very sure of his ground, he will tend to employ paragraphs of medium length. He will tend to use the more conventional paragraph structures. But in following these common-sense rules he must not conceive of paragraphs as mechanical units of even length and of homogeneous make-up. He will feel free, on occasion, to formulate paragraphs of "felt unity," relying upon his own impression of the "rightness" of the structure. For the student must never forget that the paragraph is a part—a meaningful part— of a larger structure, and therefore cannot be formulated mechanically any more than can the larger structure of which it is a part.

## APPLICATIONS

**I.** Reread the long excerpt from James Harvey Robinson's *The Mind in the Making*, pages 77-88. We have used the passage to illustrate classification and division. How are the successive paragraphs related to this general function? Are any of them constructed as classifications? Do any provide illustrations? Attempt to state the structural principles to be found in the first ten paragraphs of this section.

**II.** What structural principles are to be found in each of the following paragraphs? If you judge that the paragraph has no real structure, say so and indicate why.

1. The second of the two paragraphs from Leo Tolstoy's *War and Peace* quoted on page 133.

2. The first paragraph from Melville's "The Encantadas" quoted on page 48.

3. The second paragraph from Thomas Wolfe's *Of Time and the River* quoted on page 52.

4. The paragraph from T. H. Huxley's "The Herring" quoted on page 53.

5. The paragraph from Swift's *Gulliver's Travels* quoted on page 54.

6. The second paragraph from Melville's *Moby Dick* quoted on page 58.

7. The first paragraph from Lawrence's *Seven Pillars of Wisdom* quoted on page 309.

**III.** Reread the passage from Marquis James's *Andrew Jackson*, pages 283-86. Attempt to state the structural principle of each of the paragraphs in this piece of narrative.

## LINKING PARAGRAPHS TOGETHER

Since paragraphs are parts of a whole work, elements in an ordered sequence, it is important that they be properly linked together. Even if the chain of development embodied in the series of paragraphs has been thought out carefully, the reader will still be grateful for signposts placed to direct him. The judicious use of transitional words and phrases such as *therefore, consequently, hence, thus, accordingly, on the contrary, however, nevertheless, furthermore, finally, in the same way,* and *moreover* constitutes one way of helping the reader. The writer may also make use of the co-ordinate conjunctions *for, and, but, or,* and *nor* as explicit signs of the connection between paragraph and paragraph. Since, however, we ordinarily use these conjunctions to join the parts of a sentence, or to join sentence with sentence, we employ them less frequently to tie a paragraph to a preceding paragraph. But they can be used, though the use is more appropriate to an informal than to a formal style.

If we do provide the reader with transitional words as explicit signposts, obviously we must use them accurately. We must not begin a paragraph by writing "In the same way . . ." unless what follows *is* "in the same way"; we must not write "Consequently" unless what follows is a consequence of the preceding paragraph. For a discussion of the improper use of transitional words and phrases, see Beach's "Unripe Fruits" (p. 742).

An obvious device for linking paragraphs is the repetition of a key word or phrase. It is a useful device, particularly if we wish to avoid the formality of style suggested by the employment of transitional words, but wish also to avoid the abruptness occasioned by the use of *and, but,* and *or.* To illustrate: Christian Gauss, in his "The Threat of Science," effects the transition between his third and fourth paragraphs in this way. (We have italicized the key words here, and in the examples that follow.)

To the biologist the lion who kills many antelopes has "survival value." He is, this scientist will even tell us, a *good* lion.

When the scientist uses this word *good* we must be on our guard. He does not mean what the theologian . . .

The exact word or phrase, of course, need not be repeated. It may be varied. Here is Gauss's transition from paragraph six to seven.

[The] truths [of experimental science] are not really truths of a higher sort; they are not above ordinary truths, as the angels (if there still are angels) are over the earth; they are only the truths of science in what might be called *their state of innocence.*

For this reason experimental science should not be regarded as *wicked;* it is only *unmoral.* No harm will come so long . . .

Here is a series of three paragraphs from a story in *Time* magazine:

*A buzzard coasting* high in the air over Central America last week, would have seen nothing unusual. The mountainous, forest-matted isthmus lay quietly in the greasy November sun. Among the many human realities invisible to the buzzard were the boundary lines—the imaginary but very actual barriers that said: "This is Costa Rica; this is Guatemala; this is Nicaragua."

Far below the *coasting buzzard,* in the grey-green jungles of northern Nicaragua, more was stirring than his great bird's-eye view could catch. Snaking through the scrub, *guerrilla riflemen made short, sharp little raids* against government outposts. In and out of the piny mountain country on Nicaragua's northern flank, armed, machete-toting *men filtered mysteriously.* In Guatemala and Costa Rica dusty little *companies,* in faded denim and khaki, *marked time in the tropic heat.*

*All this scattered activity* added up to one gathering purpose. That purpose called itself the Caribbean Legion.[7]

Here is a series of three paragraphs from Dorothy Sayers's *The Mind of the Maker:*

It is for this reason that I have prefixed to this brief study of the creative mind an introductory chapter in which I have tried to make clear the difference between *fact and opinion,* and between the so-called "laws" based on *fact and opinion* respectively.

In the creeds of Christendom, we are confronted with a set of documents which purport to be, not expressions of *opinion* but statements of *fact.* Some of these *statements* are historical, and with these the present book is not concerned. Others are theological—which means that they claim to be statements of fact about the nature of God and the universe; and with a *limited number of these I propose to deal.*

[7] Courtesy of TIME, Copyright Time, Inc. 1948.

*The selected statements* are those which aim at defining the nature of God, conceived in His capacity as Creator. They were originally . . .[8]

Another obvious device for linking paragraphs is the use of *this* (*these*) and *that* (*those*); but these words must be used with care. We are frequently tempted to use them vaguely, hoping that the idea or object to which they refer will be clear from the context. Frequently it is not clear, and instead of a tight and neat coupling of the two paragraphs, we have only the vague and clumsy suggestion of a tie. For example, the second paragraph of "The Colors That Animals Can See" (p. 547) ends thus:

After we have arranged these new cards, we have not long to wait. Very soon bees arrive again, and it can be seen that they fly straight on to the blue card; none goes to the red card.

Now we might be tempted to begin the next paragraph with: "This seems to indicate two things. The first is . . ." But what the author wrote was: "This behavior of the bees seems to indicate two things. . . ." A little reflection will indicate that his judgment was sound. The author intends to state clearly a process of proof. He has been wise therefore to make very precise what "this" refers to. The mistake of vague and indefinite reference can be quite serious. It is so common an error in student themes that the student had better make sure that "this" or "that" standing at the beginning of a paragraph refer unmistakably to some specific noun.

## USE OF THE PARAGRAPH TO INDICATE DIALOGUE

There is one further and special use of the paragraph. This use is conventional, though the convention is an important and inflexible one. In writing dialogue, we begin a new paragraph with each change of speaker. (A long speech by one speaker may, of course, need to be divided into two or more paragraphs: that is, the convention does not require the converse, that each new speaker be allowed only *one* paragraph.) The utility of the convention is obvious: by beginning a new paragraph each time the speaker changes,

[8] From *The Mind of the Maker* by Dorothy Sayers, copyright, 1942, by Harcourt, Brace and Company, Inc.

we make it much easier for the reader to keep straight who is speaking. For an illustration, see page 303.

## SUMMARY

A PARAGRAPH is a unit of thought. We mark off these units of thought by indenting the first line. No precise rules govern paragraph length, but common sense dictates that very short and very long paragraphs be used rarely. A succession of very short paragraphs (or of very long paragraphs) would be of little use in indicating to the reader the divisions of the writer's thought.

Since a paragraph is a *unit* of thought, it has an ordered structure. The three great interrelated principles of order (unity, coherence, and emphasis) obviously apply to the paragraph. Now, in this text, these principles have received their fullest discussion in connection with the whole theme—in the chapters treating description, narration, exposition, and argument. But paragraphs, as meaningful parts of the whole, involve the principle of order. Paragraphs exemplify these principles in a double sense. As an individual structure the paragraph has its own unity, coherence, and emphasis. As a part of the larger structure, the paragraph contributes to the unity, coherence, and emphasis of the total composition.

The interplay between these relationships is intimate. That is why we have been able to draw from the earlier chapters, which deal with the whole theme, principles that apply to the structure of the paragraph as such. That is why these same earlier chapters furnish so many illustrations of paragraph construction. In other words, the student should realize that when he comes to this chapter on the paragraph, he already knows a great deal about the paragraph. He has actually been studying the structural principles of the paragraph all along.

As for the part-to-whole relationship (the paragraph as related to the whole composition), a further word may be said. As parts of a larger structure, paragraphs often have specialized functions. The opening paragraph (or paragraphs), for example, must introduce the whole essay; the final paragraph (or paragraphs) must bring it to a suitable conclusion. Within the essay itself, there may be many paragraphs of specialized function: one paragraph states a particular argument; another provides an illustration; still another effects a transition between two sections of the essay.

These part-to-whole relationships, least of all, however, can be studied by considering the paragraph in isolation. Here too the student will learn most by studying the paragraph in relation to the whole. (The student might look, for example, at the opening paragraphs of the various essays in the selections printed at the end of this text. From such an examination he would probably learn much more about how to construct introductory paragraphs than from any general discussion.) Study of the paragraph, therefore, leads us back to the general problems of composition. The student will provide his own best conclusion to this summary by going back to Chapter 1 and rereading pages 13-23.

## APPLICATIONS

I. The section which follows was divided by the author into five paragraphs. Try to determine where the paragraph divisions occur. Indicate the topic sentences if any. Indicate how the paragraphs are linked together: by repetition of important words or phrases, by transitional words or phrases, or by other devices.

As a man who has been cheated in business or love or any of the things that happen will toss on his bed through the sleepless night, going over each step in the transaction and saying to himself, "If I had done this," "If I had not done that," and rises with the sun, full of anger and violence and despair; so the South after the Civil War. At every crossroad, in every country store, wherever men gathered, the Confederate veteran was present to tell how the South had been—not defeated, never that—bilked, cheated, tricked out of the victory, overwhelmed. In the North, I am told, which is what we called all of America outside the South, listeners grew impatient at the talkative old man (another's victory is a bore) and walked off into the future. But for the South there was no future. Stunned by their overwhelming, men and women wandered about in a dream world, a world of incomparably brave men and women every one a Helen, and listened eagerly to the words of the old men who had returned from the bright past. Boys listened too. "If we'd just 'a had one more company, we'd 'a licked 'em," the old man said, and the boy became that company. Anger, violence, despair, all were in us and in all of us, and longing for another chance we knew would never come. (If Wilson had remembered his childhood, he might have brought peace to Germany; but Wilson was also a Southern Presbyterian, coldly violent.) We knew the chance would never come, but we got ready for it. We kept our violence in condition, by fist fights (many of my age-fellows carried brass knuckles), cutting scrapes (every one carried a knife), brawls at political rallies. (Ben Tillman often could not make himself heard above the din.) Our violence was schooled, literally, in another way. The South was, and still is, dotted with military schools, academies and colleges. Violence was also curbed, channeled, by them. When Clemson College was established in South Carolina for the training of farmer boys, some one asked Ben Tillman why he had made it military. "How'n hell do you think we could keep these wild boys down?" he asked in answer. Tillman, the first of the Southern dictators, knew what he was talking about, as he always did when it came to knowing his people. The Southerner, for all his easy ways, is quick to anger. "Techy" (touchy), "ficety" (like a fice, a mongrel pup, nervous and misunderstood), "meaner'n a blue-gum nigger" (the bite of a "blue-gum nigger" was poisonous)—these were some of the regional words to describe the extremes, but we were all, in our several ways, wild. The first task of a school was therefore to tame a boy, to match violence with violence; by means of the rod and the peach-tree switch to make of him a gentleman (chivalry is codified violence) and, hopefully a scholar. "School" meant private school, if a boy was to be prepared for college or for life—the preparations were the same. The public school, even as late as the turn of the century, was in its infancy, and there remained, for it died at the end of the eighth grade or thereabouts; also, education at public expense offended the genteel tradition.—JOHN A. RICE: *I Came Out of the Eighteenth Century*, Chap. 5.[9]

II. In the following paragraphs from the selections in the Readings, indicate the topic sentences (if any) and the devices for connecting one paragraph with another.

1. The first ten paragraphs of "It Was a Stable World" (pp. 798-803)
2. Section IV of "The Threat of Science" (pp. 672-76)
3. The first ten paragraphs of "Spanish Horses Among the Plains Tribes" (pp. 877-81)

III. The paragraphs referred to here may be said to exemplify the following structures: (a) identification and illustration, (b) comparison and contrast, (c) causal analysis, (d) frame image, and (e) disposition of details from a fixed point of view. Which paragraphs exemplify which of these methods of organization?

[9] From *I Came Out of the Eighteenth Century* by John A. Rice. Copyright, 1942, by Harper and Brothers.

1. Paragraph two in "It Was a Stable World" (p. 799)
2. Paragraph five in "It Was a Stable World" (p. 801)
3. Paragraph two in "The Webb School" (p. 859)
4. Paragraph nine in "The Threat of Science" (p. 662)
5. Paragraph two in "Wordsworth in the Tropics" (p. 762)

**IV.** Are the paragraphs in Santayana's "Dickens" (p. 749) and in Huxley's "Wordsworth in the Tropics" (p. 762) too long? Can you suggest divisions into shorter paragraphs? Are the paragraphs in "Dawn over Zero" (p. 592) too short? Can you suggest ways in which to combine them into larger paragraphs?

# CHAPTER 8

# The Sentence

OUR DISCUSSION in earlier chapters has dealt with rhetorical problems; that is, we have been concerned with making our expression clear and convincing to the reader. Our discussion of the whole theme and of its subdivisions, of the process of composition considered generally and considered in its various kinds (description, exposition, and so on), has been conducted from the point of view of rhetoric. We have asked: How can we select, arrange, and dispose our materials so as to make them register with maximum impact on the reader? Thus, we have applied the principles of rhetorical organization to the composition as a whole, to its parts (the paragraphs), and now are to apply them to its smallest part, the SENTENCE.

## RHETORIC AND GRAMMAR

But with the sentence, this smallest rhetorical unit, we encounter another problem. It is the problem of grammar. In earlier chapters we could take the problem of grammar for granted, for, since the larger units of a composition are made up of sentences, we could assume that the demands of GRAMMAR had been met. In this chapter, although we shall still be primarily concerned with how to make our sentences effective (the rhetorical problem), we shall have to touch upon specifically grammatical problems. These have to do with the rules and conventions that govern English sentence structure. We might illustrate the relation between grammar and rhetoric in this way: The *grammar* of a game of chess, say, would be the rules of the game—what moves are possible if one is to play the game fairly and correctly. The *rhetoric* of chess, on the other hand, would be the principles which govern the playing of a winning game—what moves we ought to make and in what sequence, if we hope to play effectively and well. If we are to write English effectively, we must have a knowledge of rhetoric; but if we are to write English at all, we must have a knowledge of English grammar.

In this book the student's knowledge of English grammar is assumed. The book is specifically a rhetoric, not a grammar. Yet, in the sentence, the two problems of grammar and rhetoric interpenetrate so thoroughly that it would be impractical, even if it were possible, to leave the grammatical aspect out of account.

A sentence is usually defined as a complete thought expressed through a subject and a predicate. Unfortunately, the definition is of little value to anyone who does not already know what "complete" means in this context, or who does not already know what predication is. The student using this book presumably does know; and yet it may be of some value to review the definition, particularly since we shall attempt to relate the sentence to the basic principles of rhetorical structure: unity, coherence, and emphasis. A sentence has unity (is a complete thought) and its parts cohere (that is, are related to each other in a special way so as to produce that unity). But does emphasis also figure importantly in making a sentence a sentence? It does, for every complete sentence, as we shall see, must have a special focus of interest—a specific centering of emphasis, which constitutes the nucleus around which the parts cohere.

We shall need some concrete illustrations, however, if we are to make this point clear. We have said that a sentence is a complete thought; it says something about something. If one simply says, for example, "the box," we have the "something" but we do not have the "aboutness." If one should say "the large burning box in the back yard," the "aboutness" is still lacking. The box has been named, and there is even some fullness of description, but the thought is still incomplete: we feel that nothing has been "said about" this rather fully described object. If, on the other hand, one should say "the large box burns," the "aboutness" is provided. We have a sentence. The student, however, might very well put this objection: that there is no real difference between "the large burning box"

7. Rain fell.

8. Is he to be in town?

9. That he is diligent, honest, trustworthy—traits of the highest importance.

10. While we, on the other hand, were listening to the cannonading.

11. That the rain would fall had been predicted.

12. That the rain fell in accordance with the prediction.

13. Whoever is in there, come out!

14. The so gently falling rain, which had been prayerfully awaited in every part of the region by those who had lived through the parching drouth of summer, falling now over the farms.

15. The great shaggy dog, yawning in the heat and lolling out his red tongue, walked slowly out of the kennel with an air of lazy satisfaction like that of a man surveying a deed well done.

16. Was ever a poet so trusted?

## THE FIXED WORD ORDER OF THE NORMAL SENTENCE [2]

The parts of a normal English sentence are arranged in a special way. We have first the subject, then the finite verb, then the indirect object (if any), and last the direct object or any other complement of the verb (if any).

| Subject | Verb * | Indirect object | Direct object † |
|---|---|---|---|
| James | talked. | | |
| James | told | | stories. |
| James | was telling ‡ | | stories. |
| James | told | Roger | stories. |
| James | was telling | me | that he was ill. |
| That James was ill | caused | me | anxiety. |
| James | told | Roger | to stop. |

* Finite verb, or finite verb plus verbals.

† Or other complement of the verb.

‡ was (finite verb) + telling (verbal—in this instance, a present participle).

The student will notice that in these examples we have left out all modifiers, either adjectival or adverbial. The position of modifiers will be discussed later; here we are concerned with the order

[2] For much of the material in this and the following sections of this chapter, the authors are indebted to Professor Harold Whitehall of Indiana University.

of the basic components of the sentence. What the student needs to see is that the order is a *fixed* order. We cannot say, for example, "John told stories Roger," though of course we can say, "John told stories to Roger."

The student should also observe that we have talked about the word position in the *normal* English sentence, not the average English sentence. For something more important than an average is at stake. We are concerned here with a norm, a standard pattern which is so deep-rooted in our sense of the language that most of us are quite unconscious of the fact that we observe it instinctively all the time. It is important, however, that we here see it quite consciously and explicitly, for a realization of the fact that English has a characteristic pattern of fixed word order can illuminate the deviations from this order. To sum up, in calling attention to the fixed word order we are not attempting to give the student any new information, but rather to make him notice the pattern which he has been unconsciously observing since childhood.

### VARIATIONS FROM FIXED WORD ORDER

Now, deviation from a norm is always a means of emphasis. If a man wears a red hat, he emphasizes the hat and himself. The wearing of spats on an American street, just because it deviates from the norm, calls attention to the wearer's feet, though, conversely, the *lack* of spats in a large group of people wearing spats would likewise call attention to the feet. Deviation from the fixed word positions of the sentence are emphatic as all variations from a norm tend to be emphatic. For example, compare "I do not believe that" and "That, I do not believe." The second sentence, by inverting the normal order, throws heavy emphasis on "that."

Constant emphasis, however, defeats its own end, and becomes banal and trite. Presumably the first pulp writer who wrote "Came the dawn," instead of the normal "The dawn came," was trying to secure emphasis, an emphasis which would give a certain rhetorical effect. But the writers of Hollywood in the days of silent pictures, by using "Came the dawn" over and over again, wore the caption to rags. All of which is by way of saying that we have every right to *change* the fixed word positions in order to emphasize some word, but that we vary from the normal order at our peril, and that meaningless departures from the norm make our writing empty and pretentious. Assuming, however, that we have good reason to emphasize some part of the sentence, how are the emphases secured? We have already illustrated one means, that of inversion:

> That, I do not believe.
> Books, he had read in plenty.

In interrogative sentences, of course, we want to emphasize the interrogative word or the verb. We regularly invert the order in English for a question.

> *What* does he want?
> *When* did you see him last?
> *Didn*'t you *know*?
> *Knew* you not? (archaic)

What are some of the other means for securing emphasis?

## EMPHASIS ON THE SUBJECT

Our simplest way of emphasizing the subject is to begin the sentence with "It is," "It was," and so on, or "There is," "There was," and so on. For example, compare "James told me stories" with "It was James who (that) told me stories." Or compare "A man knew seventeen languages" with "There was a man who knew seventeen languages." In each of these instances, the effect of the reformulation is to emphasize "James" and "the man" by throwing everything that follows into a subordinate clause. But it ought to be apparent that a constant and thoughtless use of "It is" and "There is" not only fails to secure emphasis but makes the sentences needlessly bumbling.

## EMPHASIS ON THE OBJECTS (OR COMPLEMENTS) OF THE VERB

If we wish to emphasize the indirect object, we put it in the position of the normal subject and make the verb passive. Thus we get, not "James told me stories" but "I was told stories by James." By a similar process, we can throw emphasis upon the direct object: "Stories were told to me by James."

Now this process of converting the object of the verb (either direct or indirect) into the subject, is so familiar that the student may well wonder that it is worth mentioning here at all, particularly in a text that is concerned with problems of rhetoric and touches upon grammatical relationships only incidentally. Yet the point involved is a very important one. If we can see that these passive constructions violate the normal English sentence pattern, it may be easier for us to see that, like all emphatic variations, they are to be used sparingly and only when we want a special emphasis on what would be, in normal order, the object of the verb. Indeed, the warning frequently given in composition books against "weak passive" constructions becomes clearer when we see that the weak passive becomes weak because it is essentially an overused, and therefore misused, *device for emphasis.*

Here are some examples of weak passives:

1. The book was picked up by me.
2. The problem of maintaining friendly relations and at the same time a proper firmness was seen.
3. The matter has been taken up for consideration, and as soon as a solution can be arrived at, settlement will be made.

Now it is apparent that in the first sentence no *emphasis* on book is intended or required. The writer has thoughtlessly drifted into the passive construction. He needs to restore the normal sentence order from which there was no good reason to depart. He should simply write "I picked up the book." (There are, of course, contexts in which *book* might deserve emphasis. One can easily imagine a story in which a character said: "But the book—not the paperweight —was picked up by *me.*")

Something more than carelessness probably accounts for the second and third examples. The real subject (what would be the subject in normal sentence order) is either vague or unknown. The writer has not troubled to define it, or else he timidly refuses to define it. Let us say that in the third sentence the true subject is "the assistant manager in charge of claims." The assistant manager shrinks from taking responsibility, or his stenographer hesitates to put him down as responsible, or feels, quite foolishly, that "we" is somehow inelegant. Thus we get the sentence as it stands, rather than "Mr. Johnson has taken the matter up and hopes to make settlement soon," or "We are considering the matter and hope to make settlement soon."

Such weak and awkward constructions have come to dominate a great deal of modern prose—especially "official" writing—writing that comes from government bureaus, business offices, and committees. The student ought to be on his guard against its influence.

We can sum up by saying that the normal word order of the English sentence is (1) subject, (2) verb, (3) indirect object (if any), and (4) direct object or other verbal complement (if any). There is nothing inelegant about this arrangement. It constitutes the basis of a sound English style. The student should keep to this normal pattern *unless he has a good reason for departing from it*. In checking the first draft of a theme it is good practice to justify every deviation from the normal sentence pattern.

## POSITION OF THE MODIFIERS

We now need to consider the position in the sentence occupied by the various modifiers—by the adjectives and adverbs, and by the phrases and clauses which function either as adjectives or adverbs. The position of some of these modifiers is rather rigidly fixed; that of others is optional, and since there is no prescribed position for them, the ordering of these "movable" modifiers is a matter of taste, emphasis, and expressiveness. We can say that the fixed modifiers are placed largely in accordance with grammatical rules; the position of the movable modifiers is assigned largely in terms of rhetorical considerations.

### FIXED MODIFIERS

Let us consider first the fixed modifiers. These include most adjectives, and phrases and clauses which have the function of adjectives. Relative clauses, adjectival phrases, and adjectival infinitives *follow* the substantive which they modify. We must write, for example:

The man *to see* is Jim.
The man *I knew* was Jim.
The man *whom I mentioned* was Jim.
The house *in the country* was for sale.

We cannot write:

The *to see* man is Jim.

or:

The *I knew* man was Jim.

Single adjectives, on the contrary, just reverse this rule. The normal position of a single adjective is *before* the substantive that it modifies. For example, we would normally write:

A *bright* day dawned.
A *long black* automobile rounded the corner.
He gave an *extended, involved,* and *tortuous* argument.

Predicate adjectives, of course, do not come under this rule. We say that they modify the substantive "through the verb," and they normally come after the verb. Consider these illustrations.

The rose was *red.*
The third night seemed *long.*
The house was *for sale.*

On occasion, however, we do reverse the normal positions. Examples will readily occur to the student. Here are a few:

Comrades *all!*
Chapter *ten.*
John the *Baptist.*
A car, *long* and *black,* rounded the corner.
A small face, *dirty,* appeared at the window.
*Black* is my true love's hair.

As we have seen earlier, variation from the norm is emphatic, and in all these illustrations the reversal of normal position has the effect of emphasizing the adjectives used.

One qualification of this principle, however, must be made. Some of the examples given seem to represent, not an emphatic variation, but the normal pattern: e.g., *chapter ten* and *John the Baptist.* But in expressions of this sort, as a little reflection will show, the adjective is important and normally requires stress. Furthermore, there are other expressions in which we normally encounter the adjective following the noun: first, certain fossilized expressions derived from French law, such as "body politic" and "heir apparent"; and second, expressions such as "the day following," "the funds available," which actually represent elliptical expressions which we would have to fill out as follows: "the day following (this day)," "the funds available (to us)."

These classes of exceptions, however, do not affect the general rule, that an adjective normally *precedes* its substantive, and that the reversal of this position throws emphasis upon the adjective.

We observed earlier that thoughtless use of emphatic position or overuse of emphatic position defeats its own ends. The principle applies to modifiers. John Bunyan, in his *Pilgrim's Progress,* used the phrase "the house beautiful." In the context provided by Bunyan the expression is well used. But, with it as model, the advertisers nowadays produce such absurdities as "the memorial park beautiful," "the body beautiful," and "the hair-do glamorous." Variation from the normal position of the adjective, like other emphatic devices, ought to be used sparingly and cautiously.

To sum up, the position of adjectives and adjectival phrases and clauses allows very little variation. The position of most adjectival modifiers is definitely fixed. The student's real problem here is to avoid clumsiness and absurdity through a careless placing of such modifiers.

In this connection, relative clauses (which we must remember are adjectival modifiers) call for a further word. Relative clauses may be *unlinked* as in the sentence "The man I knew was Jim" or *linked* as in "The man whom I knew was Jim." The *link* words are the pronouns *who* (*whom*), restricted to human beings; *which,* restricted to animals and inanimate objects; and *that,* unrestricted. A relative clause which *immediately* follows the substantive modified requires no link word; otherwise it does, and the choice of the proper link word may be necessary for clarity. Compare:

1. The man in the automobile that I recognized was Jim.

with:

2. The man in the automobile whom I recognized was Jim.

Note that sentence 1 is ambiguous as sentence 2 is not.

Relative clauses occasion difficulty in still other ways. We may make a clumsy reduplication of clauses:

The man who had just come in whom I had never met was a Mr. Rogers.

Better to write:

The new arrival, whom I had never met, was a Mr. Rogers.

or:

A Mr. Rogers, whom I had never met, had just come in.

Sometimes we carelessly make a relative clause modify a general idea which is implied but not expressed. Thus:

She had been hurt and bitterly disappointed, which accounted for her strange conduct.

Better to write:

Her hurt and bitter disappointment accounted for her strange conduct.

or:

She had been hurt and bitterly disappointed, a fact which accounted for her strange conduct.

## APPLICATIONS

In the following sentences, some of the adjectival modifiers are improperly placed. Rearrange the modifiers and, where necessary, rewrite the sentences to improve clarity and effectiveness.

1. Bird cage and parrot offered by refined young lady, having green feathers and yellow beak for what have you?—The Salt Lake *Tribune*.

2. A two-story house was for sale with green shutters.

3. A man in the army that I served with gave me this book.

4. He was badly shaken up emotionally, which caused him to lose his job.

5. It was the man I knew whom I now saw.

6. The translation, the best one, is from Latin into French.

7. The lady whom I knew from Boston has not returned.

8. Boy is missing in first pair of long pants.—The Detroit *Free Press*.

9. Rex Parsons laid an egg on our table that had been previously laid on the nest by a little white leghorn hen that was three inches in length and 6½ inches in circumference the smallest way.—The Farmington *Franklin Journal*.

10. Slowly filling with water, we saw the ship go down.

11. The ducks on the pond with ringed necks swam in lazy circles.

12. The ducks were still undisturbed on the pond; those in the nearby meadow quacked noisily.

13. In the confusion I lost my head which made me take the wrong turning.

14. Walking sedately before the bride, came her small nephew George

Slaughter 3rd, carrying the ring and two little nieces of the groom.—The Roswell *Dispatch*.

## MOVABLE MODIFIERS

The attentive student will have noticed that there is one kind of adjectival modifier, the participial phrase, that is not fixed, but is rather freely movable. Consider, for example:

*Smoking a cigarette,* James sauntered down the street.
James, *smoking a cigarette,* sauntered down the street.
James sauntered down the street, *smoking a cigarette.*

All three sentences are perfectly good English. There is no one correct position for this participial phrase. In choosing where to place it, we are governed by considerations of taste and emphasis.

Nearly all the *adverbs* and *adverbial modifiers,* moreover, are movable in this way. Here are sentences which will illustrate some of the various positions which adverbial modifiers may occupy.

1. *Because I respect him,* I gave him candid advice.
2. I gave him, *because I respect him,* candid advice.
3. I gave him candid advice *because I respect him.*
4. James, *with a low mumble,* took the letter.
5. I was *presumably* breaking the law.
6. I made, *with all the grace I could summon,* my amends.
7. There, *at ten o'clock,* I arrived *as I had been told.*
8. *At ten o'clock,* I arrived there, *as I had been told.*
9. There, *as I had been told,* I arrived *at ten o'clock.*

In these examples, the various arrangements of the movable modifiers make little difference to the general sense of the sentence; but they may make considerable difference in emphasis. Sentences 7, 8, and 9, for example, say much the same thing. But sentence 7 tends to stress the place; sentence 8, the time of arrival. Sentence 9 also emphasizes the place and suggests that the instructions had been primarily concerned with designating the place. Control of emphasis and of shadings of meaning is the mark of a skillful writer. He will place his movable modifiers carefully, not thoughtlessly.

The proper arrangement of the movable modifiers is necessary for nuance of meaning and exact emphasis, but in some instances proper arrangement may be necessary to prevent downright confusion. For example, consider this sentence:

The boy who sold the most tickets today will receive the prize. Does the sentence mean that the prize will be given today? Or that the prize will be given to the boy who sold most tickets today? If we mean the former, we should write:

The boy who sold the most tickets will be given the prize today.

or:

The prize will be given today to the boy who sold the most tickets.

If we mean the latter, we should write:

The prize will be given to the boy who sold the most tickets today.

Our illustrative sentences suggest that adverbial modifiers may occur at almost any position in the sentence: at the beginning of the sentence (1, 7, 8, and 9), at the end of the sentence (3, 7, 8, and 9), between the subject and the verb (4), between the finite verb and verbal (5), between the verb and its object (6), and between the indirect object and the direct object (2). But the last two positions are somewhat special. One would hardly write:

He sang *pleasantly* the song.

though he might write:

He sang *pleasantly* the song that I had taught him.

One would hardly write:

I gave him *quickly* candid advice.

though, as we have seen, one might write:

I gave him, *because I respect him,* candid advice.

The principle would seem to be this: that if the modifier or the direct object is sufficiently weighted with words, the modifier may precede the direct object. But the whole problem of placing the movable modifier calls for taste and tact. Even an experienced writer may need to experiment with possible positions before he feels that he has placed his movable modifiers most effectively.

One further principle emerges from a consideration of our examples. Placed before or after a sentence, movable modifiers modify the sentence as a whole; placed internally, they modify the relation between the words that precede and the words that follow them. Consider the different shadings of meaning in the following sentences:

Presumably, the thief had gained entrance through a window.
The thief, presumably, had gained entrance through a window.

In the first sentence, it is the total statement that we are to presume. In the second, the presumption is limited: what we presume is that the entrant was the thief.

There is one class of adverbial modifiers, however, which is not freely movable. These are adverbs which state a direction, adverbs like *in, back, to, up,* and *down.* These adverbs (which we may call *directives*) cannot precede a verb or verbal. For example, we can write:

James gave it *back.*

but not:

James *back* gave it.

We can write:

The water had leaked *out.*

but not:

The water had *out* leaked.

or:

The water *out* had leaked.

Moreover, these directives, if used in a series of adverbial modifiers, must precede the other adverbial modifiers. Thus:

I put the cat out last night.

not:

I put the cat last night out.

But these directive adverbs *can* precede the subject of the sentence when the verb expresses explicit motion. Thus:

*Back* ran Jim to third base when the outfielder made his throw to the catcher.

or:

*Home* the little fellow darted as fast as he could run.

These last instances reveal once more our pattern of emphatic variation: *back* and *home* which, as we have seen, normally follow the verb, are emphasized when they are placed at the beginning of the sentence.

The student already knows how to use *directives,* of course. Native speakers have *unconsciously* been using them correctly all their lives. The intention here, and elsewhere in this discussion of fixed and movable modifiers, is not to cram the student's head with sets of rules and categories of exceptions to the rules. Most native speakers observe the rules (and their exceptions) quite automatically.

But having noted the exceptions, we are allowed to sum up the general pattern in two simple statements:

*1. Adjectival modifiers are relatively fixed: variation from the normal position constitutes a means for emphasizing the modifier.*

*2. Adverbial modifiers are rather freely movable: careful placing of the modifiers constitutes a means of controlling the finer shadings of meaning.*

Moreover, the foregoing discussion sheds real illumination on the problem of the "dangling participle."

### THE DANGLING PARTICIPLE

Participles are verbal adjectives. Since they are adjectives, they must modify some substantive in the sentence. Yet, as we have seen, like adverbs, they are *movable* modifiers. This fact explains why we so easily forget that they are adjectives, and treat them as if they were truly adverbs. Here is an example:

Walking along the road, a cloud of dust obscured the neighboring fields.

Such absurdities are, as we have seen, produced by the writer's changing the construction in the course of writing the sentence. He begins with an adjectival modification and then forgets to provide a substantive for the participle to modify. The remedy, of course, is to make the construction consistent—to write:

As we walked along the road, a cloud of dust obscured the neighboring fields.

or:

Walking along the road, we encountered a cloud of dust which obscured the neighboring fields.

## APPLICATIONS

Some of the following sentences include dangling modifiers. In others, the modifiers have been shifted out of the order given by the original author. Remove dangling modifiers, and rearrange the italicized modifiers so as to improve the clarity and effectiveness of each sentence.

1. Though the Greek scientist Eratosthenes had, *with only a small error,* calculated the distance of the sun from the earth, and the earth's circumference at the Equator, his theory of a global world was received by men of common sense *with polite scorn.*

2. Singing merrily and happily, our music put the whole company into a jolly mood.

3. In a myriad private hotel rooms of a myriad hotels the Alumni Weekly Lunch is, *today,* being celebrated, *as every day.*

4. *Because their maxims would not have expressed their hearts,* they would not have been perfect moralists *then, even if their theory had been correct* (which, I think it was, *though not in statement,* in intention).

5. Thinking as hard as we could, the answer still could not be found.

6. Eight men were drowned, *however,* and *from that memory* my grandfather *at intervals all his life* suffered, and never read anything but the shipwreck of St. Paul *if asked to read the family prayers.*

7. There can be no miracles *unless there exists something else which we may call the supernatural, in addition to Nature.*

8. Calling and calling again as we wandered over the fields, not a sound was heard from the lost child.

9. Turning the corner, the gigantic skeleton of New York's newest and the world's highest building comes into view.—The New York Herald Tribune.

10. There are wild woods and mountains, marshes and heaths, even in England. But *only on sufferance* are they there, *because we have chosen to leave them their freedom, out of our good pleasure.*

11. For Nature is always alien and inhuman, *even in the temperate zone,* and diabolic *occasionally.*

## GENERAL PRINCIPLES OF SENTENCE STRUCTURE

### PARALLELISM

Thus far we have considered the structure of the sentence from one point of view: that of the arrangement of the basic constituents of the sentence, and the arrangement of the various kinds of modifiers. But there are other principles which may determine the structure of a sentence. One of these is PARALLELISM: the adjustment of grammatical pattern to rhetorical pattern. In its simplest terms, parallelism means no more than that like meanings should be put in like constructions.

The very richness of English tempts us to violate parallelism. For example, we have two noun forms of the verb. We can use the infinitive "to swim" or the gerund "swimming." Consequently, the careless writer may blunder into a sentence like this:

*To swim* and *hunting* are my favorite sports.

But the distinction between infinitive and gerund awkwardly distracts the reader from what is a co-ordinate relation. We ought to write:

*Swimming* and *hunting* are my favorite sports.

or:

*To swim* and *to hunt* are my favorite sports.

It is, however, our great variety of movable modifiers that most often leads us into this kind of blundering. We write, for example:

*Being lazy by nature* and *because I am clumsy,* I have never liked tennis.

Such violations of parallelism easily creep into first drafts—even into the first drafts of a good writer. Careful rewriting is the answer.

We must not forget, however, that the principle of parallelism may be used positively. So used, it becomes a powerful rhetorical device. By stressing parallel constructions we emphasize the ideas expressed, and we can thus play one sort of meaning off against the other. Sentences constructed on this principle are sometimes called "balanced sentences." Here are some examples:

1. As the hart panteth after the water brooks, so panteth my soul after Thee, O God.

2. He was sick of life, but he was afraid of death; and he shuddered at every sight or sound which reminded him of the inevitable hour.

3. To examine such compositions singly, cannot be required; they have doubtless brighter and darker parts; but when they are once found to be generally dull, all further labour may be spared; for to what use can the work be criticized that will not be read?

The parallel elements may be represented in the following scheme:

|   |   |   |
|---|---|---|
| 1. | as | so |
|   | hart | soul |
|   | panteth | panteth (repetition) |
|   | water brooks | Thee |
| 2. | sick | afraid |
|   | life | death |
| 3. | singly | generally |
|   | required | spared |
|   | once found | all further |
|   | be criticized | be read |

### CO-ORDINATION

Co-ordination may be regarded as an aspect of parallelism. We have seen that like meanings should be put in like constructions. By the same token, only sentence elements of like importance may be linked together as equals. Conversely, a less important element must be made subordinate to the more important. Consider the following sentence:

I stayed at home; I was ill.

What is the relation between the two statements? The writer has merely associated them. He has not defined the relation of one to the other. He might define the relationship in various ways:

Because I was ill, I stayed at home.
While I was staying at home, I was ill.
Although I stayed at home, I was ill.
Feeling ill, I stayed at home.
I stayed at home, quite ill.

Simple uncritical writing (that of a child, say) tends to present a succession of co-ordinate units: "Then the bear got hungry. He came out of his den. He remembered the honey tree. And he started walking toward the honey tree." The mature and discriminating writer indicates the relation of his statements, one to another, subordinating the less important to the more important, thus:

Having done this, she thought it prudent to drop a few words before the bishop, letting him know that she had acquainted the Puddingdale family with their good fortune so that he might perceive that he stood committed to the appointment.

The writer who points up relationships, instead of leaving them to be inferred by the reader, obviously makes the reader's task easier. He gives not only facts, but an integration of facts: the very pattern of subordination suggests an interpretation. If, however, the writer, by using subordination, assumes this burden of interpretation, he must not falsify his interpretation by careless and thoughtless subordination. He must think through the relation of part to part. Unless he thinks it through, he may write sentences like this:

My head was feeling heavy when I took an aspirin.

In this sentence the motive for the act is treated as if it were the matter of importance; the act itself has been relegated to the subordinate position. Rather than confuse the reader with a subordination which inverts the real relationship, the writer would have done better simply to have written:

My head was feeling heavy; I took an aspirin.

It is easy, of course, to see what the proper subordination would be:

Because my head was feeling heavy, I took an aspirin.

or:

When my head began to feel heavy, I took an aspirin.

Here are two further examples of improper subordination·

1. The workman snored loudly and he had a red face.

Alter to:

The workman, who had a red face, snored loudly.

or to:

The red-faced workman snored loudly.

2. Mr. Jones is our neighbor and he drove by in a large automobile.

Alter to:

Mr. Jones, who is our neighbor, drove by in a large automobile.

or to:

Mr. Jones, our neighbor, drove by in a large automobile.

Yet, though subordination is important as a means for tightening up a naïve and oversimple style, the student ought not to be browbeaten into constant subordination. In certain contexts a good writer might prefer:

The workman snored loudly. He had a red face.

This form of the statement does bring into sharp focus the detail of the red face. It might even suggest a leisurely observer, looking on with some amusement. For discussion of some other effects secured by a simple and uncomplicated style, the student might look at page 452.

We may sum up this topic as follows: Grammatical subordination must conform to the rhetorical sense; it must not mislead by inverting it. Positively, it is an important means for securing condensation. Careful subordination tends to give the sense of a thoughtful observer who has sifted his ideas and arranged them with precision.

## LOOSE SENTENCES AND PERIODIC SENTENCES

We can view sentence structure in still another way. We can distinguish between those sentences in which the sense of the sentence is held up until almost the end (PERIODIC SENTENCES), and those in which it is not held up (LOOSE SENTENCES). Holding up the sense creates suspense: we do not know how the sentence is "coming out" until we have reached, or nearly reached, the end of it. Here are some examples:

1. "It was partly at such junctures as these and partly at quite different ones that, with the turn my matters had now taken, my predicament, as I have called it, grew most sensible."—HENRY JAMES.

If we convert the sentence to loose structure, we get something like this:

With the turn my matters had now taken, my predicament, as I have called it, grew most sensible, partly at such junctures as these and partly at quite different ones.

2. "But of all those Highlanders who looked on the recent turn of fortune with painful apprehension the fiercest and the most powerful were the Macdonalds."—LORD MACAULAY

Converted to loose structure, the sentence reads:

But the Macdonalds were the fiercest and the most powerful of all those Highlanders who looked on the recent turn of fortune with painful apprehension.

The loose sentence is the "normal" sentence in English; the structure of the periodic sentence, the "abnormal." As we have seen in this chapter, deviation from the norm always tends to be emphatic. The periodic sentence, in skillful hands, is powerfully emphatic. By inversion, by use of the "It was" construction, or by interposition of movable modifiers between subject and predicate, the sentence and its primary statement are made to end together. But like all deviations from the norm, the periodic sentence—and the balanced sentence—are somewhat artificial. Overused, such sentences would soon weary.

## SENTENCE LENGTH AND SENTENCE VARIATION

How long should a sentence be? It may be as short as one word. "Go!" is a perfectly good sentence: it has a predicate with subject implied. On the other hand, a sentence may be forty or fifty words long; and by tacking on further elements with *and's* and *but's*, we could construct sentences of indefinite length. These are the possible extremes. But with the sentence, as with the paragraph, common sense and taste set reasonable limits. A succession of very short sentences tends to be monotonous. Extremely long sentences tend to bog the reader down in a quagmire of words.

This is not, of course, to say that the writer should not feel free to use a one-word sentence whenever he needs it, or even a long succession of short sentences to gain special effects (see p. 452 for an example). By the same token, he ought to feel free to use very long sentences to gain special effects. The following sentence from Lytton Strachey's *Queen Victoria* will illustrate.

Perhaps her fading mind called up once more the shadows of the past to float before it, and retraced, for the last time, the vanished visions of that long history—passing back and back, through the cloud of years, to older and ever older memories—to the spring woods at Osborne, so full of primroses for Lord Beaconsfield—to Lord Palmerston's queer clothes and high demeanour, and Albert's face under the green lamp, and Albert's first stag at Balmoral, and Albert in his blue and silver uniform, and the Baron coming in through a doorway, and Lord M. dreaming at Windsor with the rooks cawing in the elm-trees, and the Archbishop of Canterbury on his knees in the dawn, and the old King's turkey-cock ejaculations, and Uncle Leopold's soft voice at Claremont, and Lehzen with the globes, and her mother's feathers sweeping down towards her, and a great old repeater-watch of her father's in its tortoise-shell case, and a yellow rug, and some friendly flounces of sprigged muslin, and the trees and the grass at Kensington.—LYTTON STRACHEY: *Queen Victoria*, Chap. 10.[3]

Strachey is imagining what may have passed through the old Queen's dying mind as she slipped from consciousness. Moreover, he imagines the succession of memories as going backward in time, through those of adult life, to those of youth, and on back to the memories of childhood. The loosely linked series is justified on two counts: the memories are presented as those of a dying mind, and, as the memories go backward in time, they become those of a child. Thus dramatically considered, the jumping from scene to

[3] From *Queen Victoria* by Lytton Strachey, copyright, 1921, by Harcourt, Brace and Company, Inc.

scene (as suggested by the dashes) and the loose tacking on of additional scenes (by *and's*) are justified. This sentence, which closes Strachey's book with what amounts to a recapitulation of Victoria's life, is thus used to gain a special effect.

Unless, however, the writer is striving for some special effect, he ought to look with some suspicion on very short and especially on very long sentences. Two considerations demand that he be suspicious of the extremes: the normal requirements and limitations of the human mind which dictate (1) how much we can take in satisfactorily, and with satisfaction, "at one bite"; and (2) a need for variety.

Let us consider a particular case. Look back at the paragraph from Virginia Woolf quoted on page 260. These thirteen sentences range in length from three words to fifty-two. The fourth sentence is quite long; the seventh sentence, very long. But three short sentences lead up to the fourth sentence, and two short sentences separate the fourth and seventh sentences.

Santayana's "Dickens" (p. 749) will repay close study for the skill in which sentence variety is maintained. Santayana's sentences tend to be long. They are carefully constructed and are frequently quite complex. But he is careful not to tire the reader. The following passage will illustrate.

Having humility, that most liberating of sentiments, having a true vision of human existence and joy in that vision, Dickens had in a superlative degree the gift of humour, of mimicry, of unrestrained farce.

But after this sentence, we are given the simple statement:

He was the perfect comedian.

And having thus had time to catch our breaths, we are ready to go on with "When people say Dickens . . ."

Alternation of long and short sentences is but one means, however, by which to secure variety. Another, and a most important means, consists in varying the structure of the sentence. The examples from Santayana will illustrate: the sentence "He was the perfect comedian" is not only shorter than the sentence that precedes it; it represents a return to the simplest type of structure (subject + predicate + predicate complement) after the quite complex structure of the preceding sentence.

Sentences that repeat a pattern become monotonous. Here is an example:

I was twenty that April and I made the glen my book. I idled over it. I watched the rhododendron snow its petals on the dark pools that spun them round in a swirl of brown foam and beached them on a tiny coast glittering with mica and fool's gold. I got it by heart, however, the dripping rocks, the ferny grottos, the eternal freshness, the sense of loam, of deep sweet decay, of a chain of life continuous and rich with the ages. I gathered there the walking fern that walks across its little forest world by striking root with its long tips, tip to root and root to tip walking away from the localities that knew it once. I was aware that the walking fern has its oriental counterpart. I knew also that Shortia, the flower that was lost for a century after Michaux found it *"dans les hautes montagnes de Carolinie,"* has its next of kin upon the mountains of Japan. I sometimes met mountain people hunting for ginseng for the Chinese market; long ago the Chinese all but exterminated that herbalistic panacea of theirs, and now they turn for it to the only other source, the Appalachians.

The "I was—I idled—I gathered" formula is relieved somewhat by the long descriptive phrases and relative clauses. Even so, it is irritatingly monotonous. Here is the way in which Donald Culross Peattie actually wrote the passage:

The glen was my book, that April I was twenty. I idled over it, watching the rhododendron snow its petals on the dark pools that spun them round in a swirl of brown foam and beached them on a tiny coast glittering with mica and fool's gold. But I got it by heart, the dripping rocks, the ferny grottos, the eternal freshness, the sense of loam, of deep sweet decay, of a chain of life continuous and rich with the ages. The walking fern I gathered there, that walks across its little forest world by striking root with its long tips, tip to root and root to tip walking away from the localities that knew it once, has its oriental counterpart; of that I was aware. And I knew that Shortia, the flower that was lost for a century after Michaux found it, *"dans les hautes montagnes de Carolinie,"* has its next of kin upon the mountains of Japan. Sometimes I met mountain people hunting for ginseng for the Chinese market; long ago the Chinese all but exterminated that herbalistic panacea of theirs, and now they turn for it to the only other source, the Appalachians.—DONALD CULROSS PEATTIE: *Flowering Earth,* Chap. 12.[4]

[4] From *Flowering Earth* by Donald Culross Peattie. Copyright, 1939, by Donald Culross Peattie. Courtesy of G. P. Putnam's Sons.

There are many ways in which to vary sentence structure. Nearly everything said earlier in this chapter can be brought to bear on this problem. We can invert the normal pattern, or rearrange the pattern to throw emphasis on what is normally the subject or complement; we can subordinate severely or rather lightly. Most of all, we can dispose the modifiers, particularly the movable modifiers, so as to vary the pattern almost infinitely. Variety is, of course, never to be the overriding consideration. A sentence ought to take its characteristic shape primarily in its own right: the structure best adapted to its particular job. The writer will usually find that he is thoroughly occupied in discharging this obligation. Yet it is well to remind ourselves here again of the claims of the whole composition. We never write a "collection of sentences"—we write an essay, a theme, a total composition. The good sentence honors the claims exerted upon it by the total composition. And in our writing, and especially in our *rewriting,* we need to see that we have avoided irritating monotony of sentence length or of sentence structure.

## SUMMARY

A SENTENCE is a complete thought expressed through a PREDICATE. In this chapter we are primarily concerned with the sentence as a rhetorical unit: that is, with the effectiveness of various kinds of sentences. Yet the terms UNITY, COHERENCE, and EMPHASIS, though primarily rhetorical terms, have their grammatical equivalents. A sentence is more than a vague cluster of ideas: its grammatical completeness (*unity*) requires a certain kind of *coherence* of parts (subject, predicate, complements, modifiers) organized around a point of *emphasis,* a focus of interest, which is indicated by the finite verb.

In the normal sentence the basic constituents of the sentence are arranged in a fixed order:

1. Subject + verb + indirect object (if any) + direct object or other verb complements (if any)

2a. Adjectives precede the substantive they modify. (Predicate adjectives are governed by rule 1.)

2b. Adjectival phrases and clauses follow the substantive they modify.

3a. Adverbs and adverbial modifiers (plus participial phrases) are not fixed as to position, but movable.

3b. Movable modifiers placed at the beginning or end of a sentence modify the whole sentence; placed internally, they modify the relation between the words preceding and the words following them.

Deviations from the normal pattern show EMPHASIS, and like other emphatic devices are to be used sparingly and with caution.

Sentence structure also may be viewed in terms of PARALLELISM and CO-ORDINATION.

Parallelism: like ideas demand like grammatical constructions.

Co-ordination: only elements of like importance are to be linked as equals; the less important element is to be subordinated to the more important.

Violation of these principles results in sentences that are not only ineffective and awkward but grammatically incorrect. But we can *stress* these principles, if we like, for positive rhetorical effect. The consequent variation from the normal sentence is, like all departures from the norm, emphatic. The PERIODIC SENTENCE (in which the sense of the sentence is held up until the end) is emphatic in the same way and for the same reason. These more consciously rhetorical types of sentence structure quickly lose their power when overused.

The student will do well to master the normal pattern of sentence structure. There is nothing to be ashamed of in its sturdy simplicity. It will constitute, as it ought to constitute, the staple of his prose. But, just in proportion as the student grasps the normal pattern *plainly as a norm,* he is enabled to use effectively departures from the norm—both for the expressiveness of the particular sentence and for general sentence variety. He can, first of all, try to place his movable modifiers with more care. He can occasionally vary the basic pattern itself in order to emphasize a particular sentence element—the more safely if he knows that his variation is for the sake of emphasis. He can occasionally experiment with the more elaborate departures from the norm such as the balanced and periodic sentences.

## *APPLICATIONS*

**I.** Try to determine which of the following sentences are periodic in structure and which are loose. Rewrite the periodic sentences into loose sentences, and the loose into periodic. Pick out the balanced sentences, if any.

1. The power, and the restriction on it, though quite distinguishable when they do not approach each other, may yet, like the intervening colors between white and black, approach so nearly as to perplex the understanding, as colors perplex the vision in marking the distinction between them.—CHIEF JUSTICE JOHN MARSHALL.

2. Peace cannot be secured without armies; and armies must be supported at the expense of the people. It is for your sake, not for our own, that we guard the barrier of the Rhine against the ferocious Germans, who have so often attempted, and who will always desire, to exchange the solitude of their woods and morasses for the wealth and fertility of Gaul.—EDWARD GIBBON.

3. The night, the earth under her, seemed to swell and recede together with a limitless, unhurried, benign breathing.—KATHERINE ANNE PORTER.

4. And it is precisely because of this utterly unsettled and uncertain condition of philosophy at present that I regard any practical application of it to religion and conduct as exceedingly dangerous.—CHARLES S. PIERCE.

5. If we begin with certainties, we shall end in doubts; but if we begin with doubts, and are patient in them, we shall end in certainties. —FRANCIS BACON.

6. The mania for handling all the sides of every question, looking into every window, and opening every door, was, as Bluebeard judiciously pointed out to his wives, fatal to their practical usefulness in society.— HENRY ADAMS.

7. Bubbling spontaneously from the artless heart of a child or man, without egoism and full of feeling, laughter is the music of life.—WILLIAM OSLER.

8. Every night I pulled my flag down and folded it up and laid it on a shelf in my bedroom, and one morning before breakfast I found it, though I had folded it up the night before, knotted around the bottom of the flagstaff so that it was touching the grass.—W. B. YEATS.

9. The hunger and thirst for knowledge, the keen delight in the chase, the good-humored willingness to admit that the scent was false, the eager desire to get on with the work, the cheerful resolution to go back and begin again, the broad good sense, the unaffected modesty, the imper-

turbable temper, the gratitude for any little help that was given—all these will remain in my memory, though I cannot paint them for others. —F. W. MAITLAND.

10. If he be my enemy, let him triumph; if he be my friend, as I have given him no personal occasion to be otherwise, he will be glad of my repentance. It becomes me not to draw my pen in the defense of a bad cause, when I have so often drawn it for a good one.—JOHN DRYDEN.

II. The following paragraphs are taken from *Time*. *Time*-style is celebrated for its inversions of, and its drastic departures from, normal sentence order. The motive, presumably, is a desire for condensation and emphasis. Rewrite these paragraphs so as to restore normal sentence order. Can you justify the departures from normal order? Is emphasis intelligently used? Does too much emphasis result in no emphasis?

An abandoned lime quarry at Makapangsgat, Transvaal, yielded two bones last year to Dart's diggers: part of an occiput (the back part of the skull) and a lower jaw, from a pygmy moppet who had died while still getting his second teeth. Near by were many baboon skulls, bashed in from above or behind with a club which had a ridged head (the distal end of the humerus).

Most startling was Dart's evidence, from a number of charred bones, that the little man had learned to use fire. He lived in the early Ice Age, from 300,000 to 500,000 years before Peking Man, hitherto the earliest known user of fire. In honor of both his fire-bringing record and his prophetic skills, the new little man was named *Australopithecus prometheus*.[5]

III. The next paragraph is from Ring Lardner's *You Know Me, Al,* which purports to be a series of letters from Jack, the rookie pitcher, to his friend. As a revelation of character and of speech "in character," it is quite perfect. But it may provide us with a useful exercise in sentence structure and proper subordination. Rewrite it, putting it into formal English.

We was to play 2 games here and was to play 1 of them in Tacoma and the other here but it rained and so we did not play neither 1 and the people was pretty mad a bout it because I was announced to pitch and they figured probily this would be there only chance to see me in axion and they made a awful holler but Comiskey says No they would not be no game because the field neither here or in Tacoma was in no shape for a game and he would not take no chance of me pitching and may be slipping in the mud and straneing myself and then where would

[5] Courtesy of TIME, Copyright Time, Inc. 1948.

the White Sox be at next season. So we been laying a round all the p.m. and I and Dutch Schaefer had a long talk to gether while some of the rest of the boys was out buying some cloths to take on the trip and Al I bought a full dress suit of evening cloths at Portland yesterday and now I owe Callahan the money for them and am not going on no trip so probily I wont never get to ware them and it is just $45.00 throwed a way but I would rather throw $45.00 a way then go on a trip a round the world and leave my family all winter.[6]

[6] From *You Know Me, Al* by Ring Lardner, copyright, 1925, by Charles Scribner's Sons.

# CHAPTER 9

# Style

## GENERAL DEFINITION OF STYLE

WE USE the general term STYLE to indicate the manner in which something is said or done. We talk, for instance, of a pole vaulter's style; or we speak of an old style of handwriting; we talk about a coat or a dress of a certain style; and accordingly we speak of a writer's style—his manner of saying a thing—his special way of expressing an idea. But it is plain that we use the term loosely and generally. Style evidently can mean a great many different things.

A discussion of style had better begin, therefore, by making perfectly clear how the term is to be used. We have already suggested that style is used to indicate "how" a thing is said as distinguished from "what" is said. Suppose we want someone to shut the door. We can speak in a courteous or in an abrupt manner; we can make a request or a demand: we might say, "I expect you would like to close that door," or "Would you mind shutting that door," or "Shut that door now!" All three sentences have the same "content"; "what" they say is much the same; but the style, the manner, varies a great deal.

The way in which a thing is said evidently qualifies *what* is said: that is, style helps define and determine content. For the practicing writer, it is on this level that the problem of style becomes important. He cannot say accurately what he wants to say unless he also masters the "how" of saying it. This is the problem that will largely concern us in the chapters that follow. Yet we ought to mention two other senses in which we use the word *style*, if only to isolate and emphasize the basic sense.

## THREE ASPECTS OF LITERARY STYLE

First, *style* can be used to designate a manner of writing characteristic of a whole age. A writer of the sixteenth century uses a different style from that of a twentieth-century writer, or, for that matter, from a writer of the late seventeenth century. The King James Version of the Bible (1611) has "the sower went forth to sow." A modern writer would normally write "the sower went out to sow." Addison, in one of his *Spectator* papers (1711), writes: ". . . several of those Gentlemen who value themselves upon their Families, and overlook such as are bred to Trade, bear the Tools of their Forefathers in their Coats of Arms." Today we would write: ". . . gentlemen who are proud of their families and look down upon people who are in business" or perhaps "upon businessmen"; and we would have to say "on," not "in their coats of arms." Some of the writing of the past, therefore, seems as quaint to us as the fashion of dress that obtained centuries ago. This aspect of style, however, need not concern us very much. We can assume that all of us who write in the twentieth century will share certain period likenesses which will set off our writing, good and bad, from the writing of earlier periods.

Second, style can be used to designate a personal and individual manner. Two tennis players, for example, though trained under the same coach, may each have his own individual style. We may mean by style, therefore, the special way in which each writer expresses himself. We can frequently recognize something written by a friend, even though it is merely read aloud to us, because we feel that the way in which it is written reflects the friend's personality: Bill Jones would put it in just this way, whereas Jim Smith would put it in that way.

Thus far we have mentioned three levels on which one encounters the problem of style. A neat summary of the three levels is provided if we consider, in each instance, what it is that shapes the style. First, and most important, there is style as shaped by the writer's specific purpose—the choice and arrangement of words as determined by the audience addressed and the purpose at hand. Second, we have style as shaped by the writer's general environment. Third, we have style as shaped by the writer's own personality. The second of these, we have said, need not concern us very much in this book. The third is a highly pervasive thing: we shall probably do well to postpone consideration of it to Chapter 13. It is with the first—the choice and arrangement of words as an adaptation to the writer's specific purpose—that the rest of this chapter will be concerned. But at this point we ought to have a concrete illustration showing how these three levels of style are related to each other. Let us return for a moment to Bill Jones.

Our friend Bill Jones may have his own personal way of saying a thing (style as expression of personality), in spite of the fact that his way of saying it will, in some respects, resemble the way in which his contemporaries say it (style as expression of a period): but Bill Jones, nevertheless, will probably write in several different styles, as he takes into account the audience he addresses and the particular occasion on which he writes. For example, he will sometimes use a colloquial style, in conversation with his fellows; at other times, when the occasion demands a certain dignity, he may prefer to use a much more formal style. We constantly make such distinctions: a letter of application for a job demands one style; a note to an intimate friend, quite another.

## STYLE AS AN INTERPLAY OF ELEMENTS

In the essay entitled "Learned Words and Popular Words" (p. 552), Greenough and Kittredge write: "Every educated person has at least two ways of speaking his mother tongue. The first is that which he employs in his family, among his familiar friends, and on ordinary occasions. The second is that which he uses in discoursing on more complicated subjects and in addressing persons with whom he is less intimately acquainted. It is, in short, the language which he employs when he is 'on his dignity,' as he puts on evening dress when he is doing to dine. The difference between these two forms of language consists, in great measure, in a difference of vocabulary."

It should be noted that Greenough and Kittredge are careful to specify "*at least two* ways of speaking his mother tongue," for if we are to be accurate, there are many more than *two* ways of speaking it, and an even larger number of ways of writing it. Indeed, we can say that between the extremes of a highly ceremonious formality, on the one hand, and utterly intimate informality, on the other, there are hundreds of intermediate shadings. In the chapters that follow we shall want to talk about some of these shadings, and how they are produced. Greenough and Kittredge are also perfectly right in saying that it is a "difference of vocabulary" which largely determines levels of style. But, important as the choice of vocabulary is, it is only one of the many elements which go to make up a style.

The real difficulty in discussing style comes just here. Style, as was pointed out in the Introduction (p. 6), is an over-all effect. It is an effect determined by the interplay of sentence structure, vocabulary, figures of speech, rhythm, and many other elements. It is not always easy for a reader to pick out the element which is most important, or even largely important, in giving the style of the writer its special quality. It is quite impossible for a writer to produce a given quality of style by mechanically measuring out so much of this element and so much of that. A modern author has put the matter in this way: "Style is not an isolable quality of writing; it is writing itself." But if style is simply writing itself, how will it be possible to give the student any practical pointers for developing a proper style of his own? The very complexity of the interaction of form and content, element and element, may seem to render the problem hopeless.

## THE PLAN OF THE FOLLOWING CHAPTERS ON STYLE

The problem of style is certainly difficult, but it is not hopeless. Granted that the separate devices cannot finally be isolated, still nothing forbids our singling out the various elements for purposes of study. In the four chapters which follow, we shall discuss some of the more important aspects of style: DICTION (the choice of words), METAPHOR (the use of comparisons and figures of speech), TONE (the manifestation of the writer's attitude toward his material and toward his audience), and RHYTHM (the pattern of stresses and pauses); we shall also, in passing, touch on various other aspects of style. Yet, even though we must, in order to treat the subject at all, try to isolate the various means by which the writer secures his effect, we must keep reminding ourselves that they are not really "isolable." Style is an over-all quality; consequently the discussion of one aspect of style necessarily overlaps other aspects.

A concrete example will serve to illustrate this necessary over-lapping. Take the indignant expression "He is a dirty rat." This sentence is certainly a humble example of style, but it will serve. For it has a certain quality which differs, say, from "The man is treacherous," or "The man has evil intentions," and that quality is the result of a complex of elements. Diction is certainly involved, but so is metaphor: the "he" in question is not literally a small, gray-furred mammal. Attitude is plainly involved, for the sentence is not so much a proposition as an expression of feeling. One could argue that even rhythm may be involved. If we compare "He is a dirty rat" with "He is a contemptible little verminous animal," we sense the difference in effect: the second expression is less violent, more considered and calculated, more grandly contemptuous than the first. It is just possible that the more elaborate and formal rhythm of the second sentence has something to do with this effect.

To sum up, all four chapters that follow have to do with style. They constitute the divisions of a general discussion of this topic; but these chapters are not offered as a logical division of the topic. They are not that. They do not constitute an exhaustive classification, nor are they mutually exclusive. They overlap at points. Still, it can be claimed that they represent a practical classification.

The obvious point at which to begin any discussion of style is with DICTION. The choice of vocabulary is primary. Moreover, the chapter on diction necessarily lays the groundwork of the chapters that follow. The chapter on METAPHOR grows naturally out of it. For metaphor, and figures of speech generally, can be regarded as extensions of words—a stretching of words beyond their literal meanings, in order to gain further expressiveness. Through metaphor the writer transcends "dictionary" meanings, bending and shaping language to his particular purpose.

The chapter of TONE, like that on metaphor, grows out of the discussion of diction. For the chapter on tone extends the discussion of the ways in which a coloring of meaning, a shading of emphasis, a hint as to attitude, may be given, not merely by a particular word (a matter discussed under diction) but also by a whole phrase, or sentence, or the total composition.

The fourth chapter in this series, "The Final Integration," is, as its title suggests, something of a summary of the problems of style. It deals with general matters of over-all effect such as RHYTHM, but more especially with the way in which a successful style is made to bear the stamp of the writer's whole personality.

We have already said that these divisions of the general topic of style do not constitute a logical classification of the various aspects of style. The student ought at the very beginning to recognize this and to expect some necessary overlapping. But the student has it in his power to make of this necessity a virtue if he will allow the overlapping to serve as a constant reminder that "style is not an isolable quality of writing; it is writing itself."

# Diction

GOOD diction is the choice of the right words. Accurate, effective expression obviously requires the right words—the words which will represent, not nearly, not approximately, but precisely and exactly what we want to say. This is a simple rule and it covers the whole problem of writing; but in application the rule is far from simple. The good writer must choose the right words, yes; but which are the right words? The criterion for judging "rightness" is not simple but highly complex.

Now diction would be no problem if there existed for each object and each idea just one word which denoted specifically that object or idea, one name and only one name for each separate thing. Unfortunately, language is not like that. Words are not strictly denotative. Some words in English, it is true, do represent the only name we have for a particular object or substance. *Lemming,* for example, is the only specific name for a certain small mouse-like rodent; *purine* is the only specific name of a compound whose chemical formula is $C_5H_4N_4$. The ideal scientific language would be a language of pure denotation. But the language of pure science (that of mathematics, say) constitutes a very special case.

## DENOTATION AND CONNOTATION

Actually the writer faces quite another kind of situation: instead of one word and only one word for each thing, he ordinarily finds competing for his attention a number of words all of which denote exactly or approximately the same thing. Moreover, even those words which have exactly the same DENOTATION (that is, those which explicitly refer to the same thing) may have different CONNOTATIONS: they may *imply* different shadings of meaning. (Every word has one *denotation*, but probably more than one *connotation*.) For example, *brightness, radiance, effulgence, brilliance* may be said to have the same denotation, but there is a considerable difference among them in what they connote. *Radiance*, for example, implies beams radiating from a source, as the words *brilliance* or *brightness* do not. *Brilliance*, on the other hand, suggests an intensity of light which *effulgence* and *brightness* do not. Again, *brightness* is a more homely, everyday word than are *radiance, brilliance*, and *effulgence*. These are only a few suggested contrasts among the connotations of these words, all of which describe a quality of light. Varying connotations in words with the same denotation may also be illustrated from words which refer to concrete objects. Compare the simple words *bucket* and *pail*. The denotations are much the same. We might apply either word to name one and the same vessel. But in present-day America, at least, *bucket* is more likely to be the ordinary word, with associations of everyday activity, whereas *pail* will seem a little more old-fashioned and endowed with more "poetic" suggestions. It will connote for some readers a bygone era of pretty milkmaids in an idyllic setting. But not necessarily, someone will exclaim, remembering the sentimental song entitled, "The Old Oaken *Bucket*." For words change from period to period and their connotations change, as a rule, much more rapidly than do their denotations.

Words, then, are not static, changeless counters, but are affected intimately, especially on the level of connotation, by the changing, developing, restless life of the men themselves who use them. Some words wear out and lose their force. Some words go downhill and lose respectability. Other words rise in the scale, and, like *mob*, which was no better than slang in the eighteenth century, acquire respectability.

In 1710 Jonathan Swift concocted the following letter to illustrate some of the faults in the English of his day:

Sir,

I *couldn't* get the things you sent for all *about Town.*—I *thot* to *ha'* come down myself, and then *I'd ha' brout 'um;* but I *han't don't,* and I *can't do't,* that's *pozz.*—Tom begins to *g'imself airs* because *he's* going with the *plenipo's.*—'Tis said, the *French* King will *bamboozl' us agen,* which *causes many speculations.* The *Jacks,* and others of that *kidney,* are very *uppish,* and *alert upon't,* as you may see by their *phizz's.*—Will Hazzard has got the *hipps,* having lost *to the tune of* five hundr'd pound, *tho* he understands play very well, *nobody better.* He has promis't me upon *rep,* to leave off play; but you know 'tis a weakness *he's* too apt to *give into, tho* he has as much wit as any man, *nobody more.* He has lain *incog* ever since.—The *mobb's* very quiet with us now.—I believe you *thot* I *banter'd* you in my last like a *country put.*—I *sha'n't* leave Town this month, *&c.*

Swift proceeds to comment on this letter, among other things on its diction:

The third refinement observable in the letter I send you, consists in the choice of certain words invented by some *pretty* fellows; such as *banter, bamboozle, country put,* and *kidney,* as it is there applied; some of which are now struggling for the vogue, and others are in possession of it. I have done my utmost for some years past to stop the progress of *mobb* and *banter,* but have been plainly borne down by numbers, and betrayed by those who promised to assist me.

## APPLICATIONS

Read through again the letter by Swift, and then answer these questions:

1. Which of the "faults" that Swift condemned have become accepted in good English?
2. Which are still relegated to colloquial English?
3. Which words and expressions have died out completely?

The process of growth and decay in language is so strong that many words in the course of generations have shifted, not only their connotations, but their denotations as well; and some have even reversed their original meanings. Later in this chapter we shall have occasion to return to the history of words when we discuss the use of the dictionary. At this point, suffice it to say that the writer must take into account the connotations of a word as well as its precise denotation. He has the task of controlling words in two dimensions. Thus, in a romantic tale one might appropriately use the word *steed* rather than *horse.* But in ordinary contexts one certainly would not say or write, "Saddle my steed"—unless he were being deliberately playful or ironic. On the other hand there are still other contexts in which, instead of the rather neutral word, *horse*, it might be appropriate to use words like *plug* or *nag*—terms which are as derisive or humorous in tone as *steed* is poetic and "literary."

## TWO DISTINCTIONS: CONCRETE-ABSTRACT AND SPECIFIC-GENERAL

There are, of course, words whose connotations are not important. Obviously this will be true of the so-called empty words like *and, if, the, however.* But even among the "full" words, some will be much richer in connotations than others. As one would expect, the richest and most colorful words will tend to be those that are CONCRETE and SPECIFIC; the most nearly neutral and colorless, those that are ABSTRACT and GENERAL. For example, *peach, pear, quince, apple, apricot* are concrete and specific. Why do we call these words both *concrete* and *specific?* Let us take the easier distinction first. *Peach, pear, quince, apple,* and *apricot* name specific members of a class of objects, the general name of which is *fruit. Peach,* therefore, is specific; *fruit,* general. Again: *ship* is a general word, but *brig, schooner, lugger, yawl,* and *brigantine* are specific: they are members of a class of which *ship* is the class name.

But why do we call *peach, pear . . . apricot* concrete? The distinction between concrete and abstract has to do with the treatment of qualities. *Concrete* comes from a Latin word that means "grown together"; *abstract,* from another Latin word that means "taken away." The word *peach* certainly implies qualities: a certain shape, a certain color, a certain sweetness. But *peach* implies these qualities as "grown together"—as we actually find them embodied in a peach. We can, however, abstract (take away) these various qualities from the actual peach, and refer to them in isolation: *sweetness, fuzziness, softness.* If we do so, we get a set of abstract words. *Sweetness,* for instance, isolates a quality common to peaches (and to many other things): the quality is thought of as an idea in itself. To give other examples: *heat* is an abstract word, but *furnace* is concrete; *force* is abstract, but *dynamo* is concrete; *insanity* is abstract, but *madman* is concrete.

Words that refer to ideas, qualities, and characteristics *as such* are usually abstract. Words that name classes of objects and actions are usually general. Words that refer to particular objects and actions are usually concrete *and* specific. (In this connection, the student might reread the discussion of the process of abstraction on page 35.)

It ought to be plain that the two classifications just discussed are not mutually exclusive, and that consequently the same word may occupy two categories. *Peach* and *pear*, as we have seen, are concrete *and* specific. *Ship*, since it signifies an object but also names a class of objects, is both concrete and general. In the same way, abstract words may be either general or specific. *Courtesy*, *kindness*, and *bravery* are abstract words: they denote qualities of conduct. But in relation to *gentlemanliness*, another abstract word, they are specific; for *courtesy*, *kindness*, and *bravery* are specific elements of the more general virtue *gentlemanliness*. *Courtesy*, therefore, is abstract and specific; *gentlemanliness*, abstract and general.

This last example suggests a further point: *general* and *abstract* are not to be applied absolutely but in relation to other words. Some words are more general, or more abstract, than others. *Coat*, for example, is more specific than *garment*, for a coat is a kind of garment; but *coat* is, on the other hand, more general than *hunting jacket*, for a hunting jacket is a kind of coat.

## APPLICATIONS

I. Make a list of the concrete words in the passages of description quoted on pages 226, 228, and 229. Make another list of the concrete words in the passages quoted on pages 70, 77, and 106. Which tend to use the greater proportion of concrete words? Why?

II. Compare, in the matter of abstract-general and concrete-specific diction, the paragraph quoted from *Gulliver's Travels* (p. 54) and that quoted from "The Fall of the House of Usher" (p. 54). Can you account for the choice of diction in terms of what each author is trying to do? About which of the two houses described do you have the more facts? Which do you visualize the more vividly?

### THE MISUSE OF ABSTRACT AND GENERAL WORDS

Much writing that is woolly and clouded, difficult to read, clogged and ineffective, is writing that is filled with general and abstract words. For example: "Quite significantly, the emphasis is being placed upon vocational intelligence, which is based upon adequate occupational information for all pupils in secondary schools. . . . This emphasis upon vocational guidance for the purpose of making young people intelligent concerning the world of occupations and the requirements for entering occupations need not conflict seriously with other views of guidance that take into account everything pertaining to the education of the pupil."

There are a number of things wrong with this flabby statement, but, among other things, there is the large number of abstract words. The author might have written: "High schools today insist that the student learn enough about jobs to choose his own job wisely. Tommy and Mary Anne need to learn what various jobs pay, what training they require, and what kinds of people find them interesting. Tommy and Mary Anne can learn these things while they are learning the other things that schools are supposed to teach. Both kinds of learning are preparations for life, and one need not interfere with the other." The rewritten version still makes use of general and abstract words (*training, preparation,* and so on); but some of the cloudiest of the abstractions (*vocational intelligence, occupational information*) have been removed, and the rewritten version is not only simpler, but has more force.

We are not to assume, however, that concrete and specific words are somehow in themselves "better" than abstract and general words. They are better for some purposes; for others, not. Many subjects require general and abstract words.

For example, compare these two ways of saying the same thing. (1) "A child needs sympathy." (2) "A child does not like frowns. Cold looks cow him. He is fearful when he hears harsh words." The second account is long-winded; even so, the concrete words do not manage to give fully the meaning of the one abstract word *sympathy.*

Or, compare (1) "He lived in a house of medium size." (2) "His home did not have the suburban air of a bungalow, and it certainly had nothing of the rustic style of a lodge. It was much smaller than a mansion, but somewhat larger than a cottage." *Mansion, cottage, bungalow,* and *lodge* (not to mention *cabin, hut, villa,* and *château*) are overspecific for the writer's purpose here: he needs the simple, general term *house*. Our pronouns provide another illustration. The English personal pronouns sometimes prove to be overspecific. In some contexts, it would be most convenient if we had a pronoun which could mean either "he" or "she" ("his" or "her," "him" or "her"), without forcing us either to specify, or to use the masculine form with the understanding that it applied to either sex: "Someone has left his or her pen" (or "his pen").

The writer cannot, and need not try to, avoid abstract and general words. But he ought not to fall into the slovenly habit of using them without thought. In any case, he should remember that a sprinkling of concrete and specific words can be used to lighten the numbing weight of cumulative abstractions. To illustrate, compare (1) "A child needs sympathy. Tolerance of his mistakes and the sense of understanding and comradeship provide the proper stimulus for his developing personality. Conversely, an environment defective in sympathy and understanding can be positively thwarting; it can lead to repressions and thus lay the foundation for ruinous personality problems." (2) "A child needs sympathy. He didn't intend to smash the vase or to hurt the cat when he pulled its tail. Tolerance of mistakes and some sense of understanding is necessary if he is to feel that he is a comrade. Acceptance as a comrade stimulates him to become a better comrade. He grows and develops toward responsibility. But he finds it hard to grow normally in a cold and repressive atmosphere. The meaningless spanking—meaningless to him, since he had no intention of breaking the vase—drives him in on himself. He becomes confused and repressed. Some of these confusions and repressions may linger into adult life."

In choosing our words, the overriding consideration, of course, will always be the particular effect which the writer wishes to secure. Description and narration, for example, thrive on the concrete and the specific. Notice the number of concrete and specific terms in the following passage:

> He knew the inchoate sharp excitement of hot dandelions in young Spring grass at noon; the smell of cellars, cobwebs, and built-on secret earth; in July, of watermelons bedded in sweet hay, inside a farmer's covered wagon; of cantaloupe and crated peaches; and the scent of orange rind, bitter-sweet, before a fire of coals.—THOMAS WOLFE: *Look Homeward, Angel*, Chap. 8.

Exposition and argument, on the other hand, by their very nature, call for a diction in which general and abstract words are important.

Marx's interpretation of the past is explicit and realistic; his forecast of the future seems to me vague and idealistic. I have called it utopian, but you object to that word. I do not insist on it. I will even surrender the word "idealistic." But the point is this. Marx finds that in the past the effective force that has determined social change is the economic class conflict. He points out that this economic class conflict is working to undermine our capitalistic society. Very well. If then I project this explanation of social changes into the future, what does it tell me? It seems to tell me that there will be in the future what there has been in the past—an endless economic class conflict, and endless replacement of one dominant class by another, an endless transformation of institutions and ideas in accordance with the changes effected by the class conflict.—CARL BECKER: "The Marxian View of History." [1]

Scientific statements, for the reasons given on pages 34-38, may require a diction that is still more abstract and general. To cite an extreme example, "The square of the hypotenuse of a right triangle is equal to the sum of the squares of the other two sides." For its purpose, the diction here is admirable. The statement concerns itself, not with a triangular field or a triangular box or a triangular piece of metal. It deals with triangularity itself. The *right triangle* of this statement is an abstraction: so also are *square, hypotenuse,* and even *sides,* for the "sides of a right triangle" are abstractions too. They are not sides of wood or metal or plastic, but pure distances between defined points. We have here a general proposition that must hold true for all right triangles. The diction used is therefore properly abstract and general.

With terms of this extreme degree of abstraction, connotations disappear altogether. Exact science needs no colorful words. Scientific terms aspire to become pure denotations: terms that are inflexibly fixed, terms completely devoid of all blurring overtones. Science strictly conceived not only does not need connotative words; the connotations would constitute a positive nuisance.

[1] From *Every Man His Own Historian: Essays on History and Politics* by Carl L. Becker. Copyright, 1935, by F. S. Crofts & Company, Inc. Permission granted by Appleton-Century-Crofts, Inc.

# LANGUAGE GROWTH BY EXTENSION OF MEANING

We have said that a word not only has a specific meaning (denotation) but also implied meanings (connotations). The connotations are obviously less definite than the denotation, and therefore less stable and more amenable to change. In scientific language, as we have seen, the denotations are rigidly stabilized and the hazy and shifting connotations are, in so far as possible, eliminated. In a colorful and racy use of language, just the reverse is the case. The connotations are rich and important. We are tempted to use a word, not LITERALLY (that is, adhering strictly to the denotation), but FIGURATIVELY, stressing some connotation of the word. It is through such a process that words have shifted their meanings in the past; but this process of extension of meaning is constantly at work in our own time. Let us consider an illustration of the process.

## MEANINGS EXTENDED BY ANALOGY

The casual and unthinking view of language sees each word as fastened neatly and tightly to a certain specific object: "cat" means a certain kind of small, furry mammal that purrs, likes cream, and is the natural enemy of mice; "ladder" means a contraption consisting of parallel strips to which are fastened crossbars on which we rest our feet as we climb the ladder; "spade" means an instrument for digging in the earth. But words are not actually so neatly fastened to the objects for which they stand. Even when we are determined to speak forthrightly, and "call a spade a spade," we rarely do so. It is against the nature of language that we should be able to do so.

For example, Anna, who is determined to call a spade a spade, says: "I'll tell you frankly why I don't like Mary. Yesterday she saw a ladder in my stocking and a few minutes later I overheard her telling Jane that I was always slovenly. That's typical of Mary. She is a perfect cat." But obviously one is not calling a spade a *spade* when one calls a female human being a *cat*, or a special kind of unraveling in a stocking a *ladder*.

*Cat* and *ladder* are not being used literally here: their meanings have been extended on the basis of analogy. In the case of *ladder*, the extension of meaning is very easy to grasp: a "run," with the horizontal threads crossing the gap between the sides of the run, does resemble a ladder. *Cat* represents a slightly further extension: a cat, furry and soft, yet armed with sharp claws which it conceals but can bare in an instant, may be thought to resemble a woman who is outwardly friendly but is capable of inflicting wounding comments.

The situation we have just considered is thoroughly typical. Many common words have been extended from their original meanings in just this fashion. We speak of the "eye" of a needle, the "mouth" of a river, the "legs" of a chair, the "foot" of a bed. The hole in the end of a needle might have been given a special name; but instead, men called it an "eye" because of its fancied likeness to the human eye. So too with examples such as these: a *keen* mind, a *bright* disposition, a *sunny* smile, a *black* look. Someone saw an analogy between the way in which a *keen* blade cut through wood and the way in which a good mind penetrated the problem with which it was concerned. The smile obviously does not really shed sunlight, but it may seem to affect one as sunlight does, and in a way quite the opposite of the black look.

But the point to be made here does not concern the basis for the analogy, whether of physical resemblance (the *jaws* of a vice), similarity of function (*key* to a puzzle), similarity of effect (a *shining* example), or what not. The point to be made is rather that people normally use words in this way, extending, stretching, twisting their meanings so that they apply to other objects or actions or situations than those to which they originally applied. This is the METAPHORI-CAL process. The essence of metaphor inheres in this transfer of meaning—in the application of a word that literally means one thing to something else.

Thus far we have taken our illustrations from common words. But less common words and learned words will illustrate the same process of extension of meaning. Indeed, most of our words that express complex ideas and relationships have been built up out of simpler words. For example, we say "His generosity caused him to overlook my fault." *Overlook* here means to "disregard or ignore indulgently." But *overlook* is obviously made up of the simple words *look* and *over*. To look over an object may imply that one does not let his gaze rest upon that object: his eyes pass over it without noticing it. *Overlook,* then, in the sense of "disregard," is an extension and specialization of one of the implied meanings of *look over.* We have said "one of the meanings," for *look over* obviously implies other possible meanings. (Compare the archaic sense of *overlook* in the passage quoted from Addison, p. 366.) Consider the nearly parallel expression "to see over." From it we get the word *oversee.* This word normally means today *to direct, to supervise—* something quite different from "overlook." *Supervise* is built out of the same concepts as *oversee,* for *super* in Latin means *over,* and *-vise* comes from the Latin verb *videre* (past participle *visus*) which means *to see.* A bishop, by the way, is literally an *overseer.* For *bishop* comes originally from two Greek words: *epi,* which means *over,* and *skopein* which means *to look.* Thus, such diverse words as *overlook, oversee, overseer, supervise,* and *bishop* represent particular extensions of much the same primitive literal meaning.

## THE DICTIONARY: A RECORD OF MEANINGS

The etymology (that is, the derivation and history) of a word is often highly interesting in itself, but knowledge of word origins is also of great practical usefulness. The full mastery of a particular word frequently entails knowing its root meaning. Possessing that meaning, we acquire a firm grasp on its various later meanings, for we can see them as extended and specialized meanings that have grown out of the original meaning.

Here, for example, is what *The American College Dictionary* gives for the word *litter:* [2]

> **lit·ter** (lĭt′ər), *n.* **1.** things scattered about; scattered rubbish. **2.** a condition of disorder or untidiness. **3.** a number of young brought forth at one birth. **4.** a framework of canvas stretched between two parallel bars, for the transportation of the sick and the wounded. **5.** a vehicle carried by men or animals, consisting of a bed or couch, often covered and curtained, suspended between shafts. **6.** straw, hay, etc., used as bedding for animals, or as a protection for plants. **7.** the rubbish of dead leaves and twigs scattered upon the floor of the forest. —*v.t.* **8.** to strew (a place) with scattered objects. **9.** to scatter (objects) in disorder. **10.** to be strewed about (a place) in disorder (fol. by *up*). **11.** to give birth to (young): said chiefly of animals. **12.** to supply (an animal) with litter for a bed. **13.** to use (straw, hay, etc.) for litter. **14.** to cover (a floor, etc.) with litter, or straw, hay, etc. —*v.i.* **15.** to give birth to a litter. [ME *litere,* t. AF, der. *lit* bed, g. L *lectus*] —**Syn. 3.** See **brood.**

[2] From *The American College Dictionary,* ed. by Clarence L. Barnhart, copyright, 1947, by Random House, Inc.

The word is a noun (*n.*). Seven meanings for the noun are given. But the word is also a transitive verb (*v.t.*). Seven meanings are given for *litter* as a transitive verb. But *litter* is also an intransitive verb (*v.i.*), for which one meaning is given.[3] The word occurs in Middle English (ME *litere*), was taken from Anglo-French (t. AF), was derived from a word meaning bed (der. *lit* bed) and goes back finally to Latin bed, *lectus* (g. L *lectus*). Synonyms (words of nearly the same meaning) for the third meaning of *litter* will be found under *brood* (Syn. 3. See **brood**).

Let us consider the various meanings given for *litter*. At first glance there seems little to connect meaning 2, "a condition of disorder or untidiness" with 3, "a number of young brought forth at a birth," and even less with meaning 4, "a framework of canvas . . . for the transportation of the sick and the wounded." But once we grasp the fact that *litter* comes originally from a Latin word meaning *bed,* it is fairly easy to see how the various apparently unconnected meanings of *litter* developed. Meanings 4 [4] and 5 obviously refer to special sorts of portable beds; and the term *bedding* in definition 6 provides a link to meanings 12, 13, and 14. For if beds originally consisted of straw or rushes heaped together, it is easy to see how any scattering of straw or hay might come to be called a *litter,* and the process of strewing it a process of *littering.* Meanings 1, 2, 8, and 9 are obvious further extensions, for in these meanings the emphasis has been shifted from the purpose of making a kind of bed to an aimless and untidy strewing about.

Meanings 3, 11, and 15 derive from the original meaning, bed, by another chain of development. The mother animal frequently makes a sort of rude bed in which she lies to give birth, and by

[3] We have said earlier (p. 372) that every word has *one* denotation, but probably more than one connotation. Are we to regard the fifteen meanings given here for *litter* as fifteen denotations, with the further consequence that we are to think of the dictionary's account as an account of fifteen different words? Probably so, particularly in view of the fact that some of the meanings are so far apart: i.e., (1) scattered rubbish and (3) a number of young brought forth at a birth. But if we think of the original meaning (*bed*) as the denotation (p. 379), then we can understand how the fifteen meanings specified are related to this root meaning, as implied meanings (connotations) of a word are related to its denotation.

[4] The meanings are *not* numbered in the order of probable development.

association the rude bed (*litter*) comes to be used for what is found in the bed, the young animals themselves.

Let us consider one further example, this time from *Webster's Collegiate Dictionary*. Here is what the dictionary gives for the common word *sad:*

> **sad** (săd), *adj.; * SAD'DER (-ẽr); SAD'DEST.  [AS. *sæd* satisfied, sated.]  **1.** *Archaic.*  Firmly established.  **2.** Affected with or expressive of grief; downcast; gloomy.  **3.** Characterized by or associated with sorrow; melancholy; as, the *sad* light of the moon.  **4.** Afflictive; grievous.  **5.** Dull; somber; — of colors.  **6. a** Shocking; wicked; — often playfully.  **b** *Slang.* Inferior. — **Syn.** Solemn, sober; sorrowful, dejected, depressed. — **Ant.** Joyous; gay.

The word is an adjective (*adj.*). The forms of the comparative and superlative degrees are given; then its derivation (from Anglo-Saxon *saed*). Next, the dictionary lists five meanings, one of which it designates as archaic (1) and another as slang (6*b*). There follows a list of synonyms (words of approximately the same meaning) and of antonyms (words of opposed meaning).

Even so brief an account as this suggests a history of shifting meanings. Inspection of a larger dictionary such as *Webster's New International Dictionary* or the *Oxford English Dictionary* (*A New English Dictionary*), with its fuller information as to the derivation of the word and its finer discrimination of meanings (including the various earlier meanings), enables us to make out a detailed history of the meanings of the word.

*Sad* is closely related to the German word *satt* (full to repletion) and to the Latin word *satis* (enough) from which we get such modern English words as *satiate* and *satisfied*. But a man who has had a big dinner is torpid and heavy, not lively or restless, and so *sad* came to carry the suggestion of *calm, stable, earnest.* Shakespeare frequently uses it to mean the opposite of "trifling" or "frivolous." But a person who seems thus sober and serious *may* be so because he is grieved or melancholy, and the word gradually took on its modern meaning, "mournful" or "grieved." But we must not end this account without mentioning other lines of development. The sense of *torpid* or *heavy* was extended from animate beings, which can eat to repletion, to inanimate things which cannot—to bread, for example, that fails to rise, or to a heavy laundry iron. (The student should look up, in this connection, the word *sadiron*.)

Meaning 5 (dull; somber;—of colors) represents still another such extension. It means the kind of color which a sobersides (as opposed to a gay and sprightly person) would wear—dull, sober colors.

Has the process of extension now ceased? Hardly. Meaning 6*a* represents a fairly late instance of it. In mock deprecation, a young fellow might be called "a sad young dog"—as if his conduct caused horror and grief. Meaning 6*b* is a later extension still, one that has not yet been approved by the dictionary as "good English." In such a phrase as "sad sack" this meaning of *sad* has temporarily gained wide currency (though in America we tend to prefer the word *sorry:* a sorry team, a sorry outfit, a sorry job). If meaning 6*b* ever establishes itself, the dictionary will presumably remove the characterization "slang." (Some terms which began as slang have found their way into the language and into good usage; but a vastly greater number have enjoyed a brief popularity, have been discarded, and are now forgotten.)

The definition of a word is, then, a somewhat more complex business than one might suppose. There is frequently not just "the" meaning, but interrelated sets of meanings, some of which are current and some of which are not; some of which are established and some of which are not; some of which have been accepted into good society and some of which are merely clinging to the fringes of society. A word which is appropriate in one context obviously might be grossly out of place in another.

## APPLICATIONS

I. Look up the origin of the following words:

| | | |
|---|---|---|
| nostril | enthusiasm | fast (adj.) |
| aristocracy | urbane | egregious |
| plutocracy | Bible | sympathetic |
| complicate | fine (adj.) | malaria |
| thrilling | infant | starboard |
| vivid | silly | melancholy |
| gerrymander | laconic | bourgeois |

Does knowledge of its origin clarify the meaning of any word? Does it enable you to understand the relationship between current discrepant meanings (i.e., "He made a *fast* trip," and "The boat was made *fast* to the pier"; or "This *fine* print hurts my eyes" and "He was a big, *fine*, upstanding man")? Does knowledge of the origin of the word help account for such uses as "legal *infant*" and "the *Book*" (as applied to the Bible)?

II. With the help of the dictionary discriminate as carefully as you can among the words in the following groups:

1. sulky, petulant, peevish, sullen, morose, crabbed, surly
2. skeptic, infidel, atheist, freethinker, agnostic
3. reasonable, just, moderate, equitable, fair-minded, judicial
4. rebellion, revolt, insurrection, revolution
5. belief, faith, persuasion, conviction, assurance, reliance
6. sneak, skulk, slink
7. trick, fool, hoodwink, bamboozle, deceive, beguile, delude, cheat, mislead
8. brave, daring, courageous, fearless, valiant, dauntless
9. dawdle, idle, loiter, linger, lag
10. solemn, sober, serious, grave, reverential, earnest

Does a knowledge of the origin of the word throw light upon the special connotations of any of these words?

## THE COMPANY A WORD KEEPS: COLLOQUIAL, INFORMAL, AND FORMAL

Earlier, in discussing the connotations of words, we touched briefly upon the way in which connotations may determine the appropriateness of a word for a particular context (p. 373). The word *steed*, we saw, would be proper for some contexts, *nag* for others, and *horse* for still others. But the problem of appropriateness is important and deserves fuller treatment.

In the first place, there is what may be called the dignity and social standing of the word. Like human beings, a word tends to be known by the company it keeps. Words like *caboodle* and *gumption* are good colloquial words and perfectly appropriate to the informal give-and-take of conversation. But they would be out of place in a dignified and formal utterance. For example, a speech welcoming a great public figure in which he was complimented on his "statesman-like gumption" would be absurd. To take another example, many of us use the slang term *guy*, and though, like much slang, it has lost what pungency it may once have had, its rather flippant breeziness is not inappropriate in some contexts. But it would be foolish to welcome our elder statesman by complimenting him on being a "wise and venerable guy." The shoe, it is only fair to say, can pinch the other foot. Certain literary and rather highfalutin terms, in a *colloquial* context, sound just as absurd. We do not praise a friend for his "dexterity" or for his "erudition"— not at least when we meet him on the street, or chat with him across the table.

The fact that words are known by the company they keep does not, however, justify snobbishness in diction. Pomposity is, in the end, probably in even worse taste than the blurting out of a slang term on a formal occasion. Tact and common sense have to be used. But the comments made above do point to certain levels of usage of which most of us are already more or less aware. The various levels of diction (and their necessary overlappings) are conveniently represented in the following diagram: [5]

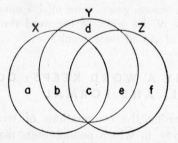

The three circles X, Y, Z, represent the three sets of language habits indicated above.

X—formal literary English, the words, the expressions, and the structures one finds in serious books.

Y—colloquial English, the words, expressions, and the structures of the informal but polite conversation of cultivated people.

Z—illiterate English, the words, the expressions, and the structures of the language of the uneducated.

b, c, and e represent the overlappings of the three types of English.

c—that which is common to all three: formal literary English, colloquial English, and illiterate English.

b—that which is common to both formal literary English and colloquial English.

e—that which is common to both colloquial English and illiterate English.

a, d, and f represent those portions of each type of English that are peculiar to that particular set of language habits.

In this matter of levels of diction, the dictionary can be of real help. It marks as such, colloquial words, slang, technical words, and so on. Yet even recourse to the dictionary is not a substitute for the

[5] From *The American College Dictionary*, ed. by Clarence L. Barnhart, copyright, 1947, by Random House, Inc.

student's developing a feeling for language. In this matter the dictionary can help, but wide reading can help even more. (The student will find the essay "Learned Words and Popular Words," page 552, pertinent to this general problem of levels of diction, and highly interesting for its own sake.)

## APPLICATIONS

**I.** The following passage is quite informal—even colloquial—in diction and expression. Rewrite the passage so as to make it as formal as possible.

I could recognize big changes from Commerce down. Beaver Dam Rock was out in the middle of the river now, and throwing a prodigious "break"; it used to be close to the shore, and boats went down outside of it. A big island that used to be away out in mid-river has retired to the Missouri shore, and boats do not go near it any more. The island called Jacket Pattern is whittled down to a wedge now, and is booked for early destruction. Goose Island is all gone but a little dab, the size of a steamboat. The perilous "Graveyard," along whose numberless wrecks we used to pick our way so slowly and gingerly, is far away from the channel now, and a terror to nobody. One of the islands formerly called the Two Sisters is gone entirely; the other, which used to lie close to the Illinois shore, is now on the Missouri side, a mile away; it is joined solidly to the shore, and it takes a sharp eye to see where the seam is—but it is Illinois ground yet, and the people who live on it have to ferry themselves over and work the Illinois roads and pay Illinois taxes: singular state of things!—SAMUEL L. CLEMENS: *Life on the Mississippi*, Chap. 15.

**II.** This passage is much more formal than that by Clemens. Attempt to rewrite the passage so as to make it less formal.

The reader has been informed, that we were running along the coast, within a mile of it, to enable us to keep sight of the land. The object of this was to make the proper landfall for running into the Gulf of Paria, on which is situated the Port of Spain, in the island of Trinidad, to which we were bound. We opened the gulf as early as nine A.M., and soon afterward identified the three islands that form the *Bocas del Drago*, or dragon's mouth. The scenery is remarkably bold and striking at the entrance of this gulf or bay. The islands rise to the height of mountains, in abrupt and sheer precipices, out of the now muddy waters—for the great Orinoco, traversing its thousands of miles of alluvial soil, disembogues near by. Indeed, we may be said to have been already within the delta of that great stream.

Memory was busy with me, as the *Sumter* passed through the Dragon's Mouth. I had made my first cruise to this identical island of Trinidad, when a green midshipman in the Federal Navy. A few years before, the elder Commodore Perry—he of Lake Erie memory—had died of yellow fever, when on a visit, in one of the small schooners of his squadron, up the Orinoco. The old sloop-of-war *Lexington,* under the mommand of Commander, now Rear-Admiral Shubrick, was sent to the Port of Spain to bring home his remains. I was one of the midshipmen of that ship. A generation had since elapsed. An infant people had, in that short space of time, grown old and decrepit, and its government had broken in twain. But there stood the everlasting mountains, as I remembered them, unchanged!—ADMIRAL RAPHAEL SEMMES: *Service Afloat,* Chap. 16.

## HOW CONNOTATIONS CONTROL MEANINGS

Thus far we have seen how connotations determine what may be called the social tone of a word. But we must go on to consider the very important way in which the connotations actually determine, though sometimes subtly, the effect of the word—that is, the way in which the connotations actually determine meaning. In our time especially, propaganda and advertising have made this whole matter very important.

A group of words having more or less the same denotation may range in their connotations from highly favorable to highly unfavorable. For example, we may call an agriculturist a "farmer," a "planter," a "tiller of the soil," or, in more exalted fashion, "the partner of Mother Nature"; but we can also refer to him as a "rube," a "hayseed," or a "hick." Few of our words merely *name* something. They imply a judgment about its value as well. They make a favorable or an unfavorable evaluation. Consider, for example, the following table of rough synonyms:

| *Favorable* | *Neutral* | *Unfavorable* |
|---|---|---|
| highest military leader- ship | general staff | army brass |
| motor sedan, cabriolet, convertible | automobile | jallopy |
| special agent | informer | stool pigeon |
| expert advisers | technical advisers | brain trust |

| *Favorable* | *Neutral* | *Unfavorable* |
| --- | --- | --- |
| cherub | child | brat |
| Democratic (or Republican) statesman | party leader | political boss |
| self-control | discipline | regimentation |

By choosing terms with the right connotations, one can easily color his whole account of a man or a happening or an idea. Much of the effectiveness of this method depends upon the fact that the writer ostensibly is only pointing to certain things, only naming them: the damaging (or ennobling) connotations are, as it were, smuggled in surreptitiously. This is the method frequently used by a writer like Westbrook Pegler or H. L. Mencken. Notice how heavily the following passage from one of Mencken's essays leans upon this device. (The italics are supplied by the present authors.)

"The ride of the Valkyrie" has a certain intrinsic value as pure music; played by a competent orchestra it may give civilized pleasure. But as it is commonly performed in an opera house, with a *posse* of fat *beldames* throwing themselves about the stage, it can produce the effect of a dose of ipecacua. The sort of person who actually delights in such spectacles is the sort of person who delights in plush furniture. Such half-wits are in a majority in every opera house west of the Rhine. They go to the opera, not to hear music, not even to hear bad music, but merely to see a more or less obscene *circus.*—H. L. MENCKEN: "Opera," *Prejudices: Second Series.*[6]

The power of connotations is also illustrated by our recourse to EUPHEMISMS. Certain words, even necessary words, which refer to unpleasant things, are avoided in favor of softening expressions or indirect references. "Bastard," in many contexts, is felt to be too brutal, and so "illegitimate" is substituted for it. Even a word like "died" may be avoided in favor of "deceased," or "passed away," or "went to his reward." Undertakers have taken to calling themselves "morticians," and butchers in some parts of the country prefer to be known as "meat-cutters." Whatever one may think of the substitutions, they at least testify to the strength of connotations, and the desire of men to avoid words with unpleasant or disparaging associations.

[6] Reprinted from *Prejudices: Second Series* by H. L. Mencken, by permission of Alfred A. Knopf, Inc. Copyright 1920 by Alfred A. Knopf, Inc. Copyright 1948 by H. L. Mencken.

Another obvious means of influencing the reader's attitude is the use of what I. A. Richards calls "projectile" adjectives: that is, adjectives which function, not so much to give an objective description, as to express the writer's or speaker's feelings. For example, a child will say "a mean *old* teacher," whether the teacher is old or young. "Beautiful," "fine," "nice," "miserable," "great," "grand" are typical projectile adjectives. The "*miserable* wretch" may actually be smiling happily. The woman who has just been called "a *great* little wife" may be large or small. *Great* and *little* here do not measure size—they are projectile adjectives.

How some of these adjectives (and the adverbs derived from them) came to acquire their expressive force involves a study of the history of the word. In nearly every case the process has been that of extension. (See p. 384, above.) The original meaning of *fine* is "finished," "brought to perfection." But the favorable associations with which we regard carefully done workmanship came to be extended to things which were not polished or intricately made. Conversely, the favorable associations aroused by *great* as it signifies the magnitude of certain objects (a great tree, a great pile of wheat) came to be extended to objects that lack magnitude. And so we can have "a great little wife" or "a fine country of mountains and forests."

Mention of the origin of projectile adjectives points to a third obvious device for influencing attitudes: the association of the thing in question with something pleasant or unpleasant, noble or ignoble. We express contempt by calling a man a "rat" or a "louse" or a "worm"; a certain admiration for his cleverness, by calling him a "fox"; hatred (and perhaps fear), by calling him a "snake." In general, the animal creation is a rich source of expressions of attitude toward other human beings, particularly of hostile or contemptuous attitudes. But we may use associations drawn from all sorts of areas: "He is a tower of strength," "He is as hard as flint," She is as neat as a pin."

Here follows the account of an incident as it might be reported by a relatively impartial writer:

Democratic [or Republican] Senator Briggs expressed surprise at being met by reporters. He told them that he had no comment to make on the "Whitlow deal." He said that he had not known that Whitlow was in the employ of General Aircraft, and observed that the suggestion that he had received favors from Whitlow was an attempt to discredit him.

How might a hostile reporter describe the incident? He would perhaps give an account something like this:

Senator Briggs, Democratic [or Republican] wheel-horse, was obviously startled to find himself confronted by newspapermen. He stubbornly refused to comment on what he called the "Whitlow deal," and professed not to have known that Whitlow was a lobbyist. The Senator complained that he was being smeared.

The second account seems to be substantially the same as the first. The "facts" are not appreciably altered. But the emotional coloring, and with it, the intended effect on the reader, have been sharply altered. The senator is now a "wheel-horse," with its suggestions of a hardened and (probably) calloused political conscience. Whitlow is a "lobbyist," and again suggestions of political corruption are insinuated. Moreover, the senator's actions and speech ("obviously startled," "stubbornly refused," "professed not to have known," and "complained") are made to suggest guilt.

Now the point in this comparison of the two accounts is not to indicate that the dryer, more objective account is necessarily "truer" and therefore to be preferred. Our estimable fictitious senator may in fact be quite guilty, and the writer of the second account may have given us the more accurate account of what actually happened in the interview. (It is even conceivable that the first account was written by a reporter who was pretty certain of the senator's guilty conduct but whose editor had ordered him to play down any suggestion of guilt. In that event, the first account would have to be regarded as the biased account.) The point to be made is this: that the coloring of attitudes in a piece of writing is extremely important, and is indeed an integral part of its "meaning." (In this general connection, the student should read "How to Detect Propaganda," p. 566.)

## APPLICATIONS

I. For the following words, try to find synonyms (or generally synonymous words or phrases) of opposite connotation:

| rebellion | harsh | dictator |
|---|---|---|
| tycoon | reformer | liberal |
| elegant | conventional | ward-leader |
| discrimination | diplomacy | theoretical |
| freedom | practical | aroma |
| police officer | vacillating | radical |
| esoteric | strait-laced | canard |

II. Alter the diction of the following passages in order to gain (a) a more favorable tone; (b) a less favorable tone. (The sample sentence, with its optional terms, will illustrate the kind of alteration which the student is to make.)

The veteran (still-youthful, aging) movie star walked (swept, minced) into the strong (brilliant, harsh) light, and paused for a moment to look at (glance at, ogle) the crowd.

1. The old woman walked up to the counter and priced the scarf. She hesitated, seemed to think for a moment, and then opened her black purse, and extracted a five-dollar bill. She laid it on the counter and began to finger the bright piece of cloth.

2. The mayor, a stocky man of middle age, stepped forward to the microphone with a sheaf of papers in his hand. He placed these on the lectern and cleared his throat. His face was serious as he began his speech.

3. Hans Eisler, alleged Communist Hollywood composer (and brother of Communist Gerhart Eisler) who had left the United States last week before deportation proceedings would have come into effect, appeared in Prague. He expressed pleasure at being able once more "to breathe the air of a friendly and enlightened country."

## WORN-OUT WORDS AND CLICHÉS

We began this chapter by saying that the problem of diction is that of finding the right words—the words which will say exactly what the writer wants to say. But we have seen that exactness in language cannot be secured simply and mechanically, that the exactness works on a number of levels. Words are not static. They are not changeless, inflexible counters. They have a history; they have biographies; and even, one is tempted to say, personalities. Most of all, since they are not changeless and inflexible, but to some extent plastic, changing their shape a little under the pressure of the context in which they occur, they offer a continual stimulus and challenge to the imagination of the writer.

The perfectly normal human habit of extending meanings beyond the "fixed" meaning has been discussed briefly. But it is an important topic and will be treated much more fully in Chapter 11 ("Metaphor"). In discussing a related topic, the way in which words may be used to imply value and to color an argument, we have laid the ground work for another important topic which will be discussed at large in Chapter 12 ("Situation and Tone"). We ought not, however, to conclude this chapter without noticing what we may call the degenerative disease that attacks and weakens language.

For as we have seen earlier, language changes, develops, grows, and by the same token, language wears out. We are not thinking, however, of the normal sloughing off of words that have died natural deaths, and now either do not occur in a modern dictionary at all, or if they do occur, are marked *obsolete* (*shoon* for *shoes*) or *archaic* (*e'en* for *even*). We are thinking rather of words that have been thoughtlessly used in particular contexts so often that they have lost nearly all their force. Whether we call these threadbare expressions "trite" or "hackneyed," or term them "stereotypes" and "clichés," is of little importance. Their common fault is this: they pretend to say more than the common expression says, and therefore call attention to their shabbiness.

## COMMON STEREOTYPES, INCLUDING SLANG

Jargon is produced by writers who do not think out what they want to say, but find a worn groove in the language down which they let their thoughts slide. Books on rhetoric sometimes supply lists of threadbare expressions against which the student is warned: "the more the merrier," "last but not least," "to trip the light fantastic toe." But hackneyed phrases of this sort have probably by now become too literary, too old-fashioned, to offer much temptation to a modern student—even to a lazy one. But stereotyping continues, and much of the writing and conversation to which we are constantly exposed is a tissue of trite expressions. The sports page, for example, will yield stereotypes in abundance. Mr. Frank Sullivan amusingly exhibits some of these in the form of question and answer.

*Q.* If [the teams] don't roll up a score what do they do?

*A.* They battle to a scoreless tie.

*Q.* What do they hang up?

*A.* A victory. Or, they pull down a victory.

*Q.* Which means that they do what to the opposing team?

*A.* They take the measure of the opposing team, or take it into camp.

*Q.* And the opposing team?

*A.* Drops a game, or bows in defeat.

*Q.* This dropping, or bowing, constitutes what kind of blow for the losing team?

*A.* It is a crushing blow to its hopes of annexing the Eastern championship. Visions of the Rose Bowl fade.

*Q.* So what follows as a result of the defeat?

*A.* A drastic shakeup follows as a result of the shellacking at the hands of Cornell last Saturday.

*Q.* And what is developed?

*A.* A new line of attack.

*Q.* Mr. Smith, how is the first quarter of a football game commonly referred to?

*A.* As the initial period.

—FRANK SULLIVAN: "Football Is King." [7]

Society page editors have their own brand of stereotypes: "social function," "society bud," "gala affair." To come closer home still, there is slang. Some slang expressions may once have been pungent and colorful. The sports writer who first described the strike-out of a slugging batter by saying "he made three dents in the atmosphere" conveyed the scene sharply and humorously. When slang is thus "tailor-made" for the occasion, it may be bright and perceptive (though, if it is still fresh and vivid, it is a question whether it ought to be viewed as "slang" at all). But as most of us use it, slang is a worn and impoverished language, not sprightly and irreverently lively, but stale and dead: "the party was a washout"; "I am fed up"; "he crabbed a lot"; "he blew his top." The real sin committed here is not so much that of bringing slang's flippant associations into a serious context. We do not often commit this fault. The real sin in using slang consists in using a thin and impoverished language.

[7] From "Football Is King," by Frank Sullivan, printed in *The Atlantic Monthly,* by permission of the author.

## JARGON: THE DEGENERATIVE DISEASE OF PROSE

We have to step up, however, to a somewhat more exalted plane to find the stereotypes which most damage modern prose and which are calculated to do the student most harm. These are such expressions as "along the lines of," "in the last analysis," "socio-economic considerations," "the world of business affairs," "according to a usually reliable source." Such locutions puff out many an official document, many a political speech, and, it must be admitted, many a professor's lecture or article.

This wordy, woolly style is sometimes called "officialese." Former Congressman Maury Maverick has recently damned it as "gobbledygook," submitting as a horrible sample the following extract:

Whereas, national defense requirements have created a shortage of corundum (as hereafter defined) for the combined needs of defense and private account, and the supply of corundum now is and will be insufficient for defense and essential civilian requirements, unless the supply of corundum is conserved and its use in certain products manufactured for civilian use is curtailed; and it is necessary in the public interest and to promote the defense of the United States, to conserve the supply and direct the distribution and use thereof. Now, therefore, it is hereby ordered that . . .

But whether we call it officialese when it emanates from some government bureau, or gobbledygook, or simply jargon, its empty wordiness is characteristic. Here are two somewhat more respectable samples culled from *College English*—a fact which should warn us that anyone can fall into jargon, even those who undertake to teach others how to write effective English.

[1] If we start at one of the extremes of the continuum, we shall find a grouping around a point of great vitality and wide appeal. Keenly aware of the painstaking scholarship and of the high creative effort that over the centuries has accumulated the body of subject matter we call "English," a group of our ablest teachers conceive their role to be to transmit this product of human endeavor, this hard-won store of learning and of art, this rich portion of man's heritage of culture, to the oncoming generations, and to imbue them with some perception of its worth.

[2] But whether we are trained statisticians or not, we can improve the results of our examination speeches and themes. First of all, we can, without great difficulty, develop better controlled problems. There are

various degrees of control possible in examination speeches and themes, and, within reasonable limits, it would seem as though the greater the control the more meaningful the test results. Complete freedom of choice of topic and material puts a premium upon accidental inspiration and upon glibness rather than thoughtfulness. A single assigned topic is palpably unfair since it may strike the interest and experience of some and yet leave others untouched.

These two passages have been somewhat unfairly taken out of context. Moreover, the topics discussed are not precisely colorful and exciting. Is it fair, then, to condemn their authors for having written jargon? How else could either writer have said what he had to say?

It is true that we have torn the passages out of context, and it is true that the subject matter is difficult. Yet even so, the symptoms of jargon are present. Consider the second excerpt: "puts a premium upon," "palpably unfair," are clearly stereotypes. Moreover, what does the author gain by specifying "without great difficulty," and "within reasonable limits"? Are these specifications necessary? Could they not be assumed? Has not the writer put them in for rhetorical purposes, that is, to "dress up" his statement, rather than to make necessary qualifications?

## JARGON: SOME ANTIDOTES

But jargon, of course, involves more than stereotypes. Jargon is nearly always compounded of clusters of general and abstract words, and though there is no certain prescription against jargon, it is easy to state one or two practical antidotes.

1. The student should try to use words that are as specific and concrete as possible; that is, he should never use a word more general and indefinite than he has to. Hazy and indefinite expressions represent the easy way out for a writer who is too timid to commit himself, or too lazy to think through what he wants to say.

2. The student should avoid stereotypes of all kinds—prefabricated phrasings which come easily to mind but which may not represent precisely his own ideas and emotions. But note this carefully: he should never avoid an *individual* word because it seems simple and common. If the sense calls for a simple, common word, it is generally best to repeat the word, if necessary, again and again. There is little to be said in favor of what is sometimes called ELE-

GANT VARIATION, that is, the substitution of some synonym in order to avoid repetition. Here is an example: "Mr. Jones was a powerful *financier*. As a *tycoon* he had a deep suspicion of socialism. He shared the feelings of his associates who were also *bankers*." The variations are irritating and can be confusing. Either recast the sentence or repeat *financier*.

On the other hand, the student should try to avoid *words strung together*—phrasings—which are common, and for that very reason, probably stereotyped. He cannot avoid all common expressions, nor should he try to avoid them, but he ought to learn to inspect them carefully before he decides to use them. If he really needs to say "along the lines of"—if something is really "in consideration of" something else and an emphasis on *consideration* is relevant—then let him use the expression by all means. But it is a good rule to remember that though he need never shy away from an individual *word* because it is common, he ought to be very shy of *phrases* that are common.

3. The student should try to use live words, remembering that finite verbs are the most powerful words that we have. We can find an instance of the failure to do so in the second sentence of the first excerpt quoted on page 395: "Keenly aware of the painstaking scholarship and of the high creative effort that over the centuries has accumulated the body of subject matter we call 'English,' a group of our ablest teachers conceive their role to be to transmit this product of human endeavor, this hard-won store of learning and of art, this rich portion of man's heritage of culture, to the oncoming generations. . . ." This sentence is packed with ideas, but the only finite verb in it (aside from *has accumulated* and *call,* in the two relative clauses) is the verb *conceive. Aware,* a participle, is made to carry the weight of the first twenty-six words; and the whole latter part of the sentence hangs from two successive infinitives, "to be to transmit." The sentence has so little stamina that it sprawls. It sprawls because the writer has starved it of finite verbs. The author might better have written: "Our ablest teachers realize what effort has gone into the making of that body of subject matter we call 'English.' They know it is a precious thing, for it embodies the effort of painstaking scholars and of great poets and novelists. They want to transmit this heritage of culture to the oncoming generations."

Finite verbs are more powerful than strings of participles, ger-
unds, or infinitives. Moreover, a specific verb is usually stronger
than a more general verb qualified by modifiers. Compare "He
walked along slowly" with "He strolled," "He sauntered," "He
dawdled," "He lagged." Frequently, it is true, we need the qualifiers.
But we ought not to forget the wealth of concreteness which the
English language possesses in its great number of verbs which
name specifically, and therefore powerfully, specific modes of action.

4. Finally, the student ought to remember that simple sentences
in normal sentence order (see p. 339) rarely degenerate into jargon.
An essay so written may be childishly simple, and it can become
monotonous; but it will seldom collapse into the spineless flabbiness
of jargon.

Jargon, however, is not to be dealt with summarily. It is our most
pervasive kind of "bad" style, and, like style in general, it is the
product of the interplay of many elements. We shall have to recur
to this topic in some of the chapters that follow, particularly in the
discussion of metaphor.

## SUMMARY

The discussion of DICTION carried on in this chapter may be summarized rather concisely since the various aspects of diction are so
closely interrelated. Words, as we have seen, are not pure DENOTA-
TIONS, that is, words are not tied to one specific meaning and only
one specific meaning. They have CONNOTATIONS as well—implied
meanings, shadings of meanings, qualities of feeling which are
associated with them. These implied meanings are naturally more
powerful in words that refer to some specific thing or action. Connotations are generally less vivid and less important in words which
are more general in their reference or which refer to some generalized quality or characteristic (abstract words).

The good writer must choose his words not only for appropriate
denotations but also for appropriate connotations. His problem, of
course, will vary with his purpose and with the occasion on which
he writes. At one extreme is technical and scientific writing in which
exact denotations are all-important and in which the writer's problem is to keep disturbing connotations out of his work. At the other
extreme is that kind of writing which attempts to give the impact

and quality of life itself. In such writing the connotations are of immense importance.

The dictionary is not merely a kind of logbook of precise meanings. As we have seen, words are really clusters of interrelated meanings. Some knowledge of how words grow, how meanings are extended, how language is constantly shifting and changing, will allow the student to make a wiser use of the dictionary and of his own personal experience of language.

From the general account of language just given, several important propositions follow.

1. The writer must be careful to choose his words in terms of their appropriateness within a particular context: some words are dignified, some "literary," some pleasantly informal, and so on.

2. Few words are simple namings. They also interpret the thing in question. They may be used to beg the question or to color an argument, as the advertiser or the propagandist has learned.

3. Everything else being equal, the writer will prefer live words to dead words or drugged words. He will avoid stereotyped phrasings of all sorts. He will avoid words which have been worn smooth by overuse in certain contexts, but he may discover that even words which seem to have lost all their vigor, if put in fresh patternings, tailor-made to his specific purpose, come alive again.

4. In general, the student will avoid wordiness, carefully choosing the right words for his purpose, and then giving these words elbow room in which to do their work.

## APPLICATIONS

I

Dear Miss Dix:

The time has come when I feel that I need some personal advice. I am a woman 32 years old. A little more than a year ago I met a man 45 years old and fell madly in love with him. I gave him his meals and was thrilled to do it. But now I wonder if I have just had a case of infatuation, for this man never pays any of the bills, or takes me to any place of amusement, or does anything to make me happy.

He says he loves me and wants to marry me some time, but when I suggest that we settle on a date, he always postpones it. Will a man who does nothing for me before marriage support me after marriage?

PERPLEXED

Answer:

Of course, he won't. The dumbest woman in the world would know that a man who grafted his living off a woman before marriage would continue his deadbeat tactics after marriage, if she only would give her brains a chance to function now and then.

Strange and unaccountable are the ways a woman's mind works its wonders to perform. Of all loathsome human beings is the male parasite who lives on women, instead of working and supporting himself, and how any woman can find anything to love in such a creature, passes all comprehension.

Don't deceive yourself into thinking that this man will ever marry you. He hasn't the slightest intention of doing so. He will leave you as soon as some woman who works a little harder and makes a little more money and is a little better graft comes along. Yet there are thousands of women who fall for this racket.

You ask if I think what you feel for this man is "infatuation"? I'd say that what ails you is just lack of plain, ordinary common sense.

List the clichés and stereotyped phrasings in Dorothy Dix's answer. Attempt to rewrite her answer in simple, clear English, free of slang and hackneyed expressions.

**II**

[Euclid] was limited by the social culture in which he lived. The Greeks did not live in a world of interest and petrol consumption and bowling analysis. Ratios were not familiar quantities. They represented a process of division which was carried out with a very stiff instrument, the abacus. Proportion did not sit lightly on Euclid's pupils. You can easily see the difficulty of Euclid's pupils. Suppose I know that the petrol consumption of a car is 35 miles to the gallon. I can get the number of miles I can run before filling up by multiplying the number of gallons in the tank by 35. I can get the number of gallons I require by dividing the number of miles I intend to run by 35. The two processes are equally easy in our arithmetic. The arithmetic of the counting frame is different. Multiplying one proper number by another always gives you an exact result which you get by repeated addition. Dividing one proper number by another means finding how many times you can take one away from the other. Usually you have some beads left over on the counting frame. You rarely get an exact answer. So division was a much more difficult process to grasp when people thought that all real numbers were proper numbers. Euclid had to devote a whole book (Book V) to illustrate the simple rules of proportion which are all summed up in the diagonal rule given in the last chapter. Draw two right-angled triangles, one with the two shorter sides 3 and 4 centimetres long, the other with the two shorter sides of 1½ and 2 inches; compare them, and you will see without difficulty that two triangles having corresponding sides whose lengths are in the same ratio is a situation no more difficult to grasp than the fact that a motor-cycle has the same petrol consumption on Good Friday and All Fools' Day.— LANCELOT HOGBEN: *Mathematics for the Million*, Chap. 4.[8]

The author of this passage is attempting to treat with some sprightliness a subject which for most people is abstruse and painfully dry. Is he successful? If so, how does his choice of diction contribute to his success? How many concrete words does Hogben use? How many abstract words? How does Hogben avoid the sense of formality? Illustrate from his choice of diction. What are the connotations of *bowling, petrol, car, tank*, and *motor-cycle*? What are the connotations of *Greeks, abacus*, and *counting frame*? Does Hogben actually want the contrast between the associations of the two groups of words? What purpose does it serve? Do the connotations of *Good Friday* and *All Fools' Day* clash? What purpose is served by this clash?

### III

Will Rogers, W. C. Fields, Wallace Beery, and other funny men have had trouble in the fourth grade. The born comedian apparently cannot take fractions seriously. Rogers used to boast that he would have become a dignified businessman if he could have mastered fourth-grade mathematics, and Fields has confided that he would have been a pillar of Philadelphia society but for the fourth grade. Beery's career was largely determined by his three years in that grade.

Beery is the best of the sheepish comics. He has never had to practise shamefacedness before a mirror. He acquired the trick in 1896, when he was the biggest boy in the fourth grade in Kansas City; he perfected it in 1899, when he was probably the biggest boy that any fourth-grade has ever known. Among his little schoolfellows he answered to the name of Jumbo. He was as happy with them as an elephant among mice. It is still recalled how at any false move his knees would tear up his desk by the roots. Some of his old classmates who whizzed through the fourth grade in a single year, and are now clerking in retail stores in Kansas City, are full of reminiscences about Wallie's dumbness and awkwardness.

[8] Reprinted from *Mathematics for the Million* by Lancelot Hogben, by permission of W. W. Norton & Company, Inc. Copyright 1937, 1940 by the publishers.

His fourth-grade experience accounts for the comic and villainous streaks in Beery, but fails to explain another set of characteristics—his ability to assume a noble stance, his occasional haughtiness and arrogance. Family pride may explain these qualities. Wallace was the son of a policeman. The extremes of his early professional career may have had something to do with his conflicting traits: he started on the stage and on the screen respectively as a chorus man and female impersonator; he had his name in lights on Broadway in 1907, when, at the age of twenty-one, he was the youngest musical-comedy star in the country. —ALVA JOHNSTON: "Jumbo." [9]

The student will probably conclude that the writing in this passage is quite effective. As prose, it is, on the whole, rather straightforward. The sentences are simple in structure. The passage may even be deceptively simple. How much of the effectiveness of this passage depends upon the choice of diction? How many hackneyed expressions are there, if any? Does the writer make use of slang? If so, is it justified? Why?

Can one literally "tear up a desk by the roots"? Is the metaphorical extension justified here? How is the metaphor (the desk is treated as if it were a tree) related to the comparison of Beery to an elephant? Is the comparison successful? How is this comparison, in turn, related to Beery's nickname?

## IV

1. In the passage quoted from *Service Afloat* (p. 387), Semmes uses the term *disembogues*. Consult the dictionary for the etymology of this word. Does the root meaning of the word indicate why Semmes chose it rather than some other for the particular passage in which it occurs?

2. In the passage quoted from *Life on the Mississippi* (p. 387), an island "has retired," another island is "booked for early destruction," the division between still another island and the mainland is a "seam." What are the literal or normal meanings of "retire to," "book for," and "seam"? Are the metaphorical extensions involved here justified? Attack or defend them.

[9] From "Jumbo" by Alva Johnston. Copyright 1935 The New Yorker Magazine, Inc. (Formerly the F-R Publishing Corporation.)

# Metaphor

## METAPHOR DEFINED

IN METAPHOR there is a transfer of meaning. We apply an old word to a new situation. Thus, as we saw in Chapter 10, we speak of the "eye" of a needle, the "legs" of a chair, the "bed" of a river. As we saw also in that chapter, language normally grows by a process of metaphorical extension. We proceed from the known to the unknown. We extend old names to new objects. But most of the illustrations of this process considered in Chapter 10 are instances of "dead" metaphor. Compare, for example, "the bed of a river" with "the dance of life." The first phrase carries no suggestion that the bed is a place of repose or that the river is sleepy! We use "bed of the river" technically, as a pure denotation from which the connotations that apply to *bed* in its usual senses are quite absent. But it is very different with the phrase "the dance of life." This metaphor is still alive. (At least Havelock Ellis, who used it as the title of one of his books, hoped that it would seem alive.) Here the connotations—the suggestions, the associations—are thoroughly relevant to Ellis's purpose. The connotations (of something rhythmic, of patterned movement, even, perhaps, of gaiety and happiness) are meant to be associated with life. We have characterized "bed of a river" as a dead metaphor, but to say "dead metaphor" is, of course, to make use of a metaphor, one based on an analogy with the animal kingdom. Animals (and vegetation, for that matter) can literally die: a metaphor cannot.

Our last metaphor, however, can illuminate the problem now being considered and may be worth a little further extension. With "dead" metaphors, we can say, *rigor mortis* has set in: they have no flexibility, no force; they have stiffened into one meaning, connotation has yielded to denotation. Metaphors that are still very much alive prove that they are alive by possessing a certain flexibility; and because they are still alive, they can be used to give color and life to a piece of writing. They can still excite the imagination.

In metaphors that are recognizably metaphors, there are, of course, varying degrees of life. The following are not very lively, but they do show that metaphor is a perfectly normal and important part of our normal speech: we say, for example, "John is a good egg," "Jane is a peach," "He ran out on the deal," "That remark threw him for a loss." Such expressions as these are rather worn and faded. But their original metaphorical character is plain enough, and we still think of them, and use them, as metaphors. The list of expressions that are badly shopworn but are still recognizably metaphors could be extended almost indefinitely: "hot as the devil," "cool as a cucumber," "independent as a hog on ice," "lazy as a dog," "crazy as a bat," and so on.

## IMPORTANCE OF METAPHOR IN EVERYDAY LANGUAGE

Our preference for the concrete and the particular, as these examples show, is not only normal; it is deeply and stubbornly rooted in the human mind. Consider the following situation: it is a hot day. We can say "It is hot" or "It is very hot" or, piling on the intensives, we can say "It is abominably and excruciatingly hot." But most of us, afflicted with the heat, will resort to metaphor of some kind: "It is hot as hell," or more elaborately, "It's hot as the hinges of hell." Evidently metaphor is felt to add forcefulness, and evidently the forcefulness has some relation to freshness of expression. The "hinges of hell" are not necessarily any hotter than other parts of hell; the precise specification and additional concreteness is an attempt to freshen the worn and dulled comparison, "as hot as hell."

That is one point, then: in metaphor, force and freshness tend to go together. Indeed, we are usually attracted to metaphor in the first place because ordinary language seems trite. A second point to be made is this: metaphor tends to accompany the expression of emotions and attitudes. A strictly scientific purpose would find entirely adequate expression in the statement that it is now 97.6 degrees Fahrenheit and that the humidity is 88.

Let us consider another simple case. Suppose one feels an especial kind of happiness and tries to express his feelings. He can say, "I feel happy." Or he can try to find a word which more accurately hits off this special feeling: *merry, gay, ecstatic, cheerful, glad, jolly,* or *joyous.* There are many synonyms for *happy,* as the dictionary will quickly reveal, and they differ in their shades of meaning. For example, *jolly* suggests a kind of heartiness and good humor that goes with comfortable living; *ecstatic* suggests some kind of transcendent experience of rapture; *gay* suggests a kind of sprightliness, a nimble lightheartedness. We shall do well to consult the dictionary to learn (or remind ourselves of) the wealth of resources at our disposal. Even so, we rarely find an adjective which exactly expresses our feelings. We tend to resort to metaphor. We say "I'm happy as a June-bug" or "I feel like a million dollars" or "I'm walking on air this morning" or "I feel like a colt in springtime," or, as a poet put it once:

> My heart is like a singing bird
>   Whose nest is in a water'd shoot;
> My heart is like an apple-tree
>   Whose boughs are bent with thick-set fruit.

If the feeling is very special or complex, we are usually *forced* to resort to metaphor. Here are the ways in which three writers of fiction express the special kind of happiness which each of their characters experiences.

The first is the happiness of a boy at the race track as he watches the horses work out.

Well, out of the stables they come and the boys are on their backs and it's lovely to be there. You hunch down on top of the fence and itch inside you. Over in the sheds the niggers giggle and sing. Bacon is being fried and coffee made. Everything smells lovely. Nothing smells better than coffee and manure and horses and niggers and bacon frying and pipes being smoked out of doors on a morning like that. It just gets you, that's what it does.—SHERWOOD ANDERSON: "I Want to Know Why." [1]

[1] From *The Triumph of the Egg* by Sherwood Anderson. Copyright 1921 by Eleanor Anderson.

What makes this passage effective is the re-creation of the scene in our imagination. This is done through the skillful use of descriptive detail: the author summons up for us the atmosphere of the race track. But he uses metaphor too—metaphor which is charged by the atmosphere. The metaphor, it is true, is scarcely declared; but it is there under the surface. The itch "inside you" is not a real itch; and "It just gets you" is a metaphor, for all the fact that it is slang. A more explicit (and highfalutin) way of saying it—the experience seizes you, or takes hold of you powerfully—reveals the metaphor clearly.

In the next example, the principal metaphor is perfectly explicit. The experience described is that of a boy in love for the first time.

> Her name sprang to my lips at moments in strange prayers and praises which I myself did not understand. My eyes were often full of tears (I could not tell why) and at times a flood from my heart seemed to pour itself out into my bosom. I thought little of the future. I did not know whether I would ever speak to her or not or, if I spoke to her, how I could tell her of my confused adoration. But my body was like a harp and her words and gestures were like fingers running upon the wires.—JAMES JOYCE: "Araby." [2]

The author uses three comparisons here: that of worship, that of a flood, and that of a harp. The second is the easiest and most obvious: the tears that well up in the boy's eyes suggest the flood metaphor. The first is the least explicit but the most pervasive: the metaphor may seem only hinted at in the phrase "strange prayers and praises"; but it is picked up once more in the phrase "confused adoration," for *adore* means literally "to pray to." This metaphor prepares for the third, the summarizing comparison: "my body was like a harp . . ." The boy responds to the loved one as a harp responds to the harpist's touch. Note that the harp comparison illuminates even "praises which I myself did not understand," for the harp as instrument cannot understand the "praise," the "adoration" which is elicited from it.

The third example describes the feelings of a shy man who has

[2] From *Dubliners* by James Joyce, copyright, 1925, by The Viking Press, Inc., and now included in *The Portable James Joyce,* published by The Viking Press, Inc., New York.

blundered into a darkened room and unexpectedly been kissed before the young woman, keeping her tryst there, has realized that he is not her lover.

At first he was tormented by shame and dread that the whole drawing-room knew that he had just been kissed and embraced by a woman. He shrank into himself and looked uneasily about him, but as he became convinced that people were dancing and talking as calmly as ever, he gave himself up entirely to the new sensation which he had never experienced before in his life. Something strange was happening to him. . . . His neck, round which soft, fragrant arms had so lately been clasped, seemed to him to be anointed with oil; on his left cheek near his moustache where the unknown had kissed him there was a faint chilly tingling sensation as from peppermint drops, and the more he rubbed the place the more distinct was the chilly sensation; all over, from head to foot, he was full of a strange new feeling which grew stronger and stronger.—ANTON CHEKHOV: "The Kiss." [3]

The man's intense emotions are treated in their vividness almost as if they were physical sensations. Notice, for example, "faint chilly tingling sensation as from peppermint drops." The comparison combines the sense of touch (chill) and taste. The sensation is slightly queer, and, to the man, troubling, and quite delightful.

## APPLICATIONS

Choose metaphors which will describe *how you felt* in the following situations. Do not necessarily take the first metaphor which comes to mind; try to avoid wornout metaphor; try to find a metaphor which describes as accurately as possible your own feelings.

1. On getting an A when you would have been happy to settle for the grade of C.
2. On getting well splashed by a passing car when on your way to an appointment.
3. On your first experience of stage fright.
4. On seeing a serious accident.
5. On first discovering that a close friend has betrayed your friendship.
6. On coming to realize that you have been guilty of a serious fault.

[3] From Anton Chekhov: *The Party and Other Stories.* Tr. Constance Garnett. Copyright, 1917 by The Macmillan Company and used with their permission.

## SLANG AS METAPHOR

In connection with metaphor it may be profitable to consider again two abuses of language, slang and jargon, which have already been touched upon in the preceding chapter (pp. 393-96). The impulse to use slang springs from our sound general preference for the concrete and the particular. Slang expressions are originally metaphors, and the problem of the misuse of slang cannot properly be solved apart from the more general problem of the use and abuse of figurative language. That is why it does very little good for the instructor to tell the student—or for the student to tell himself—not to use slang, for this advice is essentially negative. The student is right in wanting to make his writing warm, colorful, and lively. What he needs to do, therefore, is not to discard figurative language in favor of abstract expressions; but rather to inspect all his figurative language, *including slang,* in order to improve it as metaphor. He will try to eliminate all metaphors which are worn and trite, or which seem pretentious, or which are discordant with the rest of the composition. The practical result, of course, will be that in this process most of the slang will be sloughed off, but sloughed off *because it proves to be poor and ineffective metaphor,* not because it is figurative. For the good writer tries to bring his metaphors to life, and to direct and control them in that life. How to do this, of course, is a matter of craftsmanship and experience. But it is an important thing to learn, and it is our justification for devoting so much space in this text to the subject of metaphor. The student must get firmly in mind that this discussion of figurative language has not been inserted on the supposition that the student must learn to write a highfalutin and pretentious "literary" style. He needs, on the contrary, to master figurative language for the most practical of reasons.

## JARGON AND WORN-OUT METAPHOR

But why recur to the second general abuse of language, jargon, in this chapter on metaphor? What possible connection can jargon have with metaphor? The first answer to this question can be put simply: there is an important negative relation. It is the very lack of concrete words and of metaphorical vividness and particularity that makes jargon cloudy and ineffective. A primary way to avoid jargon, then, is to use concrete language—including its extension into metaphor. The spinelessness of jargon is in part the result of the writer's timid avoidance of vigorous metaphor. Even the most timid writer, however, is not actually able to avoid all metaphor; and with this observation we can give a second answer to the question. Jargon characteristically involves stereotypes of all kinds, including stereotyped and therefore lifeless metaphor. This connection of jargon with secondhand metaphor is forcefully put by the British critic, George Orwell.

Prose [nowadays] consists less and less of *words* chosen for the sake of their meaning, and more and more of *phrases* tacked together like the sections of a prefabricated henhouse. . . . There is a huge dump of worn-out metaphors which have lost all evocative power and are merely used because they save people the trouble of inventing phrases for themselves. . . . Modern writing at its worst . . . consists in gumming together long strips of words which have already been set in order by someone else.

(The student will notice that Orwell himself uses metaphor very effectively—"sections of a prefabricated henhouse," "dump of worn-out metaphors," "gumming together long strips of words." Orwell thus vividly suggests his two points of indictment: the lazy and careless craftsmanship of the writer of jargon, and the second-hand quality of the materials he uses.)

Orwell goes on to illustrate his point by suggesting how a modern writer of hand-me-down phrases would express the following passage from Ecclesiastes: "I returned, and saw under the sun, that the race is not to the swift, nor the battle to the strong, neither yet bread to the wise, nor yet riches to men of understanding, nor yet favor to men of skill; but time and chance happeneth to them all."

Such a writer, says Orwell, would probably turn it out like this: "Objective consideration of contemporary phenomena compels the conclusion that success or failure in competitive activities exhibits no tendency to be commensurate with innate capacity, but that a considerable element of the unpredictable must invariably be taken into account."

## CONFUSED METAPHOR AND HALF-DEAD METAPHOR

Orwell has hardly exaggerated, and the faults which he points out are found just as frequently in America as in Great Britain. Consider the following passages taken from recent magazines.

In the sense that we have known it in the past, American agriculture is a dying industry. The nation's largest single business still remaining in the hands of private citizens is in the midst of a scientific revolution, and the farm as an individual production unit—the final refuge from a mechanical and goose-stepped civilization—is seeing its last days. For chemistry and technology are bringing agriculture under control.

In broad terms, one may say that the farm is being wrecked by a series of three major frontal attacks, any one of which is deadly enough to have caused a serious crisis. . . .

The authors call American agriculture a "dying industry" but in the next sentence they say that it is "in the midst of a scientific revolution" and finally, that it "is seeing its last days." They attempt to give liveliness to these statements by comparing American agriculture to a dying animal; but any sense of vigor in the metaphor is pretty well lost when we have to consider agriculture first as an animal, next as a citizen living through a revolution, and finally as a "refuge from a mechanized and goose-stepped civilization." And if the reader is able to keep the metaphorical sense at all through these confusions, that sense is completely canceled out by the short statement that follows: ". . . chemistry and technology are bringing agriculture under control." An animal or a man who is dying and has seen his last days is certainly under control, and the pyramid of metaphors thus topples to a rather absurd anticlimax.

We can reconstruct the process of composition as follows: the authors were actually not sure whether they wanted the metaphors to come alive or remain decently dead. "Dying industry" they probably used as a dying metaphor—that is, they hoped that the metaphor would be lively in the first sentence, but decently dead and forgotten by the time that the reader got to the next sentence. But, in the floridly metaphorical atmosphere of the second sentence, the metaphor implicit in "dying" comes to life too—to embarrass and distract the new metaphor.

This confusion and irresponsibility in the use of metaphor is revealed in the last sentence where the authors, still anxious to maintain a kind of rhetorical liveliness, treat the farm under the figure of a war. "The farm," they say, "is being wrecked by a series of three major frontal attacks. . . ." But let us examine the figure for only a moment. There can be only one *frontal* attack on any one position. Frontal attacks must come, as the authors have themselves indicated, in "series," one after the other. It might make sense to say that the farm is being wrecked by a frontal attack which is being carried on simultaneously with attacks on either flank. Or it might make metaphorical sense to say that the farm has already sustained two damaging frontal attacks and that the third such attack is now in progress. This last statement is perhaps what the authors intended (though actually, it is very difficult to be certain as to what they did intend); but if they did intend the latter, they have been betrayed into confusion by their desire to use the "strong" word "frontal" when actually they had in mind no conception of a frontal attack as opposed to an attack from the side or from the rear.

The first essential in providing background information would be to present a comparative view of the societies of the world, from the simple primitive tribes to the complex civilized communities. Until the student is able to place data upon his own society in a comparative framework, he cannot be said to have gained any perspective or objectivity in that field. Such a cultivated emotional detachment is the first step toward understanding.

The danger of having dead and inert metaphors come to life is well illustrated by the statement "to place data upon his own society in a comparative framework." Obviously the author does not mean "to place data upon"—though the temptation to take "place upon" as a unit is almost irresistible. He meant to say that the student must place, in a comparative framework, the data that concerns his own society. But after we have made the correction, it becomes apparent that "place" is still not the word the author wanted. He would better have said that the student must *relate* data *to* a comparative scheme, or that the student must be able to *order* it *in* a comparative framework. Further confusion is promoted by the main clause of the sentence. How can placing data, or relating it, or ordering it "in a comparative framework" be said to give perspective? One may place himself at a vantage point from which he can see objects in perspective—that is, see them at a distance, from a point of view. But the metaphor of a framework, followed closely by a metaphor of getting perspective, results in a blurring and confusion of both metaphors. The "framework" has to be taken, not as a framework at all, but as an abstraction, for it behaves with embarrassment when forced into the dance of metaphors. The last sentence of the paragraph indicates what the author meant to say: that the student must stand back from—that is, detach himself from —his material so that he can see it in perspective.

Students and professors are sometimes accused of leading a cloistered existence comfortably removed from the dust and heat of everyday life. There may be some truth in that accusation, but let us remember that in the Dark Ages it was in the cloisters rather than in the market places that the flame of the spirit was kept alive. How is it faring today at Harvard and Yale, at Dartmouth and at Cornell? Are you determined to use your education merely to get a good job, marry and settle down,— in ordinary times that would be the natural aspiration,—or are some of you chafing to defend the rights of the spirit in a rapidly materializing world? Unless you are, the shadow of Hitlerism is likely to darken the world for a long time to come.

The first part of this passage echoes—and quite properly—Milton's famous remark that he could not "praise a fugitive and cloistered virtue . . . that never sallies out to seek her adversary, but slinks out of the race, where that immortal garland is to be run for, not without dust and heat." And the contrast between the cloisters and the market place again is used soundly. But the author gets into trouble when he speaks of "the rights of the spirit in a rapidly materializing world." Mediums make (or pretend to make) spirits "materialize." Does the author mean that the world too is a spirit which is being made to materialize? Or is he trying to say that the world is rapidly becoming unspiritualized—that it is preoccupied with matter as opposed to the realm of spirit? The momentary confusion is not clarified by the sentence that follows in which "the shadow of Hitlerism" is made to threaten darkness to the world. One is tempted to see Hitlerism as a shadow which is "materializing," that is, turning the world into solid murk and darkness. Actually in this case there is little difficulty in untangling the chance associations of spiritualist mediums from the rather straightforward distinction between the realm of the spirit and the realm of the material. But would not the sentence be more effective without this confusion?

The writer of the passage which follows is attempting to describe the effect of the comic books:

They defy the limits of accepted fact and convention, thus amortizing to apoplexy the ossified arteries of routine thought. But by these very tokens the picture-book fantasy cuts loose the hampering debris of art and artifice and touches the tender spots of universal human desires and aspirations, hidden customarily beneath long accumulated protective coverings of indirection and disguise.

But can one defy a limit? One can, of course, defy another person to set a limit. The comic books may break across boundaries, may exceed limits, and their authors may defy authorities to set any limits that they will respect. But here it is the comic books that are made to "defy limits," probably because the author was looking for a strong metaphor, and was willing to accept, without asking too many questions of it, the first strong metaphor that he found. The defiance hinted by the comic books has violent results. The comic books amortize the "ossified arteries of routine thought." To "amortize" is to cancel a mortgage. And "amortize" like "mortgage" is related etymologically to Latin *mors*, death. Even so, how can a defiance extinguish a mortgage on the arteries of thought—to the point of apoplexy? People who suffer from a hardening of the arteries are subject to strokes of apoplexy. Perhaps the writer is trying to say that the outrageous breaking of the conventions drives certain readers to apoplexy. But he has his apoplectic stroke affect the creaky and antiquated thoughts themselves. The result is a rather amazing mixup.

In the next sentence, the comic books, having by their defiance ruptured the arteries of conventional thought, proceed to cut loose the "debris of art and artifice." Or rather, it is the fantasy which cuts this debris loose. But "debris" means a scattered mass of materials. Can one cut a person loose from debris? Or does one not rather dig a victim *out of* the debris which has fallen upon him. And how can such debris be *worn*, as is evidently the case here, as a "protective covering"? The cutting loose of wreckage, the pulling off of a disguise, and the removal of a protective shell are thoroughly scrambled. And the confusion is not helped when we remember that the debris in question is composed of "art and artifice" and that the agent which cuts it loose is fantasy—something which one usually regards as associated with both art and artifice.

There is much to be said for a rich and concrete idiom. In return for it, we might be willing to disregard a few metaphorical loose ends. But there are limits, even though the comic books are said to defy limits. The writer here is evidently buried up to his ears in a debris which may be artifice but certainly is not art.

The excerpts examined are, we repeat, taken from "quality magazines"—the last and worst one, from the magazine published by Phi Beta Kappa. These are by no means the most absurd instances that could be collected. But they are absurd enough to indicate that "good" writers often manage their metaphors very poorly.

## APPLICATIONS

The following passages are taken from articles in reputable magazines. Make a criticism of the use of metaphor in these passages. Where the metaphors seem garbled or inappropriate, rewrite the passage, substituting consistent or appropriate metaphors.

1. Today Hitler has rolled time back to the grim days of pillage and purge, building, not a "greater Germany that will last a thousand years," but the greatest hate ever brewed in the hearts of men.

2. As his fame was slowly ascending, partly because of this social skill of his, into more illustrious circles, so was it trickling down among the more numerous obscure.

3. It's not the hurt the other fellow does you that keeps on rankling; it's the hurt you do yourself by your own remembering. That sticks in your skin and infects your mind.

I guess that's the secret of all successful forgetting. Don't let it break through your insulation at the start. Don't let it make a deep and lasting brand on the sensitive recording plate of your consciousness.

4. The emancipation of the slaves withdrew the Negroes from the maternal wing of the plantation system and threw them into the labor market.

5. Therefore, when he championed his middle class, he instinctively set his face against everything that threatened to substitute quantity for quality—against the encroachments of commerce and the new imperialism which the progressively minded among both Whigs and Tories were imbibing from Chatham. And the caveat against the dangers lurking in materialistic panaceas is not without implications that carry beyond the time and the place.

## THE FUNCTION OF METAPHOR

Thus far we have given our attention to some of the abuses of figurative language. It is high time to give a more positive account of metaphor and to show some of the uses of figurative language. After all, why do we use metaphor? What purpose does it serve? We have already assumed in earlier pages that it has its value in contributing color and liveliness, but if we are to understand why it is one of the great resources of the writer, we shall need to define more clearly what its function is. This is all the more necessary since the conventional account of the uses of metaphor is calculated to mislead. For example, we are in the habit of saying that the purpose of metaphor is (1) to illustrate or (2) to embellish; but these terms can easily suggest that figurative language is a kind of "extra" which may be usefully or gracefully "added on" to a statement, but which is never essential to the statement—never a direct part of what is being said. In accordance with this conventional view, the practical function of metaphor is to give a concrete illustration of some point which has been put more abstractly. The artistic use is to provide a pleasing decoration like an attractive wallpaper pasted onto the wall, or like a silk ribbon tied around a box of candy. But the trouble with this account is that, in either case, the figure of speech seems to be something which can be left off; and if we misconceive the purposes of metaphor by thinking of it as something external and additional, we shall never come to understand why a mastery of metaphor is absolutely essential to good writing.

## WHY SCIENTIFIC STATEMENT DOES NOT REQUIRE METAPHOR

Let us begin by disposing of a special kind of writing in which metaphor is indeed unnecessary or merely an addition. If I wish to say "2 + 2 = 4" or that "the square of the hypotenuse of a right triangle is equal to the sum of the squares of the other two sides," I shall not require metaphor. Metaphor would be in the way. Such statements as these, however, are very special: the terms used in such statements are (or aspire to be) pure denotations. If such terms have connotations at all, the connotations are surely irrelevant (see p. 378). Thus the "words" employed are not words in the usual sense. They are not capable of metaphorical extension. They are very special symbols, and the purest statements of this kind are able to dispense with words altogether: thus, $2 + 2 = 4$, or $H_2SO_4 + Fe \rightarrow FeSO_4 + H_2\uparrow$.

But important as such statements are, they represent a stringently limited discourse. Most of the discourse which interests us as human beings and which we must use as writers, goes far beyond abstract relationships of this kind. Most of our discourse has to do with the "full" world of our human experience—not the colorless, soundless, abstract world of modern physics, say, or of mathematics.[4]

## METAPHOR AS ILLUSTRATION

It ought to be noted, however, that even the scientific writer very often needs to go beyond this stringently limited abstract discourse, and even for him, metaphor, though frankly employed as illustration, may be highly necessary and useful. The following passage from Bertrand Russell's *The Scientific Outlook* will illustrate. The book is addressed to a general audience and Bertrand Russell is attempting to convince his reader that "what is actually experienced is much less than one would naturally suppose." He proceeds to analyze a typical experience for us. Here follows his analysis of what happens scientifically when we "see" someone.

You may say, for example, that you see your friend, Mr. Jones, walking along the street: but this is to go far beyond what you have any right to say. You see a succession of coloured patches, traversing a stationary background. These patches, by means of a Pavlov conditioned reflex, bring into your mind the word "Jones," and so you say you see Jones; but other people, looking out of their windows from different angles, will see something different, owing to the laws of perspective: therefore, if they are all seeing Jones, there must be as many different Joneses as there are spectators, and if there is only one true Jones, the sight of him is not vouchsafed to anybody. If we assume for a moment the truth of the account which physics gives, we shall explain what you call "seeing Jones" in some such terms as the following. Little packets of light, called "light quanta," shoot out from the sun, and some of these reach a region where there are atoms of a certain kind, composing Jones's face, and hands, and clothes. These atoms do not themselves exist, but are merely a compendious way of alluding to possible occurrences. Some of the light quanta, when they reach Jones's atoms, upset

[4] This is not, of course, to question the importance or the reality of such worlds. The scientist can deal with his material in this abstract way, and in no other way. His language is neither more nor less real than the language of the poet or novelist. It is merely different. In this general connection, the student might reread the discussion of abstract and concrete words (pp. 374-75).

their internal economy. This causes him to become sunburnt, and to manufacture vitamin D. Others are reflected, and of those that are reflected some enter your eye. They there cause a complicated disturbance of the rods and cones, which, in turn, sends a current along the optic nerve. When this current reaches the brain, it produces an event. The event which it produces is that which you call "seeing Jones." As is evident from this account, the connection of "seeing Jones" with Jones is a remote, roundabout causal connection. Jones himself, meanwhile, remains wrapped in mystery. He may be thinking about his dinner, or about how his investments have gone to pieces, or about that umbrella he lost; these thoughts are Jones, but these are not what you see.— BERTRAND RUSSELL: *The Scientific Outlook*, Chap. 3.[5]

Notice that Russell completes his analysis with the last statement of the passage; yet apparently he felt that the account might prove too technical and that his reader might fail to understand. Therefore he adds the following statement: "To say that you see Jones is no more correct than it would be, if a ball bounced off a wall in your garden and hit you, to say that the wall had hit you. Indeed, the two cases are closely analogous." Most readers will be grateful for this illustration. Most minds find abstractions so alien to them that they need a concrete statement such as the analogy provides. This is a truth which the writers of all books of scientific popularization know, and, for that matter, it is one known by every writer of directions for setting up a patent can opener. Even if the writer is able, as Bertrand Russell is able here, to state his analysis directly, the extra illustration—the concrete analogy drawn from daily experience—is helpful.

## APPLICATIONS

### I

The authors of the following passages supplied illustrative or summarizing comparisons, to make clearer or more emphatic what they had to say. In the passages printed below, these summarizing comparisons have been omitted. Try to supply an appropriate comparison.

**A.** These molecules move with very high speeds; in the ordinary air of an ordinary room, the average molecular speed is about 500 yards

[5] From *The Scientific Outlook* by Bertrand Russell, by permission of George Allen and Unwin, Ltd.

a second. This is roughly the speed of a rifle-bullet, and is rather more than the ordinary speed of sound. As we are familiar with this latter speed from everyday experience, it is easy to form some conception of molecular speeds in a gas. It is not a mere accident that molecular speeds are comparable with the speed of sound. Sound is a disturbance which one molecule passes on to another when it collides with it, rather like . . .—SIR JAMES JEANS: *The Universe Around Us*, Chap. 2.[6]

**B.** An insect, therefore, is not afraid of gravity; it can fall without danger, and can cling to the ceiling with remarkably little trouble. It can go in for elegant fantastic forms of support like that of the daddy-long-legs. But there is a force which is as formidable to an insect as gravitation to a mammal. This is surface tension. A man coming out of a bath carries with him a film of water of about one-fiftieth of an inch in thickness. This weighs about a pound. A wet mouse has to carry about its own weight of water. A wet fly has to lift many times its own weight and, as everyone knows a fly once wetted by water or any other liquid is in a very serious position indeed. An insect going for a drink is in as great danger as . . .—J. B. S. HALDANE: "On Being the Right Size."[7]

## II

In the following passages the authors have made much use of illustrative metaphor. Try to restate what is said in language as unmetaphorical as you can devise. Do not be surprised if you find that the rewritten version requires a good many more words than the original passage.

**A.** We, then, the animals, consume those stores in our restless living. Serenely the plants amass them. They turn light's active energy to food, which is potential energy stored for their own benefit. . . .

Animal life lives always in the red; the favorable balance is written on the other side of life's page, and it is written in chlorophyll. All else obeys the thermodynamic law that energy forever runs down hill, is lost and degraded. In economic language, this is the law of diminishing returns, and it is obeyed by the cooling stars as by man and all the animals. They float down its Lethe stream. Only chlorophyll fights up against the current. It is the stuff in life that rebels at death, that has never surrendered to entropy, final icy stagnation. It is the mere cob-

[6] From Sir James Jeans: *The Universe Around Us*. 4th ed. Copyright, 1944 by The Macmillan Company and used with their permission.

[7] From *Possible Worlds*, by J. B. S. Haldane, through the permission of Harper and Brothers.

web on which we are all suspended over the abyss.—DONALD CULROSS
PEATTIE: "Chlorophyll: The Sun Trap," *Flowering Earth,* Chap. 3.[8]

**B.** The paragraph beginning "In plain language," page 663. (Gauss,
"The Threat of Science")

**C.** The passage beginning "Most of the philosophical systems," page
766, and ending "of the third-floor windows," page 767.

## METAPHOR AS ESSENTIAL STATEMENT

We may sum up then by saying that in strict scientific statement metaphor has no place, and that in a less strict scientific discussion metaphor is optional and additional. It provides an illustration, and, as the example from Russell shows, this may be of great
importance. But in most of the writing with which we are concerned
—political speeches, articles on international affairs, letters to friends,
expressions of opinions, attempts to persuade or convince, essays
which invite other people to share our own experiences and valuations—in nearly all the ordinary writing which we shall do, metaphor
is not subsidiary and external but a primary device by which we
"say" what we want to say. Metaphor then is not to be thought
of as a roundabout way—an alternative way—of communicating an
experience. Often it constitutes the only possible way by which
we can convey the special quality of an experience. As one authority on language puts it: we think by proceeding from the known
to the unknown, by extending a familiar term to an unfamiliar fact
or situation. As he defines them, metaphors are "essentially discoveries of new meanings . . . by means of old names." Seen in these
terms, metaphor is not something external to thinking: it is central.
By the same token, it is not vague and emotional; it has its own
accuracy, for it frequently provides the only means by which a
thing can be "said." Metaphor is, then, an indispensable instrument
for interpreting experience.

Let us illustrate. In the sentence that follows, Helen Keller describes what tactile sensation means to a person who has always
been blind and deaf: "The immovable rock, with its juts and warped
surface, bends beneath my fingers into all manner of grooves and

[8] From *Flowering Earth,* by Donald Culross Peattie. Copyright, 1939, by
Donald Culross Peattie. Courtesy of G. P. Putnam's Sons.

hollows." The rock, of course, does not literally bend: it is "immovable." But under her sensitive fingers, which do duty for eyes, the rock itself seems to respond dynamically to her touch. For what is being described is not the fumbling of an ordinary person who is blindfolded. We are, rather, being let into Helen Keller's "world," a world of exciting qualities which most of us do not know at all. Metaphor here is the only means by which it may be made known to us. For since this world does not exist in our experience, it cannot be pointed to: it can only be created for us. (The student should compare with Helen Keller's account of touch, Bertrand Russell's account of sight, page 416. We do not have to choose one and reject the other. Both are true, but we must not confuse them. The two accounts are radically different in purpose, and therefore in method.)

Helen Keller's world may seem a special case. The world which Miss Keller knows through her finger tips obviously can be known by most of us who lack her sensitive finger tips only through analogy, suggestion, and imaginative insight. Yet the worlds of all of us are more special than we think, determined as they are by our values, moods, and emotional biases.

### SOME ILLUSTRATIONS OF ESSENTIAL, NONDECORATIVE METAPHOR

Consider what metaphor does in the following two verses from Ecclesiastes. "It is better to bear the rebuke of the wise, than for a man to hear the song of fools. For as the crackling of thorns under a pot, so is the laughter of a fool: this also is vanity."

This comparison, as we see, uses the dry, crackling sound of burning thorn branches to describe the laughter of a fool. Now, there is a certain realistic basis for the comparison. But the metaphor is far more than a phonetic description. It makes a value judgment too: the fool's laughter, it is implied, is brittle, hollow, meaningless: it is the noise that attends the going up in smoke of something quite worthless—the rubbish of dried thorn branches. This is the justification for the last clause, "this [the fool's laughter] also is a vanity." But the metaphor does much more than to "illustrate" the vanity. It is the metaphor itself that defines vanity and realizes it for us—its specious brightness, its explosive chatter, its essential emptiness.

Let us take one further example, this time from a novel. In her *Delta Wedding* Miss Eudora Welty describes the sunset as seen by a little girl through the window of a railway coach.

In the Delta the sunsets were reddest light. The sun went down lop-sided and wide as a rose on a stem in the west, and the west was a milk white edge, like the foam of the sea. The sky, the field, the little track, and the bayou, over and over—all that had been bright or dark was now one color. From the warm window sill the endless fields glowed like a hearth in firelight.—EUDORA WELTY: *Delta Wedding*, Chap. 1.[9]

Since this is a passage from a novel it is tempting to say that here surely the figurative language is merely "decorative," an attempt at a prettification of the scene. Even here, however, the metaphors have a much more important function. The sun, it is true, is compared to a conventionally pretty object, a rose. But it is here a "lopsided" rose. The "hearth" comparison is domestic rather than beautiful in its associations. Actually, the metaphors work here to create the scene and the mood. It is a particular sunset seen by a particular character at a particular time. The scene is modified by the mood which it has helped to generate; and the mood itself is the reflection of a special personality. And it is this complex of scene and mood and personality which the metaphors do so much to reveal. The special quality of redness, almost unreal—the diffused rosiness of the light—the sense of warmth—the scene perceived as something framed and set apart and remote—all of these qualities are suggested by the comparison of the sun to a lopsided rose, and of the flat and endless fields to a hearth glowing in firelight. In this total pattern of statement, "lopsided" is seen to be not merely whimsical, but to contribute its own mite of precision (the apparent distortion of the red globe of the sun as it touches the horizon) to a statement that is aiming at great precision.

A few paragraphs above we admitted that the world of Helen Keller's experience is a special world which can be conveyed to us only through suggestion and analogy. Yet a little reflection will show that the world of experience of each of us is far more special than we think, for such a world is determined by our values, moods, and emotional biases. The world as seen by the little girl in *Delta*

[9] From *Delta Wedding* by Eudora Welty, copyright, 1945, 1946, by Eudora Welty. Reprinted by permission of Harcourt, Brace and Company, Inc.

*Wedding* is thus special in this sense, and so too is that of the Hebrew preacher who speaks in Ecclesiastes. If we are to communicate our experience with any accuracy, figurative language is frequently the only way by which such experience can be conveyed at all. For by means of metaphor we grasp not only the object as an entity, but its "meaning," its value to us as well. The "thing" which Miss Welty wished to say was not that the sun was round or red or an immense globe of superhot elements some ninety-three million miles from the earth. What she wished to give us was the sun as it appeared to the child as she watched it from the window of the train. It is not the scientific sun—the abstraction taken from some book on astronomy—with which the author is concerned, but rather the sun as part of a total experience and of a very particular and special experience.

One more example, just to make sure that the last illustration, since it is from fiction, does not give the impression that metaphor is somehow "literary" and therefore unimportant. Here is the way in which "Bugs" Baer describes the collapse of a prize fighter: "Zale folded as gracefully as the Queen's fan and fell on his battered face alongside the ropes. His seconds carried him to his corner like three window-dressers packing a melted dummy off during a heat wave on the sunny side of Broadway." This description may be judged to be good writing or bad, but it is easy to see why Baer used figurative language. He was not trying to "tell" us about the scene: he was trying to make us *see* the scene, vividly, freshly, fully, as a somewhat cynical but highly interested observer might have seen it.

The nature and uses of metaphor can be further illustrated from passages quoted in the earlier chapter on description. For example, let us look again at the metaphor which Faulkner uses in his description of Miss Emily (p. 232): "She looked bloated, like a body long submerged in motionless water, and of that pallid hue." There is an analogy, of course, between the appearance of the bloated and unnaturally pallid woman and that of a drowned body. But the author might have found other analogies, superficially quite as apt. What specific function does the comparison serve? It serves to interpret the woman for us. It describes the woman but it gives more than mere physical description: it suggests that she has long been immersed in a thick, unnatural medium like water. Moreover, the water in which she has drowned is "motionless." There has been a kind of stagnation. She has been removed from the whole course of human activity.

Or consider Thoreau's comparison of the state of Massachusetts to a human body (p. 261). There is, it is true, some kind of resemblance between the shape of Cape Cod on the map and that of a bended arm. But the physical analogy is pretty well exhausted with this item; yet Thoreau goes on to give the state a "back" and "feet" and another "fist" with which the state "keeps guard the while upon her breast." Thoreau too is using his comparison to suggest that we are to conceive of the state as a human being and as an alert and vigilant human being.

## WHAT MAKES A "GOOD" METAPHOR?

In this connection we ought to note that the physical similarity of the items compared is easily overestimated in judging the value of a metaphor. In many finely effective comparisons the degree of physical similarity is not very great. Some element of resemblance, there must be, of course. But a good comparison is not necessarily one in which there is close resemblance: for "illustration," as we have seen, is not the primary purpose of metaphor. Moreover, even a great deal of dissimilarity does not necessarily render the comparison a strained or forced one.

### THE ELEMENT OF SIMILARITY IN METAPHOR

To realize this last point, let us consider one of the tritest comparisons of all: "her eyes were like stars." Far from seeming strained or overingenious, the comparison will seem to most of us entirely too simple and easy. And yet, even in this well-worn analogy, the objects compared are really very dissimilar. Certainly the human eyeball and the flaming mass of elements which make up the stars have very little in common. But if this examination, which compares the two objects as scientifically considered, seems somewhat unfair, one can go on to point out that the eyes, even those of a lovely woman, do not much resemble the glinting points of light which are the stars as we see them. The truth of the matter is that what supports this oldest and most hackneyed of comparisons is not the physical resemblances so much as the associations: the associations

of stars with brilliance, with the high and celestial. It is these associations which have made the stars seem "like" the glances of the
eyes of someone loved.

Thus, every comparison has a very important subjective element
in it: its proper task is to interpret, to evaluate—not to point to
physical analogies. Its proper function is, as we have said, to define
attitude.

Let us consider a few further illustrations: Samuel Butler, in his
satire, "Hudibras," gives this description of the dawn.

> And like a lobster, boyl'd, the morn
> From black to red began to turn.

We think of this as an absurd comparison, and so it is—appropriately so, for "Hudibras" is a humorous poem, and Butler is casting
good-humored scorn upon his hero. Why does the comparison strike
us as absurd? We are likely to say that it is absurd because the
dawn doesn't in the least resemble a boiled lobster. But the colors
to be seen in the shell of a boiled lobster may very closely resemble
the exact shade of red to be seen on some mornings. The absurdity,
then, does not come from the lack of physical resemblance: it comes
rather from the absurd contrast of the associations of cooking and
the associations of morning—the sense of fresh coolness and natural
beauty. Butler has, for humorous effect, deliberately played the
connotations of lobster-boiling against the connotations of morning. It is the clash of connotations which creates the tone (see
Chapter 11) of good-humored contempt, befitting a mock epic such
as "Hudibras." (Objectively considered, the sun looks quite as much
like the shell of a boiled lobster as it looks like Miss Welty's lopsided rose—a figure which we have seen is *not* used for ludicrous
effect.)

The principle of contrast, however, may be used for very different effects. Consider the use to which the element of contrast is put
in the following passage from Aldous Huxley's *After Many a Summer Dies the Swan:*

> In the green and shadowy translucence, two huge fish hung suspended,
> their snouts almost touching, motionless except for the occasional ripple
> of a fin and the rhythmic panting of their gills. A few inches from their
> staring eyes a rosary of bubbles streamed ceaselessly up toward the light.

The chain of bubbles may be thought to look like a string of beads, and the rapt, motionless attitude of the staring fish may allow one fancifully to see them as participants in a religious rite, staring at the string of ascending bubbles as at a rosary. (The adjectives "suspended" and "staring" and especially the phrase "streamed ceaselessly up toward the light," tend to support the analogy.) But the effect is not absurd as Butler's is: the effect is rather that of sardonic irony. A reading of the novel would indicate how the irony fits the bitter commentary which Huxley makes on his hero's morbid grasping at life.

Here is another example of a metaphor used for ironic effect, though for a still different kind of irony:

> In the rear of this row of guns stood a house, calm and white, amid bursting shells. A congregation of horses tied to a long railing, were tugging frenziedly at their bridles. Men were running hither and thither.
> —STEPHEN CRANE: *Red Badge of Courage.*

Why "a congregation of horses" rather than "a line" or "a group" of horses? *Congregation* (from Latin *congrex*) means literally a "herding together," and (though it is a somewhat pedantic application) "congregation" is thus literally accurate here. But as we commonly use the word, "congregation" implies a group of worshipers, people who have come together of their own will, though this particular "congregation" is frantically trying to get away. The contrast is an ironic one, but the author has not left his choice of the word to be justified by this obvious and rather brittle contrast: the metaphor points to a richer and larger contrast. The "congregation of horses" tied to the railing suggests the scene at some rural church where the congregation within is implied by the "congregation" of hitched horses without. The line of tied animals thus ironically suggests a peaceful scene in contrast to the actual battle which is raging around them.

### THE ELEMENT OF CONTRAST IN METAPHOR

We think of metaphors (and related figurative expressions) as "comparisons," and yet it is plain that we might as accurately refer to them as "contrasts." For the elements of dissimilarity between the terms of a metaphor may be of just as much importance as the elements of likeness. One can go further still: in an effective metaphor there must be a *considerable degree of contrast.* If we say "the river roared like a flood" or "the dog raged like a wild beast," we feel that the metaphor in each case is weak or nonexistent. A river is too much like a flood, and a dog, though a tame beast, too much resembles a wild beast. If, on the other hand, we say, "the fire roared like a flood" or "the fire raged like a wild beast," we feel that these are metaphors (even if actually rather poor metaphors). Fire and flood or fire and beast are sufficiently dissimilar for us to feel that some metaphorical transfer occurs: in these cases there are the "new namings" which constitute metaphor.

A famous English critic of the eighteenth century, Samuel Johnson, saw this point clearly in discussing a famous poetic comparison of his time. In a poem on the battle of Blenheim, the poet had compared the English general, Marlborough, to an angel "who rides in the whirlwind and directs the storm." The general himself was not engaged in dealing blows. In a sense he was above the battle. But calm and aloof, like the angel, he directed the crushing power of his regiments. Johnson's objection to the comparison was not that the poet had not described properly Marlborough's function, but rather that the functions of Marlborough and of the angel were too nearly the same for the comparison to have any imaginative quality. Whether or not Johnson was fair to the comparison in question, the student may decide for himself by looking up Addison's poem, "The Campaign." But there is no doubt at all that Johnson was entirely right about the principle involved.

We are inclined to reject what we rather awkwardly call "far-fetched" comparisons. (The term is awkward because it suggests that the terms of a good comparison are close together, though we have seen that even "eyes" and "stars" are not really very close—see p. 423.) But if comparisons must not be too "far-fetched," neither must they be too "nearly-fetched." They have to be fetched some distance if we are to have a recognizable metaphor at all.

## *APPLICATIONS*

Discuss the function performed by the metaphors in the following passages. Are the metaphors purely illustrative? Are they used to express the writer's attitude? Can you improve upon any of them?

1. Mill's comparison of the people's rulers to a weapon and to vultures (p. 698).

2. Huxley's comparison of the exhilaration of loneliness to the exhilaration produced by alcohol (p. 763).

3. Beach's comparison of Hergesheimer's carelessness in prose to that of a cultivated gentleman (p. 742).

4. Rice's comparison of Sawney Webb to an actor; of John Webb to a dramatist (p. 868).

5. Sheean's comparison of the University of Chicago library to a sunken continent (p. 876).

6. Williamson's comparison of his task of revision to that of a lumberman clearing up a forest (p. 738).

## CONSISTENCY IN METAPHOR

In this connection, it is convenient to take up the problem of consistency in metaphor. How consistent with itself need a metaphor be? The point is worth discussing because most of us have been made well aware of the absurdity of "mixed metaphors." Everyone is familiar with the Congressman's oratorical declaration: "I smell a rat. I see it floating in the air. But I shall nip it in the bud." Moreover, earlier in this chapter the absurdity of the mixed metaphors which occur in the passages on pages 410-13 has been commented upon. But it would be a mistake if the student concluded that *any* mixing of metaphors or *any* change from one metaphor to another is in itself bad.

It is perfectly true that an extended metaphor can sometimes be used for very powerful effect, and it is further true that a metaphor which suddenly, or for no apparent reason, reverses our expectations, can give us a sense of absurd confusion. But a metaphor need not be extended; and there are fine passages of prose and poetry in which the author moves rapidly from one metaphor to another. Is the following passage from *Hamlet* absurd because the metaphor is "mixed"?

> To be, or not to be—that is the question.
> Whether 'tis nobler in the mind to suffer
> The slings and arrows of outrageous fortune
> Or to take arms against a sea of troubles
> And by opposing end them. To die—to sleep—
> No more; and by a sleep to say we end
> The heartache, and the thousand natural shocks
> That flesh is heir to.

The troubles are first conceived of as missiles—"slings and arrows"—of fortune, but then they are characterized as a "sea of troubles." One can "take arms" against a contingent of bowmen, but how can one take arms against a sea? It is possible to conceive of myriad troubles as a sea; and a great armed host, with its advancing ranks and with its seemingly infinite reserves, ready to come up to replace them, may be thought of as a sea. There is a sort of link, therefore, between "slings and arrows of outrageous fortune" and "sea of troubles." Yet do we not get into an absurdity when other elements of the two figures are brought together as Shakespeare brings them together here? How can a man take arms against the sea (as one might against an army)? Only a madman would try to fight the sea, as the Irish warrior Cuchulain was fabled to have done. Perhaps so; but if so, there may be method in Hamlet's madness here (and method in Shakespeare's arrangement of metaphors). The troubles that attack Hamlet are, like the sea, infinite. He can hardly hope to conquer them. But if he advances courageously into the waves, he may "end them" nonetheless; for in swallowing *him* up, his troubles end themselves: "by the sleep [of death] . . . we end / The heartache, and the thousand natural shocks / That flesh is heir to." The figure is daring and it is difficult, but it does not involve an absurdity.

Consider another sequence of metaphors which may seem even more confusingly mixed. In the following passage Macbeth expresses his sense of the meaninglessness of life:

> . . . all our yesterdays have lighted fools
> The way to dusty death. Out, out, brief candle!
> Life's but a walking shadow; a poor player,
> That struts and frets his hour upon the stage,
> And then is heard no more: it is a tale
> Told by an idiot, full of sound and fury,
> Signifying nothing.

Here again the images may seem to have no connection with one another; but closer reading indicates that the images are knit together rather tightly.

Death is a sleep. Our bed is the dust from which we came. The sun itself is finally but a candle by which we are lighted to this bed. Macbeth, apathetic and wearied, feels ready for the bed of death, and he needs no candle to find it. He says, "Out, out, brief candle!" But the image of the candle (which one carries to light himself to bed) suggests another figure to signify the emptiness of life, the shadow. (Life has no substance; it is mere appearance.) And this figure suggests another: life is like an actor who plays a role. The actor gives us but a shadow, an appearance. Moreover, the appearance is brief: he "struts and frets" his little "hour upon the stage." With the words "And then is heard no more," we shift from a visual to an auditory figure. The actor's speech—considered coldly and in detachment, as by a spectator who has just come into the theater in the middle of the play—strikes the ear as a meaningless rant. It is like the speech of an idiot: words pour forth, there is sound and fury, but no meaning is conveyed. In this passage, then, the various metaphors are related to each other; they grow out of each other; and they enrich and develop a total meaning which is consistent with itself.

These two examples can hardly do more than suggest some of the possible justifications for certain kinds of "mixed" metaphor. The subject, moreover, is too complex for one to lay down rules which will indicate when metaphor is improperly "mixed" and when it is not. But one common-sense principle is clear enough. Looking at the problem from the standpoint of the writer, we may say that he should not arouse expectations which he does not gratify. If he leads the reader to *expect* a consistent elaboration of a figure, he becomes inconsistent at his peril.

In general, however, as writers, our best defense against absurdly mixed metaphors on the one hand, and against rigid theories of consistency on the other, is to be found in a sound conception of the function of metaphor. Let us repeat: metaphor is not a mere decoration. It is not an illustration—not a point-to-point analogical likeness. It is not an alternate naming of the thing which is chosen because it is "prettier" or "simpler." Rather it is our great instrument for interpreting the thing in question. Metaphors are new namings which seize upon the thing and interpret it lovingly, reverently, contemptuously, mockingly, coldly, or warmly as the skillful author may desire. The aptness of a comparison, therefore, cannot be determined in isolation. The author's larger purpose, and the whole context in which the comparison occurs, must be taken into account.

Because of the delicacy and the importance of these relations between the terms of a metaphor and between the metaphor and its context, we have chosen not to present the student with the classifications of figurative language that are frequently made in rhetoric books. For many of these classifications are of no fundamental importance. We have not distinguished, for example, from metaphorical language in general, SIMILE (an explicit comparison, usually announced by *like* or *as:* "she glided into the room like a swan," "as brittle as ice") or METONYMY (the use of a part to designate the whole: "he employed twenty hands on his farm"), and so on. Such classifications, in our considered opinion, are of little importance to the practicing writer.

## APPLICATIONS

I. Consider carefully the metaphors in Smith's "A Lark's Flight" on page 677. What is the justification of the author's using so much figurative language? (In this connection one might observe that Pyle's "The End in Sight," page 579, uses comparatively little metaphor. Do you see why the one writer should use so much, the other so little?)

II. Notice that Aldous Huxley, in his "Wordsworth in the Tropics," uses a rather elaborate metaphor on page 766: "rush from a dark jungle into the haven of a well-lit, commodious house." Can this be said to be a summarizing metaphor? Does this supposition account for Huxley's rather elaborate development of the metaphor? Has the metaphor been carefully prepared for? (Note the amount of forest imagery which has preceded it.) Attempt to state the point made by this elaborate comparison in nonmetaphorical language.

III. On page 800 Graves compares Rome to a "great jackdaw's nest." What is the justification of this comparison? The comparison in its associations certainly clashes with the scope and grandeur of the Roman world as described in the earlier paragraphs. Is the clash an intentional one? What purpose, if any, is served by it? Attempt to rewrite the paragraph in which the jackdaw's nest metaphor occurs, making use of some other metaphor of your own choosing in order to give another effect.

IV. Notice that neither James's "Siege of the Alamo" nor Yeats's *Reveries* uses any large amount of metaphor. Yet James is describing a vivid scene and spirited action, and Yeats is a poet. Can you account for the fact that in neither selection is there a great deal of use of metaphor? Do the metaphors that occur in these selections throw any light on this problem?

**V.** Santayana's prose will repay careful reading, for its treatment of metaphor. The student might look carefully for three things in particular: (1) the occasional extended metaphor which may dominate a whole section of the essay; (2) the revivification of what would ordinarily be dead metaphor; and (3) constant pointing up of abstractions by some concrete detail. For example, the passage beginning "In his love of roads" (p. 753) and ending "love and laughter" (p. 755) is rather abstract in its ideas. Moreover, Santayana has risked using such apparent clichés as "never see the wood for the trees," "pendulum soon swings back," or the "vain tides" of things. Mark the metaphors in this passage and attempt to state how the metaphors are related to each other. Are there any actual clichés? If there are not, what prevents some of the expressions from affecting us as clichés? What is the relation to the whole pattern of the two or three extended metaphors that occur?

## METAPHOR AND SYMBOL

There is, however, one further important relationship that ought to be specified: the relation of metaphor to SYMBOL. A symbol is a kind of sign. Thus, the flag is a symbol of the nation; the cross, of Christianity; the letter *a*, of a particular vowel sound (or actually in modern English, of a particular group of vowel sounds). Symbols of this sort are conventional and arbitrary signs. For example, it is conceivable that the United States of America might have adopted some other flag, and once we had agreed to think of it as *our* flag, that flag would have symbolized our nation just as much as Old Glory now does. The Greek letter, *alpha*, corresponds to our Roman letter *a*, though it has a somewhat different shape, thus α. Mathematical and scientific symbols likewise are conventional and arbitrary signs.

Now metaphor has nothing to do with this kind of conventional symbolism. In metaphor, as we have seen, words are not used literally but are extended beyond their conventional meanings. Yet there is another kind of symbol which is not conventional and arbitrary. Washing one's hands, for example, does not necessarily signify that one feels guilt. It usually means no more than that one wants to get his hands clean. But when Shakespeare has Lady Macbeth, in the sleep-walking scene in *Macbeth,* attempt to wash the imaginary blood from her hands, her action becomes a symbol of her feeling of guilt. The simple and ordinarily unimportant act turns into a revelation of character—becomes endowed with symbolic force. Likewise, in De Maupassant's story, "The Diamond Necklace" (p. 299), the paste diamonds come to stand for the vanity and emptiness for which Madame Loisel has sacrificed her youth. With this kind of symbolism, metaphor does have something in common. In metaphor, a word is extended to a new meaning; in this kind of symbolism, an object or incident is made to take on a larger meaning. In the simplest terms, we may say that metaphor has to do with the word (or the idea) and symbolism with the thing (or the action).

## METAPHOR AND THE CREATIVE IMAGINATION

The distinction between such created symbols and merely arbitrary symbols can throw much light on the problem of metaphor. In the first place, most of the effective symbols in literature, since they are not arbitrary signs, are instances of the metaphorical process—that is, they represent the endowing of some concrete object or incident with further meaning. In "The Diamond Necklace," for example, the revelation that the diamonds, for which so much has been sacrificed, are really paste becomes a kind of metaphor. A writer rarely finds a symbol ready-made for him: he creates his important symbols by the same process as that by which he creates his other metaphors.

In the second place, a consideration of symbols throws light on the problems that have to do with the validity of metaphor. Some objects and incidents do seem to have a "natural" symbolic meaning. Thus, blood may seem to be a natural symbol for violence; darkness, for evil; or light, for truth. In a sense blood, darkness, and light *are* such natural symbols; yet we need to observe two things: (1) the "natural" symbolism is much more vague and general than at first sight might be supposed. Blood can be used—and has been used—to symbolize a wealth of very different things: courage or heredity or race. Moreover, darkness can be used to symbolize, not evil but goodness: at least one poet has used darkness in this way. Henry Vaughan's poem "The Night" celebrates darkness as the proper time for spiritual meditation and communion.

with God. Moreover, light *can* symbolize evil: i.e., the hard, hot light of the desert can be made to suggest the mocking falsity of the mirage. (2) Even the natural and obvious symbols are ineffective unless they are presented to us freshly and dramatically. The writer cannot use them merely at the conventional level and still use them effectively. The moment that the word for the object in question has become frozen at a certain level of significance, it becomes a mere sign—an alternate name—and its emotional power has all but vanished. Thus, as we have seen, the "eye of a needle" no longer suggests any association with the human eye: "eye" has become merely the conventional name for the thread-hole. No metaphorical transfer is made: the original transfer of meaning has become fixed permanently.

The ideal scientific language, it is sometimes said, would not use metaphor at all: there would be one precise term for every object, a term which would mean only one thing. For men who are irritated by the ambiguities and confusions of metaphor, such a prospect is tempting. A few years ago, Mr. Stuart Chase (in *The Tyranny of Words*) came close to recommending that we abandon metaphor altogether in favor of a strict, unambiguous use of words. (Centuries earlier, in 1667, Thomas Sprat, the historian of the Royal Society, complimented this group of new scientists on having "exacted from all their members, a close, naked, natural way of speaking; positive expressions; clear sense; a native easiness: bringing all things as near the mathematical plainness as they can.")

But such a language, though admirable for exact scientific purposes—mathematical formulae are better still (p. 378)—would be an excessively limited instrument for other purposes. Now science properly strives toward pure notation: thus, the specific gravity of iron at 20° C. is 7.86; granite is an igneous rock; $2 + 2 = 4$. But most that we have to say is not pure notation: we want to tell a joke or to describe a knockout or to say what it feels like to be in love. Our normal discourse is "impure" with our own interpretations, evaluations, and insights. And these interpretations are too intimately related to ourselves for us to have a precise, ready-made term for each thing that we have to say. It is better to have a language which possesses flexibility—one which can be shaped and re-formed to the most special use.

## SUMMARY

METAPHOR is the use of a concrete term to signify a wider, more general relationship. Language began as metaphor. Men came to extend concrete terms by analogy to further relationships. Yet, basic as the metaphorical process is, we tend to misapprehend its real importance. We tend to think of metaphor as a kind of external decoration which may be applied or not, as the writer chooses, to the essential statement, a statement which we think of as nakedly logical.

But, just as the development of language is from the concrete to the abstract, not from the abstract to the concrete, so the normal method of composition is from the concrete to the more abstract, not from abstract schematic outlines to metaphorical expression. The compulsion to use slang, for example, is an indication of the normality of metaphor as opposed to abstract statement. For slang, though it is usually shabby and worn-out metaphor, is, nonetheless metaphor; and the impulse to use it represents a basically sound human impulse. Consequently, the most fruitful attitude toward the misuse of slang will be that which acknowledges the natural tendency toward metaphor and attempts to replace worn and inaccurate metaphor with fresh and accurate metaphor.

The misuse of metaphor is a peculiarly significant ailment of contemporary prose. It testifies, perhaps, to the fact that we have misconceived the real function of metaphor, and having misconceived it, blunder in our practice.

Since the metaphorical process is central to language, the conventional emphases on metaphor as (1) illustrative or (2) decorative go astray by suggesting that metaphor merely adds something unessential to expression. The primary function of metaphor is to interpret experience for us—to mold and control attitudes. In all discourse (except that which aspires to strict scientific notation) this interpretative element is central. Metaphor, then, is not to be thought of as a colorful but inaccurate way of saying something. What we usually have to "say" includes this aspect of interpretation, and good metaphor has therefore its own kind of accuracy.

The fact that metaphor is used primarily to control attitudes has an important bearing on the problem of the validity of metaphor.

If we misunderstand metaphor, taking it to be simply a kind of loose analogy, then the best metaphors will be those in which the items compared are physically most nearly alike; and we shall be disposed to reject all comparisons in which there is no close physical resemblance between the items compared. If, on the contrary, we see that metaphor is one of our prime instruments of interpretation, we may be prepared to admit a large interpretative (subjective) element in metaphor, and further, to understand that the element of contrast is necessary and important.

A metaphor is a kind of symbol: that is, the concrete particular comes to stand for something larger than itself. It is not, of course, an arbitrary symbol like the cross or the flag or the letter A. For when the metaphor no longer makes a transfer of meaning, it is a dead metaphor just as the arbitrary symbol is frozen to one meaning and means one, and only one, thing. But the great literary symbols (and many humbler ones in our daily experience) do not have their meaning assigned to them by an arbitrary convention. They derive their meanings from a special context—they come to mean something special and untranslatable. In this sense, they are metaphors. We may use the term *symbol* when we think of the sign itself; the term *metaphor* when we think of the process of transfer of meaning.

When men think of the neatness and logical accuracy given by scientific terms, they sometimes long for the elimination of all metaphor. But reflection indicates that such a language of terms, each frozen to one denotation, is impossible: such a language could express only "public," agreed-upon relationships. With the elimination of the possibility of metaphor we should have eliminated connotations, the whole realm of personal evaluations through language, and all those elements which make language flexible and alive. For metaphor is ultimately the power to take a given and known term and *bend* it to a fresher and richer use.

## APPLICATIONS

### I

The following metaphors are primarily *illustrative* (that is, the metaphor makes something plain by comparing it with a simpler or more familiar thing). But are they *merely* illustrative? Are any of the metaphors used to *state* a meaning as well as to *illustrate* a meaning?

Test them on this point by trying to restate precisely "the thing said" in nonmetaphorical language.

**A.** On each side of the [bee's] abdomen are four little wax-pockets situated in the joints of the hard-surfaced body; and here the supply of wax may be seen issuing, the flat, light-colored wax appearing somewhat like a letter which a man has tucked up under his waistcoat.— CHARLES D. STEWART: "The Bee's Knees."

**B.** Intellectual assimilation takes time. The mind is not to be enriched as a coal barge is loaded. Whatever is precious in a cargo is taken carefully on board and carefully placed. Whatever is delicate and fine must be received delicately, and its place in the mind thoughtfully assigned. —ARLO BATES: "Reading on the Run," *Talks on the Study of Literature.*

**C.** Bed is the perfect laboratory—just the right degree of withdrawal from the world, yet with the comforts at hand, and errands delegated to someone else. The toast crumbs, accumulating among the sheets, set up the irritation inside the shell and start the pearl growing.—E. B. WHITE: "Peavy, Book and Guitar."

**D.** When I am dead, the chance that my bones will become fossilized is very remote. Bones decay away like the rest of our bodies unless a lot of very unlikely things happen. First of all, a dead body will not leave any permanent remains in the form of a fossil unless it happens to be covered up and thus protected from decay. That is fairly easy in the case of animals in the sea. Rivers are always carrying sediment out and depositing it, and tides and currents shift the sediment and cover up the bodies of dead animals. But even in this case it is by no means likely that the bones will be fossilized. Much more probably they will gradually dissolve away and leave no trace of themselves. Fossilization is rather a complicated process. It involves the replacement of each particle of bone, as it dissolves away, by a less soluble and therefore more permanent substance. When that has happened, the chances are still very remote that anyone will find the fossil thousands or millions of years later. Our quarries and mines and cuttings are mere scratches on the surface of the earth. With terrestrial animals the chances of fossilization are still less than with marine ones. They are likely to die and decay without being covered up. It would be quite absurd to look with any great hopefulness for the fossil remains of the ancestors of any given animal. It would not simply be like looking for the proverbial pin in a haystack, for then you are supposed to have the advantage of knowing that the pin is there. But in this case you are looking for a soluble pin in a haystack in a thunderstorm, and you always have at the back of your mind the disconcerting thought that perhaps it is no longer there.—JOHN R. BAKER: "Missing Links." [10]

**E.** This man was hunting about the hotel lobby like a starved dog that has forgotten where he had buried a bone.—O. HENRY: "A Municipal Report," *Strictly Business.*

**F.** . . . [the ship's] middle structure was like a half-tide rock awash upon a coast. It was like an outlying rock with the water boiling up, streaming over, pouring off, beating round—like a rock in the surf to which shipwrecked people cling before they let go—only it rose, it sank, it rolled continuously, without respite and rest, like a rock that should have miraculously struck adrift from a coast and gone wallowing upon the sea.—JOSEPH CONRAD: *Typhoon*, Chap. 3.

## II

Do any of the following metaphors seem "far-fetched" and extravagant? Do any seem too tame and flat? What principle, if any, seems to determine the matter of acceptability?

Are any of the passages ineffective because the metaphors are "mixed"? Is it possible to shift rapidly from one metaphor to another without producing confusion? Are we never to mix metaphor? What principle, if any, seems to determine this matter?

**A.** The chickens he raised were all white meat down through the drumsticks, the cows were tended like children, and the big ram he called Goliath had horns with a curl like a morning-glory vine and could butt through an iron door. But Dan'l wasn't one of your gentleman farmers; he knew all the ways of the land, and he'd be up by candlelight to see that the chores got done. A man with the mouth of a mastiff, a brow like a mountain and eyes like burning anthracite—that was Dan'l Webster in his prime.—STEPHEN VINCENT BENÉT: "The Devil and Daniel Webster." [11]

**B.** A smile lit the eyes of the expiring Kentuck. "Dying!" he repeated; "he's a-taking me with him. Tell the boys I've got the Luck with me now"; and the strong man, clinging to the frail babe as a drowning man is said to cling to a straw, drifted away into the shadowy river that flows forever to the unknown sea.—BRET HARTE: "The Luck of Roaring Camp."

[10] From "Missing Links," by John R. Baker (in *Science in a Changing World,* ed. Mary Adams) through the permission of Appleton-Century-Crofts, Inc.

[11] From *Selected Works* of Stephen Vincent Benét published by Rinehart & Company. Copyright 1936 by Stephen Vincent Benét.

**C.** Due to the great increase in the importance of social and economic problems during the past generation, philosophy is giving more attention than heretofore to the social and economic aspects of life. Also, esthetics is receiving greater consideration as the problem of civilization's goal becomes more pressing.—JOHN GEISE: *Man and the Western World,* Chap. 21.

**D.** Over in the corner Zale was rounding as slowly as the Queen Mary docking in the Hudson. He had taken a beating that would have busted the light in a night club bass drum. . . . In the sixth both sluggers were plugging away like a thirty-six cylinder car at a gasoline pump with the motor running. Neither the car nor the pump had gained an inch. . . . The seventh was as tough a spelling bee as ever missed out on cat. They were moving around like a fiji fire dancer wearing celluloid sox. And banging both hands to the equator.—" 'Bugs' Baer Says."

**E.**                                        Take the instant way;
For honor travels in a strait so narrow,
Where one but goes abreast: keep then the path;
For emulation hath a thousand sons,
That one by one pursue: if you give way,
Or hedge aside from the direct forthright,
Like to an enter'd tide they all rush by,
And leave you hindmost:—
Or, like a gallant horse fallen in first rank,
Die there for pavement to the abject rear,
O'er-run and trampled on: Then what they do in present,
Though less than yours in past, must o'ertop yours:
For time is like a fashionable host,
That slightly shakes his parting guest by the hand;
And with his arms out-stretch'd, as he would fly,
Grasps in the comer: Welcome ever smiles,
And farewell goes out sighing.
            —SHAKESPEARE: *Troilus and Cressida,* Act III.

**F.** . . . Even with the most virtuous at the levers, how can control be exercised for the good of all when there are so many voices emerging from different conditions, inheriting different traditions, committed to different ideals, and demanding different solutions. Every man wants to realize the opportunities of human knowledge, but each is inclined to believe that all will benefit if knowledge is mobilized in the service of his ideals and his traditions. Though their powers are universal, men's values are local and mired in the mud of history. Power is too often untamed by responsibility to the world.

Few want to turn back the clock of science and technology. Most approve the trend toward an integration of the world so that its resources, its experience, its knowledge will be available to everyone, but they do not want to turn their backs entirely on the customs, the morals, the language, the institutions which they have inherited from heir ancestors. . . .—QUINCY WRIGHT: "The Universities and the World Order." [12]

**G.** But perfection has one grave defect: it is apt to be dull. Swift's prose is like a French canal, bordered with poplars, that runs through a gracious and undulating country. Its tranquil charm fills you with satisfaction, but it neither excites the emotions nor stimulates the imagination. . . . Dryden flourished at a happy moment. He had in his bones the sonorous periods and the baroque massiveness of Jacobean language and under the influence of the nimble and well-bred felicity that he learnt from the French he turned it into an instrument that was fit not only for solemn themes but also to express the light thought of the passing moment. He was the first of the rococo artists. If Swift reminds you of a French canal, Dryden recalls an English river winding its cheerful way round hills, through quietly busy towns and nestling villages, pausing now in a noble reach and then running powerfully through a woodland country. It is alive, varied, windswept; and it has the pleasant open-air smell of England.—SOMERSET MAUGHAM: *The Summing Up,* Chap. 10.[13]

**H.**     And he shall be like a tree planted by the streams of water,
        That bringeth forth its fruit in its season,
        Whose leaf also doth not wither;
        And whatsoever he doeth shall prosper.
        The wicked are not so,
        But are like the chaff which the wind driveth away.
                                    —Psalms, I:3-4.

**I.** We must be vigilantly on our guard to protect our sacred institutions against the boring from within of subversive elements, those bloodthirsty termites who like to fish in troubled waters.—From a commencement address.

### III

What is the function of each of the following metaphors? Are any of them merely decorative? What does each metaphor "say"? Try

[12] Reprinted by permission from the American Association of University Professors *Bulletin,* Spring 1947.
[13] From: *The Summing Up* by W. Somerset Maugham. Copyright 1938 by W. Somerset Maugham. Reprinted by permission of Doubleday & Company, Inc.

to restate in nonmetaphorical language the exact shade of meaning that each conveys.

**A.** The furnished room received its latest guest with a first glow of pseudo-hospitality, a hectic, haggard, perfunctory welcome like the specious smile of a demirep.—o. HENRY: "The Furnished Room."

**B.** A late moon had cut a round, white hole in the sky off to the east, shedding enough light so that down below I could see the thin smokelike scattered clouds floating half way between me and the chromium-plated highway of the Potomac.—BEIRNE LAY, JR.: *I Wanted Wings*, Chap. 9.

**C.** Her bones felt loose, and floated around in her skin, and Doctor Harry floated like a balloon around the foot of the bed. He floated and pulled down his waistcoat and swung his glasses on a cord.—KATHERINE ANNE PORTER: "The Jilting of Granny Weatherall."

**D.** Thus we see what a tree really is. It is a sheath of life spread over the dead trees of other years. Generation stands within generation, successively wrapped about. The outer life of cambium and leaf and bud uses this as a trellis to go up and reach out sunward and skyward.—CHARLES D. STEWART: "The Tree as an Invention."

**E.** And so the dance whizzed on with cumulative fury, the performers moving in their planet-like courses, direct and retrograde, from apogee to perigee, till the hands of the well-kicked clock at the bottom of the room had travelled over the circumference of an hour.—THOMAS HARDY: "The Three Strangers."

**F.** "I am sorry for everything," he said, lifting a narrow, pontifical hand, waving away vulgar human pity which always threatened, buzzing like a fly at the edges of his mind.—KATHERINE ANNE PORTER: "Hacienda."

**G.**
  Its leaps should be set
  to the flageolet;
  pillar body erect
  on a three-cornered smooth-working Chippendale
  claw—propped on hind legs, and tail as third toe,
  between leaps to its burrow.
     —MARIANNE MOORE: "The Jerboa." [14]

**H.**
       He glides
  a hundred feet or quivers about
  as charred paper behaves—full
  of feints . . .
     —MARIANNE MOORE:
      "The Frigate Pelican."

[14] The jerboa is a kind of desert rat.

I. It was followed by visits to museums, lifelessly clean and lighted evenly and pleasantly, but as though with the dull light cast by snow. . . ."—IVAN BUNIN: "The Gentleman from San Francisco."

Material for further exercises on metaphor may be found in the Applications at the end of Chapter 5, pages 256-61.

# Situation and Tone

## TONE AS THE EXPRESSION OF ATTITUDE

EVERY piece of discourse implies a particular situation. A man is attempting to convince a hostile audience; or a mother is attempting to coax a child into doing something which the child dislikes; or a legislator, who can assume agreement on ends, is trying to persuade his colleagues that certain procedures constitute the best means by which to secure these ends. Even technical treatises, which attempt no persuasion, imply a special situation: the writer assumes that he is writing for people whose interest in the truth is so absorbing that rhetorical persuasions would be unnecessary and even positively irritating.

But if every discourse implies a situation in which the writer is related to his audience, by the same token every piece of discourse implies a certain TONE. This term "tone" is based frankly on a metaphor. We all know how important in actual speech the tone of voice may be in indicating the precise meaning of the words themselves. For instance, the words "very well," uttered in a certain tone of voice, may imply enthusiastic agreement, but spoken in another tone of voice they may indicate nothing more than surly compliance. The "tone" of a piece of writing, in the same way, may show the writer's attitude, and in so doing may heavily qualify the literal meanings of the words themselves.

The importance of tone is easily illustrated by the misunderstandings which personal letters so often provoke. In conversation even a rather clumsy and inadequate knowledge of language can be so supplemented by the actual tone of the voice that little serious misunderstanding will occur. But when such a speaker writes a letter—where, of course, the "tone of voice" has to be implied by the words themselves—all sorts of misunderstandings can occur, and frequently do occur. The practiced writer, on the other hand, is able, even in this medium, to control what we have called the "tone."

Some of the more obvious devices for controlling tone have already been discussed in Chapter 10 (pp. 388-91). There we saw that diction itself is a most important means of expressing our ATTITUDES. We can refer to a policeman as an "officer" or as a "cop"; we can say "farmer" or "rube." There are other obvious means by which we express our attitudes: by adjectives ("projectile adjectives" we called them) which make direct valuations (*nice, good, fine, miserable,* and so on) and by simple comparisons which are also emotional and subjective, with little or no objective content ("He's a good egg," "She's a peach"). Such devices for indicating tone are so simple that they could be discussed, as they have been, in the chapter on diction. But tone is a pervasive thing which characterizes a whole composition, and diction, strictly considered, is only one of the many elements which the writer must manage in order to secure a proper tone. In the pages that follow we are to consider some of the larger problems.

## THE IMPORTANCE OF TONE

In most of our writing the management of tone is an important problem, for in most of our writing our attitudes are highly relevant. An important part of what we are trying to "communicate" is the attitude itself. This is true not only of poetry and fiction, it is true also of most essays, sermons, orations, and letters. It is even true of much of what we are inclined to regard as pure exposition. For even in expository writing the author is rarely content to give us mere facts, or mere propositions. He feels that to do this is to be painfully and technically "dry."

A glance at the so-called articles of information in magazines like the *Atlantic* and *Harper's* will indicate that even here the establishment of the appropriate tone is of the highest importance. For example, a typical expository article in *Harper's* (Wolfgang

Langewiesche's "Making the Airplane Behave," May 1942) makes very special use of tone, and is thus anything but a mechanically "dry" piece of exposition. The author assumes that the reader is a reasonably intelligent person who has a fairly wide acquaintance with the modern world; specifically, that he knows how to drive an automobile, that he does not have a technical equipment in physics, but that he does have enough common sense to follow a clear illustration. The exposition does not insist on technicalities any more than the writer stands on his own dignity. His attitude toward his reader is definitely informal. The tone of his article suggests that flying is interesting and important, but that the author's attitude toward it is sprightly.

How do we know all this? Well, consider the following paragraph.

You try, for instance, steep turns in a strong wind. The ship will go in some crazy, wrong-looking attitude; but when you check your instruments you find that it is doing a correct job of flying and that the seat of your pants and your eyes would have tricked you had you been allowed to do the "co-ordinating."

The informal "you try" rather than the more formal "one tries"; the phrase "the seat of your pants" rather than the more formal "tactile pressure of the plane"; the informal "tricked" rather than the more formal "deceived"—all of these point to the tone—that is, they indicate the attitude which the author is taking toward his audience and toward his subject matter.

## WHAT DETERMINES TONE?

If, however, we are to define tone as the reflection of the author's attitude, it is necessary to make a simple distinction. Tone is the reflection of the author's attitude toward what? Toward his reader? Or toward his material? For example, if one is writing about the New Deal, his attitude may be one of admiration or contempt, of approval or disapproval. That attitude will presumably color the writing and constitute one source of its tone. But there is another source to be considered: let us suppose that the writer does approve of the New Deal. When he writes to persuade a hostile audience he will probably adopt a tone quite different from that

which he uses when he addresses himself to a friendly audience.
Moreover, he may wish to take into account the fact that his reader
is a child or an adult, a banker or a welder, a New Englander or a
Midwesterner. The writer's attitude toward his reader, therefore,
may be important in determining tone.

As we shall see later, there are many kinds of writing in which
the distinction between attitude toward material and attitude toward audience has little importance. But in many kinds of writing
where there is a strong practical purpose—political speeches, sermons, advertisements, propaganda—the writer's attitude toward his
audience is of immense importance. It may be the primary determi-
nant of the tone, and indeed of the whole strategy of the rhetorical
organization.

## TONE AS AN ADJUSTMENT TO THE WRITER'S AUDIENCE

Let us consider some fairly obvious instances of tone determined
by the nature of the audience. Here is an advertisement for a
dandruff remover. Above a picture of two young women talking,
there is the caption, "It's Listerine, for you chum . . . but *quick!*
Those innocent-looking flakes and scales you see on scalp, hair or
dress-shoulders, are a warning. . . . This is no time to fool around
with smelly lotions or sticky salves that can't kill germs. You need
antiseptic action . . . and you need it quick."

The young women in the picture are clearly friends, and the
opening caption is represented as the comment of one to the other.
But the advice as given to a chum is meant to carry over to the
reader. As the advertisement frankly goes on to address the reader,
"This is no time to fool around with smelly lotions. . . . You need
antiseptic action. . . ."

What is the attitude toward the reader, then? The attitude of a
sprightly, intimate friend whose advice can be frank and straight
from the shoulder.

Let us look at another advertisement. This one, printed in color,
depicts a young woman seated on a luxurious bed looking dreamily
at a handsome blanket. The caption begins "For you to whom
beauty is a necessity. . . . Yours is a nature that thrives on beauty.
. . . Seize it as a vital factor in your daily living. To you a blanket
should be more than a source of warmth. Exquisite colors, luxuri-

ously deep-nap, rich virgin-wool loveliness—these awaken in you an emotional response far beyond the material."

These statements, of course, are not addressed merely to the young woman pictured in the advertisement. They are addressed to the reader as well, and they make certain flattering assumptions about the reader: that she is a young woman of means who is at home with the luxurious and who has a soul which deserves and requires beauty as a necessity. Coarser natures may buy blankets simply for warmth, but you, dear and lovely reader, ought to have something more—even in a blanket.

The attitude toward the reader, of course, need not be flattering. Here follows an example of a very different tone, though like the advertisements just discussed, the tone here also is primarily conditioned by the writer's attitude toward his reader. The example is a letter written by Dr. Samuel Johnson to James Macpherson. In the 1760's Macpherson had published several volumes of poetry which he claimed to have translated from Gaelic [1] originals. Dr. Samuel Johnson refused to believe in the existence of any Gaelic originals of which the disputed poems were translations. He openly pronounced his opinion that they were Macpherson's own composition. In reply to Macpherson's demands that he retract this charge Johnson wrote the following letter:

Mr. James Macpherson:

I received your foolish and impudent letter. Any violence offered me I shall do my best to repel; and what I cannot do for myself, the law shall do for me. I hope I shall never be deterred from detecting what I think to be a cheat, by the menaces of a ruffian.

What would you have me retract? I thought your book an imposture; I think it an imposture still. For this opinion I have given my reasons to the publick, which I here dare you to refute. Your rage I defy. Your abilities, since your *Homer*, [2] are not so formidable; and what I hear of your morals, inclines me to pay regard not to what you shall say, but to what you shall prove. You may print this if you will.—SAM. JOHNSON.

A most important part of this letter is the attitude taken toward Macpherson. For Johnson might have stated the "facts" in a form

---

[1] The original Celtic language of the Scottish Highlands.
[2] Macpherson had published a translation of Homer.

as simple as this: "I continue to hold the view that the Macpherson translations are fraudulent" or "I repeat that I shall not believe in any Gaelic originals until they are produced." And if we argue that Johnson's expression of fearlessness also is a "fact" with which the letter concerns itself, even this fact might have been expressed very differently: thus, "I have no intention of expressing a retraction" or "I mean to stand my ground on this matter" or "I am sorry that I can make no retraction since I feel that there is nothing to retract."

The tone is of the utmost importance, then. How shall we characterize the tone of the letter as Johnson actually wrote it? No paraphrase of the letter will do justice to the tone; and an abstract description of the tone is clumsy as well as inadequate. For the full realization of the tone, we shall have to return to the letter itself. But one can point to some important elements of the tone: a manly contempt of threats, a confidence in truth and in his own integrity, perhaps even a trace of sardonic amusement at baffled and petty rage.

The following excerpt consists of the opening paragraphs of the first of *The Drapier's Letters,* letters which Jonathan Swift wrote to the Irish people, warning them against accepting any of the coins which one William Wood had been given a patent to mint. Swift felt that acceptance and circulation of the coins would injure the economy of Ireland.

Brethren, friends, countrymen and fellow-subjects, what I intend now to say to you, is, next to your duty to God, and the care of your salvation, of the greatest concern to yourselves, and your children; your bread and clothing, and every common necessary of life entirely depend upon it. Therefore I do most earnestly exhort you as men, as Christians, as parents, and as lovers of your country, to read this paper with the utmost attention, or get it read to you by others; which that you may do at least expense, I have ordered the printer to sell it at the lowest rate.

It is a great fault among you, that when a person writes with no other intention than to do you good, you will not be at the pains to read his advices: One copy of this paper may serve a dozen of you, which will be less than a farthing apiece. It is your folly that you have no common or general interest in your view, not even the wisest among you, neither do you know or enquire, or care who are your friends, or who are your enemies.

Swift assumes that his audience is not a learned one. He adopts the simplest language. His phrase "or get it read to you" indicates that he assumes, further, that many of the people whom he wishes to reach cannot read. But in addition to the almost painful effort to make himself completely clear, Swift implies that his readers are childishly thoughtless, taking too little care of their own interests, and confused as to their real friends. The tone is one of grave and patient admonition. Swift emphasizes the importance of what he is going to say; he appeals to his readers in terms of their deepest allegiances as "Christians, as parents, and as lovers of [their] country," and patiently makes clear how little the paper will cost such readers. He does not hesitate to tax their "folly," folly which renders them blind as to who their real friends are. The last point is, of course, of crucial importance for the effectiveness of Swift's tract. For unless his readers are willing to see that he is their real friend, he can hardly expect that they will follow his advice.

## APPLICATIONS

**I.** Select five advertisements from current magazines and state what is the primary basis of the appeal made to the reader. What attitude is taken toward the reader? What statements or devices in the advertisement suggest this attitude rather than some other?

**II.** What kind of audience does Thomas Huxley address in his "The Method of Scientific Investigation" (p. 559)? How do you infer this from the tone of the essay? What adjustments to a particular audience are indicated by the style of his essay?

**III.** In his "The Decline of the Graces" (p. 730), Max Beerbohm makes a special allusion to a possible reader: "I except from my indictment any young lady who may read these words." But is the essay addressed primarily to such a young lady? To what audience is the essay addressed? What is the tone of the essay?

**IV.** What is Froude's attitude toward Mary, Queen of Scots (p. 808)? What does Meline say that Froude's attitude is (p. 817)? How does Froude's attitude qualify his style? Rewrite the paragraphs on pages 815 so as to give a neutral attitude or a more favorable attitude toward Mary.

### TONE AS AN ADJUSTMENT TO THE WRITER'S MATERIAL

It might seem appropriate, just at this point, to take up the matter of formality and informality of tone, for it would seem that the degree of formality of the utterance is largely determined by the kind of audience that the author addresses. In any event, the degree of formality is ostensibly an adjustment of manner to the audience addressed. For example, the writer may choose to treat his reader as a friend with whom he converses intimately and even casually. Or the author may choose to address him with a good deal more ceremony, respectful of his dignity and careful to take no liberties. Even so, by writing "the author may choose," we have indicated that formality or informality of tone is not determined automatically by the nature of the audience addressed. The occasion may determine the tone even more than the audience. A serious subject, for example, may call for a certain formality of tone, even though the writer is addressing friends with whom he moves on terms of intimacy; and actually the writer most often addresses a general reader whom he does not know personally, whom he may never see, and whom he chooses to approach formally or informally because of the nature of his subject and of his strategy for handling the subject.

With this matter of formality and informality, therefore, we have actually moved away from the audience as the determiner of tone into more general problems of tone, problems in which tone is shaped by other considerations.

But though we now turn to these more general problems of tone, we have probably been wise to begin with the problem in its easiest form, where there is a definite and particular audience to be placated, defied, cajoled, mollified, or in general induced to act in a certain way.

But what of the other kinds of writing in which the audience addressed is less special and in which the writer is less interested in an immediate result? What of fiction, poetry, formal essays, articles of information? Is tone of no importance in these? Quite the contrary, even though no matter of practical expedience is involved. The tone of such writing may be of immense importance, for the tone frequently suggests how we are to "take" what is said.

## TONE AS A QUALIFICATION OF MEANING

A little reflection will show that full meaning is rarely conveyed by literal statements. We constantly find that we must "read between the lines" in order to understand a letter, or to take into

account the tone of voice and the facial expressions in our conversation with a friend. To take a simple example, John tells Ben:
"You have done well"; but the simple statement can convey anything from hearty commendation to hesitant and reluctant approval, depending upon the way in which John says these words.
We can go further: "You have done well" can even mean, when
spoken in a certain tone of voice, that Ben has not done well at all,
for John may be speaking ironically.

### IRONY AS A MODE OF TONE

IRONY always involves a discrepancy between the literal meaning
of a statement and the actual meaning. The ironical statement says
one thing on the surface, in actuality something rather different.
In a lighthearted, laughingly ironical statement the literal meaning
may be only partially qualified; in a bitter and obvious irony (such
as we call SARCASM), the literal meaning may be entirely reversed.
Between delicate ironical qualification of a statement and sarcastic
reversal of a statement there are a thousand possible shadings, and
it is perhaps a pity that we do not have specific terms for them.
But on second thought, our lack of the terms may be no real handi-
cap. What is important is that we be aware of the fact of ironical
qualification. Such qualification is important, even in everyday
practical writing; and if we are to learn to write, we must learn
how to qualify our statements so as to convey precisely what we
want to say, and only what we want to say.

We can say, then, that even in writing in which there is no practical problem of adjustment to a particular audience, even in writing addressed to an ideal reader, the matter of tone is of great
consequence. In fiction, for example, mastery of tone may become
almost the whole consequence; for tone, we must remember, represents the author's total attitude as it is reflected in the work; the
tone conveys the final shadings of meaning and interpretation which
he wishes to convey.

Tone may of course be handled successfully or unsuccessfully,
and a failure in tone can be thoroughly disastrous. Let us illustrate with examples both of failure and of success.

### OVERSTATEMENT AND UNDERSTATEMENT

The following passage consists of the last two paragraphs of
Bret Harte's story, "The Outcasts of Poker Flat." In the story the

gambler and the prostitute rise to heroism as they try to shelter and protect the innocent girl who has fallen into their company when the whole party is overtaken by a severe snow storm in the mountains. The paragraphs that follow describe the last days of the two women, the innocent girl and the prostitute.

The wind lulled as if it feared to waken them. Feathery drifts of snow, shaken from the long pine boughs, flew like white-winged birds, and settled about them as they slept. The moon through the rifted clouds looked down upon what had been the camp. But all human stain, all trace of earthly travail, was hidden beneath the spotless mantle mercifully flung from above.

They slept all day that day and the next, nor did they waken when voices and footsteps broke the silence of the camp. And when pitying fingers brushed the snow from their wan faces, you could scarcely have told from the equal peace that dwelt upon them which was she that had sinned.

Here the author, in his anxiety to stress the pathos of the scene and the redemption of the fallen woman, is not content to let the scene speak for itself. The wind "lulls" the two women; the moon looks down upon them; "a spotless mantle" is "mercifully flung from above." The pseudopoetic language, the suggestion that nature mercifully hides "all human stain," the general absence of restraint and reserve—all indicate that the tone here is one of SENTIMENTAL-ITY; that is, emotion in excess of the occasion. The author wants his reader to respond powerfully and sympathetically. We are to feel the pathos of the women's death.

What was Bret Harte's own attitude? One has to conclude that either he himself was "soft" (that is, that Bret Harte was taken in by his own attempt to "work up" an effect); or else that he was cynically trying to seduce his reader into an emotional response which is not itself justified by the dramatic occasion that he provided. In either case most sensitive readers will feel that the tone is sentimental. Sentimentality usually betrays itself by a conscious strain to work up the reader's feelings. Of course, in a sense, any appeal to our emotions represents an attempt "to work up" the effect. But it is one thing to do this skillfully and legitimately by presenting a scene with imaginative power, and it is quite a different thing to cram the emotion down the reader's throat. Readers may disagree on whether the response has been evoked legitimately or illegitimately (that is, sentimentally), but the principle involved is crucial. Otherwise any writer, however tawdry or mawkish, could demand our response simply by making a direct assault on our feelings.

Contrast with the passage from Bret Harte the following passage (from Hemingway's *A Farewell to Arms*), which describes an incident in the retreat from Caporetto in World War I. The Germans have broken through the Italian lines, and the speaker, an American serving with the ambulances attached to the Italian army, has just been picked up by the Italian battle police who are questioning all who are separated from their units.

This officer too was separated from his troops. He was not allowed to make an explanation. He cried when they read the sentence from the pad of paper, and they were questioning another when they shot him. They made a point of being intent on questioning the next man while the man who had been questioned before was being shot. In this way there was obviously nothing they could do about it. I did not know whether I should wait to be questioned or make a break now. I was obviously a German in Italian uniform. I saw how their minds worked; if they had minds and if they worked. They were all young men and they were saving their country. The second army was being re-formed beyond the Tagliamento. They were executing officers of the rank of major and above who were separated from their troops. They were dealing summarily with German agitators in Italian uniform. They wore steel helmets. Only two of us had steel helmets. Some of the carabinieri had them. The other carabinieri wore the wide hat. Airplanes we called them. We stood in the rain and were taken out one at a time to be questioned and shot. So far they had shot every one they had questioned. The questioners had that beautiful detachment and devotion to stern justice of men dealing in death without being in any danger of it. They were questioning a full colonel of a line regiment.—ERNEST HEMINGWAY: *A Farewell to Arms*, Chap. 30.[3]

This passage ably illustrates the effectiveness in some contexts of UNDERSTATEMENT. The speaker's comments on the actions of his captors are studiedly dry. He allows the actions to speak for themselves, his own commentary upon them being implied by the very act of refraining from the expected comment. The short sentences, the summary style, the repetitions—all point up the irony. (Understatement is a form of irony: the ironical contrast inheres in the discrepancy between what one would be expected to say and his actual refusal to say it.) Understatement then is the staple rhetorical device here, but the irony is occasionally allowed to become overt in such a passage as "if they had minds and if they worked."

Why does the author (who has on the whole avoided detailed description) give us the detail about the steel helmets? Because it points farther the ironical contrast: the men who have been under fire have not had the protection of the helmets. The men who are questioning them with that "devotion to stern justice of men dealing in death without being in any danger of it" do not need the helmets which they wear. Indeed, the steel helmets become a kind of symbol of the men who wear them: their reasoning and their justice is "steel-headed"—in a double sense.

Repetition in this passage also becomes an important adjunct of the ironical understatement. The word "questioned" (or "questioning") for example, occurs in this passage no less than seven times. As first used, it is used innocently and normally: it merely means "interrogated," with the implication that answers are expected and that the answers given are attended to. But by the end of the passage it has become "loaded" with other meanings: it has come to mean to the speaker, and to us, "sentenced to death." That is, the "questioning" is an empty form; the answers do not matter. No one will pay attention to them anyway. But the speaker, as the narration continues, does not change his term or qualify it. He is content to continue to use the word "questioned" or "questioning," and his continuing to repeat the original word becomes thus a form of understatement.

If the tone of this excerpt from *A Farewell to Arms* can fairly be described as that of understatement, the tone of the excerpt from Bret Harte is that of OVERSTATEMENT. But we are not, of course, to conclude that understatement is always successful or that overstatement always fails. The point to be made, rather, is this: that, for the writer of fiction and poetry, tone is important, just as important as it is for the writer who wishes to produce some practical effect. True, the poet or the writer of fiction can assume a fixed audience—an ideal reader—but even so, his attitude toward his material is of the utmost importance—even if he is writing consciously only for himself. It is easy to see that the political writer, say, uses rhetorical blandishments at his peril; if he seems to play fast and loose with the truth, he may defeat his purpose by convincing his reader that he is using a specious rhetoric—trying to persuade the reader to accept a lie by playing on his emotions. But the writer of poetry and fiction, we ought to observe, does not try to win acceptance of a lie either—fiction, though not "true," is not a lie. And even though his fiction is designed to stir the reader's emotions, he is not thereby entitled to use *any* device calculated to stir the emotions. For him, too, there is a problem of integrity: the emotional response must seem to spring legitimately from the situation which he presents.

## SOME PRACTICAL DON'TS

The problem of tone, then, is most important. There are obviously too many shadings of tone for us to be able to set up an elaborate classification. But it is possible to set down a few "don'ts" which have a very general application.

1. Writing down. One must not "write down" to his audience. The sense of oversimple statement and painfully careful explanation can disgust the reader as quickly as any offense of which the writer is capable. Prose which is properly suited to an audience of eight-year-olds would prove completely tiresome, or, on the other hand, unintentionally funny, to a mature audience. Swift, for example, would have adopted a very different tone, had *The Drapier's Letters* been addressed to a lettered audience.

2. False enthusiasm. The reader is also likely to resent any hint of synthetic breeziness and false camaraderie. It is a fault into which modern advertising is tending to press the whole civilization. Bug-eyed young matrons oo-la-la-ing over the purchase of sheets or toothbrushes, and the all-too-infectious joviality of supersalesmen, more and more fill the advertisements. The student obviously wishes to gain a kind of liveliness and warmth in his style, but an artificial concoction of informality and sprightliness can be more depressing than a rather painful dryness.

3. Sentimentality. This third fault is hardly likely to appear in most simple expository writing, but as we have seen in earlier chapters there is very little writing which is "simple expository." Sentimentality may show itself as simply gushiness or as a kind of

hair-trigger emotional sensitiveness. But whatever form it takes, sentimentality always involves an implied demand, on the part of the writer, for more emotional response than the situation warrants; and it implies, on the part of the sentimental reader, a willingness to respond emotionally when the response is not actually justified.

## APPLICATIONS

**I.** Can it be said that Ernie Pyle's "The End in Sight" employs understatement? Consider in particular the description on page 581. Does the description here avoid sentimentality? Attempt to describe an accident that you have seen or some other scene that was violent or exciting, using a method of understatement. See whether you can use understatement in your description and yet make the scene vivid and moving.

**II.** In Stace's "Have Nations Any Morals?" (p. 624), the first five paragraphs deal with what is basically an ironical situation. The method of presentation, however, is not primarily ironical, but straightforward. Attempt to rewrite these five paragraphs so as to make the presentation itself ironical.

**III.** Robert Graves's "It Was a Stable World" (p. 798) may be said to be characterized by irony. What is the tone of Edward Gibbon's account of Rome (p. 784)? Graves, for example, is somewhat flippant in comparison with Gibbon's formality and solemnity. Is there any hint of irony in Gibbon's account of Rome? Compare and contrast the tone of these two selections as carefully as you can. Be specific. Give concrete illustrations.

**IV.** In Wingfield's "The Last Days" (p. 821), there is a detailed account of the queen's departure for execution. It is a scene in which nearly all present weep. Is the writer guilty of sentimentality? If the description is not sentimental, why is it not? Discuss in detail.

## SOME PRACTICAL APPLICATIONS

It scarcely needs to be said that the rules given on page 454 must not be applied mechanically. The problem of attitude is intimately bound up with the particular occasion presented, and what would be "writing down" in one situation might possibly be overwriting in another situation. Perhaps our best mode of procedure is to consider a series of examples of tone as growing out of particular situations.

## TONE IN PERSUASION

First let us consider an example of persuasive exposition. In the passage that follows, Thomas Huxley is writing for an audience of intelligent laymen about scientific method. It is a nontechnical audience, but it is an audience capable of following an argument. Huxley takes pains to make himself clear, but he is not "writing down." In this passage he is concluding his argument that parts of England were once covered by the sea, and going on to argue that the period during which they were covered by the sea must have been a very long one.

I think you will now allow that I did not overstate my case when I asserted that we have as strong grounds for believing that all the vast area of dry land, at present occupied by the chalk, was once at the bottom of the sea, as we have for any matter of history whatever; while there is no justification for any other belief.

No less certain it is that the time during which the countries we now call south-east England, France, Germany, Poland, Russia, Egypt, Arabia, Syria, were more or less completely covered by a deep sea, was of considerable duration. We have already seen that the chalk is, in places, more than a thousand feet thick. I think you will agree with me, that it must have taken some time for the skeletons of animalcules of a hundredth of an inch in diameter to heap up such a mass as that. I have said that throughout the thickness of the chalk the remains of other animals are scattered. These remains are often in the most exquisite state of preservation. The valves of the shellfishes are commonly adherent; the long spines of some of the sea-urchins, which would be detached by the smallest jar, often remain in their places. In a word, it is certain that these animals have lived and died when the place which they now occupy was the surface of as much of the chalk as had then been deposited; and that each has been covered up by the layer of *Globigerina* mud, upon which the creatures imbedded a little higher up have, in like manner, lived and died. But some of these remains prove the existence of reptiles of vast size in the chalk sea. These lived their time, and had their ancestors and descendants, which assuredly implies time, reptiles being of slow growth.—THOMAS HUXLEY: "On a Piece of Chalk," *Discourses.*

It will of course occur to the reader that Huxley might have shortened his discussion considerably by omitting such phrases as "I think that you will now allow," "I think you will agree with me," "we have already seen," "I have said that," "it is certain that." Why did he include them? He included them because he wished to re-assure his audience, to indicate to them the validity and reason-ableness of the inferences he was making, and to make certain that all seemed perfectly coherent. Such phrases, indeed, tell us a great deal about the way in which Huxley envisaged his audience and about his attitude toward that audience.

Huxley evidently respects his typical hearer, even though his hearer has no technical knowledge of geology. Huxley does not water down his conclusions for him. He refuses to overwhelm him with authority. As a matter of fact, Huxley does just the reverse of this: he presents him with the evidence, and attempts to show him why certain conclusions and only certain conclusions can be fairly inferred from the evidence. Huxley, it is obvious, has com-plete confidence in the case that he is making; but his confidence nowhere reflects itself as arrogance.

To take up one further illustration: Why does Huxley go to the pains that he does to show that the easily detached spines of some of the sea-urchins often remain in place? It is another evidence of his respect for the intelligence of his audience. He does this obviously in order to forestall the possible objection that the re-mains of the sea-urchins were thrown up on the chalk at some later date. That the spines are still in place indicates that the creatures must "have lived and died when the place that they now occupy was the surface of as much of the chalk as had then been de-posited."

The next passage will illustrate persuasive argument.

From 1937, when he made his "quarantine" speech in Chicago until the Japanese attack on Pearl Harbor, President Roosevelt struggled with the problem of making our bankrupt foreign position solvent. As early as 1937 it was clear that the American situation demanded an immediate, intensified expansion of our armed forces, the fortification of our strategic commitments in Alaska, Guam, the Philippines, and Panama, and the formation of arrangements for mutual aid with Great Britain, France, and China—our obvious allies in an attack which was being prepared against them and against us alike. But this prudent course was held to be politically imprudent. This is another way of saying that the Ameri-can people would not agree to protect their vital interests because they had no foreign policy which disclosed their vital interests.

Thus from 1937 to 1940 President Roosevelt moved anxiously and hesitantly between his knowledge of what ought to be done and his estimate of how much the people would understand what ought to be done. I shall not attempt to answer the question whether he could have made the people understand how great was their peril because their commitments were totally unbalanced. The illusions of a century stood in the way of their understanding, and it may be that no words, but only the awful experience of total war, could even partially dispel the illusion.—WALTER LIPPMANN: *U. S. Foreign Policy: Shield of the Republic*, Chap. 4.[4]

Lippmann's general thesis is that we have lacked a meaningful foreign policy for a very long time, and that our misunderstanding of the problem has been general—not confined to one party or group. The purpose of his book is to persuade the American citizen to agree with him that the problem of foreign policy has been consistently misunderstood, and to accept now a different conception of it. But Lippmann's purpose is to win over to his thesis all American citizens, not merely those that are Republicans or those that are Democrats.

In illustrating his thesis from an episode in Roosevelt's presidency, it is not to Lippmann's purpose either to attack or to defend Roosevelt. Presumably Lippmann is sympathetic with Roosevelt's dilemma. But whether he is sympathetic or whether he is not, his primary purpose in this book is to make his general point, if possible, without alienating the reader who may be enthusiastically pro-Roosevelt or bitterly anti-Roosevelt. This purpose definitely determines the tone of this passage.

How powerfully it determines the tone can easily be demonstrated by rewriting a few of the sentences. Suppose Lippmann's attitude toward Roosevelt were more sharply critical (or that Lippmann did not mind alienating the fiercely pro-Roosevelt reader). Instead of "But this prudent course was held to be politically imprudent," he might have written: "But Roosevelt held this prudent course to be politically imprudent," or more bitterly, "But Roosevelt allowed political expediency to overrule what was the prudent course for the nation." Again, in the first sentence of the second paragraph, he might have substituted for "moved anxiously and

[4] From Walter Lippmann, *Foreign Policy: Shield of the Republic* by permission of Little, Brown and Company and the Atlantic Monthly Press.

hesitantly" the one word "vacillated." In the next sentence, he might have written, not "I shall not attempt to answer the question . . . ," but "I prefer not to try to answer the question," or "Perhaps we had better leave to Roosevelt's conscience the question." Such changes as these, plus minor changes to bring the rest of the passage into line with them, would alter the tone drastically, and with it, the total import of the whole passage.

## SOME KINDS OF IRONY

In the passage that follows, the author, William Makepeace Thackeray, makes his tone clearly evident, and indeed raucously evident. The passage quoted is taken from *Vanity Fair*, Chap. 48. The author has for a moment dropped his role as narrator of the novel and describes an occasion on which he saw King George IV.

The King? There he was. Beefeaters were before the august box; the Marquis of Steyne (Lord of the Powder Closet) and other great officers of state were behind the chair on which he sate, *He* sate—florid of face, portly of person, covered with orders, and in a rich curling head of hair. How we sang, God Save Him! How the house rocked and shouted with that magnificent music. . . . Ladies wept; mothers clasped their children; some fainted with emotion. . . . Yes, we saw him. Fate cannot deprive us of *that*. Others have seen Napoleon. Some few still exist who have beheld Frederick the Great, Doctor Johnson, Marie Antoinette, etc.: be it our reasonable boast to our children that we saw George the Good, the Magnificent, the Great.

In this mock-ecstatic tribute to George IV, Thackeray makes use of an obvious sarcasm. The literal profession of his awe of the great person is completely reversed by the tone in which the profession is given. Though pretending to praise, Thackeray indicates clearly enough what his real attitude is: by his exaggerated use of capitals and italics; by his hyperbolic laudation; by the qualities which he singles out for notice—"florid of face, portly of person."

Thackeray's sarcasm is almost too obvious. It verges on the burlesque. But irony can be used in much more subtle and much more effective fashion. Notice how John Dryden uses irony in his reference to Jeremy Collier in the passage quoted below. Collier, a clergyman, had violently attacked the writers of plays, including Dryden, for their obscenity and immorality. Here follows Dryden's answer:

I shall say the less of Mr. Collier, because in many things he has taxed me justly; and I have pleaded guilty to all thoughts and expressions of mine, which can be truly argued of obscenity, profaneness, or immorality, and retract them. If he be my enemy, let him triumph; if he be my friend, as I have given him no personal occasion to be otherwise, he will be glad of my repentance. It becomes me not to draw my pen in the defense of a bad cause, when I have so often drawn it for a good one. Yet it were not difficult to prove, that in many places he has perverted my meaning by his glosses, and interpreted my words into blasphemy and bawdry, of which they were not guilty. Besides that, he is too much given to horse-play in his raillery, and comes to battle like a dictator from the plough. I will not say, *The Zeal of God's House has eaten him up;* but I am sure it has devoured some part of his good manners and civility. It might also be doubted, whether it were altogether zeal which prompted him to this rough manner of proceeding; perhaps it became not one of his function to rake into the rubbish of ancient and modern plays; a divine might have employed his pains to better purpose, than in the nastiness of Plautus and Aristophanes, whose examples, as they excuse not me, so it might be possibly supposed, that he read them not without some pleasure.

It is highly important, in view of Dryden's later sentences, that he should begin with a manly confession of his own guilt. Dryden makes his confession quietly but quite positively—"I have pleaded guilty to all thoughts . . . if he be my friend . . . he will be glad of my repentance." The next sentence—"It becomes me not to draw my pen . . ."—breathes a confidence in his own general integrity which accounts for the fact that he can afford to plead guilty, but it also looks forward to the treatment which he proposes to deal out to Collier because of the character of Collier's attack. Dryden's own counterattack is gradually developed as the paragraph goes on. It comes with deadly effect because it is made quietly and because it has been prepared for. More obvious irony would make his castigation of Collier seem heavy-handed and strained. As it is, Dryden has managed to suggest powerfully a sense of his own composure and self-confidence, and further to suggest Collier's own frenetic and bad-humored attitude.

## APPLICATIONS

**I.** The following passage constitutes the beginning of a story by Katherine Anne Porter. Try to define the tone of this passage. What is the author's attitude toward Kennerly? Toward the Indians? Is it scornful? Sympathetic? Amused? Or what?

It was worth the price of a ticket to see Kennerly take possession of the railway train among a dark inferior people. Andreyev and I trailed without plan in the wake of his gigantic progress (he was a man of ordinary height merely, physically taller by a head, perhaps, than the nearest Indian; but his moral stature in this moment was beyond calculation) through the second-class coach into which we had climbed, in our haste, by mistake. . . . Now that the true revolution of blessed memory has come and gone in Mexico, the names of many things are changed, nearly always with the view to an appearance of heightened well-being for all creatures. So you cannot ride third-class no matter how poor or humble-spirited or miserly you may be. You may go second in cheerful disorder and sociability, or first in sober ease; or, if you like, you may at great price install yourself in the stately plush of the Pullman, isolated and envied as any successful General from the north. "Ah, it is beautiful as a *pulman!*" says the middle-class Mexican when he wishes truly to praise anything. . . . There was no Pullman with this train or we should most unavoidably have been in it. Kennerly traveled like that. He strode mightily through, waving his free arm, lunging his portfolio and leather bag, stiffening his nostrils as conspicuously as he could against the smell that "poured," he said, "simply poured like mildewed pea soup!" from the teeming clutter of wet infants and draggled turkeys and indignant baby pigs and food baskets and bundles of vegetables and bales and hampers of domestic goods, each little mountain of confusion yet drawn into a unit, from the midst of which its owners glanced up casually from dark pleased faces at the passing strangers. Their pleasure had nothing to do with us. They were pleased because, sitting still, without even the effort of beating a burro, they were on the point of being carried where they wished to go, accomplishing in an hour what would otherwise have been a day's hard journey, with all their households on their backs. . . . Almost nothing can disturb their quiet ecstasy when they are finally settled among their plunder, and the engine, mysteriously and powerfully animated, draws them lightly over the miles they have so often counted step by step. And they are not troubled by the noisy white man because, by now, they are accustomed to him. White men look all much alike to the Indians, and they had seen this maddened fellow with light eyes and leather-colored hair battling his way desperately through their coach many times before. There is always one of him on every train. They watch his performance with as much attention as they can spare from their own always absorbing business; he is a part of the scene of travel.—KATHERINE ANNE PORTER: "Hacienda," *Flowering Judas and Other Stories.*[5]

**II.** The scene described below is a British club in India, some decades ago. The orchestra has just played "God Save the King." What is the author's attitude toward his fellow countrymen? The passage is obviously ironic, but what is the precise shading of irony? Is the author indignant? Mocking? Bitter? Or what?

Meanwhile the performance ended, and the amateur orchestra played the National Anthem. Conversation and billiards stopped, faces stiffened. It was the Anthem of the Army of Occupation. It reminded every member of the club that he or she was British and in exile. It produced a little sentiment and a useful accession of will-power. The meager tune, the curt series of demands on Jehovah, fused into a prayer unknown in England, and though they perceived neither Royalty nor Deity they did perceive something, they were strengthened to resist another day. They poured out, offering one another drinks.—E. M. FORSTER: *A Passage to India,* Chap. 3.[6]

**III.** The next paragraph is from Ring Lardner's *The Big Town,* Chap. 5. What is the speaker's attitude toward the Follies? Toward comedians? Toward the "big gal numbers"? What is the *author's* attitude toward his character? How do you know?

We got in the theater a half hour before the show begin. I put in the time finding out what the men will wear, and the gals looked up what scenes Ralston'd be in. He was only on once in each act. They don't waste much time on a comedian in the Follies. It don't take long to spring the two gags they can think up for him in a year, and besides, he just interferes with the big gal numbers, where Bunny Granville or somebody dreams of the different flappers he danced with at the prom, and the souvenirs they give him; and one by one the different gals writhes in, dressed like the stage director thinks they dress at the female colleges —a Wesley gal in pink tights, a Vassar dame in hula-hula, and a Smith gal with a sombrero and a sailor suit. He does a' couple of steps with them and they each hand him a flower or a vegetable to remember them by.[7]

[5] From *Flowering Judas and Other Stories* by Katherine Anne Porter, copyright, 1930, 1935, by Katherine Anne Porter. Reprinted by permission of Harcourt, Brace and Company, Inc.

[6] From *A Passage to India* by E. M. Forster, copyright, 1924, by Harcourt, Brace and Company, Inc.

[7] From *The Big Town* by Ring Lardner, copyright, 1921, by Charles Scribner's Sons.

## TONE IN PUBLIC UTTERANCE AND PRIVATE UTTERANCE

John Dryden's answer to Collier is, as we observed on page 460, a fine example of the subtlety of tone that may be achieved by a writer who can count upon cultivated readers. The public orator will usually aim at a different kind of effect and will make use of rhetorical devices appropriate to that effect. The passage which follows is the last paragraph of the now famous speech which Winston Churchill delivered before the House of Commons on June 4, 1940, just after the British Army had been successfully removed from Dunkirk.

I have, myself, full confidence that if all do their duty, if nothing is neglected, and if the best arrangements are made, as they are being made, we shall prove ourselves once again able to defend our island home, to ride out the storm of war, and to outlive the menace of tyranny, if necessary for years, if necessary alone. At any rate, that is what we are going to try to do. That is the resolve of His Majesty's Government—every man of them. That is the will of Parliament and the nation. The British Empire and the French Republic, linked together in their cause and in their need, will defend to the death their native soil, aiding each other like good comrades to the utmost of their strength. Even though large tracts of Europe and many old and famous States have fallen or may fall into the grip of the Gestapo and all the odious apparatus of Nazi rule, we shall not flag or fail. We shall go on to the end, we shall fight in France, we shall fight on the seas and oceans, we shall fight with growing confidence and growing strength in the air, we shall defend our island, whatever the cost may be, we shall fight on the beaches, we shall fight on the landing grounds, we shall fight in the fields and in the streets, we shall fight in the hills; we shall never surrender, and even if, which I do not for a moment believe, this island or a large part of it were subjugated and starving, then our Empire beyond the seas, armed and guarded by the British Fleet, would carry on the struggle, until, in God's good time, the new world, with all its power and might, steps forth to the rescue and the liberation of the old.
—WINSTON CHURCHILL: *Blood, Sweat, and Tears.*[8]

Churchill's purpose was to rally the British people in a firm determination to continue their resistance in spite of the disastrous loss of North France and the Channel ports. But he was speaking, of

[8] From *Blood, Sweat, and Tears* by Winston Churchill, copyright, 1941, by G. P. Putnam's Sons.

course, also to a world audience, an audience which also had to be
given confidence in British determination to carry on the war.
Notice the amount of repetition in this closing paragraph. Is it
justified? Why does it not grow monotonous? Would it be particularly effective in oral delivery? Notice too that the specification
of the places where the British will continue to fight makes a kind
of progression, moving from France, from which the British Army
had just been evacuated, to "our island," and then on to "our
Empire beyond the seas." Does this progression prevent the repetition of "we shall fight" from becoming monotonous? Notice too
that Churchill is willing to entertain the possibility that "this island"
may be subjugated. Does the admission of the possibility undermine the sense of resolution? Or does it strengthen it?

The student might also notice that the peroration of this speech
is closely linked to the events which had just occurred at Dunkirk
where the Navy had rendered splendid service. Does this linkage
help give new strength to the otherwise rather worn metaphor
"storm of war"? Does it help account for Churchill's putting his
mention of the British Fleet in climactic position?

This speech by Churchill represents the effect sought by the
orator on a high occasion. It is political in the best sense of the
term, for the speaker was not only speaking to an audience but
speaking consciously as the mouthpiece of a whole people. Yet the
rhetorical effect sought would be quite out of place in the passage
which follows, a passage which is also political, but "private" and
personal. It is an excerpt from one of Thomas Jefferson's letters
to his friend and former political rival, John Adams.

. . . I agree with you that there is a natural aristocracy among men. The
grounds of this are virtue and talents. Formerly, bodily powers gave
place among the *aristoi*. But, since the invention of gunpowder has armed
the weak as well as the strong with missile death, bodily strength, like
beauty, good humor, politeness, and other accomplishments, has become
but an auxiliary ground for distinction. There is also an artificial aristocracy, founded on wealth and birth, without either virtue or talents;
for with these it would belong to the first class. The natural aristocracy
I consider as the most precious gift of nature, for the instruction, the
trusts, and government of society. And, indeed, it would have been inconsistent in creation to have formed man for the social state, and not
to have provided virtue and wisdom enough to manage the concerns of

the society. May we not even say that that form of government is the best which provides the most effectually for a pure selection of these natural *aristoi* into the offices of government? The artificial aristocracy is a mischievous ingredient in government, and provision should be made to prevent its ascendancy. On the question what is the best provision, you and I differ; but we differ as rational friends, using the free exercise of our own reason, and mutually indulging its errors. You think it best to put the pseudo *aristoi* into a separate chamber of legislation, where they may be hindered from doing mischief by their co-ordinate branches, and where, also, they may be a protection to wealth against the agrarian and plundering enterprises of the majority of the people. I think that to give them power in order to prevent them from doing mischief is arming them for it, and increasing instead of remedying the evil. For, if the co-ordinate branches can arrest their action, so may they that of the co-ordinates. Mischief may be done negatively as well as positively. Of this a cabal in the Senate of the United States has furnished many proofs. Nor do I believe them necessary to protect the wealthy, because enough of these will find their way into every branch of the legislation to protect themselves. From fifteen to twenty legislatures of our own, in action for thirty years past, have proved that no fears of an equalization of property are to be apprehended from them. I think the best remedy is exactly that provided by all our constitutions, to leave to the citizens the free election and separation of the *aristoi* from the pseudo *aristoi*, of the wheat from the chaff. In general they will elect the really good and wise. In some instances, wealth may corrupt, and birth blind them; but not in sufficient degree to endanger society.

The tone of this passage is not formal and public, but informal and private, as befits a letter from a wise and seasoned statesman to a wise and seasoned friend. Jefferson disagrees with Adams, but there is no rancor in the disagreement. (They differ "as rational friends.") Indeed, the paragraph in question represents Jefferson's attempt to put their fundamental disagreement in its clearest light. He can appeal to the political experience shared by both of them, and this means that he need not go into detail with some of his illustrations. He can also count upon Adams' own sense of language and even on his knowledge of Greek; and so Jefferson uses the term *aristoi* (which means "the best") naturally and gracefully. Moreover, Jefferson does not need to identify "best." Adams will know that he means those "best fitted to hold office."

Jefferson does not claim too much. He can make reasonable concessions (note the last sentence in the excerpt), for this is not a lawyer's brief in which he must put the best possible face on the position he maintains, nor is it a public speech which must offer no loopholes to his opponents. It is a letter, a letter to a "rational friend," and the tone has the candor and the reasonableness of such a letter.

## TONE: FAMILIAR AND FORMAL

The so-called FAMILIAR ESSAY depends upon tone for its special character. Indeed, without employing the concept of tone, it is difficult to define the familiar essay at all. For the essence of the familiar essay does not reside in subject or theme or even style, if we use style in the most general sense of that term. The essence resides in a certain geniality of tone. There are familiar essays on all sorts of subjects and they make use of long sentences or short, vivid descriptions or no descriptions at all, quotations from the classic English authors or no quotations. The one matter which they have in common is a special attitude toward the audience, and variations of tone which reflect this attitude.

### THE IMPORTANCE OF TONE IN THE FAMILIAR ESSAY

In this connection consider the opening paragraphs of a celebrated familiar essay, Charles Lamb's "Mrs. Battle's Opinions on Whist."

"A clear fire, a clean hearth, and the rigour of the game." This was the celebrated *wish* of old Sarah Battle (now with God) who, next to her devotions, loved a good game at whist. She was none of your lukewarm gamesters, your half-and-half players, who have no objection to take a hand, if you want one to make up a rubber; who affirm that they have no pleasure in winning; that they like to win one game and lose another; that they can while away an hour very agreeably at a cardtable, but are indifferent whether they play or no; and will desire an adversary, who has slipped a wrong card, to take it up and play another. These insufferable triflers are the curse of a table. One of these flies will spoil a whole pot. Of such it may be said that they do not play at cards, but only play at playing at them.

Sarah Battle was none of that breed. She detested them, as I do, from her heart and soul; and would not, save upon a striking emergency, willingly seat herself at the same table with them. She loved a thorough-paced partner, a determined enemy. She took, and gave, no concessions. She hated favours. She never made a revoke, nor ever passed it over in her adversary without exacting the utmost forfeiture. She fought a good fight: cut and thrust. She held not her good sword (her cards) "like a dancer." She sate bolt upright; and neither showed you her cards, nor desired to see yours. All people have their blind side—their superstitions; and I have heard her declare, under the rose, that Hearts was her favourite suit.

What is Lamb's attitude toward his reader? Basically, the attitude assumes that the reader is a companion who is accepted on terms of friendly equality. The assumption, indeed, makes further claims still: it assumes that the reader is one of the initiate. He can be counted on to appreciate the writer's values, to respond to his jests, to understand his allusions, to take, without any urging, the writer's own attitude toward the materials with which he deals.

Because this attitude is basic, the familiar essay frequently makes use of literary allusions, quotations and semi-quotations from the classics, the more subtle forms of irony, and, in general, all the devices of indirection. Such devices can be employed because it is assumed that the reader is able to follow them, and moreover, that he will relish them. But these devices do not in themselves give us a familiar essay. Stevenson's "Pulvis et Umbra" (p. 471) is hardly an informal essay, though it contains many literary allusions; nor is Johnson's letter to Macpherson, though its tone is ironical. The informal essay requires a tone more special still.

The passage quoted from Lamb will illustrate. Lamb's implied attitude toward his reader is very different from his attitude, say, toward Mrs. Battle herself. Though Lamb obviously admires Mrs. Battle, he is capable of smiling at her too; and we are expected to join him in smiling. Mrs. Battle is presented, mock-heroically, as a warrior. She is stern; she is even grim; she lives by a strict code, insisting that her opponent live by the same, and valuing a foeman worthy of her steel. (The whist-warfare analogy, by the way, runs through the whole essay.)

In this passage she is said, in accordance with St. Paul's injunction, to have "fought a good fight"; she has the contempt of Shakespeare's battle-scarred warrior Antony for one who held his sword "like a dancer." The information that Hearts was her favorite suit

is given with the air of divulging an amiable foible in an otherwise
grim old warrior who might be thought to have had none.

But the irony generated in the cards-warfare contrast is directed
at Sarah Battle with a difference. The speaker is careful to align
himself on Sarah Battle's side. Ostensibly he agrees with her—in the
zest which he takes in mimicking the excuses of her adversaries
("they can while away an hour very agreeably at a cardtable"), in
joining in her detestation of those who "only play at playing at"
cards ("She detested them, as I do"), in the mock-reverence with
which he speaks of her ("now with God"). If, however, someone
argues that the mock-reverence is not merely mock-reverence, but
has an aspect of sincerity and affection, that is perfectly true. Sarah
Battle is described in terms of an irony so gentle that it is finally
affectionate. But this is just the point: the writer of the informal
essay makes use of a complex tone: he can assume that his audience
will be alive to nuance and inflection.

Compare in this matter of tone a modern example of the familiar
essay—on quite another topic, and in quite another style.

I see by the new Sears Roebuck catalogue that it is still possible to
buy an axle for a 1909 Model T Ford, but I am not deceived. The great
days have faded, the end is in sight. Only one page in the current
catalogue is devoted to parts and accessories for the Model T; yet everyone remembers springtimes when the Ford gadget section was larger
than men's clothing, almost as large as household furnishings. The last
Model T was built in 1927, and the car is fading from what scholars
call the American scene—which is an understatement, because to a few
million people who grew up with it, the old Ford practically *was* the
American scene.

It was the miracle God had wrought. And it was patently the sort of
thing that could only happen once. Mechanically uncanny, it was like
nothing that had ever come to the world before. Flourishing industries
rose and fell with it. As a vehicle, it was hard-working, commonplace,
heroic; and it often seemed to transmit those qualities to the persons who
rode in it. My own generation identifies it with Youth, with its gaudy,
irretrievable excitements; before it fades into the mist, I would like to
pay it the tribute of the sigh that is not a sob, and set down random
entries in a shape somewhat less cumbersome than a Sears Roebuck
catalogue.

The Model T was distinguished from all other makes of cars by the
fact that its transmission was of a type known as planetary—which was

half metaphysics, half sheer friction. Engineers accepted the word
"planetary" in its epicyclic sense, but I was always conscious that it also
means "wandering," "erratic." Because of the peculiar nature of this
planetary element, there was always, in Model T, a certain dull rapport
between engine and wheels, and, even when the car was in a state
known as neutral, it trembled with a deep imperative and tended to
inch forward. There was never a moment when the bands were not
faintly egging the machine on. In this respect it was like a horse, rolling
the bit on its tongue, and country people brought to it the same technique they used with draft animals.—LEE STROUT WHITE: "Farewell, My
Lovely." [9]

Here we feel that we are hardly asked to be on the alert for quotations from the Bible and Shakespeare. Rather it is assumed that
we are familiar with the Sears, Roebuck catalogue. (Even so, the
number of literary quotations is more important than might be
thought: the cliché "the American scene"; the first message sent
over the telegraph wires, "What hath God wrought!"; "the tribute
of a sigh" from Gray's "Elegy.") It is assumed then that the reader
will be familiar with the Sears, Roebuck catalogue and with the
Model T; but it is also assumed that, unlike the average Sears,
Roebuck reader, he will also be conversant with epicycles and
metaphysics. For unless he knows something of both, he will miss
a good deal of the humor, and he may fail to realize that the "sigh
that is not a sob" is a gentle noise, which for its full suspiration,
requires that the tongue be held in the cheek.

Certainly, to enjoy the essay the reader must be aware that the
authors lament the passing of the Model T with mock seriousness.
And, if the reader objects that, as with Lamb's essay, the seriousness of the lament has its element of sincerity, one must emphatically agree. Of course it has; but to realize this is but to realize more
fully the extent to which the author of the familiar essay takes his
reader into his confidence. We can perhaps see the matter more
clearly by discriminating the kinds of statement: direct, simple
ironical, and complex ironical. In the first, the writer states his attitude directly and straightforwardly. In the second, he states it ironically and indirectly: that is, he pretends to champion a position at
variance with his real position. In the third, the method is still more

[9] From "Farewell, My Lovely," by Lee Strout White. Copyright 1936 The
New Yorker Magazine, Inc. (Formerly The F-R Publishing Corporation.)

indirect, for here his irony partially doubles back upon itself. His attitude of affirmation and admiration is given in an indirect and ironic form, which, though the reader has learned to associate that form with negation, here carries an element of positive compliment.

## APPLICATIONS

**I.** Both Vincent Sheean (p. 870) and James Thurber (p. 722) write about their university days. Which of the two accounts has the tone of the familiar essay? Note that the answer is not quite so simple as saying that one is humorous and the other is serious. For what kind of audience is each author writing? What is the author's attitude toward his reader? What is his attitude toward himself? Write a short theme comparing and contrasting the tone of the two selections.

**II.** Two paragraphs of Charles Lamb's "Mrs. Battle's Opinions on Whist" (p. 710) have been analyzed on page 467. Reread the analysis. Compare the tone of the opening paragraphs with that of the rest of the essay. What special quality of irony is to be found in the essay? What elements of style make for such irony? Be specific.

**III.** Compare the tone of Beerbohm's "The Decline of the Graces" (p. 730) with the tone of Lamb's "Mrs. Battle's Opinions on Whist" (p. 710) and with the tone of Thurber's "The Dog That Bit People" (p. 716). What is the quality of Beerbohm's irony? Severe? Gentle? Mocking? Bitter? Or what? Does Beerbohm have any serious point to make?

**IV.** Smith's "A Lark's Flight" (p. 677), like the essays by Lamb and Beerbohm, makes an appeal to a cultivated audience. There are, for example, literary allusions, references to history, and references to folklore. But how does the tone of "A Lark's Flight" differ from that of either Lamb's or Beerbohm's essay? Can "A Lark's Flight" be called a "formal" essay in contrast to the "informality" of the other essays? If you think so, indicate why, and illustrate your point. Take into account Smith's choice of diction, the presence of irony or lack of it, and any other elements of style that you think are relevant.

**V.** Write an informal theme on one of your own college or school experiences, attempting to achieve something of the tone of Thurber's "University Days."

### TONE IN THE FORMAL ESSAY

A relative complexity of tone may, however, characterize essays which are not familiar at all. The familiar or informal essay always has as one of the ingredients of its tone an element of casualness and an acceptance of the reader on the same footing as the writer.

Stevenson's "Pulvis et Umbra," an excerpt of which follows, will illustrate the point by contrast. For in this essay Stevenson's manner suggests a kind of formality, a mounting of the rostrum, a speaking of a set piece to an audience—all of which makes his essay a formal declamation as Lamb's essay on Mrs. Battle, or the White essay on the Model T, is not.

We look for some reward of our endeavours and are disappointed; not success, not happiness, not even peace of conscience, crowns our ineffectual efforts to do well. Our frailties are invincible, our virtues barren; the battle goes sore against us to the going down of the sun. The canting moralist tells us of right and wrong; and we look abroad, even on the face of our small earth, and find them change with every climate, and no country where some action is not honoured for a virtue and none where it is not branded for a vice; and we look in our experience, and find no vital congruity in the wisest rules, but at the best a municipal fitness. It is not strange if we are tempted to despair of good. We ask too much. Our religions and moralities have been trimmed to flatter us, till they are all emasculate and sentimentalized, and only please and weaken. Truth is of a rougher strain. In the harsh face of life, faith can be read a bracing gospel. The human race is a thing more ancient than the ten commandments; and the bones and revolutions of the Kosmos, in whose joints we are but moss and fungus, more ancient still.

There is one sense, of course, in which Stevenson takes his stand on the same level as the reader. He writes "*We* look for," "*Our* frailties are invincible," "The canting moralist tells *us* of right and wrong." Stevenson thus properly includes himself in his commentary on mankind. But his essay *is* a commentary on mankind—not a casual chat with Tom, Dick, or Harry, the writer's good friend.

The tone of formal, meditated, "public" utterance reveals itself in half-a-dozen ways. To consider only a few: (1) the vocabulary is more "literary" than Stevenson would have used in an informal essay. Thus, he writes "the battle goes sore against us" rather than "the battle goes against us" or, more colloquially still, "we begin to lose out." (2) He gives us echoes of the King James Version of the Bible. Thus, "to the going down of the sun." (cf. Joshua 10:27, "And it came to pass at the time of the going down of the sun, that Joshua commanded . . .") (3) Stevenson formalizes the rhythms to give a sense of balanced antithesis, particularly in the closing sentence of the paragraph: "The human race is a thing more ancient than the ten commandments; and the bones and revolutions of the Kosmos, in whose joints we are but moss and fungus, more ancient still."

## COMPLEXITY OF TONE: WHEN, AND WHY, IT IS NECESSARY

Let us consider one more example of complexity of tone, taken this time, not from an essay either formal or informal, but from an autobiography. In the passage which follows, T. E. Lawrence describes an incident that occurred in Arabia during World War I while he was serving with the Arabs in their revolt against Turkey. The incident occurred while Lawrence was leading a raiding party of Arab tribesmen.

My followers had been quarrelling all day, and while I was lying near the rocks a shot was fired. I paid no attention; for there were hares and birds in the valley; but a little later Suleiman roused me and made me follow him across the valley to an opposite bay in the rocks, where one of the Ageyl, a Boreida man, was lying stone dead with a bullet through his temples. The shot must have been fired from close by; because the skin was burnt about the wound. The remaining Ageyl were running frantically about; and when I asked what it was, Ali, their head man, said that Hamed the Moor had done the murder. I suspected Suleiman, because of the feud between the Atban and Ageyl . . . but Ali assured me that Suleiman had been with him three hundred yards further up the valley gathering sticks when the shot was fired. I sent all out to search for Hamed, and crawled back to the baggage, feeling that it need not have happened this day of all days when I was in pain.

As I lay there I heard a rustle, and opened my eyes slowly upon Hamed's back as he stooped over his saddle-bags, which lay just beyond my rock. I covered him with a pistol and then spoke. He had put down his rifle to lift the gear: and was at my mercy till the others came. We held a court at once; and after a while Hamed confessed that, he and Salem having had words, he had seen red and shot him suddenly. Our inquiry ended. The Ageyl, as relatives of the dead man, demanded blood for blood. The others supported them; and I tried vainly to talk the gentle Ali round. My head was aching with fever and I could not think; but hardly even in health, with all eloquence, could I have begged Hamed off; for Salem had been a friendly fellow and his sudden murder a wanton crime.

COMPLEXITY OF TONE: WHEN AND WHY IT IS NECESSARY 473

Then rose up the horror which would make civilized man shun justice like a plague if he had not the needy to serve him as hangmen for wages. There were other Moroccans in our army; [Hamed the Moor was a Moroccan] and to let the Ageyl kill one in feud meant reprisals by which our unity would have been endangered. It must be a formal execution, and at last, desperately, I told Hamed that he must die for punishment, and laid the burden of his killing on myself. Perhaps they would count me not qualified for feud. At least no revenge could lie against my followers; for I was a stranger and kinless.

I made him enter a narrow gully of the spur, a dank twilight place overgrown with weeds. Its sandy bed had been pitted by trickles of water down the cliffs in the late rain. At the end it shrank to a crack a few inches wide. The walls were vertical. I stood in the entrance and gave him a few moments' delay which he spent crying on the ground. Then I made him rise and shot him through the chest. He fell down on the weeds shrieking, with the blood coming out in spurts over his clothes, and jerked about till he rolled nearly to where I was. I fired again, but was shaking so that I only broke his wrist. He went on calling out, less loudly, now lying on his back with his feet towards me, and I leant forward and shot him for the last time in the thick of his neck under the jaw. His body shivered a little, and I called the Ageyl; who buried him in the gully where he was. Afterwards the wakeful night dragged over me, till, hours before dawn, I had the men up and made them load, in my longing to be free of Wadi Kitan. They had to lift me into the saddle.—T. E. LAWRENCE: *Seven Pillars of Wisdom*, Chap. 31.[10]

What is Lawrence's attitude toward Hamed? Toward the Arabs and their blood feuds? Most of all, toward himself? Is he ashamed of himself? Proud of himself? Complacent and untroubled about himself?

One's first impression is that the incident is told with detachment and an almost studied dryness; and so, in a sense, it is. But it is evident that Lawrence is not glossing over the incident casually and briefly. He develops it, and he gives us even minute details: e.g., "bullet through his temples," "as he stooped over his saddle-bags," "shot him for the last time in the thick of his neck under the jaw." Even the scene of the execution, the gully, is described carefully and precisely: "Its sandy bed had been pitted by trickles of water down the cliffs in the late rain."

[10] From: *Seven Pillars of Wisdom* by T. E. Lawrence. Copyright 1925, 1935 by Doubleday & Company, Inc.

The narrator evidently remembers the whole incident vividly, and knows how to make the incident vivid to his reader. Why, then, is he not much more explicit about his own feelings and attitudes? Would anything have been gained if Lawrence had added a long paragraph describing the feelings that passed through his mind as he decided that he must act as executioner? Would anything have been lost? Notice that Lawrence is willing to use the word "horror," but he does not write, "As a civilized man I was overwhelmed with horror," but rather, "Then rose up the horror which would make civilized man shun justice like a plague if he had not the needy to serve him as hangmen for wages." Why does Lawrence, in this most explicit account of his own feelings, prefer the generalized statement?

A little meditation on these questions is likely to result in some such conclusion as this: that Lawrence, far from remaining cool and detached, was indeed terribly shaken by the experience, but that, nevertheless, he preferred to make his *account* of the experience as detached and objective as was possible. He chose to give a rather restrained account of his actions, leaving his reader to infer from the actions themselves what his feelings must have been. True, Lawrence once uses the word "desperately" and he refers to "the horror which would make civilized man shun justice," had he to execute justice in his own person. But these are almost the only explicit references to his feelings; and in the account of the actual execution, there are none at all.

This restraint itself has an important effect on the tone: it implies a certain modesty (his own mental anguish is not allowed to dominate the story as if Lawrence thought his anguish the important thing in the episode); it implies a certain confidence in the reader's maturity and sensitiveness—the reader need not be "told" what Lawrence was feeling. But the restraint, here, is of still further importance: the restraint manifested in Lawrence's *account* of his action is a reflection of, and a type of, the disciplined control which he imposed on his followers and on himself in the desert. The man who relates the action is the man who acted, and his manner of writing about the event suggests his attitude toward the event itself.

There is a more general conclusion about tone which may be drawn from this example, and it is a conclusion which is well worth pointing out to the student. It is this: that subtlety of attitude and complexity of attitude frequently (one is tempted to say usually) can only be suggested, not stated directly. The writer has to trust to the effect of the whole passage, or even the whole book—not to explicit statements of his feeling. This means that he has to place a good deal of reliance upon his audience. (A twelve-year-old reader might well decide, on reading the passage, that Lawrence was a callous man, or that he considered the Arabs to be bloodthirsty savages and therefore without the feelings of real human beings, or even that he got a positive satisfaction out of ridding the earth of Hamed, the wanton killer.) Finally, if the writer must trust to the maturity of his audience, he will do well to appeal to their imaginations—to make every detail sharp and concrete, as Lawrence does here—but he will wisely avoid writing down to them or attempting to play upon their heartstrings.

The examples of tone that we have considered in this chapter indicate how wide the range of tone is and how difficult it is to speak of tone abstractly and in general. For the tone of a piece of writing, as the various examples make plain, is intimately related to the occasion which calls forth the writing, and is as intimately related to the author's general purpose. In some instances the tone may be as elusive as the expression of personality itself; but it can be, as our examples have shown, of the utmost importance. It is not to be thought of as decoration—as a mere grace of style; it is an integral—sometimes the central—part of the meaning.

Our examples also indicate that the tone may be generated through all sorts of subtle devices; that, indeed, there is no set and specific way in which tone is indicated. Because of this fact it has been difficult to do full justice to the subject in this chapter, for it has been impossible to give examples of great length, and so, since tone is the quality of the whole context, the most important manifestations of tone—the tone of a whole novel or essay or history—could not be illustrated.

## APPLICATIONS

I. The problem of tone in Carl Becker's "The Marxian View of History" (p. 643) is in large part that of conveying to the reader a sense of candor and fairness. Becker's attack on Marxism will appear the more convincing if we do not feel that he is speaking as a blind and bitter partisan. This problem is in part solved by the use of the dialogue form:

each position has its proponent, and these proponents argue the matter out rationally, voicing their objections, and giving the other an opportunity for an answer. Attempt to rewrite the essays by Wiener (p. 648) and Ridenour (p. 651) in the form of a dialogue. Note that Ridenour has made your task easier by his attempt to take Wiener's points definitely into account.

**II.** What is the tone of Mitchell's essay "Mazie" (p. 830)? Notice that Mazie is portrayed with real sympathy and that the author takes her seriously as a genuine, as a "good," and, in some sense, admirable character. But in presenting her real virtues, there is no attempt to prettify or sentimentalize her. The author finds her amusing and expects us to be amused by her. It will be well worth study to notice how the account of Mazie's foibles and limitations is used to reinforce rather than to cancel out our sympathy for her. Write a theme about some "character" you have known. "Mazie" may serve as something of a model for the tone to be secured in this essay.

**III.** Is the account of the hanging in "A Lark's Flight" (p. 677) overwritten? Does the account of the hanging play too heavily upon our sympathies? Discuss in detail, taking into account not only the description of the hanging itself, but its relation to the whole essay.

## THE SPECIAL AUDIENCE AND THE IDEAL AUDIENCE

Earlier in this chapter we spoke of tone as the reflection of the author's attitude toward his audience *or* toward his material, without making any elaborate distinction between the two levels of attitude. But the student may well ask: When should attitude toward the audience dominate, and when attitude toward the material?

Writing which demands that the author take into account his particular audience is, as we have seen, always "practical" writing —writing designed to effect some definite thing. The advertiser is trying to persuade the housewife to buy something. The politician delivers a speech which he hopes will induce citizens to vote for him. Or, to take a more exalted case (for there need be no self-interest), a statesman urges a nation (through his writing and his speeches) to adopt a certain course of action. But these cases all have one thing in common: they are designed to secure a practical end. An audience is to be won to agreement or urged to action.

If such writing is to be effective, the author must, of course, keep his audience constantly in mind. An approach that is calculated to win the suffrage of one audience may very well repel another. The age, the intelligence, the amount of education, the interest, the habits and prejudices—must all be taken into account. The skillful management of such problems is an aspect of rhetoric, and for many people rhetoric has come to mean largely the art of persuasion. Rhetoric has therefore come to have something of a bad name, as if it consisted in cold-bloodedly fitting the statement to the emotional background and even to the prejudices of the audience. Certainly rhetoric is an instrument which can be used for bad ends, and a rhetorical appeal which, in its anxiety to produce an effect, ignores truth and relevance is vicious. But the fact that it may be misused does not render the instrument vicious. It may be properly used, and it is the part of common sense for a writer to take his special audience into account as he tries to gain their conviction. One may illustrate from Churchill's speech (p. 463), but one may also cite in this connection the passage from Huxley (p. 456). For Huxley, as contrasted with the ordinary mathematician or geologist, has a "practical" end in view; and by the same token, he has a special audience. The scientist acting strictly as scientist does not argue with his reader; he "just tells him." The facts speak for themselves, and in purely technical writing they are allowed to speak for themselves. But they speak fully only to a specially trained audience. In the work from which we have quoted, Huxley is writing for an audience that is not so trained, and the tone which he adopts toward his readers quite properly takes that fact into account.

The student, however, when he finds that he must address himself to a general reader rather than to some specific and quite special reader, may find that the problem of tone becomes difficult because he lacks a definite target at which to aim. Yet all good writing is addressed to a reader, even though that reader is an ideal reader, not a limited and special reader. One could argue, in fact, that because the ideal reader is ideal, his intelligence, his sensitivity, his general discrimination are to be honored and respected all the more. This is to say what has been said earlier, that we do not evade the problem of tone by addressing ourselves to the reader-in-general rather than to Tom, Dick, or Harry. In fact, the problem of tone here becomes more important, not less important. The student, however, even though agreeing with what has just been argued, may find that the ideal reader remains too shadowy to furnish him something definite to shoot at. In that case it may be of practical help, as he writes, to think of some particular person, the most intelligent and discriminating person that he knows. If he can please that person and be convincing to that person, the problem of tone will probably have been taken care of quite adequately.

There is another way of solving the problem practically: we say that the author writes for a particular audience, but he also writes for himself. There is his own sense of fitness that must be satisfied. The writer himself becomes the audience at which he aims. The question which he asks himself is not, "Have I made this convincing to Tom or to Dick or to Harry?" but rather, "Have I made this convincing to myself?"; or, to put the matter more succinctly still, "Have I made this convincing?"

In writing for this "ideal" reader, then, the author can transpose all problems of tone into the problem of handling his material itself. The problem of tone alters only when the writing is addressed specifically to Tom or to Dick—not to just any reader—and in proportion as Tom or Dick differs from the ideal reader.

Let us, however, give one further illustration of the relation between these two aspects of tone, tone as modified by the special audience, and tone as modified only by the nature of the material. Let us look back at the passage quoted from *Seven Pillars of Wisdom* (p. 472). The passage, as we saw, tells us a good deal about Lawrence's character, and it makes a commentary on a number of things: to mention only a few, on the Arabs, on justice, and on capital punishment. But as we have already observed, such writing makes its points by implication, and it requires a mature reader. For the ideal reader, no alteration of tone is required, and Lawrence has managed his problem of tone in probably the most satisfactory way possible.

But let us suppose that Lawrence were relating the episode to an audience which was complacent in its contempt for the "barbarian" Arabs. Unless his attitude toward the Arabs were to be completely distorted, Lawrence would have to alter the tone to take the prejudices of his audience into account. In particular, he would have to make much more explicit the fact that the Arabs honestly faced up to their imposition of the death penalty as the more sentimental, but ultimately more callous, citizen of England or America refuses to face it.

Or suppose that Lawrence were standing for a seat in Parliament, and a garbled account of the incident were being used against him. He might be content to rely upon the relation which he has given in *Seven Pillars*. Properly read, it shows him to be anything but calloused and insensitive. But the politician cannot afford to risk what the artist can. The objectivity of his account might have to be qualified. What his feelings and attitudes were could not safely be left to inference. Lawrence would have to state them explicitly. In general, the rewritten account would be focused not on the drama of the scene itself, but on Lawrence's personal feelings and his struggle with duty.

## SUMMARY

Every piece of discourse implies a particular situation, a situation which involves a certain kind of reader and an occasion that accounts for that reader's being addressed. Even technical writing assumes a special situation, one which involves a reader who need not be coaxed and who has an interest that transcends any particular occasion.

Just as every piece of discourse implies a particular situation, it also implies a particular TONE. "Tone" may be defined as the reflection in the writing itself of the author's ATTITUDE toward his audience and toward his material. (The term is a metaphor derived from the tone of the voice in which an utterance is made. The writer cannot indicate his attitude, as the speaker can, by the tone of *voice;* but by his choice and arrangement of words, the skillful writer can convey that attitude very precisely.)

But tone is not to be conceived of as a kind of surface refinement, a kind of external embellishment. On the contrary, it has to do with the central problem of meaning itself. Tone involves a qualification of the literal meaning, and in certain kinds of heavy irony it actually effects a complete reversal of the literal meaning. The management of tone, therefore, has everything to do with the meaning that the writer wishes to convey. Even in expository writing and in "practical" writing of all kinds, the problem of tone is most important.

Since the tone of a piece of writing is the result of the interplay of many elements—choice of words, sentence structure, sentence rhythm, metaphors—and since tone is always intimately related to a particular situation, it would be difficult to make a general classification of possible "tones." But it is easy to point out some general faults in the management of tone:

1. Writing down to one's reader.
2. False enthusiasm and synthetic cheeriness.
3. SENTIMENTALITY—which may be defined as the attempt to evoke an emotional response in excess of that warranted by the situation.

Moreover, though an elaborate classification of kinds of tone would be of little use, it will be profitable to mention several general methods of statement, important for their effect on tone.

1. OVERSTATEMENT (which may express proper emphasis, but which may produce mere inflation; sentimentality, false enthusiasm, and boring pomposity are kinds of overstatement).

2. UNDERSTATEMENT (in which less is said than might have been expected to be said).

3. IRONY (to which understatement is closely related). The essence of irony resides in the contrast between the surface meaning and the actual full meaning. The gradations of irony are almost infinite, ranging from a harsh SARCASM (in which the surface meaning is completely reversed) to the various kinds of gentle irony (in which the literal meaning is only slightly qualified by the total context). It is unfortunate that we lack terms by which to point to some of the major gradations. As a result, the term "irony" is likely to be overworked as one attempts to describe the manifold, and important, ways in which the literal meaning of a statement is qualified by the context which surrounds it. Perhaps our best practical expedient is to try to define as nearly as we can the kind of irony in each particular case: playful irony, whimsical irony, sardonic irony, quiet irony, and so on.

Thus far we have approached the general problem in terms of overstatement or understatement, or in terms of literal meaning and literal meaning qualified by context. But other approaches, of course, are possible: for example, the degree of seriousness or playfulness with which the writer makes his presentation to the reader, his gravity or his gaiety. Closely related to this distinction (though by no means to be equated with it) is the distinction between his formality or his informality.

1. Formality of tone. A formal tone implies a formal relation between writer and reader and a certain regard for forms and ceremonies.

2. Informality of tone. An informal tone implies a friendly and familiar relation between writer and reader—no standing upon forms and ceremonies. (But the informal or "familiar" essay may, on occasion, embody a serious purpose; and informality of tone is certainly not in itself to be identified with lack of seriousness.)

We have used the term "tone" rather loosely to indicate the reflection of the author's attitude toward his reader *and* also toward his material. In the act of composition the two go together so closely that it is impossible to separate them, but a practical distinction is simple and obvious. In "practical writing"—writing designed to persuade or convince a special audience—the student will find his attitude toward that special audience tends to come to the fore, and certainly it should be allowed to modify and control his method of presentation. But in imaginative writing the student addresses himself to an ideal reader—a universal reader—and, though the *general* problem of tone becomes of even greater importance, the problem of convincing his ideal reader becomes simply a part of the problem of "convincing"—convincing all readers—convincing himself.

## *APPLICATIONS*

The following are general questions which the student might well ask himself as he considers the passages quoted below. More specific questions will be found at the end of each passage or pair of passages.

*a.* What is the author's attitude toward the reader? How is this shown?

*b.* What is the author's attitude toward his material?

*c.* Are there any instances of sentimentality? In what way is this revealed? Are there any instances of other kinds of overstatement? Is the overstatement justified or unjustified?

*d.* Which of the passages, if any, makes use of understatement?

*e.* Do any of the passages make use of irony? Try to characterize the kind of irony in each case—as sarcasm, light mocking irony, bitter irony, gay irony, and so on.

*f.* Are there any passages which are toneless? Are there any which are confused in tone?

**A.** They [the Congressional sub-committee] were having a go-around in connection with the union rackets in the movie industry which P—— certainly should know all about, for he worked a long time hand in glove with three of the foulest vermin in the whole American Federation of Labor. . . . Blank was an ideal labor leader to this bellowing old four-flusher who has fattened on the toil and the sufferings of American labor for 25 years.—WESTBROOK PEGLER in a newspaper column.

What is the author's attitude toward P——? How is it indicated? Try to characterize the tone.

**B.** The style of architecture was like crazy Elizabethan half-timber work, in the elaborate Cheshire fashion, but gone gimcrack to an incredible degree. House-fronts were fretted, pierced and pargetted till they looked as though cut out of cardboard for a romantic stage-setting. Every story jutted, every window leaned one way or other; often the very walls sloped. It was like a dead city, so clean underfoot, and so quiet. Its winding, even streets were floored with damp sand solidified by time and as silent to the tread as any carpet. The lattices and wall-returns deadened all reverberation of voice. There were no carts, nor any streets wide enough for carts, no shod animals, no bustle anywhere. Everything was hushed, strained, even furtive. The doors of houses shut softly as we passed. There were no loud dogs, no crying children: indeed, except in the bazaar, still half asleep, there were few wayfarers of any kind; and the rare people we did meet, all thin, and as it were wasted by disease, with scarred, hairless faces and screwed-up eyes, slipped past us quickly and cautiously, not looking at us. Their skimp, white robes, shaven polls with little skull-caps, red cotton shoulder-shawls, and bare feet were so same as to be almost a uniform.

The atmosphere was oppressive, deadly. There seemed no life in it. It was not burning hot, but held a moisture and sense of great age and exhaustion such as seemed to belong to no other place: not a passion of smells like Smyrna, Naples or Marseilles, but a feeling of long use, of the exhalations of many people, of continued bath-heat and sweat. One would say that for years Jidda had not been swept through by a firm breeze: that its streets kept their air from year's end to year's end, from the day they were built for so long as the houses should endure.—T. E. LAWRENCE: *Seven Pillars of Wisdom,* Chap. 9.[11]

In this description we get a definite impression of Jidda. It possesses a definite quality, a special atmosphere. But what is the author's attitude

[11] From: *Seven Pillars of Wisdom* by T. E. Lawrence. Copyright 1925, 1935 by Doubleday & Company, Inc.

toward this city? Does he loathe it? Admire it? Feel affection for it? Is his writing florid? Studiedly dry? What is the tone?

**C.** Before intelligent criteria can be developed for the selection of superimposed leaders, the organization, through its professional staff, must first clearly define the objectives of its group program and establish qualifications for group leadership. Second, these objectives must be made clear to the leaders. In group work terminology the concept *socialization* appears as the central objective, but in the experience of the writer little effort has been made to define this concept so as to be understandable to the leader.—From a magazine of social research.

For what audience is this paragraph written? Has the audience been visualized by the writer? Could it be said that the writing is relatively "toneless"? If so, is its tonelessness a defect or a virtue?

**D.** Of his odes nothing favourable can be said: the sentiments commonly want force, nature, or novelty; the diction is sometimes harsh and uncouth, the stanzas ill-constructed and unpleasant, the rhymes dissonant, or unskilfully disposed, too distant from each other, or arranged with too little regard to established use, and therefore perplexing to the ear, which in a short composition has not time to grow familiar with an innovation.

To examine such compositions singly cannot be required; they have doubtless brighter and darker parts: but when they are once found to be generally dull, all further labour may be spared; for to what use can the work be criticized that will not be read.—SAMUEL JOHNSON: "Life of Akenside."

What is the author's attitude toward the poet he discusses? Does he despise him? Envy him? Feel superior to him? Or what? Is the tone bitter? Detached? Sarcastic? Judicious? Try to define it.

**E.** [The mate] felt all the majesty of his great position, and made the world feel it, too. When he gave even the simplest order, he discharged it like a blast of lightning, and sent a long reverberating peal of profanity thundering after it. I could not help contrasting the way in which the average landsman would give an order with the mate's way of doing it. If the landsman should wish the gang-plank moved a foot farther forward, he would probably say: "James, or William, one of you push that plank forward, please"; but put the mate in his place, and he would roar out: "Here, now, start that gang-plank for'ard! Lively, now! *What*'re you about! Snatch it! *snatch* it! There! there! Aft again! aft again! Don't you hear me? Dash it to dash! are you going to *sleep* over it! 'Vast heaving. 'Vast heaving, I tell you! Going to heave it clear astern? WHERE're you going with that barrel! *for'ard* with it 'fore I make you swallow it, you dash-dash-dash-*dashed* split between a tired mud-turtle and a crippled hearse-horse!" I wished I could talk like that.—SAMUEL L. CLEMENS: *Life on the Mississippi*, Chap. 5.

Characterize the tone of the mate's speech. Characterize the author's attitude *toward* the mate. Be as specific as you can.

**F.** When the quest is for a material of inexplicable behavior, of unique and spectacular qualities, water has all other chemicals licked for first place. True, it is the most abundant material on the Earth's surface. If suddenly all the water on the Earth could be broken into its constituent gases and released into the air, the atmospheric pressure (now 15 pounds) would become 6,000 pounds to the square-inch. That's how much water there is. And its quantity is increasing continually. Every fire we light, every explosion we set off, every puff of a cigarette, combines some particles of oxygen to build new water and release it to the air. Yes, water is common, and continually becoming more so.— GEORGE W. GRAY: "Little Drops of Water." [12]

For what kind of audience is this author writing? How do you know? Compare the tone of this paragraph with the tone of the passage quoted from Huxley on page 456.

**G.** Yet with unconscious irony McAllister closes his chapter called "Entering Society" with this summation: "I think the great secret of life is to be contented with the position to which it has pleased God to call you." Even Emily Post offers a few demure suggestions to the "outsider": "The better, and the only way if she has not the key of birth, is through study to make herself eligible. Meanwhile, charitable or civic work will give her interest and occupation as well as throw her with ladies of good breeding, by association with whom she cannot fail to acquire some of those qualities before which the gates of society always open." The patronage of charity, church settlement work (Episcopalian), the financial support of hospitals, clinics, and opera are probably the safest route which the newcomer can travel. After she has given her cheque for a substantial sum and shown her eagerness to work for the cause, she will be asked to become a sustaining member and sit on the board with women she has wanted to know. Probably they will begin to ask her to tea, then to large parties and luncheons, and finally to dinner. If fortune has blessed her with a small daughter, let her be sent to a fashionable day school, where she will have classmates to be invited

---

[12] From *Little Drops of Water*, by George W. Gray. Copyright, 1938, by Esquire, Inc.

to a birthday party, and given expensive souvenirs; in this way a little child may lead them. No climber should overlook the broadening influences of travel; in crossing the Atlantic, cruising the Mediterranean, or circumnavigating the globe, one may get a good table by generous tipping and promptness, and then maneuver eligible acquaintances and celebrities into sitting there. Deck stewards also can do much for one, since during the course of a long voyage propinquity is almost irresistible.— DIXON WECTER: *Saga of American Society*, Chap. 6.[13]

What is the quality of the irony employed in this passage? Define it as precisely as you can. What are some of the ironical devices employed?

**H.** None of this would have happened if he had married me, thought Mrs. Upchurch.

As she had so often insisted to a conveniently deaf Providence, she had never been immoderate, she had never even been exacting, in her demands of life. All she had ever required of a second husband was that he should be comfortably, if not amply provided for. Birth, youth, breeding, appearance, character, yes, even character—all these agreeable perquisites of marriage she would have exchanged for the consolation of an established income. But Destiny, as she had not failed to observe was often the case, had granted her every opportunity except the one she urgently needed. As an engaging widow, armed with a disenchantment so profound that it was mistaken for softness of temper, she had been approached by youth without intelligence, by appearance without character, by character without youth, by birth and breeding without another redeeming attribute; but wealth, being the one and only gift she desired, had successfully eluded her grasp. In the end, since she was as amiable as is consistent with virtue, she had thankfully ceased her struggles, and had nestled into the less lucrative, and certainly less exacting, position of mother-in-law to a rich and generous man.—ELLEN GLASGOW: *The Romantic Comedians*, Chap. 12.[14]

Compare the quality of the irony here with that in G. Are we expected to be sympathetic to Mrs. Upchurch? Does the irony qualify our sympathy? Does it eliminate sympathy?

**I.** "Now, boys," the Texan said, "who says that pony ain't worth fifteen dollars? You couldn't buy that much dynamite for just fifteen dollars. There ain't one of them can't do a mile in three minutes: turn

[13] From *The Saga of American Society* by Dixon Wector, copyright, 1937, by Charles Scribner's Sons.
[14] From *The Romantic Comedians* by Ellen Glasgow, copyright, 1926, by Ellen Glasgow. Reprinted by permission of Harcourt, Brace and Company, Inc.

them into pasture and they will board themselves; work them like hell all day and every time you think about it, lay them over the head with a single-tree and after a couple of days every jack rabbit one of them will be so tame you will have to put them out of the house at night like a cat."—WILLIAM FAULKNER: *The Hamlet*, Book IV, Chap. 1.[15]

What attitude does the Texan exhibit toward his audience? Does he expect to be believed in his recommendation of the ponies? What function is performed by his use of exaggeration? Does he appeal to the buyers' pride? To their sporting instinct?

**Ja.** It wasn't the bully amateur's world any more. Nobody knew that on armistice day, Theodore Roosevelt, happy amateur warrior with the grinning teeth, the shaking forefinger, naturalist, explorer, magazine-writer, Sundayschool teacher, cowpuncher, moralist, politician, righteous orator with a short memory, fond of denouncing liars (the Ananias Club) and having pillowfights with his children, was taken to the Roosevelt hospital gravely ill with inflammatory rheumatism.

Things weren't bully any more;

T.R. had grit;

he bore the pain, the obscurity, the sense of being forgotten as he had borne the grilling portages when he was exploring the River of Doubt, the heat, the fetid jungle mud, the infected abscess in his leg.

and died quietly in his sleep

at Sagamore Hill,

on January 6, 1919

and left on the shoulders of his sons

the white man's burden.—JOHN DOS PASSOS: "The Happy Warrior," *1919.*[16]

**Jb.** No man could have been more bitter against opponents, or more unfair to them or more ungenerous. In this department, indeed, even so gifted a specialist in dishonorable controversy as Dr. [Woodrow] Wilson has seldom surpassed him. He never stood up to a frank and chivalrous debate. He dragged herrings across the trail. He made seductive faces to the gallery. He capitalized his enormous talents as an entertainer, his rank as a national hero, his public influence and consequence. The two great law-suits in which he was engaged were screaming burlesques upon justice. He tried them in the newspapers before ever they were called; he befogged them with irrelevant issues; his appearances in court

[15] From *The Hamlet* by William Faulkner, copyright, 1940, by Random House, Inc.

[16] From *1919*, second volume of *U.S.A.* by John Dos Passos. Published by Houghton Mifflin and reprinted by permission of the author.

were not the appearances of a witness standing on a level with other witnesses, but those of a comedian sure of his crowd. He was, in his dealings with concrete men as in his dealings with men in the mass, a charlatan of the very highest skill—and there was in him, it goes without saying, the persuasive charm of the charlatan as well as the daring deviousness, the humanness of naïveté as well as the humanness of chicane. He knew how to woo—and not only boobs. He was, for all his ruses and ambuscades, a jolly fellow.—H. L. MENCKEN: "T. R. Roosevelt: An Autopsy," *Prejudices: Second Series*.[17]

Both Dos Passos and Mencken exhibit definite attitudes toward T. R. Roosevelt. Compare and contrast them. How does the attitude in each case color the writer's account. Cite specific instances.

**Ka.** How many have seen a mare or a stallion of the Only Blood go into battle? How few realize that such a horse, in full action, and especially if steel-shod as Tirade was, is one of the most dangerous fighting animals? Out in the open, fair and free, not even the grizzly of the Rockies has a chance to do better than escape alive from a horse like Tirade.

She seized the red wolf. She shook it. She gave her head and her long muscular neck a twisting flip—and hurled the wolf some ten feet into the air, straight up. The snarling, momentarily shaken into silence by the onslaught of the mare, came back in a mortal scream. The form of the wolf sprawled darkly against the darkly turbid sky, then it fell. The mare lashed out with her front feet. She hit the descending carcass with the lightning's stroke, and the lightning's sureness. . . . It was a limp mass of wind-stirred fur, neck broken, ribs broken, spine broken. The Colfax Fox lay dead upon the moor in Sor'land where he had disported when a whelpling. One of the Mountain's own was back home.

Maggie's baby was avenged. The ghosts of the two hounds that lay in a grave in a hollow in Loudoun were at rest. And the Doctor's collie rested too.

A melancholy little wind went wandering across the heath. It was a requiem. However fierce it is, . . . Nature never loses one of her types unheeded, nor leaves it to lie unmourned. Listen and you will always hear the little, keening wind—the wind that blew over Sor'land . . . the Colfax Fox's coronach.—MARGUERITE BAYLISS: *The Bolinvars*, Chap. 17.[18]

[17] From "T. R. Roosevelt: An Autopsy" by H. L. Mencken. Reprinted from *Prejudices: Second Series* by H. L. Mencken, by permission of Alfred A. Knopf, Inc. Copyright 1920 by Alfred A. Knopf, Inc. Copyright 1948 by H. L. Mencken.

[18] From *The Bolinvars* by Marguerite Bayliss. Reprinted by permission of Henry Holt and Company, Inc. Copyright, 1947, by Marguerite Bayliss.

**Kb.** This time the bear didn't strike him down. It caught the dog in both arms, almost loverlike, and they both went down. [The boy] was off the mule now. He drew back both hammers of the gun but he could see nothing but moiling spotted houndbodies until the bear surged up again. Boon was yelling something, he could not tell what; he could see Lion still clinging to the bear's throat and he saw the bear, half-erect, strike one of the hounds with one paw and hurl it five or six feet and then, rising as though it would never stop, stand erect and begin to rake at Lion's belly with his forepaws. Then Boon was running. The boy saw the gleam of the blade in his hand and watched him leap among the hounds, hurdling them, kicking them aside as he ran, and fling himself astride the bear as he had hurled himself onto the mule, his legs locked around the bear's belly, his left arm under the bear's throat where Lion clung, and the glint of the knife as it rose and fell.

It fell just once. For an instant they almost resembled a piece of statuary: the clinging dog, the bear, the man astride its back, working and probing the buried blade. Then they went down, pulled over backward by Boon's weight, Boon underneath. It was the bear's back which reappeared first but at once Boon was astride it again. He had never released the knife and again the boy saw the almost infinitesimal movement of his arm and shoulder as he probed and sought; then the bear surged erect, raising with it the man and the dog too, and turned and still carrying the man and dog it took two or three steps toward the woods on its hind feet as a man would have walked and crashed down. It didn't collapse, crumple. It fell all of a piece, as a tree falls, so that all three of them, man dog and bear, seemed to bounce once.—WILLIAM FAULKNER: "The Bear." [19]

Both Ka and Kb present the end of a long hunt. How are we supposed to feel toward the fox? Toward the bear? Are we to feel pity? Satisfaction? Triumph? How are we to feel toward the mare Tirade? Toward the dog Lion? Which passage is overwritten? Is either guilty of sentimentality? If you feel that either passage is sentimental, indicate why it is so and contrast it, on this point, with the other passage.

[19] From *Go Down Moses* by William Faulkner, copyright, 1942, by Random House, Inc.

# CHAPTER 13

# The Final
# Integration

IN THE last three chapters we have tried to deal specifically with some of the important elements of style: diction, metaphor, and tone. In this chapter our concern is rather different. We shall be primarily interested in the interplay of elements—in the total harmony which results from the blending of the various elements. Even in the preceding chapters this interplay has come in for a great deal of attention, particularly in the chapter on tone. But before we launch into a discussion of this final integration, we must take up one element of style which thus far has been merely mentioned. It is RHYTHM, the disposition of pauses and accents.

Now rhythm is a forbidding topic. A full discussion would be highly complex and would call for a separate chapter, and a long chapter at that. Our intention here, however, is much more modest. We shall treat rhythm briefly, and as merely a part of this final chapter on style. For this last procedure there is a good deal of warrant. By its very nature, rhythm can scarcely be profitably discussed in isolation. Moreover, rhythm in itself involves a rather intricate interplay of elements.

## RHYTHM

In discussing tone we pointed out that in actual conversation the tone of the voice, gesture, and facial expression supplement the words and do much to set the particular tone which the speaker intends—playfulness, seriousness, irritability, and so on. If we use the written word, however, the "tone" has to be established by the choice of words and the patterning of those words. But it will have occurred to the student that in moving from actual conversation to the written word the speaker relinquishes still another very important element—the matter of emphasis. Consider the following simple sentence: "Are you going to town?" If we stress the word *are*, the sentence becomes an emphatic question; and if we stress it heavily, it may even suggest surprise. But if we stress *you*, the question becomes centered upon whether it is *you* who are going rather than someone else. If we stress *town*, we get a third variation; the question then emphasizes the destination.

Thus the rhythmic inflection of a sentence, with its various stresses on particular words, is a very important way in which we express our meanings. When we put the sentence on paper, we can, of course, indicate something of this stress by underlining the words to be emphasized. But mere underlining is a relatively crude substitute for the living voice, and it is the mark of a clumsy writer to have to rely upon constant underlining. The skilled writer, by his control of the rhythm of his sentences, suggests where the proper emphases are to fall; for emphasis is an element of rhythm.

### RHYTHM AND CLARITY OF MEANING

Mastery of rhythm, then, is important for clarity of meaning. This is illustrated by the muddled and monotonous rhythms of technological jargon. Look back at Maury Maverick's example of gobbledygook (p. 395). Jargon of this sort is difficult to read for a variety of reasons: it is fuzzy, abstract, and dull. It lacks flavor. But it lacks clarity as well; for there are no natural emphases, no obvious points of primary stress.

Compare with the passage quoted by Maverick, the following:

Nor had Dickens any lively sense for fine art, classical tradition, science, or even the manners or feelings of the upper classes in his own time and country: in his novels we may almost say there is no army, no navy, no church, no sport, no distant travel, no daring adventure, no feeling for the watery wastes and the motley nations of the planet, and luckily, with his notion of them—no lords and ladies.—GEORGE SANTAYANA: *Soliloquies in England.*[1]

[1] From *Soliloquies in England and Later Soliloquies* by George Santayana, copyright, 1922, by Charles Scribner's Sons.

Santayana's sentence is long and relatively complex, but it is rhythmical. The heavy stresses come where they should, on words like "Dickens," "lively," "fine," "classical," "even." Moreover, phrase balances phrase: "no distant travel" balances "no daring adventure"; "watery wastes" sets off "motley nations." Even the parenthetical phrase, "with his notion of them," is prepared for. (Notice that the rhythm is destroyed if we alter the ending to read "and—with his notion of them—luckily no lords and ladies.")

We have observed that lack of rhythm is frequently a symptom of disordered discourse; an easily grasped rhythm, on the other hand, is often the sign of good order and proper disposition of words and phrases. But rhythmic quality is much more, of course, than a mere index of clarity.

Emphatic rhythms tend to accompany emotional heightening. It is no accident that eloquent prose, prose that makes a strong appeal to the feelings, tends to use clearly patterned rhythms, or that poetry is commonly written in the systematized rhythm which we call "verse." The association of formal rhythm with emotional power is based on a perfectly sound psychological fact. Fervent expression of grief, rage, or joy tends to fall into rhythmic patterns—whether it be the sobbings of a grief-stricken woman or the cursing of an irate cab driver.

## RHYTHMIC PATTERNS

In verse there is a formalizing of the rhythm to a system or pattern, and we have various ways of indicating the verse pattern. A common method is to indicate unaccented syllables by this mark ( ˘ ); accented syllables, by this ( ′ ). The stanza that follows may be marked ("scanned") thus:

To skies/ that knit/ their heart/strings right,

To fields/ that bred/ them brave,

The sav/iors come/ not home/ tonight:

Themselves/ they could/ not save.

A pair of syllables, the first unaccented, the second accented, we call an iambic foot (e.g., To skies); and we would describe the verse pattern of this stanza as iambic tetrameter (that is, a line consisting of *four* iambs) alternating with iambic trimeter (a line consisting of *three* iambs).

Now prose could be marked off (scanned) in such a fashion— even though prose is not, like verse, patterned to a certain kind of foot and divided off into lines containing a certain number of feet. For example, Mr. Gorham Munson scans a sentence of Emerson's as follows: "We knŏw/ thĕ aŭthĕntĭc/ ĕffĕcts/ ŏf thĕ trŭe fĭre/ thrŏugh ĕvĕry ŏne/ ŏf ĭts mĭllĭŏn/ dĭsgŭisĕs." The sort of metrical analysis Mr. Munson is making would involve our knowing, not only the simpler kind of metrical feet such as the iamb ("we know" is an iamb), but many very complex feet as well. "The authentic," for example, is called a *paeon*. In order to scan prose in this fashion, we should need many more technical terms than we usually need to scan verse.

Such an analysis of prose rhythm may have considerable value. But the rhythms of prose are infinite in their kinds, and some of the rhythmic effects are so subtle that an exact description requires a very complicated scheme of representation. Such a study, however, is completely beyond the range of this book; there is little practical gain in learning the definitions of such feet as the "amphibrach" and the "cretic." The student will probably feel that he has his hands full in trying to control diction, metaphor, and tone without adding another element, rhythm. Fortunately, there is a considerable kernel of truth in the statement made by the Duchess in *Alice in Wonderland*: "Take care of the sense and the sounds will take care of themselves."

## RHYTHM AS A DEVICE OF EXPRESSION

But "the sounds" can be used as a kind of test of the sense. As we have seen, limp, weak, confused rhythms are frequently a symptom of a more general confusion; and conversely, a well-defined rhythm often points to the writer's mastery of his instrument. This generalization is not to be interpreted to mean that all unemphatic rhythms are "bad" or that all elaborate and intricate rhythms are "good." The rhythm is only one of a number of devices which the writer uses. Its goodness or badness will depend upon a number of things: the writer's purpose and the adequacy of the rhythm to that purpose.

Let us consider a passage which has been studied earlier for its tone. The fact that this passage has been analyzed in earlier pages may make clearer the specific contribution of the rhythm to the total effect. At least it should serve to warn the student not to attribute the final effect to the rhythmic pattern alone.

They were executing officers of the rank of major and above who were separated from their troops. They were dealing summarily with German agitators in Italian uniform. They wore steel helmets. Only two of us had steel helmets. Some of the carabinieri had them. The other carabinieri wore the wide hat. Airplanes we called them. We stood in the rain and were taken out one at a time to be questioned and shot. So far they had shot every one they had questioned.

In this passage the sentences are short and simple, and the rhythm of the passage supports brilliantly the ironic tone of the description. The lack of variety in the rhythmic pattern makes it seem flat, almost "expressionless," and this flatness is part of the ironic understatement. Momentous and terrible things are being described, but the description is kept studiedly dry. A more varied and complex rhythm (such as usually goes with excitement) would weaken Hemingway's effect. (See p. 452 for fuller analysis of the passage.)

In contrast to this passage, compare a paragraph of description from Thackeray's *Vanity Fair.* (See also p. 459.)

The King? There he was. Beefeaters were before the august box; the Marquis of Steyne (Lord of the Powder Closet) and other great officers of state were behind the chair on which he sate, He sate—florid of face, portly of person, covered with orders, and in a rich curling head of hair. How we sang, God Save Him! How the house rocked and shouted with that magnificent music. . . . Ladies wept; mothers clasped their children; some fainted with emotion. . . . Yes, we saw him. Fate cannot deprive us of *that.* Others have seen Napoleon. Some few still exist who have beheld Frederick the Great, Doctor Johnson, Marie Antoinette, etc.: be it our reasonable boast to our children that we saw George the Good, the Magnificent, the Great.

Thackeray's mockery is reflected first in the balanced phrasings as our eyes focus on the king: "*He* sate—florid of face, portly of person, covered with orders, and in a curling head of hair." Then the rhythms become staccato, expressing the sense of mock excitement: "How we sang, God Save Him! How the house rocked and shouted with that magnificent music. . . . Ladies wept; mothers grasped their children; some fainted with emotion. . . . Yes, we saw him." The sarcasm comes to a climax in the highly formalized rhythms of the concluding sentences of the paragraph: "Be it our reasonable boast to our children that we saw George the Good, the Magnificent, the Great."

One ought not claim that the rhythm alone creates the effect, or that the rhythm is even the principal device used to achieve the effect. But certainly rhythm, in conjunction with diction, metaphor, and other devices, may become powerfully expressive. In this passage the very exaggeration of the rhythmic pattern makes its function easier to discern.

Rhythm is ordinarily used more subtly, though not for that reason less effectively. Let us look once more at the Texan's auctioneering speech (from Faulkner's *The Hamlet*) which we analyzed earlier for tone (p. 486). What part, if any, does the rhythm play in producing the effect? Does it support the tone?

"Now, boys," the Texan said, "Who says that pony ain't worth fifteen dollars? You couldn't buy that much dynamite for just fifteen dollars. There ain't one of them can't do a mile in three minutes: turn them into pasture and they will board themselves; work them like hell all day and every time you think about it, lay them over the head with a single-tree and after a couple of days every jack rabbit one of them will be so tame you will have to put them out of the house at night like a cat."

Suppose that we rewrite the last few lines to read as follows:

"Work the hell out of them every day and ever so often bust a single-tree over their heads. In a little while you'll have them all tame as tame can be. You'll have to shove 'em out of the door at night just like they was a bunch of cats."

In this version the diction has not been altered from that which the Texan might be expected to use, and the rewritten version "says" just about what the original "says"; but the rhythm has been destroyed and with it much of the flavor and nearly all of the force of the Texan's auctioneering speech.

One further passage may be quoted to indicate what complex effects can be wrought by the skillful handling of rhythm in conjunction with other devices. The passage forms the opening of W. B. Yeats's *Reveries over Childhood and Youth.*

My first memories are fragmentary and isolated and contemporaneous, as though one remembered some first moments of the Seven Days. It seems as if time had not yet been created, for all thoughts connected with emotion and place are without sequence.

I remember sitting upon somebody's knee, looking out of an Irish window at a wall covered with cracked and falling plaster, but what wall I do not remember, and being told that some relation once lived there. I am looking out of a window in London. It is at Fitzroy Road. Some boys are playing in the road and among them a boy in uniform, a telegraph boy perhaps. When I ask who the boy is, the servant tells me that he is going to blow the town up, and I go to sleep in terror.[2]

The author says that his memories of childhood are "fragmentary," "isolated," "contemporaneous," and "without sequence." So they appear in his account. There is a memory of looking out of an Irish window. Then, without any transition, Yeats presents a memory of looking out a London window. Moreover, with this second instance, he drops the statement "I remember" and reverts to the present tense: "I am looking out of a window in London." The author's purpose, obviously, is to give us the sense of contemporaneity. He tries to put himself into these memories as they rise up—chaotic, disordered, fragmentary. True, he is forced to use a man's words. "Isolated" and "contemporaneous" would not be used by a child; nor would the allusion to the Biblical Seven Days of creation occur to a child. But the author has tried to suggest the movement of the child's mind in its simple, uncritical succession of events. Most of all, he has depended upon the rhythmic pattern to suggest the slow, almost tranced movement of reverie. The student might experiment with altering the rhythm of the passage. In an altered rhythm, the sense of reverie is at once lost, and the sense of living back into one's childhood memories collapses.

## RHYTHM AS A PRACTICAL TEST OF SOUND SENTENCE PATTERN

To sum up, control of rhythm is an important resource of the skilled writer. It is a powerful means for shifting tone, for establish-

[2] From W. B. Yeats: *Reveries.* Copyright, 1916 by The Macmillan Company and used with their permission.

ing a mood, for pointing a contrast, or for heightening the appeal
to the emotions. The student may feel, however, that rhythm is
much too intricate an instrument for him to try to use *consciously*.
It probably is. We are far from suggesting that the student consciously try for rhythmic effects. Even so, a very practical use of
rhythm can be made: the student may learn to use rhythm in order
to test his composition. As he rereads it aloud he should learn to
listen for the break in the rhythm, the jangling discord, the lack
of smoothness that signals to him that something in the sentence
is awry. This comment applies particularly to the disposition of
modifiers, prepositional phrases, and the like. The student may find
that reading his composition aloud and listening to its rhythms
proves to be one of the best practical means for spotting sentence
elements that are not in the best order.

Consider the following sentence:

Oriental luxury goods—jade, silk, gold, spices, vermillion, jewels—formerly
had come by way of the Caspian Sea overland; and a few daring Greek
sea captains, now that this route had been cut by the Huns, catching
the trade winds were sailing from Red Sea ports and loading up at Ceylon.

The sentence is passable, and is not perhaps noticeably unrhythmical. But if we read this sentence in the form in which Robert Graves
actually wrote it, we shall find that it is not only clearer; it is much
more rhythmical and much easier to read:

Oriental luxury goods—jade, silk, gold, spices, vermillion, jewels—had
formerly come overland by way of the Caspian Sea and now that this
route had been cut by the Huns, a few daring Greek sea captains were
sailing from Red Sea ports, catching the trade winds and loading up
at Ceylon.

## APPLICATIONS

Consider the following sentences. Which are rhythmical? Which are
noticeably unrhythmical? Can you improve the rhythm of any of them
by a simple rearrangement of the elements of the sentence?

1. And it was then, that the *Titanic's* survivors, in all its green-white
majesty, saw the iceberg floating idly, tinted with the sunrise.

2. Indeed, much there is in Dickens which Communism would only
emphasize and render universal, if it came.

3. For good Wordsworthians a tour through Westmorland is as good as a pilgrimage to Jerusalem; a walk in the country is the equivalent of going to church.

4. A new mood of doubt, of self-questioning, creeps into the student mind and morbid introspection has no place in the cheering section or in evening campus sings.

5. In the strand, there was a long rivulet and he wondered, as he waded up its course slowly, at the endless drift of seaweed. Swaying and turning, emerald and black and russet and olive, it moved beneath the current. The water of the rivulet was dark with endless drift and mirrored the highdrifting clouds. Above him silently the clouds were drifting, and the seatangle was silently drifting below him and the grey warm air was still and in his veins a new wild life was singing.—Altered from JAMES JOYCE: *Portrait of the Artist as a Young Man.*

6. Now he entered, confident of the fidelity of his forces, the belt of woods, passed easily through it in the red illumination, climbed a fence, ran across a field, now and again turning to coquette with his responsive shadow, and so approached the blazing ruin of a dwelling. Desolation everywhere. Not a living thing was visible in all the wide glare. He cared nothing for that; the spectacle pleased, and in imitation of the wavering flames he danced with glee.—Altered from AMBROSE BIERCE: "Chickamauga."

## STYLE AS HARMONIOUS INTEGRATION

To conclude this brief note on rhythm: "Good" rhythm is rhythm which is appropriate to the passage as a whole—which contributes to the desired effect. If it functions to support that effect, it is "good." If it does not, it is "bad," no matter how soothing or lilting or beautifully harmonized it may appear in itself. The principle involved is the same principle which we have encountered earlier in discussing such topics as diction and metaphor. As we have seen, a metaphor is not to be chosen because it is beautiful in itself or is brilliant in itself. A good metaphor is rather one which "says" precisely what the composition as a whole requires at that particular point. Good diction is diction which, for the case in hand, is neither too colloquial nor too highfalutin, neither too vague nor too pedantically exact. So with rhythm. Had Hemingway used more intricate rhythms in the passage quoted on page 493, he would have impaired the effectiveness of the passage as a whole. *It is as part of the whole that any element of style is to be judged.* But what, then, of the passage from *Vanity Fair* (p. 493)? Thackeray has there used heavily formalized rhythms which are quite out of harmony with the triviality of the matters celebrated. Does this violate the principle of harmonious adaptation? Not at all, for the passage aims at a heavily ironic effect, and the absurd contrast between the exalted rhythm of the prose and the triviality of what it describes, admirably supports the ironic effect.

What has been said with reference to rhythm obviously holds for all the other elements that go to make up a style. The question to be asked is always this: Does the element in question do its particular job in the expressive pattern of the whole? In the light of this question examine the following passage, noting any disharmonious elements of whatever kind.

At latitude zero, however, the obvious is not the same as with us. Rivers imply wading, swimming, alligators. Plains mean swamps, forest, fevers. Mountains make you think of something dangerous or something just too big to get over. If you've got to go somewhere, you have to hack your way through a lot of plants and vines. "God made the country," said Cowper, in his rather too blank verse. In New Guinea he would have had his doubts; he would have longed for the man-made town.

This passage (from Huxley's "Wordsworth in the Tropics") has been garbled. The student ought to have little difficulty in seeing that the beginning and the end of this passage are similar in style, but that the middle section is an anomalous lump. The style of the first three sentences and of the last two is characterized by condensation and thoughtful arrangement. The condensed, carefully disposed style breaks down with the fourth sentence. The fourth and fifth sentences are lumbering and clumsy, vaguely indefinite in pointing toward objects, and awkwardly colloquial. Can you rewrite the sentences so as to bring them into accord with the style of the first three and the last two? Consider diction and tone particularly, and check your rewritten sentences with what Huxley actually wrote (p. 764).

What anomalies of style occur in the following passage?

A large percentage of those who returned to their ordinary pursuits were conditioned to violence, since war has to be regarded as a sort of conditioning process. This large percentage of returning veterans were also disposed to be in an angry mood because of their defeat. The farm to which a majority of them had to return proved to be not so prosperous or pleasant in reality as their memories of it under war conditions had led them to believe. Men who had been bred to the law took to the plow, and others in their several ways had to bury their ambitions and go about earning a living, and by living they meant bread and meat.

The student should compare the last sentence of this passage with the preceding sentences. The last sentence is concrete where the preceding are abstract and fuzzy. It even hints at a forceful metaphor: the soil, as it is turned over by the plow, is actually the earth covering up the plowman's ambitions. This last sentence is condensed whereas the preceding sentences are filled with distracting circumlocutions. For example, what is gained by writing "a large percentage" rather than "many"? There are contexts, to be sure, in which an exact percentage has relevance, but no figures are given here. Which is the more forceful, the simple word "many" or the phrase "a large percentage"? The student should try to rewrite the passage with a view to making the rest of the passage as concrete and specific as is the style of the last sentence. The original passage, ungarbled, may be found on page 532.

## THE INSEPARABILITY OF FORM AND CONTENT

Since a good style represents an adaptation of means to a particular purpose, all the various devices of style have to be viewed as expressive devices. That is to say, even the minor ornaments of style are, strictly speaking, not ornaments but conveyors of meaning. The general point is so important that it can stand some elaboration. Mr. W. K. Wimsatt [3] provides a neat illustration. He quotes the sentence: "to read his tales is a baptism of optimism. . . ." and goes on to comment on the nasty jingle of "-ptism" and "-ptimism." The jingling effect is, as he says, nasty "just because the two combinations so nearly strive to make these words parallel, whereas they are not; one qualifies the other." That is, the style is bad because the diction (*baptism . . . optimism*) suggests a parallelism between terms that are not parallel, and the reader feels that what

[3] *The Prose Style of Samuel Johnson*, Yale University Press, 1941, p. 13.

pretended to be an expressive element—the *-ism* link between the terms—has proved to be meaningless—even misleading. (The reader will not necessarily make this analysis, of course; he will probably merely *feel* it, hearing the *-ism* repetition as an irritating jingle.)

Mr. Wimsatt goes on to say: "The case is even plainer if we take an example of the common '-ly' jingle, 'He lived practically exclusively on milk,' and set beside it something like this: 'We are swallowed up, irreparably, irrevocably, irrecoverably, irremediably.' In the second we are not conscious of the repeated '-ly' as a jingle any more than of the repeated 'irre-.' "

Why does the second sentence not register as even more "jingling" than the first? It has not a double, but a quadruple repetition of "-ly" plus a quadruple repetition of "irre-." But it does not jingle because, to paraphrase Mr. Wimsatt, the repetitions here become a part of the structure of meaning: the words linked together by "irre-" and "-ly" *belong* together. The structure of sound effects expresses perfectly the structure of sense, which it fits like a glove.

Now the examples just given may be thought to be trivial, and perhaps they are; but the principle to which they point is all-important. One may state it in these terms: a good style is the perfect garment of its "content." It is perfectly adapted to its content, which it bodies forth and from which it may not be divorced.

We said in Chapter 9 that style has to do with "how" a thing is said rather than with "what" is said; and therefore this last remark, that a good style is the perfect garment of its content and cannot be separated from its content, may seem to offer a contradiction. There is no real contradiction, of course; for if we cannot separate, we can at least distinguish between the thought and the words, the content and the form, the what and the how. Moreover, the distinction between form and content is a useful one. But the distinction can be easily misused. It is proper, therefore, to see how much weight the distinction between form and content can bear.

In the first place, content and form never exist in separation. After all, we know *what* a writer says only through the way in which he has said it. Moreover, if we alter the *way* in which a thing is said, we have also altered, if only ever so slightly, *what* is said. (The alteration in what is said may sometimes be so slight that we feel justified in disregarding it; we may say that we have not changed the content, only the form.) But at this point we are interested in theory—not in the practice, but in the principle; and it is necessary to get the principle straight. Cardinal Newman has stated the principle very emphatically:

Thought and speech are inseparable from each other. Matter and expression are parts of one: style is the thinking out into language. . . . When we can separate light and illumination, life and motion, the convex and the concave of a curve . . . then will it be conceivable that the . . . intellect should renounce its own double.

In insisting on this inseparability of form and content, we may seem to be riding pure theory very hard. But if we can grasp the theory, several very important practical considerations follow from it. First, style is seen to be not a mere outward coating, a kind of veneer which overlies the content; for the style is the outward manifestation of the content. Second, the theory illuminates the difficulty of the writer as he gropes for proper expression. As writers, we usually feel that we know exactly what we want to say; we just can't quite find the precise words. But a little reflection will reveal that we know exactly what we want to say *only when we have found the precise words.* The truth of the matter is that we do not *really know* what we want to say as we chew the pen and try to get down on paper the next sentence of a difficult theme. The process of writing is frequently, and perhaps even usually, a process of exploration. The principle of the inseparability of style and content may indicate more clearly why this is true.

A third consideration of the greatest practical importance is this: If a good style and its matter are really inseparable, it follows that bad style always reveals itself in some sort of cleavage from its "content." Let us put the matter in this way. If a style is inseparable from its content, if it is actually the bodying forth of its content, then in so far as it does this adequately we can never call it "bad"—though of course the piece of writing in question (of which style is an aspect) may be relatively trivial. But in this last instance it will be the whole piece of writing that is trivial, not the *style as such* that is bad. The term "bad" can properly be applied to style, then, only when the style does not adequately body forth what we guess must have been the content that the writer had in mind.

To sum up: there are no devices of style that are "good," absolutely and in themselves. They become good only in so far as they are used to promote the fullest, best, most adequate expression of what is to be said. One is tempted to say, conversely, that there are no really "bad" devices—provided always that they are "English"— that is, arrangements of words which the genius of the language permits. But, and this is the point of crucial importance, *any* device, any patterning which violates the larger pattern, which works at cross purposes to it, or which is irrelevant to it—any such patterning, by "sticking out," by calling attention to itself, warns the writer to reconsider. It warns him to reconsider not only how he shall "say it" but also *what it is precisely that he has to say.* For in a good style the two are inseparable, and the very fact of their separation signals that revision is in order. To use the example already given above: the *-ly* parallel in "He lives practically exclusively on milk" *sticks out,* whereas the much heavier reiteration of the *-ly,* and the *irre-* in "We are swallowed up, irreparably, irrevocably, irrecoverably, irremediably" does not stick out: these latter repetitions become part of the pattern of meaning and seem an inevitable part of it.

### APPLICATIONS

**I.** Compare the following account with the story as told by Alexander Smith on page 688. Notice that in both accounts the facts are much the same. In comparing them, we are inclined to say that they differ merely in "style." But does not the difference in style carry with it a difference in content? What is the difference between what each version "says"? If Smith's version is to be preferred, try to indicate why, making special reference to his choice of diction, sentence structure, rhythm, and any other elements of style which seem relevant.

One Saturday night a serving girl was seated in the kitchen reading her Bible. She heard a tap at the door and the voice of her sweetheart demanding to be let in. She had not expected him to call at such an hour, but admitted him. To her surprise, he berated her for reading her Bible and was, in general, so unlike himself that she was soon terrified. Suddenly, strangest of all, he knelt down and laid his head in her lap. To her horror, she saw that his head was covered not with hair, but with moorland moss. "In God's name," she screamed, "begone!" In that instant he vanished. Clearly, to her mind, she had been visited by the devil in guise of her lover. The story is, of course, ridiculous; but the student of folklore will find the detail of moss for hair highly interesting.

For the moss suggests a figure condemned to wander the waste moors, and is thus consonant with that whole body of folklore which sees the devil as an outlaw, a kind of pariah, wandering over the waste places of the world.

II. The following paragraph represents a rewriting of the first paragraph of Joseph Mitchell's "Mazie" (p. 830). Notice that the rewritten version preserves most of the "facts" of the original, but notice further that, in the rewritten version, more than Mitchell's style has been lost. With the loss of the style, we have also lost the character of Mazie. Her personality has disappeared. Test this by stating what kind of person emerges from the rewritten version and comparing it with the person who emerges from the original version.

Mazie P. Gordon, who sells tickets at the Venice Theater, in the Bowery, is well known in that district. She has a wide acquaintance with the ne'er-do-wells of the Bowery, and many of them make free to call her by her first name. She is somewhat stern in her manner, but seems to have a real fondness for the hapless transients and habitual drunkards who are to be found in the cheaper taverns and in the dingier restaurants. At any rate, she dispenses charity to these drunkards each night, a dime here and a dime there, though the total sum dispensed may amount on some evenings to as much as fifteen dollars. Mazie Gordon is not without a sense of humor, and sometimes, with a smile, compares herself with John D. Rockefeller, since he also is celebrated for giving away dimes. Miss Gordon is blonde, and has worked as ticket seller for twenty-one years.

III. It has been said that Lamb's essay on Mrs. Battle displays a real affection toward her (p. 468). Can you rewrite the second, third, and fourth paragraphs of his essay (pp. 710 ff.) so as to preserve the essential facts and yet to convey a different conception of Sarah Battle's personality? (If the student feels that this assignment asks him to hack up a masterpiece, its underlying purpose is actually to the greater glory of the masterpiece: by this means he may come to see how important the more subtle touches of Lamb's style are.)

IV. Compare and contrast Wingfield's eye-witness account of the beheading of Mary Queen of Scots (p. 821) with the account given by Froude (p. 808). Are Meline's strictures against Froude (p. 819 f.) well taken? Does Froude's way of describing the execution embody a judgment of the Queen? Try to rewrite the passage (using Wingfield's facts) as a fervent partisan of Mary Queen of Scots might describe the execution.

## STYLE AS AN EXPRESSION OF PERSONALITY

Thus far we have primarily considered style as related to the writer's purpose, but there are other important relations to be considered, and one of them, the relation of style to the writer's personality, requires careful attention. The relation of style to personality comes up appropriately at this point, for we have just said that a good style does not call attention to itself: style and content are inseparable, and the very cleavage between them is a symptom of something's having gone wrong.

But this last point suggests further that a good style is not pretentious or affected: that it is natural and sincere, that it is the authentic expression of the writer's mind. This matter of unaffected naturalness is so important that many writers on style have emphasized it. One celebrated essay on style gives the following advice: "Be natural, be simple, be yourself: shun artifices, tricks, fashions. Gain the tone of ease, plainness, self-respect. To thine own self be true. Speak out frankly that which you have thought out in your own brain and have felt within your soul" (Frederic Harrison, "On English Prose").

This, it goes without saying, is good advice; but it does not take us very far. In the first place, like so much advice which urges us to "be ourselves," it assumes that we know what that self is. But writing is precisely the field in which it is most difficult to know oneself. One "finds himself" in a style only through exploration, and perhaps painful experiment.

In the second place, there is danger that Harrison's comment may confuse the real issue by seeming to associate "truth to self" with simplicity, plainness, and ease. If we took his advice literally, we might be tempted to throw out any style which was not thoroughly simple. Pomposity is always bad, of course; but some very fine prose is rich and complex—which is quite another thing (see "Complexity of Tone: When, and Why, It Is Necessary," p. 472).

Yet, having made these qualifications, it is proper to point out that a "good style" always does express the personality of the writer. Such self-expression is usually unconscious, however; and the student may well allow it to remain unconscious, not asking "Does this express me?" but rather "Does this say what ought to be said?"

Indeed, the student can be assured that the writer's personality always does find expression in any good style. For the style of a piece of writing is the shaping, directing, organizing force made manifest in the writing itself. The way in which the topic is approached, the kind of analyses to which it is subjected, the emphases, heavy or light, that it receives, are revealed in the style, and through the style. The style, so conceived, becomes an index of the mind and personality of the writer. A metaphor may serve to illustrate: The style of a work is not a sort of veneer glued over the outside. On the contrary, it is like the pattern of the grain in a piece of wood. It is a pattern that goes all the way through: a manifestation of the growth and development of the structure of the tree itself.

The student does not need to strive for individuality as such, since individuality must obtain in any genuine piece of work. (The grain pattern of no two trees is just alike, and human personalities are at least as various as trees.) Individuality in style is important, then, *not because it is valuable in itself, but as a symptom of the presence of something else: genuineness.*

The distinct impress which a personality gives to a style is easily demonstrated. The very structure of sentences and the handling of rhythms is tempered by the mind and personality of the writer. A child, for example, obviously will tend to use short sentences linked together by *and*'s and *but*'s and interspersed with very few subordinate clauses. Such a style thus reflects the simple, relatively uncritical response to the child's experience.

Let us go on to consider a more elaborate example, not a "natural" and naïve simplicity, but the carefully fashioned simplicity of a conscious artist. In the stories of Ernest Hemingway, the style is simple, even to the point of monotony. Most of the sentences are simple or compound. The paragraphs tend to be based upon simple sequence. In part, of course, this simplicity of style derives from the fact that Hemingway's typical characters are unsophisticated, and that they are characteristically treated in simple, fundamental situations. The uncomplicated style of the stories, therefore, is a matter of dramatic propriety: that is, the author is merely having his characters talk in the way in which they would talk.[4] But this

---

[4] This is not to say, of course, that Hemingway is simply giving a kind of transcript of actual conversation. See p. 302.

is not the whole explanation. In part, the uncomplicated style is a reflection of the sensibility of the author himself. The short, simple rhythms, the succession of co-ordinate clauses, and the general lack of subordination—all suggest a dislocated and ununified world. Hemingway is apparently trying to suggest in his style the direct experience—things as seen and felt, one after another, and not as the mind arranges and analyzes them. Consider the following paragraphs from his story, "In Another Country":

In the fall the war was always there, but we did not go to it any more. It was cold in the fall in Milan and the dark came very early. Then the electric lights came on, and it was pleasant along the streets looking in the windows. There was much game hanging outside the shops, and the snow powdered in the fur of the foxes and the wind blew their tails. The deer hung stiff and heavy and empty, and small birds blew in the wind and the wind turned their feathers. It was a cold fall and the wind came down from the mountains.

We were all at the hospital every afternoon, and there were different ways of walking across the town through the dusk to the hospital. Two of the ways were alongside canals, but they were long. Always, though, you crossed a bridge across a canal to enter the hospital. There was a choice of three bridges. On one of them a woman sold roasted chestnuts. It was warm, standing in front of her charcoal fire, and the chestnuts were warm afterward in your pocket. The hospital was very old and very beautiful, and you entered through a gate and walked across a courtyard and out a gate on the other side. There were usually funerals starting from the courtyard. Beyond the old hospital were the new brick pavilions, and there we met every afternoon and were all very polite and interested in what was the matter, and sat in the machines that were to make so much difference.

The doctor came up to the machine where I was sitting and said: "What did you like best to do before the war? Did you practise a sport?"

I said: "Yes, football."

"Good," he said. "You will be able to play football again better than ever."

My knee did not bend and the leg dropped straight from the knee to the ankle without a calf, and the machine was to bend the knee and make it move as in riding a tricycle. But it did not bend yet, and instead the machine lurched when it came to the bending part. The doctor said: "That will all pass. You are a fortunate young man. You will play football again like a champion."—ERNEST HEMINGWAY: "In Another Country." [5]

A style which involves subordination and complicated shadings of emphasis—a style which tends toward complex sentences with many qualifying clauses and phrases—implies an exercise of critical discrimination. It implies the sifting of experience through the intellect. But Hemingway, apparently, is primarily concerned with giving the immediate impact of experience rather than with analyzing and evaluating it in detail. His very style, then, seems to imply that the use of the intellect, with its careful discriminations, may blur the rendering of experience and may falsify it; and this style, taken with his basic concern for simple, and frequently, "tough" characters, seems to imply a distrust of the intellect in solving man's basic problems.

Compare with Hemingway's style that of the following passage from Henry James's *The Turn of the Screw*. An English governess is telling the story, and in this passage she is reflecting upon the housekeeper's (Mrs. Grose's) account of a former servant of the house.

I forebore, for the moment, to analyze this description further than by the reflection that a part of it applied to several members of the household, of the half-dozen maids and men who were still of our small colony. But there was everything, for our apprehension, in the lucky fact that no discomfortable legend, no perturbation of scullions, had ever, within anyone's memory, attached to the kind old place. It had neither bad name nor ill fame, and Mrs. Grose, most apparently, only desired to cling to me and to quake in silence. I even put her, the very last thing of all, to the test. It was when, at midnight, she had her hand on the schoolroom door to take leave. "I have it from you then—for it's of great importance—that he was definitely and admittedly bad."

The passage is, first of all, in character. The governess is a carefully educated woman. Her choice of words reflects her education; but it reflects also a certain primness, a certain fastidiousness. For example, she refines the phrase "no discomfortable legend," by adding an elaboration of it, "no perturbation of scullions." The structure of the sentences too reflects the governess's manner. In telling the

[5] From *Men Without Women* by Ernest Hemingway, copyright, 1927, by Charles Scribner's Sons.

story, she is re-creating events which have already happened. As she relates them, she tries to render them faithfully and exactly, but she is not being carried along by the rush of events. She has the advantage of looking back on them, and that reflection displays itself in the style. The sentences are "arranged," thought out with some care: for example, she says, "But there was everything, *for our apprehension*, in the lucky fact that. . . ." Or, she can write "I even put her, *the very last of all*, to the test."

Perhaps we ought to leave our analysis of the style at this level, and say merely that it reflects precisely the character and personality of James's chosen narrator, the governess. Yet one is tempted to try to penetrate a little deeper and find in the style something of the sensibility of James himself: if so, we should find in James's prose just the reverse of what we found in Hemingway's. We could say of this passage (and of most of Henry James's work) that the style does imply an exercise of critical discrimination, the sifting of experience through the intellect. The sentence rhythms are complex, there is a high degree of subordination, there are complicated shadings of emphasis. It is the prose of a mind which is arranging its world, by delicate adjustments and careful discriminations, into a perspective pattern.

### FURTHER EXAMPLES OF THE EXPRESSION OF THE WRITER'S PERSONALITY

These generalizations on Hemingway and James are based, of course, on each man's work as a whole, and the validity of the generalizations would require for demonstration extended passages rather than the short excerpts that we have quoted. Indeed, it is always difficult to make a convincing case for the impress of a writer's personality on his style if one has only a short excerpt to exhibit. The short passages which follow, however, may serve further to suggest some of the more obvious ways in which an author's style may reflect his personality.

Here is Donald Culross Peattie's definition of a weed. The definition is a thoroughly accurate one. (Compare it with the dictionary definition: "a plant occurring obtrusively in cultivated ground to the exclusion or injury of the desired crop.") But how lively an account it is; and how much it tells us about the personality of Peattie!

What is a weed? I have heard it said that there are sixty definitions. For me, a weed is a plant out of place. Or, less tolerantly, call it a foreign aggressor, which is a thing not so mild as a mere escape from cultivation, a visitor that sows itself innocently in a garden bed where you would not choose to plant it. Most weeds have natal countries, whence they have sortied. So Japanese honeysuckle, English plantain, Russian thistle came from lands we recognize, but others, like gypsies, have lost all record of their geographic origin. Some of them turn up in all countries, and are listed in no flora as natives. Some knock about the seaports of the world, springing up wherever ballast used to be dumped from the old sailing ships. Others prefer cities; they have lost contact with sweet soil, and lead a guttersnipe existence. A little group occurs only where wool waste is dumped, others are dooryard and pavement weeds, seeming to thrive the more as they are trod by the feet of man's generations. Some prized in an age of simpler tastes have become garden *déclassés* and street urchins; thus it comes about that the pleasant but plebeian scent of Bouncing Bet, that somewhat blowsy pink of old English gardens, is now one of the characteristic odors of American sidewalk ends, where the pavement peters out and shacks and junked cars begin.
—DONALD CULROSS PEATTIE: *Flowering Earth,* Chap. 12.[6]

The writer, as this passage indicates, evidently possesses a great deal of botanical information. He is undoubtedly familiar with the various "flora" and knows which plants are listed in them and which are not. But this passage is not intended to be a technical description; rather it is a more desultory and amiable account of weeds. Peattie is a man of perception, with senses that are keen ("the pleasant but plebeian scent of Bouncing Bet," "the characteristic odors of American sidewalk ends"). He evidently has a sense of humor. He is aware of current politics ("foreign aggressor"). He has a sense of history.

In short, in this passage we get something of the play of an informed and sensitive mind—a mind which special knowledge has not made stuffy—and of a personality which savors, with evident enjoyment, the varied and amusing world with which it is thoroughly familiar. In this connection notice how the general metaphor which treats the weed as a human being who has broken bounds runs through the whole passage, and how this metaphor is varied through the passage to express the varying aspects of weeds in gen-

[6] From *Flowering Earth,* by Donald Culross Peattie. Copyright, 1939, by Donald Culross Peattie. Courtesy of G. P. Putnam's Sons.

eral and of certain weeds in particular. One weed may be like a "foreign aggressor" to be resisted; another, like an immigrant or colonist from another land; still another, like a gypsy whose original homeland is lost in obscurity. Some weeds, like groups of immigrants, remain near the seaports where they made their first entry. But the migration of other weeds has been from country to city. They have moved in from the provinces and have become citified and now lead a "guttersnipe" existence. Still other weeds are like human beings who have come down in the world from a higher class of society, and having lost pride of class and dignity, are now happily and frowsily plebeian. The general comparison of the weed to the human migrant is flexible enough to provide quite specific illustrations of the various kinds of weeds. The metaphor not only renders the abstract definition concrete, but it suggests Peattie's own attitude toward weeds—an attitude which is one of genial and good-humored amusement.

Notice too how the diction unobtrusively but powerfully supports the variations of the basic metaphor. "Foreign aggressor" is pointed up by the use of the word "sortied." (A "sortie" suggests a military raid.) "Guttersnipe existence" sharpens the hint given by "others prefer cities." "Plebeian" and "somewhat blowsy" support and extend the suggestions made by "*déclassé*."

The diction, of course, has been chosen to do something more. Though Peattie is willing to use a technical term like *flora*, most of his words are specific and concrete. Moreover, he does not hesitate to use colloquial expressions like "knock about" and even the slang expression "peters out." Peattie is not at all like the fabled scholar who knew all the pedantic terms but could not address a dog in his own dialect. His diction is accommodated to the wholesome vulgarity of his subject. Weeds interest him, and to that interest he brings not only a fund of knowledge but all the resources of a rich personality.

The familiar essay, as we should expect, furnishes obvious examples of the reflection of personality in the style. (The familiar essay is sometimes called the "personal essay.") Here is the first paragraph of Charles Lamb's essay, "Mackery End, in Hertfordshire":

Bridget Elia has been my housekeeper for many a long year. I have obligations to Bridget, extending beyond the period of memory. We house together, old bachelor and maid, in a sort of double singleness; with such tolerable comfort, upon the whole, that I, for one, find in myself no sort of disposition to go out upon the mountains, with the rash king's offspring, to bewail my celibacy. We agree pretty well in our tastes and habits—yet so, as "with a difference." We are generally in harmony, with occasional bickerings—as it should be among near relations. Our sympathies are rather understood, than expressed; and once, upon my dissembling a tone in my voice more kind than ordinary, my cousin burst into tears, and complained that I was altered. We are both great readers in different directions. While I am hanging over (for the thousandth time) some passage in old Burton, or one of his strange contemporaries, she is abstracted in some modern tale, or adventure, whereof our common reading-table is daily fed with assiduously fresh supplies. Narrative teazes me. I have little concern in the progress of events. She must have a story—well, ill, or indifferently told—so there be life stirring in it, and plenty of good or evil accidents. The fluctuations of fortune in fiction—and almost in real life—have ceased to interest, or operate but dully upon me. Out-of-the-way humors and opinions— heads with some diverting twist in them—the oddities of authorship please me most. My cousin has a native disrelish of anything that sounds odd or bizarre. Nothing goes down with her that is quaint, irregular, or out of the road of common sympathy. She "holds Nature more clever. . . ."

Lamb begins his essay by pointing some contrasts between himself and his cousin, Bridget. They have come to know intimately, and to be reconciled to, and even to enjoy, their differences. Their tastes in literature illustrate the basic difference very well. Bridget demands in her reading a chain of narrative, a plot; but "Narrative teazes" him. He is for out-of-the-way humors and opinions, foibles, crotchets, and oddities. But notice that the prose that *tells us this* provides in itself a nice instance of Elia's taste. For his first sentence hints at a narrative, but the narrative does not develop. Indeed, with the playful phrase, "double singleness," there comes the "diverting twist" which Elia tells us he relishes. So also is the humorous collocation of King Jephthah's daughter bewailing her virginity, and the comfortable bachelor Elia, reading "for the thousandth time" some passage from Burton's *Anatomy of Melancholy*.

The structure of the sentences, with their asides and their abrupt and whimsical shifts, reflects the very traits of the personality which these sentences undertake to describe: thus, "She must have a story —well, ill, or indifferently told—so there be life stirring in it, and plenty of good or evil accidents. The fluctuations of fortune in fiction—and almost in real life—have ceased to interest, or operate but dully upon me." In short, the *way* in which Elia writes about his traits of character is an exemplification of those very traits: the style mirrors its content.

The reflection of personality in style comes out clearly if we compare the varying accounts of two writers who have the same topic. In the two passages that follow, James Boswell and Lord Macaulay discuss the personal eccentricities of the eighteenth-century critic and man of letters, Samuel Johnson. First, Boswell's account:

He had another particularity, of which none of his friends ever ventured to ask an explanation. It appeared to me as some superstitious habit, which he had contracted early, and from which he had never called upon his reason to disentangle him. This was his anxious care to go out or in at a door or passage by a certain number of steps from a certain point, or at least so that either his right or his left foot (I am not certain which) should constantly make the first actual movement when he came close to the door or passage. Thus I conjecture: for I have, upon innumerable occasions, observed him suddenly stop, and then seem to count his steps with a deep earnestness; and when he had neglected or gone wrong in this sort of magical movement, I have seen him go back again, put himself in a proper posture to begin the ceremony, and, having gone through it, break from his abstraction, walk briskly on, and join his companion. A strange instance of something of this nature, even when on horseback, happened when he was in the isle of Sky. Sir Joshua Reynolds has observed him to go a good way about, rather than cross a particular alley in Leicester-fields; but this Sir Joshua imputed to his having had some disagreeable recollection associated with it.

That the most minute singularities which belonged to him, and made very observable parts of his appearance and manner, may not be omitted, it is requisite to mention, that while talking or even musing, as he sat in his chair, he commonly held his head to one side towards his right shoulder, and shook it in a tremulous manner, moving his body backwards and forwards, and rubbing his left knee in the same direction, with the palm of his hand. In the intervals of articulating he made various sounds with his mouth, sometimes as if ruminating, or what is called chewing the cud, sometimes giving a half whistle, sometimes making his tongue play backwards from the roof of his mouth, as if clucking like a hen, and sometimes protruding it against his upper gums in front, as if pronouncing quickly under his breath, *too, too, too:*

all this accompanied sometimes with a thoughtful look, but more frequently with a smile. Generally when he had concluded a period, in the course of a dispute, by which time he was a good deal exhausted by violence and vociferation, he used to blow out his breath like a Whale. This I supposed was a relief to his lungs; and it seemed in him to be a contemptuous mode of expression, as if he had made the arguments of his opponent fly like chaff before the wind.

I am fully aware how very obvious an occasion I here give for the sneering jocularity of such as have no relish of an exact likeness: which to render complete, he who draws it must not disdain the slightest strokes. But if witlings should be inclined to attack this account, let them have the candour to quote what I have offered in my defense.— JAMES BOSWELL: "1764: Ætat 55," *Life of Johnson.*

His life during the thirty years which followed was one hard struggle with poverty. The misery of that struggle needed no aggravation, but was aggravated by the sufferings of an unsound body and an unsound mind. Before the young man left the university, his hereditary malady had broken forth in a singularly cruel form. He had become an incurable hypochondriac. He said long after that he had been mad all his life, or at least not perfectly sane; and, in truth, eccentricities less strange than his have often been thought grounds sufficient for absolving felons and for setting aside wills. His grimaces, his gestures, his mutterings, sometimes diverted and sometimes terrified people who did not know him. At a dinner table he would, in a fit of absence, stoop down and twitch off a lady's shoe. He would amaze a drawing-room by suddenly ejaculating a clause of the Lord's Prayer. He would conceive an unintelligible aversion to a particular alley, and perform a great circuit rather than see the hateful place. He would set his heart on touching every post in the streets through which he walked. If by any chance he missed a post, he would go back a hundred yards and repair the omission. Under the influence of his disease, his senses became morbidly torpid, and his imagination morbidly active. At one time he would stand poring on the town clock without being able to tell the hour. At another he would distinctly hear his mother, who was many miles off, calling him by name. But this was not the worst. A deep melancholy took possession of him, and gave a dark tinge to all his views of human nature and of human destiny. Such wretchedness as he endured has driven many men to shoot themselves or drown themselves. But he was under no temptation to commit suicide. He was sick of life, but he was afraid of death; and he shuddered at every sight or sound which reminded him of the inevitable hour. In religion he found but little comfort during his long and frequent fits of dejection; for his religion partook of his own character. The light from heaven shone on him, indeed, but not in a direct line, or with its own pure splendor. The rays had to struggle through a disturbing medium; they reached him refracted, dulled and discolored by the thick gloom which had settled on his soul; and, though they might be sufficiently clear to guide him, were too dim to cheer him.—THOMAS BABINGTON MACAULAY: "Samuel Johnson."

Lord Melbourne, a contemporary of Macaulay's, once said that he wished that he could be as cocksure of anything as Macaulay was of everything. If this is not the prose of a cocksure man, it is at least the prose of a thoroughly assured man. Macaulay has a tidy mind; he values clarity; he enjoys clean balances and antitheses. One judges that he has small patience with mysteries and mystifications. Certainly, he sees Johnson's character as plain as a pikestaff. Johnson suffered from an "unsound body and an unsound mind." His struggle aggravated his misery. His eccentricities are the product of his hereditary malady. Johnson was "sick of life." If he did not rid himself of a life he was "sick of," it was because he was "afraid" of death.

Now this is not the place in which to discuss whether or not Macaulay has oversimplified Johnson's personality. The passage has been quoted, not to throw light upon Johnson's personality, but upon Macaulay's. But some comparison with Boswell's account of Johnson's eccentricities may be of help here. Boswell agrees that Johnson was sick, but he does not say patly that he was "sick of life" (which, in Macaulay's sentence so neatly balances "afraid of death"). Moreover, Boswell, in mentioning the alley which Johnson avoided, takes pains to refer to Reynolds's conjecture that Johnson avoided it because it was for him associated with some painful memory. Boswell does not say that he agrees with Reynolds, and he frankly calls one of Johnson's eccentricities a "superstitious habit," and another a "magical movement." Still, Boswell is more tentative than Macaulay in his explanations of Johnson's conduct, just as he presents a richer and more detailed description of the eccentricities.

One must not, of course, build too much upon two rather brief passages. Even these passages, however, do present some contrasts between Boswell's personality and Macaulay's. Macaulay's is obviously the more methodical mind, the more practical mind, the more "brilliant" mind. Boswell, one would suppose, has more geniality, more sympathy, more sense of the rich sensuous detail of life, more humility before the mystery of human personality. This last comment requires the admission, of course, that Boswell, in the passage in question, is writing about his hero, Johnson. This is true enough. But the passage does not breathe uncritical hero-worship. Boswell is willing to characterize the odd action he describes as "a ceremony," and he is not unduly squeamish about his great friend's dignity when he writes "sometimes giving a half whistle, sometimes making his tongue play backwards from the roof of his mouth, as if clucking like a hen."

Boswell is neither the uncritical devotee nor the meticulous cataloguer. We get a better characterization of his interests if we read the last paragraph of his selection. Here the conscious artist is speaking. Boswell is fascinated with Johnson; he means to make us see him, even if the minuteness of the details may prompt some readers to laugh. He is the sort of man who will not be satisfied with a formula which will explain Johnson or satisfied with any mere summary of Johnson's traits. Macaulay (in the best, as well as in the worst sense) is the man who is fascinated by summaries, who sees the value of summaries, and means to give us the neatest and most pithy summary possible.

## IMPROPER INTRUSION OF THE WRITER'S PERSONALITY

The writer's own personality, then, is reflected in his writing, even though that reflection may well be unconscious. This fact offers an opportunity to consider briefly a further point which is of the utmost concern to the writer. If personality ultimately cannot be kept out of one's writing, how is the expression of the writer's personality to be controlled?

Consider the following passage from one of Dickens's novels.

She was dead. Dear, gentle, patient, noble Nell was dead. Her little bird—a poor slight thing the pressure of a finger would have crushed—was stirring nimbly in its cage; and the strong heart of its child mistress was mute and motionless for ever.

Where were the traces of her early cares, her sufferings, and fatigues? All gone. Sorrow was dead indeed in her, but peace and perfect happiness were born; imaged in her tranquil beauty and profound repose.

And still her former self lay there, unaltered in this change. Yes. The old fireside had smiled upon that same sweet face; it had passed, like a dream, through haunts of misery and care; at the door of the poor schoolmaster on the summer evening, before the furnace fire on the cold wet night, at the still bedside of the dying boy, there had been the same mild lovely look. So shall we know the angels in their majesty, after death.

The old man held one languid arm in his, and had the small hand tight folded to his breast, for warmth. It was the hand she had stretched out to him with her last smile—the hand that had led him on, through all their wanderings. Ever and anon he pressed it to his lips; then hugged it to his breast again, murmuring that it was warmer now; and, as he said it, he looked, in agony, to those who stood around, as if imploring them to help her.—CHARLES DICKENS: *The Old Curiosity Shop*, Chap. 71.

Many things could be said about this passage: its obvious sentimentality (cf. p. 451), the strain evidenced by the writer as he tries to squeeze the last drop of feeling from the scene, its shameless parading of all the clichés of tenderness, its invitation to the reader to abandon himself to the sweet sadness of little Nell's death. Yet the passage does express Dickens's own feelings, and it would probably be idle to argue that it is not a "sincere" expression of values that Dickens held very dearly. (That is, it is unlikely that Dickens was cold-bloodedly attempting to stir the reader's feelings. Dickens, too, probably felt the scene deeply, and far from cynically playing upon our feelings, is himself being swept along by his own emotions.) Even so, the passage reveals what may be called a disturbing intrusion of the author's own personality into the scene. The feeling of tenderness is not absorbed and objectified: it spills over chaotically. Compare this death scene with the following:

Snag was a crippled Negro who had caddied for my uncle when he won his first golf tournament. Cap'm John had been fond of Snag. He was fond of all Negroes, and I remember how pleased both he and Snag would be over any golf shot the two of them contrived to make. . . .

But Snag used to swim in the river. He believed it would help his undeveloped leg. He had a mongrel dog, and the two of them would swim on warm mornings up at a great sweeping bend of levee and wilderness beyond the golf course. It was on an empty Sunday morning that Snag was killed. He hadn't seen the oil tanker when she came around the bend. They were out in the middle, then, just two black specks on the yellow vastness. Then the long blast came like a mighty trumpet. They said that the nigger must have misjudged their swing.

They were already well on the turn when they saw him and they said that they eased the wheel to straighten out and pass the nigger on starboard. They said that he must have just put it to a guess and he guessed wrong, because they said that he had two-thirds of the river to swim in but that he had turned back and so they put the wheel hard to starboard and then he turned back again—the two of them, the nigger and the dog, swimming back and forth each time in a shorter arc until they could see his face stretched like laughter in the sunshine with all the white teeth, or like a grimace of joyous surprise, recognition, and with men even running forward, waving from the swinging cliff (she was high, empty) and the long trumpet blast right up to the moment he was struck and they wasted the life preserver. He was struck by the great bulging side, nearly amidship, as the wall of steel swung gatelike and fast with the wheel hard over. They saw only the hand and the vanishing gleam of teeth and then nothing.—s. s. FIELD: "Goodbye to Cap'm John." [7]

In its intention, this passage is not, to be sure, quite on the same level with that of Dickens. It is more modest in its claim on our emotions; it presumably aims at a less intense effect. Yet the man who remembers the story from his boyhood, and narrates it here, is obviously fond of Snag, and feels a sense of sorrow at his death. Moreover, the student will probably find the passage quite moving. How is the emotion which we feel kept from spilling over into sentimentality? Why does it not become excessive? In part, because the scene has been realized for us vividly in its detail; because the writer does not seem at our elbow nudging us to "emote," or suggesting what we ought to feel; because he has left us free to draw our own interpretations, confident that if the scene is fairly presented, the reader may be relied upon to respond fully and properly to it. In short, Field does not *intrude* his own personality into the scene: his relevant emotion is absorbed into the scene itself.

The sensitive artist's ability to express emotion without cramming it down our throats—without intruding his own personality into the work—may be further illustrated by excerpts from a story by Katherine Anne Porter and a story by Ernest Hemingway. In Miss Porter's story two little girls have been watching a race which their uncle's horse, Miss Lucy, has just won.

[7] From "Goodbye to Cap'm John," by S. S. Field, published by *The Southern Review*, Vol. I (1936). Courtesy of Louisiana State University Press.

The little girls sat down, feeling quite dizzy, while their father tried to pull their hats straight, and taking out his handkerchief held it to Miranda's face, saying very gently, "Here, blow your nose," and he dried her eyes while he was about it. He stood up then and shook them out of their daze. He was smiling with deep laughing wrinkles around his eyes, and spoke to them as if they were grown young ladies he was squiring around.

"Let's go out and pay our respects to Miss Lucy," he said. "She's the star of the day."

The horses were coming in, looking as if their hides had been drenched and rubbed with soap, their ribs heaving, their nostrils flaring and closing. The jockeys sat bowed and relaxed, their faces calm, moving a little at the waist with the movement of the horses. Miranda noted this for future use; that was the way you came in from a race, easy and quiet, whether you had won or lost. Miss Lucy came last, and a little handful of winners applauded her and cheered the jockey. He smiled and lifted his whip, his eyes and shriveled brown face perfectly serene. Miss Lucy was bleeding at the nose, two thick red rivulets were stiffening her tender mouth and chin, the round velvet chin that Miranda thought the nicest kind of chin in the world. Her eyes were wild and her knees were trembling, and she snored when she drew her breath.

Miranda stood staring. That was winning, too. Her heart clinched tight; that was winning, for Miss Lucy. So instantly and completely did her heart reject that victory, she did not know when it happened, but she hated it, and was ashamed that she had screamed and shed tears of joy when Miss Lucy, with her bloodied nose and bursting heart, had gone past the judges' stand a neck ahead. She felt empty and sick and held to her father's hand so hard that he shook her off a little impatiently and said, "What is the matter with you? Don't be so fidgety."—KATHERINE ANNE PORTER: "Old Mortality." [8]

In Hemingway's story, the boy is watching a race that has been "fixed."

They weren't at the post hardly any time at all when the gong started and you could see them way off across the infield all in a bunch starting on the first swing like a lot of little toy horses. I was watching them through the glasses and Kzar was running well back, with one of the bays making the pace. They swept down and around and came pounding past and Kzar was way back when they passed us and this Kircubbin

---

[8] From *Pale Horse, Pale Rider* by Katherine Anne Porter, copyright, 1939, by Katherine Anne Porter. Reprinted by permission of Harcourt, Brace and Company, Inc.

horse in front and going smooth. Gee it's awful when they go by you and then you have to watch them go farther away and get smaller and smaller and then all bunched up on the turns and then come around towards you into the stretch and you feel like swearing and goddamming worse and worse. Finally they made the last turn and came into the straightaway with this Kircubbin horse way out in front. Everybody was looking funny and saying "Kzar" in a sort of sick way and them pounding nearer down the stretch, and then something came out of the pack right into my glasses like a horse-headed yellow streak and everybody began to yell "Kzar" as though they were crazy. Kzar came on faster than I'd ever seen anything in my life and pulled up on Kircubbin that was going as fast as any black horse could go with the jock flogging hell out of him with the gad and they were right dead neck for neck for a second but Kzar seemed going about twice as fast with those great jumps and that head out—but it was while they were neck and neck that they passed the winning post and when the numbers went up in the slots the first one was 2 and that meant Kircubbin had won.

I felt all trembly and funny inside, and then we were all jammed in with the people going down stairs to stand in front of the board where they'd post what Kircubbin paid. Honest, watching the race I'd forgot how much my old man had bet on Kircubbin. I'd wanted Kzar to win so damned bad. But now it was all over it was swell to know we had a winner.

"Wasn't it a swell race, Dad?" I said to him.

He looked at me sort of funny with his derby on the back of his head. "George Gardner's a swell jockey, all right," he said. "It sure took a great jock to keep that Kzar horse from winning."—ERNEST HEMINGWAY: "My Old Man." [9]

Both passages attempt to suggest, first the excitement of the observer, and then the subsequent disappointment: in the case of the little girl, at the realization that the horse has been pushed beyond its strength and injured; in the case of the boy, at the realization that the race has been "fixed"—that the horse that should have won has been held back and cheated of its victory. Each passage reflects the dramatic character (the "personality") of the observer. This fact is, of course, primary. But it is possible to see that each passage also reflects the personality of the author. We have already commented upon the way in which the style of a typical Hemingway

[9] From *Three Stories and Ten Poems* by Ernest Hemingway, copyright, 1923, by Charles Scribner's Sons.

story is related to Hemingway's own personality (p. 507). This excerpt from "My Old Man" provides a good instance of our generalization. But what of Miss Porter's style? Can a comparable generalization be made?

Probably so. Hers is the prose of a sensitive observer. It is feminine prose (in the best sense of that term) as Hemingway's is masculine prose. But the details, rich as they are, and "naturally" as they are presented (through the eyes of the little girl), are not chaotic. They are ordered to a pattern; they are meaningful in terms of a generalization about life. This is not to say that the little girl is made to appear too wise for her years. It is rather to say that the scene is being described as remembered by a woman; that the experience of the little girl receives the benefit of subsequent maturity; that, though the scene is focused upon the child, the passage describing it is not being written by a child.

Are we to conclude, then, that both passages are autobiographical: that Miranda is taken from Miss Porter's childhood and that the boy observer in Hemingway's "My Old Man" is the boy Hemingway, or at least derives from some comparable boyhood experience of Hemingway's? Not necessarily. For the point to be made here concerns *how* a writer uses his materials—not *where* they may have come from.

## PERSONALITY CONTROLLED AND OBJECTIFIED IN THE WORK

In both passages before us the intelligence and sensitivity of the writer, his interests and values, are subordinated to the work in question. It would be more accurate to say that they are here completely *absorbed* into the story of Miranda and into the story of the boy at the race track. If there is a moral here for the writer, it is one that applies not merely to the writer of fiction. Even the essayist who writes in the first person may profit by using a comparable means of objectification and control. He may actually find it helpful to objectify and dramatize the "I" who speaks, not at all to disguise or suppress his personality, but rather to realize that personality most fully. Even Charles Lamb preferred to write as "Elia" rather than as Charles Lamb, Esq.

## APPLICATIONS

**I.** After reading Steffens's "I Get a Colt to Break In" (p. 851), attempt to describe the personality of the author that is revealed in this selection. Obviously Steffens enjoyed his colt and had a real affection for her. Does he look back at his boyhood with pleasure? Was it a happy boyhood? Does he have a sense of humor? Is he able to see the boyhood events in perspective? Try to answer these and similar questions, pointing out the specific elements of the style which give you your answers.

**II.** What sort of personality is revealed in Max Beerbohm's "The Decline of the Graces" (p. 730)? Is Beerbohm a woman-hater? Is he an old fogy? Is his sense of humor bitter, acid, playful? Point to specific passages in his essay in answering these questions.

**III.** What sort of personality is revealed in Christian Gauss's "The Threat of Science" (p. 659)? Does he hate science? Does he respect the scientist? Is he, as a professor of the humanities, insecure and uncertain in a world more and more dominated by science? Is he self-righteous? Does he make use of irony, and if so, for what reason? Try to answer these questions with specific references to the style of his essay.

**IV.** Both James Thurber (p. 722) and J. A. Rice (p. 859) write about their school days, and both write with humor. In spite of their humor (or perhaps by means of it), both make some serious criticisms of present-day American education. Consider the two essays as a revelation of personality. Compare and contrast these personalities as specifically as you can. Is either man capable of bitterness? Of righteous indignation? Would it be possible to rewrite the opening paragraphs of "The Webb School" in something of the style of Thurber's "University Days"? What would be gained? What would be lost? Attempt such a rewriting of the first three paragraphs.

**V.** Carl Becker, in his essay "The Marxian View of History," (p. 634), states certain objections to Marxism. Could it be said that the first paragraph of Santayana's "Dickens" (p. 749) *implies* certain objections to Marxist communism? What are they? Indicate specifically how they are suggested by the way in which the world of Dickens is described. Does Santayana use this comparison of a communist world and the Dickens world as a criticism of Marxism, or as a criticism of Dickens?

## STYLE CULTIVATED BY READING

Thus far in this chapter we have discussed style (1) as related to the writer's immediate purpose and (2) as related to the writer's personality. But there is a third aspect of style which ought to be discussed at least briefly: (3) style as related to the writer's linguistic environment. The first aspect of style is, of course, all-important. It is the aspect of style which concerns the writer immediately as he looks down upon the paper before him and grapples with the problem of putting his meaning adequately into words. The second aspect (style as the expression of the writer's innermost self) involves a double problem: on the one hand, that of the writer's personal integrity, and on the other, that of his originality. The third aspect of style has to do with the writer's inheritance, his relation to his linguistic tradition generally. Specifically and practically, it has a great deal to do with his reading.

One cannot learn how to write unless he learns how to read. In stressing this we are not forgetting the importance of originality or urging the student's falling into slavish imitation. For it is only through reading that we discover ourselves and find our own individual style.     .

A little reflection will show why reading is of paramount importance for writing. In the first place, we inherit language. We learn words by imitating our parents. We imitate their words, and we learn to associate meanings with these spoken sounds. As we grow, the meanings of these words are enriched, and we acquire fresh words. Moreover, we learn, again by imitation, how to arrange these words in patterns so that more precise meanings can be conveyed. A child who can merely babble a few isolated words may be able to make its wants known. When it says "water," the mother understands that it wants a drink of water. As it grows, it acquires grammatical patterns. But it learns further expressive patterns as well. The devices of style are expressive patternings. Parallelism and antithesis, for example, express relationships: they point (or should point) to elements that line up together and to others that balance each other in opposition. Stylistic arrangements *of all sorts* are thus acquired by imitation: for the process of learning by imitation is not interrupted as we learn to read.

A student who has read nothing but the local newspaper will begin by writing in the style of the local newspaper. How could he do otherwise? Anyone who can read and write has been thoroughly exposed to models of a sort. Strictly speaking, there is no such thing as a "natural" style. The only question, then, is not whether one shall or shall not be exposed to models of style. It is rather whether his experience shall include a wide range of models or be restricted to a narrow one. Ironically, it is the writer least acquainted with a variety of styles who usually turns out to be least individual in his own style. It is easy to see why this must be true. If our acquaintance with style is limited to that of the newspapers, a few popular magazines, and an occasional novel, our knowledge of the expressive possibilities of the language is so restricted that we have little range in which to make our own personalities felt.

Imitation, then, does not necessarily run counter to originality. For we must remember the terms in which our problem is set for us: we can always be as "original" as we please by using our own peculiar grammar, by assigning our own meaning to words, or, for that matter, by simply inventing a new language. The penalty for such originality is that we should not be understood. The only originality that counts, therefore, is an originality that does not deny the necessary conventional element in language. That element—though we may want to argue about its ultimate limits—is always very great. Therefore, since we can win only a cheap and worthless originality by violating the permissible modes of expression, the way to a truly individual style is through acquaintance with the whole realm of possibilities. For we do not invent words and expression: the only area in which we may display originality is in the way in which we may dispose and reorder them.

In a later section of this book (pp. 537 ff.) the importance of reading will be discussed more generally. Suffice it to say here that learning how to write goes hand in hand with learning how to read, and that a rich background in reading, far from fettering the writer to worn and dull conventionality, is his richest resource for discovering his own characteristic style.

How far back should the reading go? Can the (to our ears) quaint and obsolete style of Sir Thomas Malory aid us who are committed to the idiom of the twentieth century? Can the eighteenth-century prose of Joseph Addison be of any real utility to us in forming a style? Has not prose changed so much since the nineteenth century that a nineteenth-century style, even that of Charles Lamb, for example, seems quaint and out of place today? These are some of the questions that the student may be tempted to ask at this point.

A proper answer to these questions might take some such form as this. It is perfectly true that language changes and that writers of an earlier century can rather easily be identified through the period style which they write. It is also perfectly true that it would be absurd for a twentieth-century writer to affect the prose style, say, of a seventeenth-century writer. Naturally the student will derive most direct help from writers who are attempting to solve the typical problems of style that face a writer of our time. But even the writers of the remote past may prove to be of more direct value than a superficial opinion would indicate. For we must remember that reading is not undertaken for the sake of carbon-copy imitation. Not even the twentieth-century writer is to be read as a model to be followed slavishly. We read in order to enlarge our resources, in order to strengthen our hold on the language and its range of expressive devices; we read other writers in order to provide ourselves with the equipment which will give us the means to be more truly ourselves. Seen in these terms, imitation and originality do not war against each other; a writer may possibly find that he can learn from the prose of two centuries ago as well as from that which was written last year.

## SUMMARY

A very important element in style is RHYTHM. Rhythm depends upon the relationship of stressed and unstressed syllables. Poetry tends to employ a formalized rhythm which we call verse. Prose rhythms are much less formalized, and for that reason somewhat more difficult to describe accurately. But rhythm is frequently one of the most important expressive devices which the writer possesses. The student is not advised to try consciously for special rhythmic effects. He ought, however, to learn to recognize rhythmic defects in his own prose as symptoms of poor or defective arrangement of sentences and sentence elements.

Style involves an over-all harmony among the various expressive elements: sentence structure, diction, metaphor, rhythm, and all the rest. There are, therefore, no devices that are good in themselves, absolutely and intrinsically. Moreover, if we are to speak strictly, we shall have to regard as a bad style only that style which is at odds with itself, a style which lacks harmony among its various expressive factors. By the same token, we have to say that style and matter, form and content, are inseparable. We know what is said only through the way in which it is said; and to alter the way in which a thing is said is always to alter, if only ever so slightly, what is said. Three practical considerations follow from our realization of this inseparability of style and matter. (1) Style is not a mere veneer, a decorated surface laid over the content. (2) The writer's real difficulty in composition is finally to know what he wants to say—not, as we are tempted to think, merely how to say it. (3) Bad style always shows itself in some disharmony or cleavage between what is said and what we guess the author actually meant to say. The elements at fault call attention to themselves —"stick out."

These last considerations bear upon another aspect of style: the sincerity of the writer. We properly take originality to be a symptom of a good style. If we see that the style is not a veneer, but rather the informing principle of content, we can understand why good style is always indelibly impressed with the personality of the writer. But the student needs to be warned against any excessive striving for originality as such. It is not enough to urge him to be his unique self, for frequently he finds that true self only through a process of exploration. Originality, the impress of personality, like good rhythm, fortunately can be left to take care of itself if the writer manages to take care of what he can consciously control in his composition.

Thus far we have considered the relation of style to the writer's purpose and to the writer's own inner self. A third matter has to be considered: the relation of a writer to his linguistic environment. This amounts, in practice, to what the writer can learn from his reading, since language itself is inherited along with all of its expressive devices. The writer who strives to avoid all imitation locks himself into a narrow prison. His way to freedom and to true originality consists rather in extending his knowledge of the language and of various styles. Intelligent reading goes hand in hand with the discipline of writing.

## A MORE CONCRETE SUMMARY

If some of the matters discussed in this chapter seem rather abstract, perhaps it may be helpful to discuss them under the following

metaphor. We are familiar with "styles" of dress, and Lord Chesterfield, in a well-known pronouncement on style, defined style as "the
dress of thoughts." It probably seems natural to most of us to think
of style as a garb in which our thoughts are clothed.

Buffon, however, made a comment on style quite as famous as
that of Chesterfield. He said that "the style is the man himself."
His statement and Chesterfield's, then, seem to stand in flat contradiction. Is there a way out of the apparent contradiction? There
is, for both Chesterfield and Buffon are making use of the same
metaphor, though they use different aspects of it. Chesterfield is
presumably thinking of the writer's power to choose a proper style
and of his need to choose wisely. A man does not choose to wear
a dinner jacket for work in the garden, nor does he choose a suit
of overalls to wear to a formal dinner. There must be an accommodation of style to the occasion, and Chesterfield's statement insists
upon the necessity for careful choice. Buffon, on the other hand,
is stressing the fact that in a proper style the words do not cover
up and disguise the man; instead the style becomes an expression
of the man. The two pronouncements thus can be reconciled; for
if words may be thought of as a kind of dress, still a proper kind
of dress ought to reflect the personality of the wearer. In other
words, Buffon is not recommending that the writer walk about
*naked*, for, since, in terms of our clothes analogy, the words are the
clothing, that would be to have the writer give up words altogether.
Nor is Chesterfield, one may assume, recommending that the writer
shrivel away into a kind of tailor's dummy—that is, become merely
an animated suit of clothes.

Our clothes metaphor, then, properly understood, will carry us
a step further. It will even account for the fact that we do not
know what we want to say until, through exploration, we have
found how we are to say it. We may fit the problem to the metaphor
in this fashion. It is true that a man's "word-clothing" is not like
his naked skin, something that he is born with and cannot and
need not change. He acquires language: language is not natural
but always in some sense artificial. Nevertheless, this also needs to
be remembered: the "man" who is to be measured and clothed,
in this case, cannot turn over his measurements to a journeyman
clerk who selects from the shelves the ready-made articles, guaranteed to fit. On the contrary, an intricate and careful tailoring is

required; for we must remember that the "man" to be fitted (the "thing" to be said) is only a vague and nebulous ectoplasm *until he assumes the garments which define him and realize him.* For the thoughts, of which the words are the dress, are not defined with any precision until they have assumed their dress—until they are expressed in words.

Lastly, even the problem of reading can be fitted to the clothes metaphor. In suggesting that the student may, by intelligent reading, learn how to write, one is not suggesting that he go into a museum and choose a sixteenth-century doublet, an eighteenth-century peruke, and Dickens's nineteenth-century greatcoat. To acquire past styles in this sense would be merely to outfit oneself for a fancy-dress party. But the person who is acquainted with no styles except those of the newspaper and an occasional magazine is like a man who goes shopping in a shop so meagerly furnished that it can offer him only one shoddy suit, size 28, and one overcoat, size 42. He cannot clothe himself properly unless he has a variety of items from which to choose, a variety large enough to allow him to display real discrimination and thus dress himself not only comfortably, but also in a fashion which will express his own individual personality.

## APPLICATIONS

I. Read carefully the following illustrative passages and answer the questions after each item or group of items.

**Aa.** Southward from the Celebes Sea, toward Java and the rich oil wells of Balikpapan, the Jap drove last week. All had gone his way up to then in the Dutch Indies; nowhere had he been defeated in his Pacific battleground. Before him now was the final conquest of the Indies, perhaps a final grip on the Pacific world.

Then, for the first time in fair combat, he met the U. S. Navy. Into narrow Macassar Strait, where the warships, transports and screening planes of the Jap's convoy coursed south, steamed destroyers from Admiral Thomas C. Hart's Asiatic Fleet. U. S. cruisers and at least one U. S. submarine followed. Overhead and probably in advance of Admiral Hart's warships, the U. S. Army's Flying Fortresses and Dutch airmen in U. S.-made bombers harried the Jap's protecting planes, destroyers, cruisers.[10]

[10] Courtesy of TIME, Copyright Time, Inc. 1942.

**Ab.** Headman Luce was born in Tengchowfu, China, on April 3, 1898, the son of Henry Winters and Elizabeth Middleton Luce, Presbyterian missionaries. Very unlike the novels of Pearl Buck were his early days. Under brows too beetling for a baby, young Luce grew up inside the compound, played with his two sisters, lisped first Chinese, dreamed much of the Occident. At 14, weary of poverty, already respecting wealth and power, he sailed alone for England, entered school at St. Albans. Restless again, he came to the United States, enrolled at Hotchkiss, met up and coming young Brooklynite Briton Hadden. Both even then were troubled with an itch to harass the public. Intoned Luce years later: "We reached the conclusion that most people were not well informed and that something should be done. . . ."

First publication to inform fellowman was *Hotchkiss Weekly Record;* next *Yale Daily News,* which they turned into a tabloid; fought to double hours of military training, fought alumni who wished to change tune of Yale song from *Die Wacht am Rhein.* Traditionally unshaven, wearing high-buttoned Brooks jackets, soft white collars, cordovan shoes, no garters, Luce and Hadden were Big Men on a campus then depleted of other, older Big Men by the war. Luce, pale, intense, nervous, was Skull and Bones, Alpha Delta Phi, Phi Beta Kappa, member of the Student Council, editor of the *News;* wrote sad poems, read the *New Republic,* studied political philosophy. As successful, less earnest, more convivial, Hadden collected china dogs, made jokes. In 1920 the senior class voted Hadden Most Likely to Succeed, Luce Most Brilliant. Most Brilliant he, Luce sloped off to Christ Church, Oxford, there to study European conditions, take field trips into the churning Balkans.[11]

The first of the passages quoted above is taken from *Time* magazine and is written in *Time's* characteristic style (see p. 363). The second of the passages is from a *New Yorker* "Profile" of the owner of *Time* magazine, Henry Luce. The profile is obviously written in a parody of *Time's* style. A good parody, however, may throw light on virtues as well as defects. Write a brief description of *Time-style,* summarizing its characteristic virtues and characteristic faults.

**B.** Unjust laws exist: shall we be content to obey them, or shall we endeavor to amend them, and obey them until we have succeeded, or shall we transgress them at once? Men generally, under such a government as this, think that they ought to wait until they have persuaded the majority to alter them. They think that, if they should resist, the remedy would be worse than the evil. But it is the fault of the government itself

[11] Copyright 1936 The New Yorker Magazine, Inc. (Formerly the F-R Publishing Corporation.)

that the remedy *is* worse than the evil. *It* makes it worse. Why is it not more apt to anticipate and provide for reform? Why does it not cherish its wise minority? Why does it cry and resist before it is hurt? Why does it not encourage its citizens to be on the alert to point out its faults, and *do* better than it would have them? Why does it always crucify Christ, and excommunicate Copernicus and Luther, and pronounce Washington and Franklin rebels? . . .

If the injustice is part of the necessary friction of the machine of government, let it go, let it go: perchance it will wear smooth—certainly the machine will wear out. If the injustice has a spring, or a pulley, or a rope, or a crank, exclusively for itself, then perhaps you may consider whether the remedy will not be worse than the evil; but if it is of such a nature that it requires you to be the agent of injustice to another, then, I say, break the law. Let your life be a counter-friction to stop the machine. What I have to do is to see, at any rate, that I do not lend myself to the wrong which I condemn.

As for adopting the ways which the state has provided for remedying the evil, I know not of such ways. They take too much time, and a man's life will be gone. I have other affairs to attend to. I came into this world, not chiefly to make this a good place to live in, but to live in it, be it good or bad. A man has not everything to do, but something; and because he cannot do *everything*, it is not necessary that he should do *something* wrong. It is not my business to be petitioning the Governor or the Legislature any more than it is theirs to petition me; and if they should not hear my petition, what should I do then? But in this case the State has provided no way: its very Constitution is the evil. This may seem to be harsh and stubborn and unconciliatory; but it is to treat with the utmost kindness and consideration the only spirit that can appreciate or deserves it. So is all change for the better, like birth and death, which convulse the body.

This passage is from Henry David Thoreau's "On the Duty of Civil Disobedience." In this passage Thoreau tells us some things about himself explicitly. But he implies more. What traits of personality are reflected in the style? Describe the personality and relate it to the style as explicitly as you can.

**C.** If we watch awhile we will see a line of blackish seaweed and wet sand appearing along the edge of the water, showing that the tide has turned and begun to recede. In an hour it has ebbed a considerable distance, and if we clamber down over the great weather-worn rocks the hardy advance guard of that wonderful world of life under the water is seen. Barnacles whiten the top of every rock which is reached by the tide, although the water may cover them only a short time each day. But they flourish here in myriads, and the shorter the chance they have at the salt water the more frantically their little feathery feet clutch at the tiny food particles which float around them. These thousands of tiny turreted castles are built so closely together that many are pressed out of shape, paralleling in shape as in substance the inorganic crystals of the mineral kingdom. The valved doors are continually opening and partly closing, and if we listen quietly we can hear a perpetual shuss! shuss! Is it the creaking of the tiny hinges? As the last receding wave splashes them, they shut their folding doors over a drop or two and remain tightly closed, while perhaps ten hours of sunlight bake them, or they glisten in the moonlight for the same length of time, ready at the first touch of the returning water to open wide and welcome it.

The thought of their life history brings to mind how sadly they retrogress as they grow, hatching as minute free-swimming creatures like tiny lobsters, and gradually changing to this plant-like life, *sans* eyes, *sans* head, *sans* most everything except a stomach and a few pairs of feathery feet to kick food into it. A few pitiful traces of nerves are left them. What if there were enough ganglia to enable them to dream of their past higher life, in the long intervals of patient waiting!

A little lower down we come to the zone of mussels,—hanging in clusters like some strange sea-fruit. Each is attached by strands of thin silky cables, so tough that they often defy our utmost efforts to tear a specimen away. How secure these creatures seem, how safe from all harm, and yet they have enemies which make havoc among them. At high tide fishes come and crunch them, shells and all, and multitudes of carnivorous snails are waiting to set their file-like tongues at work, which mercilessly drill through the lime shells, bringing death in a more subtle but no less certain form. Storms may tear away the support of these poor mollusks, and the waves dash them far out of the reach of the tides, while at low water, crows and gulls use all their ingenuity to get at their toothsome flesh.—WILLIAM BEEBE: "Secrets of the Ocean," *Log of the Sun.*[12]

This passage is from a naturalist's account of the seashore. What do you learn, if anything, about the personality of the author? (In this connection, the student might look back at the analysis of Peattie's definition of a weed on p. 509.) Is the author of this passage a sensitive man? Does he have a sense of humor? What is his attitude toward the creatures that he describes? In trying to make an estimate of his personality, the student should note among other things his use of adjectives and

[12] From *The Log of the Sun* by William Beebe. Reprinted by permission of Henry Holt and Company, Inc.

adverbs: "that *wonderful* world of life," "*mercilessly* drill," "these *poor* mollusks," "their *toothsome* flesh." (Why *toothsome*, particularly since the flesh is to be devoured by *crows* and *gulls!*)

**II.** Making use of Williamson's rules ("How to Write Like a Social Scientist," p. 737) rewrite the first three paragraphs of "The Colors That Animals Can See" (p. 547). Here, for a start, is the first paragraph rewritten:

I propose in the following study to examine the question of what hues are visually significant to animals. As compared with human beings, do other mammals, and, for that matter, other creatures with visual sense organs, make fine or less fine color discriminations? In order to produce valid findings with reference to this question, scientists have performed a number of experiments. The essence of all these experiments consists in training the animals to respond to different hues, usually by associating a particular hue with some food lure to which the animal normally responds. There is a high ration of similarity between this method of testing color discrimination and experiments used in the past to test responsiveness to sound.

**III.** Test Ridenour's essay (p. 651) by Williamson's rules. Can any parts of his essay be simplified by reversing Williamson's rules?

**IV.** On page 661 of his essay, Gauss writes "The pure scientist might conceivably in his laboratory seek to discover that least stable combination of chemical elements which under given conditions would constitute the world's most powerful explosive." This essay was written in 1930. As we know, this most powerful explosive has now been found, and William L. Laurence (p. 592) describes the first practical test of it. Attempt to rewrite the passage in Laurence's essay beginning "Up it went," and going on to the end of the essay, as you would imagine Christian Gauss might have written it. (Note that the most significant part of the rewriting will consist in giving to the passage the particular inflection which Gauss might be expected to give. No new facts need be added.)

**V.** Make a careful analysis of the integration of diction, sentence structure, figurative language, rhythm, and other elements of style in the following passages. In each case, is there a real integration? Do any elements of style "stick out," resisting the general pattern of integration?
1. The last paragraph of Santayana's essay (p. 759).
2. The eighth paragraph of Sheean's essay (p. 874).
3. The sixth paragraph of Huxley's essay (p. 770).
4. The fifth paragraph of Mill's essay (p. 700).

**VI.** Select one of the following four subjects and write a theme of 500 to 700 words, imitating the style of the selection or selections listed. The imitation should not be slavish, but the student should attempt to apply to his own writing all that he can learn from his model.

1. The present state of the United States (depicted as one of stability or instability) on the model of Graves's "It Was a Stable World."

2. An essay on a favorite pet on the model of Thurber's "The Dog That Bit People."

3. A description of some simple process on the model of Fox's "The Colors That Animals Can See."

4. An account of a fire, an accident, or some violent happening on the model of Pyle's "The End in Sight."

✦

NOTE: The following is the original version of the garbled passage appearing on pp. 498-99:

There were many who came home inured to ordered violence, angry at their destiny, only to find that the farm, which had remained green and fruitful in their memory, gave them a strange welcome. Men who had been bred to the law took to the plow, and others in their several ways had to bury their ambitions and go about earning a living, and by living they meant bread and meat.—JOHN A. RICE: *I Came Out of the Eighteenth Century,* Chap. 5.

# A Book of Readings

# CONTENTS

# Introduction

A LARGE part of the material we write about is drawn from our personal experience and observation. Reporters, feature writers, essayists, and fiction writers draw heavily on actual life, as do, at times, even more technical writers, philosophers, for instance. The most important or vivid events, experienced or witnessed, are not worth much to us, however, unless we think about them. We have to see their significance before they are worth recording. And in one sense, it can even be said that they cannot be recorded at all unless we think about them, for the only thing that we can record is what we think of something, how it strikes us, how we interpret it. We cannot record the thing in its absolute purity without reference to our own response to it.

So our experience and observation are extremely important to us. But what of experience and observation that come to us secondhand, through reading? What can reading do for us? It can do many things for us, but for immediate purposes, we may list three. It can help us think. It can give us things to think about. And it can help us to express our thoughts.

Reading can help us think by giving us examples of thinking, good or bad. Obviously, the example of good thinking helps us. It gives us a model. It shows the principles of thinking in operation. But the example of bad thinking is useful, too. At least, it is useful if we read critically enough to spot it as bad. The bad thinking gives us the challenge to define the real issue, assess the evidence offered, correct the bad logic. And it may even awaken us to our own failures in thinking by showing us how some method we have employed leads to confusion. In reading, the student must try to break down what he reads into its logical divisions and state for himself the relation among these divisions. In other words, he must try to define the structure of the whole discourse.

Reading may be about anything. Every subject that conceivably interests man has been written about somewhere. So reading is the great mine of material for our thinking. It extends our limited individual experience in time and space, back into the past and outward into other places than our own. We can find out what Athens was like at the time of Plato or what London was like at the time of George III. Reading tells us what our own time and place are like. And it can put us inside the being of other people. The poem, the novel, the play, the memoir, the autobiography or biography, the philosophical treatise, the essay—almost any form of writing—can do this. Characteristically, it is the job of poetry, fiction, and drama—imaginative literature—to draw us fully into the flow of the experience of others. But in so far as our imagination, or the imagination of the writer, works on the material, any form of writing can do this. We feel that we know Macbeth or Becky Sharp better than we know our next-door neighbor, and Socrates or George Washington better than we know Calvin Coolidge. Writers have made this possible for us, Shakespeare, Thackeray, Plato, and the historians of the American Revolution.

Reading gets us out of our own time and place, out of ourselves, but it can in the end return us to ourselves and help us to define ourselves. It places us in relation to human history and human effort. It locates us on a map, as it were, of human experience, and sets up points of reference by which we can inspect ourselves. Reading ends by giving us ourselves as material for thinking.

It also gives us our own immediate world. We thought that we had that already, the home and family, the daily occupations, the familiar street, but when we come back to that world from our reading we find that it has a new look, a deeper interest, and a brighter gloss. After Sinclair Lewis's *Main Street,* Edgar Lee Masters' *Spoon River Anthology,* Thomas Wolfe's *Look Homeward, Angel,* or Sherwood Anderson's *Winesburg, Ohio,* the American small town never looks the same. After Thoreau's *Walden,* the back pasture or the creek never looks the same. Or after Charles A. Beard's *The Making of the American Constitution,* the report in the morning paper about the latest action of Congress does not look the same. Reading gives us our immediate world, because it gives us a new way of looking at that world. We can see new material in it.

Reading can help us to express our thoughts. Every selection or example in this book shows us, by its success or failure, something about the process of getting our meaning into words. With this topic, however, we return to our first topic—and also to a topic discussed on page 499, the inseparability of "form" and "content." For the way of thinking and the way of saying meet at one level and become the same thing. Can we say that we have thought something through until we have the words for it? In a kind of rough-and-ready way, we do distinguish between our idea and the words we put it into, and the distinction is useful, just as, in reading, the attempt to put the writer's idea into our own words is a useful check on our understanding. But words are the instrument of thought and there are no two ways of saying exactly the same thing. The difference may be slight in a given case, so slight that it doesn't matter, but the principle does matter. When we read we are constantly being affected by the slight qualifications of meaning and these slight qualifications are in the end of enormous importance.

When we write, if we are writing conscientiously, we keep trying to locate the right word or phrase. The thing doesn't "feel" right to us as it stands. We don't know exactly how we want to put it (in other words, we don't quite have our idea), but we are dissatisfied and keep fumbling for the right expression. We may even try to phrase to ourselves the grounds of our dissatisfaction—using words to diagnose our bad use of words—and this may help us. But we do not have the right expression until we have it, and we may have to get it by a process of trial and error, checking each try by our "feel," our hunch, continually asking ourselves the question: "Is this really what I want to say?" Sometimes we have to arrive at the right expression by some such process of elimination. For instance, when asked how he managed to get the right word, the poet A. E. Housman replied that he didn't bother so much about getting the right word; he bothered about getting rid of the wrong one.

Is there some sort of a system for reading which will help the student? There is no foolproof system. For one thing, different kinds of writing may call for different systems of reading. What may work for fiction may not, and probably will not, work for writing that is primarily expository. Moreover, a system which works for one person may not work for another. In the end the student may have to develop his own system. But any system must take into account such questions as these:

1. What is the material?
2. What understanding do I already have of such material? That is, do I have any basis for comparison and criticism?
3. What is the author's motivation? Is he trying to inform me, convince me, persuade me, or make me participate in a total, imaginative experience—the experience of a novel, say, or of a poem or play?
4. What is the author's basic idea or theme?
5. How is this idea developed in the structure of the work? In other words, what is the author's method of thinking?
6. What are the tone and style of the work? Do I understand the intention and the effect of the language as used in his work?
7. What enlightenment does the work give me? New facts? New ideas? New methods of thought? New sense of character? Deeper awareness of human experience?

Number 1 is the easiest question. The book, or whatever it is, is about something. The material (as opposed to the author's interpretation of that material—the idea or theme) may be tribal life in Polynesia, co-operative marketing, the theory of relativity, the program of the Republican Party, socialism, the nature of the good. It is fairly easy to identify the material—the "raw material"—the author worked with. Number 2 also seems easy, but it is sometimes harder than it looks. To answer these questions, the reader must look honestly into his own knowledge. It is easy to delude oneself. A person hears about something and in the end assumes that he knows something about it. But he merely has the words, and perhaps has one accidental or arbitrary interpretation. He must ask: What do I know about Polynesia? What do I know about the ways in which the good has been conceived? What are some of the problems involved in defining it? Certainly, we want to read about subjects we do not know about, and for any subject there must always be the first acquaintance. We have to start somewhere. The point is simply this: the reader must try to know where he stands, what is his own background and equipment for dealing with a subject.

Number 3 seems relatively easy, and usually is. Often an author will state quite flatly what he intends to do—to inform the reader about tribal life in Polynesia, to persuade the reader to vote the Republican ticket. But all cases are not so simple. Sometimes there are concealed motives. For instance, what seems to be a piece of history may actually be written from a point of view that would imply your adopting some attitude or line of action, here and now. The life of Abraham Lincoln might work as an appeal to support the Republican Party in the next election, or the life of George Washington might work as an argument against political co-operation with Great Britain. In both of these examples, the apparent motive would be to inform but the real motive would be to convince or persuade. Try to see whether the author has something up his sleeve.

When we deal with fiction, poetry, or drama—the kinds of writing which are art forms—the question of the author's motivation becomes even more complicated. In one sense such kinds of writing are primarily for our enjoyment. That is their distinguishing characteristic. But a great deal hinges on the word *enjoyment* here. We recognize immediately some difference between the kind of enjoyment found in a who-dun-it and that found in Shakespeare's *Romeo and Juliet*. The who-dun-it gives us the pleasure of the puzzle, the excitement of action. That is all the author commits himself to provide. *Romeo and Juliet* gives us the pleasure of a fuller acquaintance with life, a sense that experience can be rich and meaningful, a deeper understanding of human motives and problems (including our own). This does not mean that the thrill of suspense and the excitement of action are lacking, for those qualities may be present in serious literature, but it does mean that those qualities are not present for their own sakes but are part of a larger intention. The who-dun-it gives us mere entertainment. When we finish reading it we are through with it. *Romeo and Juliet* gives us artistic enjoyment, and we are never through with it. We can come back to it over and over again and find fuller significance in it and renewed enjoyment.

This is not the occasion to try to analyze the elements involved in the enjoyment of literature. But we can say here that it is a mistake to think of such enjoyment as something cut off from our other interests in the world. It involves those other interests, makes use of them, and returns us to them with more insight. On the practical side, a novel, for instance, may give us certain facts about the life and background presented, certain information about social conditions and psychology, ideas on a number of subjects. Such things have their own interest without relation to the novel in which they appear. Such things, nevertheless, are the material of fiction, and, as material, can be judged on their own merits. The picture of a social situation may be false or the ideas involved may be trivial. Or a novel which is sound in such matters may still be a very poor novel. It may not capture the sense of life in motion, the pattern of human beings acting and reacting on each other. It might not appeal to the imagination. But sound facts, true information, just and adequate pictures of the social situation are important in a work of art, even if their presence does not insure the goodness of the work as art. For our experience of a work of art is not cut off from our other and more general interests: The experience of a work of art stems from these interests.

In regard to question 4, sometimes an author will state very explicitly his main idea, or theme. This idea is to be distinguished sharply from the mere material. It is what the author *thinks about* the material, his interpretation of it, the line of action that he proposes be taken in regard to it. But sometimes he is not explicit. The reader must arrive at it by the course of the discussion. Furthermore, even if an author does state the idea, it is sometimes a good thing for the reader to put it into his own words, to state it as it would appear to him, and to try to see how it might apply to other instances and situations than those used by the author. The whole point here is for the reader to be sure that he really has the idea in its fundamental significance and in its implications.

The business of stating the theme of one of the literary art forms ordinarily is much more difficult than that of stating the theme of a piece of exposition or argument. To do this well requires a good deal of experience in reading poetry, drama, or fiction, and this is no place for such a special study. But when we read such works we can ask ourselves questions such as these: What does the author think is bad or good in human conduct? What does he think constitutes success or failure? What does he think about the relation between the individual and the group he lives with? Do his characters seem to be responsible for their own lives or do they seem to be the victims of outside forces? Is the general effect of his work brisk, humorous, satirical, serious, sad, tragic? An attempt to answer such questions may provide us with the material from which we can phrase the statement of the theme of a novel. We want, in the end, to get a statement which will indicate the author's basic view of the world, his set of values, and how they work out in human experience. In other words, we must ask: What is the essential meaning, the significance, of the novel?

Once we get such a statement framed, we shall probably consider it very poor and bare compared to, for instance, the novel itself. And the better the novel, the poorer and barer the statement of theme will appear. The theme is not the novel, the poem, or the play. The novel, poem, or play is the vital working out of the theme in its complexities of experience. If the work of art is good, it will give us the feeling of meaning in experience, and will return us, filled with that sense, to our own living.

When we think we have some grasp of the theme of the work in hand, we should try to answer question 5, to see in some detail how the theme is developed in the structure of that work. How does one idea lead to another, what is the handling of explanation or argument? Why are things put in this particular order? Do illustrations really illustrate the point intended by the author? Is the work consistent, or does it contain self-contradictions? Are the author's conclusions the only conclusions which could be derived from the evidence he presents? Questions such as these—and the student can frame others of the same sort—will give some notion of the structure of the whole.

By a parallel process we can investigate the structure of the play, poem, or piece of fiction. Poetry raises many special considerations; fiction is a little easier to handle. We can ask, for example, about the logic of the plot. Does one situation or event really lead to the next? Do the motives of the characters adequately account for the behavior of the characters? What idea does a character or event seem to embody? How do the different ideas relate to each other? How do they lead us to the theme?

As for question 6, we seem to come to this late in the day. How do we get anything from a piece of writing if we do not really understand the language? But there are degrees of understanding. After we think we have understood well enough to get the main drift—to state, for instance, the theme and to work out something of the structure of the whole composition—we can return to a closer inspection of the language itself. Upon this inspection we may find that we had not really understood many things. We may have even missed the basic notion of the whole work. So we may have to revise our answers to earlier questions.

When we read we are constantly being affected, whether we know it or not, by the slight qualifications of meaning in the language, and these slight shadings are in the end of enormous importance. Attention to such matters in our reading leads us to a skill in our own use of language. What questions can we ask ourselves to sharpen our own sensitivity to language?

For one thing, we can ask as a general question of any phrase or passage that seems interesting or important: Why is it this way and no other? The student can try to state to himself the exact significance of a word or phrase as it appears in the particular context. He can ask himself how this may differ from other uses which he has encountered. He might try to imagine what other words the writer may have originally used and discarded. Why would he have discarded them? Was the original version inaccurate, that is, was its dictionary content wrong in some degree for the purpose in hand? Was it vague, so that the reader couldn't be sure of any particular meaning? Was it ambiguous, so that the reader had a choice of different meanings and could not decide between them? Was the tone inappropriate to the occasion, or inconsistent with the rest of the composition? The student ought to try to define the tone of the whole composition and see how individual items, words, phrases, or images, contribute to this tone.

But we should never forget that we cannot deal with any part of a piece of writing in isolation. Words modify sentences, paragraphs modify other paragraphs. As readers, we are dealing with an elaborate tissue of interrelations, and the whole point of our effort is to understand this fact in a practical way. And a practical way, as opposed to a theoretical way, is the way of recognition and use. To gain this practical understanding the student will find theorizing helpful. We theorize when we try to state why a thing works the way it does, and why it succeeds or fails. But the end of your effort is not to say why. It is to appreciate and do.

The answer to the last question, number 7, really summarizes all the other answers. But it does more. It puts what the student has gained from the present work into the context of what he has gained from all his past reading and experience. It may be that he has gained nothing—for several possible reasons. The work may be bad or trivial in itself. Or the work may be good in itself, but be a thing which is too elementary for the student's present stage of maturity. Or the student may simply not be prepared to profit from the work; his background may not qualify him to grasp it. Or it may be that the student simply hasn't given enough time and effort to it. But if you discover that you have failed to gain anything from something you have read, try honestly to understand why.

The questions have been numbered, one to seven, but this does not mean that there is any order of importance here. All are important, and if you as reader cannot answer one, you probably cannot answer others. They are all interrelated, and in the end have to do with the unit which is the work. As there is no order of importance here, so there is no necessary order in which the questions should be considered. With one reservation: perhaps numbers 1 and 2 should always be first and second, and number 7 last. But the others may have to be considered in different orders at different times. Occasionally, for instance, the reader might have to work hard at the language before he could get at the theme and organization. Or he might find the reverse true. Fumble with the thing until you find a key. If one approach fails, try another. The random touch may spring the secret latch. Or long after, when you have decided that you cannot come to grips with the thing, its significance will suddenly dawn upon you.

There is one more general remark of great importance. This has to do with the speed and amount of reading. The superstition is current, particularly in schools and colleges, that speed and amount of reading are valuable in themselves. But do not believe a word of it.

It is true that there is some correlation between speed and expertness in reading. And there is some correlation between a person's intellectual resources and the amount of reading he has done. But more important than speed or amount is the quality of the reading itself. If one does not read thoughtfully, he might as well not read at all. Even if the reader amasses information from his reading, this is still true, because information without thought is dead lumber. Only thought can erect that lumber into a useful structure.

Different kinds of reading demand different speeds, and the right speed for you is the speed that allows you to get the most out of your reading. Familiar material presented in familiar patterns permits a relatively high degree of speed. A certain amount of familiar materials presented in familiar patterns comes to anyone in the course of his work. In dealing with it use what speed you can. But this kind of reading does not do the reader as much good as reading which involves unfamiliar materials presented in unfamiliar patterns. Then we have to put our minds to it and stretch our capacities. It is the hard reading—and since hard, therefore slow—that develops our own possibilities. And as a corollary to this, the amount of reading is not in itself important. A thing worth reading at all, except for mere entertainment, is probably worth reading more than once, and it is certainly worth thinking about. And it is better to read one good thing well than a dozen things in a routine, mechanical way.

If this is true for reading in general, it is especially true for the reading of poetry, fiction, and drama. There are two reasons for this. The first has to do with the handling of the material, and the second with the handling of the language. By and large, the writer of exposition or argument uses a direct method. He tries to say quite explicitly and directly what he means, to present his facts or ideas straight. This is not usually true of poetry, fiction, or drama. Or rather, what the author "means" here is different from what he means in the other type of writing. Here he is trying to capture the quality of experience, the flow of event, the colors, forms, and smells of the physical world, states of being, modes of character and motivation, as well as to give facts or ideas. Facts and ideas, as we have said, are involved here; but we do not read poetry, fiction, or drama for the facts and ideas *as such*. We read them to experience imaginatively how the facts and ideas relate to the other elements—how, for instance, ideas grow out of other elements of experience and are embodied in them. This means that the language of the art forms is of primary importance, because here the language is not *about* something but *is* something. There is a kind of parallel with painting. What is the picture without line and color—the medium in which it appears? Or what is music without the organization of sound—its medium?

# Articles of Information and Observation

## THE COLORS THAT ANIMALS CAN SEE

### H. MUNRO FOX

What colors can animals see? Is the world more brightly colored or duller to animals than it is to us? To find out the answers to these questions scientists have used a method of training the animals to come to different colors, which is similar in principle to the method used in studying the sense of hearing in animals.

Let us take bees first of all, partly because more exact scientific research has been done on the color-sense of bees than of almost any other animal. It is especially interesting to know what colors bees can see because these insects visit flowers to get sweet nectar from them to make honey, and in so doing the bees incidentally carry pollen from flower to flower. On the face of it, it would seem very likely that bees are attracted to flowers by their bright colors. But possibly it is the scents that attract the bees, or perhaps it is both color and scent. So, among other things, we want to know whether bees can really see the colors of flowers, and if so, what colors they can see. Exactly how is this found out?

A table is put in a garden, and on the table a piece of blue cardboard is placed, on which there is a watch-glass containing a drop of syrup. After a short while bees come to the syrup and suck up some of it. The bees then fly to their hive and give the syrup to other bees in the hive to make honey. Then they return to the

THE COLORS THAT ANIMALS CAN SEE: From *The Personality of Animals* by H. Munro Fox. Reprinted by permission of the author and Penguin Books, Ltd.

feeding-place which they have discovered. We let the bees go on doing this for a while, after which we take away the blue cardboard with the syrup on it. Instead of this card we now put on the table a blue card on the left side of the first feeding-place, and a red card to the right of the first feeding-place. These new cards have no syrup on them but only an empty watch-glass lying on each. Thus, the blue card is on the left, the red card on the right, and there is nothing where the first blue feeding-card used to be. After we have arranged these new cards, we have not long to wait. Very soon bees arrive again, and it can be seen that they fly straight on to the blue card; none go to the red card.

This behavior of the bees seems to indicate two things. The first is that the bees remember that blue means syrup and so they fly to the blue. Since they did not go to the place on the table where the syrup used to be, but flew to the blue card which had been placed on the left, it really was the blue card that attracted them, not the place where the syrup had previously been. We have trained the bees to come to the blue card. And the second thing our experiment seems to mean is that bees can tell blue from red.

But can they? This is not yet quite certain. The reason for our doubt is as follows. It is well known that there are a few people in the world, very few, who cannot see colors at all. These people are totally color-blind. To them all colors look like different shades of grey. They may be able to tell red from blue, because red will perhaps look darker and blue lighter in shade, but the colors are not red or blue. It might be, then, that bees are really color-blind, and that in the experiment they came to the blue card not because they saw it as blue but just because it appeared lighter in shade than the red card. Perhaps they had really been trained to come not to blue, but to the lighter of two shades. We can find out quite simply if this is so by another training experiment.

On our table in the garden we put a blue card, and all around this blue card we put a number of different grey cards. These grey cards are of all possible shades of grey, from the extremes of white to black. On each card a watch-glass is placed. The watch-glass on the blue card has some syrup in it; all the others are empty. After a short time bees find the syrup as before, and they come for it again and again. Then, after some hours, we take away the watch-glass of syrup which was on the blue card and put an empty one in its place. Now what do the bees do? They still go straight to the blue card, although there is no syrup there. They do not go to any of the grey cards, in spite of the fact that one of the grey cards is of exactly the same brightness as the blue card. Thus the bees do not mistake any shade of grey for blue. In this way we have proved that they really do see blue as a color.

We can find out in just the same way what other colors bees can see. It turns out that bees see various colors, but these insects differ from us as regards their color-sense in two very interesting ways. Suppose we train bees to come to a red card, and having done so we put the red card on the table in the garden among the set of different grey cards. This time we find that the bees mistake red for dark grey or black. They cannot distinguish between them. Thus it appears that red is not a color at all for bees; for them it is just dark grey or black. In reality further experiments have shown that bees can see red as a color but only when it is very brilliantly illuminated: They are relatively insensitive to red.

That is one strange fact: here is the other. A rainbow is red on one edge, violet on the other. Outside the violet of the rainbow there is another color which we cannot see at all. The color beyond the violet, invisible to us, is called the ultra-violet. Although invisible, we know that the ultra-violet is there because it affects a photographic plate. Now, although we are unable to see ultra-violet light, bees can do so; for them ultra-violet is a color. Thus bees see a color which we cannot even imagine. This has been found out by training bees to come for syrup to various different parts of a spectrum, or artificial rainbow, thrown by a quartz prism on a table in a dark room. In such an experiment the insects can be taught to fly to the ultra-violet, which for us is just darkness.

We will leave the bees now and turn to birds. Cocks have striking colors in their plumage—striking to us, at any rate—while hens only possess dull tints. But can hens see the colors of the cock as we can see them? Can the peahen, for instance, see the wonderful colors of the peacock? To answer this question we must know what colors a bird can actually see. This has been studied in the following manner. A lamp and prism are set up to throw a spectrum of rainbow colors on the floor of a dark room. On the different colors of the spectrum grains of corn are sprinkled, and then a hen is brought in. She pecks at the grains of corn and gobbles up all she can see. After a time we remove the hen and take note of what grains are left untouched by her. We find that the hen has eaten nearly all the grains which were in the red, in the yellow, and in the green regions of the spectrum. We find that she has taken a few of the grains in the blue light, but the hen leaves the grains in the violet untouched. This means that she cannot see the grains which are in the violet light, and she is not able to see those in the blue very well either, for she did not pick up many of them. So violet is just like black to the hen, and blue is not a very bright color.

This has been confirmed with homing pigeons on which colored spectacles were fitted; with red and yellow specs the birds flew home normally, but with green, and especially blue, they were unable to do so. A human being could see clearly through the blue celluloid of which the spectacles were made, but evidently blue is like a black-out to the bird, and it is well known that homing pigeons cannot find their way in dim light or darkness.

Other birds are like this, too, which seems strange at first, because some birds are themselves blue. The kingfisher, for instance, is blue. Are we to conclude that the kingfisher is unable to see the beautiful color of its mate? This does not follow; the kingfisher can probably see his mate's blue plumage, for our experiments do not show that birds are unable to see blue at all. Birds just do not see this color very well; for them to see blue, the blue must be intense. And indeed the color of the kingfisher is very bright. Yet it is not all birds that have such difficulty in seeing blue; owls, on the contrary, are more sensitive than we ourselves to the blue end of the spectrum.

And what can dogs see? The answer to this question is disappointing: dogs apparently see no colors. The answer is disappointing because many owners of dogs will naturally be sorry that their dogs cannot see colors which to them are beautiful. But then, they may reflect that dogs have an extraordinarily keen sense of smell. The dogs' world is rich in enjoyable smells, even if it may be colorless.

How do we know if dogs are color-blind? This has been tested in the same way that it has been discovered what dogs can hear. The attempt has been made to train dogs to salivate when they are shown certain different colors, just as they were trained so that their mouths watered when definite musical notes were sounded. Such experiments have turned out failures; it has been found impossible to make dogs distinguish colors from one another as signals for their dinner. This question requires further testing with other techniques, but so far as the available scientific evidence goes, dogs seem to be color-blind. Many dog-owners will disagree with this, being convinced that their dogs know, for instance, the color of a dress. But the evidence given for this has never been sufficiently rigid for a scientist, who is not certain that the dog did not really respond to some other clue or sign than the color—to a smell, for instance, or to the particular behavior of the wearer of the dress.

Experiments have been made, too, to test the color-sense of cats; although these experiments may not yet be conclusive, they have indicated, so far, that cats are color-blind. Different cats were trained to come for their food in response to signals of each of six different colors. But the cats always confused their particular color with one of a number of shades of grey, when these were offered at the same time as the color.

Monkeys, on the other hand, are able to distinguish colors. They have been trained successfully to go for their meal to a cupboard, the door of which was painted in a certain color, and to ignore other available cupboards with differently colored doors, in which there was no food. Apart from monkeys and apes, however, most mammals seem to be color-blind, at any rate those which have been scientifically tested. Even bulls have been shown not to see red as a color. In spite of popular belief they are not excited by red, and they cannot distinguish red from dark grey. No doubt any bright waving cloth excites a high-spirited bull.

Color-blindness in mammals, other than monkeys, is comprehensible when one considers the lives of the animals in a wild state. For nearly all wild mammals are nocturnal or crepuscular. Wolves and lions hunt mostly at night, while antelopes and wild cattle graze at night, or in the evening when colors are dim. But monkeys, in the forests where they live, are awake and about in the daytime, and there are abundant colors for them to see in the bright tropical light.

Moreover, the color-blindness of mammals other than monkeys accords with the fact that the animals themselves are more or less dull colored; their coats are brown or yellow, black or white. Only in monkeys are greens, bright reds, and blues found. These are colors which recall the brilliant tints of birds and of fish, animals which also possess color-vision.

For questions and exercises, see p. 43, p. 172, p. 330, p. 531, and p. 532.

## LEARNED WORDS AND POPULAR WORDS

### JAMES B. GREENOUGH AND GEORGE L. KITTREDGE

In every cultivated language there are two great classes of words which, taken together, comprise the whole vocabulary. First, there are those words with which we become acquainted in ordinary conversation—which we learn, that is to say, from the members of our own family and from our familiar associates, and which we should know and use even if we could not read or write. They concern the common things of life, and are the stock in trade of all who speak the language. Such words may be called "popular," since they belong to the people at large and are not the exclusive possession of a limited class.

On the other hand, our language includes a multitude of words which are comparatively seldom used in ordinary conversation. Their meanings are known to every educated person, but there is little occasion to employ them at home or in the market-place. Our first acquaintance with them comes not from our mother's lips or from the talk of our schoolmates, but from books that we read, lectures that we hear, or the more formal conversation of highly educated speakers who are discussing some particular topic in a style appropriately elevated above the habitual level of everyday life. Such words are called "learned," and the distinction between them and "popular" words is of great importance to a right understanding of linguistic process.

The difference between popular and learned words may be easily seen in a few examples. We may describe a girl as "lively" or as "vivacious." In the first case, we are using a native English formation from the familiar noun *life*. In the latter, we are using a Latin derivative which has precisely the same meaning. Yet the atmosphere of the two words is quite different. No one ever got the

LEARNED WORDS AND POPULAR WORDS: From Greenough and Kittredge: *Words and Their Ways in English Speech.* Copyright, 1901 by The Macmillan Company and used with their permission.

adjective *lively* out of a book. It is a part of everybody's vocabulary. We cannot remember a time when we did not know it, and we feel sure that we learned it long before we were able to read. On the other hand, we must have passed several years of our lives before learning the word *vivacious*. We may even remember the first time that we saw it in print or heard it from some grown-up friend who was talking over our childish heads. Both *lively* and *vivacious* are good English words, but *lively* is "popular" and *vivacious* is "learned."

From the same point of view we may contrast the following pairs of synonyms: [1] *the same, identical; speech, oration; fire, conflagration; choose, select; brave, valorous; swallowing, deglutition; striking, percussion; building, edifice; shady, umbrageous; puckery, astringent; learned, erudite; secret, cryptic; destroy, annihilate; stiff, rigid; flabby, flaccid; queer, eccentric; behead, decapitate; round, circular; thin, emaciated; fat, corpulent; truthful, veracious; try, endeavor; bit, modicum; piece, fragment; sharp, acute; crazy, maniacal; king, sovereign; book, volume; lying, mendacious; beggar, mendicant; teacher, instructor; play, drama; air, atmosphere; paint, pigment.*

The terms "popular" and "learned," as applied to words, are not absolute definitions. No two persons have the same stock of words, and the same word may be "popular" in one man's vocabulary and "learned" in another's.[2] There are also different grades of "popularity"; indeed there is in reality a continuous gradation from infantile words like *mama* and *papa* to such erudite derivatives as *concatenation* and *cataclysm*. Still, the division into "learned" and "popular" is convenient and sound. Disputes may arise as to the classification of any particular word, but there can be no difference of opinion about the general principle. We must be careful, however, to avoid misconception. When we call a word "popular," we

[1] Not all the words are exact synonyms, but that is of no importance in the present discussion.

[2] It is instructive to study one's own vocabulary from this point of view, making a list of (1) those words which we feel sure we learned in childhood, (2) those which we have learned in later life, but not from books, (3) those which have entered our vocabulary from books. We shall also find it useful to consider the difference between our reading vocabulary and our speaking vocabulary.

do not mean that it is a favorite word, but simply that it belongs to the people as a whole—that is, it is everybody's word, not the possession of a limited number. When we call a word "learned" we do not mean that it is used by scholars alone, but simply that its presence in the English vocabulary is due to books and the cultivation of literature rather than to the actual needs of ordinary conversation.

Here is one of the main differences between a cultivated and an uncultivated language. Both possess a large stock of "popular" words; but the cultivated language is also rich in "learned" words, with which the ruder tongue has not provided itself simply because it has never felt the need of them.

In English it will usually be found that the so-called learned words are of foreign origin. Most of them are derived from French or Latin, and a considerable number from Greek. The reason is obvious. The development of English literature has not been isolated, but has taken place in close connection with the earnest study of foreign literatures. Thus, in the fourteenth century, when our language was assuming substantially the shape which it now bears, the literary exponent of English life and thought, Geoffrey Chaucer, the first of our great poets, was profoundly influenced by Latin literature as well as by that of France and Italy. In the sixteenth and seventeenth centuries the Greek and Latin classics were vigorously studied by almost every English writer of any consequence, and the great authors of antiquity were regarded as models, not merely of general literary form, but of expression in all its details. These foreign influences have varied much in character and intensity. But it is safe to say that there has been no time since 1350 when English writers of the highest class have not looked to Latin, French, and Italian authors for guidance and inspiration. From 1600 to the present day the direct influence of Greek literature and philosophy has also been enormous—affecting as it has the finest spirits in a peculiarly pervasive way—and its indirect influence is quite beyond calculation. Greek civilization, we should remember, has acted upon us, not merely through Greek literature and art, but also through the medium of Latin, since the Romans borrowed their higher culture from Greece.

Now certain facts in the history of our language have made it peculiarly inclined to borrow from French and Latin. The Norman

Conquest in the eleventh century made French the language of polite society in England; and, long after the contact between Norman-French and English had ceased to be of direct significance in our linguistic development, the reading and speaking of French and the study of French literature formed an important part of the education of English-speaking men and women. When literary English was in process of formation in the fourteenth and fifteenth centuries, the authors whose works determined the cultivated vocabulary were almost as familiar with French as with their mother tongue, and it was therefore natural that they should borrow a good many French words. But these same authors were also familiar with Latin, which, though called a dead language, has always been the professional dialect of ecclesiastics and a *lingua franca* for educated men. Thus the borrowing from French and from Latin went on side by side, and it is often impossible to say from which of the two languages a particular English word is taken. The practice of naturalizing French and Latin words was, then, firmly established in the fourteenth century, and when in the sixteenth century there was a great revival of Greek studies in England, the close literary relations between Greece and Rome facilitated the adoption of a considerable number of words from the Greek. Linguistic processes are cumulative: one does not stop when another begins. Hence we find all of these influences active in increasing the modern vocabulary. In particular, the language of science has looked to Greece for its terms as the language of abstract thought has drawn its nomenclature from Latin.

It would, however, be a great mistake to suppose that all our "popular" terms are of native origin and that all foreign derivatives are "learned." The younger and less cultivated members of a community are naturally inclined to imitate the speech of the older and more cultivated. Hence, as time has passed, a great number of French and Latin words, and even some that are derived from the Greek, have made themselves quite at home in ordinary conversation. Such words, whatever their origin, are as truly popular as if they had been a part of our language from the earliest period.

Examples of such popular words of foreign derivation are the following:

From French: *army, arrest, bay, card, catch, city, chase, chimney, conveyance, deceive, entry, engine, forge, hour, letter, mantle, ma-*

*son, merchant, manner, mountain, map, move, navy, prince, pen, pencil, parlor, river, rage, soldier, second, table, veil, village.*

From Latin: *accommodate, act, add, adopt, animal, anxious, applause, arbitrate, auction, agent, calculate, cancer, circus, collapse, collision, column, congress, connect, consequence, contract, contradict, correct, creation, cucumber, curve, centennial, decorate, delicate, dentist, describe, diary, diffident, different, digest, direct, discuss, divide, educate, elect, emigrant, equal, erect, expect, extra, fact, genius, genuine, graduate, gratis, horrid, imitate, item, joke, junction, junior, major, magnificent, medicine, medium, miser, obstinate, omit, pagan, pastor, pauper, pedal, pendulum, permit, picture, plague, postpone, premium, prevent, prospect, protect, quiet, recess, recipe, reduce, regular, salute, secure, series, single, species, specimen, splendid, strict, student, subscribe, subtract, suburb, suffocate, suggest, tedious, timid, urge, vaccinate, various, ventilation, veto, victor, vim, vote.*

From Greek: *anthracite, apathy, arsenic, aster, athlete, atlas, attic, barometer, biography, calomel, catarrh, catholic, catastrophe, catechism, caustic, chemist, crisis, dialogue, diphtheria, elastic, encyclopedia, hector, homeopathy, iodine, lexicon, microscope, monotonous, myth, neuralgia, panic, panorama, photograph, skeleton, strychnine, tactics, telegraph, tonic, zoölogy.*

No language can borrow extensively from foreign sources without losing a good many words of its own. Hence, if we compare the oldest form of English (Anglo-Saxon) with our modern speech, we shall discover that many words that were common in Anglo-Saxon have gone quite out of use, being replaced by their foreign equivalents. The "learned" word has driven out the "popular" word, and has thereupon, in many cases, become "popular" itself. Thus instead of A.S. *herë* we use the French word *army;* instead of *thegn* or *thēow,* the French word *servant;* instead of *sipherë* (a compound of the Anglo-Saxon word for *ship* and that for *army*), we use *navy;* instead of *micel,* we say *large;* instead of *sigë, victory;* instead of *swīthë, very;* instead of *lāf,* we say *remainder* or *remnant,* and so on.

Curiously enough, it sometimes happens that when both the native and the foreign word still have a place in our language, the latter has become the more popular, the former being relegated to the higher or poetical style. Thus it is more natural for us to say *divide* (from L. *divido*) than *cleave* (from A.S. *clēofan*); *travel* than *fare*; [3] *river* than *stream;* *castle* than *burg;* *residence* than *dwelling;* *remain* than *abide;* *expect* than *ween;* *pupil* or *scholar* than *learner;* *destruction* than *bale;* *protect* or *defend* than *shield;* *immediately* than *straightway;* *encourage* than *hearten;* *present* than *bestow;* *firm* than *steadfast;* *direct* than *forthright;* *impetuous* than *heady;* *modest* than *shamefaced;* *prince* than *atheling;* *noise* or *tumult* or *disturbance* than *din;* *people* than *folk;* [4] *prophet* than *soothsayer;* *fate* than *weird;* *lancer* than *spearman;* *I intend* than *I am minded;* *excavate* than *delve;* *resist* than *withstand;* *beautiful* than *goodly;* *gracious* than *kindly.* The very fact that the native words belong to the older stock has made them poetical; for the language of poetry is always more archaic than that of prose.

Frequently we have kept both the native and the foreign word, but in different senses, thus increasing our vocabulary to good purpose. The foreign word may be more emphatic than the native: as in *brilliant, bright; scintillate, sparkle; astonishment, wonder; a conflagration, a fire; devour, eat up; labor, work.* Or the native word may be more emphatic than the foreign as in *stench, odor; straightforward, direct; dead, deceased; murder, homicide.* Often, however, there is a wide distinction in meaning. Thus *driver* differs from *propeller; child* from *infant; history* from *tale; book* from *volume; forehead* from *front; length* from *longitude; moony* from *lunar; sunny* from *solar; nightly* from *nocturnal; churl* from *villain; wretch* from *miser; poor man* from *pauper; run across* from *occur; run into* from *incur; fight* from *debate.*

From time to time attempts have been made to oust foreign words from our vocabulary and to replace them by native words that have become either obsolete or less usual (that is to say, less popular). Whimsical theorists have even set up the principle that no word of foreign origin should be employed when a native word of the same meaning exists. In English, however, all such efforts are predestined to failure. They result, not in a simpler and more natural style, but in something unfamiliar, fantastic, and affected. Foreign words that have long been in common use are just as much English as if they had been a part of our language from the beginning. There is

---

[3] *Fare* is still common as a noun and in figurative senses.

[4] But the irregular plural *folks* is a common colloquialism.

no rational theory on which they should be shunned. It would be just as reasonable for an Englishman whose ancestors had lived in the island ever since the time of King Alfred to disown as his countrymen the descendants of a Frenchman or a German who settled there three hundred years ago. The test of the learned or the popular character of a word is not its etymology, but the facts relating to its habitual employment by plain speakers. Nor is there any principle on which, of two expressions, that which is popular should be preferred to that which is learned or less familiar. The sole criterion of choice consists in the appropriateness of one's language to the subject or the occasion. It would be ridiculous to address a crowd of soldiers in the same language that one would employ in a council of war. It would be no less ridiculous to harangue an assembly of generals as if they were a regiment on the eve of battle. The reaction against the excessive Latinization of English is a wholesome tendency, but it becomes a mere "fad" when it is carried out in a doctrinaire manner. As Chaucer declares:

> Ek Plato seith, whoso that can him rede,
> "The wordes mot be cosin to the dede."

Every educated person has at least two ways of speaking his mother tongue. The first is that which he employs in his family, among his familiar friends, and on ordinary occasions. The second is that which he uses in discoursing on more complicated subjects and in addressing persons with whom he is less intimately acquainted. It is, in short, the language which he employs when he is "on his dignity," as he puts on evening dress when he is going to dine. The difference between these two forms of language consists, in great measure, in a difference of vocabulary. The basis of familiar words must be the same in both, but the vocabulary appropriate to the more formal occasion will include many terms which would be stilted or affected in ordinary talk. There is also considerable difference between familiar and dignified language in the manner of utterance. Contrast the rapid utterance of our everyday dialect, full of contractions and clipped forms, with the more distinct enunciation of the pulpit or the platform. Thus, in conservation, we habitually employ such contractions as *I'll, don't, won't, it's, we'd, he'd,* and the like, which we should never use in public

speaking, unless of set purpose, to give a markedly colloquial tinge
to what we have to say.

For questions and exercises, see p. 43, p. 367, and p. 387.

# THE METHOD OF SCIENTIFIC INVESTIGATION

### T. H. HUXLEY

The method of scientific investigation is nothing but the expression of the necessary mode of working of the human mind. It is
simply the mode at which all phenomena are reasoned about, rendered precise and exact. There is no more difference, but there is
just the same kind of difference, between the mental operations
of a man of science and those of an ordinary person, as there is
between the operations and methods of a baker or of a butcher
weighing out his goods in common scales, and the operations of a
chemist in performing a difficult and complex analysis by means
of his balance and finely graduated weights. It is not that the action
of the scales in the one case, and the balance in the other, differ
in the principles of their construction or manner of working; but
the beam of one is set on an infinitely finer axis than the other,
and of course turns by the addition of a much smaller weight.

You will understand this better, perhaps, if I give you some
familiar example. You have all heard it repeated, I dare say, that
men of science work by means of induction and deduction, and
that by the help of these operations, they, in a sort of sense, wring
from Nature certain other things, which are called natural laws,
and causes, and that out of these, by some cunning skill of their
own, they build up hypotheses and theories. And it is imagined by
many, that the operations of the common mind can be by no means
compared with these processes, and that they have to be acquired
by a sort of special apprenticeship to the craft. To hear all these
large words, you would think that the mind of a man of science
must be constituted differently from that of his fellow men; but if
you will not be frightened by terms, you will discover that you are
quite wrong, and that all these terrible apparatus are being used by
yourselves every day and every hour of your lives.

THE METHOD OF SCIENTIFIC INVESTIGATION: From *Collected Essays*, "Darwin-
iana," by T. H. Huxley.

There is a well-known incident in one of Molière's plays, where the author makes the hero express unbounded delight on being told that he had been talking prose during the whole of his life. In the same way, I trust that you will take comfort, and be delighted with yourselves, on the discovery that you have been acting on the principles of inductive and deductive philosophy during the same period. Probably there is not one here who has not in the course of the day had occasion to set in motion a complex train of reasoning, of the very same kind, though differing of course in degree, as that which a scientific man goes through in tracing the causes of natural phenomena.

A very trivial circumstance will serve to exemplify this. Suppose you go into a fruiterer's shop, wanting an apple—you take up one, and on biting it, you find it is sour; you look at it, and see that it is hard and green. You take up another one and that too is hard, green, and sour. The shopman offers you a third; but, before biting it, you examine it, and find that it is hard and green, and you immediately say that you will not have it, as it must be sour, like those that you have already tried.

Nothing can be more simple than that, you think; but if you will take the trouble to analyse and trace out into its logical elements what has been done by the mind, you will be greatly surprised. In the first place you have performed the operation of induction. You found that, in two experiences, hardness and greenness in apples went together with sourness. It was so in the first case, and it was confirmed by the second. True, it is a very small basis, but still it is enough to make an induction from; you generalise the facts, and you expect to find sourness in apples where you get hardness and greenness. You found upon that a general law that all hard and green apples are sour; and that, so far as it goes, is a perfect induction. Well, having got your natural law in this way, when you are offered another apple which you find is hard and green, you say, "All hard and green apples are sour; this apple is hard and green, therefore this apple is sour." That train of reasoning is what logicians call a syllogism, and has all its various parts and terms—its major premiss, its minor premiss, and its conclusion. And, by the help of further reasoning, which, if drawn out, would have to be exhibited in two or three other syllogisms, you arrive at your final determination, "I will not have that apple." So that, you see, you have, in the first place, established a law by induction, and upon that you have founded a deduction, and reasoned out the special particular case. Well now, suppose, having got your conclusion of the law, that at some time afterwards, you are discussing the qualities of apples with a friend: you will say to him, "It is a very curious thing, but I find that all hard and green apples are sour!" Your friend says to you, "But how do you know that?" You at once reply, "Oh, because I have tried them over and over again, and have always found them to be so." Well, if we were talking science instead of common sense, we should call that an experimental verification. And, if still opposed, you go further, and say, "I have heard from the people in Somersetshire and Devonshire, where a large number of apples are grown, that they have observed the same thing. It is also found to be the case in Normandy, and in North America. In short, I find it to be the universal experience of mankind wherever attention has been directed to the subject." Whereupon, your friend, unless he is a very unreasonable man, agrees with you, and is convinced that you are quite right in the conclusion you have drawn. He believes, although perhaps he does not know he believes it, that the more extensive verifications are—that the more frequently experiments have been made, and results of the same kind arrived at—that the more varied the conditions under which the same results are attained, the more certain is the ultimate conclusion, and he disputes the question no further. He sees that the experiment has been tried under all sorts of conditions, as to time, place, and people, with the same result; and he says with you, therefore, that the law you have laid down must be a good one, and he must believe it.

In science we do the same thing—the philosopher exercises precisely the same faculties, though in a much more delicate manner. In scientific inquiry it becomes a matter of duty to expose a supposed law to every possible kind of verification, and to take care, moreover, that this is done intentionally, and not left to a mere accident, as in the case of the apples. And in science, as in common life, our confidence in a law is in exact proportion to the absence of variation in the result of our experimental verifications. For instance, if you let go your grasp of an article you may have in your hand, it will immediately fall to the ground. That is a very common verification of one of the best established laws of nature—that of gravitation. The method by which men of science establish the existence of that law is exactly the same as that by which we have established the trivial proposition about the sourness of hard and green apples. But we believe it in such an extensive, thorough, and unhesitating manner because the universal experience of mankind verifies it, and we can verify it ourselves at any time; and that is the strongest possible foundation on which any natural law can rest.

So much, then, by way of proof that the method of establishing laws in science is exactly the same as that pursued in common life. Let us now turn to another matter (though really it is but another phase of the same question), and that is, the method by which, from the relations of certain phenomena, we prove that some stand in the position of causes towards the others.

I want to put the case clearly before you, and I will therefore show you what I mean by another familiar example. I will suppose that one of you, on coming down in the morning to the parlour of your house, finds that a tea-pot and some spoons which had been left in the room on the previous evening are gone—the window is open, and you observe the mark of a dirty hand on the window-frame, and perhaps, in addition to that, you notice the impress of a hob-nailed shoe on the gravel outside. All these phenomena have struck your attention instantly, and before two seconds have passed you say, "Oh, somebody has broken open the window, entered the room, and run off with the spoons and the tea-pot!" That speech is out of your mouth in a moment. And you will probably add, "I know there has; I am quite sure of it!" You mean to say exactly what you know; but in reality you are giving expression to what is, in all essential particulars, an hypothesis. You do not *know* it at all; it is nothing but an hypothesis rapidly framed in your own mind. And it is an hypothesis founded on a long train of inductions and deductions.

What are those inductions and deductions, and how have you got at this hypothesis? You have observed in the first place, that the window is open; but by a train of reasoning involving many inductions and deductions, you have probably arrived long before at the general law—and a very good one it is—that windows do not open of themselves; and you therefore conclude that something has opened the window. A second general law that you have arrived at in the same way is, that tea-pots and spoons do not go out of a window spontaneously, and you are satisfied that, as they are not now where you left them, they have been removed. In the third place, you look at the marks on the window-sill, and the shoe-marks outside, and you say that in all previous experience the former kind of mark has never been produced by anything else but the hand of a human being; and the same experience shows that no other animal but man at present wears shoes with hob-nails in them such as would produce the marks in the gravel. I do not know, even if we could discover any of those "missing links" that are talked about, that they would help us to any other conclusion! At any rate the law which states our present experience is strong enough for my present purpose. You next reach the conclusion that, as these kinds of marks have not been left by any other animal than man, or are liable to be formed in any other way than by a man's hand and shoe, the marks in question have been formed by a man in that way. You have, further, a general law, founded on observation and experience, and that, too, is I am sorry to say, a very universal and unimpeachable one—that some men are thieves; and you assume at once from all these premises—and that is what constitutes your hypothesis—that the man who made the marks outside and on the window-sill, opened the window, got into the room, and stole your tea-pot and spoons. You have now arrived at a *vera causa*—you have assumed a cause which, it is plain, is competent to produce all the phenomena you have observed. You can explain all these phenomena only by the hypothesis of a thief. But that is a hypothetical conclusion, of the justice of which you have no absolute proof at all; it is only rendered highly probable by a series of inductive and deductive reasonings.

I suppose your first action, assuming that you are a man of ordinary common sense, and that you have established this hypothesis to your own satisfaction, will very likely be to go off for the police, and set them on the track of the burglar, with the view to the recovery of your property. But just as you are starting with this object, some person comes in, and on learning what you are about, says, "My good friend, you are going on a great deal too fast. How do you know that the man who really made the marks took the spoons? It might have been a monkey that took them, and the man may have merely looked in afterwards." You would probably reply, "Well, that is all very well, but you see it is contrary to all experience of the way tea-pots and spoons are abstracted; so that, at any rate, your hypothesis is less probable than mine." While you are talking the thing over in this way, another friend arrives, one of the good kind of people that I was talking of a little while ago. And he might say, "Oh, my dear sir, you are certainly going on a great deal too fast. You are most presumptuous. You admit that all these occurrences took place when you were fast asleep, at a time when you could not possibly have known anything about what was taking place. How do you know that the laws of Nature are not suspended during the night? It may be that there has been some kind of supernatural interference in this case." In point of fact, he declares that your hypothesis is one of which you cannot at all demonstrate the truth, and that you are by no means sure that the laws of Nature are the same when you are asleep as when you are awake.

Well, now, you cannot at the moment answer that kind of reasoning. You feel that your worthy friend has you somewhat at a disadvantage. You will feel perfectly convinced in your own mind, however, that you are quite right, and you say to him, "My good friend, I can only be guided by the natural probabilities of the case, and if you will be kind enough to stand aside and permit me to pass, I will go and fetch the police." Well, we will suppose that your journey is successful, and that by good luck you meet with a policeman; that eventually the burglar is found with your property on his person, and the marks correspond to his hand and to his boots. Probably any jury would consider those facts a very good experimental verification of your hypothesis, touching the cause of the abnormal phenomena observed in your parlour, and would act accordingly.

Now, in this supposititious case, I have taken phenomena of a very common kind, in order that you might see what are the different steps in an ordinary process of reasoning, if you will only take the trouble to analyse it carefully. All the operations I have described, you will see, are involved in the mind of any man of sense in leading him to a conclusion as to the course he should take in order to make good a robbery and punish the offender. I say that you are led, in that case, to your conclusion by exactly the same train of reasoning as that which a man of science pursues when he is endeavouring to discover the origin and laws of the most occult phenomena. The process is, and always must be, the same; and precisely the same mode of reasoning was employed by Newton and Laplace in their endeavours to discover and define the causes of the movements of the heavenly bodies, as you, with your own common sense, would employ to detect a burglar. The only difference is, that the nature of the inquiry being more abstruse, every step has to be most carefully watched, so that there may not be a single crack or flaw in your hypothesis. A flaw or crack in many of the hypotheses of daily life may be of little or no moment as affecting the general correctness of the conclusions at which we may arrive; but, in a scientific inquiry, a fallacy, great or small, is always of importance, and is sure to be in the long run constantly productive of mischievous if not fatal results.

Do not allow yourselves to be misled by the common notion that an hypothesis is untrustworthy simply because it is an hypothesis. It is often urged, in respect to some scientific conclusion, that, after all, it is only an hypothesis. But what more have we to guide us in nine-tenths of the most important affairs of daily life than hypotheses, and often very ill-based ones? So that in science, where the evidence of an hypothesis is subjected to the most rigid examination, we may rightly pursue the same course. You may have hypotheses, and hypotheses. A man may say, if he likes, that the moon is made of green cheese: that is an hypothesis. But another man, who has devoted a great deal of time and attention to the subject, and availed himself of the most powerful telescopes and the results of the observations of others, declares that in his opinion it is probably composed of materials very similar to those of which our own earth is made up: and that is also only an hypothesis. But I need not tell you that there is an enormous difference in the value of the two hypotheses. That one which is based on sound scientific knowledge is sure to have a corresponding value; and that which is a mere hasty random guess is likely to have but little value. Every great step in our progress in discovering causes has been made in exactly the same way as that which I have detailed to you. A person observing the occurrence of certain facts and phenomena asks, naturally enough, what process, what kind of operation known to occur in Nature, applied to the particular case, will unravel and explain the mystery? Hence you have the scientific hypothesis; and its value will be proportionate to the care and completeness with which its basis had been tested and verified. It is in these matters as in the commonest affairs of practical life; the guess of the fool will be folly, while the guess of the wise man will contain wisdom. In all cases, you see that the value of the result depends on the patience and faithfulness with which the investigator applies to his hypothesis every possible kind of verification.

Does Huxley use many abstract words? (See p. 374.) How has he managed, with such a subject, to avoid using a heavily abstract diction? For further questions and exercises, see p. 134 and p. 448.

## HOW TO DETECT PROPAGANDA

### INSTITUTE FOR PROPAGANDA ANALYSIS

If American citizens are to have clear understanding of present-day conditions and what to do about them, they must be able to recognize propaganda, to analyze it, and to appraise it.

But what is propaganda?

As generally understood, *propaganda is expression of opinion or action by individuals or groups deliberately designed to influence opinions or actions of other individuals or groups with reference to predetermined ends.* Thus propaganda differs from scientific analysis. The propagandist is trying to "put something across," good or bad, whereas the scientist is trying to discover truth and fact. Often the propagandist does not want careful scrutiny and criticism; he wants to bring about a specific action. Because the action may be socially beneficial or socially harmful to millions of people, it is necessary to focus upon the propagandist and his activities the searchlight of scientific scrutiny. Socially desirable propaganda will not suffer from such examination, but the opposite type will be detected and revealed for what it is.

We are fooled by propaganda chiefly because we don't recognize it when we see it. It may be fun to be fooled but, as the cigarette ads used to say, it is more fun to know. We can more easily recognize propaganda when we see it if we are familiar with the seven common propaganda devices. These are:

1. The Name Calling Device
2. The Glittering Generalities Device

HOW TO DETECT PROPAGANDA: From *Propaganda Analysis,* November 1937. Copyright 1937, by The Institute for Propaganda Analysis, Inc.  •

3. The Transfer Device
4. The Testimonial Device
5. The Plain Folks Device
6. The Card Stacking Device
7. The Band Wagon Device

Why are we fooled by these devices? Because they appeal to our emotions rather than to our reason. They make us believe and do something we would not believe or do if we thought about it calmly, dispassionately. In examining these devices, note that they work most effectively at those times when we are too lazy to think for ourselves; also, they tie into emotions which sway us to be "for" or "against" nations, races, religions, ideals, economic and political policies and practices, and so on through automobiles, cigarettes, radios, toothpastes, presidents, and wars. With our emotions stirred, it may be fun to be fooled by these propaganda devices, but it is more fun and infinitely more to our own interests to know how they work.

Lincoln must have had in mind citizens who could balance their emotions with intelligence when he made his remark: ". . . but you can't fool all of the people all of the time."

### NAME CALLING

"Name Calling" is a device to make us form a judgment without examining the evidence on which it should be based. Here the propagandist appeals to our hate and fear. He does this by giving "bad names" to those individuals, groups, nations, races, policies, practices, beliefs, and ideals which he would have us condemn and reject. For centuries the name "heretic" was bad. Thousands were oppressed, tortured, or put to death as heretics. Anybody who dissented from popular or group belief or practice was in danger of being called a heretic. In the light of today's knowledge, some heresies were bad and some were good. Many of the pioneers of modern science were called heretics; witness the cases of Copernicus, Galileo, Bruno. Today's bad names include: Fascist, demagogue, dictator, Red, financial oligarchy, Communist, muckraker, alien, outside agitator, economic royalist, Utopian, rabble-rouser, troublemaker, Tory, Constitution wrecker.

"Al" Smith called Roosevelt a Communist by implication when

he said in his Liberty League speech, "There can be only one capital, Washington or Moscow." When "Al" Smith was running for the presidency many called him a tool of the Pope, saying in effect, "We must choose between Washington and Rome." That implied that Mr. Smith, if elected President, would take his orders from the Pope. Likewise Mr. Justice Hugo Black has been associated with a bad name, Ku Klux Klan. In these cases some propagandists have tried to make us form judgments without examining essential evidence and implications. "Al Smith is a Catholic. He must never be President." "Roosevelt is a Red. Defeat his program." "Hugo Black is or was a Klansman. Take him out of the Supreme Court."

Use of "bad names" without presentation of their essential meaning, without all their pertinent implications, comprises perhaps the most common of all propaganda devices. Those who want to *maintain* the status quo apply bad names to those who would change it. . . . Those who want to *change* the status quo apply bad names to those who would maintain it. For example, the *Daily Worker* and the *American Guardian* apply bad names to conservative Republicans and Democrats.

### GLITTERING GENERALITIES

"Glittering Generalities" is a device by which the propagandist identifies his program with virtue by use of "virtue words." Here he appeals to our emotions of love, generosity, and brotherhood. He uses words like truth, freedom, honor, liberty, social justice, public service, the right to work, loyalty, progress, democracy, the American way, Constitution defender. These words suggest shining ideals. All persons of good will believe in these ideals. Hence the propagandist, by identifying his individual group, nation, race, policy, practice, or belief with such ideals, seeks to win us to his cause. As Name Calling is a device to make us form a judgment to *reject and condemn*, without examining the evidence, Glittering Generalities is a device to make us *accept and approve*, without examining the evidence.

For example, use of the phrases, "the right to work" and "social justice," may be a device to make us accept programs for meeting labor-capital problems, which, if we examined them critically, we would not accept at all.

In the Name Calling and Glittering Generalities devices, words are used to stir up our emotions and to befog our thinking. In one device "bad words" are used to make us mad; in the other "good words" are used to make us glad.

The propagandist is most effective in the use of these devices when his words make us create devils to fight or gods to adore. By his use of the "bad words," we personify as a "devil" some nation, race, group, individual, policy, practice, or ideal; we are made fighting mad to destroy it. By use of "good words," we personify as a godlike idol some nation, race, group, etc. Words which are "bad" to some are "good" to others, or may be made so. Thus, to some the New Deal is "a prophecy of social salvation" while to others it is "an omen of social disaster."

From consideration of names, "bad" and "good," we pass to institutions and symbols, also "bad" and "good." We see these in the next device.

### TRANSFER

"Transfer" is a device by which the propagandist carries over the authority, sanction, and prestige of something we respect and revere to something he would have us accept. For example, most of us respect and revere our church and our nation. If the propagandist succeeds in getting church or nation to approve a campaign in behalf of some program, he thereby transfers its authority, sanction, and prestige to that program. Thus we may accept something which otherwise we might reject.

In the Transfer device, symbols are constantly used. The cross represents the Christian Church. The flag represents the nation. Cartoons like Uncle Sam represent a consensus of public opinion. Those symbols stir emotions. At their very sight, with the speed of light, is aroused the whole complex of feelings we have with respect to church or nation. A cartoonist by having Uncle Sam disapprove a budget for unemployment relief would have us feel that the whole United States disapproves relief costs. By drawing an Uncle Sam who approves the same budget, the cartoonist would have us feel that the American people approve it. Thus the Transfer device is used both for and against causes and ideas.

### TESTIMONIAL

The "Testimonial" is a device to make us accept anything from a patent medicine or a cigarette to a program of national policy. In this device the propagandist makes use of testimonials. "When I feel tired, I smoke a Camel and get the grandest 'lift.'" "We believe the John L. Lewis plan of labor organization is splendid; C.I.O. should be supported." This device works in reverse also; counter-testimonials may be employed. Seldom are these used against commercial products like patent medicines and cigarettes, but they are constantly employed in social, economic, and political issues. "We believe that the John L. Lewis plan of labor organization is bad; C.I.O. should not be supported."

### PLAIN FOLKS

"Plain Folks" is a device used by politicians, labor leaders, business men, and even by ministers and educators to win our confidence by appearing to be people like ourselves—"just plain folks among the neighbors." In election years especially do candidates show their devotion to little children and the common, homey things of life. They have front porch campaigns. For the newspaper men they raid the kitchen cupboard, finding there some of the good wife's apple pie. They go to country picnics; they attend service at the old frame church; they pitch hay and go fishing; they show their belief in home and mother. In short, they would win our votes by showing that they're just as common as the rest of us—"just plain folks"—and, therefore, wise and good. Business men often are "plain folks" with the factory hands. Even distillers use the device. "It's our family's whiskey, neighbor: and neighbor, it's your price."

### CARD STACKING

"Card Stacking" is a device in which the propagandist employs all the arts of deception to win our support for himself, his group, nation, race, policy, practice, belief, or ideal. He stacks the cards against the truth. He uses under-emphasis and over-emphasis to dodge issues and evade facts. He resorts to lies, censorship, and distortion. He omits facts. He offers false testimony. He creates a smoke screen of clamor by raising a new issue when he wants an embarrassing matter forgotten. He draws a red herring across the trail to confuse and divert those in quest of facts he does not want revealed. He makes the unreal appear real and the real appear unreal. He lets half-truth masquerade as truth. By the Card Stacking device, a mediocre candidate, through the "build-up," is made to appear an intellectual titan; an ordinary prize fighter, a probable world champion; a worthless patent medicine, a beneficent cure. By means of this device propagandists would convince us that a ruthless war of aggression is a crusade for righteousness. Some member nations of the Non-Intervention Committee send their troops to intervene in Spain. Card Stacking employs sham, hypocrisy, effrontery.

### THE BAND WAGON

The "Band Wagon" is a device to make us follow the crowd, to accept the propagandist's program en masse. Here his theme is: "Everybody's doing it." His techniques range from those of medicine show to dramatic spectacle. He hires a hall, fills a great stadium, marches a million men in parade. He employs symbols, colors, music, movement, all the dramatic arts. He appeals to the desire, common to most of us, to "follow the crowd." Because he wants us to "follow the crowd" in masses, he directs his appeal to groups held together by common ties of nationality, religion, race, environment, sex, vocation. Thus propagandists campaigning for or against a program will appeal to us as Catholics, Protestants, or Jews; as members of the Nordic race or as Negroes; as farmers or as school teachers; as housewives or as miners. All the artifices of flattery are used to harness the fears and hatreds, prejudices, and biases, convictions and ideals common to the group; thus emotion is made to push and pull the group on to the Band Wagon. In newspaper article and in the spoken word this device is also found. "Don't throw your vote away. Vote for our candidate. He's sure to win." Nearly every candidate wins in every election—before the votes are in.

### PROPAGANDA AND EMOTION

Observe that in all these devices our emotion is the stuff with which propagandists work. Without it they are helpless; with it, harnessing it to their purposes, they can make us glow with pride or burn with hatred, they can make us zealots in behalf of the program they espouse. As we said at the beginning, propaganda as generally understood is expression of opinion or action by individuals or groups with reference to predetermined ends. Without the appeal to our emotion—to our fears and to our courage, to our selfishness and unselfishness, to our loves and to our hates—propagandists would influence few opinions and few actions.

To say this is not to condemn emotion, an essential part of life, or to assert that all predetermined ends of propagandists are "bad." What we mean is that the intelligent citizen does not want propagandists to utilize his emotions, even to the attainment of "good" ends, without knowing what is going on. He does not want to be "used" in the attainment of ends he may later consider "bad." He does not want to be gullible. He does not want to be fooled. He does not want to be duped, even in a "good" cause. He wants to know the facts and among these is included the fact of the utilization of his emotions.[1]

Keeping in mind the seven common propaganda devices, turn to today's newspapers and almost immediately you can spot examples of them all. At election time or during any campaign, Plain Folks and Band Wagon are common. Card Stacking is hardest to detect because it is adroitly executed or because we lack the information necessary to nail the lie. A little practice with the daily newspapers in detecting these propaganda devices soon enables us to detect them elsewhere—in radio, news-reel, books, magazines, and in expression of labor unions, business groups, churches, schools, political parties.

[1] For better understanding of the relationship between propaganda and emotion see Chapter One of *Folkways* by William Graham Sumner. This shows why most of us tend to feel, believe, and act in traditional patterns. See also *The Mind in the Making* by James Harvey Robinson. This reveals the nature of the mind and suggests how to analyze propaganda appealing to traditional thought patterns.

Relate the seven common propaganda devices to the discussion of diction on pp. 388-91. Which devices does Pegler use in the passage quoted on p. 482? For further exercises, see p. 191 and p. 391.

# THE CAUSES OF WAR

WILL DURANT

The causes of war are psychological, biological, economic, and political—that is, they lie in the impulses of men, the competition of groups, the material needs of societies, and fluctuations of national power.

The basic causes are in ourselves, for the state is an enlarged picture of the soul. The five major instincts of mankind—food-getting, mating, parental love, fighting, and association—are the ultimate sources of war. Our inveterate habit of eating is the oldest and deepest cause of war. For thousands, perhaps millions, of years, men were uncertain of their food supply. Not knowing yet the bounty of the soil, they trusted to the fortunes of the hunt. Having captured prey, they tore or cut it to pieces, often on the spot, and gorged themselves to their cubic capacity with the raw flesh and the hot gore; how could they tell when they might eat again? Greed is eating, or hoarding, for the future; wealth is originally a hedge against starvation; war is at first a raid for food. All vices were once virtues, indispensable in the struggle for existence; they became vices only in the degree to which social order and increasing security rendered them unnecessary for survival. Once men had to chase, to kill, to grasp, to overeat, to hoard; a hundred millenniums of insecurity bred into the race those acquisitive and possessive impulses which no laws or ideals, but only centuries of security, can mitigate or destroy.

The desire for mates and the love of children write half of the private history of mankind, but they have only rarely been the direct causes of war. The fighting instinct enters more obviously into the analysis, even if it operates most freely in persons above the military age. Nature develops it vigorously as an aid in getting or keeping food or mates; it arms every animal with organs of offense and defense, and lends to the physically weaker species the advantages of cunning and association. Since, by and large, those individuals and groups survived that excelled in food-getting, mate-getting, caring for children, and fighting, these instincts have been selected and intensified with every generation, and have budded into a hundred secondary forms of acquisition, venery, kindliness, and contention.

As the quest for food has grown into the amassing of great fortunes, so the fighting instinct has swelled into the lust for power and the waging of war. The lust for power is in most men a wholesome stimulus to ambition and creation, but in exceptional men, dressed in great and lasting authority, it becomes a dangerous disease, an elephantiasis of the soul, which goads them on to fight a thousand battles by proxy. Nietzsche, nervous and sickly and disqualified for military service, thrilled at the sight and sound of cavalry galloping along a Frankfort street, and at once composed a paean in honor of war and the "will to power." Mussolini and Hitler have read Nietzsche, and may, by replacing parliaments with supermen, and the religion of peace with the religion of war, justify the gentle maniac's prediction that the future would divide history into B.N. and A.N.—Before Nietzsche and After Nietzsche. Nothing is so improbable as the future.

The instinct of flight is hardly a source of war, though war gives it an extensive field of operations. The instinct of action enters into the picture as a love of adventure, an escape from relatives and routine. A richer source is the instinct of association. Men fear solitude, and naturally seek the protection of numbers. Slowly a society develops within whose guarded frontiers men are free to live peaceably, to accumulate knowledge and goods, and to worship their gods. Since our self-love overflows into love of our parents and children, our homes and possessions, our habits and institutions, our wonted environment and transmitted faith, we form in time an emotional attachment for the nation and the civilization of which these are constituent parts; and when any of them is threatened, our instinct of pugnacity is aroused to the limit determined by the natural cowardice of mankind. Such patriotism is reasonable and necessary, for without it the group could not survive, and the individual could not survive without the group. Prejudice is fatal to philosophy, but indispensable to a people.

Put all these passions together, gather into one force the acquisitiveness, pugnacity, egoism, egotism, affection, and lust for power of a hundred million souls, and you have the psychological sources of war. It may be that these sources are not completely instinctive, not inevitably rooted in the blood; contemporary psychology is chary of instincts, and suspects that many of them are but habits formed in early years through the imitation of corrupt adults. We need not spend ourselves on the dispute, for in any case the practical problem would remain—we should still have to change the parents before we could change the children.

The experience of Russia indicates that the business of pursuing food and mates, of fighting and gathering together, of loving children and money and power, is more deeply ingrained in human character than fashionable theory believes. Or was it that the lenience of the Ogpu allowed too many adults to survive? It is hard to build tomorrow's society with the day-after-tomorrow's men. *Historia non facit saltum:* History, like nature, makes no leaps.

These psychological impulses, taken in their social mass, become the biological sources of war. The group, too, as well as the individual, can be hungry or angry, ambitious or proud; the group, too, must struggle for existence, and be eliminated or survive. The protective fertility of organisms soon multiplies mouths beyond the local food supply; the hunger of the parts, as in the body, becomes the hunger of the whole, and species wars against species, group against group, for lands or waters that may give more support to abounding life. Euripides, twenty-three hundred years ago, attributed the Trojan War to the rapid multiplication of the Greeks. "States that have a surplus population," said the ancient Stoic philosopher Chrysippus, "send great numbers out to colonies, and stir up wars against their neighbors." If that was the case when infanticide and Greek friendship were tolerated as means of controlling population, consider the results where statesmen encourage fertility. For then the birth rate must be raised to provide soldiers for war; war must be waged to conquer land for an expanding population; and population expands because the birth rate is so high. It is a very pinwheel of logic, bright and frail, a form of reasoning puzzlingly whimsical until we add its concealed premise —the will to power.

Group hunger begets group pugnacity, and pugnacity develops in the group, as in the individual, organs of protection and attack. In the group these are called armament; and when they are powerful, they may themselves, like the boy's biceptual consciousness, become a secondary source of war. On either scale some armament is necessary, for struggle is inevitable, and competition is the trade of life. The tragedy of our ideals is that we hitch them to the falling stars of equality and peace, while nature blithely bases her inescapable machinery of development upon difference and inequality of endowment and ability, upon competition and war; what chance have our ideals, nurtured in the mutual aid of the family, against that supremest court of all? Even mutual aid becomes an organ of struggle: We co-operate as individuals that we may the better compete as groups; morality and order have been developed because they strengthened the group in the inexorable competition of the world. Only when another star attacks us will the earth know internal peace; only a war of the planets can produce, for a moment, the brotherhood of man.

These psychological and biological forces are the ultimate origins of human conflict. From them flow the national rivalries that generate the proximate causes of war—those economic and political causes with which superficial analysis so readily contents itself.

The basic economic cause is rivalry for land: Land to receive a designedly expanding population, land to provide material resources, land to open up new subjects to conscription and taxation. So the ancient Greeks fought their way through the Aegean isles to the coasts of Asia Minor and the Black Sea, and through the Mediterranean to Africa, Sicily, Italy, France, and Spain; so the English spread through the world in the last two centuries; so the Italians begin to spread today. There is, in history, a law of colonial expansion almost as explosive as any law of expansion in physics: Whenever a population fails to exploit the resources of its soil, it will sooner or later be conquered by a people able to exploit those resources, and to pour them into the commerce and uses of mankind.

These ancient provocations to conquest have been sharpened and magnified by the Industrial Revolution. To make war successfully a modern nation must be wealthy; to be wealthy it must develop industry; to maintain industry it must, in most cases, import food, fuel, and raw materials; to pay for these it must export manufactured goods; to sell these it must find foreign markets; to win these it must undersell its competitors or wage successful war. As likely as not, it will make war for any of the goods it must import, or for control of the routes by which it imports them.

Even in antiquity semi-industrial Athens waged war for the control of the Aegean, the Hellespont, and the Black Sea, because it was dependent upon Russian grain; Rome had to conquer Egypt because it needed corn, and Asia Minor because it needed markets for its handicrafts and fortunes for its politicians. Egyptian wheat, Near-Eastern oil, and Indian cotton explain many a battle in British history; Spanish silver explains the wars of Rome with Carthage; Spanish copper, not Fascist theory, explains in our time the German help to the insurgent forces in Spain. Our sinless selves had a taste for sugar in 1898; and far back in 1853 we pointed our presents and cannon at a frightened shogun and persuaded him to allow a peaceful, agricultural, self-contained nation to transform itself into industrial, imperial, militaristic Japan. Those chickens have come home to roost.

The business cycle adds its own contribution to the causes of modern war. Since men are by nature unequal—some strong and some weak, some able and some (as they tell us) virtuous—it follows that in any society a majority of abilities will be possessed by a minority of men; from which it follows that sooner or later, in any society, a majority of goods will be possessed by a minority of men. But this natural concentration of wealth impedes the wide spread of purchasing power among the people; production, perpetually accelerated by invention, leaps ahead of consumption; surpluses rise and generate either depression or war. For either production must stop to let consumption catch up, or foreign markets must be found to take the surplus unbought at home. Foreign markets can be secured by underselling competitors or defeating them in war. To undersell our competitors is impractical; our standard of living is too high for that; to lower it to the level of Japan's would bring revolution; apparently the choice is between depression and war. But another depression, possibly made worse through the increased displacement of costly labor by economical machines, might also bring revolution. What is left but war—or an unprecedented change in the behavior of men?

Add a few political causes, and our recipe for war will be complete. The first law of governments is self-preservation, their second law is self-extension; their appetite grows by what they feed on, and they are seldom content. But further, the distribution of power among nations is always changing—through the discovery or development of new natural resources, through the rise or decline of population, through the weakening of religion, morals, and character, or through some other material, or biological, or psychological circumstance; and the nation that has become strong soon asserts itself over the nation that has become weak. Hence the impossibility of writing a peace pact that will perpetuate a *status quo;* hence the absurdity of Article X of the League of Nations Covenant; hence the failure of sanctions and the breakdown of the Treaty of Versailles. Excellent indeed is the peace treaty that does not generate a war.

These, then, are the causes of war. How natural it seems now, in the perspective of science and history; how ancient its sources and how inscrutable its destiny!

Is it any wonder that peace is so often but invisible war, in which the nations rest only to fight again?

Is Durant's diction prevailingly abstract or concrete? (See p. 374.) Does he ever use diction to color his argument? (See pp. 388-91.) Does he make use of much metaphor? For what purposes? (See pp. 415 ff.) For a further exercise, see p. 134.

# Reportage

## THE END IN SIGHT

ERNIE PYLE

We finally left Central Tunisia behind us and pushed north, Americans as well as British. The end of the long Tunisian trail was in sight. The kill could not be long delayed.

The British had more troops, and more experienced troops, in Tunisia than we had. In some measure we had divided the load earlier, but with the arrival of the Eighth Army the affair had become predominantly British.

It would be wrong to try to make anything sinister out of that, for it was the way it should have been. Since Montgomery had chased Rommel all the way from Egypt in one of the great military achievements of history, it was only right that the British should make the kill.

The Eighth Army was a magnificent organization. We correspondents were dazzled by its perfection. So were our troops. It must surely be one of the outstanding armies of all time. We trailed it several days up the Tunisian coast, and we came to look upon it almost with awe.

Its organization for continuous movement was so perfect that it seemed more like a big business firm than a destructive army. The men of the Eighth were brown-skinned and white-eye-browed from the desert sun. Most of them were in shorts, and they were a

THE END IN SIGHT: From *Here Is Your War* by Ernie Pyle. Copyright, 1943, by Henry Holt and Company, Inc.

healthy-looking lot. Their spirit was like a tonic. The spirit of our own troops was good, but those boys from the burning sands were throbbing with the vitality of conquerors.

They were friendly, cocky, confident. They had been three years in the desert, and they wore the expression of victory on their faces. We envied them, and were proud of them.

The north country was entirely different from the semidesert where we Americans had spent the winter. In the north the land was fertile and everything was violently green.

Northern Tunisia was all hills and valleys. There were no trees at all, but there in the spring the earth was solidly covered with deep green—pastures and freshly growing fields of grain. Small wildflowers spattered the countryside. I never saw lovelier or more gentle country. It gave a sense of peacefulness, it seemed to speak its richness. It was a full, ripe country, and there in the springtime living seemed sweet and worthwhile.

There were winding gravel roads everywhere, with many roads of fine macadam. Villages were perched on the hillsides, and some of them looked like picture postcards. It was all so different from the Tunisia we had known that all of us, driving up suddenly one sunny afternoon into that clean cool greenness, felt like holding out our arms to such verdant beauty.

Yet that peaceful green gradually turned red with blood. The roads were packed with brown-painted convoys, and the trailers sprouted long rifle barrels. The incredibly blue sky with its big white clouds was streaked with war planes in great throbbing formations. And before long the whole northeastern corner of Tunisia roared and raged with a violence utterly out of character with a landscape so rich in nature's kindness.

The only thing we could say in behalf of ourselves was that the human race even in the process of defiling beauty still has the capacity to appreciate it.

Thousands of soldiers want someday to bring their wives and children back to Tunisia, in time of peace, and take them over the battlefields we came to know so well. But except for the cities they will not find much to remind them of the ferocity that existed there.

I traveled over the Tunisian battle area—both the part we knew

so intimately because it was on our side and the part we didn't
know at all because the Germans lived there at the time.

I didn't see the sort of desolated countryside I remembered from
pictures of France in the last war. That was because the fighting
had been mobile, because neither side used permanent huge guns,
and because the country was mostly treeless and empty. But there
were some marks left.

East of El Guettar, down a broad valley through which ran a nice
macadam road, I saw dark objects sitting far off on the plain. They
were the burned-out tanks of both sides. A certain two sat close
together like twins, about a mile off the road. The immense cater-
pillar track was off one of them and it lay trailed out behind for
fifty feet. The insides were a shambles. Seared and jumbled personal
and mechanical debris was scattered around outside. Our soldiers
had already retrieved almost everything worthwhile from the German debris, but there were still big wrenches, oil-soaked gloves,
and twisted shell cases lying about.

There were many of those tanks scattered miles apart through the
valley. And in the shade of one tank, not five feet from the great
metal skeleton, was the fresh grave of a German tanker, marked by
a rough wooden cross without a name.

On the hillsides white splotches were still visible—powder marks
from our exploding artillery shells. Gnarled lengths of Signal Corps
telephone wire, too mauled to retrieve, strung for yards along the
roadsides.

There were frequent filled-in holes in the macadam where artillery or dive bombers had taken their toll. Now and then a little
graveyard with wooden crosses stood lonesomely at the roadside.
Some of the telephone poles had been chopped down. There were
clumps of empty ammunition boxes. But for all these things a
person had to look closely. There had been a holocaust but it left
only a slight permanent mark. It is difficult to disfigure acres of
marigolds and billions of blades of fresh desert grass.

Sidi bou Zid was the little white village I saw destroyed by shell-
fire back in February. It was weeks later before I could get close
enough to see the details, because the village remained German
territory for some time. It was one of the little towns I had known
so well, but when I went back it was a pitiful sight. The village
almost didn't exist. Its dozens of low stone adobe buildings, stuccoed

a snowy white, were nothing but rock piles. The village had died. The reason for the destruction was that German and American tank columns, advancing toward each other, met there. Artillery from both sides poured its long-distance fury into the town for hours. There will have to be a new Sidi bou Zid.

Faid Pass is the last pass in the Grand Dorsal before the drive eastward onto the long flat plain that leads to the Mediterranean at Sfax. For months we looked with longing eyes at Faid. A number of times we tried to take it and failed. But when the Germans' big retreat came they left Faid Pass voluntarily. And they left it so thoroughly and maliciously mined that we never dared drive off onto the shoulder of the road for fear of getting blown to kingdom come.

Our engineers went through those mine fields with electrical instruments, located the mines, and surrounded them with warning notices until they could be dug up or exploded. Those notices were of two types—either a white ribbon strung around the mine area on knee-high sticks or else stakes with oppositely pointing arrows on top. The white arrow pointing to the left meaning that side was safe, the red arrow pointing to the right meaning that side was mined.

And believe me, after seeing a few mine-wrecked trucks and jeeps, we feared mines so dreadfully that we found ourselves actually leaning away from the side of the road where the signs were, as we drove past.

I hate to think of poor little Sfax. I believe it was one of the prettiest of all the Tunisian cities we saw. Somehow it had something of Miami's Biscayne Boulevard in it, and a little of San Diego too. But it was demolished—at least the downtown business part was, for it lay right on the water front and our Allied bombers played havoc with it. The whole business section, however, was evacuated before the bombing started, so probably there was only a slight loss of life.

After the bombing, parts of Sfax looked like London during the blitz. A locomotive sprawled on its side across a sidewalk. Royal palms, uprooted, lay pitifully in the street. Little parks were no-man's-lands of craters. The macadam streets had great cracks across them. There was no square inch left unwrecked in the downtown area.

The French felt that we shouldn't have bombed Sfax, because it was French. But it was one of Germany's big supply ports, and not to have bombed it would have been cutting our own throats as well as the throats of all Frenchmen.

Kairouan was a holy city, one of the minor Meccas, but it wasn't holy to the Germans. They used it all winter as a big rail and highway supply point.

We got to Kairouan shortly after the Germans had fled before the Eighth Army. That was the first time I had been close on the heels of a reoccupation. Three of us correspondents rode into the town in jeeps, and to our astonishment found the streets lined with crowds waving and cheering and applauding each passing vehicle.

Not knowing the difference, they gave us correspondents as big a hand as the rest. And we beamed and waved back just as if we'd run the Germans out ourselves.

Kairouan had been under Axis domination for nearly three years but it was not damaged much by bombing. Therein lay a slight mix-up somewhere, for it had been reported that one of our fliers destroyed the Splendide Hotel, which housed a German headquarters. Yet the Splendide was still standing, quite unharmed.

In Kairouan we saw the first white woman most of us had seen in a long time. Three French girls stood on a street corner for hours waving and smiling at the Allied tanks and trucks as they passed through the town. One of the girls had on a blue skirt and a white blouse, which made her stand out from the others. After that episode countless soldiers told me about the wonderful girl they had seen in Kairouan. Eventually they described how she was dressed, and it always turned out to be Miss Blue-Skirt-and-White-Blouse.

That one girl, merely by standing in the street and waving, had given to scores of women-hungry men an illusion of Broadway and Main Street that they'd not known in months.

Gafsa was the southern town we took back after it had been in German hands for a couple of months. Gafsa was not much damaged by shot and shell, but it was gutted by the cruel hands of ruthless men. Whether those were the hands of Germans or Arabs I wasn't able to find out.

One French officer estimated that the Arabs of Gafsa were 85 per cent for the Germans, 5 per cent for the French, and 10 per cent indifferent. That was a testimonial to the power of German propaganda, for the Arabs are lovers of might.

At any rate, when we returned to Gafsa the streets were littered, and the homes of all the Jews and better-off French and Arabs were wrecked. Windows had been broken, rugs and all other valuables stolen, furniture smashed and thrown out into the streets for desert Arabs to steal. Marauders went into a nice little hotel, apparently with hammers, and smashed every lavatory, every mirror and every window. They smashed the mechanism of every refrigerator in town.

Their crippling of the city power plant was legitimate. But their senseless smashings and their uprooting of private gardens was barbarism, solely for barbarity's sake. . . .

For a time there I lived again with some of our American fighter pilots, and I found that the shift in balance had done as much for them as for our ground troops. They flew themselves punch-drunk in that big push, yet they flew with a dash they had never known before. For at last they were on the upper end of things.

We made great hay while the sun shone. The ground crews worked like fiends keeping the planes flyable. Pilots were going at a pace they couldn't possibly have stood very long. Some fighter pilots flew as many as five missions a day; formerly one was tops. The fighters did all kinds of work—escorting, ground sweeping, dogfighting, and even light bombing.

Let me tell you how that air superiority worked. In the old days we had sent a cover of fighters along with the bombers, but there were hardly ever enough of them. When we came into our own, we not only sent an enormous cover but we sent a second layer to cover the cover. A sort of double insulation. We didn't even stop there. We sent out groups of fighters known as "free lances," far out of sight of our bombers, just to intercept anything that might be wandering around. And to wind it all up we sent out fresh planes to meet the bombers just after they left the target, in case the regular cover of fighters might have trouble or run low on gas. They were called "delousing missions," and they scraped off any pests that got tenacious.

Both sides had kept constant airdrome patrols in the air all winter

—from two to half a dozen planes circling each airdrome constantly from dawn to dusk, to be already in the air if enemy planes appeared. After we got the upper hand, we still patrolled, but we also took on a little extra work, and this I think is the ultimate in air superiority: we patrolled the German airdromes too!

Our fighters actually patrolled one whole afternoon over a big German drome, just flying back and forth and around, and prevented every single German plane from even taking off. Of course that was an isolated case, and I'm not trying to make you believe we patrolled all the German dromes all the time, but the fact that it could happen at all was practically phenomenal.

Yes, air superiority was a wonderful thing. It was one of life's small luxuries to which I was eager to become more accustomed.

Our army in North Africa was still full of rumors. Most of them had to do with when we would go home. There was a rumor that President Roosevelt had made a radio address saying that the mothers, wives, and sweethearts of the men in North Africa were due for a big surprise as soon as the Tunisian campaign was over. The rumored remark spread and was immediately interpreted by the men as meaning that everybody was going home the minute the last German was out of Africa. Some of our troops sincerely believed that would happen.

The orange and tangerine season was over. Those richly juicy North African tangerines were one of the pleasantest things of our war over here. For months we ate them by the daily dozen. When they were all gone we went back to occasional canned fruit juice from America. And on British mess tables we found a little can of pills called ascorbic tablets, which we took daily to make up for the lack of fruits in our diet.

A new type of American ration showed up in answer to the British compo, which small groups of traveling soldiers had found so superior to anything of ours. The new stuff was called "U ration." It was wonderful. It had everything that was needed by four or five men who had to fix their own meals out on a trip.

It came in a pasteboard box inside a wooden box. Everything was done up in small cans or packets just big enough to be used up at one meal. With it came two printed menus, guides in eating the rations. I lost No. 1 but No. 2 was: Breakfast—tomato juice, whole-wheat cereal, sliced bacon, biscuits, coffee; dinner—bean soup, roast beef, quick-cooking rice, biscuits, lemonade, hard candy; supper—meat and vegetable stew, dried prunes, coffee, apricot spread.

The ration also included root beer, gumdrops, canned butter, tomato juice in powdered form, and two big envelopes of toilet paper. The tomato juice was fairly lousy, but the canned bacon was superb. God bless the U ration!

As was bound to happen in wartime, close friends sometimes disappeared. And as soon as they were gone we sat of an evening and recounted stories about them, just as we did in the old aviation days after a mail pilot didn't come back from his run.

One of my closest friends was Lieutenant Leonard Bessman, a lawyer from Milwaukee. We had almost definite proof that Bessman was captured, and not killed; so we all hoped to see him again before too long if things turned out right. I've mentioned Lennie Bessman before. Of all the soldiers I have ever known he was the most sensitive to the little beauties of war and to the big tragedy of life. Maybe that was because he was a Jew, or maybe it wasn't. I don't know.

His bravery was a byword among us long before he was captured. It was a bravery based on pure idealism—the invulnerable kind of bravery—and it was inevitable that sooner or later he would either die or fall prisoner. I never heard of anyone who didn't love and admire him.

We sat around on our cots at night and laughed about things we had heard Lennie say, because they sounded so melodramatic, yet, knowing him as we did, we knew they weren't melodramatic at all and that Lennie had meant what he said.

A good example is the day he was trapped, overwhelmed and captured. He was far up forward of our advance troops, for that was his job, and suddenly he found himself cut off, with a German tank in front of him and a machine-gun nest on his side. Lennie jumped out of his jeep, pulled his .45 and yelled at the heavily armed enemy, "Come on out and I won't shoot." In other people that would have been artificial bravado; but Lennie really meant it.

Most of us found our emotions becoming jaded as month after

month of war piled up on us, but Lennie was never jaded. He had
a facility for mirroring in his fertile mind every human thing that
crossed his path. We had a certain type of antiaircraft gun, mounted
on a half-track, which required two men to fire. The gunners sat in
two metal bucket seats just back of the guns. Lennie was lying near
this ack-ack outfit during a terrific dive-bombing and strafing, and
he kept his eyes on those two special gunners as the Stukas came
down right upon them.

The two never wavered. They sat there firing until suddenly and
in unison they toppled sideways out of their seats—dead. And all
within the same instant two more Americans rose like twins from
the bed of the half-track, took the seats just vacated by death, and
went right on with the firing. Lennie was terribly moved by that
little drama of duty automatically performed, and he almost choked
up when he told the story.

The incident that most tickled his admiration happened at the
time we had a big concentration of artillery that was giving the
Germans plenty of trouble. They couldn't locate it; so at night they
sent planes over hunting for it. Of course it was then our cue to lay
low and silent, so as not to give away our position by firing at them.

They came night after night, and never did find us. But each
night after they had circled and were finally leaving, one lone
contemptuous gunner fired one lone contemptuous shot at them,
just as if to say, "Here we are, you silly fools!"

Night after night that one gunner fired his one slapstick shot just
as they were leaving. His sauciness exalted Lennie's soul. I heard
him say, "I'd rather shake hands with that man than anybody in the
American Army. I'm going to try to find him, and even if he's a
private I'm going to salute him."

We had heard that the Germans took the few Americans captured
at El Guettar and marched them up the main street of Tunis, then
loaded them in trucks and paraded them back again, then unloaded
them and marched them through town once more—to make it look
as if there were lots of prisoners. One of Lennie's friends said he
could just see Lennie, on his third compulsory trip down the main
street of Tunis, screwing up his nose in the special mask of comic
disgust which was one of his little habits, and observing, "Seems
as if I've seen this before somewhere."

✦

Another friend, whom I've already mentioned, was also among the missing. He, too, we knew almost definitely, was a prisoner. He was Captain Tony Lumpkin, of Mexico, Missouri. Tony was headquarters commandant of a certain outfit—a headquarters commandant being a sort of militarized hotel manager.

Just before he disappeared Tony got to going by the nickname of "Noah" Lumpkin, because he always seemed to pick out such a miserably wet place for a command post. On their last move before he was captured, the commanding general—a swell guy with a sense of humor—called Captain Lumpkin over, stood with him outside a tent looking out over the watery landscape, and congratulated him on locating them in the center of such a beautiful lake.

Tony Lumpkin needn't have been captured at all if he had been content to stick to his comparatively safe "hotel managing." But he wanted to get a crack at the Jerries himself. He was an expert gunner, and he finally talked the commander into letting him take five men and a small gun on wheels and go out to see what he could pick off.

The first day they got one German truck plus something that turned out later to be a camel, although it looked like a truck at the distance they were firing from. The second day they moved farther into the mountains to get into a better shooting position, but bagged nothing. On the third day they went even farther into the hills, hunting a perfect spot for firing.

Captain Lumpkin used to share a tent with Major Chuck Miller of Detroit, and with their assistant, Corporal William Nikolin of Indianapolis, both of whom I've mentioned, they formed an intimate little family.

That third night Major Miller came in late. He was astonished, and a little bit concerned, to see Tony's cot empty. When he woke up next morning there was still no Tony. Major Miller went to the general and got permission to start out with a squad of his own military police and hunt for his lost companion.

They covered all the ground Tony had covered, and finally, by studying the terrain and talking with others who had been near by, and interviewing German prisoners, they pieced together what had happened. The hill that Captain Lumpkin had been trying to get to had been simply lousy with German machine gunners. The Germans saw him all the time. They sent out a party that worked behind and surrounded him. A German who was captured later said that a captain with a tommy gun killed one German and wounded another before being taken.

There wasn't grief in the little Lumpkin-Miller-Nikolin family, but there was a terrible vacancy. "We were a perfect team," Major Miller said. "Tony was slow and easygoing, and I'm big and lose my temper too quickly. We balanced each other. I'd keep him pepped up and he'd calm me down. We sure miss him, don't we, Nicky?"

That spring I was away from the front lines for a while, living with other troops, and considerable fighting took place while I was gone. When I got ready to return to my old friends at the front I wondered if I would sense any change in them. I did, and definitely.

The most vivid change was the casual and workshop manner in which they talked about killing. They had made the psychological transition from their normal belief that taking human life was sinful, over to a new professional outlook where killing was a craft. No longer was there anything morally wrong about killing. In fact, it was an admirable thing.

I think I was so impressed by that new attitude because it hadn't been necessary for me to make that change along with them. As a noncombatant, my own life was in danger only by occasional chance or circumstance. Consequently I didn't need to think of killing in personal terms, and killing to me was still murder.

Even after a winter of living with wholesale death and vile destruction, it was only spasmodically that I seemed capable of realizing how real and how awful the war was. My emotions seemed dead and crusty when presented with the tangibles of war. I found I could look on rows of fresh graves without a lump in my throat. Somehow I could look on mutilated bodies without flinching or feeling deeply.

It was only when I sat alone away from it all or lay at night in my bedroll, re-creating what I had seen, thinking and thinking and thinking, that at last the enormity of all those newly dead struck like a living nightmare. Then there were times when I felt I couldn't stand it and would have to leave.

But to the fighting soldier that phase of the war was behind. It was left behind after his first battle. His blood was up. He was fighting for his life, and killing then for him was as much a profession as writing was for me.

He wanted to kill individually or in vast numbers. He wanted to see the Germans overrun, mangled, butchered in the Tunisian trap. He spoke excitedly of seeing great heaps of dead, of our bombers sinking whole shiploads of fleeing men, of Germans by the thousands dying miserably in a final Tunisian holocaust of their own creation.

In that one respect the front-line soldier differed from all the rest of us. All the rest of us—you and me and even the thousands of soldiers behind the lines in Africa—we wanted terribly yet only academically for the war to be over. The front-line soldier wanted it to be terminated by the physical process of his destroying enough Germans to end it. He was truly at war. The rest of us, no matter how hard we worked, were not. Say what you will, nothing can make a complete soldier except battle experience.

In the semifinals—the cleaning out of Central Tunisia—we had large units in battle for the first time. Frankly, they didn't all excel. Their own commanders admitted it, and admirably they didn't try to alibi. The British had to help us out a few times, but neither American nor British commanders were worried about that, for there was no lack of bravery. There was only lack of experience. They all knew we would do better the next time.

The First Infantry Division was an example of what our American units could do after they had gone through the mill of experience. Those boys did themselves proud in the semifinals. Everybody spoke about it. Our casualties included few taken prisoners. All the other casualties were wounded or died fighting. "They never gave an inch," a general said. "They died right in their foxholes."

I heard of a high British officer who went over the battlefield just after the action was over. American boys were still lying dead in their foxholes, their rifles still grasped in firing position in their dead hands. And the veteran English soldier remarked time and again, in a sort of hushed eulogy spoken only to himself, "Brave men. Brave men!"

We moved one afternoon to a new position just a few miles behind the invisible line of armor that separated us from the Germans in Northern Tunisia. Nothing happened that first night that was spectacular, yet somehow the whole night became obsessed with a spookiness that leaves it standing like a landmark in my memory.

We had been at the new camp about an hour and were still setting up our tents when German planes appeared overhead. We stopped work to watch them. It was the usual display of darting planes, with the conglomerate sounds of ack-ack on the ground and in the sky. Suddenly we realized that one plane was diving straight at us, and we made a mad scramble for foxholes. Two officer friends of mine had dug a three-foot hole and set their tent over it. They made for their tent, and I was tramping on their heels. The tent flap wouldn't come open, and we wound up in a silly heap. Finally it did open, and we all dived through the narrow opening at once.

We lay there in the hole, face down, as the plane came smack overhead with a terrible roar. We were all drawn up inside, waiting for the blow. Explosions around us were shatteringly loud, and yet when it was all over we couldn't find any bomb holes or anybody hurt. But we could have found a lot of nervous people.

Dusk came on, and with dusk began the steady boom of big guns in the mountains ahead of us. They weren't near enough for the sound to be crashing. Rather it was like the lonely roll of an approaching thunderstorm—a sound which since childhood has always made me sad with a kind of portent of inevitable doom.

We went to bed in our tents. A near-by farmyard was full of dogs and they began a howling that lasted all night. The roll of artillery was constant. It never stopped for twenty-four hours. Once in a while there were nearer shots which might have been German patrols, or might not. We lay uneasily in our cots. Sleep wouldn't come. We turned and turned. I snapped on a flashlight.

"What time is it?" asked Chris Cunningham from the next cot.

"Quarter to one," I answered. "Haven't you been asleep?"

He hadn't.

A plane droned faintly in the distance and came nearer and nearer until it was overhead. "Is that a Jerry or a Beaufighter?" Chris asked out of the darkness.

"It hasn't got that throb-throb to it;" I said, "so it must be a Beaufighter. But hell, I never can tell really. Don't know what it is."

The plane passed on, out of hearing. The artillery rolled and rolled. A nearer shot went off uncannily somewhere in the darkness. Some guinea hens set up a terrific cackling. I remember that just before dusk a soldier had shot at a snake in our new camp, and they had thought it was a cobra. And we'd just heard our first stories of scorpions. I began to feel creepy and wondered if our tent flaps were tight.

Another plane throbbed in the sky, and we lay listening with an awful anticipation. One of the dogs suddenly broke into a frenzied barking and went tearing through our little camp as if chasing a demon. My mind seemed to lose all sense of proportion, and I got jumpy and mad at myself.

Concussion ghosts, traveling in waves, touched our tent walls and made them quiver. Ghosts were shaking the ground ever so lightly. Ghosts were stirring the dogs to hysteria. Ghosts were wandering in the sky, peering for us cringing in our hide-outs. Ghosts were everywhere, and their hordes were multiplying as every hour added its production of new battlefield dead.

We lay and thought of the graveyards and the dirty men and the shocking blast of the big guns, and we couldn't sleep.

"What time is it?" came out of darkness from the next cot. I snapped on the flashlight.

"Half past four, and for God's sake go to sleep!"

Finally just before dawn we did sleep, in spite of everything.

Next morning we spoke around among ourselves and found that all of us had tossed away all night. It was an unexplainable thing. For all of us had been through greater danger. On another night the roll of the guns would have lulled us to sleep.

It was just that on some nights the air became sick and there was an unspoken contagion of spiritual dread, and we were little boys again, lost in the dark.

For questions and exercises, see p. 430, p. 455, and p. 532.

# DAWN OVER ZERO

## WILLIAM L. LAURENCE

The Atomic Age began at exactly 5.30 mountain war time on the morning of July 16, 1945, on a stretch of semi-desert land about

DAWN OVER ZERO: Reprinted from *Dawn over Zero* by William L. Laurence, by permission of Alfred A. Knopf, Inc. Copyright 1946 by William L. Laurence.

fifty air-line miles from Alamogordo, New Mexico, just a few minutes before the dawn of a new day on that part of the earth. At that great moment in history, ranking with the moment when man first put fire to work for him, the vast energy locked within the heart of the atoms of matter was released for the first time in a burst of flame such as had never before been seen on this planet, illuminating earth and sky, for a brief span that seemed eternal, with the light of many super-suns.

The elemental flame, first fire ever made on earth that did not have its origin in the sun, came from the explosion of the first atomic bomb. It was a full-dress rehearsal preparatory to dropping the bomb over Hiroshima and Nagasaki—and other Japanese military targets, had Japan refused to accept the Potsdam Declaration for her surrender.

The rehearsal marked the climax in the penultimate act of one of the greatest dramas in our history and the history of civilized man—a drama in which our scientists, under the direction of the Army Corps of Engineers, were working against time to create an atomic bomb ahead of our German enemy. The collapse of Germany marked the end of the first act of this drama. The successful completion of our task, in the greatest challenge by man to nature so far, brought down the curtain on the second act. The grand finale came three weeks afterward in the skies over Japan, with a swift descent of the curtain on the greatest war in history.

The atomic flash in New Mexico came as a great affirmation to the prodigious labors of our scientists during the past four years. It came as the affirmative answer to the until then unanswered question: "Will it work?"

With the flash came a delayed roll of mighty thunder, heard, just as the flash was seen, for hundreds of miles. The roar echoed and reverberated from the distant hills and the Sierra Oscuro range near by, sounding as though it came from some supramundane source as well as from the bowels of the earth. The hills said yes and the mountains chimed in yes. It was as if the earth had spoken and the suddenly iridescent clouds and sky had joined in one affirmative answer. Atomic energy—yes. It was like the grand finale of a mighty symphony of the elements, fascinating and terrifying, uplifting and crushing, ominous, devastating, full of great promise and great forebodings.

I watched the birth of the era of atomic power from the slope of a hill in the desert land of New Mexico, on the northwestern corner of the Alamogordo Air Base, about 125 miles southeast of Albuquerque. The hill, named Compania Hill for the occasion, was twenty miles to the northwest of Zero, the code name given to the spot chosen for the atomic bomb test. The area embracing Zero and Compania Hill, twenty-four miles long and eighteen miles wide, had the code name Trinity.

I joined a caravan of three busses, three automobiles, and a truck carrying radio equipment at 11 P.M. on Sunday, July 15, at Albuquerque. There were about ninety of us in that strange caravan, traveling silently and in the utmost secrecy through the night on probably as unusual an adventure as any in our day. With the exception of myself the caravan consisted of scientists from the highly secret atomic bomb research and development center in the mesas and canyons of New Mexico, twenty-five miles northwest of Santa Fe, where we solved the secret of translating the fabulous energy of the atom into the mightiest weapon ever made by man. It was from there that the caravan set out at 5.30 that Sunday afternoon for its destination, 212 miles to the south.

The caravan wound its way slowly over the tortuous roads overlooking the precipitous canyons of northern New Mexico, passing through Espagnola, Santa Fe, and Bernalillo, arriving at Albuquerque at about 10 P.M. Here it was joined by Sir James Chadwick, who won the Nobel Prize and knighthood for his discovery of the neutron, the key that unlocks the atom; Professor Ernest O. Lawrence of the University of California, master atom-smasher, who won the Nobel Prize for his discovery of the cyclotron; Professor Edwin M. McMillan, also of the University of California, one of the discoverers of plutonium, the new atomic energy element; and several others from the atomic bomb center, who, like me, had arrived during the afternoon.

The night was dark with black clouds, and not a star could be seen. Occasionally a bolt of lightning would rend the sky and reveal for an instant the flat semi-desert landscape, rich with historic lore of past adventure. We rolled along on U. S. Highway 85, running between Albuquerque and El Paso, through sleeping ancient Spanish-American towns, their windows dark, their streets deserted— towns with music in their names, Los Lunas, Belen, Bernardo, Alamillo, Socorro, San Antonio. At San Antonio we turned east and crossed "the bridge on the Rio Grande with the detour in the middle of it." From there we traveled ten and one half miles eastward on U. S. Highway 380, and then turned south on a specially built dirt road, running for twenty-five miles to the base camp at Trinity.

The end of our trail was reached after we had covered about five and one fifth miles on the dirt road. Here we saw the first signs of life since leaving Albuquerque about three hours earlier, a line of silent men dressed in helmets. A little farther on, a detachment of military police examined our special credentials. We got out of the busses and looked around us. The night was still pitch-black save for an occasional flash of lightning in the eastern sky, outlining for a brief instant the Sierra Oscuro Range directly ahead of us. We were in the middle of the New Mexico desert, miles away from nowhere, with hardly a sign of life, not even a blinking light on the distant horizon. This was to be our caravansary until the zero hour.

From a distance to the southeast the beam of a searchlight probed the clouds. This gave us our first sense of orientation. The bomb-test site, Zero, was a little to the left of the searchlight beam, twenty miles away. With the darkness and the waiting in the chill of the desert the tension became almost unendurable.

We gathered in a circle to listen to directions on what we were to do at the time of the test, directions read aloud by the light of a flashlight:

At a short signal of the siren at minus five minutes to zero, "all personnel whose duties did not specifically require otherwise" were to prepare "a suitable place to lie down on." At a long signal of the siren at minus two minutes to zero, "all personnel whose duties did not specifically require otherwise" were to "lie prone on the ground immediately, the face and eyes directed toward the ground and with the head away from Zero. Do not watch for the flash directly," the directions read, "but turn over after it has occurred and watch the cloud. Stay on the ground until the blast wave has passed (two minutes). At two short blasts of the siren, indicating the passing of all hazard from light and blast, all personnel will prepare to leave as soon as possible.

"The hazard from blast is reduced by lying down on the ground in such a manner that flying rocks, glass and other objects do not intervene between the source of blast and the individual. Open all car windows.

"The hazard from light injury to eyes is reduced by shielding the closed eyes with the bended arms and lying face down on the ground. If the first flash is viewed a 'blind spot' may prevent your seeing the rest of the show.

"The hazard from ultraviolet light injuries to the skin is best overcome by wearing long trousers and shirts with long sleeves."

David Dow, assistant to the scientific director of the Atomic Bomb Development Center, handed each of us a flat piece of colored glass such as is used by arc welders to shield their eyes. Dr. Edward Teller of George Washington University cautioned us against sunburn. Someone produced sunburn lotion and passed it around. It was an eerie sight to see a number of our highest-ranking scientists seriously rubbing sunburn lotion on their faces and hands in the pitch-blackness of the night, twenty miles away from the expected flash. These were the men who, more than anybody else, knew the potentialities of atomic energy on the loose. It gave one an inkling of their confidence in their handiwork.

The bomb was set on a structural steel tower one hundred feet high. Ten miles away to the southwest was the base camp. This was G.H.Q. for the scientific high command, of which Professor Kenneth T. Bainbridge of Harvard University was field commander. Here were erected barracks to serve as living-quarters for the scientists, a mess hall, a commissary, a post exchange, and other buildings. Here the vanguard of the atomists, headed by Professor J. R. Oppenheimer of the University of California, scientific director of the Atomic Bomb Project, lived like soldiers at the front, supervising the enormously complicated details involved in the epoch-making tests.

Here early that Sunday afternoon gathered Major General Leslie R. Groves, commander in chief of the Atomic Bomb Project; Brigadier General T. F. Farrell, hero of World War I, General Groves's deputy; Professor Enrico Fermi, Nobel Prize winner and one of the leaders in the project; President James Bryant Conant of Harvard; Dr. Vannevar Bush, director of the Office of Scientific Research and Development; Dean Richard C. Tolman of the California Institute of Technology; Professor R. F. Bacher of Cornell; Colonel Stafford L. Warren, University of Rochester radiologist;

and about a hundred and fifty other leaders in the atomic bomb program.

At the Base Camp was a dry, abandoned reservoir, about five hundred feet square, surrounded by a mound of earth about eight feet high. Within this mound bulldozers dug a series of slit trenches, each about three feet deep, seven feet wide, and twenty-five feet long. At a command over the radio at zero minus one minute all observers at Base Camp, lay down in their assigned trenches, "face and eyes directed toward the ground and with the head away from Zero." But most of us on Compania Hill remained on our feet.

Three other posts had been established, south, north, and west of Zero, each at a distance of 10,000 yards (5.7 miles). These were known, respectively, as South-10,000, North-10,000, and West-10,000, or S-10, N-10, and W-10. Here the shelters were much more elaborate—wooden structures, their walls reinforced by cement, buried under a massive layer of earth.

S-10 was the control center. Here Professor Oppenheimer, as scientific commander in chief, and his field commander, Professor Bainbridge, issued orders and synchronized the activities of the other sites. Here the signal was given and a complex of mechanisms was set in motion that resulted in the greatest burst of energy ever released by man on earth up to that time. No switch was pulled, no button pressed, to light this first cosmic fire on this planet.

At forty-five seconds to zero, set for 5.30 o'clock, young Dr. Joseph L. McKibben of the University of California, at a signal from Professor Bainbridge, activated a master robot that set off a series of other robots, until, at last, strategically spaced electrons moved to the proper place at the proper split second.

Forty-five seconds passed and the moment was zero.

Meanwhile at our observation post on Compania Hill the atmosphere had grown tenser as the zero hour approached. We had spent the first part of our stay eating an early morning picnic breakfast that we had taken along with us. It had grown cold in the desert, and many of us, lightly clad, shivered. Occasionally a drizzle came down, and the intermittent flashes of lightning made us turn apprehensive glances toward Zero. We had had some disturbing reports that the test might be called off because of the weather. The radio we had brought with us for communication with Base Camp kept going out of order, and when we had finally repaired it some blatant band would drown out the news we wanted to hear. We knew there were two specially equipped B-29 Superfortresses high over head to make observations and recordings in the upper atmosphere, but we could neither see nor hear them. We kept gazing through the blackness.

Suddenly, at 5.29.50, as we stood huddled around our radio, we heard a voice ringing through the darkness, sounding as though it had come from above the clouds: "Zero minus ten seconds!" A green flare flashed out through the clouds, descended slowly, opened, grew dim, and vanished into the darkness.

The voice from the clouds boomed out again: "Zero minus three seconds!" Another green flare came down. Silence reigned over the desert. We kept moving in small groups in the direction of Zero. From the east came the first faint signs of dawn.

And just at that instant there rose from the bowels of the earth a light not of this world, the light of many suns in one. It was a sunrise such as the world had never seen, a great green super-sun climbing in a fraction of a second to a height of more than eight thousand feet, rising ever higher until it touched the clouds, lighting up earth and sky all around with a dazzling luminosity.

Up it went, a great ball of fire about a mile in diameter, changing colors as it kept shooting upward, from deep purple to orange, expanding, growing bigger, rising as it expanded, an elemental force freed from its bonds after being chained for billions of years. For a fleeting instant the color was unearthly green, such as one sees only in the corona of the sun during a total eclipse. It was as though the earth had opened and the skies had split. One felt as though one were present at the moment of creation when God said: "Let there be light."

To another observer, Professor George B. Kistiakowsky of Harvard, the spectacle was "the nearest thing to doomsday that one could possibly imagine. I am sure," he said, "that at the end of the world—in the last millisecond of the earth's existence—the last man will see what we have just seen!"

A great cloud rose from the ground and followed the trail of the great sun. At first it was a giant column, which soon took the shape of a supramundane mushroom. For a fleeting instant it took the form of the Statue of Liberty magnified many times. Up it went, higher, higher, a giant mountain born in a few seconds instead of millions of years, quivering convulsively. It touched the multicolored clouds, pushed its summit through them, kept rising until it reached a height of 41,000 feet, 12,000 feet higher than the earth's highest mountain.

All through this very short but extremely long time-interval not a sound was heard. I could see the silhouettes of human forms motionless in little groups, like desert plants in the dark. The newborn mountain in the distance, a giant among the pygmies of the Sierra Oscuro Range, stood leaning at an angle against the clouds, a vibrant volcano spouting fire to the sky.

Then out of the great silence came a mighty thunder. For a brief interval the phenomena we had seen as light repeated themselves in terms of sound. It was the blast from thousands of blockbusters going off simultaneously at one spot. The thunder reverberated all through the desert, bounced back and forth from the Sierra Oscuro, echo upon echo. The ground trembled under our feet as in an earthquake. A wave of hot wind was felt by many of us just before the blast and warned us of its coming.

The big boom came about one hundred seconds after the great flash—the first cry of a newborn world. It brought the silent, motionless silhouettes to life, gave them a voice. A loud cry filled the air. The little groups that had hitherto stood rooted to the earth like desert plants broke into a dance—the rhythm of primitive man dancing at one of his fire festivals at the coming of spring. They clapped their hands as they leaped from the ground—earthbound man symbolizing the birth of a new force that for the first time gives man means to free himself from the gravitational pull of the earth that holds him down.

The dance of the primitive man lasted but a few seconds, during which an evolutionary period of about 10,000 years had been telescoped. Primitive man was metamorphosed into modern man—shaking hands, slapping his fellow on the back, all laughing like happy children.

The sun was just rising above the horizon as our caravan started on its way back to Albuquerque and Los Alamos. We looked at it through our dark lenses to compare it with what we had seen.

"The sun can't hold a candle to it!" one of us remarked.

For questions and exercises, see p. 197, p. 301, p. 334, and p. 531.

## THE HICKMAN STORY

### JOHN BARTLOW MARTIN

The oldest son of the Hickman family, Willis, twenty years old, went to the barber shop after work and got home about 8:15, and then they all were home who were coming home that night, the seven children and the parents. Another son was working. The father, James Hickman, a cleancut Negro of thirty-nine, serious of mien and small but tightly-knit of body, was getting ready to go to his night job. He "had bad feet" and he sent Willis to the floor below to get a bucket of water to bathe them. (The Hickmans had no running water in their attic room atop the tenement.) About nine o'clock Hickman left for the steelmill. He was the head of this family.

Willis, and Charles, who was nineteen, and their mother helped the younger children with their lessons. The three in school—Leslie, fourteen, Elzena, nine, and Sylvester, seven—were really studying and Velvena was playing at studying, though she was only four. After half an hour Mrs. Hickman, a thin quiet woman, went to bed. Soon the four younger children crawled in with her. Willis and Charles got into the other bed, first turning off the kerosene heater, cookstove, and lamp. They all fell asleep. It was then about 10:00 P.M. on January 16, 1947.

An hour and a half later Mrs. Hickman was wakened by fire. "I heard the paper popping" in the ceiling. She ran to the door to the only stairway and "the fire and the smoke hit me, fire came right to me, in the face," and she slammed the door and went to get the children up. Charles leaped through the fiery doorway naked and escaped down the stairs. Mrs. Hickman was about to collapse. Willis wakened; "fire was over my head, in the door, I threw the cover back, and burned my hand." He rolled out of bed, crawled beneath the smoke to the front window, kicked it out, started out, hesitated, looked back.

Dimly through the smoke and flame he saw his mother huddled in the corner near her four smallest children. The flames were upon them. He pulled her to the window. It was three floors straight down the bare face of the old brick tenement to the street. He straddled the sill and hung her outside and told her to kick out the glass on the third floor below. She was too short, so Willis climbed out and, hanging by one hand, lowered her down. She scrambled to the second-floor window. He grabbled the third-floor window frame, but it gave way and he fell to the ground, breaking his collar bone and leaving her dangling. A man below yelled to her to let go, and she did, and he caught her. Later a fire chief said, "I cannot understand how she escaped . . . it was a miracle," and the coroner said, "The Lord was with her." But her four children were dead.

The night was cold, snow lay on the ground, but a great crowd gathered, this was a slum fire. Other tenants of the building streamed out, maybe forty of them. Neighbors took Mrs. Hickman and Willis to the hospital. The fire chief recalled, "It was a holocaust, it was one mass of fire rolling across that roof." But the firemen put it out in five minutes. Soon the street in the slum was deserted again.

Hours later, about 7:30 in the morning, gray daylight, a man alone came walking up the street, James Hickman the father. He had been told at work that he "had trouble in my home." Out in front of the tenement a man was tinkering with an automobile, he had the hood up, and another man was pouring water over the steps of the building. Hickman started upstairs, ". . . a policeman hailed me and asked where I was going. I said I was going upstairs where I live. 'You can't go up there,' he said. 'Man, you tell me I can't go up there, what's the trouble? I am James Hickman, I live there.'" The policeman asked cautiously what floor he lived on. "I said the fourth and he said, 'Ah, you can't go up there, we had a big fire.' I asked him where were my children, he said he didn't know." Another tenant had appeared. "He said, 'Mr. Hickman, I hate to tell you this, four of your children is burnt to death.' And I weakened down to the ground." They carried him into the basement. Presently, Hickman recalls, "My mind referred back." He remembered that his landlord David Coleman, had threatened to burn down the building if the tenants didn't clear out. A neighbor recalls, "Mr. Hickman was walking back and forth. He said nothing. There were tears in his eyes. Mr. Hickman looked pretty bad, like he was losing his mind. After about one half-hour, some officers helped Mr. Hickman away."

Our story is about James Hickman, a Negro. It is about his landlord, David Coleman, likewise a Negro, and their combat. It is also about slums and housing and race discrimination, the plight of the Negroes in the northern ghettos, the segregation that keeps them there and generates explosions, explosions like this fire and what came after it.

James Hickman, a man of rich brown color, was born February 19, 1907, "in the country" near Louisville, Mississippi. His mother and father were sharecroppers raising cotton and corn. They lived in a four-room shack. He was the youngest of four children; one was killed, the others left. At ten he went to work in the fields. At twelve he experienced a religious conversion. Forever after he was deeply religious. His mother and father separated when he was fourteen and he quit school. At sixteen he married a neighbor girl, Annie Davis. They lived with his mother and took care of her; she had tuberculosis. (She died in 1926 and for half a year Hickman grieved.) Their first child was born on August 2, 1924. They named her Arlene and Hickman made a vow to God: "I was the head of this family and had to make a support for them, I was a guardian to see for them as long as the days I should live on the land." He was then seventeen.

They moved to Fern Spring, "sharecropping cotton and corn, and vegtables for ourselves," his wife remembers. "We started farming at sun-up and stopped at sun-down. We were in the hilly part of Mississippi. I chopped cotton myself. . . ." They moved often, making a crop and giving birth to a child, then moving on, trying to better their lot. Some owners were fair, some were not. "We never could own the land." They moved to the Delta, land of milk and honey. They farmed the Delta seventeen years. One year, 1942, they made $935 their greatest earnings in the South. Before the war they often made only $100, one year $28, some years nothing at all. When they had a bad year "the bossmen . . . claimed that the cotton prices had failed." "When we got paid, Smith and Wiggins took their money first for food, clothes, fertilizer." Hickman says, "The landlord furnished everything. But you pays for it. And he don't work."

After the children were eight or nine, they rarely attended school more than four or five months a year, sometimes only one; for if the parents didn't send them to the fields, Hickman recalls, "the landlord'd be a-grumblin'. He'd say, get 'em busy, your grass is growin', this, that, or else he'd put a bunch in the fields, and it'd come out of your pay in the fall. Work is all they look for you to do. They don't look for no school. The plow and hoe and such'll keep knowledge out of a person's head." Mrs. Hickman says, "We was very anxious to get up North where they had the opportunity to go to school and all these privileges," meaning by "privileges" freedom for a black person.

Nine children were born and the Hickmans reared them all, an achievement for Negroes in the South. One, Corene, was born blind and never talked, the only one afflicted. Hickman said, "We couldn't help her but I loved her just like I loved the rest of them." Hickman was stern with his children but he loved them with a surpassing love. Upon the birth of each he repeated his vow to God to protect them and set them free. He wanted to take them North. He felt they were destined for great things. The ones born first disappointed him. "The oldest one was taken in the Army. The next one was kicked out of school. The daughter married. I said all right. These youngest children—I had told them all one night—'It seems like I can see a future for you.' I see in those four children that they possibly would be great men and great women some day. . . . I had a vision and the spirit said they would be great."

The Navy ordered Hickman to report for induction April 12, 1944, but the day before, men of his age were exempted "until further notice." He didn't know what to do, but the North had been tugging at him for a long time, so he went up there, worked ten months in a shipyard, went back South, then in the spring of 1945 went alone to Chicago, intending to find a job and a home and to bring his family North to stay.

How did Chicago look to this countryman? He'd visited Southern cities, but Chicago was different. Bigger, of course, but more than that. "Here, it was quite different when I'd see peoples riding in the cars together, buses—in the banks and post office colored would be working," he said recently in his slow, deep, deliberate voice. His oldest daughter, who had married, was living in Chicago, and Hickman stayed with her. "A gentleman picking up labor carried us over to a place to work"; Hickman thought it was the factory where his son-in-law worked but it was the stockyards, and he left. He got a job at Wisconsin Steel, far out at the Indiana line. He worked "on the crib," guiding the hot steel as it came off the hotbed. He was paid about $1.25 an hour, an awful lot to him. Better still, "I could see what I was gittin'. On the farm I'd be charged for a lot of things, I couldn't see what it was for. In the factory work it comes to my hand."

But soon the pleasures of earning good money and riding white men's buses palled. "I would see so many old raggedy buildings I'd say my goodness, I see so many nice buildings and then others just propped, folks livin' in just to have some place to live." He was hunting a place for his family. Finding one proved difficult. Hickman was bucking what may be the nation's worst housing problem.

Chicago's Black Belt is a narrow strip of land seven miles long and a mile and a half wide on the South Side, in spots almost—but not quite—touching the gilded lakefront. This is America's second biggest Negro city. Here, and in several scattered communities, dwell 400,000 Negroes, a tenth of Chicago's population. When a housing project of 1,658 units was opened in 1941, more than 19,000 people applied to live in it. Since then about 100,000 more Negroes, drawn by the war boom and Northern freedom, have come to live in Chicago. Why do they all crowd into this one area? Poverty? Yes, to a certain extent; but well-to-do Negroes live here too. The law? No, our laws imply the opposite, freedom. Ethnological attraction, then, which draws any immigrant group together? Again, yes, to a certain extent. Ah, but here we can see the truth: the European immigrants, as their earnings and adaptation increased, scattered throughout the city, disappearing into the general population. "Disappearing"—how can a black man disappear? He is not wanted. He is condemned to inhabit the areas that nobody else wants. Around the Negroes we have welded an iron ring of restrictive covenants and less formalized segregation enforced by violence. Thus trapped they turn upon one another. In this artificially restricted market, people of means bid high for hovels; rentals skyrocket; landlords gouge. Some of the landlords are white, some are black, all profit by the race-hate that makes their hovels desired. The Black Belt landlords squeeze tighter, and sometimes an eruptions occurs, as in the Hickman case.

James Hickman got off the night shift at 7:00 A.M. "I would leave the job and just ride, hunting for a place for my folks," till dark, rest a few hours, then go back to work. "Ride and ride, walk and walk. I'd knock on a door and ask. Workin' and lookin'." Ignorant of Chicago, he often got into strange neighborhoods. "Sometimes I'd get to where they wasn't nothin' but white folks, I'd be the only colored man walkin' down the street. I'd see houses and I didn't know who was living there till I'd knock on the door and they'd say white folks only. They'd tell me which hundred block was for the colored. I'd catch the car and go back and get off there." Did he experience any unpleasantness? "My race talked more rougher than the other race. I was born in a country where there's nothin' but white folks and I knowed how to talk and carry myself and they treated me mighty fine."

He found plenty of empty flats. "But they didn't want nobody with children." Even a public housing project refused him because he had so many children. Real estate offices took his money and produced nothing. Their usual fee was between $1 and $5 "to enlist," plus a month's rent if they found you a place. One landlord wanted to rent a four-room flat for $45 a month and sell the furniture for $1,200. Another asked "a thousand dollars down and $55 for twenty-five years, I didn't have that kind of money." But he had saved $260 since coming to Chicago and he was willing to pay up to $100 a month rent.

After six months, a barber offered to rent him a room in his own house. Hickman paid him a month's rent, $30, and sent train fare to his wife. She arrived with all the children on January 10, 1946, and Hickman met them at the station and took them out to their daughter's flat. Next day their furniture arrived from Mississippi, all their belongings, "meat and lard and everything but bread."

But the barber said the room wasn't ready yet. They put their furniture in their daughter's basement. Time passed. The Hickmans began looking for another place. A "real estate" lady found them one and they gave her $25 and paid the landlady $25 but the landlady returned their money; they couldn't have the apartment. They resumed their search, streetcars, pavements, want ads, realtors, all spring long. In June the barber called: they could have the room. They hired a truck for $18 and took their belongings to the barber's home. The barber's wife met them. She said they couldn't move in;

"she was the boss." They went away. They put the furniture in a warehouse. And started all over again, looking.

Hickman's daughter's landlord said there were too many of them, they'd have to get out. "We scattered," he recalls. On August 19, their daughter heard about a five-room basement flat where children were acceptable. Immediately Mr. and Mrs. Hickman caught a streetcar to the real estate office, paid $5 a room "for listing"— $23 cash and $2 owed—received the landlord's address, 2720 Prairie and hurried there by taxi. It proved to be a stone relic of the Gold Coast's splendor, drawing rooms and even butler's pantries now rented out as "apartments." Far at the back, in a recess dark even at noonday, lived the man the Hickmans had come to see, David Coleman. He only rented a room here, this was not his building. He took them outdoors to talk things over. They sat down in his half-brother's two-tone Buick taxicab parked in the glass-strewn street in front of the mansion's big iron gates.

Coleman was a very black man, twenty-five years old, about five-feet-ten, solidly built. He asked $200 rent in advance. Hickman said he couldn't pay so much. Coleman asked if he could pay $150. "Then he stopped, he looked at me, he said you look like I see you somewhere Hickman." They had lived only about three miles apart in the Delta. Coleman said. "Well now. Maybe we can get together. You can give me $100, can't you?" Hickman said he could but he wanted to see the apartment first. The three of them caught a streetcar.

II

Now David Coleman had been born January 12, 1922, at a flag-stop on the railroad in the Mississippi Delta. He was the last of eleven children; all but three of them died in infancy. "They just died," his mother says. "I don't know what of." He went to the fields full-time at twelve; later got a job driving a truck; married and had a child; and in 1943, lured by tales of freedom and high wartime wages, drove with his family to Chicago. They got along fine. The mother says, "We had a good job and a place to live. Nobody can do better." They came earlier than the Hickmans, before the housing screws were tightened quite so much, and they had fewer children. Coleman's wife died in bearing his second child. He married again; learned arc welding and once earned $2.10

an hour; liked to think of himself as a business man and tried to dress like one.

In July 1946, he met a woman with a building to sell. He borrowed money and leased the building and later he bought it "on contract" for $8,000, paying $300 down, the rest monthly. He had a lot of trouble over this deal, as we shall see; indeed it led to his death.

The building is on the West Side in an area once called Little Italy but now almost solidly Negro except for a few Mexicans. The best buildings are the churches and the factories. The buildings where people live are high brick tenements, patched-up wooden tenements, sheds. In between are vast wastelands, desolate open areas where buildings have collapsed or been torn down, the excavations partly filled with rubble. Broad Roosevelt Road, busy with traffic, cuts the section cleanly. A half block south is Washburne Street, our scene. It is a quiet street. A man is sitting idly on the iron railing in front of a house, tossing a pair of dice in the air and catching them, and a woman is sweeping the sidewalk with a broom, and now and then a child skates past, and that is all. The doorways of many houses are open, open onto a black void, the doors may be open or they may have vanished, and the houses look abandoned; but a woman is leaning on the railing, a hint of humanity packed inside. At the streetcorners are a Jewish delicatessen, a drugstore selling "Dream Books," the Temptation Cleaners, the iron structure of the El. In midblock, one of many in a row, is No. 1733, David Coleman's building. It is old, perhaps forty or fifty years old. It is huge and narrow—it stands three stories high above an English basement but, built on a twenty-five-foot lot, it is only thirty-one brick lengths wide. Two perpendicular rows of windows run up its face; in each is a panel of stained glass. To reach the upstairs flats you have to walk down a narrow gangway and enter a doorway halfway back along the side.

It was to this building on August 20, 1946, that David Coleman, as landlord, took Mr. and Mrs. Hickman. He showed them the basement apartment, offered at $50 a month. Hickman recalls, ". . . the water was half a leg deep in the basement . . . no windows, no lights, no nothing in there." A man who has since visited it says, "It was a woodshed really. The only impression it made on me was, this is how rats live." Hickman said it wouldn't do. Coleman said that in nine days a flat on the second floor would be available at $50 a month, and in the meantime they could have a room in the attic for $6 a week. Hickman testified later: "We walked up the stairs, it was so dark . . . we almost had to feel our way. . . . I am walking around looking at it, I don't like this. She said, I don't neither but surely we can stay here because we ain't got no place." They went outdoors and Hickman paid Coleman $30 "to hold us." He went to the South Side, withdrew $70 from his postal savings, and took it to Coleman. He got his furniture out of storage and that night he and his wife hired a taxi and took their six youngest children there—the two older boys moved in later—and they all slept there that night.

And so now, after more than a year, they had a home. It was an attic room about fourteen by twenty-one feet but the roof sloped so that you could stand up only in a fourteen-foot-square space. The three smallest children slept with Mr. and Mrs. Hickman and the rest slept in the other bed. There was no electricity; they used a kerosene lamp. There was no gas; they used a stove and heater burning kerosene. There was one window. There was no water; they had to go down to the third floor to use the toilet or to get water for washing or cooking. But it was shelter, and a place they could all be together with their things. And it was, they thought, only temporary.

The nine days passed, however, and ten more, and Hickman asked Coleman about the second-floor flat. "He said, Hickman wait until the 18th and if those folks don't move out, I'll give you back your $100." Hickman agreed. But "on September 18th, he dodged me." Hickman began to suspect a runaround. Other tenants told him they'd had trouble with Coleman. On September 22 Hickman caught up with Coleman. He asked for his $100 so he could use it to find another place to live. Coleman replied, "I won't pay you until I get ready." Hickman recalls, "I said I'd go to the law and make him give it back. He said he had a man on the East Side ready to burn the place up if . . . I had him arrested. . . . He said go ahead and have me arrested, I would be sorry. And," Hickman now says, "I really was sorry." But that day he said nothing, he went back upstairs. "I looked at my family, looked at my small children. . . . I . . . told my wife what David Coleman told me downstairs, I said I wanted peace, I have lived in peace forty years,

I asked her if there was laws in Chicago to take care of men like that, she said yes." On September 24 they got a warrant for Coleman's arrest. But the police never served it.

Coleman had leased the building July 27 from the owner, Mrs. Mary Porter Adams, a county social worker. About October 7 he took possession under his purchase contract. He had paid a rather high price and to meet the monthly payments he decided to cut the building up into more lucrative "kitchenette" apartments. He sent a contractor to the building, but the tenants obstructed him. Coleman arrived. An argument ensued. If he wanted to cut up the flats, they said, he would have to have the court evict them first. One recalled later, "He said: 'I am the owner, I don't have to go to court to do that, I will get everybody out of here when I want to if it takes fire.'"

Another family man, Albert Jones, had rented the dismal basement for $300, six months at $50 a month. Coleman had promised to repair it but he didn't. The main water line into the building was broken and so the water ran onto the floor of Jones's "apartment"; to alleviate this condition the other tenants turned off the main valve outside the building, and by prearrangement one of them would go outdoors and turn on the valve for a few minutes each day while the others flushed all the toilets and drew water into slop jars and buckets.

The Hickmans took their blind backward child, Corene, to a State hospital at Lincoln, Illinois. That left nine Hickmans in the room. "I worried about it night and day. I didn't want to bring them up in such living conditions." Hickman later testified that he never had lived so poorly in Mississippi as he had to live in Chicago.

Coleman refused to make repairs. Perhaps he hoped that hardship would drive the tenants out. Many bitter wrangles ensued. The tenants appealed to the OPA, the police, the fire department, the board of health, the water inspector. The only results: a policeman "come and looked and said it was awful," and the waterman shut off the water (probably because the bill wasn't paid). Nor was all this anything new; one tenant said, "We had been calling [the authorities] for the last few years," and violation of fire or building regulations—including insufficient fire exits—had been charged to various owners of this building but only one fine—of $25—had been levied. In December 1946, after a routine department inspection, Mrs. Adams was ordered to make certain repairs and to re-move papers, lumber, rags, and combustible rubbish, and a little later the city building department ordered her and Coleman to exterminate rats, reduce illegal overcrowding, repair the plumb-ing, and place "premises in habitable condition or vacate same." But nothing was done and there was no evidence that the building department took any steps toward enforcement—until after the fire.

As we have seen, Coleman bought the building on a shoestring. In November he leased it to Anthony Lee Barnett, Jr., who paid him $425. But then Barnett discovered that Jones already had a lease on the basement and Hickman had a $100 claim, so Barnett went to the State's Attorney and was advised to get a warrant for Coleman's arrest. Coleman fell behind in his monthly payments to Mrs. Adams. She visited the building about January 1, 1947, and was surprised to learn of Barnett's lease. The thing was a terrible muddle. That Sunday there was a fire in the flue. It did little dam-age but it aroused the tenants. They telephoned Mrs. Adams. She too wanted to get them out. One of them testified that she said, "Well, you are not paying enough rent there. . . . I am not going to fix anything. . . . It is not my fault because you got chil-dren. . . . Just find yourself another place." Another tenant told Mrs. Adams he was going to have the plumbing fixed "and pay it out of the rents." She sent him an eviction notice. She told the Hickmans there were too many of them in one room. Hickman said he didn't know what to do; and she suggested he find another home.

That same week the fire chief, on a routine inspection, found nineteen people living in the attic: another family had moved into the rear room. The chief ordered this other family out, and they went.

On three nights that week the Hickmans heard "somebody tip-ping up the stairs to the door and tipping down." Hickman asked his wife, "I wonder what they are up to. Do you reckon that some-body would burn us up here?" Coleman had lived for a time in a small room at the head of the stairs and had left an old bed frame and mattress and a trunk; now he came up and moved his trunk away. But he left the old bed frame and the mattress, the mattress rolled up in the corner. A week later the fire started where the mattress was.

III

Hickman was at work when the fire occurred. The police telephoned the steelmill and the foreman called for Hickman and a white man named Hicks went home by mistake. Not till almost 4:00 A.M. did they reach the right person. They told him he was wanted at the DesPlaines Street police station. The streetcar motorman told him where to get off but it was the wrong place and he walked around, lost. A man told him to go back to State Street and take a car up to Roosevelt Road and transfer. He still couldn't find the station so he went home.

The police investigation was lackadaisical (a deputy coroner remarked: "If this fire happened over on Sheridan Road some place, we would have half the police force in here"). Coleman denied having threatened to burn the building. There was no direct evidence that he had set it afire. But nobody could figure out an innocent origin and evidence indicated a strong possibility of arson. In the little room at the head of the stairs, investigators found a five-gallon can that nobody in the building recognized and it was half full of kerosene; one witness had seen a strange man running down the stairs the night of the fire; Coleman had removed his trunk a week earlier; firemen thought the fire moved suspiciously fast. But the coroner's jury, while "vigorously" condemning the condition of the building, confessed itself unable to determine whether the fire was accident or arson and recommended that the State's Attorney investigate further. The State's Attorney's investigation was feeble. The Coroner dropped the case. Nothing at all resulted. In April Coleman was fined $350 and costs and Mrs. Adams was fined $250 and costs for violations of the city building code—charges that could have been instituted months earlier, before the fire, but were not.

Hickman was convinced that Coleman had fired the building. And he felt justice had not been done. He was bitter. "Paper was made to burn, coal and rags. Not people. People wasn't made to burn." His son Willis remembers, "Before the fire he was outgoing. Not after the fire. He wouldn't eat. He had nothing to say. He would sit with his eyes closed, but was not asleep." One night in April, Willis heard him in the bedroom, "talkin' to Elzena," the child of nine who had burned to death, and to Velvena, the dead child of four. He talked "at first faintly and then excitedly." Then he jumped out of bed and cried, "The Lord have mercy," and ran from the room.

People of sympathy had got the Hickmans into a housing project, and Hickman had gone back to work, but his wife remembers, "He used to carry on practically every day. He would come home from work, sit down, and start talking about the children. 'My children got no cause to be dead. Other children are playing. My children have a right to play too. They didn't do any harm.' The more we talked about it, the more I would get worried. He would say: 'I know what Coleman told me. After he said it would happen, it did happen.'" Coleman's threat "went through my mind like a clock, over and over again." He bought a thirty-two caliber automatic pistol, telling his wife it was "for home use"; he always had kept a gun around the house. A strike at the steelmill July 10 made him idle. He brooded more. "When I looked around, the oldest ones was gone and the youngest ones were too. It used to be if we wanted a drink of water the baby would get it. Now there was no one there. No one to say: 'Daddy have you any candy?' There would be no happiness again until I would get in camp with God." He and his wife were officers of the Liberty Baptist Church. On July 15, Hickman said, "I got no mind to go to church," but they went. His wife recalls, "We had a Morning Star Club meeting." They got home about midnight. Hickman went to bed, got up, went into the boys' room, looked at them sleeping, looked at the pictures of the dead children. He got out his gun and polished it. He "turned the radio on—it didn't play so good. I started a verse to a hymn. I walked back and sat down on the studio couch. When I got to summing up my life, I saw my life was unhappy. I was in grief and sorrow." Next morning, his wife recalls, "he got up quiet."

Hickman remembers that day: "I drunk a half a cup of tea and part of a sandwich, I was filled up. I wasn't mad, I wasn't glad, I walked in the . . . living room, I reached under the bed in the cash box, I took the key off my side and unlocked it, reached in for this automatic, picked it up and laid it down. You just got to go through with it. I laid it down again. I walked back and sat down beside my wife, I ain't spoke nothing to her. I walked back to the cash box, I picked up this gun, I knocked the safety off of it and wanted to see if it would hang. I put it back down, I can't go through with this. The voice kept speaking, you know your promise." The "promise" was the vow he had made to God to protect his children. "The third time I picked up this gun, I put eight in the magazine, knocked the safety off and threw one in the barrel." Still he paced the house and yard in torment; once he got a block away. But he came back: "The word was so sharp it was cutting like a two edge sword. . . . The third time I didn't return no more."

He caught a bus, transferred to a streetcar, and got off at 26th and Indiana. Coleman lived a few blocks away. "I stood there on the street. I didn't want to go through with what it was telling me. . . . [But] this was a vow that I made to this family in 1923 . . . and the answer is I wouldn't back up. So I walked on down to Prairie." It was a little before 1:00 P.M. Out in front of the big dilapidated mansion at 2720 Prairie, David Coleman was sitting behind the wheel of his half-brother's big Buick taxicab, reading a newspaper, reading aloud an account of a raid to Percy Brown, who was leaning through the window.

Hickman came up the sidewalk. "He had some rent tickets in his lap . . . I walked up to him and spoke to him and friendly talked. I wanted peace with all mankind. 'How do you do, how are you feeling this morning, Coleman?' 'What do you want with me?' 'I come to ask you something about this arrest warrant, of the $100 and causing this disturbance,'" that is, the fire. Coleman replied, "Yes, but I ain't going to pay you." Hickman recalls, "My mind got scattered. I took out my automatic and blazed him twice. He said: 'I'll pay you.' I said: 'It's too late now. God is my secret judge.' I said: 'You started that fire.' He said: 'Yes, I did.' I shot him twice more. . . . I thought he was dead." He wasn't but he died three days later.

Hickman walked down the street and away, the automatic still in his hand. He missed a streetcar, walked on, farther than he needed. "I had put a heavy load down and a big weight fell off of me and I felt light." He took a streetcar home and asked his son Charles, "Where is your mother?" "He said, 'down to Arlene's.' I said, 'Tell her to come here, I got something to tell her,' so she came. . . . She said . . . 'They will find you.' 'I know.'" He waited till 4:15 P.M. before the Homicide Squad arrived. They arrested him and took his gun. He confessed immediately. A coroner's jury bound him to the Grand Jury, which indicted him for first degree murder. He was jailed without bond. He had no money for a lawyer. It looked like at least fourteen years in the penitentiary and he could have been electrocuted.

IV

But suddenly to his rescue came some citizens—an organizer for the Socialist Workers party, Mike Bartell, and two labor union men, Willoughby Abner, a Negro and first vice president of the central CIO Council in Chicago, and Charles Chiakulas, president of the United Auto Workers (CIO) local. (Hickman was not then a CIO member.) Bartell had visited Hickman the day after the fire and at his behest a civil-rights lawyer, M. J. Myer, had represented Hickman at the inquest (subsequently, when Mrs. Adams had filed suits to evict the other tenants who kept on living in the burned building without paying rent, Myer and Leon M. Despres represented them, presenting the interesting defense that the building was unfit for human habitation and therefore no rent was due). Now Abner, Chiakulas, and Bartell formed a Hickman Defense Committee.

Myer, Despres, and William H. Temple agreed to defend Hickman. Abner recalls "We had two objectives—to raise money for the defense and to educate the public to the horrible conditions these people lived in and the tragedies that can result." Others active were the Reverend James Luther Adams, a Unitarian minister and a board member of the Independent Voters of Illinois; Gerald Bullock, chairman of the Committee on Racial Equality; Franklin Field, a unionist active in the AVC; and Sidney Lens, head of an AF of L local. Many such groups degenerate into luncheons and resolutions. Hickman's defenders worked hard, effectively, fast, and according to plan. One traveled all over the East on $100, setting up local committees. They held rallies (Tallulah Bankhead, the actress, appeared) and put donation jars in Black Belt stores. Each member obtained mailing lists, publicity, and money from organizations he had access to.

Hickman's trial began on November 10, 1947, before a white judge and a white jury, with four white lawyers out of five on both sides. The prosecution proved that Hickman killed Coleman, the defense claimed he did so while temporarily insane. Hickman himself occupied the witness chair for a day and a half, a small black man behind an oak panel, speaking freely in flowing narrative, sometimes in language almost biblical.

He said: "My feelings was that I was mistreated without a cause. I felt that my children was without a guardian, that they suffered death, that they ought to be free on land and living."

He said: "This was God fixed this. I had raised these children up and God knowed that vow I made to him . . . that these children was a generation to be raised up. God wasn't pleased what happened to them."

His lawyer asked him about blind Corene who had been taken to an institution: "Mr. Hickman, while you were up in the attic before the fire, did one of the children leave the family and go live elsewhere?" and he said, "Leave the family? Yes, sir," and the lawyer said, "Will you describe her—when was she born, what happened to her?" and Hickman began, "She was born in June and she was beautiful."

His lawyer asked him to describe "your feelings" between the fire and the shooting, and he replied: "I had two sons and two daughters who would some day been great men and women, some day they would have married, some day they would have been fathers or mothers of children; these children would have children and then these children would have children and another generation of Hickmans could raise up and enjoy peace."

The jury was out for nineteen hours and then reported hopeless disagreement. All six men and one woman reportedly voted for acquittal, the other five women were for conviction. The jury was discharged. Hickman was sent back to jail to await a new trial.

But by this time the Hickman Defense Committee's work had taken hold. Letters were rolling in on the State's Attorney from all over the United States. The Defense Committee finally reached an agreement with Assistant State's Attorney Samuel L. Freedman, and on December 16 Judge Rudolph F. Desort dismissed the murder charge, found Hickman guilty of manslaughter and placed him on probation for two years. A few hours later Hickman went home to his family for Christmas.

Before disbanding, the Defense Committee held its only luncheon meeting. Abner, a quiet softspoken man, recalls, "Mr. and Mrs. Hickman thanked us from the bottom of their hearts, said they were very grateful." Abner said recently, "I don't know—at the start, you knew the thing was there, you couldn't just sit back and do nothing about it, it got inside you. We really felt good when it was over. It shows everything isn't in vain, it isn't all injustice, people will rally, it shows what can be done."

Not quite everybody had rallied. Some organizations declined to do so. The Communists and the organizations they control or influence would not participate. The American Civil Liberties Union felt that no civil-rights issue was involved and the National Association for the Advancement of Colored People that no race issue was involved. Attorney Myer said recently, "Sure Hickman and Coleman were both Negroes—but there wouldn't have been any fire or shooting either if it hadn't been for restrictive covenants and the Negro slums."

And in truth Coleman as well as Hickman seems the victim of a system. The system of segregation that creates such tremendous housing pressures also creates opportunity for men weak by nature to exploit their fellows. Coleman happened to be black but it was white man's race prejudice that enabled him to exploit Hickman. And he was only the last of many men who had oppressed Hickman because of Hickman's color. The white planters of Mississippi had driven him to Chicago. Here Coleman took over. And he was able to take over because of the prejudice of Northern whites. The North had failed the Negro no less than the South, there is no place in this country for a black man to go. In Chicago after the 1917-18 war the tremendous population pressure burst the bounds of the Black Belt despite bombings, arsons, and a major race riot. The same thing is happening today. And the greater the pressure of the blacks, the greater white resistance—more hurried meetings of "improvement" associations to draw new restrictive covenants, more rocks and bombs and "Molotov cocktails" thrown at newly-purchased Negro homes, more suspect fires that already within the past three years have killed a score of Negroes, more "streetcar incidents" and "bathing beach incidents," more political speeches promising "racial purity." Even the government's efforts in the Negroes' behalf, public housing, have been resisted stoutly. It is profitable to rent firetraps. The vested—and highly respectable—real estate interests of this city draw the iron ring ever tighter. (Who cares if they are corroding away the heart of the city? They also are pandering to our own prejudices.) Chicago's postwar housing record is one of complete failure; indeed, despite innumerable editorials and civic luncheons, bond issues, and tub-thumping, in 1946 the city actually lost more dwelling units through fire and simple decay than it erected. The housing problem is bad everywhere in America; in no major city is it worse than in Chicago, and Negroes are at the bottom of the heap because we put them there and we keep them there. Now after a "people's war" Negroes are becoming restive; and on at least one occasion since V-J Day only Negro restraint has prevented a major race riot; and the Mayor's Commission on Human Relations, which has done much to ease the dangerous tensions, has warned: "Unless more homes are provided, no one, regardless of good will or police power, can check the social conflicts which are inherent in this situation . . . we have all of the ingredients for social destruction."

The Defense Committee helped to get Hickman a new job. He and his wife and the remaining children, the three boys, eighteen, twenty, and twenty-two, are living in a housing project near the airport, close to another project where in 1946 one of Chicago's most dangerous race flare-ups occurred. They intend to stay in Chicago. Mrs. Hickman says, "I like Chicago. I used to like it very much when I had my children."

A year after the fire the old building at 1733 Washburne was deserted. After the shooting the tenants had quit resisting eviction and moved away, and almost at once another fire gutted the building. The windows have been boarded up, the attic is open to the weather, charred black timbers and jagged bricks and boards askew against the sky. In the alley dirty newspapers blow gently by a wrecked car, a woman is burning trash in a salamander, and in the center lies a dead rat. On a little mound of rubble behind 1733, an old Negro squats amid piles of junk, hat brim up, shoes broken, denim jacket patched; he is tending a little fire to burn the wood from barrel hoops, burning tin cans and buckets clean with fire. He moved here in 1919 from the South Side, the only Negro in his block, and for a time white kids broke his windows, "though I guess their folks put them up to it." It isn't as nice here as on the South

Side. Why do people move over here? "Looking for some place to go." There's talk that the owner of 1733 is going to fix the building up and sell it. Will people live in it? "Sure," and he laughs. "If they fix it up, they'll soon be lined up here, putting in their application. People got no place to go."

What is the tone of this article? In framing your answer, ask yourself the questions listed on p. 481. For further exercises, see p. 131 and p. 293.

# THE ASSAULT ON MT. EVEREST

### JAMES ULLMAN

At last, however, the route up the wall was completed. The body of climbers retired to Camp III, at its foot, for a much-needed rest, leaving Hazard and twelve porters in the newly established camp on the col. During the night the mercury fell to twenty-four below zero and at dawn a heavy snowfall began; but Geoffrey Bruce and Odell nevertheless decided to ascend to the col. They did not get far. Halfway up they encountered Hazard and eight of the porters coming down. They were near collapse after the night of frightful cold and wind on the exposed col. Worse yet, four of the porters were still up above, having absolutely refused to budge downward over the treacherous fresh snow of the chimney.

A sombre council of war ensued at Camp III. Snow and wind were now driving down the mountain in wild blasts, and it was obvious that the marooned men could not survive for long. All plans had to be set aside and every effort devoted to getting them down.

What followed constitutes one of the most remarkable and courageous rescues in mountaineering annals. Mallory, Norton and Somervell, the three outstanding climbers of the expedition, fought their way up the ice-wall and came out at last upon a steep snow-slope a short distance below the top and immediately above a gaping crevasse. At the top of the slope the porters huddled, half-dead from exposure, but afraid to move. The snow between them and the rescuing party was loose and powdery, liable to crumble away at any moment.

At this point Somervell insisted on taking the lead. Roping up, he crept toward the porters along the upper lip of the crevasse, while Mallory and Norton payed out behind him. But the rope's two hundred feet were not enough; when he had reached its end he was still ten yards short of the men. There was nothing for it but that they must risk the unbridged stretch on their own. After long persuasion two of them began edging across. And made it. Somervell passed them along the rope to Mallory and Norton. Then the other two started over, but at their first step the snow gave way and they began sliding toward the abyss below. Only a patch of solid snow saved them. They brought up at the very edge of the crevasse, gasping, shaken, unable to move an inch.

Now Somervell called into action all his superb talents as a mountaineer. He jammed his ice-ax into the snow and, untying the rope from his waist, passed it around the ax and strained it to its fullest length. Then he lowered himself down the slope until he was clinging to its last strands with one hand. With the other he reached out and, while the snow shuddered ominously underfoot, seized each porter in turn by the scruff of the neck and hauled him up to safety. Within a few hours climbers and porters were back in Camp III, all of them still alive, but little more.

After this harrowing experience a few days' rest at lower altitudes was absolutely necessary, and for the second time in two weeks the Everesters found themselves driven back to the base camp. Their situation could scarcely have been more discouraging. They had planned to be on the northeast ridge by the middle of May, and now it was already June and no man had yet set foot on the mountain proper. In another ten days, at most, the monsoon would blow in and all hope of success would be gone. They must strike hard and strike fast, or go down again to defeat.

The next week witnessed climbing such as the world has never seen before.

The plan called for an assault in continuous waves, each climbing party consisting of two men, each attempt to begin the day after the preceding one. The base of operations was to be Camp IV on the North Col. Camp V was to be set up on the ridge, near the site of the 1922 bivouac, and a sixth camp higher yet—as near to the summit as the porters could possibly take it. The climbers believed that the establishment of Camp VI was the key to the ascent; the experiences of the previous expedition had convinced them that the top could be reached only if the final "dash" were reduced to not more than 2000 feet. In the first fine weather they had experienced in weeks the band of determined men struggled back up the glaciers.

Mallory and Geoffrey Bruce were chosen for the first attack. With Odell, Irvine and nine porters they reached the North Col safely, spent the night there, and the next morning struck out up the ridge, accompanied by eight of the "tigers." [1] Odell, Irvine and one helper remained on the col in support. The climbers made good progress the first day and set up their tents at 25,300 feet—a mere 200 feet lower than the highest camp in 1922. A night of zero cold and shrieking wind, however, was too much for the porters, and the next morning no amount of persuasion would induce them to go higher. Seething with frustration, Mallory and Bruce were forced to descend with them.

Meanwhile the second team of Norton and Somervell, had started up the col, according to plan. They passed the first party on the way down, reached Camp V and spent the night there. In the morning their porters, too, refused at first to go on, but after four solid hours of urging three of them at last agreed to make a try. The work they subsequently did that day has seldom been matched anywhere, for endurance, courage, and loyalty. Step by gasping step they struggled upward with their packs—freezing, leaden-footed, choking for air—until at last Camp VI was pitched at the amazing altitude of 26,800 feet. Their task completed, they then descended to the North Col, to be hailed as heroes by all below: Lhakpa Chede, Napoo Yishay and Semchumbi, greatest of all "tigers."

That night Norton and Somervell slept in a single tiny tent, higher than men had ever slept before. Their hearts now were pounding with more than the mere physical strain of their exertions: the long dreamed-of summit loomed in the darkness only 2300 feet above them; victory was at last within their reach. Carefully, for the hundredth time, they reviewed their plans for the final day. There were two opinions in the expedition as to the best route to be followed. Mallory and some of the others were in favor of ascending straight to the northeast shoulder and then following the crest of the main east ridge to the base of the summit pyramid. Norton

[1] Native porters who excelled at mountaineering were called "tigers."

and Somervell, however, believed that by keeping a few hundred feet below the ridge they would not only find easier climbing, but also escape the full fury of the west wind; and it was this route that they now determined to take.

Dawn of the next day broke clear and still. By full sunrise they were on their way, creeping upward and to the west over steeply tilted, snow-powdered slabs. As they had hoped, they were protected from the wind, but the cold was bitter and both men coughed and gasped in the thin, freezing air. They could take only a dozen steps in succession before pausing to rest. While moving, they were forced to take from four to ten breaths for each single step. Yet they kept going for five hours: to 27,000 feet—27,500—28,000—

At noon Somervell succumbed. His throat was a throbbing knot of pain and it was only by the most violent effort that he was able to breathe at all. Another few minutes of the ordeal would have been the end of him. Sinking down on a small ledge in a paroxysm of coughing, he gestured to his companion to go on alone.

With the last ounce of his strength Norton tried. An hour's climbing brought him to a great couloir, or gully, which cuts the upper slopes of Everest below the summit pyramid and the precipices of the north face below. The couloir was filled with soft, loose snow, and a slip would have meant a 10,000-foot plunge to the Rongbuk Glacier. Norton crossed it safely, but, clinging feebly to the ledges on the far side, he knew that the game was up. His head and heart were pounding as if any moment they might literally explode. In addition, he had begun to see double, and his leaden feet would no longer move where his will directed them. In his clouded consciousness he was just able to realize that to climb farther would be to die.

For a few moments Norton stood motionless. He was at an altitude of 28,126 feet—higher than any man had ever stood before; so high that the greatest mountain range on earth, spreading endlessly to the horizon, seemed flattened out before him. Only a few yards above him began the culminating pyramid of Everest. To his aching eyes it seemed to present an easy slope—a mere thousand feet of almost snow-free slanting rock beckoning him upward to the shining goal. If only his body possessed the strength of his will; if only he were more than human—

Somehow Norton and Somervell got down the terrible slopes of

Everest. By nine-thirty that night they were back in the North Col
camp in the ministering hands of their companions, safe, but more
dead than alive. Somervell was a seriously sick man. Norton was
suffering the tortures of snow-blindness and did not regain his sight
for several days. Both had given all they had. That it was not
enough is surely no reflection on two of the most determined and
courageous mountaineers who ever lived.

Norton and Somervell's assault was the next-to-last in the adventure of 1924. One more was to come—and, with it, mystery and
tragedy.

Bitterly chagrined at the failure of his first effort, Mallory was
determined to have one last fling before the monsoon struck. Everest
was *his* mountain, more than any other man's. He had pioneered
the way to it and blazed the trail to its heights; his flaming spirit
had been the principal driving force behind each assault; the conquest of the summit was the great dream of his life. His companions,
watching him now, realized that he was preparing for his mightiest
effort.

Mallory moved with characteristic speed. With young Andrew
Irvine as partner he started upward from the col the day after Norton and Somervell had descended. They spent the first night at
Camp V and the second at Camp VI, at 26,800 feet. Unlike Norton
and Somervell, they planned to use oxygen on the final dash and to
follow the crest of the northeast ridge instead of traversing the
north face to the couloir. The ridge appeared to present more
formidable climbing difficulties than the lower route, particularly
near the base of the summit pyramid where it buckled upward in
two great rock-towers which the Everesters called the First and
Second Steps. Mallory, however, was all for the frontal attack and
had frequently expressed the belief that the steps could be sur-
mounted. The last "tigers" descending that night from the highest
camp to the col brought word that both climbers were in good
condition and full of hope for success.

One man only was to have another glimpse of Mallory and Irvine.

On the morning of June eighth—the day set for the assault on
the summit—Odell, the geologist, who had spent the night alone at
Camp V, set out for Camp VI with a rucksack of food. The day was
as warm and windless as any the expedition had experienced, but
a thin gray mist clung to the upper reaches of the mountain, and

Odell could see little of what lay above him. Presently, however, he scaled the top of a small crag at about 26,000 feet, and, standing there, he stopped and stared. For a moment the mist cleared. The whole summit ridge and final pyramid of Everest were unveiled, and high above him, on the very crest of the ridge, he saw two tiny figures outlined against the sky. They appeared to be at the base of one of the great steps, not more than seven or eight hundred feet below the final pinnacle. As Odell watched, the figures moved slowly upward. Then, as suddenly as it had parted, the mist closed in again, and they were gone.

The feats of endurance that Odell performed during the next forty-eight hours are unsurpassed by those of any mountaineer. That same day he went to Camp VI with his load of provisions, and then even higher, watching and waiting. But the mountain-top remained veiled in mist and there was no sign of the climbers returning. As night came on, he descended all the way to the col, only to start off again the following dawn. Camp V was empty. He spent a solitary night there in sub-zero cold and the next morning ascended again to Camp VI. It was empty too. With sinking heart he struggled upward for another thousand feet, searching and shouting, to the very limit of human endurance. The only answering sound was the deep moaning of the wind. The great peak above him loomed bleakly in the sky, wrapped in the loneliness and desolation of the ages. All hope was gone. Odell descended to the highest camp and signalled the tidings of tragedy to the watchers far below.

So ended the second attempt on Everest—and, with it, the lives of two brave men. The bodies of George Mallory and Andrew Irvine lie somewhere in the vast wilderness of rock and ice that guards the summit of the world. Where and how death overtook them, no one knows. And whether victory came before the end, no one knows either. Our last glimpse of them is through Odell's eyes —two tiny specks against the sky, fighting upward.

The rest is mystery.

Is this account "overwritten"? (See pp. 452-54.) If not, indicate why not. Comment on the diction. Is it for the most part concrete? (See p. 374.) Are many of the terms technical? (See p. 38.) Can you justify the choice of diction?

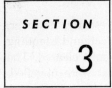

# SECTION 3

# Articles of Prop-
# aganda and Opinion

## HAVE NATIONS ANY MORALS?

### W. T. STACE

International morality may seem a figment of the imagination. It is bad enough to talk morals to the individual man in connection with his individual affairs. Tell the businessman that he ought to behave with Christian unselfishness towards his competitors and you are likely to appear intolerably smug or perhaps merely irrelevant and absurd. There is a story—perhaps it is quite apocryphal— that Carl Frederick Taeusch, Professor of Business Ethics at Harvard, was introduced to Samuel Alexander, the English philosopher, who was very deaf. The introducer said, "This is Professor Taeusch, Professor of Business Ethics at Harvard." Alexander said, "What?" The introducer shouted, "Professor of Business Ethics at Harvard." "It's no use," said Alexander. "I can't hear. It sounds to me just like 'Professor of Business Ethics at Harvard.'" Alexander thought, evidently, that "business ethics" is a contradiction in terms.

Well, if talking morals at the private individual often seems irrelevant or smug, how much more would this seem to be true if one were to talk morals at the nations. Would there be any sense in saying to the nations: "You ought to behave to one another like Christian saints"? How childishly unrealistic that sounds. Is it not an axiom that nations, in their dealings with one another, are guided

HAVE NATIONS ANY MORALS?: Originally printed in *The Atlantic Monthly*, November 1945. Reprinted here by permission of the author and *The Atlantic Monthly*.

and must be guided solely by considerations of national self-interest? And if so, what room is there here for talk about moral principles?

Now it has always struck me that there is a curious contradiction at this point in our international thinking. On the one hand, we keep repeating glibly this saying that states in their international actions are and must be governed exclusively by national self-interest. This idea is not only popular: it reaches the highest circles of our government. Some time ago a British Minister, Oliver Lyttelton, actually had the effrontery to accuse America of entering the war not wholly out of self-interest, but partly out of a generous feeling of sympathy for those nations, including the British, who had been attacked by the Nazis! He suggested that this American attitude and the actions which resulted from it had been partly responsible for Japan's decision to attack America. Secretary Cordell Hull was furious. He thundered from Washington that America had no such motives. American action and the American attitude had been entirely correct; that is, America had been motivated exclusively by considerations of self-defense—which is to say, self-interest. The British government, pursuing its policy of appeasing America, thereupon compelled Oliver Lyttelton abjectly to apologize. Thus this slogan about national self-interest is a fixed part of our international thinking.

But, on the other hand, we also talk loudly about morals in international affairs. Did we not say that there were moral issues involved in the war? Did we not claim that we were fighting for justice? Do we not say that Nazism is the repudiation of international justice, of international morals? Do we not say that we want to establish an international order based on law and justice, and not, as our enemies would have it, on the law of the jungle?

Also we high-mindedly disapprove of imperialism, and we lecture the British about keeping their promises to the Indians in India or to the Jews in Palestine. But why in the world should we disapprove of imperialism? And why in the world should the British keep their promises? There is implied in these attitudes a belief that moral principles ought to have some place in national actions.

Again, there actually exists a body of rules and principles called "international law," and *some* nations *sometimes* observe *some* of its provisions. But this international law is hardly law at all in the sense in which Acts of Congress are laws. For Acts of Congress are enforceable by sanctions. Congress does not merely exhort you to pay your income tax. It tells you that if you don't, something extremely unpleasant will happen to you. The existence of a sanction, of some way of enforcing a law, is part of the essence of law. But there is no way of enforcing international law except the crude way of reprisals. Therefore, international law is not in the full sense law, although it is true that courts adjudicate on it. What is it, then? It is mainly moral exhortation. It is a body of *moral* principles which civilized nations have agreed that they ought to follow, and which some of them do follow in some respects.

The theory that nations must act exclusively from national self-interest is identical with the theory that in international affairs the law of the jungle should prevail. It was, incidentally, Hitler's theory. That does not necessarily make it wrong, but what I am pointing out is the utter muddle-headedness of our American thinking, which believes two flatly contradictory principles.

## II

The atomic bomb, besides exploding Japanese cities, may possibly explode some of our incredibly foolish notions. We think that nations ought not to be moral—for this is the plain meaning of our chatter about self-interest as the only proper motive of nations. Well, we had better change our opinion and change it fast. Otherwise there may be no nations left to have any self-interest. I propose to show that this opinion is false—that not only *ought* nations to be moved by moral forces, but in point of fact they *are* moved by them already.

Let us take first what would seem to be the hardest case, that of the Germans. Moral forces, we might say, have not operated in their international actions in any way. But I think this is a mistaken view.

Hitler in *Mein Kampf* says repeatedly that force of arms will succeed only if it is inspired by some ideal. People will not fight, he says—or at least will not fight successfully—unless they believe that they are fighting for some great idea, for some ideal, for some just cause. They will not fight for merely selfish and material ends. Hitler was a much better psychologist than some of our statesmen. He knew that he could not make the German people fight simply out of self-interest. If he had said to them simply, "By means of a vast spilling of our blood we can conquer the earth and make everyone on earth slave for us. And then we shall all be twice as rich as we are now. We shall all eat twice as much. And those who now can drink only beer will all be able to drink champagne," not a German would have followed him. He had, on the contrary, to impregnate the German mind with a moral, ideal, and even mystical creed. He had to invent something like a new *Weltanschauung*,[1] even a new religion. He had to persuade the German people that they were called on to sacrifice their blood for a *noble* cause.

You will say, of course, that Hitler's ideas were in fact not moral but diabolical, that his *Weltanschauung* was false, that the ideals he fostered were in fact profoundly immoral. But I do not think this is correct. It may have been a false morality that animated the German people, but it was a morality. It was certainly not mere self-interest. It contains the ideas of nobility and heroism—and these, however distorted their application, are moral ideas. The point is that Hitler had to make the Germans believe they were struggling towards a higher world morality—however hideously false that morality may in fact have been.

Now let us take another case, that of England during the first World War. In 1914 when the Germans invaded Belgium, British national self-interest was involved. It was contrary to British interests that the powerful German nation should control the Channel ports and the Continental shores opposite Britain. Also it would destroy the balance of power. But Sir Edward Grey put the matter to the British nation mainly (though not exclusively) as a moral issue. Germany was breaking her solemn promises and was oppressing a little nation whose neutrality Britain as well as Germany was pledged to defend. Why did Sir Edward Grey put it thus? Because he knew, as Hitler knew later, that a nation will not be moved to the supreme effort of war by mere material self-interest, but only when the people feel themselves inspired by a moral purpose.

At this point the cynic, who knows all the answers, will say, "It is evident that the real cause of Britain's going to war in 1914 was self-interest, and Sir Edward Grey knew this, but had to delude the British into believing they had a moral cause, just as later Hitler

---

[1] A "world view," a philosophical attitude.

had to delude the Germans." I think this is cheap cynicism for two reasons.

In the first place, it is an open question how far the leaders of a self-respecting nation ever deliberately delude the nation and invent moral issues in which they do not believe. I should say that Sir Edward Grey probably himself believed both that it was Britain's self-interest to go to war and that it was her moral duty to do so, but that he was a good enough psychologist to know that he must play up the moral issue rather than the self-interest. I think he believed in the moral justice of the British cause as much as anyone else and that he was perfectly sincere in his insistence upon this. And even Hitler, I should say, at the time he wrote *Mein Kampf*, believed in his so-called higher German morality.

In the second place, even if I am wrong about this, even if we represent the leaders of nations, including Sir Edward Grey, and Hitler, and perhaps Wilson and Franklin D. Roosevelt, as a pack of cynical hypocrites who in their hearts believed in nothing but selfishness between nations,. but deluded their people with talk of moral ideas—even if we believe this, I say, it does not in any way lessen the force of my argument. Rather, it strengthens it. For it is an admission that the nations, the *peoples* of the world, are moved by moral ideas and moral forces, that moral ideals do enter into the motivation of their actions in regard to each other. It is therefore utterly false to say that the motives of international action are purely those of self-interest. And this assertion will remain true even if we hold that the moral forces acting in these peoples are merely used by their leaders to steer the nations into those courses which the leaders think they should, from their national self-interest, follow. Moral ideas are not only relevant to the international scene but are profoundly powerful in it.

### III

There used to be, among economists, an absurd abstraction called "the economic man." The economic man was governed solely by considerations of profit and loss—that is, by self-interest. His mind was nothing but a calculating machine. It added up the probable profits and losses of a proposed action, and if the calculation showed a balance of profit to himself, he acted. If not, not. And no consideration other than profit and loss moved him in the slightest degree.

Economists have now given up the idea of the economic man. It involved a fantastic oversimplification of human nature. Human beings are simply not like that. No businessman, even the most hardheaded, is a mere calculating machine of profit and loss. All sorts of other motives, some generous, some ungenerous, some indifferent, irrelevant, or merely whimsical, enter in. Even if he allows his liking for a friend to deflect his action by a hair's breadth—to make him contented, for example, with a profit of only a thousand dollars where he might have made a thousand dollars and fifty cents by ruining his friend—even this trivial deflection of his action by a slight feeling of generosity to a friend takes him out of the class of purely economic men, since it means that his action is in some degree motivated by moral impulses—for generosity and friendship are moral impulses.

Now this absurd abstraction of the economic man, long out of date in economics, pops up again in our international thinking in the form of the doctrine that foreign policy is and ought to be governed only by national self-interest. This is just as much an oversimplification of the psychology of nations as the economic man was of the psychology of individuals, and it is the same oversimplification. The motives of nations, as of individual men, are extraordinarily mixed and complicated, and somewhere in the mixture you will always find moral ideas working.

The element of truth in the current belief that nations have no morals seems to me to be this: the level of morals as practiced by individual human beings between themselves is relatively high; the level of morals as practiced by nations between themselves is deplorably low. There *is* such a thing as international morality. That is to say, moral forces do operate on the international plane. But the *standard* of morals as between nations is much lower than the *standard* of morals practiced by decent people towards each other in the sphere of individual action.

It is this fact which gives rise to statements that moral ideas do not apply to nations at all, and that nations act purely from self-interest. These statements are to be explained simply as exaggerations. We see the deplorably low level of international morality, and then we make wild statements denying altogether its existence or even its possibility.

Why is there this vast difference between the ethical standards of individuals and the ethical standards of states? There are several reasons. One is the mere fact that other nations are at a distance from us. We cannot easily wrong a person on our doorstep, where we see the results of what we do, but we can more easily act with indifference, or even brutality, when the victims are thousands of miles away and we do not see the results of our actions.

But the reason which is more relevant to my topic is the following: Individuals act within a community of individuals, the state. But nations do not act within a community of nations. There is no world state or super-state. The morality of individuals is embodied in institutions, of which the chief is the state, but which also include all sorts of other institutions, such as the family, the churches, the universities, schools, unions, societies of all kinds, even social clubs. The morality of the individual is at every point created for him, upheld, inspired, supported by the whole social organism of which he forms a part. His morality is objectified in these institutions. But there is no nation of nations, no state of states, no institution in which international morality can organize and objectify itself. Therefore, international morality inevitably remains at a low level, because it lacks the necessary organs and instruments by which to realize itself.

Several consequences follow. First, the low level of international morals is not due to any inherent non-moral character of the nation or the state as such. It is not because in the nature of things the state is super-moral or sub-moral or outside morality, or that morality does not apply to it. Men collected into a nation have the same moral feelings and moral natures as do the individuals who compose the collection. But as nations they lack the institutions, especially the institution of a great overall state, in which their moral natures can express and objectify themselves.

Second, you cannot have a very high level of international morality until you do have a world state. And in the peace after this war it is foolish to expect ideal solutions. Some people are shocked by what they consider the unjust treatment of Poland or by some other feature of the proposed peace settlement. But the general problem of the control and government of human beings everywhere, even within an organized community, is to leaven the vast inert bulk of human indifference and even wickedness with that bare modicum of morality and justice which it will stand. That is why the law of a country always lags behind the moral sense of its best citizens. It cannot enforce the highest standards of its best citizens, but only the much lower standards which practically all its citizens, even those who are most undeveloped morally, will support. If it tries to aim higher than that, the law is flouted and breaks down.

How much more true will this be in the international sphere, where there is no government to enforce any law. To be more specific, if you try to force on a country like Russia some law or principle which that country is not ready to accept, then that country will flout your law and your principle. And the result will be, not merely that law breaks down in that instance, but that all respect for law is gone, and that it breaks down everywhere all over the world. And then your entire peace breaks down.

IV

As to the world state, without which I say you can never get a high level of international morality, I have no doubt that it will some day come. It is in the direct line of human evolution. Smaller wholes coalesce into larger wholes. There are unicellular organisms. Then single cells coalesce into multicellular organisms. Individual multicellular organisms coalesce into families, families into tribes, tribes into nations. The evolutionary process would not naturally stop till it ends in the organization of all men into a single society.

But that is a long way off. Perhaps in five hundred years, perhaps even in a hundred years, we might have a world state. Possibly the atomic bomb will quicken this slow rate of development. At any rate it is no use writing of what may happen in a remote future. Let us consider merely the decade or so which lies directly in front of us.

The problem of the immediate future is: Admitting that we cannot yet have a world state, and that a very high level of international morals is impossible without it, how, in these circumstances, can we gradually raise the level of international morals? I think that there are just three principles we should try to apply. And I will say a few words about each of them.

The first principle is that we should, as a nation, place ourselves always on the side of justice, in every dispute, and endeavor by our example to influence others to do the same. In general, the American people already instinctively do this. The practical difficulty, of course, is to know which *is* the side of justice. And here we are often likely, through ignorance of complicated sets of facts about remote countries, to go astray. But even if in the particular case we may be partly ignorant or even mistaken about a situation, the fact that we stand for just solutions in general will exercise a great weight.

For instance, in the matter of India. We place ourselves on the side of freedom for the Indians. The British reply that they are as anxious for Indian freedom as we are, but that we do not understand the complexity of the problem. This charge is in general true. We are most of us woefully ignorant of even the most elementary facts of the extraordinarily complex Indian situation. But even though we underestimate the immense problem which India presents to the British, and thereby in our words and thoughts often do some injustice to our British friends, yet the fact that we do stand for Indian freedom puts the pressure in the right direction. It tends to force the British to solve those problems which otherwise they, even if we grant their good intentions, might well give up as insoluble. If we keep up this pressure, even though it be sometimes in rather an ignorant way, these problems will in the end be solved.

The second principle is that we should try to persuade nations that national self-interest is in the long run best served by international justice and morality rather than by the law of the jungle. Perhaps we need to preach this more to ourselves than to other people, certainly as much. It is the failure to understand this principle which produces isolationism.

I do not mean to suggest that one can attain the highest standard of morals by basing morality on self-interest. It is not true that they always coincide. The world's moral giants and teachers, the saints, the martyrs, the moral heroes, to whom we look up as the best of our kind, were never made merely by taking a long view of their own interests. The cynical opinion that the good man is merely more clever at advancing his own interests than the bad man, but that they both aim exclusively at their own interests, is psychologically false. But then, we are not hoping at present to produce a world of heroically moral nations. We are trying to inject a bare minimum of morality into the international chaos. And at that low level of morals at which we are compelled to operate, it is roughly true that intelligent self-interest and decent behavior coincide. For example, you do produce a relatively decent level of business ethics by getting businessmen to see that honesty is the best policy. The same will be true in the international sphere.

The third principle is that we should support all international organizations which tend toward common action and the submergence of individual national interests in a larger whole. But here we find ourselves involved in a difficulty which is something like a vicious circle. The reason we cannot attain a high level of international morality is that there is no world state. But then, the reason we cannot, at present, get a world state is that our level of international morals is so low.

I have already exhibited the first half of this circle. I will say a word about the second. Why can we not get a world state now?

The League of Nations was not a world state, but it was a move in that direction. The reason why the League of Nations broke down was not that its instrument or its machinery was faulty. It was a very good instrument; it was very good machinery. It broke down partly because it was not supported by all the great powers, and partly because even those powers which did join it were not willing to back it to the extent of risking what they believed to be their individual national interests for the sake of the interests of the community of nations. To be specific, they would not enforce the necessary sanctions in the cases of Manchuria and Ethiopia because they did not see that their own interests were immediately involved. But morality, if it means anything, means the merging of your individual interests in the interests of the community. So it comes to this: the League broke down because the level of international morals was so low.

v

What, then, are we to do to get out of this circle? We can't have a high level of morals until we get a world state. And we can't have a world state till we get a higher level of morals. There is nothing we can do in these circumstances except try to get rid of old habits of thought. We are still, all of us, everywhere in the world, in the grip of old habits of thought, carried over from the day when the nations were relatively independent or self-dependent, into an age in which they have become, whether they like it or not, interdependent. Our habit is to think in national terms only, whereas we have to learn to think in international terms.

The practical problem is, not to explain this idea—any child can understand it; it is not even to get people to believe the idea—most of us believe it now; it is to get our own people, and the peoples of the world, so soaked with this idea that they naturally and instinctively act from it—that acting from it goes with the grain of their minds, not against the grain. The achievement of this result almost involves implanting a new instinct, and is a problem of education, of conditioning.

In the early days of August, immediately after the first use of the atomic bomb, President Truman warned the Japanese that they had still time to save themselves, but that the time was short. He might as well have addressed these words to the American, or any other, nation. How long have we been living in a fool's paradise, imagining that we can shape our world policy by nothing save our own narrow interests conceived as independent of the interests of other nations? In the next war, if we allow one to come, we may be "vaporized" en masse by uranium rockets fired from a distance of thousands of miles, almost before we know that we are at war.

There is only one way out. We have to learn the lesson that nations, deserting their petty ideas of sovereignty, prestige, national self-interest, must combine to act together for the common good of humanity—which is the meaning of acting morally. There is still time to learn this lesson. *But the time is short.*

For questions and exercises, see p. 172, p. 205, p. 212, and p. 455.

## THE MARXIAN VIEW OF HISTORY

### CARL L. BECKER

I sometimes find myself discussing communism with those who profess that faith; and not infrequently I note an implicit assumption on their part that I, as an intelligent person with some knowledge of history, ought either, (1) to refute the Marxian philosophy

THE MARXIAN VIEW OF HISTORY: From *Every Man His Own Historian: Essays on History and Politics* by Carl L. Becker. Copyright, 1935, by F. S. Crofts Co., Inc. Permission granted by Appleton-Century-Crofts, Inc.

of history, or (2) in all honesty to support the communist cause. In such discussions I have maintained, (1) that an intelligent person may regard the Marxian philosophy of history as an illuminating interpretation of the past without subscribing to it as a law of history, and (2) that even if convinced that the Marxian doctrine is a valid law of history, one might still with excellent reasons refuse to support the communist cause. Such discussions, developed more fully and presented more formally, may for convenience be put in the form of a discussion between a communist and a liberal.

COMMUNIST: Don't you think, Professor, that history proves that social progress, or change if you prefer, is the result of an inevitable class-conflict?

LIBERAL: Put in that precise way, no. I can't see that history proves anything except that what happened did happen, or that anything is inevitable except what happened; but what happened is precisely the question at issue. In using the words "prove" and "inevitable" you are, as the logicians say, begging the question.

COMMUNIST: I don't insist on those precise words.

LIBERAL: Very well. I agree then that history does support, or can easily be made to support, the Marxian doctrine in a general way. For example, in the middle ages the chief source of wealth was certainly land; and it is obvious that at that time the land-owning aristocracy was the ruling class. No great ingenuity is required to show that political, social, and religious customs and ideas at that time were suited to maintaining the political and economic ascendancy of the aristocracy. Likewise, it is obvious that during the last three centuries land has gradually been replaced by capital as the chief source of wealth; and the history of this time may easily be regarded as a conflict between the middle-class capitalist and the land-owning aristocracy, as a result of which the former have replaced the latter as the ruling class and have substituted, in their interest, a new set of institutions and ideas (representative government, individual liberty, popular sovereignty, free competition) for the old. Yes, as an interpretation of the last thousand years of European history, the Marxian theory is most illuminating.

COMMUNIST: Isn't it a bit more than merely illuminating? Can you deny that it is a more convincing and realistic interpretation than any other?

LIBERAL: I could very easily deny it, but I have no wish to do so. Let us admit that it is the most convincing interpretation. I will go farther. For purposes of argument I will admit that it is the only valid interpretation.

COMMUNIST: Very well then. If you admit that Marx has correctly interpreted the past, why not admit that he has correctly interpreted the future? Why not admit that just as the bourgeois-capitalist class displaced the land-owning aristocracy as the ruling class, so the proletariat will in its turn replace the bourgeois-capitalist class? And if they do so, isn't it reasonable to suppose that the characteristic ideas of the present society (representative government, freedom of speech, *laissez-faire*) will in turn give way to others suited to the interests of the proletariat?

LIBERAL: If I accept Marx's interpretation of the past it is because I know what it is, and can test it. If I hesitate to accept his interpretation of the future it is partly because I do not know precisely what it is, and partly because, even if I know what it is, I cannot test it. I willingly admit that the future will, in some way that can after the event be rationalized, resemble the past. Certainly change is the law of life, and it is obvious that the institutions and the ideas of the nineteenth century, which were so well suited to the interests of the capitalist class, will not suffice without modification for the needs of the complex mechanized society of the twentieth. I willingly admit also that the ideas and institutions of today will be changed in such a way as to conform more closely with the economic interests of the workers, the mass of the people, the proletariat. But that is not to say that the change will come about in the way predicted by Marx, or that the result will be the sort of utopia predicted by him.

COMMUNIST: Utopia! I am not aware that Marx predicted any utopia.

LIBERAL: Well, let us say that he didn't. What then did he predict?

COMMUNIST: He predicted that the capitalist régime would by its own nature destroy itself. Its nature is to be ruthlessly competitive, so that in any industrial society the tendency is for wealth to be more highly concentrated in the hands of the few, while the mass of the people tend to fall to the condition of wage slaves. When this process reaches a certain point, the system breaks down, as it is now breaking down because it has deprived the people of the means of buying the commodities which it is the sole aim of the capitalistic class to make and sell for a profit. When the system ceases to work the people will necessarily take control, and, since it is their interest to do so, they will establish a classless society based upon the common ownership of instruments of production, and a more equitable distribution of the product. This is the social revolution that Marx predicted, and it has already begun—in Russia.

LIBERAL: In Russia, yes. In Russia, that is to say, not the most highly industrialized society but the least highly industrialized society. That is surely not according to Marx.

COMMUNIST: No, it is not. But you cannot maintain that because Marx's prediction is not verified in every detail it is not therefore valid in its general outline. The Great War created a special set of circumstances which were peculiarly favorable to the social revolution in Russia.

LIBERAL: Very true. The social revolution clearly occurred before its time in Russia. Providence, or Dialectic Materialism, or whatever it is that regulates social changes, certainly did a very curious thing in bringing the social revolution to Russia before it brought it to more highly industrialized countries, such as England. For my part, I don't think the Russian revolution does anything to verify the predictions of Marx; to me it indicates only that in a country in which the people were accustomed to being ruled by a dictatorship, a country moreover in which the prevailing form of dictatorship was especially corrupt and incompetent, it was very easy to establish a dictatorship of a different sort. But let that pass. My reluctance to accept the Marxian doctrine arises from something far more fundamental than the Russian accident. There are two difficulties which have always troubled me. Perhaps you can solve them. One is that it is extremely difficult to predict the future on the basis of past experience; or rather it is extremely easy to find in the past support for diverse predictions of the future. The other difficulty is to understand why a persistent economic class conflict in the past justifies us in predicting a classless society in the future.

As to the first difficulty. What little I know of history makes me chary of any prediction as to the form which social institutions will take in the future. Especially so when such predictions, based upon a realistic view of the past, take an idealistic view of the future. During the last two thousand years all the saints and sages of the world, deploring greed and strife, poverty and injustice, have looked forward to the time when a more just society would be established. They have many times predicted the coming of a classless society in which everyone would have enough; but the course of events has never yet verified their hopes. This generalization is as solidly based on historical fact as any that Marx has made, and it is more widely based; and if I am to judge the future by the past, I see no reason for discarding this generalization for that which Marx offers me. The less so, since Marx's interpretation of the past, if projected into the future, seems to refute his own prediction.

COMMUNIST: I don't understand that.

LIBERAL: Perhaps it will become clear if I elaborate the second difficulty I just mentioned. Marx's interpretation of the past is explicit and realistic; his forecast of the future seems to me vague and idealistic. I have called it utopian, but you object to that word. I do not insist on it. I will even surrender the word "idealistic." But the point is this. Marx finds that in the past the effective force that has determined social change is the economic class conflict. He points out that this economic class conflict explains the rise of the present capitalistic society. He shows, or at least his disciples show, how this economic class conflict is working to undermine our capitalistic society. Very well. If then I project this explanation of social changes into the future, what does it tell me? It seems to tell me that there will be in the future what there has been in the past—an endless economic class conflict, an endless replacement of one dominant class by another, an endless transformation of institutions and ideas in accordance with the changes effected by the class conflict. But this is not what Marx predicts. What he predicts is the end of the economic class conflict, the establishment of a classless society. What you and he are asking me to accept is an explanation of history that will explain it only up to a certain point. Marx criticised Hegel for that very weakness. Hegel explained past history as a transformation effected by the Transcendent Idea realizing itself in the actual events of history; according to him the great objective of history was the complete realization of the Idea in the form of Freedom, and this great objective had already been in some sense attained in the Prussian state. Marx wanted to know what the Transcendent Idea would find to do in the future, now that it was entirely realized. That is a sound criticism. Now, my difficulty is to know how Marx has improved on Hegel. To be sure Marx does not say that the great objective of history has already been attained. He says the economic class conflict will bring about another social revolution. But after the social revolution, what then? What becomes of the economic class conflict after the revolution has established a classless society? I can't find that it will have anything more to do than Hegel's Transcendent Idea. A law of history which, at some determinate moment, ceases to explain history, a law of history which is required, at the appropriate moment, to commit hari-kari on the doorstep of the ideal, surely leaves something to be desired.

COMMUNIST: Well, that's a point. But really, Professor, you know very well that this objection has been noted before, and that there is a good answer to it. Marx was not so blind as to overlook it. How could he have done so, since he pointed out that very weakness in Hegel's philosophy of history?

LIBERAL: I should be glad to learn how Marx avoids that difficulty.

COMMUNIST: I am not sure that Marx does altogether avoid it. But you must allow Marxian Philosophy to be elaborated and interpreted by his followers in the light of later experience. You have no objection to that?

LIBERAL: None at all. We must by all means discuss Marxianism at its best, as it is now interpreted by the most expert exegesis available.

COMMUNIST: Very well. According to a recent interpreter of Marxianism, history is explainable in terms of a dialectic of transformation, in which conflicts appear only to be resolved in a higher synthesis. This conflict is not necessarily always an economic class conflict. After the classless society is established the conflict will continue, but on a different level. According to Professor Sidney Hook, a recent interpreter of Marx, the dialectic in a communistic, classless society, will not be "historically conditioned in the same sense" as in earlier times. "It finds expression . . . on a more elevated plane. Although in advance no one can describe the detailed forms it will take, it is clear that its general locus is individual and personal." In other words, having solved the economic problem by establishing a classless society, men will be occupied with the higher, spiritual problems of human development.

LIBERAL: Well, I must confess that this greatly surprises me. A while back you would not allow me to apply the term "utopian" to the future society predicted by Marx, and yet this sounds to me very similar to all the utopian societies I ever heard of. Throughout the past men have been engaged in brutal conflict for material gain; but this brutal conflict is somehow to bring about a classless society in which men will suddenly change their natures and devote themselves to the nobler things of life. A dialectic materialism will be replaced by what we may call a dialectic spiritualism; or to put it in simple English, conflict will cease on the economic plane, and continue only on the moral plane.

Well, it may be so; and if it should turn out so, it would be grand. I point out merely that this is what all the idealistic prophets of the world have always hoped would happen. It is what the early prophets of democracy predicted. It is what all humane liberals may hope for. But what I don't understand is how the Marxian philosophy permits us to hope for it. I suppose it to be a fundamental tenet of Marxian philosophy that the conduct of men is strictly conditioned; and if their conduct in the past has been strictly conditioned by the economic class conflict, how can it cease to be so conditioned in the future?

COMMUNIST: Your difficulty arises from a false assumption—an assumption that is made by many of the hostile critics of Marx. The assumption is that Marx accepted the nineteenth-century doctrine of mechanistic determinism. That is not so. Marx always insisted that "man makes his own history." He contributes something novel to the conditions that determine his own conduct. Marx says explicitly: "By acting on the external world man changes his own nature." This means that man can, by acquiring knowledge, modify his environment, and so modify also his own ways of submitting to the environment. Therefore it is quite possible that men might for a very long time submit blindly to the influence of the economic class conflict; for a long time, but not necessarily forever; since, having become aware that they had been in the past submitting to the economic class conflict, they would, in the future, even if they submitted to it, not be submitting to it blindly. This awareness that their conduct has been determined by the economic class conflict, becomes a new element in the conditions, and so changes the conditions that will determine men's conduct in the future. One might say that the great object of Marx was just this: to make men aware of the conditions that made social revolutions in the past, so that in the coming social revolution, being aware of what was happening, they could consciously direct it. To quote once more from Professor Sidney Hook: "Once man acquires control of the conditions of social life, he can consciously make over his own nature in accordance with a morally free will, in contradistinction to men in the past, whose nature has been unconsciously made over by the economically determined will of the economic class."

LIBERAL: I see; at least I think so, in spite of Professor Hook's somewhat obscure academic phraseology. But what it comes to, I suppose, is this. In the physical world a law operates forever in the same way because the physical object is not aware of, and is indifferent to, what happens. A billiard ball (to use the classic example) has no desire to make over its nature. But man is aware of, and is not indifferent to, what happens. His acts are indeed strictly conditioned, but as soon as he becomes aware of what it is that conditions them, his awareness enables him to react differently; his acts are then not less strictly conditioned than formerly, but his own awareness becomes a new element that changes and complicates the conditions. For a long time men may worship the sun; when they become aware of the influences that make them worship the sun, this awareness may become an influence that will make them cease to worship the sun. Freedom of the will, as Engels said, is no more than man's knowledge that his acts are conditioned.

Very well, Marx then (or perhaps his disciples) applies this principle of freedom to the social changes or revolutions that occur in history. In the past, social revolutions have been conditioned by the economic class conflict. As long as men are not aware of this fact, social revolutions will continue to be conditioned by the economic class conflict. But when men become fully aware, through the great discovery of Marx, that social revolutions in the past have been conditioned by the class conflict, this knowledge will enable them to react differently—to react in such a way as to abolish the class conflict. This, I take it, is how you interpret Marx.

COMMUNIST: Yes, that is right.

LIBERAL: Well, I agree with this idea of free will. It seems to me obvious that as men acquire knowledge of the influences that determine their acts, this knowledge becomes a new influence that enables them to act differently. But if we accept this principle it seems odd to me that men shouldn't have acquired, before the time of Marx, some knowledge of the fact that their conduct was determined by the economic class conflict. I should have supposed that this element of awareness would have been steadily modifying the conditions that determine social change from the time of the Neanderthal man down to the present. How does it happen that this element has had no appreciable influence up to the time of Marx? Marx must have been a much greater man than I have always thought—a veritable Messiah, who at a single stroke has given mankind this epoch-making revelation that is to transform so radically the conditions that determine human history. I find it difficult to believe that knowledge has been steadily modifying the economic influences that have determined social changes in the past, and that in the future further knowledge, knowledge unknown to Marx, will continue to modify those influences in ways not dreamed of by Marx.

But that is a minor point. Let us assume that up to the time of Marx men have been submitting blindly to the economic class conflict, and that now, thanks to Marx, they are in the way of becoming aware of that fact, and that being aware of it they are in a position to modify profoundly the conditions that will determine social changes. What then? Well, it seems to me that this great revolution made by Marx is precisely what makes it impossible for him to predict the character of the coming social revolution. If we did not know that social changes had been conditioned by the economic class conflict, the coming social revolution would presumably follow the course of previous ones, in which case no classless society would emerge from it. But since we do know that social revolutions in the past were conditioned by the class conflict, this very knowledge, according to Marx, will make the coming social revolution follow some different course, in which case we may hope, but cannot be sure, that a classless society will emerge from it. In short, in so far as Marx has made men aware of the influence of the economic class conflict in the past, he has destroyed the very conditions that would have enabled him to predict the nature of the social revolution in the future. If Marx wished to predict correctly the nature of the coming social revolution, he should not have told us what it is that makes social revolutions: since he has told us, the secret is out, and hence no one can predict it. The great secret is out, thanks to Marx, and this knowledge will enable us to make of the coming social revolution something different than it otherwise would have been. Marxian philosophy presents his disciples with a dilemma which they either do not see or refuse to meet. It is this. Either social changes are always determined by the same conditions, in which case we may be sure that the coming social revolution will be similar to those in the past—it will transform the present class conflict only to create the conditions that will issue in a new one. Or else knowledge of the conditions that have determined social revolutions in the past introduces a novel influence in the conditions that will determine social revolutions in the future, in which case we cannot predict with any certainty the nature of those revolutions. The profound conviction of Communists that the proletariat is destined to establish a classless society on the ruins of the present capitalistic régime is not justified by Marxian philosophy: if you interpret Marx in terms of mechanistic determinism, this profound communist conviction is a pure delusion; on the other hand, if you interpret Marx in terms of free will, this conviction is no more than splendid hope. That is why I cannot accept the Marxian philosophy as a law of history.

COMMUNIST: Very well. Suppose, for purposes of argument, that the communist conviction is only a splendid hope. You yourself have said that the present capitalist régime must be changed in such a way as to harmonize better with the interests of the mass of the people, the proletariat. That is just what the Communists want. Since you sympathize with their object and believe that it will in some measure be realized, why not join the Communists and help to realize this splendid hope?

LIBERAL: I refuse to join the Communists because, while I sympathize with their desire to make a better world for the mass of the people, I have no faith in the methods which they propose for obtaining this object. If I understand them, they claim that nothing really worth while can be done until conditions are ripe for the application of the revolutionary technique. When that time comes, they propose, following the example of the Bolshevists in Russia, to seize control of the government, forcibly expropriate the bourgeois class, and ruthlessly suppress the expression of all opinion that a dictatorial government judges to be hostile to the welfare of the community of workers.

Now I have no faith in force and repression as the *primary* means of achieving the good life. I am not as yet a non-resistant pacifist. Any government is probably better than none, and all governments rest at last on force. But I believe that the essential test of civilized society is the extent to which law and public authority rest on free discussion and voluntary consent. A resort to force as a means of obtaining consent may be sometimes necessary to prevent a society from falling into virtual anarchy, but the resort to force in place of persuasion is so far a confession of failure. I have no faith in the possibility of abolishing oppression by oppressing oppressors. I have no faith in the infallibility of any man, or of any group of men, or of the doctrines or dogmas of any man or group of men, except in so far as they can stand the test of free criticism and analysis. I agree with Pascal that "thought makes the dignity of man"; and I believe therefore that all the great and permanently valuable achievements of civilization have been won by the free play of intelligence in opposition to, or in spite of, the pressure of mass emotion and the effort of organized authority to enforce conformity in conduct and opinion. I do not believe that there has been, or that there will be, a high civilization in any country in which the mind of man is limited to the expression of ideas authorized by public authority. Dictatorship is as old as European society; and whether it be the dictatorship of a Stalin, a Mussolini, or a Hitler, it does not become something new and admirable by being dressed up in a new and mystical ideology. I recognize it as a possibility that our modern, complex, machine civilization may so far fall into confusion that a dictatorship will in fact replace the present régime; but I refuse to recognize this outcome as inherently desirable, and I refuse to join in any effort to make it inevitable.

This is why I do not join the Communists. I believe that profound changes in our economic and industrial system are necessary; but I believe that they can and I hope that they will be made, in this country, without resorting to violent revolution, without resorting to dictatorship, without abandoning our traditional reliance on free discussion and criticism of public authority and of the measures it proposes for the solution of social ills. And there is nothing in the Marxian philosophy, as you expound it, that makes it illogical for me to take this position. According to you, now that Marx has made us aware of the influence of the economic class conflict in the past, this very awareness will enable us to master and modify the class conflict in the future. I agree. But why is it necessary to assume that this knowledge which Marx has revealed to us is the exclusive possession of the proletariat? After all, the bourgeoisie have a certain amount of intelligence. They can read Marx, or at least Sidney Hook. They can observe what has occurred in Russia, in Italy, in Germany. It is possible for them, too, to understand that the capitalist competitive system is in a fair way of destroying itself. Marxian doctrine tells me that capitalists, like proletarians, are motivated by their economic class interest; it does not tell me that they, any more than the proletarians, must forever be motivated by a blind illusion as to what that interest is. At the present moment it obviously is not to the interest of the capitalist class that the mass of the people should be without the means of buying the goods which the capitalist class produces in order to sell. It is still possible that the capitalist system in this country, subjected to the pressure of economic necessity and the force of public discontent, may by reasonably peaceful procedure be sufficiently transformed into a coordinated and planned economic system to make it, not a utopia indeed, but at least a decently workable system. And a decently workable system which preserves our traditional liberty of discussion and criticism will, in my opinion, be superior in the long run to any system that can be established by the repressive measures now employed by the Communists of Russia, the Fascists of Italy, or the Nazis of Germany.

COMMUNIST: A decently workable system. That's certainly vague enough—as vague as Marx's idealistic society of the future which you derided. No doubt a decently workable system is one which you would prefer to something which you don't like, such as the Russian communist state.

LIBERAL: It is. But you must permit me to prefer a decently workable system which I like to a decently workable system which

I don't like. You can hardly expect me to become a Communist until I am convinced that communism would be preferable to the system under which I live.

COMMUNIST: No. But you have already admitted that the "decently workable system" which you hope will be established may fail to be established—that the present system may end in a dictatorship. That I think is the more probable outcome. It is likely that in the long run the capitalist class, confronted by the rising power of the proletariat, will resort to force, as it has done in Italy and Germany. If then you are faced with the alternative of supporting a dictatorship of the proletariat or a dictatorship of the bourgeoisie what will you do? What then will become of freedom of speech and the appeal to persuasion? Since you sympathize with the objectives of the Communist, will you not then be forced to join them? Why wait till then? Why not join now the side which is bound to win in the long run because it is in harmony with the dominant trend of social forces?

LIBERAL: I do not admit that communism is necessarily in harmony with the dominant trend of social forces. I see that when it suits your argument you, like most Communists, fall back on the doctrine of a fatalistic determinism which makes the communist revolution inevitable whatever men do about it; but when your argument requires another doctrine you admit that the social revolution may be mastered and directed by the conscious purposes of men. You ought really to accept one doctrine or the other, and stick to it. But no matter. Accept one doctrine or both, as you like. In either case I see no good reason for joining the Communists. If the communist revolution is inevitable, whatever men do about it, why do anything? Why join either side, if you know beforehand that one side is bound to win anyway? But if the communist revolution is not inevitable, then the proletariat can indeed do something to hasten it, and by the same token the bourgeoisie can do something to retard it. And in that case why should I join the Communists? I am a professor; and the Communists are never weary of telling me that professors as a class support the capitalistic régime because it is their economic interest to do so. Very well, I will be a sufficiently good Marxian to accept the doctrine that men's actions are motivated by their economic class interest. If then my economic interests are bound up with the capitalist régime, and I can do something to retard the communist revolution, I should be, according to Marx himself, a poor humanitarian fool to desert my class and work for a revolution which, if successful, would ruthlessly suppress me. As a liberal humanitarian, or a Christian mystic, I might logically sacrifice myself and my class for the welfare of the masses; but as a Marxian that would be to adopt the very "utopian" attitude which Marx never ceased to ridicule. You really ask too much. The Marxian philosophy teaches me either that the communist revolution is inevitable, in which case I merely resign myself to it: or else it teaches me that the communist revolution can be hastened or retarded by the conscious efforts of men, in which case I stick to my class and do what I can to retard it. In either case I have the profound consolation of knowing that my conduct is based on the solid foundation of the Marxian philosophy of history.

These, you are to understand, are choices logically open to me on the assumption that I accept the Marxian philosophy of history. But life is less simple than logic. In logic you can present me with clear-cut alternatives. You ask me whether I will "choose" to support the dictatorship of the proletariat or the dictatorship of the bourgeoisie, quite as if some day, the two contending parties being lined up in battle array on a *champs de mars,* I should be asked to step out and join one side or the other. In actual life it does not seem to me that I am ever confronted with choices as simple or as dramatically staged as that. When I voted for Mr. Roosevelt (if I *did* vote for him—I can't be sure now) I made a choice, without being certain (any more than Mr. Roosevelt himself was) what would come of it. I am now "supporting" (so far as I am supporting anything) the Roosevelt administration, and it is possible that in 1936 I shall vote for the reelection of Mr. Roosevelt. Does this mean that I am "choosing" to support a fascist rather than a communistic regime? Thoroughgoing Communists appear to know that I am: the New Deal, they say, is obviously an American species of fascist technique. But I am sufficiently naive not to be aware of having made any choice between communism and fascism. And very glad I am that it is so. I should dislike very much to be confronted with a clear-cut choice between a dictatorship of the proletariat and a dictatorship of the bourgeoisie. I should be inclined to say, "A plague on both your houses!"

I find Mussolini as offensive as Stalin, and Hitler more offensive than either.

COMMUNIST: That is all very well, but a real revolution is not impossible. There are plenty of Russians who could assure you that the alternative you so much dislike has been presented to them in a quite sufficiently clear-cut and dramatic manner. If it should be similarly presented in this country, it seems to me that you would, however much you might dislike it, have to choose one side or the other.

LIBERAL: Not necessarily. There would still be another possibility.

COMMUNIST: What would that be?

LIBERAL: I might still refuse to join either side. I might persist in the futility of expressing my faith in the superior virtues of persuasion.

COMMUNIST: That would have serious consequences for you. You would be suppressed.

LIBERAL: True enough. But I might accept the consequences. I might choose to be suppressed rather than to support what I object to. In short, I might, as a last refuge from imbecility, become a Christian and practise the precept that it is better to suffer evil than to do it.

COMMUNIST: That would be to fall back upon a far more mystical type of idealism than Marx ever contemplated, and I fail to see that it would get you anywhere.

LIBERAL: I dare say it wouldn't. But as I said before, I am a professor, and a professor, as the German proverb has it, is "a man who thinks otherwise": if he is not permitted to talk freely he cannot get anywhere anyway.

For questions and exercises, see p. 140, p. 166, p. 205, p. 212, p. 475, and p. 521.

## A SCIENTIST REBELS

### NORBERT WIENER

[Editor's note from *The Atlantic Monthly*] The letter which follows was addressed by one of our ranking mathematicians to a research sci-

A SCIENTIST REBELS: Originally printed in *The Atlantic Monthly*, January 1947. Reprinted here by permission of the author and *The Atlantic Monthly*. Dr. Wiener is associated with the Massachusetts Institute of Technology.

entist of a great aircraft corporation, who had asked him for the technical account of a certain line of research he had conducted in the war. Professor Wiener's indignation at being requested to participate in indiscriminate rearmament, less than two years after victory, is typical of many American scientists who served their country faithfully during the war.

Professor of Mathematics in one of our great Eastern institutions, Norbert Wiener was born in Columbia, Missouri, in 1894, the son of Leo Wiener, Professor of Slavic Languages at Harvard University. He took his doctorate at Harvard and did his graduate work in England and in Göttingen. Today he is esteemed one of the world's foremost mathematical analysts. His ideas played a significant part in the development of the theories of communication and control which were essential in winning the war.—THE EDITOR

Sir:—

I have received from you a note in which you state that you are engaged in a project concerning controlled missiles, and in which you request a copy of a paper which I wrote for the National Defense Research Committee during the war.

As the paper is the property of a government organization, you are of course at complete liberty to turn to that government organization for such information as I could give you. If it is out of print, as you say, and they desire to make it available for you, there are doubtless proper avenues of approach to them.

When, however, you turn to me for information concerning controlled missiles, there are several considerations which determine my reply. In the past, the comity of scholars has made it a custom to furnish scientific information to any person seriously seeking it. However, we must face these facts: The policy of the government itself during and after the war, say in the bombing of Hiroshima and Nagasaki, has made it clear that to provide scientific information is not a necessarily innocent act, and may entail the gravest consequences. One therefore cannot escape reconsidering the established custom of the scientist to give information to every person who may inquire of him. The interchange of ideas which is one of the great traditions of science must of course receive certain limitations when the scientist becomes an arbiter of life and death.

For the sake, however, of the scientist and the public, these limitations should be as intelligent as possible. The measures taken

during the war by our military agencies, in restricting the free intercourse among scientists on related projects or even on the same
project, have gone so far that it is clear that if continued in time
of peace this policy will lead to the total irresponsibility of the
scientist, and ultimately to the death of science. Both of these are
disastrous for our civilization, and entail grave and immediate peril
for the public.

I realize, of course, that I am acting as the censor of my own
ideas, and it may sound arbitrary, but I will not accept a censorship in which I do not participate. The experience of the scientists
who have worked on the atomic bomb has indicated that in any
investigation of this kind the scientist ends by putting unlimited
powers in the hands of the people whom he is least inclined to trust
with their use. It is perfectly clear also that to disseminate information about a weapon in the present state of our civilization is
to make it practically certain that that weapon will be used. In that
respect the controlled missile represents the still imperfect supplement to the atom bomb and to bacterial warfare.

The practical use of guided missiles can only be to kill foreign
civilians indiscriminately, and it furnishes no protection whatsoever
to civilians in this country. I cannot conceive a situation in which
such weapons can produce any effect other than extending the
kamikaze way of fighting to whole nations. Their possession can do
nothing but endanger us by encouraging the tragic insolence of
the military mind.

If therefore I do not desire to participate in the bombing or
poisoning of defenseless peoples—and I most certainly do not—I
must take a serious responsibility as to those to whom I disclose my
scientific ideas. Since it is obvious that with sufficient effort you
can obtain my material, even though it is out of print, I can only
protest *pro forma* in refusing to give you any information concerning my past work. However, I rejoice at the fact that my
material is not readily available, inasmuch as it gives me the
opportunity to raise this serious moral issue. I do not expect to
publish any future work of mine which may do damage in the
hands of irresponsible militarists.

I am taking the liberty of calling this letter to the attention of
other people in scientific work. I believe it is only proper that they

should know of it in order to make their own independent decisions, if similar situations should confront them.

NORBERT WIENER

For questions and exercises, see p. 197, p. 324, and p. 476.

## THE SCIENTIST FIGHTS FOR PEACE

### LOUIS N. RIDENOUR

[Editor's note from *The Atlantic Monthly*] What is the scientist's duty towards the state today? This question which has troubled the conscience of many of the most brilliant physicists in the country—men who worked with utmost loyalty in the national defense and for the Office of Scientific Research and Development during the war years—was driven home by Norbert Wiener, one of our ranking mathematicians, in his letter, "A Scientist Rebels," which appeared in the January *Atlantic*.

Professor Wiener declined to have anything further to do with death-dealing research. His reasoning does not satisfy Louis N. Ridenour, who was Adviser on Radar to General Spaatz; who is Dean of the Graduate College at the University of Illinois; and who believes that scientists of every stripe have a larger duty to mankind than merely abstaining.—THE EDITOR

Now that the war is officially over, everyone seems to be trying to guarantee the peace in his own individual way. The wrangles and name-calling among the various peace-lovers parallel some of the worst features of a war, though they stop short of bloodletting.

I am sure that there are few people who love peace more devoutly, or who wish more profoundly to guarantee and preserve it, than Norbert Wiener. Yet I find myself in violent disagreement with his views as stated in his letter, "A Scientist Rebels." The issues involved are so important that the point of view of a scientist opposed to Wiener should be clearly stated.

Fundamentally, our disagreement turns on two points.

The first concerns the social responsibility of the scientist. Wiener clearly believes that the scientist is the armorer of modern war, and as such holds a responsibility of unique importance. I feel that

THE SCIENTIST FIGHTS FOR PEACE: Originally printed in *The Atlantic Monthly*, May 1947. Reprinted here by permission of the author and *The Atlantic Monthly*.

the social responsibility of the scientist is unique in no important way. It is identical with the social responsibility of every other thinking man, except for one special and temporary thing. It is necessary today to educate the non-scientific public to the Promethean nature of atomic energy and the true character of science (for example, that it contains no secrets). This education must be done, so that all the people can participate in the decisions they will have to make concerning the organization of society in such a form that wars become less likely.

This educational job is splendidly begun by our government with the publication of the Smyth Report—a step that has recently been criticized by men who do not understand the meaning and the scope of the stupendous educational enterprise we have only just begun. Such an attitude toward the publication of the Smyth Report is the best possible evidence that, if the instruction of all people in these matters is not done promptly and well, we shall continue to wriggle out of the thinking that is demanded of us, using the well-worn old loopholes: "Not such a terrible weapon"; "Every offensive weapon brings a countermeasure"; "We'll keep the secret"; "We'll keep ahead in armaments"; "Let's have a cheap preventive war"; and so on.

Secondly, Wiener wishes to dissociate himself utterly from any activity connected with preparation for war, even to the extent of doing everything he can to make those preparations ineffective. I regard it as deplorable that our nation is preparing for war, and I prefer to leave to others the actual work involved; but so long as it is the policy of our nation to prepare for war, I shall certainly not attempt to impede such preparations. In fact, I have tried to help them by pointing out a way in which our anxiety to increase our military strength is harming our potential military performance: the hysterical insistence on secrecy in nuclear physics is slowing our progress in that field. I conceive the duty of the peace-lover to be that of working for a world in which national arms are no longer desired by a majority of the people of this country or of the world. Meanwhile, I do not believe in the wisdom, propriety, or effectiveness of attempts to sabotage the preparation of arms when these arms are as widely believed to be necessary as they are today.

Wiener's views in these matters are best stated in his own words.

The occasion for the letter that was printed in the January *Atlantic* was that Wiener had been asked, by an employee of an aircraft company engaged in work on guided missiles, for a copy of a National Defense Research Committee report he had written during the war. This report was out of print, and Wiener's correspondent had assumed that the simplest way to get a copy was to appeal to the author. In denying the request, Wiener said:—

The policy of the government itself during and after the war . . . has made it clear that to provide scientific information is not a necessarily innocent act . . . The interchange of ideas which is one of the great traditions of science must of course receive certain limitations when the scientist becomes an arbiter of life and death. . . .

The measures taken during the war by our military agencies, in restricting the free intercourse among scientists . . . [will] if continued in time of peace . . . lead to the total irresponsibility of the scientist, and ultimately to the death of science. Both of these are disastrous for our civilization, and entail grave and immediate peril for the public. . . .

I will not accept a censorship in which I do not participate. . . . To disseminate information about a weapon in the present state of our civilization is to make it practically certain that that weapon will be used. . . .

The practical use of guided missiles can only be to kill foreign civilians indiscriminately. . . . Their possession can do nothing but endanger us by encouraging the tragic insolence of the military mind. . . .

I do not expect to publish any future work of mine which may do damage in the hands of irresponsible militarists.

No doubt Wiener's letter sounded eminently sensible, and even lofty, to many who read it. The motives that lie back of it are certainly lofty, and with them I have no quarrel. But the assumptions on which it rests are open to the gravest question. Wiener encourages his readers to believe that, since technology is the daughter of science, and war is increasingly shaped by technology, the scientist has a unique moral and social responsibility. He must guide his work along peaceful channels; he must suppress such of his findings as apply to war.

This simply does not fit with the basic character of science. By definition, science consists of a completely open-minded probing into the unknown. No man can say what will be found as the result of a given investigation; and certainly no man can predict the nature of the practical engineering outcome of a given scientific investigation. Lee De Forest, the inventor of the three-electrode vacuum tube that is the basis of all present-day electronics, is said to be appalled at the babel and cacophony his invention has loosed upon the world. But De Forest was an inventor, not a scientist. The inventor or the engineer knows the goal of his work; the scientist has no goal but truth. He may have a preconception, based on existing theory, of what he will find in a given experiment, but he is ready to discard this in a moment if his results fail to bear it out.

To continue with our example, then: if De Forest is amazed at the results his invention has brought, imagine how Clerk Maxwell and Heinrich Hertz would feel if they could spend a day with the networks. Before Maxwell, the notion of electro-magnetic radiation—radio waves—had never been conceived; before Hertz, radio waves had never knowingly been generated by man. With sufficient imagination, De Forest might have foreseen mass entertainment as the result of his improvement in the existing wireless communication art. It is altogether unthinkable that either Maxwell or Hertz could have had the slightest notion that he was providing a medium for the advertising of soap.

This essential unknowability of the practical ends of scientific investigation makes it senseless to speak, as some do, of "the planning of science for human betterment." This bit of Marxist doctrine is widely met nowadays, even in the best circles, and Professor Wiener does himself and his colleagues a disservice by embracing it. Since we cannot guess how technology will use the still unknown results of a proposed scientific investigation, we must therefore conclude that either science as a whole is good for mankind or it is not. We can "plan" science only to the extent of turning it off or on. Since science, through technology, really means material civilization, the question becomes: Is material civilization good for mankind or is it not? There are arguments on both sides of that question, but clearly its resolution is by no means the concern of the scientist alone.

Other meaningless phrases are finding their way into conversation and the public prints. According to this country's announced policy for the international control of atomic energy, we desire "the interchange of scientific information for peaceful purposes."

What can this possibly mean? Either scientific information is exchanged or it is not. No man can say what the practical effect of such interchange will be, and the nature of that effect depends fundamentally upon political and social factors, not upon the nature of the scientific information that is exchanged.

What I have said thus far about the unknowability of goal applies to science. What of technology, which by definition has a definable goal? Should an effort be made to guide technology toward peaceful ends? Professor Wiener thinks that it should. While objecting to the military interference with scientific publication that took place during the war and is still going on, he himself feels competent to perform intelligent censorship. He proposes to perform this censorship on the basis of the practical use that is contemplated for his own ideas. He states flatly, for example, that the only possible use of guided missiles is to murder foreign civilians indiscriminately.

Overlooking the astonishing lack of logic that is involved in imposing one's own censorship while simultaneously rejecting that of others, I feel that Wiener is wrong in this attitude. In a peaceful world, work even on guided missiles would proceed, though not on the same scale or with such desperate intensity as now. Guided missiles would be developed for a wholly peaceful and scientific purpose, not a military one. Given peace, they will carry man's instruments, and finally man himself, through outer space to the planets and the stars.

Here, as before—here even in the branch of engineering that Wiener regards as the farthest-north of militarism—here still the principle holds. If the world is "postured for peace," as the Senators say (some of them say it in a way which implies that the posture involves a barrel), science, technology, and the useful arts contribute to the enrichment and the improvement of peaceful life. If the world is racked with suspicion, preparing for war, or in the throes of combat, the identical arts, techniques, skills, and individuals will contribute to the frightfulness and the horror of war. The decision rests on the contemporary character of world thought and world organization.

This is the basis for my assertion that the "social responsibility of the scientist" is identical with the social responsibility of every thinking man. Each must do his best to make sure that science, the canning industry, young men, the railroads—in short, the entire fabric of our society—are used for harmless and laudable purposes, and not for war. This desirable end can be attained only in a world where measures short of war are applied to solve international frictions. The scientist can no more choose whether he works for war or for peace than the Western Electric Company can choose whether the telephone instruments it manufactures are used on domestic circuits or as Army phones on a field of battle. The scientist does science, and Western Electric makes telephones. The use of either product is determined by society as a whole.

Anyone who feels a *special* sense of guilt because he helped create an atomic bomb, or anyone who believes that the creators of the atomic bomb should feel so, is confusing two quite different things. He is identifying the profound immorality of murder with the relatively insignificant matter of improving the means of murder. God told Moses, "Thou shalt not kill"—not "Thou shalt not kill with atomic energy, for that is so effective as to be sinful." The immorality of war is shared by all. Technical improvements in weapons can influence only the logistics and the strategy of any war that may occur; whether a war occurs or not is the crucial matter, and this is determined by the current "posture" of the world.

Among the social and political factors that influence the posture of the world at any given time, the state of armament of the nations is of great importance. So is the rate at which this state of armament is increasing or decreasing. There is some evidence to suggest that arms beget war, and presumably this is what causes Wiener and others of similar views to do personally whatever they can to retard the arming of our nation. Wiener's refusal to supply the report for which he was asked, though a purely formal matter, can only be regarded as an action taken in the belief that arms are bad in themselves, and that the more feebly this nation is armed, the less likely is war. Such a belief may be partly or entirely correct. I simply do not know whether, in a feral world, it is wiser for a nation to be strong or to be weak. And since I do not know, I do not feel it my privilege, much less my duty, to challenge by individual action the clear decision in favor of armaments that has been made by our government.

By coincidence, Wiener's position in this particular matter bears a very close relationship to an important misconception widely held among those having no knowledge of science. The latter view can be called, for short, the small-war philosophy. The small-war men desire to restrain technology (which they often miscall "science") with a view to making the next war as much like the last as possible. The bombs that dropped on North America in World War II were few and small, the reasoning runs. If we can only stop weapon development at its present level, the coming war will leave our children the chance to live it through.

There are two important defects in this reasoning. First, it cannot work. Under present political arrangements, the only weapon development it lies in our power to stop is that of our own country, and stopping this could in no way guarantee that World War III would resemble World War II. Second, the small-war philosophy entirely misses the moral point; one war differs from another by not one whit of principle. The effectiveness of the weapons used in a war in no way increases or diminishes the moral guilt of murder.

I am dubious of proposals for instant unilateral disarmament and uncompromising individual pacifism. It seems to me that this country offers the best current approximation to freedom of the individual, under law, that can be found anywhere in our admittedly imperfect world. The status of the individual in our society contrasts markedly with the freedom that the individual is said to enjoy in Russia. I recognize fully that most of the desirable freedoms of the individual would be submerged, even in this country, if we had another war; but I feel that the tradition of their former existence would bring them back, if we had a succeeding peace. Given lasting peace, I am sure that the freedom of the individual would emerge everywhere in the world, under any form of government whatever; because the craving for this freedom is one of the basic human hungers, and our present peaceful technology is so abundant that we can fill even this expensive appetite, if war can be avoided. Even though I am thus convinced that freedom of the individual will appear eventually under any form of government, I am interested in preserving the form that has so far afforded the greatest freedom: our own.

Thus it seems to me deplorable but understandable that this country, while desiring and working toward peace, feels it necessary to be strong in a military sense. I shall be seriously worried about our arms only if we commence to put reliance in them as our guarantee of peace. Armaments are neither designed for this role nor useful in it. So long as we continue in a sincere effort to create a successful world organization by participation in and modification of the United Nations, it is idle to object to our possession of arms in a world of the present sort. Worse, it may be dangerous as well. I am sure that we should be regarded as a nation of lunatics if we engaged today in any thorough unilateral disarmament.

The scientist, on whom so much attention has focused for the past year and a half, is in a difficult position at the present time. Because he wishes to re-establish the traditional internationalism of his profession, he is a Communist. Because he served his country well in the war just past, he is an irresponsible armsmonger, with a childish delight in frightful new technical weapons. Because he is concerned over the damage that an uncritical policy of continued secrecy can do to our scientific and technological progress as a nation—whether for peace or war—he is an idealist who wants to give the bomb to Russia, and he "nauseates" Mr. Baruch. Because some scientists, such as Wiener, are devout pacifists, the scientist is an un-American fellow who cannot be trusted. Because certain other scientists are still working for the Army and Navy, helping to arm our nation in accordance with the overwhelmingly expressed desire of the people of the country, science is the whore of the military. Because, among the perhaps ten thousand scientists and engineers who had contact with the atomic energy project, one has been convicted of a breach of secrecy, scientists are Red spies.

What I am claiming here is that scientists are people like everybody else. In common with all other citizens of the world, they have a heavy responsibility to work toward a world-wide political organization, social philosophy, and public morality that can be adequate to prevent wars between nations. To suggest that the scientist has an outstanding responsibility in terms of this entirely unscientific problem is misleading and harmful, for it encourages the lazy to fob their own responsibility off onto someone else. Wiener, in the name of science, is cheerfully accepting a unique social responsibility, while lasting peace demands that the responsibility be shared by all.

Finally, I reject the defeatist withdrawal from the world as it is, that is implicit in Wiener's letter. The only hope for man today is to work for a better world within the framework of what we have, imperfect as this is. It *can* be improved, and such improvement must arise not from withdrawal, but from intelligent and vigorous participation in existing affairs. Most scientists stand ready to do their part.

For questions and exercises, see p. 172, p. 197, p. 476, and p. 531.

## THE THREAT OF SCIENCE

### CHRISTIAN GAUSS

There is a wide-spread belief fostered occasionally by scientists themselves that if we will but allow science fullest freedom it will eventually make us all healthy and wealthy and wise. There is little doubt that up to a certain point it can make us healthy and wealthy. If we pass over, for the moment, the question whether the health which science can give us is only physical (and not moral) health, we will all readily admit that a clearer understanding of the processes of nature and the sources of physical power can certainly save us from many ills. Science can and has eliminated many diseases and much useless motion. No one under a scientific dispensation will waste his time and effort in praying for rain or in attempting, as they did in Homer, to stop the flow of blood by incantation. It can increase and has increased immeasurably our mastery of nature. It makes us far more efficient. Whether it can really increase our mastery of human nature and thus make us wise and good is a different question. Scientists sometimes tell us that it can. In any attempt to predict our future under science this is really a much more important question than the first, for if without changing your man you place at his disposal a ton of TNT or only a sawed-off shotgun and an armored car, you may make life far more dangerous than if you had left your untutored savage with only his primitive battering-ram and his relatively harmless bow and arrow.

The academic mind is inclined to call a man wise if he understands things like the Bohr atom and the Einstein theory. That, too,

THE THREAT OF SCIENCE: Originally printed in *Scribner's Magazine* and later incorporated in *A Primer for Tomorrow*, copyright, 1935, by Charles Scribner's Sons. Reprinted here by permission of the author and *Scribner's Magazine*.

is a mistake. He is not really wise; he is only intelligent. The normal, ordinary human being must express himself by his acts. Even a recluse is involved in countless enterprises and relationships with others. If we say a man is wise we mean that whatever his theoretical beliefs, in the conduct of his life he chooses sane courses of action. If the scientist cannot help him to do this it is as much a superstition to expect unaided science to give us a safe and happy future as it was for our ancestors to believe in witch-doctors or to pray for rain.

There are times when the discouraged student of religion, of history, and of letters is tempted to rise up and call his brother who works in the laboratory blessed. Among scholars the experimental scientist is a privileged character. He is allowed to live and work in a world that knows not sin nor evil. Like Adam and Eve he lives in a Garden of Eden. Trinitrotoluol is not evil because it explodes. Hydrogen sulphide is not unclean because it smells badly. The lion is not wicked because he kills the antelope. He is only leonine. That is what lions do for a living. To the biologist the lion who kills many antelopes has "survival value." He is, this scientist will even tell us, a good lion.

When the scientist uses this word *good* we must be upon our guard. He does not mean what the theologian, the moralist, the artist, or even the ordinary man means by that word. His lion, for instance, is frankly predatory. To Dante he was the personification of pride, the most deadly of all the sins, and quite evidently he fiercely seeks his own. If the biologist should invent a science for lions, a leonine science (and knowing his ingenuity I do not put it beyond him), it would make life easier for lions. It would increase their number, eliminate waste motion in their technic of pouncing upon antelopes. In the biologist's way of looking at things, it would make them better lions but from any outside non-scientific point of view, that of antelopes, for instance, it would not make lions better. It would change only their outward habits, not their inner natures. So it is perhaps with our science in general, and if it is to be the only force operative upon humanity then to the end of time we shall have to carry with us into no matter how roseate a future only the same old Adam.

If to avoid confusion we must be on our guard when he uses the word *good*, much the same is true when he uses certain other words like *pure,* even when he uses them in his really fine phrase, pure science.

In the first instance pure science, of course, means disinterested, not applied, science. The more competent scientists when on their guard never pretend that it means anything more. It is a really noble conception, science divorced from any consideration of its useful or profitable applications. The ordinary man must be cautious, however, and not conclude that science because "pure" somehow gives us a higher kind of truth than that revealed by just plain ordinary religion or art or philosophy. The devotees of these latter studies are assumed, sometimes even by scientists, to have been laggard and never to have pushed their subjects to this twenty-four carat stage of ultimate purity. There may be an error in all this, for it must be remembered and emphasized that science becomes pure only when it has been divorced also from any consideration of social and moral welfare. The pure scientist might conceivably in his laboratory seek to discover that least stable combination of chemical elements which under given conditions would constitute the world's most powerful explosive. This deadly formula would then be available for those who apply to more practical uses the findings of pure science. Its truths are not really truths of a higher sort; they are not above ordinary truths, as the angels (if there still are angels) are over the earth; they are only the truths of science in what might be called their state of innocence.

For this reason experimental science should not be regarded as wicked; it is only unmoral. No harm will come so long as we all remember that it has little relation to what the ordinary man regards as beautiful, or holy, or good. Such extraneous considerations of beauty and holiness and goodness are really impurities in science at its highest stage. They are, however, probably still aspects of truth and it might in one sense almost be said that pure science gives us impure truth, or perhaps rather, truth mutilated; truth from which certain elements that under ideal conditions enter into its fulness have of necessity been cut off.

II

The dispensation to live and work in a world where he might disregard the good, the holy, and the beautiful, at first granted rather grudgingly, is now on the whole conceded with enthusiasm. Society is asked to adopt a policy of laissez-faire just as it was asked to do by economists in the beginnings of industrialism and "big business." This means, for instance, that in case geologists reach conclusions at variance with those held by the church, their teaching should not be suppressed. If the biologist in dealing with sex finds it necessary to lift a social taboo and discovers that "nature has no reward for chastity," and other facts about generation which in the hands of the loose-living may conceivably effect an increase in sensuality, divorce, and the instability of the family, no ban should be placed upon him. If the physicist discovers new sources of energy that may be readily released for destructive purposes, he should not be held accountable for their use. Scientists should remember that the concession given to them by society is probably the largest ever granted to any group or caste. Although it has subjected the regulative forces of civilizations to a strain severe at times almost to the breaking-point, let me hasten to add that I believe the freedom accorded has been fully justified.

Clear-thinking men, including many great scientists, recognized that, for reasons which will be set forth later, science could not hope to give us a religion; they also realized, particularly after the failure of Zola's "experimental novel" and his school of naturalism, that it could not give us an art. Although there were those who tried to bring over the biologist's conception of the predatory "good lion" as a guide in human affairs and though mistaken political scientists sought to justify Germany's invasion of Belgium in 1914 by invoking Darwin's "the survival of the fittest," it was generally recognized that science could not give us a system of human conduct, and that even excellent science could and did often make despicable morality. The unmoral world of nature, with which science can deal so fruitfully, is after all not the world of religion, of art, of morals, and of man. So long as this was recognized by theologians, artists, moralists and the ordinary man on the one side, and by scientists on the other, there could be no serious trouble and the various civilizing agencies might hope to go along in concert. There have lately been signs in many quarters that science is increasing its pretensions and is now insisting that it be accepted as the preceptor of humanity in matters of morals. A clash therefore seems inevitable.

In plain language what, then, is an experimental or physical scientist? He is a man who disentangles forces and phenomena and decides which are the same and which are different. His business is to count and calculate them. He is primarily a measurer. An experiment is a query put to nature and a really great scientist of this school, like Mr. Millikan, for instance, is one who knows how to put to her a proper question. We do not mean by this that nature is finicky or has any sense of what Victorians used to call the proprieties. She has not. A proper question is only one of the kind which nature can answer. Is this hydrogen or helium? Is this light or electricity? He himself must refrain from answering, for in a successful experiment it is nature that answers and her answer will be the same if called for by any man of any nationality in any country in the world. The scientists measure and record and their procedure is perfect in proportion as it has been effectively sterilized against what might be called such personal contact and contamination. Mathematics has provided them all with a common recording instrument. Since they have all followed this same procedure of sterilization against human deviation and error; since they are all measuring the same clearly defined forces and substances, each worker contributes to the general fund of results and modern science has become the greatest international co-operative enterprise of all time. It would be folly to disparage the wonderful results which, in pursuing this method, scientists have achieved. Sensible men are not inclined to do this. The great danger is not that modern civilization will interfere with the scientist but that the scientist may quite unwittingly interfere with modern civilization.

A good many years ago I attended a course of lectures on philology, the science of language. The professor was occasionally compelled to reach out for examples into common speech and to take words which were rarely or never printed and whose normal development had therefore never been arrested by their appearance on the printed page. As a well-mannered gentleman, he never used these expressions; but as a scientist he did so without a blush. The gentleman and the scientist were two distinct persons, Doctor Jekyll and Mr. Hyde, and the gentleman used to apologize for the scientist in a formula: "Gentlemen," he would tell us, "there is nothing obscene in philology or medicine." He was quite right.

Philology and medicine pronounce no judgments in this field. It is beyond their competence. Neither, he might have added, does mathematics or physics or chemistry or biology or geology. Quite evidently there are certain questions which the scientist can answer and certain others which he cannot. Among these latter are questions as important as the following: Is this holy or is this obscene? Is this beautiful or is this ugly? Is this good or is this evil? These are questions which nature cannot answer and they are questions which must be answered by man, not as a part of nature but as a personality. Though the heart of human life lies behind such answers, science here can give us little help. Marvellous as its results have been in its own field, that field is limited.

Someone will object that I am considering only the physical sciences and that I am overlooking certain other important scientific studies. At the risk of incurring further disapproval, let me venture a little farther and say that the so-called social scientists, the historian, the economist, and sociologist are not really scientists in any proper or exclusive sense. In certain sections of their fields, their assembling of facts, their counting and their computations, they do and they should use scientific method and they should apply it with the utmost rigor. They can, of course, go beyond that section of their subject which is amenable to scientific treatment and I believe they should do so, but when the social scientist passes any judgment whatever on what is just or unjust, good or bad, he steps out of science. It should console him more than it now does to know that by this same act he steps over into philosophy. This used to be a quite creditable profession and until recently we called, for instance, the fruitful study of politics not political science but political philosophy. It would help to clear the air if we did so again.

### III

We have said that the pretensions of scientists to competence in this field which is not theirs are increasing. Doctor Millikan, winner of the Nobel Prize and President of the American Association for the Advancement of Science, recently delivered an address, "Alleged Sins of Science." [1] The title is itself misleading and withal a bit

[1] Published in *Scribner's Magazine* for February 1930.

pretentious. Science, the mouthpiece of nature, is, as we have seen, impersonal. It is the codified body of answers which nature gives. Nature is not moral; it knows neither good nor evil, and science being soulless is, humanly speaking, innocent. It cannot commit one least little sin. That is why the Sins of Science, real or alleged, are like the snakes of Ireland. They should be dismissed even by scientists quite as summarily. We should remember, however, that the individual scientist, being human, has an immeasurable advantage over his subject. He can sin and sometimes does.

The great benefits which science has conferred are plain to all. They are perhaps too manifest. It has added incalculably to the convenience, to the comfort, to the wealth and health, of millions, by revealing to them another world quite outside their own upon which they can draw. So far as the man in the street is concerned today, it is as if a millionaire uncle whom he had never known had suddenly died and left him, in a bank of whose existence he was previously ignorant, an almost inexhaustible fortune upon which he could check at will. Science can increase this already befuddled heir's credit upon his bank but it cannot effectively direct him in spending it. In any civilization or social order the newly rich are always a problem. By creating so many of them at once science is not only a social asset but also a social liability. The newly rich individual may of course spend his substance in riotous living. He may, in vulgar language, go to the devil, and as these beneficiaries of science are now the vast majority of our population they may conceivably carry us all, including the scientists, to the devil with them. Many scientists, nevertheless, believe that the cure for too much science is more science. Here I believe they are wrong.

When, in attempting to limit their field, I described scientists as primarily measurers, I need hardly say that I meant no disparagement. Some of the noblest work of man in our time has been done by Mr. Millikan himself and precisely in this line, and as I think of him and of his work I am moved to apply to him the great Frenchman's tribute, "What arouses my admiration is not that the heavens are so vast but that man has measured them."

If I unreservedly congratulate Mr. Millikan as a man of science, with his confidence in the future of our civilization under science, I must disagree quite as unreservedly. "Any effort," he tells us, "to suppress or impede the growth of science, which means to the

scientist merely the growth of man's understanding of *his* world
and hence *his ability to live wisely in it*, is to him (the scientist) an
unpardonable sin or at least not the work of an understanding
mind." We are asked to concede that "the final service of science"
is to teach man to live wisely, not in the world of nature but in his
(man's) world. Let us stop to ask ourselves what experience and
history tell us. Lincoln, most of us would admit, lived wisely in
his world; so did Washington, so did St. Francis of Assisi, so did
Confucius, so did Christ, so did Socrates. In what way, we ask,
could science have helped them to have lived more wisely in their
respective worlds? Modern science is really quite young, amazingly
so. Mr. Eddington tells us it dates from 1917. Before that a great
many of the most eminent scientists believed that this world was
a solid lump of matter made up of solid atoms. This was, we are
told today, a gross, if a scientific, superstition. Yet many of the
scientists who believed this, which was quite the opposite of what
Mr. Millikan and the spiritual scientists of today believe, could, and
we hope sometimes did, live quite wisely in that odd and scientifically incorrect world of theirs. This is because the world in which
man the person lives as distinguished from that in which man the
thing exists is one governed not by scientific but by moral principles. If we are to accept Mr. Millikan's view we may soon learn
that Socrates and Christ and Confucius and St. Francis and Washington, who were all of them hopelessly unscientific, must now be
cast aside as quite misleading guides. Wisdom in living is not to
be learned from them but somehow from present science and its
future discoveries. Here the student of the humanities and the
historian disagree sharply. The sphere in which as individual
human beings we live really impinges very little upon the sphere
of Mr. Millikan's symbolic and ingenious atoms. This is most fortunate, for no civilization can possibly transform itself as rapidly as
science changes its fundamental conceptions. Fourteen years ago
the views of scientists on these matters were quite different and
there is no telling but that fourteen years from now they may be
quite as different again. A social system or code of morals cannot be
changed as rapidly as this; otherwise we should not know when
we went to bed at night what would be moral in the morning. They
cannot change so rapidly just because they are far more central
to civilization than any purely scientific conceptions. Man's frailty

is such and his dependence upon custom so great that his world can stand only a limited amount of renovation at a time. To make it possible for a social, a moral system, a civilization to endure at all, there must be stabilizing forces which are not scientific and the world up to the present has been wise not to accept Galileo and Kepler and Newton and Darwin and Einstein, great scientists though they were, as its stabilizing forces. That scientifically ignorant Confucius who held that he who conquereth himself is greater than he who taketh a city, is a far safer teacher for mankind than the great scientist Darwin.

Mathematics is, of course, the most perfect of the sciences. It lies behind them all. It is their impassive bookkeeper, their recording angel, if they have one. That is why it has proved so admirable an instrument for research. Like every science, however, it is valid only when we are dealing with things between which there is nothing in the nature of a moral or spiritual bond. A city or a nation is not a sum of similar individuals, it is not a census merely. That illusive factor which we call morale and which is recognized as important even in the winning of wars cannot be explained by mathematical processes. A man and his friend, a father and his son, a husband and his wife, though they count as two in a census, are not merely two human beings. One and one may constitute here not two but a quite different unity. I do not wish to slip over into this dangerous field of mysticism and shall merely repeat what a German poet once said, "I feel that my conviction gains infinitely when it is shared by a single other human soul." He was, of course, not mathematical but he may have been not altogether wrong. It is disconcerting relationships of this sort that force the student of human conduct to consider other factors than the mathematical or scientific, properly so called.

A little farther along in Mr. Millikan's creed we are told that if we are to "be asked deliberately to shut our eyes to truth or to be deterred by fear from searching for it, we might as well, so says that scientist, give up the effort at intelligent living altogether and go back to savagery."

As this is a scientist's creed we may take it that he means by truth the truth of science. We must, however, remind the overzealous that the necessary alternative to less science is not savagery. There are other cherishable forms of truth at which highly civilized

men have warmed their hands. Homer had no experimental knowledge and yet his parting of Hector and Andromache is still true
and beautiful, far more so than anything in that naturalistic school
of literature which took its principles directly from the sciences.
Epictetus and Confucius and St. Francis were not savages. Socrates
could probably not have passed high-school algebra, had never
heard of a negative quantity or mathematical infinity and probably
believed like all our ancestors until 1850 that heat was a substance.
Yet he apprehended the truths of a great art and a great philosophy,
lived wisely and well in his world and was done to death by an
intolerant demos, a peril from which science has not yet delivered
us. It was possible to bear the burden of life, even to live wisely
and quite comfortably in ages that knew not plush nor rubber nor
whirling electrons. Mr. Millikan in his defense makes much of the
great services to modern life of the Ford motor-car. We may leave
as an open question whether this, especially that ugly machine,
Model T, should be regarded as a real index of civilization or only
as a triumph of modern science. The Athenian who knew Homer,
the Parthenon, Socrates, and the tragedies of Sophocles and who
believed that only a thing of beauty was an everlasting possession
might conceivably have rejected it on appearance alone. Homer's
poems, furthermore, were not only great works of art, they were
a healthy stabilizing influence and fixed the customs and morals
for that Greek civilization which was one of humanity's greatest
triumphs.

Mr. Millikan assumes that somehow science is to provide what
might be called this steadying influence. He contrasts with evident
satisfaction "the bleary-eyed, ruby-nosed old soak who thirty years
ago sat on the driver's seat of the average cab in London or New
York with the highly skilled chauffeur of today, alert, self-respecting, sober, intelligent, and well dressed. The change is striking," he
tells us, "and the improvement enormous."

Let us not allow ourselves to become bemused by the contemplation of this mirage of progress. Science has done both more and
less than this. All cab and bus drivers were not bleary-eyed old
soaks thirty years ago. Walt Whitman learned much poetry from
some of them. There were, of course, drunkards and wastrels and
where science has been the only influence operative they are now
a far greater menace than they were then. The real successor of

the drunken cab-driver is not the sober, self-respecting chauffeur, however well dressed. His lineal descendant through science is the gunman in bullet-proof vest with the machine-gun and the armored car. He is not morally better than his predecessor and he is socially much more dangerous, for he has greater speed and power at his command, thanks to science. It is just because we have made it possible for him with this greater speed to elude the police that we probably have that increase in lawlessness, of which Mr. Millikan quite inconsistently complains. It may have to be counted in as one of the by-products of modern science which alone made it possible.

Just as Mr. Millikan believes that the drunken cab-driver has been scientifically extirpated so he tells us that war is now in process of being abolished chiefly by "this relentless advance of science, *its most powerful enemy.*"

Mr. Millikan goes on to tell us that "steel does indeed make bayonets, but it also makes ploughshares and railroads and automobiles and sewing-machines and threshers, and a thousand other things whose uses constitute the strongest existing diverter of human energies from the destructive to the peaceful arts." This rapid manufacture of motor-cars, threshers, fertilizers, and explosives to Mr. Millikan as to many others is a promise of peace. He forgets, however, that manufacturers do not give away these scientifically invented blessings. They strive to sell them to each other and to other nations in a struggle almost as fierce as war. Science does not lessen, it increases, this competition. That overproduction which it has made possible and the consequent need for markets helped create that tension which resulted in the last war and it may conceivably result in the next. Science is neither the friend nor the "enemy" of war. It has no such human attributes. Its products may, alas, be the cause of conflict. In his exaggerated faith in the friendliness of science Mr. Millikan goes out of his way to tell us of the failures of religion and of philosophy and of social ethics. "War," he tells us, "has existed in spite of religion, in spite of philosophy and in spite of social ethics and in spite of humanitarianism and the Golden Rule since the days of the caveman because, in accordance with the evolutionary philosophy of modern science, and simply because, it had survival value."

When Mr. Millikan, and I cite his argument only as the most

illustrious example of too common a fallacy, proposes to have science solve a moral problem like war because as he sees it the other civilizing agencies have failed to do so, he is, from the standpoint of the historian, guilty of one of the most serious sins of the scientist. Wars have never been ended merely by increasing wages and multiplying creature comforts and the most prosperous peoples have waged the most deadly ones. Not until the scientist gives up this talk of survival value, which in this connection is only biological jargon, and realizes that what we need is a moral and not a scientific judgment, can we hope to get anywhere with our problem. When studied from the standpoint of those judgments which religion or politics and philosophy have pronounced upon war we may find that they have not really been and are not now as impotent as the scientist so naïvely believes.

In the past, historians tell us, men made war for their families, for their tribe, later for their king, for their religion, for their nation. They met, to be sure, to kill or to be killed, and this was ugly. Yet the courage and valor of each helped his tribe, his religion, his nation, to prevail. This was self-sacrifice and as such beautiful, even moral, and in part at least it redeemed the ugliness of combat. The poet, priest, and moralist recognized that religion and country are more valuable than the individual life. There really were good wars. Perhaps, alas, for so much evil, many wars were good, and the Latin poet quite properly said, "Dulce et decorum est pro patria mori." Art was not impotent even though it passed a favorable judgment. It was not necessarily a false one, which only a wiser science can supersede. Human experience approved it. To meet one's antagonist in mortal combat, to lose, even to die for something higher than one's self, and if one triumphed to win through greater skill and valor, this is not, in a world where conflict of good and evil is the rule, morally reprehensible. Science made only one contribution to this problem. Its service was to make wars different and far more deadly. It is not, however, for this reason that wars may end. What science is doing perhaps disastrously for the arts and crafts may haply here be turned to man's advantage. From the standpoint of the artist and moralist it has made all wars bad. There can under science be no good wars. Human valor, high heroism and willingness to sacrifice oneself have become negligible factors. They cannot win the scientific wars of tomorrow.

A chivalrous soldier of the crude, old-fashioned struggles could distinguish between a civilian woman and an enemy combatant. A poison gas and long-range gun cannot. If France should again imagine Germany her enemy, small squadrons of French bombers might conceivably slink through darkened skies and drop upon a German concentration point those new perfected gas bombs which would paralyze unwitting thousands who, whether cowards or heroes, would have never a chance to resist. Guns on French soil might kill women and children in churches at Frankfort or Darmstadt, as the German "Big Bertha" at St. Gobain killed unseen women seventy miles away on Good Friday in the church of St. Gervais. The swifter plane, the deadlier gas or the longer-range gun would not necessarily even be the result of the ingenuity of any Frenchman. They might be the earlier invention of Germans themselves or of Italians or Americans friendly to Germany. It is no longer a struggle of persons, but of impersonal forces. Thus is the new welter of scientific warfare stripped of its last shred of redeeming heroism, self-sacrifice, and courage. If in the popular estimation the aviators in the last war were regarded as its greatest heroes it was because each single flier matched his individual prowess against an individual enemy and in such combat there still lingered a little of that chivalry which once made war morally tolerable. Yet even individual combat between aviators will henceforth mean little. The artist, if not the scientist, already recognizes this. At the front, if again there is one, men will not die contending with their human antagonists in prowess and daring. They must die at night when no enemy is stirring, in trenches and dugouts, like rats in a trap. This is the lesson, if scientists will but listen, that the artists are trying to teach us. This is what Remarque in "All Quiet on the Western Front," Hemingway in "A Farewell to Arms," Sherriff in "Journey's End" have already discovered. Science has dehumanized wars and in making them scientific has from the artist's and the moralist's standpoint made all of them ugly and meaningless and the remedy is not to be found in Mr. Millikan's fond hope that these deadlier instruments will automatically be diverted to the uses of peace but in more art and respect for that enlightened moral judgment which science cannot give. Whatever it may do for us, the safety factor for our modern civilization does not lie along scientific lines but in a more imaginative and comprehensive grasp by artists, preachers, and philosophers, of the moral hazards involved in each new scientific transformation.

What we really need is a careful and critical evaluation from other than the scientific point of view of what science has done. It has justified itself, enjoys enormous credit and authority. It can now take care of itself and needs no further stimulation. As one practical measure in the interest of the stability of our civilization, I would suggest that some part of the enormous' profits which it has created for industry and commerce be devoted to the advancement of art, religion, political philosophy, and the humanities which, relatively weak though they are, are still the only agencies that can prevent a social order from being shaken to pieces in an age of too rapid change.

IV

We know very little about civilization. Although there are very few things we can safely say about it, one of them is probably this. Science alone cannot save it. Civilization involves so many things that, as we have intimated, it has been possible to constitute some quite satisfactory ones without science at all. This was true of the Chinese and Hindu, even the Greek and the Roman. We have had so little regard for oriental systems and they enjoy so little credit in an age of science that we may disregard them here. The historian can, however, say quite confidently that if Greek and Roman civilization perished it was certainly not for lack of science but quite possibly for lack of an adequate religion. Russia has produced some really admirable scientists like Pavloff and the throes through which she is passing today are not caused by lack of science—the accumulated scientific knowledge of our western world is open to her— but rather by overconfidence in it and by an irreligious and an unphilosophical acceptance of conceptions invented by so-called political scientists like Marx.

Scientists make much of the fact that their conceptions now are not materialistic but spiritualistic, and assume that this of itself will revivify religion. It is a vain hope, a dangerous illusion. The Bohr atom, though much more ingenious than its scientific predecessor, is not one whit more friendly or essentially divine. God for the modern scientist, as scientist, is and always must be as He was for

La Place, a useless hypothesis. It will not help religion as a binding civilizing force to learn that God, as one of our scientific philosophers has called Him, is the principle of concretion in the universe. This will not greatly hearten unhappy mankind. Science makes no moment, and if it is to remain free it cannot make moment, of good and evil. It can analyze substances and forces but cannot find for us the root of the humanly desirable. It can rid us of some superstitions. Mr. Eddington tells us, for instance, that we must give up the idea of a Heaven in space but not in time. It is inconsistent with the space-time conceptions of modern science. Geologists and biologists have long since told us that we must give up the idea of a world created in six days. Science may force us to take out of religion many incidental things. But there is one thing which science cannot put into religion and one thing which religion can never get out of science and it is the one thing needful. Any God who is to be of any use to civilization, to suffering humanity, or to religion must have in some way or other some at least of the attributes not of a substance or of a force but of a person. He must be interested as science is not, in good and evil, beautiful and ugly, holy and obscene. It is conceivable that in the future we may have to learn to do without religion; it is certain that science as such can never give us one. Let us face the facts and admit as some scientists do not that there are some services to civilization which science cannot render.

In its callow days, modern science used to amuse itself by frightening the rest of us with its bogies, its hobgoblins. The earth was slowly cooling off and after a time would cease to be able to support life. The glacial age would return. The coal supply, the oil supply was slowly being exhausted. The sum of energy was being forever diminished and we were running into an inevitable doom. It produced mummies at the modern feast to warn us not to enter upon any too long hopes. This was not really a bad idea. It might be well to do so again and there is another adverse fate which may conceivably lie in wait for us which scientists might possibly suggest. It is not pleasant to contemplate. Science may conceivably destroy itself. The really serious danger may be one which science has itself created and which its every advance irresistibly and inevitably multiplies.

A single workman by merely pressing a button may now send

along a wire the power of fifty thousand horses. The wisest citizen of Athens and Rome never had any such agency at his command. A single malcontent lighting a fuse may virtually blow up a city as he did who set off the explosives on the ship that ruined Halifax. A determined group, numerically a much smaller group than formerly, could quite easily paralyze an entire community and destroy half its citizens. A Sioux with his bow and arrow was no such threat to a frontier blockhouse. As we have seen, science has made modern industry and modern warfare much more scientific. Other agencies if encouraged may conceivably forefend the peril of international warfare but science has made and is continuing to make any possible future political revolution far more effective and deadly. We are fortunate that we have not yet had such an upheaval. Let us hope we never will but let us remember, particularly in our optimistic enthusiasm, that this is after all only a hope. History warns us to be circumspect, for we have had revolts against particular types of civilization in the past. Our own is not yet proof against all possible human discontents. Science for all her great services cannot pluck from the heart of man a rooted sorrow or a deep-seated grievance, even a mistaken one.

Victor Hugo says somewhere that just as a banker on the verge of bankruptcy gives a great banquet to re-establish his credit, so the Lord on rare and desperate occasions is forced to give his doubting Thomases a revolution. It would almost seem to be a way that civilizations have followed. Men fight for religions, political, and social rights and their conception of these changes most rapidly in periods like ours in which an agency like science has modified customs and the way of life. They fight as in peasants' wars for the redistribution of property. Their notions must not be changed too precipitately, for a civilization is only a very nice adjustment and balance of forces of which science is but one. Let me repeat that we have not yet had such a scientific revolution. Béla Kun, the Spartacists, and the sovietists are not revolutionists of this most dangerous type. They were not really protesting against a scientific civilization; they were fighting only for the control of it. There have, however, been revolutions when fairly large sections of a population protested against a religious or a social, or a political order. Men in the past, the fairly recent past, have risen against what they believed to be the iniquities of their institutions, their church, their government. In such cases they resort to all the forces at their command. The French people in 1789 quite unexpectedly did this and a little later half-organized mobs protested against the churches and attempted to do away with them since they believed them instruments of oppression. They did their best to ruin the cathedrals of France, yet old-fashioned stonemasonry alone was proof against them. With their utmost efforts and all the destructive forces at their disposal they succeeded only in ruining the portals of Notre Dame and beheading in other parts of France some really beautiful statues. In the revolution of the *Communards* of Paris in 1871 they protested against centralized governmental agencies. They succeeded only in burning down the Tuileries, doing minor damage and overturning the Vendome Column. They did this clumsily with ropes. They could not even destroy it and one of their leaders was Courbet, that naturalistic painter whose art and whose citizenship had been much influenced by science. Let us admit that they were all mistaken but let us also admit that what was true for Tennyson is no longer true for us. He told us, and it was consoling to believe, that Galahad's strength was as the strength of ten because his heart was pure. Science has changed all that. Any man's strength may be as the strength of ten thousand not because his heart is pure but only because science which knows not good nor evil has given it to any who may wish to use it.

I have said there are few things which we can safely say about civilizations. In conclusion I shall risk one more. A social political system, a civilization in other words, falls when the accumulated discontents which it has engendered are stronger than the forces upon which the remaining contented members of society can draw to hold the protestants in effective check. Now the fiercest, the most subversive, most implacable discontents have been aroused when an individual, no matter how prosperous, feels that his moral rights have been invaded and his claims upon justice denied. It is particularly necessary that we be upon our guard now that we have placed such excessive and destructive power within the reach of smaller minorities. We must respond to a new challenge and obviate any such possible threat. Not every one is happy in our modern age and ways and an American poet has warned us that "factory windows are always broken." Science itself cannot defend us against this danger which it has raised. To do so we must greatly strengthen those stabilizing forces like an adequate art and literature, a sound religion, a sane moral and political philosophy, the only agencies which have yet been found to make consistently for social justice and for life's larger and least perturbable satisfactions.

For questions and exercises, see p. 140, p. 197, p. 325, p. 328, p. 333, p. 334, p. 419, p. 521, and p. 531.

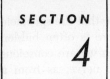

# Essays Formal
# and Informal

## A LARK'S FLIGHT

### ALEXANDER SMITH

Rightly or wrongly, during the last twenty or thirty years a
strong feeling has grown up in the public mind against the principle, and a still stronger feeling against the practice, of capital
punishments. Many people who will admit that the execution of
the murderer may be, abstractly considered, just enough, sincerely
doubt whether such execution be expedient, and are in their own
minds perfectly certain that it cannot fail to demoralise the spectators. In consequence of this, executions have become rare; and it
is quite clear that many scoundrels, well worthy of the noose, con-
trive to escape it. When, on the occasion of a wretch being turned
off, the spectators are few, it is remarked by the newspapers that
the mob is beginning to lose its proverbial cruelty, and to be stirred
by humane pulses; when they are numerous, and especially when
girls and women form a majority, the circumstance is noticed and
deplored. It is plain enough that, if the newspaper considered such
an exhibition beneficial, it would not lament over a few thousand
eager witnesses: if the sermon be edifying, you cannot have too
large a congregation; if you teach a moral lesson in a grand, impressive way, it is difficult to see how you can have too many
pupils. Of course, neither the justice nor the expediency of capital
punishments falls to be discussed here. This, however, may be said,
that the popular feeling against them may not be so admirable a

A LARK'S FLIGHT: *From Dreamthorp* by Alexander Smith.

proof of enlightenment as many believe. It is true that the spectacle is painful, horrible; but in pain and horror there is often hidden a certain salutariness, and the repulsion of which we are conscious is as likely to arise from debilitation of public nerve, as from a higher reach of public feeling. To my own thinking, it is out of this pain and hatefulness that an execution becomes invested with an ideal grandeur. It is sheer horror to all concerned—sheriffs, halbert-men, chaplain, spectators, Jack Ketch,[1] and culprit; but out of all this, and towering behind the vulgar and hideous accessories of the scaffold, gleams the majesty of implacable law. When every other fine morning a dozen cut-purses were hanged at Tyburn, and when such sights did not run very strongly against the popular current, the spectacle *was* vulgar, and could be of use only to the possible cut-purses congregated around the foot of the scaffold. Now, when the law has become so far merciful; when the punishment of death is reserved for the murderer; when he can be condemned only on the clearest evidence; when, as the days draw slowly on to doom, the frightful event impending over one stricken wretch throws its shadow over the heart of every man, woman, and child in the great city; and when the official persons whose duty it is to see the letter of the law carried out perform that duty at the expense of personal pain, a public execution is not vulgar, it becomes positively sublime. It is dreadful, of course; but its dreadfulness melts into pure aw-fulness. The attention is taken off the criminal, and is lost in a sense of the grandeur of justice; and the spectator who beholds an execu-tion, solely as it appears to the eye, without recognition of the idea which towers behind it, must be a very unspiritual and unimagina-tive spectator indeed.

It is taken for granted that the spectators of public executions—the artizans and country people who take up their stations over-night as close to the barriers as possible, and the wealthier classes who occupy hired windows and employ opera-glasses—are merely drawn together by a morbid relish for horrible sights. He is a bold man who will stand forward as the advocate of such persons—so completely is the popular mind made up as to their tastes and motives. It is not disputed that the large body of the mob, and of

[1] Jack Ketch (d. 1686) was a notorious executioner of the seventeenth cen-tury. His name is used allusively for any official executioner.

the occupants of windows, have been drawn together by an appetite for excitement; but it is quite possible that many come there from an impulse altogether different. Just consider the nature of the expected sight—a man in tolerable health probably, in possession of all his faculties, perfectly able to realise his position, conscious that for him this world and the next are so near that only a few seconds divide them—such a man stands in the seeing of several thousand eyes. He is so peculiarly circumstanced, so utterly lonely —hearing the tolling of his own death-bell, yet living, wearing the mourning clothes for his own funeral—that he holds the multitude together by a shuddering fascination. The sight is a peculiar one, you must admit, and every peculiarity has its attractions. Your volcano is more attractive than your ordinary mountain. Then consider the unappeasable curiosity as to death which haunts every human being, and how pathetic that curiosity is, in so far as it suggests our own ignorance and helplessness, and we see at once that people *may* flock to public executions for other purposes than the gratification of morbid tastes: that they would pluck if they could some little knowledge of what death is; that imaginatively they attempt to reach to it, to touch and handle it through an experience which is not their own. It is some obscure desire of this kind, a movement of curiosity not altogether ignoble, but in some degree pathetic; some rude attempt of the imagination to wrest from the death of the criminal information as to the great secret in which each is profoundly interested, which draws around the scaffold people from the country harvest-fields, and from the streets and alleys of the town. Nothing interests men so much as death. Age cannot wither it, nor custom stale it. "A greater crowd would come to see me hanged," Cromwell is reported to have said when the populace came forth on a public occasion. The Lord Protector was right in a sense of which, perhaps, at the moment he was not aware. Death is greater than official position. When a man has to die, he may safely dispense with stars and ribbands. He is invested with a greater dignity than is held in the gift of kings. A greater crowd *would* have gathered to see Cromwell hanged, but the compliment would have been paid to death rather than to Cromwell. Never were the motions of Charles I so scrutinised as when he stood for a few moments on the scaffold that winter morning at Whitehall. King Louis was no great orator usually, but when on

January 2, 1793, he attempted to speak a few words in the Place de la Revolution, it was found necessary to drown his voice in a harsh roll of soldiers' drums. Not without a meaning do people come forth to see men die. We stand in the valley, they on the hilltop, and on their faces strikes the light of the other world, and from some sign or signal of theirs we attempt to discover or extract a hint of what it is all like.

To be publicly put to death, for whatever reason, must ever be a serious matter. It is always bitter, but there are degrees in its bitterness. It is easy to die like Stephen with an opened heaven above you, crowded with angel faces. It is easy to die like Balmerino [2] with a chivalrous sigh for the White Rose, and an audible "God bless King James." Such men die for a cause in which they glory, and are supported thereby; they are conducted to the portals of the next world by the angels, Faith, Pity, Admiration. But it is not easy to die in expiation of a crime like murder, which engirdles you with trembling and horror even in the loneliest places, which cuts you off from the sympathies of your kind, which reduces the universe to two elements—a sense of personal identity, and a memory of guilt. In so dying, there must be inconceivable bitterness; a man can have no other support than what strength he may pluck from despair, or from the iron with which nature may have originally braced heart and nerve. Yet, taken as a whole, criminals on the scaffold comport themselves creditably. They look Death in the face when he wears his cruelest aspect, and if they flinch somewhat, they can at least bear to look. I believe that, for the criminal, execution within the prison walls, with no witnesses save some half-dozen official persons, would be infinitely more terrible than execution in the presence of a curious, glaring mob. The daylight and the publicity are alien elements, which wean the man a little from himself. He steadies his dizzy brain on the crowd beneath and around him. He has his last part to play, and his manhood rallies to play it well. Nay, so subtly is vanity intertwined with our motives, the noblest and the most ignoble, that I can fancy a poor wretch with the noose dangling at his ear, and with barely five minutes to live, soothed somewhat with the idea that his firm-

[2] James Elphinstone, 1st Baron Balmerino (1553?-1612), secretary of state for Scotland under James I (then James VI of Scotland); though condemned to death, he was subsequently released.

ness and composure will earn him the approbation, perhaps the pity, of the spectators. He would take with him, if he could, the good opinion of his fellows. This composure of criminals puzzles one. Have they looked at death so long and closely, that familiarity has robbed it of terror? Has life treated them so harshly, that they are tolerably well pleased to be quit of it on any terms? Or is the whole thing mere blind stupor and delirium, in which thought is paralysed, and the man an automaton? Speculation is useless. The fact remains that criminals for the most part die well and bravely. It is said that the championship of England was to be decided at some little distance from London on the morning of the day on which Thurtell was executed, and that, when he came out on the scaffold, he inquired privily of the executioner if the result had yet become known. Jack Ketch was not aware, and Thurtell expressed his regret that the ceremony in which he was chief actor should take place so inconveniently early in the day. Think of a poor Thurtell forced to take his long journey an hour, perhaps, before the arrival of intelligence so important!

More than twenty years ago I saw two men executed, and the impression then made remains fresh to this day. For this there were many reasons. The deed for which the men suffered created an immense sensation. They were hanged on the spot where the murder was committed—on a rising ground, some four miles north-east of the city; and as an attempt at rescue was apprehended, there was a considerable display of military force on the occasion. And when, in the dead silence of thousands, the criminals stood beneath the halters, an incident occurred, quite natural and slight in itself, but when taken in connexion with the business then proceeding, so unutterably tragic, so overwhelming in its pathetic suggestion of contrast, that the feeling of it has never departed, and never will. At the time, too, I speak of, I was very young; the world was like a die newly cut, whose every impression is fresh and vivid.

While the railway which connects two northern capitals was being built, two brothers from Ireland, named Doolan, were engaged upon it in the capacity of navvies. For some fault or negligence, one of the brothers was dismissed by the overseer—a Mr. Green—of that particular portion of the line on which they were employed. The dismissed brother went off in search of work, and the brother who remained—Dennis was the Christian name of him

—brooded over this supposed wrong, and in his dull, twilighted brain revolved projects of vengeance. He did not absolutely mean to take Green's life, but he meant to thrash him to within an inch of it. Dennis, anxious to thrash Green, but not quite seeing his way to it, opened his mind one afternoon, when work was over, to his friends—fellow-Irishmen and navvies—Messrs. Redding and Hickie. These took up Doolan's wrong as their own, and that evening, by the dull light of a bothy [3] fire, they held a rude parliament, discussing ways and means of revenge. It was arranged that Green should be thrashed—the amount of thrashing left an open question, to be decided, unhappily, when the blood was up and the cinder of rage blown into a flame. Hickie's spirit was found not to be a mounting one, and it was arranged that the active partners in the game should be Doolan and Redding. Doolan, as the aggrieved party, was to strike the first blow, and Redding, as the aggrieved party's particular friend, asked and obtained permission to strike the second. The main conspirators, with a fine regard for the feelings of the weaker Hickie, allowed him to provide the weapons of assault—so that by some slight filament of aid he might connect himself with the good cause. The unambitious Hickie at once applied himself to his duty. He went out, and in due time returned with two sufficient iron pokers. The weapons were examined, approved of, and carefully laid aside. Doolan, Redding, and Hickie ate their suppers, and retired to their several couches to sleep, peacefully enough no doubt. About the same time, too, Green, the English overseer, threw down his weary limbs, and entered on his last sleep—little dreaming what the morning had in store for him.

Uprose the sun, and uprose Doolan and Redding, and dressed, and thrust each his sufficient iron poker up the sleeve of his blouse, and went forth. They took up their station on a temporary wooden bridge which spanned the line, and waited there. Across the bridge, as was expected, did Green ultimately come. He gave them good morning; asked, "why they were loafing about?" received no very pertinent answer, perhaps did not care to receive one; whistled— the unsuspecting man!—thrust his hands into his breeches pockets, turned his back on them, and leaned over the railing of the bridge,

[3] *bothy:* hut (Scot.)

inspecting the progress of the works beneath. The temptation was really too great. What could wild Irish flesh and blood do? In a moment out from the sleeve of Doolan's blouse came the hidden poker, and the first blow was struck, bringing Green to the ground. The friendly Redding, who had bargained for the second, and who, naturally enough, was in fear of being cut out altogether, jumped on the prostrate man, and fulfilled his share of the bargain with a will. It was Redding it was supposed who sped the unhappy Green. They overdid their work—like young authors—giving many more blows than were sufficient, and then fled. The works, of course, were that morning in consternation. Redding and Hickie were, if I remember rightly, apprehended in the course of the day. Doolan got off, leaving no trace of his whereabouts.

These particulars were all learned subsequently. The first intimation which we schoolboys received of anything unusual having occurred, was the sight of a detachment of soldiers with fixed bayonets, trousers rolled up over muddy boots, marching past the front of the Cathedral hurriedly home to barracks. This was a circumstance somewhat unusual. We had, of course, frequently seen a couple of soldiers trudging along with sloped muskets, and that cruel glitter of steel which no one of us could look upon quite unmoved; but in such cases, the deserter walking between them in his shirt-sleeves, his pinioned hands covered from public gaze by the loose folds of his great-coat, explained everything. But from the hurried march of these mud-splashed men nothing could be gathered, and we were left to speculate upon its meaning. Gradually, however, before the evening fell, the rumour of a murder having been committed spread through the city, and with that I instinctively connected the apparition of the file of muddy soldiers. Next day, murder was in every mouth. My schoolfellows talked of it to the detriment of their lessons; it flavoured the tobacco of the fustian artizan as he smoked to work after breakfast; it walked on Change amongst the merchants. It was known that two of the persons implicated had been captured, but that the other, and guiltiest, was still at large; and in a few days out on every piece of boarding and blank wall came the "Hue and cry"—describing Doolan like a photograph, to the colour and cut of his whiskers, and offering £100 as reward for his apprehension, or for such information as would lead to his apprehension—like a silent, implacable bloodhound following close on the track of the murderer. This terrible broadsheet I read, was certain that *he* had read it also, and fancy ran riot over the ghastly fact. For him no hope, no rest, no peace, no touch of hands gentler than the hangman's; all the world is after him like a roaring prairie of flame! I thought of Doolan, weary, foot-sore, heart-sore, entering some quiet village of an evening; and to quench his thirst, going up to the public well, around which the gossips are talking, and hearing that they were talking of *him;* and seeing from the well itself, ᴎ glaring upon him, as if conscious of his presence, with a hundred eyes of vengeance. I thought of him asleep in out-houses, and starting up in wild dreams of the policeman's hand upon his shoulder fifty times ere morning. He had committed the crime of Cain, and the weird of Cain he had to endure. But yesterday innocent, how unimportant; today bloody-handed, the whole world is talking of him, and everything he touches, the very bed he sleeps on, steals from him his secret, and is eager to betray!

Doolan was finally captured in Liverpool, and in the Spring Assize the three men were brought to trial. The jury found them guilty, but recommended Hickie to mercy on account of some supposed weakness of mind on his part. Sentence was, of course, pronounced with the usual solemnities. They were set apart to die; and when snug abed o'nights—for imagination is most mightily moved by contrast—I crept into their desolate hearts, and tasted a misery which was not my own. As already said, Hickie was recommended to mercy, and the recommendation was ultimately in the proper quarter given effect to.

The evening before the execution has arrived, and the reader has now to imagine the early May sunset falling pleasantly on the outskirts of the city. The houses looking out upon an open square or space, have little plots of garden-ground in their fronts, in which mahogany-coloured wallflowers and mealy auriculas are growing. The side of this square, along which the City Road stretches northward, is occupied by a blind asylum, a brick building, the bricks painted red and picked out with white, after the tidy English fashion, and a high white cemetery wall, over which peers the spire of the Gothic Cathedral; and beyond that, on the other side of the ravine, rising out of a populous city of the dead, a stone John Knox looks down on the Cathedral, a Bible clutched in his

outstretched and menacing hand. On all this the May sunset is striking, dressing everything in its warm, pleasant pink, lingering in the
tufts of foliage that nestle around the asylum, and dipping the
building itself one half in light, one half in tender shade. This
open space or square is an excellent place for the games of us boys,
and "Prisoners' Base" is being carried out with as much earnestness
as the business of life now by those of us who are left. The girls,
too, have their games of a quiet kind, which we hold in huge scorn
and contempt. In two files, linked arm-in-arm, they alternately
dance towards each other and then retire, singing the while, in their
clear, girlish treble, verses, the meaning and pertinence of which
time has worn away—"The Campsie Duke's a-riding, a-riding, a-riding," being the oft-recurring "owercome" or refrain. All this is going
on in the pleasant sunset light, when by the apparition of certain
waggons coming up from the city, piled high with blocks and
beams, and guarded by a dozen dragoons, on whose brazen helmets the sunset danced, every game is dismembered, and we are
in a moment a mere mixed mob of boys and girls, flocking around
to stare and wonder. Just at this place something went wrong with
one of the waggon wheels, and the procession came to a stop.
A crowd collected, and we heard some of the grown-up people say
that the scaffold was being carried out for the ceremony of tomorrow. Then, more intensely than ever, one realised the condition of the doomed men. *We* were at our happy games in the sunset, *they* were entering on their last night on earth. After hammer-
ing and delay the wheel was put to rights, the sunset died out,
waggons and dragoons got into motion and disappeared; and all
the night through, whether awake or asleep, I saw the torches
burning, and heard the hammers clinking, and witnessed as clearly
as if I had been an onlooker, the horrid structure rising, till it
stood complete, with a huge cross-beam from which two empty
halters hung, in the early morning light.

Next morning the whole city was in commotion. Whether the
authorities were apprehensive that a rescue would be attempted,
or were anxious merely to strike terror into the hundreds of wild
Irishry engaged on the railway, I cannot say; in any case, there was
a display of military force quite unusual. The carriage in which
the criminals—Catholics both—and their attendant priests were
seated, was guarded by soldiers with fixed bayonets; indeed, the

whole regiment then lying in the city was massed in front and
behind, with a cold, frightful glitter of steel. Besides the foot soldiers, there were dragoons, and two pieces of cannon; a whole
little army, in fact. With a slenderer force battles have been won
which have made a mark in history. What did the prisoners think
of their strange importance, and of the tramp and hurly-burly all
around? When the procession moved out of the city, it seemed to
draw with it almost the entire population; and when once the
country roads were reached, the crowd spread over the fields on
either side, ruthlessly treading down the tender wheat braird. I got
a glimpse of the doomed, blanched faces which had haunted me so
long, at the turn of the road, where, for the first time, the black
cross-beam with its empty halters first became visible to them.
Both turned and regarded it with a long, steady look; that done,
they again bent their heads attentively to the words of the clergyman. I suppose in that long, eager, fascinated gaze they practically
*died*—that for them death had no additional bitterness. When the
mound was reached on which the scaffold stood, there was immense
confusion. Around it a wide space was kept clear by the military;
the cannon were placed in position; out flashed the swords of the
dragoons; beneath and around on every side was the crowd. Between two brass helmets I could see the scaffold clearly enough,
and when in a little while the men, bareheaded and with their
attendants, appeared upon it, the surging crowd became stiffened
with fear and awe. And now it was that the incident so simple, so
natural, so much in the ordinary course of things, and yet so frightful in its tragic suggestions, took place. Be it remembered that the
season was early May, that the day was fine, that the wheat-fields
were clothing themselves in the green of the young crop, and that
around the scaffold, standing on a sunny mound, a wide space was
kept clear. When the men appeared beneath the beam, each under
his proper halter, there was a dead silence—every one was gazing
too intently to whisper to his neighbour even. Just then, out of the
grassy space at the foot of the scaffold, in the dead silence audible
to all, a lark rose from the side of its nest, and went singing upward in its happy flight. O heaven! how did that song translate
itself into dying ears? Did it bring in one wild burning moment
father, and mother, and poor Irish cabin, and prayers said at bed-
time, and the smell of turf fires, and innocent sweet-hearting, and

rising and setting suns? Did it—but the dragoon's horse has become restive, and his brass helmet bobs up and down and blots everything; and there is a sharp sound, and I feel the great crowd heave and swing, and hear it torn by a sharp shiver of pity, and the men whom I saw so near but a moment ago are at immeasurable distance, and have solved the great enigma—and the lark has not yet finished his flight: you can see and hear him yonder in the fringe of a white May cloud.

This ghastly lark's flight, when the circumstances are taken into consideration, is, I am inclined to think, more terrible than anything of the same kind which I have encountered in books. The artistic uses of contrast as background and accompaniment, are well known to nature and the poets. Joy is continually worked on sorrow, sorrow on joy; riot is framed in peace, peace in riot. Lear and the Fool always go together. Trafalgar is being fought while Napoleon is sitting on horseback watching the Austrian army laying down its arms at Ulm. In Hood's poem, it is when looking on the released schoolboys at their games that Eugene Aram remembers he is a murderer. And these two poor Irish labourers could not die without hearing a lark singing in their ears. It is Nature's fashion. She never quite goes along with us. She is sombre at weddings, sunny at funerals, and she frowns on ninety-nine out of a hundred picnics.

There is a stronger element of terror in this incident of the lark than in any story of a similar kind I can remember.

A good story is told of an Irish gentleman—still known in London society—who inherited the family estates and the family banshee. The estates he lost—no uncommon circumstance in the history of Irish gentlemen—but the banshee, who expected no favours, stuck to him in his adversity, and crossed the channel with him, making herself known only on occasions of deathbeds and sharp family misfortunes. This gentleman had an ear, and, seated one night at the opera, the *keen* [4]—heard once or twice before on memorable occasions—thrilled through the din of the orchestra and the passion of the singers. He hurried home of course, found his immediate family well, but on the morrow a telegram arrived with the announcement of a brother's death. Surely of all superstitions that is the most imposing which makes the other world interested in the

[4] *keen:* lamentation or dirge for the dead.

events which befall our mortal lot. For the mere pomp and pride
of it, your ghost is worth a dozen retainers, and it is entirely inex-
pensive. The peculiarity and supernatural worth of this story lies
in the idea of the old wail piercing through the sweet entanglement
of stringed instruments and extinguishing Grisi.[5] Modern circumstances and luxury crack, as it were, and reveal for a moment misty
and aboriginal time big with portent. There is a ridiculous Scotch
story in which one gruesome touch lives. A clergyman's female
servant was seated in the kitchen one Saturday night reading the
Scriptures, when she was somewhat startled by hearing at the door
the tap and voice of her sweetheart. Not expecting him, and the
hour being somewhat late, she opened it in astonishment, and was
still more astonished to hear him on entering abuse Scripture-
reading. He behaved altogether in an unprecedented manner, and
in many ways terrified the poor girl. Ultimately he knelt before her,
and laid his head on her lap. You can fancy her consternation when
glancing down she discovered that, *instead of hair, the head was
covered with the moss of the moorland.* By a sacred name she
adjured him to tell who he was, and in a moment the figure was
gone. It was the Fiend, of course—diminished sadly since Milton
saw him bridge chaos—fallen from worlds to kitchen-wenches. But
just think how in the story, in half-pity, in half-terror, the popular
feeling of homelessness, of being outcast, of being unsheltered as
waste and desert places, has incarnated itself in that strange covering of the head. It is a true supernatural touch. One other story I
have heard in the misty Hebrides: A Skye gentleman was riding
along an empty moorland road. All at once, as if it had sprung from
the ground, the empty road was crowded by a funeral procession.
Instinctively he drew his horse to a side to let it pass, which it did
without sound of voice, without tread of foot. Then he knew it was
an apparition. Staring on it, he knew every person who either bore
the corpse or who walked behind as mourners. There were the
neighbouring proprietors at whose houses he dined, there were
the members of his own kirk-session, there were the men to whom
he was wont to give good-morning when he met them on the road
or at market. Unable to discover his own image in the throng, he
was inwardly marvelling whose funeral it *could* be, when the troop

[5] Giulia Grisi (1811-69), Italian opera singer.

of spectres vanished, and the road was empty as before. Then, remembering that the coffin had an invisible occupant, he cried out, "It is my funeral!" and, with all his strength taken out of him, rode home to die. All these stories have their own touches of terror; yet I am inclined to think that my lark rising from the scaffold foot, and singing to two such auditors, is more terrible than any of them.

For questions and exercises, see p. 430, p. 470, p. 476, and p. 502.

# WHAT IS A UNIVERSITY?

### JOHN HENRY NEWMAN

If I were asked to describe as briefly and popularly as I could, what a University was, I should draw my answer from its ancient designation of a *Studium Generale* or "School of Universal Learning." This description implies the assemblage of strangers from all parts in one spot;—*from all parts;* else, how will you find professors and students for every department of knowledge? and *in one spot;* else, how can there be any school at all? Accordingly, in its simple and rudimental form, it is a school of knowledge of every kind, consisting of teachers and learners from every quarter. Many things are requisite to complete and satisfy the idea embodied in this description; but such as this a University seems to be in its essence, a place for the communication and circulation of thought, by means of personal intercourse, through a wide extent of country.

There is nothing far-fetched or unreasonable in the idea thus presented to us; and if this be a University, then a University does but contemplate a necessity of our nature, and is but one specimen in a particular medium, out of many which might be adduced in others, of a provision for that necessity. Mutual education, in a large sense of the word, is one of the great and incessant occupations of human society, carried on partly with set purpose, and partly not. One generation forms another; and the existing generation is ever acting and reacting upon itself in the persons of its individual members. Now, in this process, books, I need scarcely say, that is, the *litera scripta,* are one special instrument. It is true; and emphati-

WHAT IS A UNIVERSITY?: From *Rise and Progress of Universities* by John Henry Newman.

cally so in this age. Considering the prodigious powers of the press, and how they are developed at this time in the never-intermitting issue of periodicals, tracts, pamphlets, works in series, and light literature, we must allow there never was a time which promised fairer for dispensing with every other means of information and instruction. What can we want more, you will say, for the intellectual education of the whole man, and for every man, than so exuberant and diversified and persistent a promulgation of all kinds of knowledge? Why, you will ask, need we go up to knowledge, when knowledge comes down to us? The Sibyl wrote her prophecies upon the leaves of the forest, and wasted them; but here such careless profusion might be prudently indulged, for it can be afforded without loss, in consequence of the almost fabulous fecundity of the instrument which these latter ages have invented. We have sermons in stones, and books in the running brooks; works larger and more comprehensive than those which have gained for ancients an immortality, issue forth every morning, and are projected onwards to the ends of the earth at the rate of hundreds of miles a day. Our seats are strewed, our pavements are powdered, with swarms of little tracts; and the very bricks of our city walls preach wisdom, by informing us by their placards where we can at once cheaply purchase it.

I allow all this, and much more; such certainly is our popular education, and its effects are remarkable. Nevertheless, after all, even in this age, whenever men are really serious about getting what, in the language of trade, is called "a good article," when they aim at something precise, something refined, something really luminous, something really large, something choice, they go to another market; they avail themselves, in some shape or other, of the rival method, the ancient method, of oral instruction, of present communication between man and man, of teachers instead of learning, of the personal influence of a master, and the humble initiation of a disciple, and, in consequence, of great centres of pilgrimage and throng, which such a method of education necessarily involves. This, I think, will be found to hold good in all those departments or aspects of society, which possess an interest sufficient to bind men together, or to constitute what is called "a world." It holds in the political world, and in the high world, and in the religious world; and it holds also in the literary and scientific world.

If the actions of men may be taken as any test of their convictions, then we have reason for saying this, viz.—that the province and the inestimable benefit of the *litera scripta* is that of being a record of truth, and an authority of appeal, and an instrument of teaching in the hands of a teacher; but that, if we wish to become exact and fully furnished in any branch of knowledge which is diversified and complicated, we must consult the living man and listen to his living voice. I am not bound to investigate the cause of this, and anything I may say will, I am conscious, be short of its full analysis—perhaps we may suggest, that no books can get through the number of minute questions which it is possible to ask on any extended subject, or can hit upon the very difficulties which are severally felt by each reader in succession. Or again, that no book can convey the special spirit and delicate peculiarities of its subject with that rapidity and certainty which attend on the sympathy of mind with mind, through the eyes, the look, the accent, and the manner, in casual expressions thrown off at the moment, and the unstudied turns of familiar conversation. But I am already dwelling too long on what is but an incidental portion of my main subject. Whatever be the cause, the fact is undeniable. The general principles of any study you may learn by books at home; but the detail, the colour, the tone, the air, the life which makes it live in us, you must catch all these from those in whom it lives already. You must imitate the student in French or German, who is not content with his grammar, but goes to Paris or Dresden: you must take example from the young artist, who aspires to visit the great Masters in Florence and in Rome. Till we have discovered some intellectual daguerreotype, which takes off the course of thought, and the form, lineaments, and features of truth, as completely and minutely, as the optical instrument reproduces the sensible object, we must come to the teachers of wisdom to learn wisdom, we must repair to the fountain, and drink there. Portions of it may go from thence to the ends of the earth by means of books; but the fulness is in one place alone. It is in such assemblages and congregations of intellect that books themselves, the masterpieces of human genius, are written, or at least originated.

The principle on which I have been insisting is so obvious, and instances in point are so ready, that I should think it tiresome to proceed with the subject, except that one or two illustrations may serve to explain my own language about it, which may not have done justice to the doctrine which it has been intended to enforce.

For instance, the polished manners and high-bred bearing which are so difficult of attainment, and so strictly personal when attained,—which are so much admired in society, from society are acquired. All that goes to constitute a gentleman—the carriage, gait, address, gestures, voice; the ease, the self-possession, the courtesy, the power of conversing, the talent of not offending; the lofty principle, the delicacy of thought, the happiness of expression, the taste and propriety, the generosity and forbearance, the candour and consideration, the openness of hand;—these qualities, some of them come by nature, some of them may be found in any rank, some of them are a direct precept of Christianity; but the full assemblage of them, bound up in the unity of an individual character, do we expect they can be learned from books? Are they not necessarily acquired, where they are to be found, in high society? The very nature of the case leads us to say so; you cannot fence without an antagonist, nor challenge all comers in disputation before you have supported a thesis; and in like manner, it stands to reason, you cannot learn to converse till you have the world to converse with; you cannot unlearn your natural bashfulness, or awkwardness, or stiffness, or other besetting deformity, till you serve your time in some school of manners. Well, and is it not so in matter of fact? The metropolis, the court, the great houses of the land, are the centres to which at stated times the country comes up, as to shrines of refinement and good taste; and then in due time the country goes back again home, enriched with a portion of the social accomplishments, which those very visits serve to call out and heighten in the gracious dispensers of them. We are unable to conceive how the "gentlemanlike" can otherwise be maintained; and maintained in this way it is.

And now a second instance: and here too I am going to speak without personal experience of the subject I am introducing. I admit I have not been in Parliament, any more than I have figured in the *beau monde;* yet I cannot but think that statesmanship, as well as high breeding, is learned, not by books, but in certain centres of education. If it be not presumption to say so, Parliament puts a clever man *au courant* with politics and affairs of state in a way surprising to himself. A member of the Legislature, if tolerably observant, begins to see things with new eyes, even though his views undergo no change. Words have a meaning now, and ideas a reality, such as they had not before. He hears a vast deal in public speeches and private conversation, which is never put into print. The bearings of measures and events, the action of parties, and the persons of friends and enemies, are brought out to the man who is in the midst of them with a distinctness, which the most diligent perusal of newspapers will fail to impart to them. It is access to the fountain-heads of political wisdom and experience, it is daily intercourse, of one kind or another, with the multitude who go up to them, it is familiarity with business, it is access to the contributions of fact and opinion thrown together by many witnesses from many quarters, which does this for him. However, I need not account for a fact, to which it is sufficient to appeal; that the Houses of Parliament and the atmosphere around them are a sort of University of politics.

As regards the world of science, we find a remarkable instance of the principle which I am illustrating, in the periodical meetings for its advance, which have arisen in the course of the last twenty years, such as the British Association. Such gatherings would to many persons appear at first sight simply preposterous. Above all subjects of study, Science is conveyed, is propagated, by books, or by private teaching; experiments and investigations are conducted in silence; discoveries are made in solitude. What have philosophers to do with festive celebrities, and panegyrical solemnities with mathematical and physical truth? Yet on a closer attention to the subject, it is found that not even scientific thought can dispense with the suggestions, the instruction, the stimulus, the sympathy, the intercourse with mankind on a large scale, which such meetings secure. A fine time of year is chosen, when days are long, skies are bright, the earth smiles, and all nature rejoices; a city or town is taken by turns, of ancient name or modern opulence, where buildings are spacious and hospitality hearty. The novelty of place and circumstance, the excitement of strange, or the refreshment of well-known faces, the majesty of rank or of genius, the amiable charities of men pleased both with themselves and with each other; the elevated spirits, the circulation of thought, the curiosity; the morning sections, the outdoor exercise, the well-furnished, well-earned board, the not ungraceful hilarity, the evening circle; the

brilliant lecture, the discussions or collisions or guesses of great
men one with another, the narratives of scientific processes, of
hopes, disappointments, conflicts, and successes, the splendid eulogistic orations; these and the like constituents of the annual celebration, are considered to do something real and substantial for the
advance of knowledge which can be done in no other way. Of
course they can but be occasional; they answer to the annual Act,
or Commencement, or Commemoration of a University, not to its
ordinary condition; but they are of a University nature; and I can
well believe in their utility. They issue in the promotion of a certain
living and, as it were, bodily communication of knowledge from
one to another, of a general interchange of ideas, and a comparison
and adjustment of science with science, of an enlargement of mind,
intellectual and social, of an ardent love of the particular study,
which may be chosen by each individual, and a noble devotion to
its interests.

Such meetings, I repeat, are but periodical, and only partially
represent the idea of a University. The bustle and whirl which
are their usual concomitants, are in ill keeping with the order and
gravity of earnest intellectual education. We desiderate means of
instruction which involve no interruption of our ordinary habits;
nor need we seek it long, for the natural course of things brings it
about, while we debate over it. In every great country, the metropolis itself becomes a sort of necessary University, whether we will
or no. As the chief city is the seat of the court, of high society, of
politics, and of law, so as a matter of course is it the seat of letters
also; and at this time, for a long term of years, London and Paris
are in fact and in operation Universities, though in Paris its famous
University is no more, and in London a University scarcely exists
except as a board of administration. The newspapers, magazines,
reviews, journals, and periodicals of all kinds, the publishing trade,
the libraries, museums, and academies there found, the learned and
scientific societies, necessarily invest it with the functions of a University; and that atmosphere of intellect, which in a former age
hung over Oxford or Bologna or Salamanca, has, with the change
of times, moved away to the centre of civil government. Thither
come up youths from all parts of the country, the students of law,
medicine, and the fine arts, and the *employés* and *attachés* of
literature. There they live, as chance determines; and they are

satisfied with their temporary home, for they find in it all that was promised to them there. They have not come in vain, as far as their own object in coming is concerned. They have not learned any particular religion, but they have learned their own particular profession well. They have, moreover, become acquainted with the habits, manners, and opinions of their place of sojourn, and done their part in maintaining the tradition of them. We cannot then be without virtual Universities; a metropolis is such: the simple question is, whether the education sought and given should be based on principle, formed upon rule, directed to the highest ends, or left to the random succession of masters and schools, one after another, with a melancholy waste of thought and an extreme hazard of truth.

Religious teaching itself affords us an illustration of our subject to a certain point. It does not indeed seat itself merely in centres of the world; this is impossible from the nature of the case. It is intended for the many not the few; its subject matter is truth necessary for us, not truth recondite and rare; but it concurs in the principle of a University so far as this, that its great instrument, or rather organ, has ever been that which nature prescribes in all education, the personal presence of a teacher, or, in theological language, Oral Tradition. It is the living voice, the breathing form, the expressive countenance, which preaches, which catechises. Truth, a subtle, invisible, manifold spirit, is poured into the mind of the scholar by his eyes and ears, through his affections, imagination, and reason; it is poured into his mind and is sealed up there in perpetuity, by propounding and repeating it, by questioning and requestioning, by correcting and explaining, by progressing and then recurring to first principles, by all those ways which are implied in the word "catechising." In the first ages, it was a work of long time; months, sometimes years, were devoted to the arduous task of disabusing the mind of the incipient Christian of its pagan errors, and of moulding it upon the Christian faith. The Scriptures indeed were at hand for the study of those who could avail themselves of them; but St. Irenæus does not hesitate to speak of whole races, who had been converted to Christianity, without being able to read them. To be unable to read or write was in those times no evidence of want of learning: the hermits of the desert were, in this sense of the word, illiterate; yet the great St. Anthony, though he

knew not letters, was a match in disputation for the learned philosophers who came to try him. Didymus again, the great Alexandrian theologian, was blind. The ancient discipline, called the
*Disciplina Arcani,* involved the same principle. The more sacred
doctrines of Revelation were not committed to books but passed on
by successive tradition. The teaching on the Blessed Trinity and
the Eucharist appears to have been so handed down for some hundred years; and when at length reduced to writing, it has filled
many folios, yet has not been exhausted.

But I have said more than enough in illustration; I end as I
began—a University is a place of concourse, whither students come
from every quarter for every kind of knowledge. You cannot have
the best of every kind everywhere; you must go to some great city
or emporium for it. There you have all the choicest productions
of nature and art all together, which you find each in its own
separate place elsewhere. All the riches of the land, and of the
earth, are carried up thither; there are the best markets, and there
the best workmen. It is the centre of trade, the supreme court of
fashion, the umpire of rival talents, and the standard of things rare
and precious. It is the place for seeing galleries of first-rate pictures,
and for hearing wonderful voices and performers of transcendent
skill. It is the place for great preachers, great orators, great nobles,
great statesmen. In the nature of things, greatness and unity go
together; excellence implies a centre. And such, for the third or
fourth time, is a University; I hope I do not weary out the reader
by repeating it. It is the place to which a thousand schools make
contributions; in which the intellect may safely range and speculate, sure to find its equal in some antagonist activity, and its judge
in the tribunal of truth. It is a place where inquiry is pushed forward, and discoveries verified and perfected, and rashness rendered
innocuous, and error exposed, by the collision of mind with mind,
and knowledge with knowledge. It is the place where the professor
becomes eloquent, and is a missionary and a preacher, displaying
his science in its most complete and most winning form, pouring
it forth with the zeal of enthusiasm, and lighting up his own love
of it in the breasts of his hearers. It is the place where the catechist
makes good his ground as he goes, treading in the truth day by day
into the ready memory, and wedging and tightening it into the
expanding reason. It is a place which wins the admiration of the

young by its celebrity, kindles the affections of the middle-aged by
its beauty, and rivets the fidelity of the old by its associations. It is
a seat of wisdom, a light of the world, a minister of the faith, an
Alma Mater of the rising generation. It is this and a great deal more,
and demands a somewhat better head and hand than mine to
describe it well.

Such is a University in its idea and in its purpose; such in good
measure has it before now been in fact. Shall it ever be again? We
are going forward in the strength of the Cross, under the patronage
of the Blessed Virgin, in the name of St. Patrick, to attempt it.

For questions and exercises, see pp. 102-04, p. 139, and p. 323.

# ON LIBERTY

### JOHN STUART MILL

The subject of this Essay is not the so-called Liberty of the Will,
so unfortunately opposed to the misnamed doctrine of Philosophical
Necessity; but Civil, or Social Liberty: the nature and limits of the
power which can be legitimately exercised by society over the
individual. A question seldom stated, and hardly ever discussed,
in general terms, but which profoundly influences the practical
controversies of the age by its latent presence, and is likely soon
to make itself recognized as the vital question of the future. It is
so far from being new, that, in a certain sense, it has divided mankind, almost from the remotest ages; but in the stage of progress
into which the more civilized portions of the species have now
entered, it presents itself under new conditions, and requires a
different and more fundamental treatment.

The struggle between Liberty and Authority is the most conspicuous feature in the portions of history with which we are
earliest familiar, particularly in that of Greece, Rome, and England.
But in the old times this contest was between subjects, or some
classes of subjects, and the government. By liberty was meant
protection against the tyranny of the political rulers. The rulers
were conceived (except in some of the popular governments of
Greece) as in a necessarily antagonistic position to the people

ON LIBERTY, by John Stuart Mill, Chap. 1.

whom they ruled. They consisted of a governing One, or a governing tribe or caste, who derived their authority from inheritance or conquest; who, at all events, did not hold it at the pleasure of the governed, and whose supremacy men did not venture, perhaps did not desire, to contest, whatever precautions might be taken against its oppressive exercise. Their power was regarded as necessary, but also as highly dangerous; as a weapon which they would attempt to use against their subjects, no less than against external enemies. To prevent the weaker members of the community from being preyed upon by innumerable vultures, it was needful that there should be an animal of prey stronger than the rest, commissioned to keep them down. But as the king of the vultures would be no less bent upon preying on the flock than any of the minor harpies, it was indispensable to be in a perpetual attitude of defence against his beak and claws. The aim, therefore, of patriots, was to set limits to the power which the ruler should be suffered to exercise over the community; and this limitation was what they meant by liberty. It was attempted in two ways. First, by obtaining a recognition of certain immunities, called political liberties or rights, which it was to be regarded as a breach of duty in the ruler to infringe, and which, if he did infringe, specific resistance, or general rebellion, was held to be justifiable. A second, and generally a later expedient, was the establishment of constitutional checks; by which the consent of the community, or of a body of some sort supposed to represent its interests, was made a necessary condition to some of the more important acts of the governing power. To the first of these modes of limitations, the ruling power, in most European countries, was compelled, more or less, to submit. It was not so with the second; and, to attain this, or when already in some degree possessed, to attain it more completely, became everywhere the principal object of the lovers of liberty. And so long as mankind were content to combat one enemy by another, and to be ruled by a master, on condition of being guaranteed more or less efficaciously against his tyranny, they did not carry their aspirations beyond this point.

A time, however, came, in the progress of human affairs, when men ceased to think it a necessity of nature that their governors should be an independent power, opposed in interest to themselves.

It appeared to them much better that the various magistrates of the State should be their tenants or delegates, revocable at their pleasure. In that way alone, it seemed, could they have complete security that the powers of government would never be abused to their disadvantage. By degrees this new demand for elective and temporary rulers became the prominent object of the exertions of the popular party, wherever any such party existed; and superseded, to a considerable extent, the previous efforts to limit the power of rulers. As the struggle proceeded for making the ruling power emanate from the periodical choice of the ruled, some persons began to think that too much importance had been attached to the limitation of the power itself. *That* (it might seem) was a resource against rulers whose interests were habitually opposed to those of the people. What was now wanted was, that the rulers should be identified with the people; that their interest and will should be the interest and will of the nation. The nation did not need to be protected against its own will. There was no fear of its tyrannizing over itself. Let the rulers be effectually responsible to it, promptly removable by it, and it could afford to trust them with power of which it could itself dictate the use to be made. Their power was but the nation's own power, concentrated, and in a form convenient for exercise. This mode of thought, or rather perhaps of feeling, was common among the last generation of European liberalism, in the Continental section of which it still apparently predominates. Those who admit any limit to what a government may do, except in the case of such governments as they think ought not to exist, stand out as brilliant exceptions among the political thinkers of the Continent. A similar tone of sentiment might by this time have been prevalent in our own country, if the circumstances which for a time encouraged it had continued unaltered.

But, in political and philosophical theories, as well as in persons, success discloses faults and infirmities which failure might have concealed from observation. The notion, that the people have no need to limit their power over themselves, might seem axiomatic, when popular government was a thing only dreamed about, or read of as having existed at some distant period of the past. Neither was that notion necessarily disturbed by such temporary aberrations as those of the French Revolution, the worst of which were the work of an usurping few, and which, in any case, belonged,

not to the permanent working of popular institutions, but to a
sudden and convulsive outbreak against monarchical and aristo-
cratic despotism. In time, however, a democratic republic came to
occupy a large portion of the earth's surface, and made itself felt
as one of the most powerful members of the community of nations;
and elective and responsible government became subject to the
observations and criticisms which wait upon a great existing fact.
It was now perceived that such phrases as "self-government," and
"the power of the people over themselves," do not express the true
state of the case. The "people" who exercise the power are not
always the same people with those over whom it is exercised; and
the "self-government" spoken of is not the government of each
by himself, but of each by all the rest. The will of the people,
moreover, practically means the will of the most numerous or the
most active *part* of the people; the majority, or those who succeed
in making themselves accepted as the majority; the people, consequently, *may* desire to oppress a part of their number; and precautions are as much needed against this as against any other abuse
of power. The limitation, therefore, of the power of government
over individuals, loses none of its importance when the holders
of power are regularly accountable to the community, that is, to
the strongest party therein. This view of things, recommending
itself equally to the intelligence of thinkers and to the inclination
of those important classes in European society to whose real or
supposed interests democracy is adverse, has had no difficulty in
establishing itself; and in political speculations "the tyranny of the
majority" is now generally included among the evils against which
society requires to be on its guard.

Like other tyrannies, the tyranny of the majority was at first,
and is still vulgarly, held in dread, chiefly as operating through the
acts of the public authorities. But reflecting persons perceived that
when society is itself the tyrant—society collectively, over the separate individuals who compose it—its means of tyrannizing are not
restricted to the acts which it may do by the hands of its political
functionaries. Society can and does execute its own mandates: and
if it issues wrong mandates instead of right, or any mandates at all
in things with which it ought not to meddle, it practises a social
tyranny more formidable than many kinds of political oppression,
since, though not usually upheld by such extreme penalties, it

leaves fewer means of escape, penetrating much more deeply into the details of life, and enslaving the soul itself. Protection therefore against the tyranny of the magistrate is not enough: there needs protection also against the tyranny of the prevailing opinion and feeling; against the tendency of society to impose, by other means than civil penalties, its own ideas and practices as rules of conduct on those who dissent from them; to fetter the development, and, if possible, prevent the formation, of any individuality not in harmony with its ways, and compel all characters to fashion themselves upon the model of its own. There is a limit to the legitimate interference of collective opinion with individual independence: and to find that limit, and maintain it against encroachment, is as indispensable to a good condition of human affairs, as protection against political despotism.

But though this proposition is not likely to be contested in general terms, the practical question, where to place the limit—how to make the fitting adjustment between individual independence and social control—is a subject on which nearly everything remains to be done. All that makes existence valuable to any one, depends on the enforcement of restraints upon the actions of other people. Some rules of conduct, therefore, must be imposed, by law in the first place, and by opinion on many things which are not fit subjects for the operation of law. What these rules should be, is the principal question in human affairs; but if we except a few of the most obvious cases, it is one of those which least progress has been made in resolving. No two ages, and scarcely any two countries, have decided it alike; and the decision of one age or country is a wonder to another. Yet the people of any given age and country no more suspect any difficulty in it, than if it were a subject on which mankind has always been agreed. The rules which obtain among themselves appear to themselves self-evident and self-justifying. This all but universal illusion is one of the examples of the whole magical influence of custom, which is not only, as the proverb says, a second nature, but is continually mistaken for the first. The effect of custom, in preventing any misgiving respecting the rules of conduct which mankind impose on one another, is all the more complete because the subject is one on which it is not generally considered necessary that reasons should be given, either by one person to others, or by each to himself. People are

accustomed to believe, and have been encouraged in the belief by
some who aspire to the character of philosophers, that their feelings, on subjects of this nature, are better than reasons, and render
reasons unnecessary. The practical principle which guides them to
their opinions on the regulation of human conduct, is the feeling
in each person's mind that everybody should be required to act
as he, and those with whom he sympathizes, would like them to
act. No one, indeed, acknowledges to himself that his standard of
judgment is his own liking; but an opinion on a point of conduct,
not supported by reasons, can only count as one person's preference; and if the reasons, when given, are a mere appeal to a
similar preference felt by other people, it is still only many people's
liking instead of one. To an ordinary man, however, his own
preference, thus supported, is not only a perfectly satisfactory
reason, but the only one he generally has for any of his notions
of morality, taste, or propriety, which are not expressly written
in his religious creed; and his chief guide in the interpretation even
of that. Men's opinions, accordingly, on what is laudable or blame-
able, are affected by all the multifarious causes which influence
their wishes in regard to the conduct of others, and which are as
numerous as those which determine their wishes on any other subject. Sometimes their reason—at other times their prejudices or
superstitions: often their social affections, not seldom their anti-
social ones, their envy or jealousy, their arrogance or contemptuous-
ness: but most commonly, their desires or fears for themselves—
their legitimate or illegitimate self-interest. Wherever there is an
ascendant class, a large portion of the morality of the country
emanates from its class interests, and its feelings of class superiority.
The morality between Spartans and Helots, between planters and
Negroes, between princes and subjects, between nobles and rotu-
riers, between men and women, has been for the most part the
creation of these class interests and feelings: and the sentiments
thus generated, react in turn upon the moral feelings of the members of the ascendant class, in their relations among themselves.
Where, on the other hand, a class, formerly ascendant, has lost its
ascendancy, or where its ascendancy is unpopular, the prevailing
moral sentiments frequently bear the impress of an impatient dislike of superiority. Another grand determining principle of the rules
of conduct, both in act and forbearance, which have been enforced

by law or opinion, has been the servility of mankind towards the supposed preferences or aversions of their temporal masters, or of their gods. This servility, though essentially selfish, is not hypocrisy; it gives rise to perfectly genuine sentiments of abhorrence; it made men burn magicians and heretics. Among so many baser influences, the general and obvious interests of society have of course had a share, and a large one, in the direction of the moral sentiments: less, however, as a matter of reason, and on their own account, than as a consequence of the sympathies and antipathies which grew out of them: and sympathies and antipathies which had little or nothing to do with the interests of society, have made themselves felt in the establishment of moralities with quite as great force.

The likings and dislikings of society, or of some powerful portion of it, are thus the main thing which has practically determined the rules laid down for general observance, under the penalties of law or opinion. And in general, those who have been in advance of society in thought and feeling, have left this condition of things unassailed in principle, however they may have come into conflict with it in some of its details. They have occupied themselves rather in inquiring what things society ought to like or dislike, than in questioning whether its likings or dislikings should be a law to individuals. They preferred endeavoring to alter the feelings of mankind on the particular points on which they were themselves heretical, rather than make common cause in defence of freedom, with heretics generally. The only case in which the higher ground has been taken on principle and maintained with consistency, by any but an individual here and there, is that of religious belief: a case instructive in many ways, and not least so as forming a most striking instance of the fallibility of what is called the moral sense: for the *odium theologicum,* in a sincere bigot, is one of the most unequivocal cases of moral feeling. Those who first broke the yoke of what called itself the Universal Church, were in general as little willing to permit difference of religious opinion as that church itself. But when the heat of the conflict was over, without giving a complete victory to any party, and each church or sect was reduced to limit its hopes to retaining possession of the ground it already occupied; minorities, seeing that they had no chance of becoming majorities, were under the necessity of pleading to those whom they could not convert, for permission to differ. It is accordingly on this battle-field, almost solely, that the rights of the individual against society have been asserted on broad grounds of principle, and the claim of society to exercise authority over dissentients, openly controverted. The great writers to whom the world owes what religious liberty it possesses, have mostly asserted freedom of conscience as an indefeasible right, and denied absolutely that a human being is accountable to others for his religious belief. Yet so natural to mankind is intolerance in whatever they really care about, that religious freedom has hardly anywhere been practically realized, except where religious indifference, which dislikes to have its peace disturbed by theological quarrels, has added its weight to the scale. In the minds of almost all religious persons, even in the most tolerant countries, the duty of toleration is admitted with tacit reserves. One person will bear with dissent in matters of church government, but not of dogma; another can tolerate everybody, short of a Papist or an Unitarian; another, every one who believes in revealed religion; a few extend their charity a little further, but stop at the belief in a God and in a future state. Wherever the sentiment of the majority is still genuine and intense, it is found to have abated little of its claim to be obeyed.

In England, from the peculiar circumstances of our political history, though the yoke of opinion is perhaps heavier, that of law is lighter, than in most other countries of Europe; and there is considerable jealousy of direct interference, by the legislative or executive power, with private conduct; not so much from any just regard for the independence of the individual, as from the still subsisting habit of looking on the government as representing an opposite interest to the public. The majority have not yet learnt to feel the power of the government their power, or its opinions their opinions. When they do so, individual liberty will probably be as much exposed to invasion from the government, as it already is from public opinion. But, as yet, there is a considerable amount of feeling ready to be called forth against any attempt of the law to control individuals in things in which they have not hitherto been accustomed to be controlled by it; and this with very little discrimination as to whether the matter is, or is not, within the legitimate sphere of legal control; insomuch that the feeling, highly salutary on the whole, is perhaps quite as often misplaced as well grounded in the particular instances of its application. There is, in fact, no recognised principle by which the propriety or impropriety of government interference is customarily tested. People decide according to their personal preferences. Some, whenever they see any good to be done, or evil to be remedied, would willingly instigate the government to undertake the business; while others prefer to bear almost any amount of social evil, rather than add one to the departments of human interests amenable to government control. And men range themselves on one or the other side in any particular case, according to this general direction of their sentiments; or according to the degree of interest which they feel in the particular thing which it is proposed that the government should do; or according to the belief they entertain that the government would, or would not, do it in the manner they prefer; but very rarely on account of any opinion to which they consistently adhere, as to what things are fit to be done by a government. And it seems to me that in consequence of this absence of rule or principle, one side is at present as often wrong as the other; the interference of government is, with about equal frequency, improperly invoked and improperly condemned.

The object of this Essay is to assert one very simple principle, as entitled to govern absolutely the dealings of society with the individual in the way of compulsion and control, whether the means used be physical force in the form of legal penalties, or the moral coercion of public opinion. That principle is, that the sole end for which mankind are warranted, individually or collectively, in interfering with the liberty of action of any of their number, is self-protection. That the only purpose for which power can be rightfully exercised over any member of a civilized community, against his will, is to prevent harm to others. His own good, either physical or moral, is not a sufficient warrant. He cannot rightfully be compelled to do or forbear because it will be better for him to do so, because it will make him happier, because, in the opinions of others, to do so would be wise, or even right. These are good reasons for remonstrating with him, or reasoning with him, or persuading him, or entreating him, but not for compelling him, or visiting him with any evil, in case he do otherwise. To justify that, the conduct from which it is desired to deter him, must be calculated to produce evil to some one else. The only part of the conduct of any one, for which he is amenable to society, is that which concerns others.

In the part which merely concerns himself, his independence is, of right, absolute. Over himself, over his own body and mind, the individual is sovereign.

It is, perhaps, hardly necessary to say that this doctrine is meant to apply only to human beings in the maturity of their faculties. We are not speaking of children, or of young persons below the age which the law may fix as that of manhood or womanhood. Those who are still in a state to require being taken care of by others, must be protected against their own actions as well as against external injury. For the same reason, we may leave out of consideration those backward states of society in which the race itself may be considered as in its nonage. The early difficulties in the way of spontaneous progress are so great that there is seldom any choice of means for overcoming them; and a ruler full of the spirit of improvement is warranted in the use of any expedients that will attain an end, perhaps otherwise unattainable. Despotism is a legitimate mode of government in dealing with barbarians, provided the end be their improvement, and the means justified by actually effecting that end. Liberty, as a principle, has no application to any state of things anterior to the time when mankind have become capable of being improved by free and equal discussion. Until then, there is nothing for them but implicit obedience to an Akbar or a Charlemagne, if they are so fortunate as to find one. But as soon as mankind have attained the capacity of being guided to their own improvement by conviction or persuasion (a period long since reached in all nations with whom we need here concern ourselves), compulsion, either in the direct form or in that of pains and penalties for non-compliance, is no longer admissible as a means to their own good, and justifiable only for the security of others.

It is proper to state that I forego any advantage which could be derived to my argument from the idea of abstract right, as a thing independent of utility. I regard utility as the ultimate appeal on all ethical questions; but it must be utility in the largest sense, grounded on the permanent interests of man as a progressive being. Those interests, I contend, authorize the subjection of individual spontaneity to external control, only in respect to those actions of each, which concern the interest of other people. If any one does an act hurtful to others, there is a *prima facie* case for punishing him, by law. or, where legal penalties are not safely applicable,

by general disapprobation. There are also many positive acts for
the benefit of others, which he may rightfully be compelled to
perform; such as, to give evidence in a court of justice; to bear his
fair share in the common defence, or in any other joint work
necessary to the interest of the society of which he enjoys the
protection; and to perform certain acts of individual beneficence,
such as saving a fellow creature's life, or interposing to protect the
defenceless against ill-usage, things which whenever it is obviously
a man's duty to do, he may rightfully be made responsible to society
for not doing. A person may cause evil to others not only by his
actions but by his inaction, and in either case he is justly accountable to them for the injury. The latter case, it is true, requires a
much more cautious exercise of compulsion than the former. To
make any one answerable for doing evil to others is the rule; to
make him answerable for not preventing evil, is, comparatively
speaking, the exception. Yet there are many cases clear enough
and grave enough to justify that exception. In all things which
regard the external relations to the individual, he is *de jure* amenable to those whose interests are concerned, and if need be, to
society as their protector. There are often good reasons for not
holding him to the responsibility; but these reasons must arise
from the special expediencies of the case: either because it is a
kind of case in which he is on the whole likely to act better, when
left to his own discretion, than when controlled in any way in
which society have it in their power to control him; or because the
attempt to exercise control would produce other evils, greater than
those which it would prevent. When such reasons as these preclude
the enforcement of responsibility, the conscience of the agent himself should step into the vacant judgment seat, and protect those
interests of others which have no external protection; judging himself all the more rigidly, because the case does not admit of his
being made accountable to the judgment of his fellow-creatures.

But there is a sphere of action in which society, as distinguished
from the individual, has, if any, only an indirect interest; comprehending all that portion of a person's life and conduct which affects
only himself, or if it also affects others, only with their free, voluntary, and undeceived consent and participation. When I say only
himself, I mean directly, and in the first instance: for whatever
affects himself, may affect others *through* himself; and the objec-

tion which may be grounded on this contingency will receive consideration in the sequel. This, then, is the appropriate region of human liberty. It comprises, first, the inward domain of consciousness; demanding liberty of conscience, in the most comprehensive sense; liberty of thought and feeling; absolute freedom of opinion and sentiment on all subjects, practical or speculative, scientific, moral, or theological. The liberty of expressing and publishing opinions may seem to fall under a different principle, since it belongs to that part of the conduct of an individual which concerns other people; but, being almost of as much importance as the liberty of thought itself, and resting in great part on the same reasons, is practically inseparable from it. Secondly, the principle requires liberty of tastes and pursuits; of framing the plan of our life to suit our own character; of doing as we like, subject to such consequences as may follow: without impediment from our fellow creatures, so long as what we do does not harm them, even though they should think our conduct foolish, perverse, or wrong. Thirdly, from this liberty of each individual, follows the liberty, within the same limits, of combination among individuals; freedom to unite, for any purpose not involving harm to others: the persons combining being supposed to be of full age, and not forced or deceived.

No society in which these liberties are not, on the whole, respected, is free, whatever may be its form of government; and none is completely free in which they do not exist absolute and unqualified. The only freedom which deserves the name, is that of pursuing our own good in our own way, so long as we do not attempt to deprive others of theirs, or impede their efforts to obtain it. Each is the proper guardian of his own health, whether bodily, or mental and spiritual. Mankind are greater gainers by suffering each other to live as seems good to themselves, than by compelling each to live as seems good to the rest.

Though this doctrine is anything but new, and, to some persons, may have the air of a truism, there is no doctrine which stands more directly opposed to the general tendency of existing opinion and practice. Society has expended fully as much effort in the attempt (according to its lights) to compel people to conform to its notions of personal, as of social excellence. The ancient commonwealths thought themselves entitled to practise, and the ancient philosophers countenanced, the regulation of every part of private conduct by public authority, on the ground that the State had a deep interest in the whole bodily and mental discipline of every one of its citizens; a mode of thinking which may have been admissible in small republics surrounded by powerful enemies, in constant peril of being subverted by foreign attack or internal commotion, and to which even a short interval of relaxed energy and self-command might so easily be fatal, that they could not afford to wait for the salutary permanent effects of freedom. In the modern world, the greater size of political communities, and, above all, the separation between spiritual and temporal authority (which placed the direction of men's consciences in other hands than those which controlled their worldly affairs), prevented so great an interference by law in the details of private life; but the engines of moral repression have been wielded more strenuously against divergence from the reigning opinion in self-regarding, than even in social matters; religion, the most powerful of the elements which have entered into the formation of moral feeling, having almost always been governed either by the ambition of a hierarchy, seeking control over every department of human conduct, or by the spirit of Puritanism. And some of those modern reformers who have placed themselves in strongest opposition to the religions of the past, have been no way behind either churches or sects in their assertion of the right of spiritual domination: M. Comte, in particular, whose social system, as unfolded in his *Traité de Politique Positive,* aims at establishing (though by moral more than legal appliances) a despotism of society over the individual, surpassing anything contemplated in the political ideal of the most rigid disciplinarian among the ancient philosophers.

Apart from the peculiar tenets of individual thinkers, there is also in the world at large an increasing inclination to stretch unduly the powers of society over the individual, both by the force of opinion and even by that of legislation: and as the tendency of all the changes taking place in the world is to strengthen society, and diminish the power of the individual, this encroachment is not one of the evils which tend spontaneously to disappear, but, on the contrary, to grow more and more formidable. The disposition of mankind, whether as rulers or as fellow-citizens, to impose their own opinions and inclinations as a rule of conduct on others, is so energetically supported by some of the best and by some of the worst feelings incident to human nature, that it is hardly ever kept under restraint by anything but want of power; and as the power is not declining, but growing, unless a strong barrier of moral conviction can be raised against the mischief, we must expect, in the present circumstances of the world, to see it increase.

For questions and exercises, see pp. 101-04, p. 139, p. 426, and p. 531.

## MRS. BATTLE'S OPINIONS ON WHIST

### CHARLES LAMB

"A clear fire, a clean hearth, and the rigour of the game." This was the celebrated *wish* of old Sarah Battle (now with God) who, next to her devotions, loved a good game at whist. She was none of your lukewarm gamesters, your half-and-half players, who have no objection to take a hand, if you want one to make up a rubber; who affirm that they have no pleasure in winning; that they like to win one game and lose another; that they can while away an hour very agreeably at a card-table, but are indifferent whether they play or no; and will desire an adversary, who has slipt a wrong card, to take it up and play another. These insufferable triflers are the curse of a table. One of these flies will spoil a whole pot. Of such it may be said, that they do not play at cards, but only play at playing at them.

Sarah Battle was none of that breed. She detested them, as I do, from her heart and soul; and would not, save upon a striking emergency, willingly seat herself at the same table with them. She loved a thorough-paced partner, a determined enemy. She took, and gave, no concessions. She hated favours. She never made a revoke, nor ever passed it over in her adversary without exacting the utmost forfeiture. She fought a good fight: cut and thrust. She held not her good sword (her cards) "like a dancer." She sate bolt upright; and neither showed you her cards, nor desired to see yours. All people have their blind side—their superstitions; and I have heard her declare, under the rose, that Hearts was her favourite suit.

I never in my life—and I knew Sarah Battle many of the best years of it—saw her take out her snuff-box when it was her turn to play; or snuff a candle in the middle of a game; or ring for a servant,

MRS. BATTLE'S OPINIONS ON WHIST: From *The Essays of Elia* by Charles Lamb.

till it was fairly over. She never introduced, or connived at, miscellaneous conversation during its process. As she emphatically observed, cards were cards: and if I ever saw unmingled distaste in her fine last-century countenance, it was at the airs of a young gentleman of a literary turn, who had been with difficulty persuaded to take a hand; and who, in his excess of candour, declared, that he thought there was no harm in unbending the mind now and then, after serious studies, in recreations of that kind! She could not bear to have her noble occupation, to which she wound up her faculties, considered in that light. It was her business, her duty, the thing she came into the world to do—and she did it. She unbent her mind afterwards—over a book.

Pope was her favourite author: his *Rape of the Lock* her favourite work. She once did me the favour to play over with me (with the cards) his celebrated game of Ombre in that poem; and to explain to me how far it agreed with, and in what points it would differ from, Tradille. Her illustrations were apposite and poignant; and I had the pleasure of sending the substance of them to Mr. Bowles: but I suppose they came too late to be inserted among his ingenious notes upon that author.

Quadrille, she has often told me, was her first love; but whist had engaged her maturer esteem. The former, she said, was showy and specious, and likely to allure young persons. The uncertainty and quick shifting of partners—a thing which the constancy of whist abhors; the dazzling supremacy and regal investiture of Spadille—absurd, as she justly observed, in the pure aristocracy of whist, where his crown and garter gave him no proper power above his brother-nobility of the Aces—the giddy vanity, so taking to the inexperienced, of playing alone—above all, the overpowering attractions of a *Sans Prendre Vole*—to the triumph of which there is certainly nothing parallel or approaching, in the contingencies of whist—all these, she would say, make quadrille a game of captivation to the young and enthusiastic. But whist was the *solider* game: that was her word. It was a long meal; not like quadrille, a feast of snatches. One or two rubbers might co-extend in duration with an evening. They gave time to form rooted friendships, to cultivate steady enmities. She despised the chance-started, capricious, and ever fluctuating alliances of the other. The skirmishes of quadrille, she would say, reminded her of the petty ephem-

eral embroilments of the little Italian states, depicted by Machi-
avel; perpetually changing postures and connections; bitter foes
today, sugared darlings tomorrow; kissing and scratching in a
breath—but the wars of whist were comparable to the long, steady,
deep-rooted, rational antipathies of the Great French and English
nations.

A grave simplicity was what she chiefly admired in her favourite
game. There was nothing silly in it, like the nob in cribbage—
nothing superfluous. No *flushes*—that most irrational of all pleas
that a reasonable being can set up—that anyone should claim
four by virtue of holding cards of the same mark and colour, without reference to the playing of the game, or the individual worth
or pretensions of the cards themselves! She held this to be a
solecism; as pitiful an ambition at cards as alliteration is in authorship. She despised superficiality, and looked deeper than the colour
of things. Suits were soldiers, she would say, and must have a
uniformity of array to distinguish them: but what should we say
to the foolish squire, who should claim a merit for dressing up his
tenantry in red jackets, that never were to be marshalled—never to
take the field?—She even wished that whist were more simple than
it is; and, in my mind, would have stripped it of some appendages,
which, in the state of human frailty, may be venially, and even
commendably, allowed of. She saw no reason for the deciding
of the trump by the turn of a card. Why not one suit always
trumps?—Why two colours, when the mark of the suits would have
sufficiently distinguished them without it?—

"But the eye, my dear Madam, is agreeably refreshed with the
variety. Man is not a creature of pure reason—he must have his
senses delightfully appealed to. We see it in the Roman Catholic
countries, where the music and the paintings draw in many to
worship, whom your quaker spirit of unsensualising would have
kept out.—You, yourself, have a pretty collection of paintings—
but confess to me, whether, walking in your gallery at Sandham,
among those clear Vandykes, or among the Paul Potters in the ante-
room, you ever felt your bosom glow with an elegant delight, at all
comparable to *that* you have it in your power to experience most
evenings over a well-arranged assortment of the court cards?—the
pretty antic habits, like heralds in a procession—the gay triumph-

assuring scarlets—the contrasting deadly-killing sables—the "hoary majesty of spades"—Pam in all his glory!—

"All these might be dispensed with; and, with their naked names upon the drab pasteboard, the game might go on very well, pictureless. But the *beauty* of the cards would be extinguished for ever. Stripped of all that is imaginative in them, they must degenerate into mere gambling.—Imagine a full deal board, or drum head, to spread them on, instead of that nice verdant carpet (next to nature's), fittest arena for those courtly combatants to play their gallant jousts and tourneys in!—Exchange those delicately turned ivory markers—(work of Chinese artist, unconscious of their symbol—or as profanely slighting their true application as the arrantest Ephesian journeyman that turned out those little shrines for the goddess) —exchange them for little bits of leather (our ancestors' money), or chalk and a slate!"—

The old lady, with a smile, confessed the soundness of my logic; and to her approbation of my arguments on her favourite topic that evening, I have always fancied myself indebted for the legacy of a curious cribbage board, made of the finest Sienna marble, which her maternal uncle (Old Walter Plumer, whom I have elsewhere celebrated) brought with him from Florence—this, and a trifle of five hundred pounds came to me at her death.

The former bequest (which I do not least value) I have kept with religious care; though she herself, to confess a truth, was never greatly taken with cribbage. It was an essentially vulgar game, I have heard her say—disputing with her uncle, who was very partial to it. She could never heartily bring her mouth to pronounce "*go,*" or "*that's a go.*" She called it an ungrammatical game. The pegging teased her. I once knew her to forfeit a rubber (a five dollar stake), because she would not take advantage of the turn-up knave, which would have given it her, but which she must have claimed by the disgraceful tenure of declaring "*two for his heels.*" There is something extremely genteel in this sort of self-denial. Sarah Battle was a gentlewoman born.

Piquet she held the best game at the cards for two persons, though she would ridicule the pedantry of the terms—such as pique—repique—the capot—they savoured (she thought) of affectation. But games for two, or even three, she never greatly cared for. She loved the quadrate, or square. She would argue thus—

Cards are warfare: the ends are gain with glory. But cards are war, in disguise of a sport: when single adversaries encounter, the ends proposed are too palpable. By themselves, it is too close a fight: with spectators, it is not much bettered. No looker-on can be interested, except for a bet, and then it is a mere affair of money; he cares not for your luck *sympathetically,* or for your play.—Three are still worse; a mere naked war of every man against every man, as in cribbage, without league or alliance; or a rotation of petty and contradictory interests, a succession of heartless leagues, and not much more hearty infractions of them, as in tradrille. But in square games (*she meant whist*) all that is possible to be attained in card-playing is accomplished. There are incentives of profit with honour, common to every species—though the *latter* can be very imperfectly enjoyed in those other games where the spectator is only feebly a participator. But the parties in whist are spectators and principals too. They are a theatre to themselves, and a looker-on is not wanted. He is rather worse than nothing, and an impertinence. Whist abhors neutrality, or interests beyond its sphere. You glory in some surprising stroke of skill, or fortune, not because a cold—or even an interested—by-stander witnesses it, but because your *partner* sympathises in the contingency. You win for two. Two are exalted. Two again are mortified; which divides their disgrace, as the conjunction doubles (by taking off the invidiousness) your glories. Two losing to two are better reconciled, than one to one in that close butchery. The hostile feeling is weakened by multiplying the channels. War becomes a civil game.—By such reasonings as these the old lady was accustomed to defend her favourite pastime.

No inducement could ever prevail upon her to play at any game where chance entered into the composition, *for nothing.* Chance, she would argue—and here again, admire the subtlety of her conclusion!—chance is nothing, but where something else depends upon it. It is obvious, that cannot be *glory.* What rational cause of exultation could it give a man to turn up size ace a hundred times together by himself? or before spectators, where no stake was depending?—Make a lottery of a hundred thousand tickets with but one fortunate number—and what possible principle of our nature, except stupid wonderment, could it gratify to gain that number as many times successively, without a prize?—Therefore she disliked the mixture of chance in backgammon, where it was not played for money. She called it foolish, and those people idiots, who were taken with a lucky hit under such circumstances. Games of pure skill were as little to her fancy. Played for a stake, they were a mere system of over-reaching. Played for glory, they were a mere setting of one man's wit—his memory, or combination-faculty rather —against another's; like a mock-engagement at a review, bloodless and profitless.—She could not conceive a *game* wanting the spritely infusion of chance—the handsome excuses of good fortune. Two people playing at chess in a corner of a room whilst whist was stirring in the centre, would inspire her with unsufferable horror and ennui. Those well-cut similitudes of Castles, and Knights, the *imagery* of the board, she would argue (and I think in this case justly), were entirely misplaced, and senseless. Those hard-head contests can in no instance ally with the fancy. They reject form and colour. A pencil and dry slate (she used to say) were the proper arena for such combatants.

To those puny objectors against cards, as nurturing the bad passions, she would retort, that man is a gaming animal. He must be always trying to get the better in something or other—that this passion can scarcely be more safely expended than upon a game at cards: that cards are a temporary illusion; in truth, a mere drama; for we do but *play* at being mightily concerned, where a few idle shillings are at stake, yet, during the illusion, we *are* as mightily concerned as those whose stake is crowns and kingdoms. They are a sort of dream-fighting; much ado; great battling, and little blood shed; mighty means for disproportioned ends; quite as diverting, and a great deal more innoxious, than many of those more serious *games* of life, which men play, without esteeming them to be such.—

With great deference to the old lady's judgment on these matters, I think I have experienced some moments in my life, when playing at cards *for nothing* has even been agreeable. When I am in sickness, or not in the best spirits, I sometimes call for the cards, and play a game at piquet *for love* with my cousin Bridget— Bridget Elia.

I grant there is something sneaking in it: but with a toothache, or a sprained ankle—when you are subdued and humble—you are glad to put up with an inferior spring of action.

There is some thing in nature, I am convinced, as *sick* whist.—
I grant it is not the highest style of man—I deprecate the manes
of Sarah Battle—she lives not, alas! to whom I should apologise.—

At such times, those *terms* which my old friend objected to, come
in as something admissible.—I love to get a tierce or a quatorze,
though they mean nothing. I am subdued to an inferior interest.
Those shadows of winning amuse me.

That last game I had with my sweet cousin (I capotted her)—
(dare I tell thee how foolish I am?)—I wished it might have lasted
for ever, though we gained nothing, and lost nothing, though it
was a mere shade of play: I would be content to go on in that
idle folly for ever. The pipkin should be ever boiling, that was to
prepare the gentle lenitive to my foot, which Bridget was doomed
to apply after the game was over: and as I do not much relish
appliances, there it should ever bubble. Bridget and I should be
ever playing.

For questions and exercises, see p. 311, p. 470, and p. 503.

## THE DOG THAT BIT PEOPLE

### JAMES THURBER

Probably no one man should have as many dogs in his life as I
have had, but there was more pleasure than distress in them
for me except in the case of an Airedale named Muggs. He gave
me more trouble than all the other fifty-four or -five put together,
although my moment of keenest embarrassment was the time a
Scotch terrier named Jeannie, who had just had six puppies in the
clothes closet of a fourth floor apartment in New York, had the
unexpected seventh and last at the corner of Eleventh Street and
Fifth Avenue during a walk she had insisted on taking. Then, too,
there was the prize winning French poodle, a great big black
poodle—none of your little, untroublesome white miniatures—who
got sick riding in the rumble seat of a car with me on her way
to the Greenwich Dog Show. She had a red rubber bib tucked
around her throat and, since a rain storm came up when we were
half way through the Bronx, I had to hold over her a small green

THE DOG THAT BIT PEOPLE: Permission the author. Copyright 1933 James
Thurber. In *My Life and Hard Times*, Harper and Bros.

umbrella, really more of a parasol. The rain beat down fearfully and suddenly the driver of the car drove into a big garage, filled with mechanics. It happened so quickly that I forgot to put the umbrella down and I will always remember, with sickening distress, the look of incredulity mixed with hatred that came over the face of the particular hardened garage man that came over to see what we wanted, when he took a look at me and the poodle. All garage men, and people of that intolerant stripe, hate poodles with their curious hair cut, especially the pom-poms that you got to leave on their hips if you expect the dogs to win a prize.

But the Airedale, as I have said, was the worst of all my dogs. He really wasn't my dog, as a matter of fact: I came home from a vacation one summer to find that my brother Roy had bought him while I was away. A big, burly, choleric dog, he always acted as if he thought I wasn't one of the family. There was a slight advantage in being one of the family, for he didn't bite the family as often as he bit strangers. Still, in the years that we had him he bit everybody but mother, and he made a pass at her once but missed. That was during the month when we suddenly had mice, and Muggs refused to do anything about them. Nobody ever had mice exactly like the mice we had that month. They acted like pet mice, almost like mice somebody had trained. They were so friendly that one night when mother entertained at dinner the Friraliras, a club she and my father had belonged to for twenty years, she put down a lot of little dishes with food in them on the pantry floor so that the mice would be satisfied with that and wouldn't come into the dining room. Muggs stayed out in the pantry with the mice, lying on the floor, growling to himself—not at the mice, but about all the people in the next room that he would have liked to get at. Mother slipped out into the pantry once to see how everything was going. Everything was going fine. It made her so mad to see Muggs lying there, oblivious of the mice—they came running up to her—that she slapped him and he slashed at her, but didn't make it. He was sorry immediately, mother said. He was always sorry, she said, after he bit someone, but we could not understand how she figured this out. He didn't act sorry.

Mother used to send a box of candy every Christmas to the people the Airedale bit. The list finally contained forty or more names. Nobody could understand why we didn't get rid of the dog. I didn't understand it very well myself, but we didn't get rid of him. I think that one or two people tried to poison Muggs—he acted poisoned once in a while—and old Major Moberly fired at him once with his service revolver near the Seneca Hotel in East Broad Street—but Muggs lived to be almost eleven years old and even when he could hardly get around he bit a Congressman who had called to see my father on business. My mother had never

*Nobody knew exactly what
was the matter with him.*

liked the Congressman—she said the signs of his horoscope showed he couldn't be trusted (he was Saturn with the moon in Virgo)—but she sent him a box of candy that Christmas. He sent it right back, probably because he suspected it was trick candy. Mother persuaded herself it was all for the best that the dog had bitten him, even though father lost an important business association because of it. "I wouldn't be associated with such a man," mother said. "Muggs could read him like a book."

We used to take turns feeding Muggs to be on his good side, but that didn't always work. He was never in a very good humor, even after a meal. Nobody knew exactly what the was the matter with him, but whatever it was it made him irascible, especially in the mornings. Roy never felt very well in the morning, either, especially before breakfast, and once when he came downstairs and found that Muggs had moodily chewed up the morning paper he hit him in the face with a grapefruit and then jumped up on the dining room table, scattering dishes and silverware and spilling the coffee. Muggs' first free leap carried him all the way across the table and into a brass fire screen in front of the gas grate but he was back on his feet in a moment and in the end he got Roy and gave him a pretty vicious bite in the leg. Then he was all over it; he never bit anyone more than once at a time. Mother always mentioned that as an argument in his favor; she said he had a quick temper but that he didn't hold a grudge. She was forever defending him. I think she liked him because he wasn't well. "He's not strong," she would say, pityingly, but that was inaccurate; he may not have been well but he was terribly strong.

One time my mother went to the Chittenden Hotel to call on a woman mental healer who was lecturing in Columbus on the subject of "Harmonious Vibrations." She wanted to find out if it was possible to get harmonious vibrations into a dog. "He's a large tan-colored Airedale," mother explained. The woman said that she had never treated a dog but she advised my mother to hold the thought that he did not bite and would not bite. Mother was holding the thought the very next morning when Muggs got the iceman but she blamed that slip-up on the iceman. "If you didn't think he would bite you, he wouldn't," mother told him. He stomped out of the house in a terrible jangle of vibrations.

One morning when Muggs bit me slightly, more or less in passing, I reached down and grabbed his short stumpy tail and hoisted him into the air. It was a foolhardy thing to do and the last time I saw my mother, about six months ago, she said she didn't know what possessed me. I don't either, except that I was pretty mad. As long as I held the dog off the floor by his tail he couldn't get at me, but he twisted and jerked so, snarling all the time, that I realized I couldn't hold him that way very long. I carried him to the kitchen and flung him onto the floor and shut the door on him just as he crashed against it. But I forgot about the backstairs. Muggs went up the backstairs and down the frontstairs and had me cornered in the living room. I managed to get up onto the mantelpiece above the fireplace, but it gave way and came down with a tremendous crash throwing a large marble clock, several vases, and myself heavily to the floor. Muggs was so alarmed by the racket that when I picked myself up he had disappeared. We couldn't find him anywhere, although we whistled and shouted, until old Mrs. Detweiler called after dinner that night. Muggs had bitten her once, in the leg, and she came into the living room only after we assured her that Muggs had run away. She had just seated

*Lots of people reported
our dog to the police.*

herself when, with a great growling and scratching of claws, Muggs emerged from under a davenport where he had been quietly hiding all the time, and bit her again. Mother examined the bite and put arnica on it and told Mrs. Detweiler that it was only a bruise. "He just bumped you," she said. But Mrs. Detweiler left the house in a nasty state of mind.

Lots of people reported our Airedale to the police but my father held a municipal office at the time and was on friendly terms with the police. Even so, the cops had been out a couple of times— once when Muggs bit Mrs. Rufus Sturtevant and again when he bit Lieutenant-Governor Malloy—but mother told them that it hadn't been Muggs' fault but the fault of the people who were bitten. "When he starts for them, they scream," she explained, "and that excites him." The cops suggested that it might be a good idea to tie the dog up, but mother said that it mortified him to be tied up and that he wouldn't eat when he was tied up.

Muggs at his meals was an unusual sight. Because of the fact that if you reached toward the floor he would bite you, we usually put his food plate on top of an old kitchen table with a bench alongside the table. Muggs would stand on the bench and eat. I remember that my mother's Uncle Horatio, who boasted that he was the third man up Missionary Ridge, was splutteringly indignant when he found out that we fed the dog on a table because we were afraid to put his plate on the floor. He said he wasn't afraid of any dog that ever lived and that he would put the dog's plate on the floor if we would give it to him. Roy said that if Uncle Horatio had fed Muggs on the ground just before the battle he would have been the first man up Missionary Ridge. Uncle Horatio was furious. "Bring him in! Bring him in now!" he shouted. "I'll feed the —— on the floor!" Roy was all for giving him a chance, but my father wouldn't hear of it. He said that Muggs had already been fed. "I'll feed him again!" bawled Uncle Horatio. We had quite a time quieting him.

In his last year Muggs used to spend practically all of his time outdoors. He didn't like to stay in the house for some reason or other—perhaps it held too many unpleasant memories for him. Anyway, it was hard to get him to come in and as a result the garbage man, the iceman, and the laundryman wouldn't come near the house. We had to haul the garbage down to the corner, take the laundry out and bring it back, and meet the iceman a block from home. After this had gone on for some time we hit on an ingenious arrangement for getting the dog in the house so that we could lock him up while the gas meter was read, and so on. Muggs was afraid of only one thing, an electrical storm. Thunder and lightning frightened him out of his senses (I think he thought a storm had broken the day the mantelpiece fell). He would rush into the house and hide under a bed or in a clothes closet. So we fixed up a thunder machine out of a long narrow piece of sheet iron with a wooden handle on one end. Mother would shake this vigorously when she wanted to get Muggs into the house. It made an excellent imitation of thunder, but I suppose it was the most roundabout system for running a household that was ever devised. It took a lot out of mother.

A few months before Muggs died, he got to "seeing things." He would rise slowly from the floor, growling low, and stalk stiff-legged and menacing toward nothing at all. Sometimes the Thing would be just a little to the right or left of a visitor. Once a Fuller Brush salesman got hysterics. Muggs came wandering into the room like Hamlet following his father's ghost. His eyes were fixed on a spot just to the left of the Fuller Brush man, who stood it until Muggs was about three slow, creeping paces from him. Then he shouted. Muggs wavered on past him into the hallway grumbling to himself but the Fuller man went on shouting. I think mother had to throw a pan of cold water on him before he stopped. That was the way she used to stop us boys when we got into fights.

Muggs died quite suddenly one night. Mother wanted to bury him in the family lot under a marble stone with some such inscription as "Flights of angels sing thee to thy rest" but we persuaded her it was against the law. In the end we just put up a smooth board above his grave along a lonely road. On the board I wrote with an indelible pencil "Cave Canem." Mother was quite pleased with the simple classic dignity of the old Latin epitaph.

For questions and exercises, see p. 470 and p. 532.

## UNIVERSITY DAYS

### JAMES THURBER

I passed all the other courses that I took at my University, but I could never pass botany. This was because all botany students had to spend several hours a week in a laboratory looking through a microscope at plant cells, and I could never see through a microscope. I never once saw a cell through a microscope. This used to enrage my instructor. He would wander around the laboratory pleased with the progress all the students were making in drawing the involved and, so I am told, interesting structure of flower cells, until he came to me. I would just be standing there. "I can't see anything," I would say. He would begin patiently enough,

UNIVERSITY DAYS: Permission the author. Copyright 1933 James Thurber. Originally published in *The New Yorker*.

explaining how anybody can see through a microscope, but he would always end up in a fury, claiming that I could *too* see through a microscope but just pretended that I couldn't. "It takes away from the beauty of flowers anyway," I used to tell him. "We are not concerned with beauty in this course," he would say. "We are concerned solely with what I may call the *mechanics* of flars." "Well," I'd say, "I can't see anything." "Try it just once again," he'd say, and I would put my eye to the microscope and see nothing at all, except now and again a nebulous milky substance—a phenomenon of maladjustment. You were supposed to see a vivid, restless clockwork of sharply defined plant cells. "I see what looks like a lot of milk," I would tell him. This, he claimed, was the result of my not having adjusted the microscope properly, so he would readjust it for me, or rather, for himself. And I would look again and see milk.

I finally took a deferred pass, as they called it, and waited a year and tried again. (You had to pass one of the biological sciences or you couldn't graduate.) The professor had come back from vacation brown as a berry, bright-eyed, and eager to explain cell-structure again to his classes. "Well," he said to me, cheerily, when we met in the first laboratory hour of the semester, "we're going to see cells this time, aren't we?" "Yes, sir," I said. Students to right of me and to left of me and in front of me were seeing cells; what's more, they were quietly drawing pictures of them in their notebooks. Of course, I didn't see anything.

"We'll try it," the professor said to me, grimly, "with every adjustment of the microscope known to man. As God is my witness, I'll arrange this glass so that you see cells through it or I'll give up teaching. In twenty-two years of botany, I—" He cut off abruptly for he was beginning to quiver all over, like Lionel Barrymore, and he genuinely wished to hold onto his temper; his scenes with me had taken a great deal out of him.

So we tried it with every adjustment of the microscope known to man. With only one of them did I see anything but blackness or the familiar lacteal opacity, and that time I saw, to my pleasure and amazement, a variegated constellation of flecks, specks, and dots. These I hastily drew. The instructor, noting my activity, came back from an adjoining desk, a smile on his lips and his eyebrows high in hope. He looked at my cell drawing. "What's that?" he

*He was beginning to quiver all over like Lionel Barrymore.*

demanded, with a hint of a squeal in his voice. "That's what I saw," I said. "You didn't, you didn't, you *didn't!*" he screamed, losing control of his temper instantly, and he bent over and squinted into the microscope. His head snapped up. "That's your eye!" he shouted. "You've fixed the lens so that it reflects! You've drawn your eye!"

Another course that I didn't like, but somehow managed to pass, was economics. I went to that class straight from the botany class, which didn't help me any in understanding either subject. I used to get them mixed up. But not as mixed up as another student in my economics class who came there direct from a physics laboratory. He was a tackle on the football team, named Bolenciecwcz. At that time Ohio State University had one of the best football teams in the country, and Bolenciecwcz was one of its outstanding stars. In order to be eligible to play it was necessary for him to keep up in his studies, a very difficult matter, for while he was not dumber than an ox he was not any smarter. Most of his professors were lenient and helped him along. None gave him more hints, in answering questions, or asked him simpler ones than the economics professor, a thin, timid man named Bassum. One day when we were on the subject of transportation and distribution, it came Bolenciecwcz's turn to answer a question. "Name one means of transportation," the professor said to him. No light came into the big tackle's eyes. "Just any means of transportation," said the professor. Bolenciecwcz sat staring at him. "That is," pursued the professor, "any medium, agency, or method of going from one place to another." Bolenciecwcz had the look of a man who is being led into a trap. "You may choose among steam, horse-drawn, or electrically propelled vehicles," said the instructor. "I might suggest the one which we commonly take in making long journeys across land." There was a profound silence in which everybody stirred uneasily, including Bolenciecwcz and Mr. Bassum. Mr. Bassum abruptly broke this silence in an amazing manner. "Choo-choo-choo," he said, in a low voice, and turned instantly scarlet. He glanced appealingly around the room. All of us, of course, shared Mr. Bassum's desire that Bolenciecwcz should stay abreast of the class in economics, for the Illinois game, one of the hardest and most important of the season, was only a week off. "Toot, toot, too-toooooooot!" some student with a deep voice moaned, and we all looked encouragingly at Bolenciecwcz. Somebody else gave a fine imitation of a locomotive letting off steam. Mr. Bassum himself rounded off the little show. "Ding, dong, ding, dong," he said, hopefully. Bolenciecwcz was staring at the floor now, trying to

*Bolenciecwcz was trying to think.*

think, his great brow furrowed, his huge hands rubbing together, his face red.

"How did you come to college this year, Mr. Bolenciecwcz?" asked the professor. "*Chuf*fa chuffa, *chuf*fa chuffa."

"M'father sent me," said the football player.

"What on?" asked Bassum.

"I git an 'lowance," said the tackle, in a low, husky voice, obviously embarrassed.

"No, no," said Bassum. "Name a means of transportation. What did you *ride* here on?"

"Train," said Bolenciecwcz.

"Quite right," said the professor. "Now, Mr. Nugent, will you tell us—"

If I went through anguish in botany and economics—for different reasons—gymnasium work was even worse. I don't even like to think about it. They wouldn't let you play games or join in the exercises with your glasses on and I couldn't see with mine off. I bumped into professors, horizontal bars, agricultural students, and swinging iron rings. Not being able to see, I could take it but I couldn't dish it out. Also, in order to pass gymnasium (and you had to pass it to graduate) you had to learn to swim if you didn't know how. I didn't like the swimming pool, I didn't like swimming, and I didn't like the swimming instructor, and after all these years I still don't. I never swam but I passed my gym work anyway, by having another student give my gymnasium number (978) and swim across the pool in my place. He was a quiet, amiable blond youth, number 473, and he would have seen through a microscope for me if we could have got away with it, but we couldn't get away with it. Another thing I didn't like about gymnasium work was that they made you strip the day you registered. It is impossible for me to be happy when I am stripped and being asked a lot of questions. Still, I did better than a lanky agricultural student who was cross-examined just before I was. They asked each student what college he was in—that is, whether Arts, Engineering, Commerce, or Agriculture. "What college are you in?" the instructor snapped at the youth in front of me. "Ohio State University," he said promptly.

It wasn't that agricultural student but it was another a whole lot like him who decided to take up journalism, possibly on the ground that when farming went to hell he could fall back on newspaper work. He didn't realize, of course, that that would be very much like falling back full-length on a kit of carpenter's tools. Haskins didn't seem cut out for journalism, being too embarrassed to talk to anybody and unable to use a typewriter, but the editor of the college paper assigned him to the cow barns, the sheep house, the horse pavilion, and the animal husbandry department generally. This was a genuinely big "beat," for it took up five times as much ground and got ten times as great a legislative appropriation as the College of Liberal Arts. The agricultural student knew animals, but nevertheless his stories were dull and colorlessly written. He took all afternoon on each of them, on account of having to hunt for each letter on the typewriter. Once in a while he had to ask somebody to help him hunt. "C" and "L," in particular, were hard letters for him to find. His editor finally got pretty much annoyed at the farmer-journalist because his pieces were so uninteresting. "See here, Haskins," he snapped at him one day. "Why is it we never have anything hot from you on the horse pavilion? Here we have two hundred head of horses on this campus—more than any other university in the Western Conference except Purdue—and yet you never get any real low-down on them. Now shoot over to the horse barns and dig up something lively." Haskins shambled out and came back in about an hour; he said he had something. "Well, start it off snappily," said the editor. "Something people will read." Haskins set to work and in a couple of hours brought a sheet of typewritten paper to the desk; it was a two-hundred-word story about some disease that had broken out among the horses. Its opening sentence was simple but arresting. It read: "Who has noticed the sores on the tops of the horses in the animal husbandry building?"

Ohio State was a land grant university and therefore two years of military drill was compulsory. We drilled with old Springfield rifles and studied the tactics of the Civil War even though the World War was going on at the time. At 11 o'clock each morning thousands of freshmen and sophomores used to deploy over the campus, moodily creeping up on the old chemistry building. It was good training for the kind of warfare that was waged at Shiloh but it had no connection with what was going on in Europe. Some people used to think there was German money behind it, but they didn't dare say so or they would have been thrown in jail as German spies. It was a period of muddy thought and marked, I believe, the decline of higher education in the Middle West.

As a soldier I was never any good at all. Most of the cadets were glumly indifferent soldiers, but I was no good at all. Once General Littlefield, who was commandant of the cadet corps, popped up in front of me during regimental drill and snapped, "You are the main trouble with this university!" I think he meant that my type was the main trouble with the university but he may have meant me individually. I was mediocre at drill, certainly—that is, until my senior year. By that time I had drilled longer than anybody else in the Western Conference, having failed at military at the end of each preceding year so that I had to do it all over again. I was the only senior still in uniform. The uniform which, when new, had made me look like an interurban railway conductor, now that it had become faded and too tight, made me look like Bert Williams in his bellboy act. This had a definitely bad effect on my morale. Even so, I had become by sheer practise little short of wonderful at squad manoeuvres.

One day General Littlefield picked our company out of the whole regiment and tried to get it mixed up by putting it through one movement after another as fast as we could execute them: squads right, squads left, squads on right into line, squads right about, squads left front into line, etc. In about three minutes one hundred and nine men were marching in one direction and I was marching away from them at an angle of forty degrees, all alone. "Company, halt!" shouted General Littlefield. "That man is the only man who has it right!" I was made a corporal for my achievement.

The next day General Littlefield summoned me to his office. He was swatting flies when I went in. I was silent and he was silent, too, for a long time. I don't think he remembered me or why he had sent for me, but he didn't want to admit it. He swatted some more flies, keeping his eyes on them narrowly before he let go with the swatter. "Button up your coat!" he snapped. Looking back on it now I can see that he meant me although he was looking at a fly, but I just stood there. Another fly came to rest on a paper in front of the general and began rubbing its hind legs together. The general lifted the swatter cautiously. I moved restlessly and the fly flew away. "You startled him!" barked General Littlefield, looking at me severely. I said I was sorry. "That won't help the situation!" snapped the general, with cold military logic. I didn't see what I could do except offer to chase some more flies toward his desk, but I didn't say anything. He stared out the window at the faraway figures of co-eds crossing the campus toward the library. Finally, he told me I could go. So I went. He either didn't know which cadet I was or else he forgot what he wanted to see me about. It may have been that he wished to apologize for having called me the main trouble with the university; or maybe he had decided to compliment me on my brilliant drilling of the day before and then at the last minute decided not to. I don't know. I don't think about it much any more.

For questions and exercises, see p. 470 and p. 521.

## THE DECLINE OF THE GRACES

### MAX BEERBOHM

Have you read *The Young Lady's Book?* You have had plenty of time to do so, for it was published in 1829. It was described by the two anonymous Gentlewomen who compiled it as "A Manual for Elegant Recreations, Exercises, and Pursuits." You wonder they had nothing better to think of? You suspect them of having been triflers? They were not, believe me. They were careful to explain, at the outset, that the Virtues of Character were what a young lady should most assiduously cultivate. They, in their day, laboring under the shadow of the eighteenth century, had somehow in themselves that high moral fervor which marks the opening of the twentieth century, and is said to have come in with Mr. George Bernard Shaw. But, unlike us, they were not concerned wholly with the inward and spiritual side of life. They cared for the material surface, too. They were learned in the frills and furbelows of things. They gave, indeed, a whole chapter to "Embroidery." Another they gave to "Archery," another to "The Aviary," another to "The Escrutoire." Young ladies do not now keep birds, nor shoot with bow and arrow; but they do still, in some measure, write letters; and so, for sake of historical comparison, let me give you a glance at "The Escrutoire." It is not light reading.

> For careless scrawls ye boast of no pretence;
> Fair Russell wrote, as well as spoke, with sense.

Thus is the chapter headed, with a delightful little wood-engraving of "Fair Russell," looking preeminently sensible, at her desk, to prepare the reader for the imminent welter of rules for "decorous composition." Not that pedantry is approved. "Ease and simplicity, an even flow of unlabored diction, and an artless arrangement of

THE DECLINE OF THE GRACES: From *Yet Again* by Max Beerbohm. Reprinted by permission of the author.

obvious sentiments" is the ideal to be striven for. "A metaphor may be used with advantage" by any young lady, but only "if it occur naturally." And "allusions are elegant," but only "when introduced with ease, and when they are well understood by those to whom they are addressed." "An antithesis renders a passage piquant"; but the dire results of a too-frequent indulgence in it are relentlessly set forth. Pages and pages are devoted to a minute survey of the pitfalls of punctuation. But when the young lady of that period had skirted all these, and had observed all the manifold rules of calligraphy that were laid down for her, she was not, even then, out of the wood. Very special stress was laid on "the use of the seal." Bitter scorn was poured on young ladies who misused the seal. "It is a habit of some to thrust the wax into the flame of the candle, and the moment a morsel of it is melted, to daub it on the paper; and when an unsightly mass is gathered together, to pass the seal over the tongue with ridiculous haste—press it with all the strength which the sealing party possesses—and the result is, an impression which raises a blush on her cheek."

Well! The young ladies of that day were ever expected to exhibit sensibility, and used to blush, just as they wept or fainted, for very slight causes. Their tears and their swoons did not necessarily betoken much grief or agitation; nor did a rush of color to the cheek mean necessarily that they were overwhelmed with shame. To exhibit various emotions in the drawing-room was one of the Elegant Exercises in which these young ladies were drilled thoroughly. And their habit of simulation was so rooted in sense of duty that it merged into sincerity. If a young lady did not swoon at the breakfast-table when her Papa read aloud from *The Times* that the Duke of Wellington was suffering from a slight chill, the chances were that she would swoon quite unaffectedly when she realized her omission. Even so, we may be sure that a young lady whose cheek burned not at sight of the letter she had sealed untidily—"unworthily" the Manual calls it—would anon be blushing for her shamelessness. Such a thing as the blurring of the family crest, or as the pollution of the profile of Pallas Athene with the smoke of the taper, was hardly, indeed, one of those "very slight causes" to which I have referred. The Georgian young lady was imbued through and through with the sense that it was her duty to be gracefully efficient in whatsoever she set her hand to. To the

young lady of today, belike, she will seem accordingly ridiculous
—seem poor-spirited, and a pettifogger. True, she set her hand to
no grandiose tasks. She was not allowed to become a hospital
nurse, for example, or an actress. The young lady of today, when
she hears in herself a "vocation" for tending the sick, would willingly, without an instant's preparation, assume responsibility for
the lives of a whole ward at St. Thomas's. This responsibility is not,
however, thrust on her. She has to submit to a long and tedious
course of training before she may do so much as smooth a pillow.
The boards of the theatre are less jealously hedged in than those
of the hospital. If your young lady have a wealthy father, and
retain her schoolroom faculty for learning poetry by heart, there
is no power on earth to prevent her from making her debut, somewhere, as Juliet—if she be so inclined; and such is usually her inclination. That her voice is untrained, that she cannot scan blank-
verse, that she cannot gesticulate with grace and propriety nor
move with propriety and grace across the stage, matters not a little
bit—to our young lady. "Feeling," she will say, "is everything";
and, of course, she, at the age of eighteen, has more feeling than
Juliet, that "flapper," could have had. All those other things—those
little technical tricks—"can be picked up," or "will come." But no;
I misrepresent our young lady. If she be conscious that there are
such tricks to be played, she despises them. When, later, she finds
the need to learn them, she still despises them. It seems to her
ridiculous that one should not speak and comport oneself as art-
lessly on the stage as one does off it. The notion of speaking or
comporting oneself with conscious art in real life would seem to
her quite monstrous. It would puzzle her as much as her grandmother would have been puzzled by the contrary notion.

Personally, I range myself on the grandmother's side. I take my
stand shoulder to shoulder with the Graces. On the banner that
I wave is embroidered a device of prunes and prisms.

I am no blind fanatic, however. I admit that artlessness is a
charming idea. I admit that it is sometimes charming as a reality.
I applaud it (all the more heartily because it is rare) in children.
But then, children, like the young of all animals whatsoever, have a
natural grace. As a rule, they begin to show it in their third year,
and to lose it in their ninth. Within that span of six years, they
can be charming without intention; and their so frequent failure

in charm is due to their voluntary or enforced imitation of the ways of their elders. In Georgian and Early Victorian days the imitation was always enforced. Grown-up people had good manners, and wished to see them reflected in the young. Nowadays, the imitation is always voluntary. Grown-up people have no manners at all; whereas they certainly have a very keen taste for the intrinsic charm of children. They wish children to be perfectly natural. That is (aesthetically, at least) an admirable wish. My complaint against these grown-up people is, that they themselves, whom time has robbed of their natural grace as surely as it robs the other animals, are content to be perfectly natural. This contentment I deplore, and am keen to disturb.

I except from my indictment any young lady who may read these words. I will assume that she differs from the rest of the human race, and has not, never had, anything to learn in the art of conversing prettily, of entering or leaving a room or a vehicle gracefully, of writing appropriate letters, *et patati et patata*. I will assume that all these accomplishments came naturally to her. She will now be in a mood to accept my proposition that of her contemporaries none seems to have been so lucky as herself. She will agree with me that other girls need training. She will not deny that grace in the little affairs of life is a thing which has to be learned. Some girls have a far greater aptitude for learning it than others; but, with one exception, no girls have it in them from the outset. It is a not less complicated thing than is the art of acting, or of nursing the sick, and needs for the acquirement of it a not less laborious preparation.

Is it worth the trouble? Certainly the trouble is not taken. The "finishing school," wherein young ladies were taught to be graceful, is a thing of the past. It must have been a dismal place; but the dismalness of it—the strain of it—was the measure of its indispensability. There I beg the question. Is grace itself indispensable? Certainly it has been dispensed with. It isn't reckoned with. To sit perfectly mute "in company," or to chatter on at the top of one's voice; to shriek with laughter; to fling oneself into a room and dash oneself out of it; to collapse on chairs or sofas; to sprawl across tables; to slam doors; to write, without punctuation, notes that only an expert in handwriting could read, and only an expert in misspelling could understand; to hustle, to bounce, to go straight ahead

—to be, let us say, perfectly natural in the midst of an artificial civilization, is an ideal which the young ladies of today are neither publicly nor privately discouraged from cherishing. The word "cherishing" implies a softness of which they are not guilty. I hasten to substitute "pursuing." If these young ladies were not in the aforesaid midst of an artificial civilization, I should be the last to discourage their pursuit. If they were Amazons, for example, spending their lives beneath the sky, in tilth of stubborn fields, and in armed conflict with fierce men, it would be unreasonable to expect of them any sacrifice to the Graces. But they are exposed to no such hardships. They have really a very comfortable sort of life. They are not expected to be useful. (I am writing all the time, of course, about the young ladies in the affluent classes.) And it seems to me that they, in payment of their debt to Fate, ought to occupy the time that is on their hands by becoming ornamental and increasing the world's store of beauty. In a sense, certainly, they are ornamental. It is a strange fact, and an ironic, that they spend quite five times the annual amount that was spent by their grandmothers on personal adornment. If they can afford it, well and good: let us have no sumptuary law. But plenty of pretty dresses will not suffice. Pretty manners are needed with them, and are prettier than they.

I had forgotten men. Every defect that I had noted in the modern young woman is not less notable in the modern young man. Briefly, he is a boor. If it is true that "manners makyth man," one doubts whether the British race can be perpetuated. The young Englishman of today is inferior to savages and to beasts of the field in that they are eager to show themselves in an agreeable and seductive light to the females of their kind, whilst he regards any such effort as beneath his dignity. Not that he cultivates dignity in demeanor. He merely slouches. Unlike his feminine counterpart, he lets his raiment match his manners. Observe him any afternoon, as he passes down Piccadilly, sullenly, with his shoulders humped, and his hat clapped to the back of his head, and his cigarette dangling almost vertically from his lips. It seems only appropriate that his hat is a billycock, and his shirt a flannel one, and that his boots are brown ones. Thus attired, he is on his way to pay a visit of ceremony to some house at which he has recently dined. No; that is the sort of visit he never pays. (I must confess I don't myself.) But one remembers the time when no self-respecting youth would

have shown himself in Piccadilly without the vesture appropriate
to that august highway. Nowadays there is no care for appearances.
Comfort is the one aim. Any care for appearances is regarded
rather as a sign of effeminacy. Yet never, in any other age of the
world's history has it been regarded so. Indeed, elaborate dressing
used to be deemed by philosophers an outcome of the sex-instinct.
It was supposed that men dressed themselves finely in order to
attract the admiration of women, just as peacocks spread their
plumage with a similar purpose. Nor do I jettison the old theory.
The declension of masculine attire in England began soon after
the time when statistics were beginning to show the great numeri-
cal preponderance of women over men; and is it fanciful to trace
the one fact to the other? Surely not. I do not say that either sex
is attracted to the other by elaborate attire. But I believe that each
sex, consciously or unconsciously, uses this elaboration for this very
purpose. Thus the over-dressed maiden of today and the ill-dressed
youth are but symbols of the balance of our population. The one
is pleading, the other scorning. "Take me!" is the message borne
by the furs and the pearls and the old lace. "I'll see about that when
I've had a look round!" is the not pretty answer conveyed by the
billycock and the flannel shirt.

I dare say that fine manners, like fine clothes, are one of the
stratagems of sex. This theory squares at once with the modern
young man's lack of manners. But how about the modern young
woman's not less obvious lack? Well, the theory will square with
that, too. The modern young woman's gracelessness may be due
to her conviction that men like a girl to be thoroughly natural. She
knows that they have a very high opinion of themselves; and what,
thinks she, more natural than that they should esteem her in proportion to her power of reproducing the qualities that are most
salient in themselves? Men, she perceives, are clumsy, and talk
aloud, and have no drawing-room accomplishments, and are rude;
and she proceeds to model herself on them. Let us not blame her.
Let us blame rather her parents or guardians, who, though they
well know that a masculine girl attracts no man, leave her to the
devices of her own inexperience. Girls ought not to be allowed,
as they are, to run wild. So soon as they have lost the natural grace
of childhood, they should be initiated into that course of artificial
training through which their grandmothers passed before them,

and in virtue of which their grandmothers were pleasing. This will not, of course, ensure husbands for them all; but it will certainly tend to increase the number of marriages. Nor is it primarily for that sociological reason that I plead for a return to the old system of education. I plead for it, first and last, on aesthetic grounds. Let the Graces be cultivated for their own sweet sake.

The difficulty is, how to begin. The mothers of the rising generation were brought up in the unregenerate way. Their scraps of oral tradition will need to be supplemented by much research. I advise them to start their quest by reading *The Young Lady's Book*. Exactly the right spirit is therein enshrined, though of the substance there is much that could not be well applied to our own day. That chapter on "The Escrutoire," for example, belongs to a day that cannot be recalled. We can get rid of bad manners, but we cannot substitute the Sedan-chair for the motor-car; and the penny post, with telephones and telegrams, has, in our own beautiful phrase, "come to stay," and has elbowed the art of letter-writing irrevocably from among us. But notes are still written; and there is no reason why they should not be written well. Has the mantle of those anonymous gentlewomen who wrote *The Young Lady's Book* fallen on no one? Will no one revise that "Manual of Elegant Recreations, Exercises, and Pursuits," adapting it to present needs? . . . A few hints as to Deportment in the Motor-Car; the exact Angle whereat to hold the Receiver of a Telephone, and the exact Key wherein to pitch the Voice; the Conduct of a Cigarette. . . . I see a wide and golden vista.

For questions and exercises, see p. 448, p. 470, and p. 521.

# Criticism

## HOW TO WRITE LIKE A SOCIAL SCIENTIST

### SAMUEL T. WILLIAMSON

During my years as an editor, I have seen probably hundreds of job applicants who were either just out of College or in their senior year. All wanted "to write." Many brought letters from their teachers. But I do not recall one letter announcing that its bearer could write what he wished to say with clarity and directness, with economy of words, and with pleasing variety of sentence structure.

Most of these young men and women could not write plain English. Apparently their noses had not been rubbed in the drudgery of putting one simple well-chosen word behind the other. If this was true of teachers' pets, what about the rest? What about those going into business and industry? Or those going into professions? What about those who remain at college—first for a Master of Arts degree, then an instructorship combined with work for a Ph.D., then perhaps an assistant professorship, next a full professorship and finally, as an academic crown of laurel, appointment as head of a department or as dean of a faculty.

Certainly, faculty members of a front-rank university should be better able to express themselves than those they teach. Assume that those in the English department have this ability. Can the same be said of the social scientists—economists, sociologists, and authori-

HOW TO WRITE LIKE A SOCIAL SCIENTIST: Originally printed in *The Saturday Review of Literature*, October 4, 1947. Reprinted here by permission of *The Saturday Review of Literature*.

ties on government? We need today as we never needed so urgently before all the understanding they can give us of problems of earning a living, caring for our fellows, and governing ourselves. Too many of them, I find, can't write as well as their students.

I am still convalescing from overexposure some time ago to products of the academic mind. One of the foundations engaged me to edit manuscripts of a socio-economic research report designed for the thoughtful citizen as well as for the specialist. My expectations were not high—no deathless prose, merely a sturdy, no-nonsense report of explorers into the wilderness of statistics and half-known fact. I knew from experience that economic necessity compels many a professional writer to be a cream-skimmer and a gatherer of easily obtainable material; for unless his publishers will stand the extra cost, he cannot afford the exhaustive investigation which endowed research makes possible. Although I did not expect fine writing from a trained, professional researcher, I did assume that a careful fact-finder would write carefully.

And so, anticipating no literary treat, I plunged into the forest of words of my first manuscript. My weapons were a sturdy eraser and several batteries of sharpened pencils. My armor was a thesaurus. And if I should become lost, a near-by public library was a landmark, and the Encyclopedia of Social Sciences on its reference shelves was an ever-ready guide.

Instead of big trees, I found underbrush. Cutting through involved, lumbering sentences was bad enough, but the real chore was removal of the burdocks of excessive verbiage which clung to the manuscript. Nothing was big or large; in my author's lexicon, it was "substantial." When he meant "much," he wrote "to a substantially high degree." If some event took place in the early 1920's, he put it "in the early part of the decade of the twenties." And instead of "that depends," my author wrote, "any answer to this question must bear in mind certain peculiar characteristics of the industry."

So it went for 30,000 words. The pile of verbal burdocks grew— sometimes twelve words from a twenty-word sentence. The shortened version of 20,000 words was perhaps no more thrilling than the original report; but it was terser and crisper. It took less time to read and it could be understood quicker. That was all I could do. As S. S. McClure once said to me, "An editor can improve a manuscript, but he cannot put in what isn't there."

I did not know the author I was editing; after what I did to his copy it may be just as well that we have not met. Aside from his cat-chasing-its-own-tail verbosity, he was a competent enough workman. Apparently he is well thought of. He had his doctorate, he is a trained researcher and a pupil of an eminent professor. He has held a number of fellowships and he has performed competently several jobs of economic research. But, after this long academic preparation for what was to be his life work, it is a mystery why so little attention was given to acquiring use of simple English.

Later, when I encountered other manuscripts, I found I had been too hard on this promising Ph.D. Tone-deaf as he was to words, his report was a lighthouse of clarity among the chapters turned in by his so-called academic betters. These brethren—and sister'n—who contributed the remainder of the foundation's study were professors and assistant professors in our foremost colleges and universities. The names of one or two are occasionally in newspaper headlines. All of them had, as the professorial term has it, "published."

Anyone who edits copy, regardless of whether it is good or bad, discovers in a manuscript certain pet phrases, little quirks of style and other individual traits of its author. But in the series I edited, all twenty reports read alike. Their words would be found in any English dictionary, grammar was beyond criticism, but long passages in these reports demanded not only editing but actual translation. For hours at a time, I floundered in brier patches like this: "In eliminating wage changes due to purely transitory conditions, collective bargaining has eliminated one of the important causes of industrial conflict, for changes under such conditions are almost always followed by a reaction when normal conditions appear."

I am not picking on my little group of social scientists. They are merely members of a caste; they are so used to taking in each other's literary washing that it has become a habit for them to clothe their thoughts in the same smothering verbal garments. Nor are they any worse than most of their colleagues, for example:

In the long run, developments in transportation, housing, optimum size of plant, etc., might tend to induce an industrial and demographic pattern similar to the one that consciousness of vulnerability would dictate. Such a tendency might be advanced by public persuasion and governmental inducement, and advanced more effectively if the causes of urbanization had been carefully studied.

Such pedantic Choctaw may be all right as a sort of code language or shorthand of social science to circulate among initiates, but its perpetrators have no right to impose it on others. The tragedy is that its users appear to be under the impression that it is good English usage.

Father, forgive them; for they know not what they do! There once was a time when everyday folk spoke one language, and learned men wrote another. It was called the Dark Ages. The world is in such a state that we may return to the Dark Ages if we do not acquire wisdom. If social scientists have answers to our problems yet feel under no obligation to make themselves understood, then we laymen must learn their language. This may take some practice, but practice should become perfect by following six simple rules of the guild of social science writers. Examples which I give are sound and well tested: they come from manuscripts I edited.

*Rule 1. Never use a short word when you can think of a long one.* Never say "now," but "currently." It is not "soon" but "presently." You did not have "enough" but a "sufficiency." Never do you come to the "end" but to the "termination." This rule is basic.

*Rule 2. Never use one word when you can use two or more.* Eschew "probably." Write, "it is improbable," and raise this to "it is not improbable." Then you'll be able to parlay "probably" into "available evidence would tend to indicate that it is not unreasonable to suppose."

*Rule 3. Put one-syllable thoughts into polysyllabic terms.* Instead of observing that a work force might be bigger and better, write, "In addition to quantitative enlargement, it is not improbable that there is need also for qualitative improvement in the personnel of the service." If you have discovered that musicians out of practice can't hold jobs, report that "the fact of rapid deterioration of musical skill when not in use soon converts the employed into the unemployable." Resist the impulse to say that much men's clothing is machine made. Put it thus: "Nearly all operations in the industry lend themselves to performance by machine, and all grades of men's clothing sold in significant quantity involve a very substantial amount of machine work."

*Rule 4. Put the obvious in terms of the unintelligible.* When you write that "the product of the activity of janitors is expended in the identical locality in which that activity takes place," your lay reader is in for a time of it. After an hour's puzzlement, he may conclude that janitors' sweepings are thrown on the town dump. See what you can do with this: "Each article sent to the cleaner is handled separately." You become a member of the guild in good standing if you put it like this: "Within the cleaning plant proper the business of the industry involves several well-defined processes, which, from the economic point of view, may be characterized simply by saying that most of them require separate handling of each individual garment or piece of material to be cleaned."

*Rule 5. Announce what you are going to say before you say it.* This pitcher's wind-up technique before hurling towards—not at— home plate has two varieties. First is the quick wind-up: "In the following section the policies of the administration will be considered." Then you become strong enough for the contortionist wind-up: "Perhaps more important, therefore, than the question of what standards are in a particular case, there are the questions of the extent of observance of these standards and the methods of their enforcement." Also you can play with reversing Rule 5 and *say what you have said after you have said it.*

*Rule 6. Defend your style as "scientific."* Look down on—not up to—clear simple English. Sneer at it as "popular." Scorn it as "journalistic." Explain your failure to put more mental sweat into your writing on the ground that "the social scientists who want to be scientific believe that we can have scientific description of human behavior and trustworthy predictions in the scientific sense only as we build adequate taxonomic systems for observable phenomena and symbolic systems for the manipulation of ideal and abstract entities."

For this explanation I am indebted to Lyman Bryson in the *Saturday Review of Literature* article (Oct. 13, 1945) "Writers: Enemies of Social Science." Standing on ground considerably of his own choosing, Mr. Bryson argued against judging social science writing by literary standards.

Social scientists are not criticized because they are not literary artists. The trouble with social science does not lie in its special vocabulary. Those words are doubtless chosen with great care. The trouble is that too few social scientists take enough care with words outside their special vocabularies.

It is not too much to expect that teachers should be more competent in the art of explanation than those they teach. Teachers of social sciences diligently try to acquire knowledge: too few exert themselves enough to impart it intelligently.

Too long has this been excused as "the academic mind." It should be called by what it is: intellectual laziness and grubby-mindedness.

For questions and exercises, see p. 427 and p. 531.

## UNRIPE FRUITS

### Incoherence in the Philosopher: Mr. John Dewey

#### J. W. BEACH

Half of the absurdities of Mr. Hergesheimer arise from affectation working hand and hand with carelessness. He affects the careless manner of a cultivated gentleman and expert in writing, a sort of Lord Byron of prose, improvising his oriental tales while making his toilet before his looking-glass. Different as is Professor Dewey—worlds distant from Mr. Hergesheimer in subject matter and tone—yet there is here, too, I suspect a certain pride of carelessness. Mr. Dewey is the champion of the natural and instinctive as against the pedantic and formally logical in thought and conduct. And there may be some connection between his general attitude toward life and thought, and the carelessness which often makes him such hard reading. I am greatly in sympathy with many of the opinions of Mr. Dewey, and I recognize his very great reputation among American philosophers. But his extreme want of precision in writing makes me uneasy—it makes me wonder if there is something unsound about his thinking. If that is so, his eminence among American thinkers, the readiness with which he is generally accepted as a profound thinker, would be a measure of what we lack in the way of critical culture.

UNRIPE FRUITS: From *The Outlook for American Prose* by J. W. Beach. Reprinted by permission of The University of Chicago Press.

As an example of Mr. Dewey's writing, I shall cite a somewhat lengthy passage taken from his interesting book on *Human Nature and Conduct*. It is from the first chapter, in which Mr. Dewey is setting forth the idea that standards in conduct are the product of social conditions, and particularly that rules of conduct, codes of morality, are often the means by which the ruling caste enforces its own will upon the subject castes and thereby establishes its supremacy. Mr. Dewey goes on to point out the need for a scientific study of human nature if we are to have a proper understanding of such rules of conduct. I shall first quote as it stands one continuous passage in which he develops this phase of the theme. I shall then offer a new rendering of the passage, including such changes as are necessary to make the author's meaning intelligible to the ordinary reader, putting in italics those sentences or phrases which represent a radical alteration of the original or which have been supplied for the sake of clearness. And then I shall go on to analyze a few sentences of the original in order to show the complicated process of reconstruction which it is necessary for any reader to go through in order to arrive at the author's meaning. If it is objected that this is nothing more or less than a pedantic re-writing of a theme such as is proper in college classes in composition, I can only say that that is precisely my business in life and the way in which I justify my existence in so far as I do so at all.

Here, then, is the passage from Mr. Dewey.

But no matter how much men in authority have turned moral rules into an agency of class supremacy, any theory which attributes the origin of rule to deliberate design is false. To take advantage of conditions after they have come into existence is one thing; to create them for the sake of an advantage to accrue is quite another thing. We must go back to the bare fact of social division into superior and inferior. To say that accident produced social conditions is to perceive that they were not produced by intelligence. Lack of understanding of human nature is the primary cause of disregard of it. Lack of insight always ends in despising or else unreasoned admiration. When men had no scientific knowledge of physical nature they either passively submitted to it or sought to control it magically. What cannot be understood cannot be managed intelligently. It has to be forced into subjection from without. The opaqueness of human nature to reason is equivalent to a belief in its intrinsic irregularity. Hence a decline in the authority of social oligarchy was accompanied by a rise of scientific interest in human nature. This means that the make-up and working of human forces affords a basis for moral ideas and ideals. Our science of human nature in comparison with physical sciences is rudimentary, and morals which are concerned with the health, efficiency and happiness of a development of human nature are correspondingly elementary. These pages are a discussion of some phases of the ethical change involved in positive respect for human nature when the latter is associated with scientific knowledge.

Now let us try to put into clear and coherent terms what Professor Dewey seems to mean:

But no matter how much men in authority have turned moral rules into an agency of class supremacy, *it would be a mistake to suppose that these rules were created originally with the* deliberate design *of using them for this purpose.* It is one thing to take advantage of conditions after they have come into existence; it is quite another thing to create them for the sake of an advantage to accrue. *To understand a system of morals,* we must go back to the division into classes—into superior and inferior. *We shall find that social conditions grew up spontaneously, and that is as much as to say that they were not the product of deliberate thought. Just the contrary, they were the product of a want of intelligence in interpreting human nature. Human nature was disregarded in framing moral rules because it was not understood.* Lack of insight *into anything* leads to its being despised or else admired unreasonably. *It is so with* physical nature; when man had no knowledge of it, they either passively submitted to it or sought to control it magically. What cannot be understood cannot be understood intelligently. It has to be forced into subjection from without. *In the case of* human nature, *the difficulty of understanding it leads to the assumption that it is essentially arbitrary in its action, only to be controlled from without. This is the assumption of all social oligarchy, and it is an assumption which social oligarchy finds it to its advantage to maintain. And this in turn prevents the growth of any scientific study of human nature. But* a decline in the authority of social oligarchy is *naturally* accompanied by the rise of *that* scientific interest in human nature *to which social oligarchy has been opposed. The scientific assumption is that the principles of morality should be sought in the very constitution of human nature, and based on a study of* the make-up and *actual* working of human forces. *It must be acknowledged that,* in comparison with the physical sciences, our science of human nature is rudimentary, and morals—*which are concerned with the development of human nature into something* healthful, efficient and happy—are correspondingly elementary. These pages *will be taken up with* a discussion of some phases of the ethical change involved in *that* respect for human nature *which results from its being studied in connection* with scientific knowledge *in general*.

It would be too long an undertaking to explain the necessity of the several dozen changes made in order that the course of this thought may be clear to the reader, if indeed I have succeeded in making it clear. But it would be worth our while to analyze, through several sentences, the process of trial and error, of guess and reconstruction, in which the reader must at every point engage in order to make any connected sense. Let us begin with the sentence a little below the middle of the passage, "The opaqueness of human nature to reason is equivalent to a belief in its intrinsic irregularity." The first thing the reader does instinctively is to get rid of the words "equivalent to." No fact about human nature is equivalent to any belief about it. Facts are one thing, beliefs another. The general connection makes the reader understand that the author means to say, "The opaqueness of human nature to reason leads to a belief in its intrinsic irregularity." The reader then approaches the phrase, "the opaqueness of human nature to reason." He first translates the figurative phrase into one more consistent with English idiom, and has, "the imperviousness of human nature to reason." He supposes it to mean the fact that human nature is dense and irrational, that reason cannot penetrate into it. And so he reads, for simplification, "The irrationality of human nature leads to a belief in its intrinsic irregularity." But that, in the particular connection, makes no sense, and the reader tries again. He takes his cue from the statement two sentences back that what cannot be understood cannot be managed intelligently. Perhaps the author means, not the imperviousness of human nature to reason in the abstract, the irrationality of human nature, but its imperviousness to the understanding of the observer—the difficulty of understanding it. So he tries that. "The difficulty of understanding human nature leads to a belief in its intrinsic irregularity." That does make sense in the connection, providing one develops a little the connotations of the word "irregularity." A thing that is irregular is arbitrary in its action, not to be controlled by reference to its own laws, but only to be forced into subjection from without. So the reader puts the sentence into a form that will suggest that connection, and he proceeds to the following sentence: "The difficulty of understanding human nature leads to an assumption that it is essentially irregular, or arbitrary, in its action. Hence a decline in the authority of social oligarchy was accompanied by a rise of scientific interest in human nature."

Here the reader is plunged into very great difficulties by the use of the logical connective "hence." He does not yet know that Mr. Dewey is particularly cavalier in the use of just this category of words which imply the strictest of logical bonds—that when he uses "in short" very likely he is not summing up the points already made but proceeding to add a new one; that when he says "therefore" he may be meaning "on the other hand." And so the reader takes the word "hence" in its strict sense, and tries to understand how it can be that "since the difficulty of understanding human nature leads to the assumption that it is arbitrary in its action, therefore the decline in the authority of social oligarchy was accompanied by a rise of scientific interest in human nature." He understands the contention that it is the social oligarchs who fail to understand human nature and who, assuming that it is arbitrary in its action, find that they can control it only by forcing it into subjection from without. He can also understand how a rise in scientific interest in human nature would result in a better understanding of it and would consequently undermine the authority of the social oligarchs. But he cannot see that the decline in the authority of the oligarchs would be accompanied by a spontaneous rise of scientific interest in human nature. It must be that some step in the chain of reasoning has been omitted. Perhaps Mr. Dewey means to say that the social oligarchs, finding it to their personal advantage to maintain the supposition that human nature is essentially arbitrary, instinctively discourage the rise of scientific interest in human nature for fear that it will undermine their prestige, and that consequently the rise of scientific interest in human nature is delayed until, through other causes, their authority begins to decline. In that case the missing link will have to be supplied by the reader.

The difficulty of understanding human nature leads to the assumption that it is essentially arbitrary in its action, only to be controlled by being forced into subjection from without. This is the assumption of all social oligarchy, and it is an assumption which all social oligarchy finds it to its own advantage to maintain. And this in turn prevents the growth of any scientific study of human nature. But the decline in the authority of social oligarchy was naturally accompanied by the rise of that scientific interest in human nature to which the social oligarchy had been opposed.

Now I do not guarantee that I have correctly rendered the thought of Mr. Dewey, nor even that what I have made of his passage is logical and consistent with itself. But I know that I have done the best I could, the best that a careful and diligent study of his writing makes possible. And I do not think that the difficulty lies in the subject matter, that Mr. Dewey is hard to read because he deals in difficult and abstruse matters. In general, the points he has to make are comparatively simple ones. But my impression is that he has not always thought them out to a clear issue, and still less has he taken pains to put them in terms that will make them clear to his reader.

I am not at present concerned with the lack of elegance that everywhere characterizes the writing of Mr. Dewey. It may be said that he is dealing with matters of practical importance, and that he has not time to concern himself with the luxuries and refinements of artistic writing. What I am considering is a lack of clearness, a lack of precision; and this looks in two directions. It makes hard reading; that is the rhetorical side of the matter. And I fear that it often implies confusion in the thought; and that looks back to the logical side of the matter, and tends to make us skeptical even as to the soundness and validity of his argument. It may be the pedantry of a student of rhetoric, but I cannot help suspecting that a writer who is constantly guilty of looseness in expression in detail may be sometimes guilty of looseness of thinking in the large.

It would take a long time for me to justify my statement that Mr. Dewey is constantly guilty of looseness in expression, but I will give an example or two of his want of precision in the use of synonyms. The word "quality" and the word "trait" are not words of such vague and all-inclusive meaning as many people seem to suppose; and it is evidence of unnecessary indolence of mind to use them to cover all the meanings of character, capacity, feature, circumstance, habit, faculty, etc., which Mr. Dewey does use them to cover. "The only way to achieve *traits* of carefulness," writes Mr. Dewey in *How We Think*, "The only way to achieve *traits* of carefulness, thoroughness, and continuity (traits that are, as we have seen, the elements of the 'logical') is by exercising these *traits* from the beginning." He means presumably, "The only way to acquire *habits* of carefulness, etc.," and "exercising these *faculties*." In another more extensive passage in the same book he uses "qualities" and "traits" interchangeably to designate the features, the facts, items, or circumstances connected with a certain boat by which one arrives at the conclusion that a certain object on the boat is or is not a flagpole.

Suppose we symbolize the *qualities* that suggest *flagpole* by the letters *a, b, c;* those that oppose this suggestion by the letters *p, q, r.* There is, of course, nothing inconsistent in the *qualities* themselves; but in pulling the mind to different and incongruous conclusions they conflict—hence the problem. Here the object is the discovery of some object (*O*), of which *a, b, c,* and *p, q, r,* may all be appropriate *traits*—just as, in our first case, it is to discover a course of action which will combine existing conditions and a remoter result in a single whole. The method of solution is also the same; discovery of intermediate *qualities* (the position of the pilot house, of the pole, the need of an index to the boat's direction) symbolized by *d, g, l, o,* which bind together otherwise incompatible *traits*.

Now these passages, typical of Mr. Dewey's way of writing in general, are taken from his elementary treatise, *How We Think,* a manual widely used in classes in education and logic. They represent the carefully considered writing of an educational expert, of a recognized authority on logic, a leader of the American Intelligentsia. He is a writer whose work is eagerly accepted by our most influential weekly reviews, and I think he may be taken as representative of American prose-writing of a serious character. The average untrained writer cannot surely be expected to do better than this scholar appointed to the highest posts in several of our greatest universities. As Chaucer has it, "And if gold rust, what shall iron do?" And so we have a plain indication of one of the reasons for the inferiority of American prose-writing to that of England or France. It is a simple lack of intellectual discipline.

For questions and exercises, see p. 328 and p. 427.

# DICKENS

## GEORGE SANTAYANA

If Christendom should lose everything that is now in the melting-pot, human life would still remain amiable and quite adequately human. I draw this comforting assurance from the pages of Dickens. Who could not be happy in his world? Yet there is nothing essential to it which the most destructive revolution would be able to destroy. People would still be as different, as absurd, and as charming as are his characters; the springs of kindness and folly in their lives would not be dried up. Indeed, there is much in Dickens which communism, if it came, would only emphasize and render universal. Those schools, those poorhouses, those prisons, with those surviving shreds of family life in them, show us what in the coming age (with some sanitary improvements) would be—the nursery and home of everybody. Everybody would be a waif, like Oliver Twist, like Smike, like Pip, and like David Copperfield; and amongst the agents and underlings of social government, to whom all these waifs would be entrusted, there would surely be a goodly sprinkling of Pecksniffs, Squeerses and Fangs; whilst the Fagins would be everywhere commissioners of the people. Nor would there fail to be, in high places and in low, the occasional sparkle of some Pickwick or Cheeryble Brothers or Sam Weller or Mark Tapley; and the voluble Flora Finchings would be everywhere in evidence, and the strong-minded Betsy Trotwoods in office. There would also be, among the inefficient, many a Dora and Agnes and Little Emily—with her charm but without her tragedy, since this is one of the things which the promised social reform would happily render impossible; I mean, by removing all the disgrace of it. The only element in the world of Dickens which would become obsolete would be the setting, the atmosphere of material instrumentalities and arrangements, as travelling by coach is obsolete; but travelling by rail, by motor, or by airship will emotionally be much the same thing. It is worth noting how such instrumentalities, which absorb modern life, are admired and enjoyed by Dickens, as they were by Homer. The poets ought not to be afraid of them; they exercise

DICKENS: From *Soliloquies in England and Later Soliloquies* by George Santayana. Reprinted by permission of Charles Scribner's Sons.

the mind congenially, and can be played with joyfully. Consider
the black ships and the chariots of Homer, the coaches and river-
boats of Dickens, and the aeroplanes of today; to what would an
unspoiled young mind turn with more interest? Dickens tells us
little of English sports, but he shares the sporting nature of the
Englishman, to whom the whole material world is a playing-field,
the scene giving ample scope to his love of action, legality, and
pleasant achievement. His art is to sport according to the rules of
the game, and to do things for the sake of doing them, rather than
for any ulterior motive.

It is remarkable, in spite of his ardent simplicity and openness
of heart, how insensible Dickens was to the greater themes of the
human imagination—religion, science, politics, art. He was a waif
himself, and utterly disinherited. For example, the terrible heritage
of contentious religions which fills the world seems not to exist for
him. In this matter he was like a sensitive child, with a most religious disposition, but no religious ideas. Perhaps, properly speaking, he had no *ideas* on any subject; what he had was a vast sympathetic participation in the daily life of mankind; and what he
saw of ancient institutions made him hate them, as needless sources
of oppression, misery, selfishness, and rancour. His one political
passion was philanthropy, genuine but felt only on its negative,
reforming side; of positive utopias or enthusiasms we hear nothing.
The political background of Christendom is only, so to speak, an
old faded back-drop for his stage; a castle, a frigate, a gallows,
and a large female angel with white wings standing above an
orphan by an open grave—a decoration which has to serve for all
the melodramas in his theatre, intellectually so provincial and poor.
Common life as it is lived was varied and lovable enough for
Dickens, if only the pests and cruelties could be removed from it.
Suffering wounded him, but not vulgarity; whatever pleased his
senses and whatever shocked them filled his mind alike with
romantic wonder, with the endless delight of observation. Vulgarity
—and what can we relish, if we recoil at vulgarity?—was innocent
and amusing; in fact, for the humorist, it was the spice of life. There
was more piety in being human than in being pious. In reviving
Christmas, Dickens transformed it from the celebration of a metaphysical mystery into a feast of overflowing simple kindness and
good cheer; the church bells were still there—in the orchestra; and

the angels of Bethlehem were still there—painted on the back curtain.
Churches, in his novels, are vague, desolate places where one has
ghastly experiences, and where only the pew-opener is human; and
such religious and political conflicts as he depicts in *Barnaby Rudge*
and in *A Tale of Two Cities* are street brawls and prison scenes
and conspiracies in taverns, without any indication of the contrasts
in mind or interests between the opposed parties. Nor had Dickens
any lively sense for fine art, classical tradition, science, or even
the manners and feelings of the upper classes in his own time and
country: in his novels we may almost say there is no army, no
navy, no church, no sport, no distant travel, no daring adventure,
no feeling for the watery wastes and the motley nations of the
planet, and—luckily, with his notion of them—no lords and ladies.
Even love of the traditional sort is hardly in Dickens's sphere—
I mean the soldierly passion in which a rather rakish gallantry was
sobered by devotion, and loyalty rested on pride. In Dickens love
is sentimental or benevolent or merry or sneaking or canine; in his
last book he was going to describe a love that was passionate and
criminal; but love for him was never chivalrous, never poetical.
What he paints most tragically is a quasi-paternal devotion in the
old to the young, the love of Mr. Peggotty for Little Emily, or
of Solomon Gills for Walter Gay. A series of shabby little adventures, such as might absorb the interest of an average youth, were
romantic enough for Dickens.

I say he was disinterested, but he inherited the most terrible
negations. Religion lay on him like the weight of the atmosphere
sixteen pounds to the square inch, yet never noticed nor mentioned.
He lived and wrote in the shadow of the most awful prohibitions.
Hearts petrified by legality and falsified by worldliness offered,
indeed, a good subject for a novelist, and Dickens availed himself
of it to the extent of always contrasting natural goodness and happiness with whatever is morose; and his morose people were wicked,
not virtuous in their own way; so that the protest of his temperament against his environment never took a radical form nor went
back to first principles. He needed to feel, in his writing, that he
was carrying the sympathies of every man with him. In him conscience was single, and he could not conceive how it could ever
be divided in other men. He denounced scandals without exposing
shams, and conformed willingly and scrupulously to the proprieties.

Lady Dedlock's secret, for instance, he treats as if it were the sin of Adam, remote, mysterious, inexpiable. Mrs. Dombey is not allowed to deceive her husband except by pretending to deceive him. The seduction of Little Emily is left out altogether, with the whole character of Steerforth, the development of which would have been so important in the moral experience of David Copperfield himself. But it is not public prejudice alone that plays the censor over Dickens's art; his own kindness and even weakness of heart act sometimes as marplots. The character of Miss Mowcher, for example, so brilliantly introduced, was evidently intended to be shady, and to play a very important part in the story; but its original in real life, which was recognized, had to be conciliated, and the sequel was omitted and patched up with an apology— itself admirable—for the poor dwarf. Such a sacrifice does honour to Dickens's heart; but artists should meditate on their works in time, and it is easy to remove any too great likeness in a portrait by a few touches making it more consistent than real people are apt to be; and in this case, if the little creature had been really guilty, how much more subtle and tragic her apology for herself might have been, like that of the bastard Edmund in *King Lear!* So, too, in *Dombey and Son,* Dickens could not bear to let Walter Gay turn out badly, as he had been meant to do, and to break his uncle's heart as well as the heroine's; he was accordingly transformed into a stage hero miraculously saved from shipwreck, and Florence was not allowed to reward the admirable Toots, as she should have done, with her trembling hand. But Dickens was no free artist; he had more genius than taste, a warm fancy not aided by a thorough understanding of complex characters. He worked under pressure for money and applause, and often had to cheapen in execution what his inspiration had so vividly conceived.

What, then, is left, if Dickens had all these limitations? In our romantic disgust we might be tempted to say, Nothing. But in fact almost everything is left, almost everything that counts in the daily life of mankind, or that by its presence or absence can determine whether life shall be worth living or not; because a simple good life is worth living, and an elaborate bad life is not. There remains in the first place eating and drinking; relished not bestially, but humanly, jovially, as the sane and exhilarating basis for everything else. This is a sound English beginning; but the immediate sequel,

as the England of that day presented it to Dickens, is no less delightful. There is the ruddy glow of the hearth; the sparkle of
glasses and brasses and well-scrubbed pewter; the savoury fumes
of the hot punch, after the tingle of the wintry air; the coaching
scenes, the motley figures and absurd incidents of travel; the changing sights and joys of the road. And then, to balance this, the traffic
of ports and cities, the hubbub of crowded streets, the luxury of
shop windows and of palaces not to be entered; the procession
of the passers-by, shabby or ludicrously genteel; the dingy look and
musty smell of their lodgings; the labyrinth of back-alleys, courts,
and mews, with their crying children, and scolding old women,
and listless, half-drunken loiterers. These sights, like fables, have
a sort of moral in them to which Dickens was very sensitive; the
important airs of nobodies on great occasions, the sadness and pre-
occupation of the great as they hasten by in their mourning or on
their pressing affairs; the sadly comic characters of the tavern; the
diligence of shop-keepers, like squirrels turning in their cages; the
children peeping out everywhere like grass in an untrodden street;
the charm of humble things, the nobleness of humble people, the
horror of crime, the ghastliness of vice, the deft hand and shining
face of virtue passing through the midst of it all; and finally a
fresh wind of indifference and change blowing across our troubles
and clearing the most lurid sky.

I do not know whether it was Christian charity or naturalistic
insight, or a mixture of both (for they are closely akin) that attracted
Dickens particularly to the deformed, the half-witted, the abandoned, or those impeded or misunderstood by virtue of some singular inner consecration. The visible moral of these things, when
brutal prejudice does not blind us to it, comes very near to true
philosophy; one turn of the screw, one flash of reflection, and we
have understood nature and human morality and the relation
between them.

In his love of roads and wayfarers, of river-ports and wharves
and the idle or sinister figures that lounge about them, Dickens was
like Walt Whitman; and I think a second Dickens may any day
appear in America, when it is possible in that land of hurry to
reach the same degree of saturation, the same unquestioning pleasure in the familiar facts. The spirit of Dickens would be better able
to do justice to America than was that of Walt Whitman; because

America, although it may seem nothing but a noisy nebula to the impressionist, is not a nebula but a concourse of very distinct individual bodies, natural and social, each with its definite interests and story. Walt Whitman had a sort of transcendental philosophy which swallowed the universe whole, supposing there was a universal spirit in things identical with the absolute spirit that observed them; but Dickens was innocent of any clap-trap, and remained a true spirit in his own person. Kindly and clear-sighted, but self-identical and unequivocally human, he glided through the slums like one of his own little heroes, uncontaminated by their squalor and confusion, courageous and firm in his clear allegiances amid the flux of things, a pale angel at the Carnival, his heart aflame, his voice always flute-like in its tenderness and warning. This is the true relation of spirit to existence, not the other which confuses them; for this earth (I cannot speak for the Universe at large) has no spirit of its own, but brings forth spirits only at certain points, in the hearts and brains of frail living creatures, who like insects flit through it, buzzing and gathering what sweets they can; and it is the spaces they traverse in this career, charged with their own moral burden, that they can report on or describe, not things rolling on to infinity in their vain tides. To be hypnotized by that flood would be a heathen idolatry. Accordingly Walt Whitman, in his comprehensive democratic vistas, could never see the trees for the wood, and remained incapable, for all his diffuse love of the human herd, of ever painting a character or telling a story; the very things in which Dickens was a master. It is this life of the individual, as it may be lived in a given nation, that determines the whole value of that nation to the poet, to the moralist, and to the judicious historian. But for the excellence of the typical single life, no nation deserves to be remembered more than the sands of the sea; and America will not be a success, if every American is a failure.

Dickens entered the theatre of this world by the stage door; the shabby little adventures of the actors in their private capacity replace for him the mock tragedies which they enact before a dreaming public. Mediocrity of circumstances and mediocrity of soul for ever return to the centre of his stage; a more wretched or a grander existence is sometimes broached, but the pendulum soon swings back, and we return, with the relief with which we put on our slippers after the most romantic excursion, to a golden mediocrity—to mutton and beer, and to love and babies in a suburban villa with one frowsy maid. Dickens is the poet of those acres of yellow brick streets which the traveller sees from the railway viaducts as he approaches London; they need a poet, and they deserve one, since a complete human life may very well be lived there. Their little excitements and sorrows, their hopes and humours are like those of the Wooden Midshipman in *Dombey and Son;* but the sea is not far off, and the sky—Dickens never forgets it— is above all those brief troubles. He had a sentiment in the presence of this vast flatness of human fates, in spite of their individual pungency, which I think might well be the dominant sentiment of mankind in the future; a sense of happy freedom in littleness, an open-eyed reverence and religion without words. This universal human anonymity is like a sea, an infinitive democratic desert, chock-full and yet the very image of emptiness, with nothing in it for the mind, except, as the Moslems say, the presence of Allah. Awe is the counterpart of humility—and this is perhaps religion enough. The atom in the universal vortex ought to be humble; he ought to see that, materially, he doesn't much matter, and that morally his loves are merely his own, without authority over the universe. He can admit without obloquy that he is what he is; and he can rejoice in his own being, and in that of all other things in so far as he can share it sympathetically. The apportionment of existence and of fortune is in Other Hands; his own portion is contentment, vision, love, and laughter.

Having humility, that most liberating of sentiments, having a true vision of human existence and joy in that vision, Dickens had in a superlative degree the gift of humour, of mimicry, of unrestrained farce. He was the perfect comedian. When people say Dickens exaggerates, it seems to me they can have no eyes and no ears. They probably have only *notions* of what things and people are; they accept them conventionally, at their diplomatic value. Their minds run on in the region of discourse, where there are masks only and no faces, ideas and no facts; they have little sense for those living grimaces that play from moment to moment upon the countenance of the world. The world is a perpetual caricature of itself; at every moment it is the mockery and the contradiction of what it is pretending to be. But as it nevertheless intends all the time to be something different and highly dignified, at the next moment it corrects and checks and tries to cover up the absurd thing it was; so that a conventional world, a world of masks, is superimposed on the reality, and passes in every sphere of human interest for the reality itself. Humour is the perception of this illusion, the fact allowed to pierce here and there through the convention, whilst the convention continues to be maintained, as if we had not observed its absurdity. Pure comedy is more radical, cruder, in a certain sense less human; because comedy throws the convention over altogether, revels for a moment in the fact, There take that! That's what you really are! At this the polite world pretends to laugh, not tolerantly as it does at humour, but a little angrily. It does not like to see itself by chance in the glass, without having had time to compose its features for demure self-contemplation. "What a bad mirror," it exclaims; "it must be convex or concave; for surely I never looked like that. Mere caricature, farce, and horse play. Dickens exaggerates; *I* never was so sentimental as that; *I* never saw anything so dreadful; *I* don't believe there were ever any people like Quilp, or Squeers, or Serjeant Buzfuz." But the polite world is lying; there *are* such people; we are such people ourselves in our true moments, in our veritable impulses; but we are careful to stifle and to hide those moments from ourselves and from the world; to purse and pucker ourselves into the mask of our conventional personality; and so simpering, we profess that it is very coarse and inartistic of Dickens to undo our life's work for us in an instant, and remind us of what we are. And as to other people, though we may allow that considered superficially they are often absurd, we do not wish to dwell on their eccentricities nor to mimic them. On the contrary, it is good manners to look away quickly, to suppress a smile, and to say to ourselves that the ludicrous figure in the street is not at all comic, but a dull ordinary Christian, and that it is foolish to give any importance to the fact that its hat has blown off, that it has slipped on an orange-peel and unintentionally sat on the pavement, that it has a pimple on its nose, that its one tooth projects over its lower lip, that it is angry with things in general, and that it is looking everywhere for the penny which it holds tightly in its hand. That may fairly represent the moral condition of most of us at most times; but we do not want to think of it; we do not want to see; we gloss the fact over; we console ourselves before we are grieved, and reassert our composure before we have laughed. We are afraid, ashamed, anxious to be spared. What displeases us in Dickens is that he does not spare us; he mimics things to the full; he dilates and exhausts and repeats; he wallows. He is too intent on the passing experience to look over his shoulder, and consider whether we have not already understood, and had enough. He is not thinking of us; he is obeying the impulse of the passion, the person, or the story he is enacting. This faculty, which renders him a consummate comedian, is just what alienated from him a later generation in which people of taste were aesthetes and virtuous people were higher snobs; they wanted a mincing art, and he gave them copious improvisation, they wanted analysis and development, and he gave them absolute comedy. I must confess, though the fault is mine and not his, that sometimes his absoluteness is too much for me. When I come to the death of Little Nell, or to What the Waves were always Saying, or even to the incorrigible perversities of the pretty Dora, I skip. I can't take my liquor neat in such draughts, and my inner man says to Dickens, Please don't. But then I am a coward in so many ways! There are so many things in this world that I skip, as I skip the undiluted Dickens! When I reach Dover on a rough day, I wait there until the Channel is smoother; am I not travelling for pleasure? But my prudence does not blind me to the admirable virtue of the sailors that cross in all weathers, not even to the automatic determination of the seasick ladies, who might so easily have followed my example, if they were not the slaves of their railway tickets and of their labelled luggage. They are loyal to their tour, and I to my philosophy. Yet as wrapped in my great-coat and sure of a good dinner, I pace the windy pier and soliloquize, I feel the superiority of the bluff tar, glad of breeze, stretching a firm arm to the unsteady passenger, and watching with a masterful thrill of emotion the home cliffs receding and the foreign coasts ahead. It is only courage (which Dickens had without knowing it) and universal kindness (which he knew he had) that are requisite to nerve us for a true vision of this world. And as some of us are cowards about crossing the Channel, and others about "crossing the bar," so almost everybody is a coward about his own humanity. We do not consent to be absurd, though absurd we are. We have no fundamental humility. We do not wish the moments of our lives to be caught by a quick eye in their grotesque initiative, and to be pilloried in this way before our own eyes. For that reason we don't like Dickens, and don't like comedy, and don't like the truth. Dickens could don the comic mask with innocent courage; he could wear it with a grace, ease, and irresistible vivacity seldom given to men. We must go back for anything like it to the very greatest comic poets, to Shakespeare or to Aristophanes. Who else, for instance, could have penned this:

"It was all Mrs. Bumble. She *would* do it," urged Mr. Bumble; first looking around to ascertain that his partner had left the room.

"That is no excuse," replied Mr. Brownlow. "You were present on the occasion of the destruction of these trinkets, and indeed are the more guilty of the two, in the eye of the law; for the law supposes that your wife acts under your direction."

"If the law supposes that," said Mr. Bumble, squeezing his hat emphatically in both hands, "the law is a ass, a idiot. If that's the eye of the law, the law is a bachelor; and the worst I wish the law is, that his eye may be opened by experience—by experience."

Laying great stress on the repetition of these two words, Mr. Bumble fixed his hat on very tight, and putting his hands in his pockets, followed his helpmate downstairs.

This is high comedy; the irresistible, absurd, intense dream of the old fool, personifying the law in order to convince and to punish it. I can understand that this sort of thing should not be common in English literature, nor much relished; because pure comedy is scornful, merciless, devastating, holding no door open to anything beyond. Cultivated English feeling winces at this brutality, although the common people love it in clowns and in puppet shows; and I think they are right, Dickens, who surely was tender enough, had so irresistible a comic genius that it carried him beyond the gentle humour which most Englishmen possess to the absolute grotesque reality. Squeers, for instance, when he sips the wretched dilution which he has prepared for his starved and shivering little pupils, smacks his lips and cries: "Here's a richness!" It is savage comedy; humour would come in if we understood (what Dickens does not tell us) that the little creatures were duly impressed and thought the thin liquid truly delicious. I suspect that English sensibility prefers the humour and wit of Hamlet to the pure comedy of Falstaff; and that even in Aristophanes it seeks

consolation in the lyrical poetry for the flaying of human life in
the comedy itself. Tastes are free; but we should not deny that in
merciless and rollicking comedy life is caught in the act. The most
grotesque creatures of Dickens are not exaggerations or mockeries
of something other than themselves; they arise because nature
generates them, like toadstools; they exist because they can't help
it, as we all do. The fact that these perfectly self-justified beings
are absurd appears only by comparison, and from outside; circumstances or the expectations of other people, make them ridiculous
and force them to contradict themselves; but in nature it is no
crime to be exceptional. Often, but for the savagery of the average
man, it would not even be a misfortune. The sleepy fat boy in
*Pickwick* looks less foolish; but in himself he is no more foolish,
no less solidly justified, than a pumpkin lying on the ground.
Toots seems ridiculous; and we laugh heartily at his incoherence,
his beautiful waistcoats, and his extreme modesty; but when did
anybody more obviously grow into what he is because he couldn't
grow otherwise? So with Mr. Pickwick, and Sam Weller, and Mrs.
Gamp, and Micawber, and all the rest of this wonderful gallery;
they are ridiculous only by accident, and in the context in which
they never intended to appear. If Oedipus and Lear and Cleopatra
do not seem ridiculous, it is only because tragic reflection had taken
them out of the context in which, in real life, they would have
figured. If we saw them as facts, and not as emanations of a poet's
dream, we should laugh at them till doomsday; what grotesque
presumption, what silly whims, what mad contradiction of the
simplest realities! Yet we should not laugh at them without feeling
how real their griefs were; as real and terrible as the griefs of
children and dreams. But facts, however serious inwardly, are
always absurd outwardly; and the just critic of life sees both truths
at once, as Cervantes did in *Don Quixote*. A pompous idealist who
does not see the ridiculous in *all* things is the dupe of his sympathy
and abstraction; and a clown, who does not see that these ridiculous
figures are living quite in earnest, is the dupe of his egotism.
Dickens saw the absurdity, and understood the life; and I think he
was a good philosopher.

It is usual to compare Dickens with Thackeray, which is like
comparing the grape with the gooseberry; there are obvious points
of resemblance, and the gooseberry has some superior qualities of

its own; but you can't make red wine with it. The wine of Dickens is of the richest, the purest, the sweetest, the most fortifying to the blood; there is distilled in it, with the perfection of comedy, the perfection of morals. I do not mean, of course, that Dickens appreciated all the values that human life has or might have; that is beyond any man. Even the greatest philosophers, such as Aristotle, have not always much imagination to conceive forms of happiness or folly other than those which their age or their temperament reveals to them; their insight runs only to discovering the *principle* of happiness, that it is the spontaneous life of any sort harmonized with circumstances. The sympathies and imagination of Dickens, vivid in their sphere, were no less limited in range; and of course it was not his business to find philosophic formulas; nevertheless I call his the perfection of morals for two reasons: that he put the distinction between good and evil in the right place, and that he felt this distinction intensely. A moralist might have excellent judgement, he might see what sort of life is spontaneous in a given being and how far it may be harmonized with circumstances, yet his heart might remain cold, he might not suffer nor rejoice with the suffering or joy he foresaw. Humanitarians like Bentham and Mill, who talked about the greatest happiness of the greatest number, might conceivably be moral prigs in their own persons, and they might have been chilled to the bone in their theoretic love of mankind, if they had had the wit to imagine in what, as a matter of fact, the majority would place their happiness. Even if their theory had been correct (which I think it was in intention, though not in statement) they would then not have been perfect moralists, because their maxims would not have expressed their hearts. In expressing their hearts, they ought to have embraced one of those forms of "idealism" by which men fortify themselves in their bitter passions or in their helpless commitments; for they do not wish mankind to be happy in its own way, but in theirs. Dickens was not one of those moralists who summon every man to do himself the greatest violence so that he may not offend them, nor defeat their ideals. Love of the good of others is something that shines in every page of Dickens with a truly celestial splendour. How entirely limpid is his sympathy with life—a sympathy uncontaminated by dogma or pedantry or snobbery or bias of any kind! How generous is this keen, light spirit, how pure this open heart! And yet, in spite of this extreme sensibility, not the least wobbling; no deviation from a just severity of judgement, from an uncompromising distinction between white and black. And this happens as it ought to happen; sympathy is not checked by a flatly contrary prejudice or commandment, by some categorical imperative irrelevant to human nature; the check, like the cheer, comes by tracing the course of spontaneous impulse and circumstances that inexorably lead it to success or to failure. There is a bed to this stream, freely as the water may flow; when it comes to this precipice it must leap, when it runs over these pebbles it must sing, and when it spreads into that marsh it must become livid and malarial. The very sympathy with human impulse quickens in Dickens the sense of danger; his very joy in joy makes him stern to what kills it. How admirably drawn are his surly villains! No rhetorical vilification of them, as in a sermon; no exaggeration of their qualms or fears; rather a sense of how obvious and human all their courses seem from their point of view; and yet no sentimental apology for them, no romantic worship of rebels in their madness or crime. The pity of it, the waste of it all, are seen not by a second vision but by the same original vision which revealed the lure and the drift of the passion. Vice is a monster here of such sorry mien, that the longer we see it the more we deplore it; that other sort of vice which Pope found so seductive was perhaps only some innocent impulse artificially suppressed, and called a vice because it broke out inconveniently and displeased the company. True vice is human nature strangled by the suicide of attempting the impossible. Those so self-justified villains of Dickens never elude their fates. Bill Sikes is not let off, neither is Nancy; the oddly benevolent Magwitch does not escape from the net, nor does the unfortunate young Richard Carstone, victim of the Circumlocution Office. The horror and ugliness of their fall are rendered with the hand of a master; we see here, as in the world, that in spite of the romanticists it is not virtue to rush enthusiastically along any road. I think Dickens is one of the best friends mankind has ever had. He has held the mirror up to nature, and of its reflected fragments has composed a fresh world, where the men and women differ from real people only in that they live in a literary medium, so that all ages and places may know them. And they are worth knowing, just as one's neighbours are, for their picturesque characters and their pathetic fates. Their names should be in every child's mouth; they ought to be adopted members of every household. Their stories cause the merriest and the sweetest chimes to ring in the fancy, without confusing our moral judgement or alienating our interest from the motley commonplaces of daily life. In every English-speaking home, in the four quarters of the globe, parents and children will do well to read Dickens aloud of a winter's evening; they will love winter, and one another, and God the better for it. What a wreath that will be of ever-fresh holly, thick with bright berries, to hang to this poet's memory—the very crown he would have chosen!

For questions and exercises, see p. 334, p. 358, p. 431, p. 521, and p. 531.

# WORDSWORTH IN THE TROPICS

## ALDOUS HUXLEY

In the neighbourhood of latitude fifty north, and for the last hundred years or thereabouts, it has been an axiom that Nature is divine and morally uplifting. For good Wordsworthians—and most serious-minded people are now Wordsworthians, either by direct inspiration or at second hand—a walk in the country is the equivalent of going to church, a tour through Westmorland is as good as a pilgrimage to Jerusalem. To commune with the fields and waters, the woodlands and the hills, is to commune, according to our modern and northern ideas, with the visible manifestations of the "Wisdom and Spirit of the Universe."

The Wordsworthian who exports this pantheistic worship of Nature to the tropics is liable to have his religious convictions somewhat rudely disturbed. Nature, under a vertical sun, and nourished by the equatorial rains, is not at all like that chaste, mild deity who presides over the *Gemütlichkeit,* the prettiness, the cosy sublimities of the Lake District. The worst that Wordsworth's goddess ever did to him was to make him hear

> Low breathings coming after me, and sounds
> Of undistinguishable motion, steps
> Almost as silent as the turf they trod;

WORDSWORTH IN THE TROPICS: From *Do What You Will* by Aldous Huxley. Copyright, 1929, by Aldous Huxley.

was to make him realize, in the shape of "a huge peak, black and huge," the existence of "unknown modes of being." He seems to have imagined that this was the worst Nature *could* do. A few weeks in Malaya or Borneo would have undeceived him. Wandering in the hothouse darkness of the jungle, he would not have felt so serenely certain of those "Presences of Nature," those "Souls of Lonely Places," which he was in the habit of worshipping on the shores of Windermere and Rydal. The sparse inhabitants of the equatorial forest are all believers in devils. When one has visited, in even the most superficial manner, the places where they live, it is difficult not to share their faith. The jungle is marvellous, fantastic, beautiful; but it is also terrifying, it is also profoundly sinister. There is something in what, for lack of a better word, we must call the character of great forests—even in those of temperate lands—which is foreign, appalling, fundamentally and utterly inimical to intruding man. The life of those vast masses of swarming vegetation is alien to the human spirit and hostile to it. Meredith, in his "Woods of Westermaine," has tried reassuringly to persuade us that our terrors are unnecessary, that the hostility of these vegetable forces is more apparent than real, and that if we will but trust Nature we shall find our fears transformed into serenity, joy, and rapture. This may be sound philosophy in the neighbourhood of Dorking; but it begins to be dubious even in the forests of Germany—there is too much of them for a human being to feel himself at ease within their enormous glooms; and when the woods of Borneo are substituted for those of Westermaine, Meredith's comforting doctrine becomes frankly ridiculous.

It is not the sense of solitude that distresses the wanderer in equatorial jungles. Loneliness is bearable enough—for a time, at any rate. There is something actually rather stimulating and exciting about being in an empty place where there is no life but one's own. Taken in reasonably small doses, the Sahara exhilarates, like alcohol. Too much of it, however (I speak, at any rate, for myself), has the depressing effect of the second bottle of Burgundy. But in any case it is not loneliness that oppresses the equatorial traveller: it is too much company; it is the uneasy feeling that he is an alien in the midst of an innumerable throng of hostile beings. To us who live beneath a temperate sky and in the age of Henry Ford, the worship of Nature comes almost naturally. It is easy to love a feeble and already conquered enemy. But an enemy with whom one is still at war, an unconquered, unconquerable, ceaselessly active enemy—no; one does not, one should not, love him. One respects him, perhaps; one has a salutary fear of him; and one goes on fighting. In our latitudes the hosts of Nature have mostly been vanquished and enslaved. Some few detachments, it is true, still hold the field against us. There are wild woods and mountains, marshes and heaths, even in England. But they are there only on sufferance, because we have chosen, out of our good pleasure, to leave them their freedom. It has not been worth our while to reduce them to slavery. We love them because we are the masters, because we know that at any moment we can overcome them as we overcame their fellows. The inhabitants of the tropics have no such comforting reasons for adoring the sinister forces which hem them in on every side. For us, the notion "river" implies (how obviously!) the notion "bridge." When we think of a plain, we think of agriculture, towns, and good roads. The corollary of mountain is tunnel; of swamp, an embankment; of distance, a railway. At latitude zero, however, the obvious is not the same as with us. Rivers imply wading, swimming, alligators. Plains mean swamps, forests, fevers. Mountains are either dangerous or impassable. To travel is to hack one's way laboriously through a tangled, prickly, and venomous darkness. "God made the country," said Cowper, in his rather too blank verse. In New Guinea he would have had his doubts; he would have longed for the man-made town.

The Wordsworthian adoration of Nature has two principal defects. The first, as we have seen, is that it is only possible in a country where Nature has been nearly or quite enslaved to man. The second is that it is only possible for those who are prepared to falsify their immediate intuitions of Nature. For Nature, even in the temperate zone, is always alien and inhuman, and occasionally diabolic. Meredith explicitly invites us to explain any unpleasant experiences away. We are to interpret them, Pangloss fashion, in terms of a preconceived philosophy; after which, all will surely be for the best in the best of all possible Westermaines. Less openly, Wordsworth asks us to make the same falsification of immediate experience. It is only very occasionally that he admits the existence in the world around him of those "unknown modes of

being" of which our immediate intuitions of things make us so dis-
quietingly aware. Normally what he does is to pump the dangerous Unknown out of Nature and refill the emptied forms of hills
and woods, flowers and waters, with something more reassuringly
familiar—with humanity, with Anglicanism. He will not admit that
a yellow primrose is simply a yellow primrose—beautiful, but essentially strange, having its own alien life apart. He wants it to possess
some sort of soul, to exist humanly, not simply flowerily. He wants
the earth to be more than earthy, to be a divine person. But the
life of vegetation is radically unlike the life of man: the earth has
a mode of being that is certainly not the mode of being of a person. "Let Nature be your teacher," says Wordsworth. The advice
is excellent. But how strangely he himself puts it into practice! Instead of listening humbly to what the teacher says, he shuts his
ears and himself dictates the lesson he desires to hear. The pupil
knows better than his master; the worshipper substitutes his own
oracles for those of the god. Instead of accepting the lesson as it
is given to his immediate intuitions, he distorts it rationalistically
into the likeness of a parson's sermon or a professorial lecture. Our
direct intuitions of Nature tell us that the world is bottomlessly
strange: alien, even when it is kind and beautiful; having innumerable modes of being that are not our modes; always mysteriously not personal, not conscious, not moral; often hostile and
sinister; sometimes even unimaginably, because inhumanly, evil.
In his youth, it would seem, Wordsworth left his direct intuitions
of the world unwarped.

> The sounding cataract
> Haunted me like a passion: the tall rock,
> The mountains, and the deep and gloomy wood,
> Their colours and their forms, were then to me
> An appetite; a feeling and a love,
> That had no need of a remoter charm,
> By thought supplied, nor any interest
> Unborrowed from the eye.

As the years passed, however, he began to interpret them in terms
of a preconceived philosophy. Procrustes-like, he tortured his feelings and perceptions until they fitted his system. By the time he
was thirty,

The immeasurable height
Of woods decaying, never to be decayed,
The stationary blasts of waterfalls—
The torrents shooting from the clear blue sky,
The rocks that muttered close upon our ears,
Black drizzling crags that spake by the wayside
As if a voice were in them, the sick sight
And giddy prospect of the raving stream,
The unfettered clouds and regions of the heavens,
Tumult and peace, the darkness and the light—
Were all like workings of one mind, the features
Of the same face, blossoms upon one tree,
Characters of the great Apocalypse,
The types and symbols of eternity,
Of first, and last, and midst, and without end.

"Something far more deeply interfused" had made its appearance on the Wordsworthian scene. The god of Anglicanism had crept under the skin of things, and all the stimulatingly inhuman strangeness of Nature had become as flatly familiar as a page from a textbook of metaphysics or theology. As familiar and as safely simple. Pantheistically interpreted, our intuitions of Nature's endless varieties of impersonal mysteriousness lose all their exciting and disturbing quality. It makes the world seem delightfully cosy, if you can pretend that all the many alien things about you are really only manifestations of one person. It is fear of the labyrinthine flux and complexity of phenomena that has driven men to philosophy, to science, to theology—fear of the complex reality driving them to invent a simpler, more manageable, and, therefore, consoling fiction. For simple, in comparison with the external reality of which we have direct intuitions, childishly simple is even the most elaborate and subtle system devised by the human mind. Most of the philosophical systems hitherto popular have not been subtle and elaborate even by human standards. Even by human standards they have been crude, bald, preposterously straightforward. Hence their popularity. Their simplicity has rendered them instantly comprehensible. Weary with much wandering in the maze of phenomena, frightened by the inhospitable strangeness of the world, men have rushed into the systems prepared for them by philosophers and founders of religions, as they would rush from a dark jungle into the haven of a well-lit, commodious house. With a sigh of relief and a thankful feeling that here at last is their true home, they settle down in their snug metaphysical villa and go to sleep. And how furious they are when any one comes rudely knocking at the door to tell them that their villa is jerry-built, dilapidated, unfit for human habitation, even non-existent! Men have been burnt at the stake for even venturing to criticize the colour of the front door or the shape of the third-floor windows.

That man must build himself some sort of metaphysical shelter in the midst of the jungle of immediately apprehended reality is obvious. No practical activity, no scientific research, no speculation is possible without some preliminary hypothesis about the nature and the purpose of things. The human mind cannot deal with the universe directly, nor even with its own immediate intuitions of the universe. Whenever it is a question of thinking about the world or of practically modifying it, men can only work on a symbolic plan of the universe, only on a simplified two-dimensional map of things abstracted by the mind out of the complex and multifarious reality of the immediate intuition. History shows that these hypotheses about the nature of things are valuable even when, as later experience reveals, they are false. Man approaches the unattainable truth through a succession of errors. Confronted by the strange complexity of things, he invents, quite arbitrarily, a simple hypothesis to explain and justify the world. Having invented, he proceeds to act and think in terms of this hypothesis, as though it were correct. Experience gradually shows him where his hypothesis is unsatisfactory and how it should be modified. Thus, great scientific discoveries have been made by man seeking to verify quite erroneous theories about the nature of things. The discoveries have necessitated a modification of the original hypotheses, and further discoveries have been made in the effort to verify the modifications —discoveries which, in their turn, have led to yet further modifications. And so on, indefinitely. Philosophical and religious hypotheses, being less susceptible of experimental verification than the hypotheses of science, have undergone far less modification. For example, the pantheistic hypothesis of Wordsworth is an ancient doctrine, which human experience has hardly modified throughout history. And rightly, no doubt. For it is obvious that there must be some sort of unity underlying the diversity of phenomena; for if there were not, the world would be quite unknowable. Indeed, it is precisely in the knowableness of things, in the very fact that they are known, that their fundamental unity consists. The world which we know, and which our minds have fabricated out of goodness knows what mysterious things in themselves, possesses the unity which our minds have imposed upon it. It is part of our thought, hence fundamentally homogeneous. Yes, the world is obviously one. But at the same time it is no less obviously diverse. For if the world were absolutely one, it would no longer be knowable, it would cease to exist. Thought must be divided against itself before it can come to any knowledge of itself. Absolute oneness is absolute nothingness: homogeneous perfection, as the Hindus perceived and courageously recognized, is equivalent to nonexistence, is nirvana. The Christian idea of a perfect heaven that is something other than a non-existence is a contradiction in terms. The world in which we live may be fundamentally one, but it is a unity divided up into a great many diverse fragments. A tree, a table, a newspaper, a piece of artificial silk are all made of wood. But they are, none the less, distinct and separate objects. It is the same with the world at large. Our immediate intuitions are of diversity. We have only to open our eyes to recognize a multitude of different phenomena. These intuitions of diversity are as correct, as well justified, as is our intellectual conviction of the fundamental homogeneity of the various parts of the world with one another and with ourselves. Circumstances have led humanity to set an ever-increasing premium on the conscious and intellectual comprehension of things. Modern man's besetting temptation is to sacrifice his direct perceptions and spontaneous feelings to his reasoned reflections; to prefer in all circumstances the verdict of his intellect to that of his immediate intuitions. "L'homme est visiblement fait pour penser," says Pascal; "c'est toute sa dignité et toute son mérite; et tout son devoir est de penser comme il faut." Noble words; but do they happen to be true? Pascal seems to forget that man has something else to do besides think: he must live. Living may not be so dignified or so meritorious as thinking (particularly when you happen to be, like Pascal, a chronic invalid); but it is, perhaps unfortunately, a necessary process. If one would live well, one must live completely, with the whole being— with the body and the instincts, as well as with the conscious mind.

A life lived, as far as may be, exclusively from the consciousness and in accordance with the considered judgments of the intellect, is a stunted life, a half-dead life. This is a fact that can be confirmed by daily observation. But consciousness, the intellect, the spirit, have acquired an inordinate prestige; and such is men's snobbish respect for authority, such is their pedantic desire to be consistent, that they go on doing their best to lead the exclusively conscious, spiritual, and intellectual life, in spite of its manifest disadvantages. To know is pleasant; it is exciting to be conscious; the intellect is a valuable instrument, and for certain purposes the hypotheses which it fabricates are of great practical value. Quite true. But, therefore, say the moralists and men of science, drawing conclusions only justified by their desire for consistency, therefore *all* life should be lived from the head, consciously, *all* phenomena should at *all* times be interpreted in terms of the intellect's hypotheses. The religious teachers are of a slightly different opinion. All life, according to them, should be lived spiritually, not intellectually. Why? On the grounds, as we discover when we push our analysis far enough, that certain occasional psychological states, currently called spiritual, are extremely agreeable and have valuable consequences in the realm of social behaviour. The unprejudiced observer finds it hard to understand why these people should set such store by consistency of thought and action. Because oysters are occasionally pleasant, it does not follow that one should make of oysters one's exclusive diet. Nor should one take castor-oil every day because castor-oil is occasionally good for one. Too much consistency is as bad for the mind as it is for the body. Consistency is contrary to nature, contrary to life. The only completely consistent people are the dead. Consistent intellectualism and spirituality may be socially valuable, up to a point; but they make, gradually, for individual death. And individual death, when the slow murder has been consummated, is finally social death. So that the social utility of pure intellectualism and pure spirituality is only apparent and temporary. What is needed is, as ever, a compromise. Life must be lived in different ways at different moments. The only satisfactory way of existing in the modern, highly specialized world is to live with two personalities. A Dr. Jekyll that does the metaphysical and scientific thinking, that transacts business in the city, adds up figures, designs machines, and so forth. And a natural, spontaneous Mr. Hyde to do the physical, instinctive living in the intervals of work. The two personalities should lead their unconnected lives apart, without poaching on one another's preserves or inquiring too closely into one another's activities. Only by living discretely and inconsistently can we preserve both the man and the citizen, both the intellectual and the spontaneous animal being, alive within us. The solution may not be very satisfactory; but it is, I believe now (though once I thought differently), the best that, in the modern circumstances, can be devised.

The poet's place, it seems to me, is with the Mr. Hydes of human nature. He should be, as Blake remarked of Milton, "of the devil's party without knowing it"—or preferably with the full consciousness of being of the devil's party. There are so many intellectual and moral angels battling for rationalism, good citizenship, and pure spirituality; so many and such eminent ones, so very vocal and authoritative! The poor devil in man needs all the support and advocacy he can get. The artist is his natural champion. When an artist deserts to the side of the angels, it is the most odious of treasons. How unforgivable, for example, is Tolstoy! Tolstoy, the perfect Mr. Hyde, the complete embodiment, if ever there was one, of non-intellectual, non-moral, instinctive life—Tolstoy, who betrayed his own nature, betrayed his art, betrayed life itself, in order to fight against the devil's party of his earlier allegiances, under the standard of Dr. Jesus-Jekyll. Wordsworth's betrayal was not so spectacular: he was never so wholly of the devil's party as Tolstoy. Still, it was bad enough. It is difficult to forgive him for so utterly repenting his youthful passions and enthusiasms, and becoming, personally as well as politically, the anglican tory. One remembers B. R. Haydon's account of the poet's reactions to that charming classical sculpture of Cupid and Psyche. "The devils!" he said malignantly, after a long-drawn contemplation of their marble embrace. "The devils!" And he was not using the word in the complimentary sense in which I have employed it here: he was expressing his hatred of passion and life, he was damning the young man he had himself been—the young man who had hailed the French Revolution with delight and begotten an illegitimate child. From being an ardent lover of the nymphs, he had become one of those all too numerous

woodmen who expel
Love's gentle dryads from the haunts of life,
And vex the nightingales in every dell.

Yes, even the nightingales he vexed. Even the nightingales, though
the poor birds can never, like those all too human dryads, have led
him into sexual temptation. Even the innocuous nightingales were
moralized, spiritualized, turned into citizens and anglicans—and
along with the nightingales, the whole of animate and inanimate
Nature.

The change in Wordsworth's attitude towards Nature is sympto·
matic of his general apostasy. Beginning as what I may call a
natural aesthete, he transformed himself, in the course of years, into
a moralist, a thinker. He used his intellect to distort his exquisitely
acute and subtle intuitions of the world, to explain away their often
disquieting strangeness, to simplify them into a comfortable metaphysical unreality. Nature had endowed him with the poet's gift
of seeing more than ordinarily far into the brick walls of external
reality, of intuitively comprehending the character of the bricks, of
feeling the quality of their being, and establishing the appropriate
relationship with them. But he preferred to think his gifts away. He
preferred, in the interests of a preconceived religious theory, to
ignore the disquieting strangeness of things, to interpret the impersonal diversity of Nature in terms of a divine, anglican unity.
He chose, in a word, to be a philosopher, comfortably at home
with a man-made and, therefore, thoroughly comprehensible system, rather than a poet adventuring for adventure's sake through
the mysterious world revealed by his direct and undistorted intuitions.

It is a pity that he never travelled beyond the boundaries of
Europe. A voyage through the tropics would have cured him of his
too easy and comfortable pantheism. A few months in the jungle
would have convinced him that the diversity and utter strangeness
of Nature are at least as real and significant as its intellectually·
discovered unity. Nor would he have felt so certain, in the damp
and stifling darkness, among the leeches and the malevolently
tangled rattans, of the divinely anglican character of that fundamental unity. He would have learned once more to treat Nature
naturally, as he treated it in his youth; to react to it spontaneously,

loving where love was the appropriate emotion, fearing, hating, fighting whenever Nature presented itself to his intuition as being, not merely strange, but hostile, inhumanly evil. A voyage would have taught him this. But Wordsworth never left his native continent. Europe is so well gardened that it resembles a work of art, a scientific theory, a neat metaphysical system. Man has re-created Europe in his own image. Its tamed and temperate Nature confirmed Wordsworth in his philosophizings. The poet, the devil's partisan were doomed; the angels triumphed. Alas!

For questions and exercises, see p. 212, p. 334, p. 419, p. 427, p. 430, and p. 531.

# History

## SIEGE OF THE ALAMO

MARQUIS JAMES

At Bexar was a handful of men under Travis who was doing his best to augment his force. Jim Bowie joined the garrison with a small following which, until the fighting started, rather increased Travis's difficulties than otherwise. James Bowie was not the man he had once been—the half-legendary figure whose tremendous exploits were a tradition from St. Louis to Mexico City. In the old days Bowie was a power in Northern Mexico. He had married the daughter of a grandee and, turning his abilities to less spectacular pursuits, accumulated a fortune and his family lived like royalty. Just when his wild days seemed behind him, a plague swept Bowie's beautiful wife and their children into the grave and the lion-hearted Jim almost died of grief. Nothing mattered after that. Life became a quest for activity to turn his mind from his loss. Abandoning his property, he threw himself into the Texas struggle and supported Houston in the contest that had demoralized the Texas army. With little left but blind courage and a name at which enemies still trembled, Jim Bowie then decided to stand by the wreck. His enormous form was gaunt and worn, his blue eyes unnaturally bright from the fever of tuberculosis. Whipping up his flagging forces with whisky, Jim Bowie had plunged into Bexar, determined to sell his life dearly. He could not have come to a better place.

## II

Some other recruits, dressed in fringed buckskins, rode into town and, in the drawl of a southern mountaineer, their spokesman said they wanted to fight. This was Davy Crockett with his twelve Tennesseeans. Davy had been a Tennessee congressman from a backwoods district. With a good head and an amusing way about him, he had become something of a national figure. Unfortunately he committed the error of opposing Andrew Jackson and this had lost him his seat in Congress. Texas was in the public eye and Davy had come on looking for excitement.

A few other volunteers straggled in, bringing Travis's command to the neighborhood of one hundred and forty-five men who, on February twenty-third, awaited the return of Scouts Sutherland and Smith with an indifference born of a picturesque contempt for peril. They did not have long to wait. The two horsemen were seen returning at a dead run across the plain.

Travis immediately gave orders to evacuate Bexar and occupy the Alamo Mission beyond the eastern purlieus of the town. From the way his scouts were riding, Travis knew the Mexican army was coming. Travis now had one hundred and fifty men, having gathered up a few loyal native Mexicans in the town. His first—and last— impulse was to fight.

Sutherland and Smith found their comrades in a fever of preparation to defend the Alamo. The scouts said they had seen fifteen hundred troops drawn up in line of battle, with an officer riding up and down, flourishing a sword and exhorting his men with oratory. Doctor Sutherland had injured his knee during the reconnaissance and could not walk without assistance. But he could ride and, at three o'clock in the afternoon, he sped through the Alamo gate with a message to the "Citizens of Gonzales," a little town fifty miles to the eastward. "The enemy in large force is in sight. We want men and provisions. Send them to us. We . . . are determined to defend the Alamo to the last. Give us assistance."

The message had not been long on its way when the Mexican troops filed into Bexar. A picket on the Alamo wall announced the approach of a horseman under a flag of truce. Travis suspected the object of his visit. He sent Major Morris and Captain Marten to meet the flag. These officers received Santa Anna's demand of surrender "at discretion." They gave Travis's answer. It was a refusal—which Travis rendered the more emphatic by sending a cannon ball into the town when the Mexican emissary had withdrawn. Santa Anna replied by raising the red flag of No Quarter over the tower of San Fernando and opening on the Texans with a mortar battery. The siege of the Alamo had begun.

The following day Travis spared another of his precious men to carry to the outside world a message that has been called the most heroic in American history.

> Commandancy of the Alamo
> Bexar
> Feby 24th, 1836

To the People of Texas and All Americans in the World—

Fellow Citizens and Compatriots: I am besieged with a thousand or more of the Mexicans under Santa Anna. I have sustained a continual Bombardment and cannonade for 24 hours and have not lost a man. The enemy has demanded a surrender at discretion, other wise, the garrison are to be put to the sword, if the fort is taken. I have answered the demand with a cannon shot, and our flag still waves proudly from the wall. *I shall never surrender or retreat.* Then, I call on you in the name of Liberty, of patriotism and everything dear to the American character, to come to our aid with all dispatch. The enemy is receiving reinforcements daily and will no doubt increase to three or four thousand in four or five days. If this call is neglected, I am determined to sustain myself as long as possible and die like a soldier who never forgets what is due his honor and that of his country. VICTORY or DEATH.

> WILLIAM BARRET TRAVIS
> Lt. Col. Comdt.

P.S. The Lord is on our side. When the enemy appeared in sight we had not three bushels of corn. We have since found in deserted houses 80 to 90 bushels and got into the walls 20 to 30 head of Beeves.

### III

The Alamo, which means the cottonwood tree, was a mission more than one hundred years old—a large and strong establishment with superior advantages of defense. Its size was an embarrass-

ment, however. There was a stone church, partly unroofed in previous fighting, with walls four feet thick, and two stoutly walled
enclosures adjoining. The smaller of these enclosures was the convent yard; the larger, more than two acres in extent, the general
plaza of the mission. Built against the walls of these enclosures
were several stone buildings—a convent, a hospital, barracks, a
prison. The walls varied in height from five to twenty-two feet and
to defend them Travis mounted eighteen guns. At intervals scaf-
folds were built for riflemen. The defensive arrangements were intelligently supervised by an engineer named Jameson, but neither
scientific skill nor valor could make up for the lack of men. To
garrison works so extensive required a thousand troops.

Travis knew that everything depended on reenforcements, and
they must come soon. Battalion after battalion of Mexican troops
showed themselves on the prairie, and began to encircle the Alamo
beyond the range of its guns. Batteries were pushed up and the
bombardment grew heavier. Parties of Texans sallied from the
walls to gather fire-wood and to harass the Mexican artillerymen
with rifle-fire.

To whom was the beleaguered commander to appeal for aid?
Travis knew something of the confusion existing in the Texan civil
government, but this situation was more serious than he imagined.
After taking away Governor Smith's authority, the Council members had fallen to quarreling among themselves. Unable to assemble
a quorum of their own number, the Council thus deprived Texas
of even the name of a government, and left the bewildered little
bands, called the army, to shift for themselves.

Travis was shifting. The largest and best equipped body of
troops in Texas was the four hundred and twenty men under James
W. Fannin at Goliad, one hundred and fifty miles away. In the
squabble that had disorganized Texas, Fannin had been a leader
of the clique against Sam Houston, while Travis had supported
Houston. Nevertheless, Travis appealed to Fannin. That officer
received the letter on February twenty-fifth, the third day of the
siege. Three days later he carefully packed his baggage wagons
and began a leisurely march toward the Alamo.

Travis sent other messages elsewhere and Henry Smith, the
deposed Governor, scattered a heart-rending call far and wide.
But Smith was not the type of leader to rally men for a desperate

throw. The response to Travis's heroic appeals likewise was a disappointment, a black disappointment, to the besieged garrison. After seven days and seven nights of fighting not a man had come to join the defenders. But on the eighth day of battle, March first, at three o'clock in the morning, faithful Scout John W. Smith piloted through the enemy lines thirty-two settlers from Gonzales —practically all in the town who were able to bear arms. Twenty of them had left wives and children behind. The weary garrison received these recruits with a cheer. The outside world heard from at last! Hope was revived for Fannin, whose force would surely turn the tide of battle. The watch on the parapet strained his eyes at the southern prairie, but he saw only ever-increasing numbers of Mexicans methodically throwing up works behind which to maneuver with greater safety and precision.

The Gonzales men raised the strength of the Alamo defenders to about one hundred and eighty-three, not counting some twenty refugees from Bexar, mostly women and children and two or three Negro slaves. So far the Texans had lost the services of only one man—Jim Bowie, who had fallen from a scaffold while helping to mount a gun. With a fight at hand Bowie and Travis had composed their differences. The main difficulty between these officers was that each had red hair. Jim Bowie crippled was still worth a half-dozen ordinary men and he hobbled about ready for the finish fight until a piercing "norther" brought on pneumonia. Half-delirious Jim was carried to a cot and nursed by a sister of his late wife who was among the refugees.

IV

The Texans suffered greatly from fatigue and loss of sleep, practically the whole command being on duty constantly. The bombardment was continuous and two hundred shells had fallen within the enclosures. The Texans replied with artillery and rifle-fire from the walls, but their ammunition was low and they saved it for the general assault they knew must come. With the red flag of No Quarter snapping in the north wind, the Texans witnessed every hour new preparations for this attack. The Mexicans were advancing batteries on all sides of the Alamo. Sallying parties of Texans made these maneuvers expensive to the enemy, but Santa Anna had men to spare and he used them. The long hunting rifles of the

Texans would no sooner clear out one parcel of gunners than another squad would appear to carry on the work.

During the tenth day of the siege, March third, the enemy bombardment increased in violence and a hostile battery was planted within pistol shot of the north wall. On that day Travis received has last news from the outside. It was brought by James Butler Bonham, a colonel in the Texas military establishment before dissension had demoralized it, and now serving as a volunteer scout under Lieutenant Colonel Travis. He had carried the Commandant's message to Fannin and, regardless of what Fannin intended to do, returned alone to stand with his comrades. Bonham's report of the mission to Fannin was a blow. While the whole truth of Fannin's behavior was never known to the Alamo's defenders, Bonham left Travis with little hope of aid from the source on which the garrison had built such high expectations. Fannin's half-hearted march toward the Alamo had ended within an hour after it began. One baggage wagon broke down and Fannin had returned to camp at Goliad, without so much as sending a messenger to warn Travis to try to escape.

Fannin could have got word to Travis in time to enable him to retreat. Whether Travis would have done this is a question. The chances are he would not for, even after Bonham arrived, the escape of the garrison was possible. There would have been a fight, but most of them could have got away. But Travis had said, "I shall never surrender or retreat," and he kept his word. The men who remained with him remained on those terms. A story that has been published many times relates that Travis called his men together and drew a line on the ground with his sword. Those wishing to stay were invited to step across the line. The tradition is that Jim Bowie had his cot carried over the line and every man, save one, followed him. The story, like much Alamo literature, is legend, not history.

In any event the fact stands that no man deserted the twenty-eight-year-old leader, although abundant opportunity presented. William Barret Travis lives in the history of the world for his thirteen-day defense of the Alamo. It is his sole claim to a renowned memory, and it is enough. The feat has few parallels in any annals. Bands of men have died, before and since, to show devotion to a cause or their loyalty to a leader they had long known and served, but this was not strictly the case of the Alamo. Texans were fighting Mexican tyranny—technically, that is. Actually most of them were fighting for the thrill of it, for fancied riches in the form of land, or because they were under the spell of professional adventurers who dominated a large part of the Texan stage. Travis, however, was no professional adventurer, which gentry, as a class, do not die needlessly for a cause. Neither had he any special claim on the loyalty of the men who followed him at the Alamo. Most of these men were unknown to him and he to them. His rank did not impress them, for Texans cared nothing for rank and proved it on every occasion. With them it was the man that counted—and Travis was the man.

### v

Bonham came in at eleven o'clock in the morning. There was still a chance—a bare chance—of help from without. Three days before, March first, an attempt to reorganize the Texas civil government had been scheduled to be made at the town of Washington-on-the-Brazos, two hundred and twenty-five miles away. After talking to Bonham, Travis prepared appeals to the leaders at Washington, writing all afternoon amid a cannonade and constant interruptions by his lieutenants with more bad news: the ring of investing troops was drawing closer. The appeals of Travis embodied a temperate account of the action to date.

"The spirits of my men are still high," he wrote, "although they have had much to depress them. We have contended for ten days against an enemy whose number are variously estimated at from fifteen hundred to six thousand men. . . . A reinforcement of about one thousand men is now entering Bexar, from the west."

Col. Fannin is said to be on the march to this place with reinforcements, but I fear it is not true, as I have repeatedly sent to him for aid without receiving any. . . . I look to the colonies alone for aid; unless it arrives soon, I shall have to fight the enemy on his own terms. I will, however, do the best I can . . . and although we may be sacrificed . . . the victory will cost the enemy so dear, that it will be worse for him than defeat. I hope your honorable body will hasten on reinforcements. . . . Our supply of ammunition is limited. . . . The bearer of this will give your honorable body a statement more in detail, should he escape through the enemy's lines. God and Texas—Victory or Death.

When his official communications were finished, Travis wrote to a friend to "take care of my little boy."

Night came on. The Commandant handed his letters to Captain Albert Marten and wished him well. Marten stole through the gate into the shadows. The last of Travis's soldiers had left the Alamo.

The next day the Mexicans kept up a heavy fire of artillery, the Texans replying occasionally. The day after that, Saturday, March fifth, the bombardment eased off in the afternoon and by ten o'clock at night it had stopped altogether. Travis suspected a ruse and posted all his men, who loaded their rifles and their guns and began their twelfth night of vigil. Since the siege had begun there had been no reliefs. The entire command had been continuously on duty. Beef and cornbread had been served on the walls. This was the sole ration. There was no coffee, which would have helped to keep the men awake, and sleep was an enemy more dreaded than the Mexicans. For days men had been dozing in snatches at their guns during the thunder of bombardment. Now the roar had ceased, a silence almost tangible, a starlit southern night: the defenders of the Alamo leaned against their guns—and slept.

At two o'clock on Saturday afternoon, Santa Anna called his commanding officers to headquarters in Bexar. He distributed copies of a general order. "The time has come to strike a decisive blow upon the enemy occupying the fortress of the Alamo. . . . Tomorrow at 4 o'clock A.M., the columns of attack shall be stationed at musket shot distance from the first entrenchments, ready for the charge, which shall commence at a signal to be given with the bugle."

The attacking columns would be four in number—one to storm each side of the Alamo simultaneously. They would be composed of fourteen hundred infantry who had enjoyed three days' rest. "The first column will carry ten ladders, two crowbars and two axes; the second, ten ladders; the third, six ladders; and the fourth, two ladders. The men carrying the ladders will sling their guns on their shoulders, to be enabled to place the ladders wherever they may be required. The men will wear neither overcoats nor blankets, or anything that will impede the rapidity of their motions. The men will have the chin straps of their caps down. . . . The arms, principally the bayonets, should be in perfect order." Behind the attacking infantry and the infantry reserve, cavalry would prowl the country to see that no man in the Alamo escaped.

VI

At four o'clock in the morning the moon had risen. A mild radiance softly outlined the irregular white walls of the fortress which betrayed not the slightest sign of life. Santa Anna's orders had been carried out exactly. Noiselessly, each column of assault had taken its places to encircle the Alamo. The signal bugle sounded and the Mexican band struck up the savage air of *Deguelo,* or *Cutthroat.* The troops gave a cheer for Santa Anna and advanced at a run.

Not until the charging assailants were within easy rifle range did a sound come from the walls of the Alamo. Then a flash, a roar and a pungent curtain of smoke. The Texans had let loose their guns loaded with grape-shot and scrap iron. They followed with a deadly fire of musketry. Gaps were torn in the attackers' ranks, but the impetus of the charge carried it on.

The Texans defending the north wall sent up an exultant shout. The column of attack in front of them had recoiled and was in full retreat. East, west, and south Travis's men took heart and increased their fire. The east column faltered and fell back. The west fell back. The panic spread to the south column, which had reached the walls; it broke and fled. The moonlit plain was dotted with the vague shapes of the fallen. Among the slain was Colonel Francisco Duque, commander of the north column, wounded and then trampled to death trying to stem the rout of his men.

The first assault on the Alamo had failed.

The confused masses were reformed into battalions. Battalions were regrouped for attack, commanding officers riding up and down, heartening their men. The eastern sky was growing gray and the stars were fading when the four columns again sprang forward over the pallid plain and the corpses of the dead. Once more the dim advancing lines were staggered by a broadside from the walls. The north column recoiled, the west column retired, the east column was routed. Colonel José Vincente Minon's sturdy south column tottered, but came on and applied its scaling ladders to the walls. The retreating east column veered to the right and the west column to the left. These spontaneous movements had the effect of reenforcing the flanks of the north column which, though stopped, held its ground. Officers grasped the situation and drove this combined force against the north wall in the face of a furious fire. The wall was reached, but the assailants had no will left to try to scale it. They broke and fled. On the south side the fighting was hand to hand. The Mexicans climbed their ladders, but the Texans beat them back with clubbed rifles and bowie knives.

The second assault had failed.

The break of day looked upon preparations within and without the Alamo for a renewal of the struggle. Travis and his band were in hard case. Their guns were hot and ammunition nearly gone. There had been few casualties but the men were very weary. Had the Mexicans launched their first attack as quietly as they had moved into position for it, that onslaught might have told the tale, as the Texans were sound asleep. The three pickets stationed outside the walls to observe the enemy must have been bayonetted for they gave no warning. The alarm was given by a captain on the walls. Travis was on his feet instantly. Snatching up a rifle and his sword he called to Joe, his Negro servant, and ran across the plaza to a cannon at the northwest corner of the wall. "Come on, boys, the Mexicans are here!" The cheer for Santa Anna and the notes of *Deguelo* helped to rouse the men. A clink of equipment, the pit-pat of running feet and the ghostly lines took shape in the moonlight.

After two repulses the Mexican officers had some difficulty getting their men in a mood for a third attack. But the ranks were reformed, the bugle sounded and the wave surged forward, officers beating the laggards with the flats of swords. Profiting by experience, the Mexicans varied their mode of assault. Having met with no success on the fronts assigned to them, the east and west columns swung over and joined the north column to storm that rampart. The consolidated force charged across the space swept by the Texans' cannon and reached the shadow of the wall where the cannon could not be trained to play upon them. "Nor could the defenders use their muskets with accuracy," wrote a Mexican general, "because the wall having no inner banquette, they had, in order to deliver their fire, to stand on top where they could not live for a second."

The wall was cleared and the scaling ladders flung up. Mexicans tumbled over "like sheep," according to Travis's Joe. The Commander of the Alamo fell with a ball through his head as he stood behind a useless cannon and made ready to fire his rifle. The Texans met the onrush with rifles, pistols, knives and their fists, but the Mexicans were too numerous. The defenders retreated across the plaza to the barracks that formed the east wall and to the church, also on the east side.

Meantime the southern column, which had always struck vigorous blows, breached the wall and came through. A desperate fight ensued. The Mexicans fell in heaps. The Texans took refuge in a barrack building forming the west wall of the plaza and fought from room to room until not a man of their number remained alive.

On the east side of the plaza the fight went on in the barracks there. The Mexicans ended it when they dragged inside a howitzer filled with grape, which they fired through the length of the building. Fifteen Texans were found dead in front of the gun and forty Mexicans behind it. This building was used as a hospital and according to one account, Jim Bowie perished there propped up on his cot and defending himself with two pistols.

The last point taken was the church. With his rifle "Betsy," Davy Crockett and the twelve from Tennessee held the inner gate to the little churchyard, firing until they no longer had time to load. Then clubbing their rifles and drawing hunting knives from their belts, they dispatched twenty-five more of the enemy before the last backwoodsman fell. Inside the church there was a brief struggle. The most plausible account says that Bowie died there, whence he had been carried so that his sister-in-law might attend him. Both versions of Bowie's death declare that he fought from his bed to the last and that his body was pitched about on the bayonets of the soldiers.

It had been agreed that the last Texan soldier alive should blow up the powder magazine in the church. A Mexican shot down Major Robert Evans as he attempted to apply a match. This seemed to complete the conquest. Across the corpse-strewn floor in a far corner huddled a little knot of women and children and a few slaves. The soldiers began to fling them about roughly. Mrs. A. M. Dickinson, the wife of a lieutenant who had perished on the walls, held her fifteen-months-old baby girl at her breast. At the woman's side crouched young Asa Walker, a wounded gunner.

Mrs. Dickinson pleaded for his life, but the Mexicans ran him
through, tossing "his body on their bayonets as a farmer would
handle a bundle of hay."

The slanting sunlight, driving through holes in the roof, made
irregular islands on the bloodstained western walls. It was eight
o'clock in the morning and the Alamo had fallen.

Does James make his narrative vivid? How? What is the "point" of his
narrative? For further exercises, see p. 289, p. 301, and p. 430.

## THE EXTENT AND MILITARY FORCE OF THE EMPIRE IN THE AGE OF THE ANTONINES

EDWARD GIBBON

In the second century of the Christian Era, the Empire of Rome
comprehended the fairest part of the earth, and the most civilised
portion of mankind. The frontiers of that extensive monarchy were
guarded by ancient renown and disciplined valour. The gentle but
powerful influence of laws and manners had gradually cemented
the union of the provinces. Their peaceful inhabitants enjoyed and
abused the advantages of wealth and luxury. The image of a free
constitution was preserved with decent reverence: the Roman senate appeared to possess the sovereign authority, and devolved on
the emperors all the executive powers of government. During a
happy period (A.D. 98-180) of more than fourscore years, the public
administration was conducted by the virtue and abilities of Nerva,
Trajan, Hadrian, and the two Antonines. It is the design of this,
and of the two succeeding chapters, to describe the prosperous
condition of their empire; and afterwards, from the death of Marcus Antoninus, to deduce the most important circumstances of its
decline and fall; a revolution which will ever be remembered, and
is still felt by the nations of the earth.

The principal conquests of the Romans were achieved under the
republic; and the emperors, for the most part, were satisfied with
preserving those dominions which had been acquired by the policy
of the senate, the active emulation of the consuls, and the martial
enthusiasm of the people. The seven first centuries were filled with

THE EXTENT AND MILITARY FORCE OF THE EMPIRE: From *The History of the
Decline and Fall of the Roman Empire* by Edward Gibbon.

a rapid succession of triumphs; but it was reserved for Augustus to relinquish the ambitious design of subduing the whole earth, and to introduce a spirit of moderation into the public councils. Inclined to peace by his temper and situation, it was easy for him to discover that Rome, in her present exalted situation, had much less to hope than to fear from the chance of arms; and that, in the prosecution of remote wars, the undertaking became every day more difficult, the event more doubtful, and the possession more precarious, and less beneficial. The experience of Augustus added weight to these salutary reflections, and effectually convinced him that, by the prudent vigour of his counsels, it would be easy to secure every concession which the safety or the dignity of Rome might require from the most formidable Barbarians. Instead of exposing his person and his legions to the arrows of the Parthians, he obtained, by an honourable treaty, the restitution of the standards and prisoners which had been taken in the defeat of Crassus.

His generals, in the early part of his reign, attempted the reduction of Æthiopia and Arabia Felix. They marched near a thousand miles to the south of the tropic; but the heat of the climate soon repelled the invaders, and protected the unwarlike natives of those sequestered regions. The northern countries of Europe scarcely deserved the expense and labour of conquest. The forests and morasses of Germany were filled with a hardy race of barbarians, who despised life when it was separated from freedom; and though, on the first attack, they seemed to yield to the weight of the Roman power, they soon, by a signal act of despair, regained their independence, and reminded Augustus of the vicissitude of fortune. On the death of that emperor, his testament was publicly read in the senate. He bequeathed, as a valuable legacy to his successors, the advice of confining the empire within those limits, which Nature seemed to have placed as its permanent bulwarks and boundaries; on the west the Atlantic ocean; the Rhine and Danube on the north; the Euphrates on the east; and towards the south, the sandy deserts of Arabia and Africa.

Happily for the repose of mankind, the moderate system recommended by the wisdom of Augustus, was adopted by the fears and vices of his immediate successors. Engaged in the pursuit of pleasure, or in the exercise of tyranny, the first Cæsars seldom showed themselves to the armies, or to the provinces; nor were they disposed to suffer, that those triumphs which *their* indolence neglected should be usurped by the conduct and valour of their lieutenants. The military fame of a subject was considered as an insolent invasion of the Imperial prerogative; and it became the duty, as well as interest, of every Roman general, to guard the frontiers intrusted to his care, without aspiring to conquests which might have proved no less fatal to himself than to the vanquished barbarians.

The only accession which the Roman empire received, during the first century of the Christian era, was the province of Britain. In this single instance the successors of Cæsar and Augustus were persuaded to follow the example of the former, rather than the precept of the latter. The proximity of its situation to the coast of Gaul seemed to invite their arms; the pleasing, though doubtful intelligence, of a pearl fishery, attracted their avarice; and as Britain was viewed in the light of a distinct and insulated world, the conquest scarcely formed any exception to the general system of continental measures. After a war of about forty years, undertaken by the most stupid, maintained by the most dissolute, and terminated by the most timid of all the emperors, the far greater part of the island submitted to the Roman yoke. The various tribes of Britons possessed valour without conduct, and the love of freedom without the spirit of union. They took up arms with savage fierceness; they laid them down, or turned them against each other with wild inconstancy; and while they fought singly, they were successively subdued. Neither the fortitude of Caractacus, nor the despair of Boadicea, nor the fanaticism of the Druids, could avert the slavery of their country, or resist the steady progress of the Imperial generals, who maintained the national glory, when the throne was disgraced by the weakest, or the most vicious of mankind. At the very time when Domitian, confined to his palace, felt the terrors which he inspired; his legions, under the command of the virtuous Agricola, defeated the collected force of the Caledonians at the foot of the Grampian hills; and his fleets, venturing to explore an unknown and dangerous navigation, displayed the Roman arms round every part of the island. The conquest of Britain was considered as already achieved; and it was the design of Agricola to complete and ensure his success by the easy reduction of Ireland, for which in his opinion, one legion and a few auxiliaries were sufficient. The western isle might be improved into a valuable possession, and the Britons would wear their chains with the less reluctance, if the prospect and example of freedom were on every side removed from before their eyes.

But the superior merit of Agricola soon occasioned his removal from the government of Britain; and for ever disappointed this rational, though extensive scheme of conquest. Before his departure, the prudent general had provided for security as well as for dominion. He had observed that the island is almost divided into two unequal parts by the opposite gulfs, or, as they are now called, the Friths of Scotland. Across the narrow interval of about forty miles, he had drawn a line of military stations, which was afterwards fortified in the reign of Antoninus Pius, by a turf rampart erected on foundations of stone. This wall of Antoninus, at a small distance beyond the modern cities of Edinburgh and Glasgow, was fixed as the limit of the Roman province. The native Caledonians preserved in the northern extremity of the island their wild independence, for which they were not less indebted to their poverty than to their valour. Their incursions were frequently repelled and chastised; but their country was never subdued. The masters of the fairest and most wealthy climates of the globe turned with contempt from gloomy hills assailed by the winter tempest, from lakes concealed in a blue mist, and from cold and lonely heaths, over which the deer of the forest were chased by a troop of naked barbarians.

Such was the state of the Roman frontiers, and such the maxims of the Imperial policy, from the death of Augustus to the accession of Trajan. That virtuous and active prince had received the education of a soldier, and possessed the talents of a general. The peaceful system of his predecessors was interrupted by scenes of war and conquest; and the legions, after a long interval, beheld a military emperor at their head. The first exploits of Trajan were against the Dacians, the most warlike of men, who dwelt beyond the Danube, and who, during the reign of Domitian, had insulted with impunity the Majesty of Rome. To the strength and fierceness of barbarians, they added a contempt for life, which was derived from a warm persuasion of the immortality and transmigration of the soul. Decebalus, the Dacian king, approved himself a rival not unworthy of Trajan; nor did he despair of his own and the public fortune, till, by the confession of his enemies, he had exhausted every resource both of valour and policy. This memorable war, with a very short suspension of hostilities, lasted five years; and as the emperor could exert, without control, the whole force of the state, it was terminated by an absolute submission of the barbarians. The new province of Dacia, which formed a second exception to the precept of Augustus, was about 1300 miles in circumference. Its natural boundaries were the Dniester, the Teyss [Theiss modern form], or Tibiscus, the Lower Danube, and the Euxine Sea. The vestiges of a military road may still be traced from the banks of the Danube to the neighbourhood of Bender, a place famous in modern history, and the actual frontier of the Turkish and Russian empires.

Trajan was ambitious of fame; and as long as mankind shall continue to bestow more liberal applause on their destroyers than on their benefactors, the thirst of military glory will ever be the vice of the most exalted characters. The praises of Alexander, transmitted by a succession of poets and historians, had kindled a dangerous emulation in the mind of Trajan. Like him the Roman emperor undertook an expedition against the nations of the east, but he lamented with a sigh, that his advanced age scarcely left him any hopes of equalling the renown of the son of Philip. Yet the success of Trajan, however transient, was rapid and specious. The degenerate Parthians, broken by intestine discord, fled before his arms. He descended the river Tigris in triumph, from the mountains of Armenia to the Persian gulf. He enjoyed the honour of being the first, as he was the last, of the Roman generals, who ever navigated that remote sea. His fleets ravaged the coasts of Arabia; and Trajan vainly flattered himself that he was approaching towards the confines of India. Every day the astonished senate received the intelligence of new names and new nations, that acknowledged his sway. They were informed that the kings of Bosphorus, Colchos, Iberia, Albania, Osrhoene, and even the Parthian monarch himself, had accepted their diadems from the hands of the emperor; that the independent tribes of the Median and Carduchian hills had implored his protection; and that the rich countries of Armenia, Mesopotamia, and Assyria, were reduced into the state of provinces. But the death of Trajan soon clouded the splendid prospect; and it was justly to be dreaded, that so many distant nations would throw off the unaccustomed yoke, when they were no longer restrained by the powerful hand which had imposed it.

It was an ancient tradition, that when the Capitol was founded by one of the Roman kings, the god Terminus (who presided over boundaries, and was represented according to the fashion of that age by a large stone) alone, among all the inferior deities, refused to yield his place to Jupiter himself. A favourable inference was drawn from his obstinacy, which was interpreted by the augurs as a sure presage that the boundaries of the Roman power would never recede. During many ages, the prediction, as it is usual, contributed to its own accomplishment. But though Terminus had resisted the majesty of Jupiter, he submitted to the authority of the emperor Hadrian. The resignation of all the eastern conquests of Trajan was the first measure of his reign. He restored to the Parthians the election of an independent sovereign, withdrew the Roman garrisons from the provinces of Armenia, Mesopotamia, and Assyria, and, in compliance with the precept of Augustus, once more established the Euphrates as the frontier of the empire. Censure, which arraigns the public actions and the private motives of princes, has ascribed to envy, a conduct, which might be attributed to the prudence and moderation of Hadrian. The various character of that emperor, capable, by turns, of the meanest and the most generous sentiments, may afford some colour to the suspicion. It was, however, scarcely in his power to place the superiority of his predecessor in a more conspicuous light, than by thus confessing himself unequal to the task of defending the conquests of Trajan.

The martial and ambitious spirit of Trajan formed a very singular contrast with the moderation of his successor. The restless activity of Hadrian was not less remarkable, when compared with the gentle repose of Antoninus Pius. The life of the former was almost a perpetual journey; and as he possessed the various talents of the soldier, the statesman, and the scholar, he gratified his curiosity in the discharge of his duty. Careless of the difference of seasons and of climates, he marched on foot, and bare-headed, over the snows of Caledonia, and the sultry plains of the Upper Egypt; nor was there a province of the empire which, in the course of his reign, was not honoured with the presence of the monarch. But the tranquil life of Antoninus Pius was spent in the bosom of Italy; and, during the twenty-three years that he directed the public administration, the longest journeys of that amiable prince extended no farther than from his palace in Rome to the retirement of his Lanuvian Villa.

Notwithstanding this difference in their personal conduct, the general system of Augustus was equally adopted and uniformly pursued by Hadrian and by the two Antonines. They persisted in the design of maintaining the dignity of the empire, without attempting to enlarge its limits. By every honourable expedient they invited the friendship of the barbarians; and endeavoured to convince mankind that the Roman power, raised above the temptation of conquest, was actuated only by the love of order and justice. During a long period of forty-three years their virtuous labours were crowned with success; and if we except a few slight hostilities that served to exercise the legions of the frontier, the reigns of Hadrian and Antoninus Pius offer the fair prospect of universal peace. The Roman name was revered among the most remote nations of the earth. The fiercest barbarians frequently submitted their differences to the arbitration of the emperor; and we are informed by a contemporary historian, that he had seen ambassadors who were refused the honour which they came to solicit, of being admitted into the rank of subjects.

The terror of the Roman arms added weight and dignity to the moderation of the emperors. They preserved peace by a constant preparation for war; and while justice regulated their conduct, they announced to the nations on their confines that they were as little disposed to endure as to offer an injury. The military strength, which it had been sufficient for Hadrian and the elder Antoninus to display, was exerted against the Parthians and the Germans by the emperor Marcus. The hostilities of the barbarians provoked the resentment of that philosophic monarch, and, in the prosecution of a just defence, Marcus and his generals obtained many signal victories, both on the Euphrates and on the Danube. The military establishment of the Roman empire, which thus assured either its tranquillity or success, will now become the proper and important object of our attention.

In the purer ages of the commonwealth, the use of arms was reserved for those ranks of citizens who had a country to love, a property to defend, and some share in enacting those laws, which it was their interest, as well as duty, to maintain. But in proportion as the public freedom was lost in extent of conquest, war was gradually improved into an art, and degraded into a trade. The legions themselves, even at the time when they were recruited in the most distant provinces, were supposed to consist of Roman citizens. That distinction was generally considered either as a legal qualification or as a proper recompense for the soldier; but a more serious regard was paid to the essential merit of age, strength, and military stature. In all levies, a just preference was given to the climates of the North over those of the South: the race of men born to the exercise of arms was sought for in the country rather than in cities; and it was very reasonably presumed, that the hardy occupations of smiths, carpenters, and huntsmen, would supply more vigour and resolution than the sedentary trades which are employed in the service of luxury. After every qualification of property had been laid aside, the armies of the Roman emperors were still commanded, for the most part, by officers of a liberal birth and education; but the common soldiers, like the mercenary troops of modern Europe, were drawn from the meanest, and very frequently from the most profligate, of mankind.

That public virtue which among the ancients was denominated patriotism, is derived from a strong sense of our own interest in the preservation and prosperity of the free government of which we are members. Such a sentiment, which had rendered the legions of the republic almost invincible, could make but a very feeble impression on the mercenary servants of a despotic prince; and it became necessary to supply that defect by other motives, of a different, but not less forcible nature; honour and religion. The peasant, or mechanic, imbibed the useful prejudice that he was advanced to the more dignified profession of arms, in which his rank and reputation would depend on his own valour; and that, although the prowess of a private soldier must often escape the notice of fame, his own behaviour might sometimes confer glory or disgrace on the company, the legion, or even the army, to whose honours he was associated. On his first entrance into the service, an oath was administered to him, with every circumstance of solemnity. He promised never to desert his standard, to submit his own will to the commands of his leaders, and to sacrifice his life for the safety of the emperor and the empire. The attachment of the Roman troops to their standards was inspired by the united influence of religion and of honour. The golden eagle, which glittered in the front of the legion, was the object of their fondest devotion; nor was it esteemed less impious than it was ignominious, to abandon that sacred ensign in the hour of danger. These motives, which derived their strength from the imagination, were enforced by fears and hopes of a more substantial kind. Regular pay, occasional donatives, and a stated recompense, after the appointed time of service, alleviated the hardships of the military life, whilst, on the other hand, it was impossible for cowardice or disobedience to escape the severest punishment. The centurions were authorised to chastise with blows, the generals had a right to punish with death; and it was an inflexible maxim of Roman discipline, that a good soldier should dread his officers far more than the enemy. From such laudable arts did the valour of the Imperial troops receive a degree of firmness and docility, unattainable by the impetuous and irregular passions of barbarians.

And yet so sensible were the Romans of the imperfection of valour without skill and practice, that, in their language, the name of an army was borrowed from the word which signified exercise. Military exercises were the important and unremitted object of their discipline. The recruits and young soldiers were constantly trained both in the morning and in the evening, nor was age or knowledge allowed to excuse the veterans from the daily repetition of what they had completely learnt. Large sheds were erected in the winter-quarters of the troops, that their useful labours might not receive any interruption from the most tempestuous weather; and it was carefully observed, that the arms destined to this imitation of war, should be of double the weight which was required in real action. It is not the purpose of this work to enter into any minute description of the Roman exercises. We shall only remark, that they comprehended whatever could add strength to the body, activity to the limbs, or grace to the motions. The soldiers were diligently instructed to march, to run, to leap, to swim, to carry heavy burdens, to handle every species of arms that was used either for offence or for defence, either in distant engagement or in a closer onset; to form a variety of evolutions; and to move to the sound of flutes, in the Pyrrhic or martial dance. In the midst of peace, the Roman troops familiarised themselves with the practice of war; and it is prettily remarked by an ancient historian who had fought against them, that the effusion of blood was the only circumstance which distinguished a field of battle from a field of exercise. It was the policy of the ablest generals, and even of the emperors themselves, to encourage these military studies by their presence and example; and we are informed that Hadrian, as well as Trajan, frequently condescended to instruct the unexperienced soldiers, to reward the diligent, and sometimes to dispute with them the prize of superior strength or dexterity. Under the reigns of those princes, the science of tactics was cultivated with success; and as long as the empire retained any vigour, their military instructions were respected as the most perfect model of Roman discipline.

Nine centuries of war had gradually introduced into the service many alterations and improvements. The legions, as they are described by Polybius, in the time of the Punic wars, differed very materially from those which achieved the victories of Cæsar, or defended the monarchy of Hadrian and the Antonines. The constitution of the Imperial legion may be described in a few words. The heavy-armed infantry, which composed its principal strength, was divided into ten cohorts, and fifty-five companies, under the orders of a correspondent number of tribunes and centurions. The first cohort, which always claimed the post of honour and the custody of the eagle, was formed of eleven hundred and five soldiers, the most approved for valour and fidelity. The remaining nine cohorts consisted each of five hundred and fifty-five; and the whole body of legionary infantry amounted to six thousand one hundred men. Their arms were uniform, and admirably adapted to the nature of their service: an open helmet, with a lofty crest; a breastplate, or coat of mail; greaves on their legs, and an ample buckler on their left arm. The buckler was of an oblong and concave figure, four feet in length, and two and an half in breadth, framed of a light wood, covered with a bull's hide, and strongly guarded with plates of brass. Besides a lighter spear, the legionary soldier grasped in his right hand the formidable *pilum*, a ponderous javelin, whose utmost length was about six feet, and which was terminated by a massy triangular point of steel of eighteen inches. This instrument was indeed much inferior to our modern fire-arms; since it was exhausted by a single discharge, at the distance of only ten or twelve paces. Yet when it was launched by a firm and skilful hand, there was not any cavalry that durst venture within its reach, nor any shield or corslet that could sustain the impetuosity of its weight. As soon as the Roman had darted his *pilum*, he drew his sword, and rushed forwards to close with the enemy. His sword was a short well-tempered Spanish blade, that carried a double edge, and was alike suited to the purpose of striking or of pushing; but the soldier was always instructed to prefer the latter use of his weapon, as his own body remained less exposed, whilst he inflicted a more dangerous wound on his adversary. The legion was usually drawn up eight deep; and the regular distance of three feet was left between the files as well as ranks. A body of troops, habituated to preserve this open order, in a long front and a rapid charge, found themselves prepared to execute every disposition which the circumstances of war, or the skill of their leader, might suggest. The soldier possessed a free space for his arms and motions, and sufficient intervals were allowed, through which seasonable reinforcements might be introduced to the relief of the exhausted combatants. The tactics of the Greeks and Macedonians were formed on very different principles. The strength of the phalanx depended on sixteen ranks of long pikes, wedged together in the closest array. But it was soon discovered by reflection, as well by the event, that the strength of the phalanx was unable to contend with the activity of the legion.

The cavalry, without which the force of the legion would have remained imperfect, was divided into ten troops or squadrons; the first, as the companion of the first cohort, consisted of an hundred and thirty-two men; whilst each of the other nine amounted only to sixty-six. The entire establishment formed a regiment, if we may use the modern expression, of seven hundred and twenty-six horse, naturally connected with its respective legion, but occasionally separated to act in the line, and to compose a part of the wings of the army. The cavalry of the emperors was no longer composed, like that of the ancient republic, of the noblest youths of Rome and Italy, who, by performing their military service on horseback, prepared themselves for the offices of senator and consul; and solicited, by deeds of valour, the future suffrages of their countrymen. Since the alteration of manners and government, the most wealthy of the equestrian order were engaged in the administration of justice, and of the revenue; and whenever they embraced the profession of arms, they were immediately intrusted with a troop

# HISTORY

of horse, or a cohort of foot. Trajan and Hadrian formed their cavalry from the same provinces, and the same class of their subjects, which recruited the ranks of the legion. The horses were bred, for the most part, in Spain or Cappadocia. The Roman troopers despised the complete armour with which the cavalry of the East was encumbered. *Their* more useful arms consisted in a helmet, an oblong shield, light boots, and a coat of mail. A javelin, and a long broadsword, were their principal weapons of offence. The use of lances and of iron maces they seem to have borrowed from the barbarians.

The safety and honour of the empire were principally intrusted to the legions, but the policy of Rome condescended to adopt every useful instrument of war. Considerable levies were regularly made among the provincials, who had not yet deserved the honourable distinction of Romans. Many dependant princes and communities, dispersed round the frontiers, were permitted, for a while, to hold their freedom and security by the tenure of military service. Even select troops of hostile barbarians were frequently compelled or persuaded to consume their dangerous valour in remote climates, and for the benefit of the state. All these were included under the general name of auxiliaries; and howsoever they might vary according to the difference of times and circumstances, their numbers were seldom much inferior to those of the legions themselves. Among the auxiliaries, the bravest and most faithful bands were placed under the command of præfects and centurions, and severely trained in the arts of Roman discipline; but the far greater part retained those arms, to which the nature of their country, or their early habits of life, more peculiarly adapted them. By this institution each legion, to whom a certain proportion of auxiliaries was allotted, contained within itself every species of lighter troops, and of missile weapons; and was capable of encountering every nation, with the advantages of its respective arms and discipline. Nor was the legion destitute of what, in modern language, would be styled a train of artillery. It consisted in ten military engines of the largest, and fifty-five of a smaller size; but all of which, either in an oblique or horizontal manner, discharged stones and darts with irresistible violence.

The camp of a Roman legion presented the appearance of a fortified city. As soon as the space was marked out, the pioneers carefully levelled the ground, and removed every impediment that might interrupt its perfect regularity. Its form was an exact quadrangle; and we may calculate that a square of about seven hundred yards was sufficient for the encampment of twenty thousand Romans; though a similar number of our own troops would expose to the enemy a front of more than treble that extent. In the midst of the camp, the prætorium, or general's quarters, rose above the others; the cavalry, the infantry, and the auxiliaries occupied their respective stations; the streets were broad and perfectly straight, and a vacant space of two hundred feet was left on all sides, between the tents and the rampart. The rampart itself was usually twelve feet high, armed with a line of strong and intricate palisades, and defended by a ditch of twelve feet in depth as well as in breadth. This important labour was performed by the hands of the legionaries themselves, to whom the use of the spade and the pick-axe was no less familiar than that of the sword or *pilum*. Active valour may often be the present of nature; but such patient diligence can be the fruit only of habit and discipline.

Whenever the trumpet gave the signal of departure, the camp was almost instantly broke up, and the troops fell into their ranks without delay or confusion. Besides their arms, which the legionaries scarcely considered as an encumbrance, they were laden with their kitchen furniture, the instruments of fortification, and the provision of many days. Under this weight, which would oppress the delicacy of a modern soldier, they were trained by a regular step to advance, in about six hours, near twenty miles. On the appearance of an enemy, they threw aside their baggage, and by easy and rapid evolutions converted the column of march into an order of battle. The slingers and archers skirmished in the front; the auxiliaries formed the first line, and were seconded or sustained by the strength of the legions: the cavalry covered the flanks, and the military engines were placed in the rear.

Such were the arts of war by which the Roman emperors defended their extensive conquests, and preserved a military spirit, at a time when every other virtue was oppressed by luxury and despotism. If, in the consideration of their armies, we pass from their discipline to their numbers, we shall not find it easy to define them with any tolerable accuracy. We may compute, however, that the legion, which was itself a body of six thousand eight hundred and thirty-one Romans, might, with its attendant auxiliaries, amount to about twelve thousand five hundred men. The peace establishment of Hadrian and his successors was composed of no less than thirty of these formidable brigades; and most probably formed a standing force of three hundred and seventy-five thousand men. Instead of being confined within the walls of fortified cities, which the Romans considered as the refuge of weakness or pusillanimity, the legions were encamped on the banks of the great rivers, and along the frontiers of the barbarians. As their stations, for the most part, remained fixed and permanent, we may venture to describe the distribution of the troops. Three legions were sufficient for Britain. The principal strength lay upon the Rhine and Danube, and consisted of sixteen legions, in the following proportions: two in the Lower and three in the Upper Germany; one in Rhætia, one in Noricum, four in Pannonia, three in Mæsia, and two in Dacia. The defence of the Euphrates was entrusted to eight legions, six of whom were planted in Syria, and the other two in Cappadocia. With regard to Egypt, Africa, and Spain, as they were far removed from any important scene of war, a single legion maintained the domestic tranquillity of each of those great provinces. Even Italy was not left destitute of a military force. Above twenty thousand chosen soldiers, distinguished by the titles of City Cohorts and Prætorian Guards, watched over the safety of the monarch and the capital. As the authors of almost every revolution that distracted the empire, the Prætorians will, very soon, and very loudly, demand our attention; but in their arms and institution, we cannot find any circumstance which discriminated them from the legions, unless it were a more splendid appearance, and a less rigid discipline.

The navy maintained by the emperors might seem inadequate to their greatness; but it was fully sufficient for every useful purpose of government. The ambition of the Romans was confined to the land; nor was that warlike people ever actuated by the enterprising spirit which had prompted the navigators of Tyre, of Carthage, and even of Marseilles, to enlarge the bounds of the world, and to explore the most remote coasts of the ocean. To the Romans the ocean remained an object of terror rather than of curiosity; the whole extent of the Mediterranean, after the destruction of Carthage, and the extirpation of the pirates, was included within their provinces. The policy of the emperors was directed only to preserve the peaceful dominion of that sea, and to protect the commerce of their subjects. With these moderate views, Augustus stationed two permanent fleets in the most convenient ports of Italy, the one at Ravenna, on the Adriatic, the other at Misenum, in the bay of Naples. Experience seems at length to have convinced the ancients, that as soon as their galleys exceeded two, or at the most three ranks of oars, they were suited rather for vain pomp than for real service. Augustus himself, in the victory of Actium, had seen the superiority of his own light frigates (they were called Liburnians) over the lofty but unwieldy castles of his rival. Of these Liburnians he composed the two fleets of Ravenna and Misenum, destined to command, the one the eastern, the other the western division of the Mediterranean; and to each of the squadrons he attached a body of several thousand marines. Besides these two ports, which may be considered as the principal seats of the Roman navy, a very considerable force was stationed at Frejus, on the coast of Provence, and the Euxine was guarded by forty ships, and three thousand soldiers. To all these we add the fleet which preserved the communication between Gaul and Britain, and a great number of vessels constantly maintained on the Rhine and Danube, to harass the country, or to intercept the passage of the barbarians. If we review this general state of the Imperial forces; of the cavalry as well as infantry; of the legions, the auxiliaries, the guards, and the navy; the most liberal computation will not allow us to fix the entire establishment by sea and by land at more than four hundred and fifty thousand men; a military power, which, however formidable it may seem, was equalled by a monarch of the last century, whose kingdom was confined within a single province of the Roman empire.

What are the basic principles of organization in this account? Is this account primarily expository or descriptive or what? Find examples of the balanced sentence and the periodic sentence. Does Gibbon use these sentence types to the point of monotony? For a further exercise, see p. 455.

# IT WAS A STABLE WORLD

## ROBERT GRAVES

The world was stable—a compact world of manageable size, centrally governed—a Mediterranean world with Imperial Rome as

IT WAS A STABLE WORLD: Originally printed in *The Cornhill*. Reprinted by permission of the author.

the hub, the smoke of sacrifice reeking from a thousand altars and the heavenly bodies circling in foreseeable fashion overhead. True, there was another world that began at the River Euphrates, the Eastern world into which Alexander the Great had freakishly broken three centuries before. But the Romans had left it alone since losing 30,000 men at Carrhae in an attempt to advance their frontiers at Parthian expense. Oriental luxury goods—jade, silk, gold, spices, vermillion, jewels—had formerly come overland by way of the Caspian Sea and now that this route had been cut by the Huns, a few daring Greek sea-captains were sailing from Red Sea ports, catching the trade winds and loading up at Ceylon. But commercial relations were chancy.

Northward, dense forests swarming with uncivilised, red-haired, beer-swilling Germans; and foggy Britain with its chariot fighters who seemed to have stepped from the pages of Homer; and the bleak steppes of Russia peopled by mare-milking nomad Scythians. Westward, the Ocean, supposedly extending to the point where it spilt over into nothingness. Nobody had thought it worth while to test the truth of the Greek legend that far out lay a chain of islands where coconuts grew on palms and life was indolent and merry. Southward, marvellous Africa, of which only the nearest regions had been explored; from beyond came rumours of burning deserts, pigmies, camel-leopards and marshes full of cranes. Though the Greek scientist Eratosthenes had calculated the distance of the sun from the earth, and the earth's circumference at the Equator, with only a small error, his theory of a global world was received with polite scorn by men of common sense: how could there be a Southern Hemisphere? An Egyptian admiral had once been sent out from Suez as a punishment for insubordination, with orders to follow the African coast as far as it went; after three years he had returned by way of Gibraltar claiming to have circumnavigated the continent. But that was centuries back, and the fellow had been put to death for an impious report that at the Southern Cape the sun had been rising in the wrong quarter of the sky. For the ordinary Roman citizen, the earth was still as flat as the palm of his hand.

"Midmost is safest," the Romans said—a dull, unadventurous, home-loving race, who hated the sea, preferred walking to riding, and thought banishment from their country scarcely preferable to death. They had become masters of the world against their real inclinations: the incentive to expand had not been patriotism or a self-imposed civilising mission, as was later alleged, but family rivalry sharpened by greed. The Republican institution of the "triumph" was to blame. While there was a Sacred King at Rome he won his title by marrying the queen's daughter or younger female relative, not by being the former king's eldest son; but in a prolonged struggle for the succession at the death of King Tullius all the royal princesses were either defiled or killed. This unfortunate accident—not "a burning love of freedom"—ended the monarchy. However, in the Republic that took its place, the Senate might decree one great privilege of the former king to honour commanders-in-chief who conquered an enemy state: to ride in triumph through Rome, with the captured gods—that is, their sacred statues—carried on carts behind him, himself impersonating and possessed by, the scarlet-faced Oak-god Mars, patron of shepherds. Republican commanders-in-chief, who were also judges of the Supreme Court, could be appointed only from the nobility, and it was rivalry between these noble families as to which could secure most triumphs that started Roman imperialism. For the commoners who did the fighting the rewards were loot, glory, decorations for valour and farm-lands in the conquered country upon their discharge.

The technique of expansion was simple. *Divide et impera:* enter into solemn treaty with a neighbouring country, foment internal disorder, intervene in support of the weaker side on the ground that Roman honour was involved, replace the legitimate ruler with a puppet, giving him the status of subject ally; later, goad him into rebellion, seize and sack the country, burn down the temples and carry off the captive gods to adorn a triumph. Conquered territories were put under the control of a provincial governor-general, an ex-commander-in-chief, who garrisoned it, levied taxes, set up courts of summary justice, and linked the new frontiers with the old by so-called Roman roads—usually built up by Greek engineers and native forced labour. Established social and religious practices were permitted so long as they did not threaten Roman administration or offend against the broad-minded Roman standards of good taste. The new province presently became a spring-board for further aggression.

Rome was now a great jackdaw's nest, with temples and mansions newly built in solid vulgar, imitation-Greek architectural style—

much of it concrete with a thin marble facing—stuffed with loot
from more ancient and beautiful cities. Typical scenes of "the
grandeur that was Rome" at the sack of Corinth. A group of smoke-
blackened Roman infantrymen squatting on a priceless old master—
Aristides's *The God Dionysus*—and shooting craps for possession
of sacred chalices looted from Dionysus's temple. Others hacking
souvenirs from the most famous relic of antiquity, the stern of the
ship *Argo* which had brought back the Golden Fleece from the
Caucasus more than a thousand years before. The Army commander impressing on the transport captains detailed to convey
unique works of art back to Rome—"Mind you, my men, anything
you lose you'll have to replace."

The prisoners captured in these wars became slaves. The chief
cause of Rome's industrial backwardness was not lack of inventive-
ness but the remarkable cheapness of highly skilled slave labour.
A first-class smith or weaver or potter could often be bought for
about the same price that a good dairy cow would fetch nowadays,
and was not much more expensive to keep. (For that matter, a
Greek school-master or a qualified doctor could be bought for only
a few pounds more.) In the Mediterranean the winter, in general,
is short and mild, and the Romans could import unlimited cheap
grain from Egypt, Libya and Tripoli—it was not for some centuries
that overcultivation made a dust-bowl of the whole North African
coast. Olive-oil, dried fish, chickpeas, wine, and fruit were also in
plentiful supply. Corn-mills driven by water power had been known
for some generations, yet were little used: it was a principle of
industrial economy to keep one's slaves, especially women, in good
physical condition by making them do their daily pull at the lever
of a hand-mill. And though the carpenter had developed into a
highly skilled cabinet-maker, three more centuries passed before
the principle of the watermill was combined with that of the saw.
Still more remarkable, the steam-engine had been invented by one
Ctesibius—who also invented a water-clock and a hydraulic organ
—and a working model had long been on show in the lighthouse
at Alexandria where it was used as a donkey-engine. Capitalists
were unimpressed: "Introduce mechanical hauling into industry
and encourage laziness in the workers." In the same spirit the Emperor Tiberius, Augustus's successor, put to death an inventor who
brought him a specimen of unbreakable and malleable glass: the

discovery would have thrown the jewelry trade into disorder and depreciated the value of gold bullion.

On the whole, slaves were treated well and encouraged to hard work and obedience by being given occasional tips and allowed to earn money in their off hours. Eventually they could hope to buy themselves free, though still owing certain duties as freedmen to their masters; and their children would be free-born. It was dangerous to starve slaves or flog them too freely; indeed, gross cruelty to a slave was now a penal offence. This lesson had been learned in the great Slave Revolt under the gladiator Spartacus two generations before, which had all but succeeded in making the slaves their masters' masters. Slavery was now regarded by industrialists as a safeguard against the pretensions of the free-born working classes, who could not compete in price against well-organised and highly financed slave labour. Strikes of working-men were exceptional: as when the Levite bakers in the Temple at Jerusalem walked out on being refused a 100 per cent rise in pay. The High Priest tried to break the strike by importing bakers from the rival Jewish Temple at Leontopolis in Egypt, but their shew-bread was not up to Jerusalem standard and the strikers gained their demands.

At the apex of the social pyramid, which was still nominally Republican, stood the Emperor Augustus. As leader of the winning side in the Civil Wars, caused by murderous rivalry between noble families, he had been invested with temporary dictatorial powers, religious as well as civil, which he often undertook to relinquish when the time should be ripe; but it never was. Under him in descending order of importance came the remains of the nobility, who formed a rubber-stamp Senate and from whom all high-ranking Army officers and Government officials were drawn; next, the Knights, merchant families eligible for less distinguished offices; next, the free-born Roman citizens with full civil rights, including that of voting at the free democratic elections which no longer took place, and exemption from the servile punishment of crucifixion. After these, free-born foreigners with more limited right; then freed-men; lastly, slaves.

In the higher income groups the birth-rate fell steadily despite bachelor taxes and personal appeals for fertility by the Emperor. Few society women could be bothered to bear children in any

quantity and preferred to let their husbands amuse themselves in
sporting-houses or with Greek mistresses. The society woman's day
was a full one: "Madam, your warm cinnamon milk, and the bath
is ready." "Madam, the masseuse, the chiropodist, the hair-dresser."
"The jeweller has called to show madam the Indian emeralds." "The
chief chef wishes to ask madam's advice about the wild-boar steaks.
He is of opinion that they should hang a day or two longer." "Has
madam decided after all to attend the wedding of her third cousin,
the Lady Metella? It is today." "Madam's pet monkey has, I regret
to report, been at his tricks again in the master's study. Yes, madam,
I have squared the master's secretary and, please, he has undertaken to procure madam a copy of the charming bawdy little Greek
novel that she picked up at Corbulo's yesterday." "My Lady Len-
tula's compliments and will madam confirm last night's bet of one
thousand gold pieces to three hundred against Leek Green in the
second race tomorrow?"

There was constant recruitment of the nobility from the merchant
class, and rich commoners went up into the merchant class and
were privileged to wear a gold thumb-ring and sit in seats reserved
for them at the theatre immediately behind the nobility. Morals
among the less fortunately born were based largely on social ambition. Conviction for petty felonies disqualified a man from membership of the social clubs of his class; serious felony degraded
him. There was also a vague fear that crimes, even when successfully concealed, might be punished in a shadowy Hell with perpetual tortures. Belief in the islands of Elysium, where virtue was
rewarded with a life of perpetual bliss, was still vague; besides,
Homer had made it clear that these abodes were reserved for
royalty. Ordinary citizens became twittering ghosts and went down
to Hell, and stayed there except for an annual ticket-of-leave holiday between owl-cry and cock-crow, when their pious descendants
put food out for them to lick at, and themselves kept carefully
indoors.

Among the governing classes superstitious fear of evil omens,
ghosts, and bogeys contrasted with the fashionable scepticism about
the gods. However, the majesty of Law and the sanctity of treaties
depended in theory on the official Olympian cult, and so did the
complicated system of national holidays and popular entertainments. Jokes at the expense of cross, lecherous old Father Jupiter,

his shrewish wife Juno, and his clever unmarried daughter Minerva —the Roman trinity—were confined to intimate gatherings. But gods and goddesses, so far from being jealous guardians of family morals, permitted and even demanded periodical orgies of drunkenness and sexual promiscuity as healthy vents for popular emotion. Their images also presided at the wild-beast shows, chariot races, gladiatorial fights, dances, plays, musical entertainments and displays of juggling and contortionism, arranged in their honour by endowed priesthoods.

There was no system of public education even for the free-born except in Greek cities that still prided themselves on their high standard of culture, and among the Jews everywhere, for whom attendance at the synagogue school was now a religious obligation. Elsewhere, reading, writing, and arithmetic were luxuries reserved for the governing and mercantile classes with their stewards, secretaries, accountants, and agents. The Jews were at once a comfort and a worry to the central government. Though industrious, law-abiding and peaceful wherever they were left alone, they were not merely a nation of perhaps three and a half millions settled in Palestine under the rule of Herod the Great, a petty king appointed by the Emperor, with a tribal god, a Temple, and established festivals. They were also a huge religious fraternity, including a great many converts of non-Jewish race, whose first article of faith was that there was only one God, and the intimate contact with Goddess-worshippers was disgusting and sinful. Far more Jews lived outside Palestine than in it, spread about in small or large communities from one end of the world to another and over the edge of the world in Babylonia. They constituted a serious obstacle to the Imperial policy of encouraging provincials to pay divine honours to the Emperor, but were still allowed perfect religious freedom. The distinction between Semites and Europeans had not yet been drawn; for the Spartans who were pure Greeks, officially claimed cousinship with the Jews in virtue of a common descent from Abraham. There was, however, strong local jealousy of Jews who had broken into Greek commercial spheres, with which went resentment of them as over-righteous spoilsports.

Colour was no problem. If the question had even arisen—but it never did—whether the black races were inferior to the white the answer would immediately have been found in Homer, who was quoted as an inspired authority in all matters of general morality: "Homer relates that the blessed gods themselves used to pay complimentary visits to the Blameless Ethiopians." Colour was not popularly associated with slavery, since slaves were for the most part white, and nothing prevented coloured monarchs from owning white slaves if honestly come by. Nor was miscegenation frowned upon. Augustus rewarded his ally King Juba II, a Moor, with the hand of Selene, the beautiful daughter of Cleopatra, the Greek queen of Egypt, and his own late brother-in-law Mark Antony.

The Romans were oddly backward in military development, except in the arts of entrenchment, siege warfare and infantry drill with javelin and stabbing-sword. They never practised archery even for sport, or formed their own cavalry units, but relied for flank protection of their solid, slow-moving infantry masses on allied lancers and horse-archers, including many coloured squadrons. To join the Army usually meant staying with one's regiment until the age of sixty, and campaigning was arduous, especially against active and light-armed foresters or mountaineers. The soldier's load weighed more than eighty pounds, which he had to hump for fifteen or twenty miles a day in all weathers; rations were poor, comforts few, pay irregular, floggings frequent. But peacetime garrison duty in big frontier camps was pleasant enough. A regiment kept the same station for generations, and the camp gradually developed into a city as camp-followers set up general stores under the protection of the fortifications, and soldiers married native women and built permanent huts. In remote outposts of the Empire time dragged. Last year an inscription was found on the site of a small Roman camp on the Libyan frontier to this effect "The Company commander fears that it will be a long time before their promised relief arrives from Rome; meanwhile the company have made the best of a bad job and hereby dedicate this commodious swimming-pool to the Goddess of Army Welfare."

The swimming-pool was a Greek institution. It was from the Greeks that the Romans had learned practically all they knew: law, literary technique, public speaking, philosophy, engineering, music, medicine, mathematics, astronomy, stagecraft and acting, domestic and industrial science, sanitation, and athletics. But, with a few notable exceptions, they were all barbarians at heart, and in athletics, for example, showed no innate sense of sportsmanship or any appreciation of the finer points of play. In the public ring they abandoned the Greek style of boxing with light leather gloves in favour of Mack Sennett knuckle-dusters studded with iron points with which outsize heavy-weights slogged great chunks off one another.

No great epidemics of plague, typhus, and cholera, such as ravaged Europe in the Middle Ages, are recorded in this epoch. Well-regulated water supply and sewage system in cities, official supervision of foodstuffs and wine exposed for sale, and a general determination to enjoy life to the full while it lasted: all this increased popular resistance to disease. Medicine, too, was in a saner state than it reached again before the nineteenth century: cures were effected by tried herbal remedies, fomentations, dieting, exercise, massage, and spa waters. Greek surgeons following in the wake of Roman armies had got a better knowledge of the interior of the human body from battlefield observation than hitherto from dissection of Egyptian mummies in the Alexandrian medical school; and dentists undertook fillings and complicated bridge work as well as extractions. Mail and transport services ran smoothly throughout the Empire; the insurance rate for shipping was low, now that piracy had been suppressed, and losses by burglary and fire were infrequent. Bureaucracy had just begun rearing its anonymous head: the Emperor Augustus, grown too old and weary to undertake all the official business that falls to a dictator, allowed his ex-slave secretariat to issue minutes, demands, and routine orders under his seal.

Typical success story: M. Fullanus Atrox, grandson of a Sicilian slave, has made money in hogs, invested it in a suburban tile-factory and tenement-rents in a central block at Rome. He now sells a half interest in the factory, which is placing heavy orders in Spain and North Africa, buys a villa near Naples with central heating, baths, a picture gallery, formal gardens, stabling, twenty acres of good land and accommodation for fifty slaves—the very villa where his father once stoked the furnace. He marks the happy occasion by presenting a solid gold salver engraved with poplar leaves to the nearby temple of Hercules—it will create a good impression locally. At the same time he sends his son to the university of Athens.

It was a stable world. But the farther from the hub one went the uglier grew the scene, especially after Augustus's succession by less humane and energetic Emperors. When the poorly paid Roman armies of occupation were quartered in the provinces of Asia Minor and Syria, the rich man was bled but the poor man was skinned. Banditry, beggary, blackmail, and squalor abounded. Conditions were as bad after the death of Herod the Great in the Protectorate of Judaea, where communism was already in operation among the ascetic communities of the Dead Sea area, and in the Native State of Galilee. The cost of living in Galilee, during Jesus's Ministry, was excessively high. Everything was taxed separately: houses, land, fruit trees, cattle, carts, fishing-boats, market produce, salt. There was also a poll-tax, a road tax, and taxes on exports and imports. Worse: the collection of taxes was leased to private financiers and sub-leased by them to contractors who had to buy police protection at a high cost. The Disciples were poor working-men with dependents. When they were on the road their annual out-of-pocket account—apart even from money handed out to the distressed—can hardly have grossed less than £3,000. But out they went, two by two, deploring the instability of a world that was based on greed, lovelessness, and the power of the sword. Unexpectedly, St. Luke mentions among their financial backers the wife of a high finance officer of the rapacious Native Court.

For questions and exercises, see p. 212, p. 333, p. 334, p. 430, p. 455, and p. 532.

# Biography and Shorter Sketches

## THE EXECUTION OF MARY QUEEN OF SCOTS

JAMES ANTHONY FROUDE

Briefly, solemnly, and sternly they [Lords Kent [1] and Shrewsbury [2]] delivered their awful message. They informed her [Mary Queen of Scots] that they had received a commission under the great seal to see her executed, and she was told that she must prepare to suffer on the following morning.

She was dreadfully agitated. For a moment she refused to believe them. Then, as the truth forced itself upon her, tossing her head in disdain and struggling to control herself, she called her physician and began to speak to him of money that was owed to her in France. At last it seems that she broke down altogether, and they left her with a fear either that she would destroy herself in the night, or that she would refuse to come to the scaffold, and that it might be necessary to drag her there by violence.

The end had come. She had long professed to expect it, but the clearest expectation is not certainty. The scene for which she had

---

[1] One of the thirteen barons who had sat, with other officials, in the trial of Mary at Fotheringay, October 14 and 15, 1586.

[2] George Talbot, 6th Earl of Shrewsbury (1528?-90) had been chosen by Queen Elizabeth to be the keeper of Mary Queen of Scots, who remained his ward at Tutbury, Chatsworth, Sheffield Castle, and other of his country places from 1569 to 1584.

THE EXECUTION OF MARY QUEEN OF SCOTS: From *History of England from the Fall of Wolsey to the Defeat of the Spanish Armada* by James Anthony Froude.

affected to prepare she was to encounter in its dread reality, and all her busy schemes, her dreams of vengeance, her visions of a revolution, with herself ascending out of the convulsion and seating herself on her rival's throne—all were gone. She had played deep, and the dice had gone against her.

Yet in death, if she encountered it bravely, victory was still possible. Could she but sustain to the last the character of a calumniated suppliant accepting heroically for God's sake and her creed's the concluding stroke of a long series of wrongs, she might stir a tempest of indignation which, if it could not save herself, might at least overwhelm her enemy. Persisting, as she persisted to the last, in denying all knowledge of Babington,[3] it would be affectation to credit her with a genuine feeling of religion; but the imperfection of her motive exalts the greatness of her fortitude. To an impassioned believer death is comparatively easy.

Her chaplain was lodged in a separate part of the castle. The Commissioners, who were as anxious that her execution should wear its real character as she was herself determined to convert it into a martyrdom, refused, perhaps unwisely, to allow him access to her, and offered her again the assistance of an Anglican Dean. They gave her an advantage over them which she did not fail to use. She would not let the Dean come near her. She sent a note to the chaplain telling him that she had meant to receive the sacrament, but as it might not be she must content herself with a general confession. She bade him watch through the night and pray for her. In the morning when she was brought out she might perhaps see him, and receive his blessing on her knees. She supped cheerfully, giving her last meal with her attendants a character of sacred parting; afterwards she drew aside her apothecary, M. Gorion, and asked him if she might depend upon his fidelity: when he satisfied her that she might trust him, she said she had a letter and two

---

[3] Anthony Babington (1561-86), a Roman Catholic, had been page to Mary Stuart, had made friends at the court of Elizabeth, had travelled on the continent, and had been induced by a Catholic priest to organize a conspiracy to murder Elizabeth and release Mary (1586); he was caught by Walsingham's spies, and after attempting to save himself by giving information, fled in disguise, but was finally captured, imprisoned in the Tower, and executed with the other conspirators.

diamonds which she wished to send to Mendoza.[4] He undertook
to melt some drug and conceal them in it where they would never
be looked for, and promised to deliver them faithfully. One of the
jewels was for Mendoza himself; the other and the largest was for
Philip.[5] It was to be a sign that she was dying for the truth, and
was meant also to bespeak his care for her friends and servants.
Every one of them so far as she was able, without forgetting a
name, she commended to his liberality. Arundel,[6] Paget,[7] Morgan,[8]
the Archbishop of Glasgow, Westmoreland,[9] Throgmorton,[10] the
Bishop of Ross,[11] her two secretaries, the ladies who had shared
the trials of her imprisonment, she remembered them all, and specified the sums which she desired Philip to bestow on them. And as
Mary Stuart then and throughout her life never lacked gratitude
to those who had been true to her, so then as always she remembered her enemies. There was no cant about her, no unreal talk of
forgiveness of injuries. She bade Gorion tell Philip it was her last
prayer that he should persevere, notwithstanding her death, in the
invasion of England. It was God's quarrel, she said, and worthy of
his greatness: and as soon as he had conquered it, she desired him

[4] The Spanish ambassador to London; after intrigues with the Jesuits, and
after suspicious connections with Mary Stuart, he was ordered to leave England
(1584), and became Minister at Paris, under Henry III.

[5] Philip II of Spain (1527-98).

[6] The Earl of Arundel (1557-95) had turned Roman Catholic, was suspected
of complicity in Throgmorton's plot, was imprisoned, and after a release, was
again in prison during the execution of Mary Stuart.

[7] Thomas Paget, 3rd Baron Paget (d. 1590) had fled to the continent on
the discovery of Throgmorton's plot, and died in Brussels.

[8] Thomas Morgan (1543-1606?) had helped organize the Babington plot.

[9] Charles Neville, 6th Earl of Westmoreland (1543-1601) had attempted to
release Mary Stuart in 1569.

[10] Francis Throgmorton (or Throckmorton) (1554-84), student of the Inner
Temple, and a zealous Catholic, had engaged abroad in plots against the
English government, and was arrested in England while organizing communications between Mary Queen of Scots and Mendoza and Thomas Morgan in Paris;
incriminating documents were found in his house, he confessed under torture
to furthering French designs on England, and was executed at Tyburn.

[11] John Leslie, Bishop of Ross (1527-96), had been employed in France
about the person of Queen Mary, and was her chief adviser on ecclesiastical
policy; later ambassador to Queen Elizabeth, he had to leave England (1573)
because of his connection with the Ridolfi plot (1571).

not to forget how she had been treated by Cecil,[12] and Leicester,[13] and Walsingham; [14] by Lord Huntingdon,[15] who had ill-used her fifteen years before at Tutbury; by Sir Amyas Paulet,[16] and Secretary Wade.[17]

Her last night was a busy one. As she said herself there was much to be done and the time was short. A few lines to the King of France were dated two hours after midnight. They were to insist for the last time that she was innocent of the conspiracy, that she was dying for religion, and for having asserted her right to the crown; and to beg that out of the sum which he owed her, her servants' wages might be paid, and masses provided for her soul. After this she slept for three or four hours, and then rose and with the most elaborate care prepared to encounter the end.

At eight in the morning the Provost-marshal knocked at the outer door which communicated with her suite of apartments. It was locked and no one answered, and he went back in some trepidation lest the fears might prove true which had been entertained the preceding evening. On his returning with the Sheriff, however, a few minutes later, the door was open, and they were confronted with the tall' majestic figure of Mary Stuart standing before them in splendour. The plain gray dress had been exchanged for a robe of black satin; her jacket was of black satin also, looped and slashed and trimmed with velvet. Her false hair was arranged studiously with a coif, and over her head and falling down over her back

---

[12] William Cecil, Baron Burghley (1520-98), powerful and wily statesman of the day, had organized a secret-police system to detect plots against Queen Elizabeth; he was largely responsible for the execution of Mary Stuart.

[13] The Earl of Leicester (1532?-88), one of Elizabeth's favorites, had been proposed by the Queen as a possible husband for Mary Stuart.

[14] Sir Francis Walsingham (1530?-90), great Elizabethan statesman, organized his own secret service to discover Spanish and Jesuit plots against England; he secured the conviction and execution of Mary Stuart.

[15] Henry Hastings, 3rd Earl of Huntingdon (1535-95) had been associated with Lord Shrewsbury in the custody of Mary Stuart (1569-70).

[16] Sir Amyas Paulet (or Poulet) (1536?-88) puritanical keeper of Mary Stuart in 1585; he had custody of her at Tutbury, Chartley, and Fotheringay; he assisted in the inspection of her correspondence and, as a commissioner on her trial, vehemently urged her execution.

[17] Sir William Wade (or Waad) (1546-1623) was clerk of the Privy Council; he had seized Mary's papers in 1586.

was a white veil of delicate lawn. A crucifix of gold hung from her neck. In her hand she held a crucifix of ivory, and a number of jewelled Paternosters was attached to her girdle. Led by two of Paulet's gentlemen, the Sheriff walking before her, she passed to the chamber of presence in which she had been tried, where Shrewsbury, Kent, Paulet, Drury,[18] and others were waiting to receive her. Andrew Melville, Sir Robert's [19] brother, who had been master of her household, was kneeling in tears. "Melville," she said, "you should rather rejoice than weep that the end of my troubles is come. Tell my friends I die a true Catholic. Commend me to my son. Tell him I have done nothing to prejudice his kingdom of Scotland, and so good Melville, farewell." She kissed him, and turning asked for her chaplain Du Preau. He was not present. There had been a fear of some religious melodrama which it was thought well to avoid. Her ladies, who had attempted to follow her, had been kept back also. She could not afford to leave the account of her death to be reported by enemies and Puritans, and she required assistance for the scene which she meditated. Missing them she asked the reason of their absence, and said she wished them to see her die. Kent said he feared they might scream or faint, or attempt perhaps to dip their handkerchiefs in her blood. She undertook that they should be quiet and obedient. "The Queen," she said, "would never deny her so slight a request"; and when Kent still hesitated, she added with tears, "You know I am cousin to your Queen, of the blood of Henry the Seventh, a married Queen of France, and anointed Queen of Scotland." [20]

It was impossible to refuse. She was allowed to take six of her own people with her, and select them herself. She chose her physician Burgoyne, Andrew Melville, the apothecary Gorion, and her surgeon, with two ladies, Elizabeth Kennedy and Curle's young wife Barbara Mowbray, whose child she had baptized.

"Allons donc," she then said—"Let us go," and passing out attended by the Earls, and leaning on the arm of an officer of the guard, she

[18] Sir Drue Drury (1531?-1617), courtier, joint-warder of Mary Stuart.

[19] Robert Melville, 1st Baron Melville (1527-1621), privy councilor, had entreated Queen Elizabeth for Mary Stuart's life.

[20] Mary was the great-granddaughter of Henry VII; she became Queen of France on her marriage to Francis II (1558); her grandmother was a sister of Henry VIII, the father of Elizabeth.

descended the great staircase to the hall. The news had spread far through the country. Thousands of people were collected outside the walls. About three hundred knights and gentlemen of the county had been admitted to witness the execution. The tables and forms had been removed, and a great wood fire was blazing in the chimney. At the upper end of the hall, above the fire-place, but near it, stood the scaffold, twelve feet square and two feet and a half high. It was covered with black cloth; a low rail ran round it covered with black cloth also, and the Sheriff's guard of halberdiers were ranged on the floor below on the four sides to keep off the crowd. On the scaffold was the block, black like the rest; a square black cushion was placed behind it, and behind the cushion a black chair; on the right were two other chairs for the Earls. The axe leant against the rail, and two masked figures stood like mutes on either side at the back. The Queen of Scots as she swept in seemed as if coming to take a part in some solemn pageant. Not a muscle of her face could be seen to quiver; she ascended the scaffold with absolute composure, looked round her smiling, and sate down. Shrewsbury and Kent followed and took their places, the Sheriff stood at her left hand, and Beale [21] then mounted a platform and read the warrant aloud.

In all the assembly Mary Stuart appeared the person least interested in the words which were consigning her to death.

"Madam," said Lord Shrewsbury to her, when the reading was ended, "you hear what we are commanded to do."

"You will do your duty," she answered, and rose as if to kneel and pray.

The Dean of Peterborough, Dr. Fletcher,[22] approached the rail. "Madam," he began, with a low obeisance, "the Queen's most excellent Majesty"; "Madam, the Queen's most excellent Majesty"—thrice he commenced his sentence, wanting words to pursue it. When he repeated the words a fourth time, she cut him short.

"Mr. Dean," she said, "I am a Catholic, and must die a Catholic. It is useless to attempt to move me, and your prayers will avail me but little."

[21] Robert Beale (1541-1601) had been Walsingham's secretary, and had been engaged in negotiating with Mary between 1581 and 1584.

[22] Richard Fletcher (d. 1596) became Dean of Peterborough in 1583; he had drawn up an account of Mary's examination at Fotheringay.

"Change your opinion, Madam," he cried, his tongue being loosed at last; "repent of your sins, settle your faith in Christ, by him to be saved."

"Trouble not yourself further, Mr. Dean," she answered; "I am settled in my own faith, for which I mean to shed my blood."

"I am sorry, Madam," said Shrewsbury, "to see you so addicted to Popery."

"That image of Christ you hold there," said Kent, "will not profit you if he be not engraved in your heart."

She did not reply, and turning her back on Fletcher, knelt for her own devotions.

He had been evidently instructed to impair the Catholic complexion of the scene, and the Queen of Scots was determined that he should not succeed. When she knelt he commenced an extempore prayer in which the assembly joined. As his voice sounded out in the hall she raised her own, reciting with powerful deep-chested tones the penitential Psalms in Latin, introducing English sentences at intervals that the audience might know what she was saying, and praying with especial distinctness for her Holy Father the Pope.

From time to time, with conspicuous vehemence, she struck the crucifix against her bosom, and then, as the Dean gave up the struggle, leaving her Latin, she prayed in English wholly, still clear and loud. She prayed for the Church which she had been ready to betray, for her son, whom she had disinherited, for the Queen whom she had endeavoured to murder. She prayed God to avert his wrath from England, that England which she had sent a last message to Philip to beseech him to invade.[23] She forgave her enemies, whom she had invited Philip not to forget, and then, praying to the saints to intercede for her with Christ, and kissing the crucifix and crossing her own breast, "Even as thy arms, O Jesus," she cried, "were spread upon the cross, so receive me into thy mercy and forgive my sins."

With these words she rose; the black mutes stepped forward, and in the usual form begged her forgiveness.

"I forgive you," she said, "for now I hope you shall end all my troubles." They offered their help in arranging her dress. "Truly,

---

[23] Mary had proposed to both the pope and Philip II, of (Catholic) Spain, a conquest of England, and had superintended the details of a projected invasion under the direction of the Duke of Guise.

my lords," she said with a smile to the Earls, "I never had such grooms waiting on me before." Her ladies were allowed to come up upon the scaffold to assist her; for the work to be done was considerable, and had been prepared with no common thought.

She laid her crucifix on her chair. The chief executioner took it as a perquisite, but was ordered instantly to lay it down. The lawn veil was lifted carefully off, not to disturb the hair, and was hung upon the rail. The black robe was next removed. Below it was a petticoat of crimson velvet. The black jacket followed, and under the jacket was a body of crimson satin. One of her ladies handed her a pair of crimson sleeves, with which she hastily covered her arms; and thus she stood on the black scaffold with the black figures all around her, blood-red from head to foot.

Her reasons for adopting so extraordinary a costume must be left to conjecture. It is only certain that it must have been carefully studied, and that the pictorial effect must have been appalling.

The women, whose firmness had hitherto borne the trial, began now to give way, spasmodic sobs bursting from them which they could not check. "Ne criez vous," she said, "j'ay promis pour vous." [24] Struggling bravely, they crossed their breasts again and again, she crossing them in turn and bidding them pray for her. Then she knelt on the cushion. Barbara Mowbray bound her eyes with a handkerchief. "Adieu," she said, smiling for the last time and waving her hand to them, "Adieu, au revoir." They stepped back from off the scaffold and left her alone. On her knees she repeated the Psalm, In te, Domine, confido, "In Thee, O Lord, have I put my trust." Her shoulders being exposed, two scars became visible, one on either side, and the Earls being now a little behind her, Kent pointed to them with his white wand and looked inquiringly at his companion. Shrewsbury whispered that they were the remains of two abscesses from which she had suffered while living with him at Sheffield.

When the psalm was finished she felt for the block, and laying down her head muttered: "In manus, Domine tuas, commendo animam meam." [25] The hard wood seemed to hurt her, for she placed her hands under her neck. The executioners gently removed them,

---

[24] "Do not weep; I have promised for you."
[25] "Into thy hands, O Lord, I commend my spirit." (Cf. *Luke*, 23:46.)

lest they should deaden the blow, and then one of them holding
her slightly, the other raised the axe and struck. The scene had been
too trying even for the practised headsman of the Tower. His arm
wandered. The blow fell on the knot of the handkerchief, and
scarcely broke the skin. She neither spoke nor moved. He struck
again, this time effectively. The head hung by a shred of skin,
which he divided without withdrawing the axe; and at once a meta-
morphosis was witnessed, strange as was ever wrought by wand of
fabled enchanter. The coif fell off and the false plaits. The laboured
illusion vanished. The lady who had knelt before the block was in
the maturity of grace and loveliness. The executioner, when he
raised the head, as usual, to shew it to the crowd, exposed the
withered features of a grizzled, wrinkled old woman.

"So perish all enemies of the Queen," said the Dean of Peterborough. A loud Amen rose over the hall. "Such end," said the Earl
of Kent, rising and standing over the body, "to the Queen's and the
Gospel's enemies."

Orders had been given that everything which she had worn
should be immediately destroyed, that no relics should be carried
off to work imaginary miracles. Sentinels stood at the door who
allowed no one to pass out without permission; and after the first
pause, the Earls still keeping their places, the body was stripped.
It then appeared that a favourite lapdog had followed its mistress
unperceived, and was concealed under her clothes; when discovered
it gave a short cry, and seated itself between the head and the neck,
from which the blood was still flowing. It was carried away and
carefully washed, and then beads, Paternoster, handkerchief—each
particle of dress which the blood had touched—with the cloth on
the block and on the scaffold, was burnt in the hall fire in the
presence of the crowd. The scaffold itself was next removed: a brief
account of the execution was drawn up, with which Henry Talbot,
Lord Shrewsbury's son, was sent to London, and then every one
was dismissed. Silence settled down on Fotheringay, and the last
scene of the life of Mary Stuart, in which tragedy and melodrama
were so strangely intermingled, was over.

For questions and exercises, see p. 172, p. 273, p. 293, p. 311, p. 448, and
p. 503.

## HISTORIAN AND HEADSMAN

### JAMES MELINE

It is so painful to dwell upon the words and actions of a poor woman in her moments of misery.—*History of England* by J. A. Froude, Vol. II, p. 455.

It is a miserable duty to be compelled to search for these indications of human infirmities; above all, when they are the infirmities of a lady whose faults, let them have been what they would, were so fearfully and terribly expiated.—*History of England* by J. A. Froude, Vol. I, p. 179.

We have already stated that a serious objection to Mr. Froude as a historian is his total want of a uniform standard of justice, of the ethical principle which estimates actions as they are in themselves and not in the light of personal like or dislike of his historical personages. Read the two passages which head this chapter. They are specimens of the "outbursts of the truest pathos," of "tender human sympathy," so lauded by one of his admirers. The historian penned them with reference to the case of Anne Boleyn, and when we reach his narrative of Mary Stuart's death we find that they are not the expression of any abiding sentiment or belief, but mere specimens of rhetoric *de circonstance,* to be classed among those elaborate impromptus carefully labored at leisure with which he ornaments his pages. When he tells us of Mary Stuart's death, we find that so far from being painful to him it affords him the most exquisite delight "to dwell upon the words and actions of a poor woman in her moments of misery"; and we further find that, not content with the record of her words and actions as furnished by history, he finds it expedient to invent others in order to prolong and, if possible, heighten his pleasure.

Hollow brass and tinkling cymbal too is his "miserable duty to be compelled to search for human infirmities, *above all when they are the infirmities of a lady,*" etc., when we find him complacently inviting his readers to join with him in the gaze of the two brutal earls at the scars left by illness on the shoulders of the helpless victim.

If Mr. Froude really believes the Queen of Scots to be the guilty

HISTORIAN AND HEADSMAN: From *Mary Queen of Scots* by James Meline.

woman he describes—and we seriously doubt it; if he attaches any
serious signification to the vituperative abuse he showers upon her
throughout his work, we can well imagine the bitter disappointment
which must have seized him when, contemplating his victim at the
hour of death and on the edge of the grave, he beholds her raised
so infinitely above her persecutors by her dignity and Christian
resignation. We can well understand, too, how at the spectacle of
what his more conscientious ally (Burton) calls the "noble simplicity
of her expiation," this disappointment should deepen into an angry
rage that seeks revenge. That revenge—the only one in his power—
he has taken.

Friends and enemies of Mary Stuart—sympathisers, proclaimers
of her guilt, and advocates of her innocence—have written concerning that most remarkable death scene, of which several descriptions
have come down to us; but no such strange and shocking narrative
as that of Mr. Froude has ever grieved the judicious and blotted
the page of history. His pen alone was equal to such a performance.
It is one of the monstrosities of modern literature, and stands on
"a bad eminence."

There was no refinement of cruelty, there was no excess of brutality left uninflicted on that unfortunate woman as she stood facing
the axe and the block. One would think that the veriest ruffian
stained with a thousand crimes would, in that hour supreme, be
permitted to seek and enjoy unmolested whatever to him might
constitute spiritual consolation. But it was not allowed this dying
woman. The only religious aid she required was denied her, although her almoner was in the house. A man whose services she
declined, bellowed his remonstrances and warnings in her ear, telling her—by way of encouragement—that she was damned. "He had
been evidently instructed to impair the Catholic complexion of the
scene," suggests Mr. Froude. We think it highly probable, inasmuch
as the official report states that, "according to a direction that he
had received the night before, he would have made a Godly
admonition," etc. From Kent and Shrewsbury there was nought
for this unhappy woman but inhumanity and insult. And all this
seems to our historian not only eminently proper, but immensely
gratifying.

Sensible to the last, he keeps up his "masking and mumming,
with inference, supposition, and insinuation, with forced citations,

and patched references." His narrative of the execution is little more than a paraphrase of the account written to Burghley by Richard Wigmore [Wingfield], who was Cecil's secret agent and present at the scene.[1] But the reader must not suppose from the fact that he was a sort of spy and that his account appears from the paraphrase to be so heartless and cynical, that this man Wigmore was utterly vile. He would not seem so if Mr. Froude had not carefully eliminated from his letter every passage and expression, which rendered justice to Mary Stuart's dignity and Christian resignation. . . .

Characteristically ingenious is the device of Mr. Froude to carry out and give force to his dramatic theory by dwelling on Mary's rich dress and false hair. If Mary had arrayed herself otherwise than she did, her costume might have been properly criticised as singular and affected. It was in strict conformity with the fashion of the age, of which rich dress was a characteristic. When Elizabeth died, she left eighty *atiers* or wigs ornamented with jewels. They formed at the time a part of every lady's wardrobe, and were of various colors. Mary's omission to wear one would have been thought strange. She had that morning told her women to "dress her as for a festival." Their choice of garments was naturally for the richest from an assortment by no means large. It appears that under her black robe Mary Stuart wore a sort of black jacket. Both these were taken off preparatory to the execution, and under them appeared a body of crimson satin, which with her petticoat of crimson, and a pair of crimson sleeves handed her by one of her ladies, to cover her naked arms, made the dress all red—"blood-red from head to foot," as Mr. Froude states it in his delight. We are further informed that this was all done with design, and that the "pictorial effect must have been appalling." We venture to surmise that a Christian about to stand in the presence of God has but little room in his or her mind for "pictorial effects," and that Mary Stuart's thoughts in that last hour of her life were not for this world. But see how powerless is any reasonable surmise in the presence of Mr. Froude's positive knowledge, for we have his assurance that she gave the subject of this underclothing careful study, and had her own motives for adopting it. Listen. "Her reasons for adopting

[1] To this are added a few details from other sources.

so extraordinary a costume must be left to conjecture. *It is only certain* [2] *that it must have been carefully studied,"* etc. (XII, 359.) When the head of the victim was laid on the block, the executioner, a stalwart man, brought down his axe; but it was an uncertainly directed blow and only inflicted a ghastly wound. We have already cited the passage from Mr. Froude's favorite "Vray Rapport" which relates to this incident.[3] He does not see that passage. It is a well established principle of that historian that no one who comes in hostile contact with Mary Stuart shall be capable of error. And so we are told: "The blow fell on the knot of the handkerchief, and scarcely broke the skin."

But the gratification, the joy manifested throughout this narrative of brutality, bigotry, and blood, culminates in delight when he tells us—

"The laboured illusion vanished. The lady who had knelt before the block was in the maturity of grace and loveliness. The executioner, when he raised the head, as usual, to shew it to the crowd, exposed the withered features of a grizzled, wrinkled old woman."

We are inclined to believe that what was seen was a face whose features were yet convulsed by the agonizing suffering from the executioner's first blow.

When Mary Stuart bowed her head to the axe which should end her sufferings, the executioner remarked that her fingers were upon the block in such a position under her neck, that when he struck, they would be cut off. The man's trade was death, his calling brutal, his occupation bloody. But he had no desire needlessly to multiply the horror of the scene by maiming and mangling even a body which must the next instant, be a lifeless corpse; and he gently removed the hands.

The example of this social pariah should have commended itself to Mr. Froude, for whom it is not enough that this woman should be made to suffer for a crime of which she was innocent—not enough that inhuman men should mock her infirmities in that awful

---

[2] A distinguished English historian aptly remarks that "Intuitive certainty is beyond the reach of argument." (*J. A. Froude,* Vol. XII, p. 311.) But this is said in connection with a stern rebuke administered by him to persons pretending to interpret the motives of Queen Elizabeth—"those to whom it has been given to have a perfect insight into the motives of human actions."

[3] The passage in which this occurs has been omitted from this selection.

moment—not enough that in her preparation for death she should be denied the consolations of her own faith—not enough that a religious bigot should be ordered to thrust himself between the victim and her Maker—not enough that she should receive vociferous assurance that her damnation was certain.

Not enough all this. He must do more. He is determined that Mary Stuart shall not thus escape him, and—standing on this side of a grave, cold in the shadow of three hundred years—we shudder as we see him warm up to his ghoul-like task, travestie her bearing, mock her words, inventory her garments, play the costumer, degrade the historian into a man-milliner, and—falsifying her motives —blasphemously challenge as dramatic affectation the last appeal of a poor soul to God, betraying a revolting satisfaction in her suffering, positive delight in the discovery that she was no longer in the maturity of grace and loveliness, and, with a hideous leer, call on his readers to feast with him their gaze on the withered features of a wrinkled old woman, assuring them, meanwhile, that she leaves the world with a lie on her lips!

We shrink from the revolting horror of the picture as we wonder at its mendacity.

Decidedly, the headsman with his bloody axe rises in our gaze, beside this historian, to the full proportions of one of nature's noblemen.

For questions and exercises, see p. 172, p. 448, and p. 503.

# THE LAST DAYS

### RICHARD WINGFIELD

A true narracíon of the execution of Mary late Queene of Scotland within the castle of Fortheringhaie the eight of ffeb—Anno Domini one thousand and five hundred and eighty sixe.

Directed to the right honorable Sir William Cecill Knight Lord Burleigh Lord highe Treasurer of England.

By R. W. The Epistle Dedicatorie. To the right honorable Sir William Cecill Knight Lord Burleigh Lord highe Treasurer of England.

THE LAST DAYS: *Narration of the last days of the Queen of Scots.* British Museum MSS. *Caligula* C. IX.

It maie please your good Lordship to be advertised that according as your honor gave me in command, I have heere sett downe in writing the true order and manner of the execucion of Mary last Queene of Scotland the eight day of ffebruary last past in the great hall within the Castle of Fotheringhaie together with the relacion of all such speeches and actions spoken and done by the said same Scottish Queene or anie others and all other circumstances and proceedings concerning the same from and after the deliverie of the said Queene to, Thomas Andrewes Esquire highe Sheriffe for her Majesties Countie of Norffolke vnto the end of said Execucion as followeth.

The execucion of Mary late Queene of Scotland.

It being certified the sixt of ffebruarie last to the said Queene by the right honorable the Earle of Kent the Earle of Shrewsbury and also by Sir Amyas Pawlett and Sir Drewe Drury her governors that she was to prepare herself to dye the eighte daie of ffebruary next, she seemed not to be in anie terror for ought that appeared by anie her outward iestures or behavior, other than mervailing she should dye, but rather wth smiling cheere and pleasaunt countenaunce disgested and accepted the said ordination of preparacion to her (as she saide) vnexpected execucion, sayeing that her death should be wellcome vnto her seeing that her Majestie was so resolved. And that that soule were too farr vnworthie the fruicion of the ioye of heaven forever, whose body in this world would not be content to endure the stroke of the execucion for a moment, and that spoken she wept bitterly and became silent.

The said eighte daie of ffebruarie being come, and the time and place appointed for the execucion as aforesaid.

The said Queene of Scotts being of stature tall, of body corpulent, round shouldered, her face fatt and broade double chinned and hazel eyed her borrowed hair aburne her attire was this.

On her head she had a dressing of Lawne edged with bone lace a pomander chaine, and an agnus dei about her necke, a Crusifixe in her hande a paire of beades at her girdle with a golden crosse at th' end of them, a vaille of lawne fastened to her cawle bowed out with wiar edged rounde about with bone lace, her gowne was of blacke Sattin printed with a traine and long sleeves to the grownd sett with acorne buttons of jett trimmed with pearle and shorte sleeves of blacke sattin cutt, with a pair of sleeves of purple vellvett whole vnder them. Her Kertle whole of figured blacke sattin, her petticote vpperbodie vnlaced in the backe of crimson sattin, and her petticote skirtes of crimson vellvett her shoes of spanish lether with the rough side outwarde, a paire of silke garters coloured greene, her stockinges worsted coloured watchett clocked with silver, and edged in the topps with silver, and next her legges a paire of Jersey hose white.

This Queene thus apparrelled in a kinde of ioye, without anie desire of differing of matters or time departed her Chamber, and very willinglie bended her steps towardes the place of execucion, being gentlie supported out of her said Chamber into and [sic] entrie next the said great hall by two of Sir Amyas Pawlettes chiefe gentlemen, Mr. Andrewes the highe Sheriffe goeing before her in which entrie the honorable the Earle of Kent, and the Earle of Shrewesbury Commissioners appointed by her Majestie for her said execucion, together with the two governors of her person Sir Amyas Pawlett and Sir Drew Drewrie, and divers other Knightes and gentlemen of good accompt did meete her, where they founde one of the said Queenes servants named Meluin kneeling on his knees to the said Queene his Mistres, wringing his handes and shedding tears vsed then and there theis wordes vnto her. Ah Madam vnhappie me, what man on earth was ever before the messenger of such important sorrowe and heavines, as I shalbe, when I shall reporte that my good and gratious Queene and Mistres is beheaded in England.

The saide teares prevented him of further speaking, whereupon the said Queene powring out her dyeing teares this answered him.

My good servant cease to lament for thou hast cause rather to ioye than to morne for nowe shalt thou see Marie Stewart's troubles receive their longe expected end and determinacion, ffor knowe (said she) good servant all the world is but vanitie and subiect still to more sorrowes than an whole ocian of teare can bewaile. But I praie thee (said she) carrie this message from me, That I doe die a true woman to my religion and like a true Queene of Scotland and ffraunce. But God forgive them (said she) that they have longe desired mine end, and thirsted for my blood as the hart for the water brookes.

Oh God (said she) thou art the author of all truth and truth itself knoweth the inner Chamber of my thoughtes, howe that I was ever

willing that England and Scotland should be vnited together, well
(said she) then commend me to my sonne and tells him that I haue
not done anie thing preiudiciall to the state and kingdome of Scotland, and so resolving herself againe to teares said good Meluin
farewell and with weeping eyes her cheekes all besprinkled wth
teares as they were kissed him sayeing once again farewell good
Meluin and pray for thy Mistres and Queene and then she turned
herself to the Lordes and tolde them that she had certaine requestes
to make vnto them, one was for a some of monie, which the said
Sir Amyas Pawlett knewe of, to be paid to one Curle her servant.
Next that her poore servantes might have and enioje that with
quietnes which she had given them by her wills and testament,
and that they might be favourablie entreated, and to send them
saflie into their Countries and this to doe my verie good Lord I doe
coniure you.

Answere was made to this effect by Sir Amyas Pawlett, I am not
forgettfull of the mony your grace doth speake of and therefore
(said he) your grace shall not need to rest in suspense of the not
performing your request.

And then she said there rested yett one requaest which she would
make vnto the Lordes, and that was this, That it would please them
to permitt her poore distressed servantes to be present about her
at her death, that their eyes might beholde and their harts be witnesses howe patientlie their Queen and Mistres should endure her
execucion that thereby they might be able to make relacion when
they come into their Countries, That she died a true constant
Catholique to her religion.

Then the Earle of Kent answered thus Madam that which you
haue desired cannot be convienientlie graunted, for if it should it
were to be feared lest some of them with speeches or other behavior would both be greivous to your Grace and vnpleasing to
vs and our companie, whereof we haue some experience. ffor yf
such an accesse should be allowed they would not sticke to putt
some superstitious trumpery in practize and it were but in dipping
their handkershiffes in your graces blood which were very vnmeete
for vs to give allowaunce.

My Lord said the Queene of Scottes I will give my word although
it be but dead, that they shall not deserve blame in anie the actions
you have named, but also poore soules it would doe them good

to bid their Mistres farewell. And I hope said she further to the Earle of Kent, your Mistres meaning her Majestie being a maiden Queene, will vouchsafe in regard of womanhood, that I shall have some of my owne people about me at my death.

And I knowe said she her Majestie hath not given anie such straight comission, but that you might graunt me a request of farre greater curtesy then this if I were a woman of farr meaner calling then the Queene of Scottes, and then perceiving she could not obtaine her request wthout some difficultie, of meere greife burst into teares sayeing.

I am Cosen to your Queene and descended from the blood royall of King Henrie the seaventh and a married Queene of ffraunce and an anonyted Queene of Scotland.

At which time upon great consultation betweene the two Earles and others in comission it was permitted that she should have some of her servantes about her as before she had instantlie desired and entreted and withall did desire her to make choise of half a dozen of her best beloved men and women and then of her men she chose Meluin, her Apothecarie, her Surgeon and one other old man besides, and of her Women she chose those as did vse to lye in her Chamber.

After this the said Queene being supported by Sir Amyas Pawlettes gentlemen as aforesaid and Meluin carrying vp her trayne being accompanied wth the Earle of Kentes gentlemen and the Sheriffe goeing before her as aforesaid passed out of th'entrie into the hall within the said Castle of ffotheringhaie before mentioned with an unapauled countenaunce stept up to the scaffold in the said hall then and there made for her death being twoe foote highe and twelve foote broade wth railes round about, hanged and covered with blacke.

Then haveing the stoole brought her she satt downe, on the right hand of her there stood the Earle of Kent and the Earle of Shrewsbury and on the lefte hande Mr. Andrews the Sheriffe, and opposite before her stood the two executioners and round about the scaffold stood gentlemen and others. Then silence being made the Queenes Maiesties comission for her execution was read openly by Mr. Beale clarke of the Counsell which done the people with a loude voice cried God saue the Queene. During the reading of which comission, the said Queene was very silent listening vnto it with so careles a regard as if it had not concerned her at all, nay rather wth so maerry and cheerfull countenannce, as if it had bin a pardon from her Majestie and with all vsed such a straungnes in her wordes and deedes, as yf she had never known anie of the assemblie nor had bin anie thing seene in the English language.

Then Mr. Doctor fffletcher deane of Peterborough standing directlie before her without the railes bending his body with great reverence vttered this exhortation following. . . . [The Dean's speech is omitted.]

Trouble not yourself Mr. Deane nor me for knowe that I am settled in the auncient Catholique & romaine religion, and in defence thereof by Godes grace I meane to spend my blood. Then said Mr. Deane Maddam channge your opinion & repent you your former wickednes & settle you vpon this ground that onlie in Christ Jesus you hope to be saved.

Then she answered and said with great earnestnes.

Good Mr. Deane trouble not yourself anie more about this matter ffor knowe I was borne in this religion I have lived in this religion, & am resolved to dye in this religion.

Then said the two Earles (when they sawe howe vnconformable she was to the hearing of Mr. Deanes good exhortation) Maddam we will praie for your grace that if it stand with Godes will, you maie haue your heart enlightened with the true knowledg of God & his word, & so die therein.

Then answered the said Queene my Lordes if you will praie with me, I will even from my harte thank you, & think myself greatly favored by you. But to joine with you in prayer my Lordes after your manner, whoe are not one & same religion with me, it were a sinne and I will not.

Then the Lordes called for Mr. Deane againe & bid him saye on or speake what he thought good, wherevpon the said Mr. Deane kneeling vpon the scaffold staires began this prayer following. . . . [The prayer is omitted.]

All the assenblie saveing the said Queene & her servantes said the prayer after Mr. Deane during the saying of which prayer the Queene herself satt vpon a stoole, haveing about her neck an Agnus dei, in one of her handes a Crusifix at her girdle a paire of beades with a golden crosse at the end of them, wth a lattine booke of vaine prayers in her other hand.

Thus furnished with her superstitious trumpery without anie regard had to that which Mr. Dean said Began very fastlie with teares & a loude voice to praye in lattine, & in the middest of her praying by reason of overmuch weeping and mourning as it seemed she began to slide of her stoole, at which time kneeling againe said divers other prayers in lattine. And so she left praying before Mr. Dean. When Mr. Deane had done she prayed in english for Christes afflicted Church, & for an end of her troubles, for her sonne & for the Queenes Majestie and desired God that she might prosper and serve God aright, that spoken she said she hoped to be saved by & in the blood of Jesus Christ, at the foote of whose Crucifixe holding that vp which she had in her hand she would shed her blood.

Then said the Earle of Kent, Maddam I beseech you settle Jesus Christ in your hart as you did before and leave the adiction of those popish trumperies to themselves.

She seemed little or nothing at all to regard the good Councell of the said Earle of Kent, but went forward with her prayers, and in the conclusion thereof in English, desired God that it would please him to avert his wroth from this Iland, & that he would give vnto it grace & forgiveness of sinnes.

Then she said that she forgave all her enemies with all her harte, which had long sought her blood & desired God to convert them to the truth, this done she desired all saintes to make intercession for her to the Savior of the world Jesus Christ.

Then she began to kisse her Crusifix & to crosse herself saying theis words. Even as thy armes o Jesus Christ were spred here vp̄on the crosse so receive me I beseech thee into thine armes of mercy, & forgive me all my sinns. And so ended.

Then the two executioners kneeled downe and desired her to forgive them for her death. She answered I forgive you with all my harte for I hope this death shall give an end to all my troubles.

Then she with her two women began to disrobe her & then she laide her crusifix vpon the stoole one of her executioners tooke from her necke the Agnus dei & and then she began to laye holde of it, sayeing she would give it to one of her women, and withall toulde her executioner that he should have mony for it.

Then she suffered them with her two women to take of her Chaine of pomander beades & of all her other apparell & that with a kinde of gladness & smileing she began to make herself vnready putting of a paire of sleeves wth her owne handes which the two executioners had rudely before bin taking of & that with such speed as if she longed to have bin gone out of the world. During all theis actions of disrobing of the said Queene she never altered her countenaunce but smileing as it were said, she never had such groomes before to make her vnready, nor ever did put of her clothes before such a company.

At length she being vntired & vnapparrelled of such & so much of her attire & apparell as was convenient saveing her petticote & kertle, her two women lookeing upon her burst out into a very great & pittifull shrieking & when their crying began to decline they crossed themselves and prayed in lattin.

Then the said Queene turning herself to them and seeing them in such a mournfull & lamentable plight imbraced them & said theis wordes in french. . . . & so crossed & kissed them and bad them pray for her & not to be mournfull, for said she this daie I trust shall your Mistreses troubles end then with a smileing countenaunce she turned herself to her men servantes Meluin & the reste standing vpon a bench near the scaffold who were sometimes weeping and sometimes crying out aloude & continually crossing themselves prayed in lattin. And the said Queene thus turned vnto them did herself likewise Cross them and badd them farewell, & prayed them to pray for her even vnto the last houre, this done, one of her women haveing a Corpus Christie cloth lapped it up three-cornerwise & kissed it, & put it over the face of her Mistres & pinned it fast vpon the call of her head.

Then the two women mournfully departed from her, & then the said Queene kneeled down vpon the cushion, at which time, and very resolutely, & without anie token of feare she spake aloude this psalme in lattin. In te domine confido ne confundar in eternum.

Then groeping for the block she laide downe her head putting her chinne over the block wth both her hands wch holding them still had been cut of had they not bin espied.

Then she laide herself vpon the blocke most quietlie, & stretching out her armes and legges cryed out In manus tuas domine three or foure times, & at the laste with one of the executioners helde her slightlie with one of his handes, the other gave two strookes with an axe before he cutt of her head, & yet left a little gristle behinde at which time she made verie small noyse & stirred not any parte of herself from the place where she laye.

Then the executioner that cutt of her head lifted it vp & bad God save the Queene. Then her dressing of lawne fell of from her head which appeared as gray as if she had bin threescore and tenn yeares old polled very short, her face being in a moment so much altered from the forme which she had when she was alive as fewe could remember, by her dead face. Her lipps stirred up & downe almost a quarter of an hower after her head was cut off.

Then said Mr. Deane so perish all the Queenes enemies.

Then after the Earle of Kent came to the dead bodye & standing over it wth a loude voice said likewise, such an end happen to all the Queenes and the gospelles enemies.

Then one of her executioners plucking of her garters espied her little dogge which was crept vnder her clothes which could not be gotten forth but with force & afterwardes coould not depart from her dead corpes, but came and laye betweene her head and shoulders a thing dilligently noted.

The same dogg being imbrued wth her blood was carried awaie & washed as all thinges els were that had anie blood on them, the executioners were sent awaie with mony for their fees, not haveing anie thing that belonged vnto her.

Afterwardes everyone was commanded forth of the hall saveing the sheriffe & his men, whoe carried her up into a greate Chamber made ready for the surgeons to embalme her and was embalmed.

And thus I hope (my very good Lord) I have certified your honor of all actions matters and circumstances as did proceed from her or anie others at her death, wherein I dare promise vnto your good Lordshipp (yf not in some better or worse words then were spoken somewhat I am mistaken) in matter I have not anie whitt offended.

Howbeit I will not so iustefy my duty herein but that in many thinges might well have bin omitted, as not worthy noting, yett because yt is your Lordshipps faulte, to desire to know all, & so I have certified all it is an offence pardonable. So restinge at your honors further commandement, I take my leave this XI. of ffebruary Anno 1586.

Your honors in all humble service to be commanded.

finis   .        R. W.

For questions and exercises, see p. 172, p. 273, p. 311, p. 455, and p. 503.

# MAZIE

### JOSEPH MITCHELL

A bossy, yellow-haired blonde named Mazie P. Gordon is a celebrity on the Bowery. In the nickel-a-drink saloons and in the all-night restaurants which specialize in pig snouts and cabbage at a dime a platter, she is known by her first name. She makes a round of these establishments practically every night, and drunken bums sometimes come up behind her, slap her on the back, and call her sweetheart. This never annoys her. She has a wry but genuine fondness for bums and is undoubtedly acquainted with more of them than any other person in the city. Each day she gives them between five and fifteen dollars in small change, which is a lot of money on the Bowery. "In my time I been as free with my dimes as old John D. himself," she says. Mazie has presided for twenty-one years over the ticket cage of the Venice Theatre, at 209 Park Row, a few doors west of Chatham Square, where the Bowery begins.

The Venice is a small, seedy moving-picture theatre, which opens at 8 A.M. and closes at midnight. It is a dime house. For this sum a customer sees two features, a newsreel, a cartoon, a short, and a serial episode. The Venice is not a "scratch house." In fact, it is highly esteemed by its customers, because its seats get a scrubbing at least once a week. Mazie brags that it is as sanitary as the Paramount. "Nobody ever got loused up in the Venice," she says. On the Bowery, cheap movies rank just below cheap alcohol as an escape, and most bums are movie fans. In the clientele of the Venice they are numerous. The Venice is also frequented by people from the tenement neighborhoods in the vicinity of Chatham Square, such as Chinatown, the Little Italy on lower Mulberry Street, and the Spanish section on Cherry Street. Two-thirds of its customers are males. Children and most women sit in a reserved section under the eyes of a matron. Once, in an elegant mood, Mazie boasted that she never admits intoxicated persons. "When do you consider a person intoxicated?" she was asked. Mazie snickered. "When he

MAZIE: From *McSorley's Wonderful Saloon* by Joseph Mitchell. Reprinted by permission of the Publishers, Duell, Sloan and Pearce, Inc. Copyright 1940, 1943 by Joseph Mitchell. Originally published in *The New Yorker*.

has to get down on all fours and crawl," she said. In any case, there
are drunks in practically every Venice audience. When the liquor
in them dies down they become fretful and mumble to themselves,
and during romantic pictures they make loud, utterly frank remarks to the actors on the screen, but by and large they are not
as troublesome as a class of bums Mazie calls "the stiffs." These
are the most listless of bums. They are blank-eyed and slow-moving, and they have no strong desire for anything but sleep. Some are
able to doze while leaning against a wall, even in freezing weather.
Many stiffs habitually go into the Venice early in the day and
slumber in their seats until they are driven out at midnight. "Some
days I don't know which this is, a movie-pitcher theatre or a flophouse," Mazie once remarked. "Other day I told the manager
pitchers with shooting in them are bad for business. They wake
up the customers."

Most Bowery movie houses employ bouncers. At the Venice,
Mazie is the bouncer. She tells intimates that she feels fighting is
unladylike but she considers it her duty to throw at least one customer out of the theatre every day. "If I didn't put my foot down,
the customers would take the place," she says. "I don't get any fun
out of fighting. I always lose my temper. When I start swinging, I
taste blood, and I can't stop. Sometimes I get beside myself. Also,
a lot of the bums are so weak they don't fight back, and that makes
me feel like a heel." Mazie is small, but she is wiry and fearless,
and she has a frightening voice. Her ticket cage is in the shadow
of the tracks of the City Hall spur of the Third Avenue elevated
line, and two decades of talking above the screeching of the trains
have left her with a rasping bass, with which she can dominate men
twice her size. Now and then, in the Venice, a stiff throws his head
back and begins to snore so blatantly that he can be heard all over
the place, especially during tense moments in the picture. When
this happens, or when one of the drunks gets into a bellowing
mood, the women and children in the reserved section stamp on
the floor and chant, "Mazie! Mazie! We want Mazie!" The instant
this chant goes up, the matron hastens out to the lobby and raps
on the side window of Mazie's cage. Mazie locks the cash drawer,
grabs a bludgeon she keeps around, made of a couple of copies
of *True Romances* rolled up tightly and held together by rubber
bands, and strides into the theatre. As she goes down the aisle,

peering this way and that, women and children jump to their feet, point fingers in the direction of the offender, and cry, "There he is, Mazie! There he is!" Mazie gives the man a resounding whack on the head with her bludgeon and keeps on whacking until he seems willing to behave. Between blows, she threatens him with worse punishment. Her threats are fierce and not altogether coherent. "Outa here on a stretcher!" she yells. "Knock your eyeballs out! Big baboon! Every tooth in your head! Bone in your body!" The women and children enjoy this, particularly if Mazie gets the wrong man, as she sometimes does. In action, Mazie is an alarming sight. Her face becomes flushed, her hair flies every which way, and her slip begins to show. If a man defends himself or is otherwise contrary, she harries him out of his seat and drives him from the theatre. As he scampers up the aisle, with Mazie right behind him, whacking away, the women and children applaud.

Mazie's animosity toward a stiff or a drunk usually lasts until she has driven him out to the sidewalk. Then, almost invariably, she becomes contrite and apologetic. "Look, buddy, I'm sorry," she said one afternoon recently to a drunk she had chased out because he had been screaming "Sissy! Sissy!" at George Raft during the showing of a prison picture called "Each Dawn I Die." "If you didn't see the whole show," she continued, "you can go back in." "Hell, Mazie," said the drunk, "I seen it three times." "Here, then," she said, handing him a dime. "Go get yourself a drink." Although the drunk's ears were still red from Mazie's blows, he grinned. "You got a heart of gold, Mazie," he said. "You my sweetheart." "O.K., buddy," Mazie said, stepping back into the cage. "You quit acting like a god-damn jackass and I'll be your sweetheart."

The Venice is a family enterprise. It is owned by Mazie and two sisters—Rosie, the widow of a horse-race gambler, and Jeanie, an acrobatic dancer. Mazie's sisters let her run things to suit herself. She is profoundly uninterested in moving pictures and is seldom able to sit through one. "They make me sick," she says. Consequently, she employs a manager and leaves the selection and ordering of films entirely up to him. For a theatre of its class, the Venice is prosperous, and Mazie could afford to hire a ticket girl and take things easy, but she enjoys the job and will not relinquish it, as her sisters often urge her to do. From her cage she has a good view of Chatham Square, which is the favorite promenade of

Bowery drunks and eccentrics. "The things I see, by God, you wouldn't believe it," she says proudly. When she catches sight of a person she knows among the passers-by, she sticks her face up to the round hole in the front window of her cage and shouts a greeting. Sometimes she discusses exceedingly personal matters with people out on the sidewalk. "Hey there, Squatty," she yelled one afternoon to a dreamy-eyed little man, "I thought you was in Bellevue." "I was, Mazie," the man said. "They turned me loose yesterday." "Where'd they put you this time—the drunk ward or the nut ward?" "I was in with the drunks this time." "How'd they treat you?" "They didn't do me no harm, I guess." "You get drunk last night, Squatty?" "Sure did. "Guess you had to celebrate." "Sure did." "Well, take care of yourself, Squatty." "Thanks, Mazie. You do the same."

Sitting majestically in her cage like a raffish queen, Mazie is one of the few pleasant sights of the Bowery. She is a short, bosomy woman in her middle forties. Some people believe she has a blurry resemblance to Mae West. Her hair is the color of sulphur. Her face is dead white, and she wears a smudge of rouge the size of a silver dollar on each cheek. Her eyes are sleepy and droopy-lidded. On duty, she often wears a green celluloid eyeshade. She almost always has a cigarette hanging from a corner of her mouth, and this makes her look haughty. Like a movie croupier, she can smoke a cigarette down to the end and not take it from her mouth once, even while talking. She has a deep cigarette cough; she smokes three and a half packs a day and says tobacco is murdering her. On her right hand she wears four diamond rings. She likes vigorous colors, and her dresses are spectacular; they come from shops on Division Street. The glass-topped Bowery and Chinatown rubberneck wagons often park in front of the Venice, and now and then a band of sightseers stand on the sidewalk and stare at Mazie. She despises sightseers and says they give the Bowery a black eye. Sometimes she thumbs her nose at them. Actually, however, she does not mind being stared at. "People walk past here just to give me the eye," she once said. "I got a public of my own, just like a god-damn movie-pitcher star."

Mazie is a talkative woman, and on most subjects she is exceedingly frank, but she rarely says anything about her private life, and some people on the Bowery consider her a mystery woman. A

man who had been stopping by to chat with her several times a
week for years suddenly realized recently that he did not know
whether she was Miss or Mrs. Gordon. "You ever been married,
Mazie?" he asked. "That's for me to know, you to find out," she
said sharply. A moment later she added, "I'll ask you this. Do I
look and act like a girl that never had a date?" People around
Chatham Square believe, among other things, that she was a belly
dancer in the Hurtig & Seamon burlesque houses when she was a
young woman, which isn't true. They claim, with not much relevance, that she gives her spare money to bums because she was
once disappointed in a love affair. Furthermore, they believe she
was born in Chinatown. Actually, she is a native of Boston, a fact
which gives her a lot of satisfaction. Every winter she takes a week
off and spends it in Boston, just walking around. She believes the
people of Boston are superior to the people elsewhere. One night a
blind-drunk bum stumbled into an "L" pillar in front of the Venice,
skinning his nose, and she rushed out and dragged him into her
lobby. Then she went into a nearby saloon and yelled, "Gimme
some hot water and a clean rag!" "You want to take a bath, Mazie?"
asked the bartender. This remark enraged her. "Don't you talk like
that to me, you yellow-bellied jerk," she said. "I come from Boston,
and I'm a lady."

Mazie says her real name is Mazie Phillips, but she will not tell
anything about her parents. Her intimates say that around 1903,
when she was a schoolgirl in Boston, her older sister, Rosie, came
to New York and married Louis Gordon, an East Side gambler
and promoter. They established a home on Grand Street, and a few
years later Mazie and her younger sister, Jeanie, came to live with
them. The family of Belle Baker, the vaudeville singer, lived nearby
on Chrystie Street. Irving Becker, Belle's brother, now the manager
of a road company of "Tobacco Road," once had a job loading
rifles in a shooting gallery Gordon operated at Grand Street and the
Bowery. "We and the Gordons were great friends," Becker said
recently. "Louie Gordon was as fine a gambler as the East Side
ever produced. He was a big, stately gentleman and he gave to the
poor, and the bankroll he carried a billy goat couldn't swallow it.
He hung around race tracks, but he would gamble on anything.
He made a lot of money on horses and invested it in Coney Island.
He and his brother, Leo, helped back the original Luna Park, which

opened in 1903. He was one of those silent gamblers. He never said nothing about himself. He gave everybody a fair shake, and he didn't have a thing to hide, but he just never said nothing about himself. All the Gordons were that way."

In 1914, Gordon opened a moving-picture theatre in a building he owned on Park Row, naming it the Venice, after an Italian restaurant in Coney Island whose spaghetti he liked. After operating it four years, he found that it kept him away from the tracks and he gave it to Rosie, who had been working in the ticket cage. The next year he sold his Bowery shooting gallery, in which, for several months, Mazie had been running a candy-and-root-beer concession. Rosie did not like selling tickets, so Mazie took her job. Around this time, Mazie began calling herself Mazie Gordon. She will not explain why she took her brother-in-law's name. "That's my business," she says. The Gordons left Grand Street in the early twenties, moving to a house on Surf Avenue in Coney. Mazie continued to live with them. Louis was away much of the time, following the horses. Mazie says that once, after a good season in Saratoga, he gave her a Stutz which, with accessories, cost $5,000. She used to ride down to Coney in the Stutz every night after work; one of the ushers at the Venice was her chauffeur. In October, 1932, Louis fell dead of a heart attack at the Empire City race track. Mazie and her sisters left Coney Island a few years later and returned to the East Side, eventually taking an apartment together in Knickerbocker Village, four blocks from the Venice. They live quietly. Rosie, a taciturn, sad-eyed woman, looks after property left by her husband. Besides her interest in the Venice, this property includes a number of lots along the boardwalk in Coney and an ancient red-brick tenement at 9 James Street, a block from the Venice. This tenement has sixteen cold-water flats, all occupied by unmarried Chinese men. Jeanie, a handsome young woman, boasts that she has gone to the West Coast and back ten times while working in vaudeville as an acrobatic dancer. Now and then she spells Mazie in the cage at the Venice.

Mazie's hours would kill most women. She works seven days a week, seldom taking a day off, and is usually on duty from 9:30 A.M. until 11 P.M. Her cage is not much more spacious than a telephone booth, but she long ago learned how to make herself comfortable in it. She sits on two thick pillows in a swivel chair and wears bedroom slippers. In summer she keeps an electric fan, aimed upward, on the floor, replacing it in winter with an electric heater. When the weather is especially cold she brings her dog, Fluffy, an old, wheezy Pomeranian bitch, to the theatre. She lets Fluffy sleep in her lap, and this keeps both of them warm. Mazie makes change as automatically as she breathes, and she finds time for many domestic chores while on duty. She mends clothes, puts red polish on her fingernails, reads a little, and occasionally spends half an hour or so cleaning her diamonds with a scrap of chamois skin. On rainy days she sends out for her meals, eating them right in the cage. She uses the marble change counter for a table. Once, hunched over a plate of roast-beef hash, she looked up and said to a visitor, "I do light housekeeping in here." When she gets thirsty she sends an usher across the street to the King Kong Bar & Grill for a cardboard container of beer. She used to keep a bottle of Canadian whiskey, which she calls "smoke," hidden in her cash drawer, but since an appendix operation in 1939 she has limited herself to celery tonic and beer.

There are two cluttered shelves on one wall of her cage. On the bottom shelf are a glass jar of "jawbreakers," a kind of hard candy which she passes out to children, a clamshell that serves as an ashtray, a hind leg of a rabbit, a stack of paper towels, and a box of soap. When a bum with an exceptionally grimy face steps up to buy a ticket, Mazie places a towel and a cake of soap before him and says, "Look, buddy, I'll make a bargain with you. If you'll take this and go in the gents' room and wash your face, I'll let you in free." Few bums are offended by this offer; most of them accept willingly. Occasionally she gives one fifteen cents and sends him to a barber college on Chatham Square for a shave and a haircut. If she is in a good humor, Mazie will admit a bum free without much argument. However, she says she can tell a bum by the look in his eyes, and ordinary citizens who have heard of her generosity and try to get passed in outrage her. "If you haven't got any money," she tells such people, "go steal a watch."

On Mazie's top shelf is a pile of paper-backed books, which includes "Old Gipsy Nan's Fortune Teller and Dream Book," "Prince Ali Five Star Dream Book," and "Madame Fu Futtam's Spiritual Magical Dream Book." Mazie is deeply interested in dreams, although at times she seems a little ashamed of it. "A dream just means you et something that didn't agree with you," she sometimes says, rather defiantly. Nevertheless, she makes a practice of remembering them and spends hours hunting through her books for satisfactory interpretations. Also on her top shelf are a rosary, some back numbers of a religious periodical called the *Messenger of the Sacred Heart*, and a worn copy of "Spiritual Reflections for Sisters," by the Reverend Charles J. Mullaly, S.J., which she borrowed from an Italian nun, one of the Daughters of Mary Help of Christians, who conduct a school in Chinatown. Lately Mazie has been reading a page of this book every day. She says that she understands hardly any of it but that reading it makes her feel good. Mazie is not a Catholic; she is Jewish, but she has been entranced by Roman Catholicism for many years. One of her oldest friends in the neighborhood is Monsignor William E. Cashin, rector of St. Andrews', the little church back of the Municipal Building. She frequently shows up for the Night Workers' Mass, which is said every Sunday at 2:30 A.M. in St. Andrews' by Monsignor Cashin. She sits in a middle pew with her head bowed. Surrounded by policemen, firemen, scrubwomen, telephone girls, nurses, printers, and similar night workers who regularly attend the mass, she feels at home. On the way out she always slips a dollar bill into the poor box. Now and then she calls on the Monsignor and has a long talk with him, and whenever he takes a walk on the Bowery he pauses at her cage and passes the time of day.

Mazie also knows two mothers superior quite well. The rosary she keeps in her cage is a present from the Sisters of Our Lady of Christian Doctrine, who run Madonna House, a settlement on Cherry Street. Sister Margaret, the superior there, has known Mazie for years and has made an attempt to understand her. "On the Bowery it's probably an asset to have a reputation for toughness," Sister Margaret once told a friend, "and I'm afraid Mazie tries to give people the worst possible impression of herself, just for self-protection. She isn't really tough. At heart, she's good and kind. We can always count on her for help. A few weeks ago there was a fire in an Italian tenement near here. One of the families in it had a new baby. It was late at night and we didn't know exactly how to help them. Two of the sisters went to Mazie, and she came right down and found the family a new flat and gave the mother some money." Mazie's favorite saint is St. John Bosco.

There is a statue of him in a niche in the steeple of the weather-beaten Church of the Transfiguration in Chinatown. At night the saint can be clearly seen by the light of the galaxy of neon signs on the chop-suey joints which surround the church. When she passes through Mott Street, Mazie looks up at the saint and crosses herself. "I asked a sister once if it was O.K. for me to give myself a cross, and she told me it was," Mazie says.

Mazie became interested in Catholicism in the winter of 1920. A drug addict on Mulberry Street, a prostitute with two small daughters, came to her cage one night and asked for help. The woman said her children were starving. "I knew this babe was a junky," Mazie says, "and I followed her home just to see was she lying about her kids. She had two kids all right, and they were starving in this crummy little room. I tried to get everybody to do something—the cops, the Welfare, the so-called missions on the Bowery that the Methodists run or whatever to hell they are. But all these people said the girl was a junky. That excused them from lifting a hand. So I seen two nuns on the street, and they went up there with me. Between us, we got the woman straightened out. I liked the nuns. They seemed real human. Ever since then I been interested in the Cat'lic Church."

Mazie does not spend much time at home, so she encourages people to visit her while she is working. Her visitors stand around in the lobby at the rear door of her cage. She frequently gets so interested in a caller that she swings completely around in her swivel chair and presents her back to customers, who have to shout and rap on the window before she will turn and sell them tickets. In the morning, practically all of her visitors are bums with hang-overs who come to her, scratching themselves and twitching, and ask for money with which to get their first drinks of the day. She passes out dimes regularly to about twenty-five of these men. Because of this, she is disliked by many of the hard-shell evangelists who hold hymn-singings in the gutters of the Bowery every evening. One of them, a grim, elderly woman, came to the cage not long ago and shook a finger at Mazie. "We sacrifice our nights to come down here and encourage these unfortunates to turn over a new leaf," she said. "Then you give them money and they begin using intoxicants all over again." When Mazie is faced with such a situation, she makes irrelevant or vulgar remarks until the complainant leaves. On this occasion she leaned forward and said, "Par'n me, Madam, but it sounds like your guts are growling. What you need is a beer."

Few of the men to whom Mazie gives money for eye-openers are companionable. They take her dimes with quivering fingers, mutter a word of thanks, and hurry off. Two of them, however, invariably linger a while. They have become close friends of Mazie's. One is a courtly old Irishman named Pop, and the other is an addled, sardonic little man who says he is a poet and whom Mazie calls Eddie Guest. She says she likes Pop because he is so cheerful and Eddie Guest because he is so sad. "I come from a devout family of teetotallers," Pop once said. "They was thirteen in the family, and they called me the weakling because I got drunk on Saturday nights. Well, they're all under the sod. Woodrow Wilson was President when the last one died, and I'm still here drinking good liquor and winking at the pretty girls." "That's right, Pop," Mazie said. Pop works bus stops. He approaches people waiting on corners for a bus and asks for a nickel with which to get uptown or downtown, as the case may be. When he gets a nickel, he touches his hat and hurries off to the next bus stop. At night he sings ballads in Irish gin mills on Third Avenue. Mazie thinks he has a beautiful baritone, and every morning, in return for her dime, he favors her with two or three ballads. Her favorites—she hums them—are "Whiskey, You're the Divil," "The Garden Where the Praties Grow," "Tiddly-Aye-Aye for the One-Eyed Reilly," and "The Widow McGinnis's Pig." Sometimes Pop dances a jig on the tiled floor of the lobby. "Pop's a better show than I got inside." Mazie says on these occasions.

Eddie Guest is a gloomy, defeated, ex-Greenwich Village poet who has been around the Bowery off and on for eight or nine years. He mutters poetry to himself constantly and is taken to Bellevue for observation about once a year. He carries all his possessions in a greasy beach bag and sleeps in flophouses, never staying in one two nights in succession, because, he says, he doesn't want his enemies to know where he is. During the day he wanders in and out of various downtown branches of the Public Library. At the Venice one night he saw "The River," the moving picture in which the names of the tributaries of the Mississippi were made into a poem. When he came out he stopped at Mazie's cage, spread his arms, and recited the names of many of the walk-up hotels on the Bowery. "The Alabama Hotel, the Comet, and the Uncle Sam House," he said, in a declamatory voice, "the Dandy, the Defender, the Niagara, the Owl, the Victoria House and the Grand Windsor Hotel, the Houston, the Mascot, the Palace, the Progress, the Palma House and the White House Hotel, the Newport, the Crystal, the Lion and the Marathon. All flophouses. All on the Bowery. Each and all my home, sweet home." For some reason, Mazie thought this was extraordinarily funny. Now, each morning, in order to get a dime, Eddie Guest is obliged to recite this chant for her. It always causes her to slap her right thigh, throw her head back, and guffaw. Both Eddie Guest and Mazie can be grimly and rather pointlessly amused by the signs over flophouse entrances and by the bills of fare lettered in white on the windows of pig-snout restaurants. When Mazie passes the Victoria House and sees its sign, "ROOMS WITH ELECTRIC LIGHTS, 30c," or when she looks at the window of the Greek's on Chatham Square, "Snouts with French fry Pots & coffee, T, or buttermilk, 10c," she always snickers. Mazie has considerable respect for Eddie Guest but thinks he is kidding when he calls himself a poet. Once he read to her part of a completely unintelligible poem about civilization in the United States, on which he says he has been working for twenty years and which he calls "No Rags, No Bones, No Bottles Today." "If that's a poem," Mazie said when he had finished, "I'm the Queen of Sweden."

Mazie's afternoon visitors are far more respectable than the morning ones. The people who stopped by to talk with her between noon and 6 P.M. one Saturday included Monsignor Cashin, Fannie Hurst, two detectives from the Oak Street station, a flashily dressed young Chinese gambler whom Mazie calls Fu Manchu and who is a power in Tze Far, the Chinatown version of the numbers lottery; two nuns from Madonna House, who wanted to thank her for buying a phonograph for the girls' club at their settlement; a talkative girl from Atlanta, Georgia, called Bingo, once a hostess in a Broadway taxi-dance hall and now the common-law wife of the chef of a chop-suey restaurant on Mott Street; the bartender of a Chatham Square saloon, who asked her to interpret a dream for him; and the clerk of a flophouse, who came to tell her that a bum named Tex had hanged himself in the washroom the night before. When she was told about Tex, Mazie nodded sagely and said, as she always does when she hears about the death of someone she has known, "Well, we all got to go sooner or later. You can't live forever. When your number's up, rich or poor, you got to go." Most of the visitors on that afternoon happened to be old friends of Mazie's. Miss Hurst, for example, she has known for eleven years. She calls her Fannie and likes to tell about their first meeting.

"One night," she says, "a swell-looking dame came to my cage and said she often walks on the Bowery and would like to meet me. She said her name was Fannie Hurst. 'Pleased to meet you, Fannie,' I said. 'My name is Mary Pickford.' It turned out she really was Fannie Hurst. At first I thought she was going to put me in a book, and I didn't go for her. Since she promised not to write no books about me, we been pals." Miss Hurst visits Mazie frequently. Each time she comes, Mazie looks at her dress, fingers the material, asks how much it cost, tells her she got gypped, and advises her to try one of the shops on Division Street. Miss Hurst does not mind this. "I admire Mazie," she said. "She is the most compassionate person I've ever known. No matter how filthy or drunk or evil-smelling a bum may be, she treats him as an equal." Until recently, Miss Hurst occasionally took friends down to meet Mazie. "I'm afraid they looked on her as just another Bowery curiosity," she says. "So I don't take people down any more. I used to invite Mazie to parties at my house. She always accepted but never came. I think she's still a little suspicious of me, although I've never written a line about her and never intend to. I simply look upon her as a friend."

From callers like Fu Manchu and Bingo, Mazie hears considerable gossip about the sleazy underworld of Chinatown. She says she never repeats such gossip, not even to her sisters. Detectives know that she has many Chinese friends and sometimes stop at her cage and ask apparently innocent questions about them; she shrugs her shoulders and says, "No spik English." In general, however, she coöperates with the police. Drunken tourists often come down to Bowery joints to see life, and when she notices them stumbling around Chatham Square she telephones the Oak Street station. "Such dopes are always getting rolled by bums," she says. "I got no sympathy for out-of-towners, but bums are the clumsiest thieves in the world. They always get caught, and it's best to get temptation out of their way." Although her language frequently shocks the Oak Street cops, they admire Mazie. Detective Kain, for instance, says that she has "the roughest tongue and the softest heart in the Third Precinct." "She knows this neighborhood like a farmer knows his farm," he says. "I believe she's got the second sight. If anything out of the way is happening anywhere along the Bowery, she senses it."

Detective Kain has for some time been trying to solve a mystery in which Mazie is involved. Mazie has a telephone in her booth, of course, and in June, 1929, a man whose voice she did not recognize began calling her daily at 5 P.M., asking for a date or making cryptic remarks, such as "They got the road closed, Mazie. They won't let nobody through." After three months he stopped calling. Then, around Christmas of the following year, he began again. He has been calling intermittently ever since. "I won't hear from him for maybe six months," Mazie says. "Then, one day around five, the phone will ring and this voice will say, 'All the clocks have stopped running' or 'Mazie, they cut down the big oak tree' or some other dopey remark. He never says more than a few words, and when I say something he hangs right up. One afternoon he gave me the shakes. He called up and said, 'Mazie, I got a nephew studying to be an undertaker and he needs somebody to practice on.' Then he hung up. A minute later he called again and said, 'You'll do! You'll do!' Somehow, I get to feeling he's across the street in a booth. The worst thing is I suspect every stranger that buys a ticket. I strike up conversations with strangers just to see if I can find one who talks like him. I think he's trying to drive me crazy." Among her friends, Mazie refers to her caller as The Man. If she has visitors around five o'clock and the telephone rings, she says, "Pick up the receiver and see what The Man has to say this time." Fannie Hurst once listened. "It was macabre," she said. Detective Kain has listened often, has warned the man, and has tried vainly to trace the calls. Mazie's number has been changed repeatedly, but that does no good.

Mazie closes her cage shortly after 11 P.M., when the final show is under way, and goes to an all-night diner near Brooklyn Bridge, where she glances through the *Daily News* while having a couple of cups of coffee and a honey bun. The only things in the *News* that she regularly reads from beginning to end are the comics, the "Voice of the People," and "The Inquiring Fotographer." She says she doesn't read political or war stories because she can't understand them and because they make her blue. "The world is all bitched up," she once said. "Always was, always will be." "Do you really believe that?" she was asked. "No," she said, after a moment of deliberation, "I guess I don't." She spends half an hour in the diner. Then, practically every night, before going home to bed, she makes a Samaritan tour of the Bowery and its environs. She carries an umbrella and a large handbag, which contains a flashlight, a number of cakes of soap of the size found in hotel bathrooms, and a supply of nickels, dimes, and quarters.

If it is a cold night, she goes first to an alley near the steps leading to the footwalk of Manhattan Bridge. Bums like to keep fires going in discarded oil drums in this alley. She distributes some change. Then she inspects Columbus Park, a block west of Chatham Square, where every winter a few bums pass out on benches and die of exposure. The police say Mazie has rescued scores of men in this park. Then, passing through Chinatown, she returns to the Bowery and heads uptown, pausing whenever she recognizes a bum and giving him enough money for a meal, a drink, or a flop. Frequently, in addition to small change, she gives a bum a cake of soap. "*Please* use it, buddy," she says pleadingly. Here and there she gets out her flashlight and peers into a doorway. She pays particular attention to the drunken or exhausted bums who sleep in doorways, on loading platforms, and on sidewalks. She always tries to arouse them and stake them to flops. In warm weather, if they don't seem disposed to stir, she leaves them where they are. "A sidewalk is about as nice as a flophouse cot in the summertime," she says. "You may get up stiff, but you won't get up crummy." In the winter, however, she badgers them until they awaken. She punches them in the ribs with her umbrella and, if necessary, gets down on her knees and slaps their faces. "When a bum is sleeping off his load, you could saw off his leg and he wouldn't notice nothing," she says. Sometimes a bum who has been awakened by Mazie tries to take a poke at her. When this happens, she assumes a spraddle-legged stance, like a fencer, and jabs the air viciously with her umbrella. "Stand back," she cries, "or I'll put your eyes out." If a man is too weak, sodden, or spiritless to get up, Mazie grabs his elbows and heaves him to his feet. Holding him erect, she guides him to the nearest flophouse and pulls and pushes him up the stairs to the lobby. She pays the clerk for the man's lodging (thirty cents is the customary price) and insists on his having at least two blankets. Then, with the help of the clerk or the bouncer, she takes off the man's shoes, unbuttons his collar, loosens his belt, and puts him to bed with his clothes on. This is usually a tumultuous process, and sometimes many of the lodgers are awakened. They stick their heads out of the doors of their cubicles. "It's Mazie!" they shout. "Hello, Mazie!" Now and then an emotional bum will walk out in his underwear and insist on shaking Mazie's hand. "God bless you, Mazie, old girl!" he will cry. Mazie does not approve of such antics. "Go back to bed, you old goat," she says. If she is acquainted with the clerk and trusts him, she leaves some change with him and asks that it be given to the bum when he wakes up. Flophouses are for-men-only establishments, and Mazie is the only female who has ever crossed the threshold of many of them.

At least a couple of times a week, Mazie finds injured men lying in the street. On these occasions she telephones Police Headquarters and asks for an ambulance from Gouverneur or Beekman Street, the hospitals which take care of most Bowery cases. She knows many of the drivers from these hospitals by name and orders them around. Police say she summons more ambulances than any other private citizen in town, and she is proud of this. "I don't over-do it," she says. "Unless a man is all stove-up and bloody, I don't put in a call, but if I had my way, the wagons would be rolling all night long. There's hardly a bum on the Bowery who don't belong in a hospital."

On her walk, Mazie usually tries to steer clear of other well-known nocturnal Bowery characters. Among these are the Widow Woman and the Crybaby. The Crybaby is an old mission bum who sits on the curb for hours with his feet in the gutter, sobbing brokenly. Once Mazie nudged him on the shoulder and asked, "What's the matter with you?" "I committed the unforgivable sin," he said. Mazie asked him what the sin consisted of, and he began a theological description of it which she didn't understand and which she interrupted after a few minutes, remarking, "Hell, Crybaby, you didn't commit no sin. You just prob'ly got the stomach ulsters." The Widow Woman is a bent, whining crone who wears a mourning veil, a Queen Mary hat, and a rusty black coat, and comes hobbling down the Bowery around midnight giving bums little slips of paper on which are scribbled such statements as "God is love" and "The fires of Hell will burn forever." Mazie is afraid of her. "The Widow Woman gives me the creeps," she says. "She walks like a woman and she dresses like a woman, but when she talks I get the feeling that she's a man."

Most nights, before going home to bed, which is usually around two o'clock, Mazie makes brief stops in several saloons and all-night restaurants. She does not mind the reek of stale beer, greasy cabbage, and disinfectant in them. "After you been around the Bowery a few years, your nose gets all wore out," she says. She goes into these places not to eat or drink but to gossip with bartenders and countermen and to listen to the conversation of drunken bums. She has found that bums do not talk much about sex, sports, politics, or business, the normal saloon topics. She says most of them are far too undernourished to have any interest in sex. They talk, instead, about what big shots they were before they hit the Bowery. Although their stories fascinate her, Mazie is generally cynical. "To hear them tell it," she says, "all the bums on the Bowery were knocking off millions down in Wall Street when they were young, else they were senators, else they were the general manager of something real big, but, poor fellers, the most of them they wasn't ever nothing but drunks."

Notice how much descriptive writing there is in this essay. Is the description made vivid? In this connection, consider the kind of diction (concrete, realistic, and so on) that the author uses. Consider also how the author effects his transitions from paragraph to paragraph. Is this skillfully done? For further exercises, see p. 476 and p. 503.

SECTION

8

# Autobiography

## REVERIES OVER CHILDHOOD

### W. B. YEATS

One day some one spoke to me of the voice of conscience, and as I brooded over the phrase I came to think that my soul, because I did not hear an articulate voice, was lost. I had some wretched days until being alone with one of my aunts I heard a whisper in my ear, "What a tease you are!" At first I thought my aunt must have spoken, but when I found she had not, I concluded it was the voice of my conscience and was happy again. From that day the voice has come to me at moments of crisis, but now it is a voice in my head that is sudden and startling. It does not tell me what to do, but often reproves me. It will say perhaps, "That is unjust" of some thought; and once when I complained that a prayer had not been heard, it said, "You have been helped." I had a little flagstaff in front of the house and a red flag with the Union Jack in the corner. Every night I pulled my flag down and folded it up and laid it on a shelf in my bedroom, and one morning before breakfast I found it, though I knew I had folded it up the night before, knotted round the bottom of the flagstaff so that it was touching the grass. I must have heard the servants talking of the faeries, for I concluded at once that a faery had tied those four knots and from that on believed that one had whispered in my

ear. I have been told, though I do not remember it myself, that I
saw, whether once or many times I do not know, a supernatural
bird in the corner of the room. Once too I was driving with my
grandmother a little after dark close to the Channel that runs for
some five miles from Sligo to the sea, and my grandmother showed
me the red light of an outward-bound steamer and told me that
my grandfather was on board, and that night in my sleep I
screamed out and described the steamer's wreck. The next morning
my grandfather arrived on a blind horse found for him by grateful
passengers. He had, as I remember the story, been asleep when
the Captain aroused him to say they were going on the rocks. He
said, "Have you tried sail on her?" and judging from some answer
that the captain was demoralised, took over the command and,
when the ship could not be saved, got the crew and passengers
into the boats. His own boat was upset and he saved himself and
some others by swimming; some women had drifted ashore, buoyed
up by their crinolines. "I was not so much afraid of the sea as of
that terrible man with his oar," was the comment of a schoolmaster
who was among the survivors. Eight men were, however, drowned
and my grandfather suffered from that memory at intervals all his
life, and if asked to read family prayers never read anything but
the shipwreck of St. Paul.

I remember the dogs more clearly than any one except my grandfather and grandmother. The black hairy one had no tail because
it had been sliced off, if I was told the truth, by a railway train. I
think I followed at their heels more than they did at mine, and that
their journeys ended at a rabbit-warren behind the garden; and
sometimes they had savage fights, the black hairy dog, being well
protected by its hair, suffering least. I can remember one so savage
that the white dog would not take his teeth out of the black dog's
hair till the coachman hung them over the side of a water-butt,
one outside and one in the water. My grandmother once told the
coachman to cut the hair like a lion's hair and, after a long consultation with the stable-boy, he cut it all over the head and shoulders
and left it on the lower part of the body. The dog disappeared for
a few days, and I did not doubt that its heart was broken.

There was a large garden behind the house, full of apple trees,
with flower-beds and grass-plots in the centre, and two figure-
heads of ships, one among the strawberry plants under a wall cov-

ered with fruit trees and one among the flowers. The one among
the flowers was a white lady in flowing robes, while the other, a
stalwart man in uniform, had been taken from a three-masted ship
of my grandfather's called the *Russia,* and there was a belief
among the servants that the stalwart man represented the Tsar and
had been presented by the Tsar himself. The avenue, or as they
say in England the drive, that went from the hall door through a
clump of big trees to an insignificant gate and a road bordered by
broken and dirty cottages, was but two or three hundred yards, and
I often thought it should have been made to wind more, for I
judged people's social importance mainly by the length of their
avenues. This idea may have come from the stable-boy, for he
was my principal friend. He had a book of Orange rhymes, and the
days when we read them together in the hay-loft gave me the
pleasure of rhyme for the first time. Later on I can remember being
told, when there was a rumour of a Fenian rising, that rifles had
been served out to the Orangemen; and presently, when I had begun to dream of my future life, I thought I would like to die fighting like the Fenians. I was to build a very fast and beautiful ship
and to have under my command a company of young men who
were always to be in training like athletes and so become as brave
and handsome as the young men in the story-books, and there was
to be a big battle on the sea-shore near Rosses and I was to be
killed. I collected little bits of wood and piled them in the corner
of the yard, and there was an old rotten log in a distant field I
often went to look at because I thought it would go a long way in
the making of the ship. All my dreams were of ships; and one day
a sea-captain who had come to dine with my grandfather put a
hand on each side of my head and lifted me up to show me Africa,
and another day a sea-captain pointed to the smoke from the
pern mill on the quays rising up beyond the trees of the lawn, as
though it came from a mountain, and asked me if Ben Bulben was a
burning mountain.

Once every few months I used to go to Rosses Point or Ballisodare to see another little boy, who had a piebald pony that had
once been in a circus and sometimes forgot where it was and went
round and round. He was George Middleton, son of my great-uncle
William Middleton. Old Middleton had bought land, then believed
a safe investment, at Ballisodare and at Rosses, and spent the

winter at Ballisodare and the summer at Rosses. The Middleton
and Pollexfen flour mills were at Ballisodare, and a great salmon
weir, rapids and a waterfall, but it was more often at Rosses that
I saw my cousin. We rowed in the river-mouth or were taken sailing
in a heavy slow schooner yacht or in a big ship's boat that had been
rigged and decked. There were great cellars under the house, for
it had been a smuggler's house a hundred years before, and sometimes three loud raps would come upon the drawing-room window
at sun-down, setting all the dogs barking: some dead smuggler
giving his accustomed signal. One night I heard them very distinctly and my cousins often heard them, and later on my sister.
A pilot had told me that, after dreaming three times of a treasure
buried in my uncle's garden, he had climbed the wall in the middle
of the night and begun to dig but grew disheartened "because
there was so much earth." I told somebody what he had said and
was told that it was well he did not find it, for it was guarded by a
spirit that looked like a flat iron. At Ballisodare there was a cleft
among the rocks that I passed with terror because I believed that
a murderous monster lived there that made a buzzing sound like a
bee.

It was through the Middletons perhaps that I got my interest in
country stories, and certainly the first faery stories that I heard
were in the cottages about their houses. The Middletons took the
nearest for friends and were always in and out of the cottages of
pilots and of tenants. They were practical, always doing something
with their hands, making boats, feeding chickens, and without
ambition. One of them had designed a steamer many years before
my birth and, long after I had grown to manhood, one could hear
it—it had some sort of obsolete engine—many miles off wheezing
in the Channel like an asthmatic person. It had been built on the
lake and dragged through the town by many horses, stopping before the windows where my mother was learning her lessons, and
plunging the whole school into candle-light for five days, and was
still patched and repatched mainly because it was believed to be
a bringer of good luck. It had been called after the betrothed of
its builder *Janet,* long corrupted into the more familiar *Jennet,*
and the betrothed died in my youth, having passed her eightieth
year and been her husband's plague because of the violence of her
temper. Another Middleton who was but a year or two older than

myself used to shock me by running after hens to know by their feel if they were on the point of dropping an egg. They let their houses decay and the glass fall from the windows of their greenhouses, but one among them at any rate had the second sight. They were liked but had not the pride and reserve, the sense of decorum and order, the instinctive playing before themselves that belongs to those who strike the popular imagination.

Sometimes my grandmother would bring me to see some old Sligo gentlewoman whose garden ran down to the river, ending there in a low wall full of wallflowers, and I would sit up upon my chair, very bored, while my elders ate their seed-cake and drank their sherry. My walks with the servants were more interesting; sometimes we would pass a little fat girl and a servant persuaded me to write her a love-letter, and the next time she passed she put her tongue out. But it was the servant's stories that interested me. At such and such a corner a man had got a shilling from a drill sergeant by standing in a barrel and had then rolled out of it and shown his crippled legs. And in such and such a house an old woman had hid herself under the bed of her guests, an officer and his wife, and on hearing them abuse her beaten them with a broomstick. All the well-known families had their grotesque or tragic or romantic legends, and I often said to myself how terrible it would be to go away and die where nobody would know my story. Years afterwards, when I was ten or twelve years old and in London, I would remember Sligo with tears, and when I began to write, it was there I hoped to find my audience. Next to Merville where I lived, was another tree-surrounded house where I sometimes went to see a little boy who stayed there occasionally with his grandmother, whose name I forget and who seemed to me kind and friendly, though when I went to see her in my thirteenth or fourteenth year I discovered that she only cared for very little boys. When the visitors called I hid in the hay-loft and lay hidden behind the great heap of hay while a servant was calling my name in the yard.

I do not know how old I was (for all these events seem at the same distance) when I was made drunk. I had been out yachting with an uncle and my cousins and it had come on very rough. I had lain on deck between the mast and the bowsprit and a wave had burst over me and I had seen green water over my head. I was very proud and very wet. When we got into Rosses again, I was dressed up in an older boy's clothes so that the trousers came down below my boots and a pilot gave me a little raw whiskey. I drove home on an outside car and was so pleased with the strange state in which I found myself that for all my uncle could do, I cried to every passer-by that I was drunk, and went on crying it through the town and everywhere until I was put to bed by my grandmother and given something to drink that tasted of black currants and so fell asleep.

Compare and contrast the diction used in this excerpt with that used in "Mazie." Account for the differences. For exercises, see p. 301 and p. 430.


# I GET A COLT TO BREAK IN

## LINCOLN STEFFENS

Colonel Carter gave me a colt. I had my pony, and my father meanwhile had bought a pair of black carriage horses and a cow, all of which I had to attend to when we had no "man." And servants were hard to get and keep in those days; the women married, and the men soon quit service to seize opportunities always opening. My hands were pretty full, and so was the stable. But Colonel Carter seemed to think that he had promised me a horse. He had not; I would have known it if he had. No matter. He thought he had, and maybe he did promise himself to give me one. That was enough. The kind of man that led immigrant trains across the continent and delivered them safe, sound, and together where he promised would keep his word. One day he drove over from Stockton, leading a two-year-old which he brought to our front door and turned over to me as mine. Such a horse!

She was a cream-colored mare with a black forelock, mane, and tail and a black stripe along the middle of her back. Tall, slender, high-spirited, I thought then—I think now that she was the most beautiful of horses. Colonel Carter had bred and reared her with me and my uses in mind. She was a careful cross of a mustang mare and a thoroughbred stallion, with the stamina of the wild horse and the speed and grace of the racer. And she had a sense of

I GET A COLT TO BREAK IN: From *The Autobiography of Lincoln Steffens*, copyright, 1931, by Harcourt, Brace and Company, Inc.

fun. As Colonel Carter got down out of his buggy and went up
to her, she snorted, reared, flung her head high in the air, and,
coming down beside him, tucked her nose affectionately under his
arm.

"I have handled her a lot," he said. "She is kind as a kitten, but
she is as sensitive as a lady. You can spoil her by one mistake. If
you ever lose your temper, if you ever abuse her, she will be ruined
for ever. And she is unbroken. I might have had her broken to
ride for you, but I didn't want to. I want you to do it. I have taught
her to lead, as you see; had to, to get her over here. But here she is,
an unbroken colt; yours. You take and you break her. You're only
a boy, but if you break this colt right, you'll be a man—a young man,
but a man. And I'll tell you how."

Now, out west, as everybody knows, they break in a horse by
riding out to him in his wild state, lassooing, throwing, and sad-
dling him; then they let him up, frightened and shocked, with a
yelling broncho-buster astride of him. The wild beast bucks, the
cowboy drives his spurs into him, and off they go, jumping, kicking,
rearing, falling, till by the weight of the man, the lash, and the
rowels, the horse is broken—in body and spirit. This was not the
way I was to break my colt.

"You must break her to ride without her ever knowing it," Colonel Carter said. "You feed and you clean her—you; not the stable
man. You lead her out to water and to walk. You put her on a long
rope and let her play, calling her to you and gently pulling on the
rope. Then you turn her loose in the grass lot there and, when she
has romped till tired, call her. If she won't come, leave her. When
she wants water or food, she will run to your call, and you will pet
and feed and care for her." He went on for half an hour, advising me
in great detail how to proceed. I wanted to begin right away. He
laughed. He let me lead her around to the stable, water her, and
put her in the stable and feed her.

There I saw my pony. My father, sisters, and Colonel Carter
saw me stop and look at my pony.

"What'll you do with him?" one of my sisters asked. I was bewildered for a moment. What should I do with the little red horse?
I decided at once.

"You can have him," I said to my sisters.

"No," said Colonel Carter, "not yet. You can give your sisters the pony by and by, but you'll need him till you have taught the colt to carry you and a saddle—months; and you must not hurry. You must learn patience, and you will if you give the colt time to learn it, too. Patience and control. You can't control a young horse unless you can control yourself. Can you shoot?" he asked suddenly.

I couldn't. I had a gun and I had used it some, but it was a rifle, and I could not bring down with it such game as there was around Sacramento—birds and hares. Colonel Carter looked at my father, and I caught the look. So did my father. I soon had a shotgun. But at the time Colonel Carter turned to me and said:

"Can't shoot straight, eh? Do you know what that means? That means that you can't control a gun, and that means that you can't control yourself, your eye, your hands, your nerves. You are wriggling now. I tell you that a good shot is always a good man. He may be a 'bad man' too, but he is quiet, strong, steady in speech, gait, and mind. No matter, though. If you break in this colt right, if you teach her her paces, she will teach you to shoot and be quiet."

He went off downtown with my father, and I started away with my colt. I fed, I led, I cleaned her, gently, as if she were made of glass; she was playful and willing, a delight. When Colonel Carter came home with my father for supper, he questioned me.

"You should not have worked her today," he said. "She has come all the way from Stockton and must be tired. Yes, yes, she would not show fatigue; too fine for that, and too young to be wise. You have got to think for her, consider her as you would your sisters."

Sisters! I thought; I had never considered my sisters. I did not say that, but Colonel Carter laughed and nodded to my sisters. It was just as if he had read my thought. But he went on to draw on my imagination a centaur; the colt as a horse's body—me, a boy, as the head and brains of one united creature. I liked that. I would be that. I and the colt: a centaur.

After Colonel Carter was gone home I went to work on my new horse. The old one, the pony, I used only for business: to go to fires, to see my friends, run errands, and go hunting with my new shotgun. But the game that had all my attention was the breaking in of the colt, the beautiful cream-colored mare, who soon knew me—and my pockets. I carried sugar to reward her when she did right, and she discovered where I carried it; so did the pony, and when I was busy they would push their noses into my pockets, both of which were torn down a good deal of the time. But the colt learned. I taught her to run around a circle, turn and go the other way at a signal. My sisters helped me. I held the long rope and the whip (for signaling), while one of the girls led the colt; it was hard work for them, but they took it in turns. One would lead the colt round and round till I snapped the whip; then she would turn, turning the colt, till the colt did it all by herself. And she was very quick. She shook hands with each of her four feet. She let us run under her, back and forth. She was slow only to carry me. Following Colonel Carter's instructions, I began by laying my arm or a surcingle over her back. If she trembled, I drew it slowly off. When she could abide it, I tried buckling it, tighter and tighter. I laid over her, too, a blanket, folded at first, then open, and, at last, I slipped up on her myself, sat there a second, and as she trembled, slid off. My sisters held her for me, and when I could get up and sit there a moment or two, I tied her at a block, and we, my sisters and I, made a procession of mounting and dismounting. She soon got used to this and would let us slide off over her rump, but it was a long, long time before she would carry me.

That we practiced by leading her along a high curb where I could get on as she walked, ride a few steps, and then, as she felt me and crouched, slip off. She never did learn to carry a girl on her back; my sisters had to lead her while I rode. This was not purposeful. I don't know just how it happened, but I do remember the first time I rode on my colt all the way around the lot and how, when I put one of the girls up, she refused to repeat. She shuddered, shook and frightened them off.

While we were breaking in the colt a circus came to town. The ring was across the street from our house. Wonderful! I lived in that circus for a week. I saw the show but once, but I marked the horse-trainers, and in the mornings when they were not too busy I told them about my colt, showed her to them, and asked them how to train her to do circus tricks. With their hints I taught the colt to stand up on her hind legs, kneel, lie down, and balance on a small box. This last was easier than it looked. I put her first on a low big box and taught her to turn on it; then got a little smaller box upon which she repeated what she did on the big one. By and by we had her so that she would step up on a high box so small that her four feet were almost touching, and there also she would turn.

The circus man gave me one hint that was worth all the other tricks put together. "You catch her doing something of herself that looks good," he said, "and then you keep her at it." It was thus that I taught her to bow to people. The first day I rode her out on to the streets was a proud one for me and for the colt, too, apparently. She did not walk, she danced; perhaps she was excited, nervous; anyhow I liked the way she threw up her head, champed at her bit, and went dancing and prancing down the street. Everybody stopped to watch us, and so, when she began to sober down, I picked her up again with my heel and rein, saying, "Here's people, Lady," and she would show off to my delight. By constant repetition I had her so trained that she would single-foot, head down, along a country road till we came to a house or a group of people. Then I'd say, "People, Lady," and up would go her head, and her feet would dance.

But the trick that set the town talking was her bowing to any one I spoke to. "Lennie Steffens' horse bows to you," people said, and she did. I never told how it was done; by accident. Dogs used to run out at us, and the colt enjoyed it; she kicked at them sometimes with both hind hoofs. I joined her in the game, and being able to look behind me more conveniently than she could, I watched the dogs until they were in range, then gave the colt a signal to kick. "Kick, gal," I'd say, and tap her ribs with my heels. We used to get dogs together that way; the colt would kick them over and over and leave them yelping in the road. Well, one day when I met a girl I knew I lifted my hat, probably muttered a "Good day," and I must have touched the colt with my heel. Anyway, she dropped her head and kicked—not much; there was no dog near; so she had responded to my unexpected signal by what looked like a bow. I caught the idea and kept her at it. Whenever I wanted to bow to a girl or anybody else, instead of saying "Good day," I muttered "Kick, gal," spurred her lightly, and—the whole centaur bowed and was covered with glory and conceit.

Yes, conceit. I was full of it, and the colt was quite as bad. One day my chum Hjalmar came into town on his Black Bess, blanketed. She had had a great fistule cut out of her shoulder and had to be kept warm. I expected to see her weak and dull, but no, the good old mare was champing and dancing, like my colt.

"What is it makes her so?" I asked, and Hjalmar said he didn't know, but he thought she was proud of the blanket. A great idea. I had a gaudy horse blanket. I put it on the colt and I could hardly hold her. We rode down the main street together, both horses and both boys, so full of vanity that everybody stopped to smile. We thought they admired, and maybe they did. But some boys on the street gave us another angle. They, too, stopped and looked, and as we passed, one of them said, "Think you're hell, don't you?"

Spoilsport!

We did, as a matter of fact; we thought we were hell. The recognition of it dashed us for a moment; not for long, and the horses paid no heed. We pranced, the black and the yellow, all the way down J Street, up K Street, and agreed that we'd do it again, often. Only, I said, we wouldn't use blankets. If the horses were proud of a blanket, they'd be proud of anything unusually conspicuous. We tried a flower next time. I fixed a big rose on my colt's bridle just under her ear and it was great—she pranced downtown with her head turned, literally, to show off her flower. We had to change the decorations from time to time, put on a ribbon, or a bell, or a feather, but, really it was not necessary for my horse. Old Black Bess needed an incentive to act up, but all I had to do to my horse was to pick up the reins, touch her with my heel, and say, "People"; she would dance from one side of the street to the other, asking to be admired. As she was. As we were.

I would ride down to my father's store, jump off my prancing colt in the middle of the street, and run up into the shop. The colt, free, would stop short, turn, and follow me right up on the sidewalk, unless I bade her wait. If any one approached her while I was gone, she would snort, rear, and strike. No stranger could get near her. She became a frightened, frightening animal, and yet when I came into sight she would run to me, put her head down, and as I straddled her neck, she would throw up her head and pitch me into my seat, facing backward, of course. I whirled around right, and off we'd go, the vainest boy and the proudest horse in the State.

"Hey, give me a ride, will you?" some boy would ask.

"Sure," I'd say, and jump down and watch that boy try to catch and mount my colt. He couldn't. Once a cowboy wanted to try her, and he caught her; he dodged her forefoot, grabbed the reins, and in one spring was on her back. I never did that again. My colt reared, then bucked, and, as the cowboy kept his seat, she shuddered, sank to the ground, and rolled over. He slipped aside and would have risen with her, but I was alarmed and begged him not to. She got up at my touch and followed me so close that she stepped on my heel and hurt me. The cowboy saw the point.

"If I were you, kid," he said, "I'd never let anybody mount that colt. She's too good."

That, I think, was the only mistake I made in the rearing of Colonel Carter's gift-horse. My father differed from me. He discovered another error or sin, and thrashed me for it. My practice was to work hard on a trick, privately, and when it was perfect, let him see it. I would have the horse out in our vacant lot doing it as he came home to supper. One evening, as he approached the house, I was standing, whip in hand, while the colt, quite free, was stepping carefully over the bodies of a lot of girls, all my sisters and all their girl friends. (Grace Gallatin, later Mrs. Thompson-Seton, was among them.) My father did not express the admiration I expected; he was frightened and furious. "Stop that," he called, and he came running around into the lot, took the whip, and lashed me with it. I tried to explain; the girls tried to help me explain.

I had seen in the circus a horse that stepped thus over a row of prostrate clowns. It looked dangerous for the clowns, but the trainer had told me how to do it. You begin with logs, laid out a certain distance apart; the horse walks over them under your lead, and whenever he touches one you rebuke him. By and by he will learn to step with such care that he never trips. Then you substitute clowns. I had no clowns, but I did get logs, and with the girls helping, we taught the colt to step over the obstacles even at a trot. Walking, she touched nothing. All ready thus with the logs, I had my sisters lie down in the grass, and again and again the colt stepped over and among them. None was ever touched. My father would not listen to any of this; he just walloped me, and when he was tired or satisfied and I was in tears, I blubbered a short excuse: "They were only girls." And he whipped me some more.

My father was not given to whipping; he did it very seldom, but he did it hard when he did it at all. My mother was just the opposite. She did not whip me, but she often smacked me, and she had a most annoying habit of thumping me on the head with her thimbled finger. This I resented more than my father's thorough-going thrashings, and I can tell why now. I would be playing Napoleon and as I was reviewing my Old Guard, she would crack my skull with that thimble. No doubt I was in the way; it took a lot of furniture and sisters to represent properly a victorious army; and you might think as my mother did that a thimble is a small weapon. But imagine Napoleon at the height of his power, the ruler of the world on parade, getting a sharp rap on his crown from a woman's thimble. No. My father's way was more appropriate. It was hard. "I'll attend to you in the morning," he would say, and I lay awake wondering which of my crimes he had discovered. I know what it is to be sentenced to be shot at sunrise. And it hurt, in the morning, when he was not angry but very fresh and strong. But you see, he walloped me in my own person; he never humiliated Napoleon or my knighthood, as my mother did. And I learned something from his discipline, something useful.

I learned what tyranny is and the pain of being misunderstood and wronged, or, if you please, understood and set right; they are all pretty much the same. He and most parents and teachers do not break in their boys as carefully as I broke in my colt. They haven't the time that I had, and they have not some other incentives I had. I saw this that day when I rubbed my sore legs. He had to explain to my indignant mother what had happened. When he had told it his way, I gave my version: how long and cautiously I had been teaching my horse to walk over logs and girls. And having shown how sure I was of myself and my colt, while my mother was boring into his silence with one of her reproachful looks, I said something that hit my father hard.

"I taught the colt that trick, I have taught her all that you see she knows, without whipping her. I have never struck her; not once. Colonel Carter said I mustn't, and I haven't."

And my mother, backing me up, gave him a rap: "There," she said, "I told you so." He walked off, looking like a thimble-rapped Napoleon.

Characterize the tone of this account. Contrast the tone with that of "Reveries Over Childhood." For further exercises, see p. 273, p. 289, and p. 521.

# THE WEBB SCHOOL

## JOHN A. RICE

I felt miserable all the way from Montgomery to Bell Buckle. That is all I remember, that and a little sharing of misery with other boys, when I changed trains at Nashville and started on the last long-short lap. The train stopped at the depot, indistinguishable from a thousand others with its grey sanded paint of years before, its signs "White" and "Colored," its spittoons and cinders. I followed the herd up the hill and was greeted by a boy some thirty years old, "Son Will" as he was called behind his back, Sawney's eldest and mouthpiece for routine. I was to live at the home of Dr. Hatch, he told me, some distance beyond the school, in a room with three other boys, sleeping two in a bed. (Double beds were the rule in the South.)

Dr. and Mrs. Hatch have long since gone to their reward and have, I hope, got their deserts. He was a mean old man who spat on the floor wherever he might be sitting, and bullied whom he could. His wife was the sort of woman who has lived with that sort of man forty years, patient, kindly, slowly moved to anger, but bitter when she was. She earned their living by taking ten boys as boarders, the most the school would allow in one house; cooked, cleaned house, kept the garden, and did everything else that had to be done, while her husband sat and chewed. He was the first shiftless white man I had ever seen close up. I had known shiftless Negroes, but their shiftlessness had content, was firmly grounded in purpose, a bold assertion of their right to be themselves. I am sure that Dr. Hatch—he had been an M.D. we were told by his wife, but she spoke as if she herself didn't believe it—if he could have known, absolutely and without a shadow of a doubt, that he would be allowed to spend eternity as he pleased, sitting and spitting, he would have been dead by the time the messenger of bright doom had got the words out of his mouth.

The boys, my fellow boarders, have as people almost faded. One, as I recall, was the son of a lawyer, another of a doctor; the fathers of the rest were small-town merchants. They represented in little the school at large, except for a few farmer boys from near-by, and about a dozen girls from the village.

On my first morning a roommate, Tom Stokes, who had been there the year before, offered to be my guide. To get to the school we skirted a pond and crossed by means of a crudely built stile the fence that surrounded the grounds—campus would have been too fancy a name. This stile was the first lesson in the customs, traditions, ways of the school, that looked senseless at first and yet were packed with sense. The rule, strictly enforced, Tom explained, was that, wherever a boy climbed a fence, at that point he should build a stile. The building would help him to remember, as I often heard Sawney say afterwards, that a boy in a hurry climbing a fence—and a boy was usually in a hurry, after a ball, or escape—bent the wires, the next boy bent them more, and so until the fence was down. A boy-built stile every twenty feet or so was witness to the honored rule. The grounds were divided into four sections, known as Senior, Junior, Caesar, Beginners, the names of the four classes to which they were allotted.

There were three buildings, a large one in the center of the grounds with two classrooms and one huge room called the Big Room; another building was the Junior Room; and the third was the Senior Room, which was also the library. They were built of Southern long-leaf pine mellowed by almost half a century to a deep brown, with cracks under and around doors and windows through which the wind blew serenely cold on a winter day. Pot-bellied iron stoves, heated red-hot, shed warmth for at most five feet.

When a boy was not in class, he could go where he pleased on his own grounds, or stay in his classroom, sit where he pleased and talk. Most of the boys, when they had been in the school for a while and it began to look as if they might stay—the turnover was large—bought themselves chairs and carved their names on the backs. They added to comfort, tilted against wall or tree. If a boy strayed off his grounds or did any of the things that a boy does when he wants to be different, he was put on "exile," the most dreaded punishment in school. He was required to sit in a room other than his own and not allowed to speak to anyone; but—and this was bitter—he could be spoken to, and was.

Trees were sacred, Tom went on to say. They were not to be carved or injured in any other way; one must not even pull a leaf.

Sawney knew the boys' and grownups' careless habit of pulling leaves, for no reason at all except to be doing something with the hands while walking or talking. When a boy pulled a leaf he was reported by a fellow student, whoever saw him, or he had the choice of reporting himself, a choice, when taken, regarded with approval. In the case of leaf pulling the penalty was always the same: plant a tree. In tree-planting time a boy toiled all day Saturday picking out a likely sapling, digging it up, hauling it to the grounds, and planting it where he was told. That made sense, as all the rules made sense. . . . If two boys wanted to fight, they should do so, by all means, provided they were of the same size, but it must be without onlookers; they, the onlookers, got a thrashing. To be invited "to the woods" showed that one's adversary meant business. . . . Stay on your own grounds among members of your own class. . . . Don't go off your premises at night (no Southern boy needed to be told the reason). . . . No smoking outside one's room; chew, if you must. . . . If you carved a desk, the desk was yours; the school would prefer a new one, uncarved. Some boys lived on an allowance next to nothing for a year, paying for a desk. Sawney boasted that he knew all the tricks; when a boy pulled a new one, he said to him, with dry respect, "My son, you are too slick," and required the boy to follow him around all day, going home only to sleep: to the post office, to the depot to inquire for a package he knew wasn't there, a stop at every store to chat with a townsman, trips to the barn, to the hayfield, until by suppertime the boy was ready to drop with fatigue. The old man really was tough.

Boys, and the young generally, back into an explanation. They are poets still, their minds unbound by logic, and poets are impatient of exposition. My guide was a poet, and into my bewildered ear poured jumbled information in a foreign vocabulary, "over," "exile," "dink," "trap," "slide," "books," "holiday." The last sounded familiar, and I supposed he meant Christmas and such; but no; about once a month, when the day was fair and the work in the school had been good, Sawney stepped onto the platform and said, "You may have the day," and boys exploded from doors and windows. When Tom stopped to show me how to make a shinny stick—shinny was primitive hockey—by bending down a hickory

sapling and building a fire to set the crook, he saw incomprehension
in my face and laughed. Once or twice in the history of the school,
he said, there had been a teacher who was not a graduate: he had
given up in despair; the whole thing was too intricate.

The routine, however, was easily understood: chapel first thing
in the morning, lasting from ten minutes to an hour or even more,
if Sawney happened to be talkative that day; after chapel the first
class (Greek for me, with John Webb, "Old Jack," for I was to be
a junior); an interval of about an hour and then the second class,
Latin for everybody. At noon we went to our boardinghouses for
lunch—dinner we called it, and it was—and at two o'clock the last
class met, math. At around three o'clock we were dismissed and the
rest of the day and night was ours. But when Tom went on to tell
me of other things, I got lost again. And yet, when I had lived myself
into the school, everything became as simple as child's play, and
it was just that, as anyone can testify who has ever tried to learn
a game from children.

The teacher in the school, it seemed, was not strictly speaking
a teacher at all: he was a kind of referee, for the classes of the first
three years were conducted under the "head and foot," or "trap-
ping," system, something like a spelling bee, and all the teacher
had to do was to settle the disputes between boys as to who had
answered a question right, and thrash the ones who missed the
most often. But to explain how it worked baffled Tom, as it baffles
me. I have tried it on friends, and lost them all. That was Webb
School, as simple as child's play, and intricate beyond explication.

In later years, when I bore the dubious title of educator, and at
last was tagged with the still more dubious "Progressive," I visited
schools and listened to breathless accounts of the latest thing. I
could match them point by point from the Webb School I knew
as a student, and then go them one better—two better, for the school
had both order and intellectual backbone. As to the rest, its government was for boys as no school I have since seen. Sawney Webb
had once had an active mind, and an intuitive knowledge of boys
and their ways. He grew to be a tyrant, filled with his own glory,
but once in a while there was a flash of the young man he had been.
A boy ran away and the teachers were frantic. "Go down to where
the railroad track crosses the creek," he said; "you'll probably find

him there," and there the boy was. Sawney laughed and said, "A lonely boy can't stand quiet. He's got to see something moving."

This was the story that began to unfold as we climbed one of the stiles and walked along the path toward the Big Room, where presently the whole school would assemble.

When we got near the main building an older boy came up to me and asked, "Are you John Andrew Rice?" When I nodded, he said, "Mr. Sawney wants to speak to you," and he led me to a beech tree near the entrance to the grounds, a permanent stile of sturdy steps. Here a man in his sixties sat in a split-bottomed chair tilted against the tree; sat and spat, for he chewed tobacco all the time, and when he talked irrelevantly punctuated his speech with "p'too" as he got rid of particles that had become separated from the main quid. I was so scared that I hardly heard what he said, and disconcerted because he never looked my way nor turned his head.

"Are you—p'too—John Andrew—p'too—Rice?" "Yes, Sir," I said. "Your step—p'too—mother was Miss Darnell." I was about to speak, but he went on without noticing me, p'tooing every third word or so. As one will be charmed by a speech defect and hear nothing, so I was caught by his small explosions and still more engaged when he pulled out a gold toothpick and began to add particles of food to the tobacco. But I got the drift. I had listened to enough sermons to do that while fixing my attention elsewhere. He was praising my mother, whom he was careful to call my stepmother, in words out of an old phrase book. Finally I heard, "You may go," and he sent me away without a look. I was to learn that he never looked at anyone to whom he was speaking except at the end of a castigation, when he suddenly turned and drove it home with his colorless grey eyes.

He had a kind of face I had never seen before. The space from the top of his forehead, where his hair had once stopped—and now a few hairs marked the place, like the last trees at timber line—from this spot to the tip of his nose was a perfect arc, an arc that was repeated in reverse by the curve from nostrils to tip of his short grey beard. His mouth, seen from the side, was a grim gash. In the year 1933 I saw him, long dead, again, when I made my first trip to Connecticut. On every street corner, in every town, stood

Sawney Webb—a Connecticut Yankee in Tennessee, though his an-
cestry was North Carolinian for generations.

While I stood and pulled my jerky nerves together, I saw Sawney
get up from his chair, go outside the grounds through the gate next
to the Senior Room, and around to the stile beyond. There the
teachers were waiting for him to give the signal to go over the stile.
From where I stood I could not see them clearly but I could count
them, four, and Sawney was the fifth. Every school I had known
had been skimpy in the number of its teachers; but even so I wondered how four teachers could manage more than two hundred
boys, for Sawney himself taught no longer. Then, somewhere along
my thoughts, he put his foot on the bottom step of the stile, and
immediately from every side the boys cried, "Over!" and came
running from all parts of the grounds and crowded into the Big
Room, some of last year's carelessly climbing in through the windows. By the time Sawney and the other teachers had walked along
the gravel path that led from the main stile, the Big Room was full
of boys, and noisy boys; but when they filed through the door,
Sawney in the lead, there was instant silence. They filed onto the
platform, and while the others took their seats, Sawney picked up
the Bible.

I had found a place on one of the long benches that sat one behind the other from the edge of the platform to the back of the
long wooden room. I looked up and waited.

II

John Webb had a wisdom bump in the middle of his forehead,
the size of half a walnut. That was the first thing I noticed about
him, and the last, when ten years later I told him good-by. We
were many then, we who had gathered to give thanks that he had
lived; but on this morning, when I first saw him I was alone, completely, stranger in a world of others' friends. Then I looked up
and saw John Webb's wisdom bump. Later on I was to see his
face, and the eyes behind the glasses, and the grey beard that one
day was pointed and another club, for he trimmed it with a
pair of pocket scissors as he sat and talked to himself; but in the
moment I saw only the wisdom bump set in a full forehead, and

I knew that here was something special, here was a man and a man to know.

He sat cross-legged at the left end of the narrow bench that ran along the back of the platform, his right hand resting on his knee and his face turned toward the window. His brother had just finished reading from the haphazard opening of the Bible and praying in the flat voice of long custom, and was now talking to us, repeating his thoughts of years before in words that then sounded new and exciting but would, within a short time, scratch like a worn-out record. John Webb sat detached with eyes fixed on the window. Presently his lips began to move. Last year's boys passed the word along, "Old Jack's talking to himself again."

An hour later I heard his voice. In a room—the Junior Room—full of noise, of boys greeting and slapping backs and guffawing, suddenly through the uproar a voice pierced, almost a whisper, "Take your seats, please," and there was instant silence. I never learned how he did it, how he thrust through the cacophony of ordinary speech and brought his listeners to awful silence. It always worked the same way, whether in schoolroom or parlor, or on a public platform—but this was seldom, for he distrusted speakers' speech. Even the noise of clacking women was not proof against his quiet voice. He spoke, and they listened.

At first I thought him impassive; but in time I learned to read him. The wrinkles in his face were a clue to his thoughts. There was one at the corner of his right eye that was a book of contempt, and others near his lips that deepened when he was moved by goodness in what he read. And then there was the surest clue, his voice. At first it sounded monotonous, or impassive as his face to the casual listener, but in time one began to hear the cadences and overtones, and in and through it all the counterpoint of thought. It was as simple as Bach, and as intricate. Silence was also speech with him. In my last year in the school, when we seniors spent our indoor time in the library, which was also his classroom, he often sat without speaking for long minutes, choosing in our sight the exactly right colors from the palette of speech. Sometimes, when we could hardly longer bear the suspense, he would smile slightly and say, "You may go to dinner now." We smiled at his slyness, for we somehow knew the thoughts that had been going through his

great head, and what he would have said. He had the wisdom seldom to complete a thought for others.

In the intervals between recitations—he taught the seniors everything, math, Greek, Latin, English, history, everything, and things
that have no name—he sat in a split-bottom chair in the middle of
the room and read or talked aloud to himself. When we saw that
his lips were not moving, we went to him with questions which he
tried to avoid answering. If it was a technical point, we were
shamed into research. One morning he asked us to account for a
certain Greek accent, and, when no one could answer, he dismissed
the class and told us to come back when we knew. We spent a
morning searching, frantic, dogged, desperate, and when our inner
clocks told us that it was long past dinnertime, he called dryly,
"Books!" (This was the signal for the beginning of recitation.) When
we had taken our places in a circle, he asked, "Has any one found
the answer?" Our defeated silence told the story. He laughed and
said, "It's a misprint. . . ."

Sometimes he set tasks that only the best could perform, without
bringing shame to those who could not. Somehow he knew when
to call out all one's strength, and he also knew the exact moment.
I am a loafer by nature, and it used to worry him at times, but he
had the patience to wait. He knew that patience is a goad. One day
he told me to translate a passage from Vergil. How he knew that
his patience had got on my nerves I never discovered, but at just
the right moment he called on me and I answered with a translation
that I had worked at and polished until it glittered. There was in
the class no envy, only admiration which one could feel in the air.
Finally, he spoke and quietly suggested one or two improvements.
Then, after another silence, he said, "You know, John Andrew, it
is my job to criticize." That is still the highest praise I have ever
heard.

In autumn and spring and on warm days in winter we sat outside
under the trees in groups of threes and fours and studied together,
or read, or talked. Our talk would have sounded strange to Mr.
Chips or Mr. Kipling. It was never about games, for we played no
other schools, and such games as we had were simple; the sun set
on our empire and we were content to have it so; and school spirit,

about which one reads much in sentimental records, was unknown
to us by name.

Aside from the meaningless noises made by all companies, we
talked about what we were learning, and much about what had
happened in the debating societies last Saturday night and what
would happen next, and who would be elected public debaters at
the end of the year. This was long before the present fashion in
debate—the lowest known form of intellectual perversion. We took
the side we believed in and defended it with complete passion and
ignorance; but we were learning to handle ideas and fix our prejudices, and what else is a school for?

In the South nearly all conversation is personal; a Southerner can
hardly think any other way; ideas come to him wrapped up in
people, and so with us. Besides ourselves, the most interesting
packages were Sawney and Old Jack, and we debated about them.
Our talk would have shocked the younger boys, who looked on
Sawney as a hero and would not know Old Jack until junior year,
when they would begin with Greek. Among the seniors, however,
there were few all-out champions of Sawney, only the vegetative
minds; we knew him too well and too thoroughly. With Old Jack
it was different; here was exploration, with clouds of awe still trail-
ing from earlier years but with lightness too, for there was deep-
running laughter in him and we shared its freedom.

Sawney's brutality set our own quivering for action, and frightened us a little. His sayings, by which he was known everywhere—
"Don't do things on the sly," and its variant, "Never do a thing that
you would be ashamed to have the keen sunlight of publicity shine
on"—we recognized as good advice, albeit somewhat difficult to
follow, and pleasant variations from parental admonitions. There
was a lot too about obedience being the first virtue, and not bringing grey hairs in sorrow to the grave. But he was a man of action,
and we liked that; if only he had not bragged so much and flung
his wounded arm in our faces and told so often of breaking the ice
to take his morning bath. One got the impression that the war had
been fought amid snow and ice, and that there was something immoral about warm water.

Sawney was a disciplinarian of outward order, and frightened or
shamed the young into a similitude of goodness; John Webb's was
an inner discipline, of the mind and spirit, grounded in freedom.

Pupils who in after years had become inured to injustice in themselves and others, told with delight of the thrashings they had got from Sawney and were sorry they had not learned from him the whole lesson of caution; others, fewer these, had another sorrow, and delight.

Sawney was an actor; John Webb was a dramatist. The persons of his plays were ideas, for his plays were plays of the mind. If he had written for the stage, his characters would have been his ideas clothed in men, just as Shaw's people are each something else of Shaw, who rediscovered what the Greeks knew without learning. This made him incapable of acting, that is, repeating, and peculiarly unable to act the parts that he himself had created, for he knew that language could die and meaning with it, and a thing said three times is no longer true. That was why, when he had to say the same words over again, for the student must hear familiar words, he set them each time in a new frame, for his own relief. He was quick to see and approve a new garment in his brother's tattered wardrobe. Sometimes Sawney would be droning along, when suddenly the man who had made up these speeches came to life again and wrote a new part for himself. Then John Webb would listen. He would turn his head from looking out the window, and if what Sawney said was funny, he would pat his knee and laugh; if serious, take the idea and begin working on it, to reject it or remake it for himself.

He never mentioned personal hygiene and he had no sayings; he met every moment as if it was brand new, took us behind words to meaning, and flung them away when they had served their use. We lacked the skill in hearing to repeat the lightening movement of his thought; it was like wit, which needs its setting. In other ways he was elusive, and he never stated his case. We knew him as a man of peace and grace, but we were not yet ready for peace and were unaware of the grace that was in us. We believed that, with rugged effort, we could all be Sawney's, and soon; but Old Jack's nature was out of our youthful reach; he was always drawing us into manhood while we were still half child and clinging tearfully to our state. Sawney's world was not really different from the world we knew, except that all the fun was taken out; Old Jack's was a kind of dream in which were all the good things of the present and many more as yet unseen, only felt. But, we learned from him, it was to be found not by effort, and this was a first-class puzzle. All this we said or skirted around, but in the language of youth: silence, a word or two, embarrassment, laughter, and lots of scorn.

We were in green pastures. The years before had been taken up with rigid drill in the skeleton of knowledge, grammar, the manipulative side of math, and dates and such, memory work. Now we were getting at meaning, which is a leisurely delight; beginning to chew on ideas, for we were eager to emerge into manhood, where ideas were important. Most of us would go to college, and looked with hopeful eyes over the fence to that lush carpet of freedom. Not that we were discontent, but we knew there were still better days to come. We would become philosophers, whether lawyer, doctor, preacher; one hoped to spend his life in the realm of pure meaning—he would be a Doctor of Philosophy; and one wanted some day to sit tilted in a split-bottom chair and be wise that way.

Through the open windows of the library there came a single word, spoken only once, and stopped our talk: "Books," and we picked up our chairs, dragged them in, and ranged ourselves in a circle with imitative tilt. The class might continue for two hours or last no more than five minutes. It depended, whether we were ready to learn; or there might be visitors. John Webb was no strutting actor; teaching was an intimate impersonal thing to him, as learning had become to us. Sometimes we found him with a book in his hand; sometimes he sat for a minute unoccupied, got up, went to the shelves and pulled down a book. We gratefully stored our texts and tablets under our chairs and waited.

The school library was an expression, in choice and arrangement, of the man himself. The books were not adolescent, nor for adolescents, for he knew the young want to grow. He chose mainly what he liked to read himself, and they were put on the shelves in some spiritual order that would make a student of "library science" shudder. The *Origin of Species* might sit between the poems of Keats and Lane's Latin Grammar and be none the worse for the company. He was no Aristotelian; he knew the limits, and poison, of classification.

In his own home his study was across the hall from the sitting room, and here he sat and read aloud. The talk of the family or visitors never distracted him; he was listening to his author. It might be Greek or some other foreign language, but he liked English best, and, for the full range of its expression, prose best of all. Except rarely, his reading was to and for himself, but any might come and listen. The four-year-old son of a neighbor came frequently and sat attentive while his patron read Burke, or Stevenson, or the prose of Matthew Arnold. It made no difference to the small listener. He had come for an hour of music.

The arrangement of his own was the same as in the school library, until his daughter and her new husband, a college professor addicted to order, rearranged his books for him by some system of classification. Thereafter he spent most of his time in the sitting room with whatever book he had been able to rescue from the maze of logic.

Legends grow up about a teacher—if not, he is none. It was said that many universities had tried to persuade John Webb to leave school teaching and become a professor. This was untrue, or at least exaggerated for even at that time, the end of the last and the first of this century, the universities were no place for a teacher; the scholar was what they wanted, scholar in their sense, he who pursues truth for his own sake. John Webb was called erudite, and he was, though certainly he did not know the traditional twenty-three languages with which he was credited. The boys said his wisdom bump was a bulge of his brain, like the extra walnut in an overloaded sack, and were ready to believe the whispered story that Old Jack had once "gone off his head." Didn't he talk to himself? In this report there may have been some truth: the wise are sometimes called mad in a world of fools. The ancients were more discerning. They called them blessed.

For questions and exercises, see p. 311, p. 333, p. 334, p. 427, and p. 521.

## THE MODERN GOTHIC

### VINCENT SHEEAN

In the spring of 1919 . . . I went back to the University and stayed on throughout the summer to make up for lost time. My education up to then had been a sorry failure. I had never made

THE MODERN GOTHIC: From *Personal History* by Vincent Sheean. Copyright 1934, 1935 by Vincent Sheean. Reprinted by permission of Doubleday & Company, Inc.

any headway with science, mathematics or the classical languages. Of the first two I remembered nothing; of the second I remembered just one Greek sentence, *enteuthen exelaunei* ("and the next day he marched onward")—this not because it had any stirring significance for me, but because it marked the welcome end of nearly every chapter in the Anabasis.

I had derived, it was true, considerable pleasure of a low order from some other academic pursuits in my first two years of college. I had come to the University knowing some Italian, German, and French (particularly French), and could easily make a better showing in these subjects than my contemporaries. My favourite trick had been to register for courses in which I was unlikely to encounter anything I did not already know. Such conduct was lazy and dishonest, but you could make out a good case for the theory that young people were all lazy and dishonest when they could be. Certainly what the undergraduates called "snaps" (i.e., courses easy to get through without undue effort) were always crowded in my day at the University. The football players, the social lights, the pretty co-eds, and all the other students who regarded study as an inconvenient detail in college life, rushed to inscribe themselves for "snap" courses. I was in a more advantageous position than some of my fellows for wasting time, since more courses were "snaps" for me. I could go to a series of lectures on Victorian Prose, for example, and be confident of hearing nothing new; similarly, in French, with the novels of Victor Hugo or the plays of Molière. I had read altogether too much in the two languages, thanks to a bookish childhood. There was thus a group of studies open to me at the University in which I could, without working or learning, impress my instructors sufficiently to make a good record.

More than two years of my three and a half at the University of Chicago had already been wasted in this way. It was a kind of confidence game of which the victim was, of course, myself. I did well enough in the subjects I already knew to make up for my failures in the subjects I did not know and was too lazy to study. I was too undisciplined, too indolent, and too dishonest to force myself to learn what did not interest me. And it was not until that summer of 1919 that I began to realize the silliness of such an approach to what ought to be one of the great experiences of a life. The University of Chicago in summer was invaded by hordes of earnest men and women from the smaller colleges and schools of the Middle West, working towards their master's or doctor's degree. These thin, spectacled myrmidons, humpbacked from carrying armfuls of books up and down academic steps for many years, filled the cool gray corridors and covered the green lawns I had always thought reserved for pretty girls and long-legged youths. The summer school, I discovered, was an altogether different affair from the ordinary academic year. If you tried to talk to a summer student during a lecture, a cold glance through glittering spectacles was the only reply. The brilliant hot sun of a Chicago July threw into merciless relief all the unloveliness of these dank visitors from the provincial colleges of Indiana, Wisconsin, Illinois, Iowa, and Minnesota. Their presence was somehow unbecoming, both to their surroundings and to the general fitness of things. I resented them for two or three weeks, and on the few occasions when I saw my vacationing friends, the undergraduates who had finished their college year in June, we were exceedingly witty about the looks, manners, lives, and minds of the pitiable summer students. There were probably not half a dozen of these bookworms, we calculated, who could dance the fox trot decently.

But as the summer study advanced I became more and more uncomfortable about them. They were not beautiful, but neither were they ignorant. They were always putting me to shame, somehow or other. I was not to remember much about most of the studies of that summer; only one was vivid in retrospect. It was a fairly advanced course in French—the poetry of Victor Hugo, all of it, including every pitiless line of *La Légende des Siècles*. The instructor was a visiting bigwig from one of the Eastern universities, a Frenchman with a German name. He used to conduct the course in an informal fashion, lecturing some of the time, reading occasionally, and starting discussions whenever the spirit moved him. It was assumed that students in such a course as this would be mature and educated enough to know something besides the actual subject matter itself. Comparisons were always popping up, were constantly invited. Most of the students—there may have been twelve or fifteen, men and women—were well past thirty, and probably all of them taught French literature somewhere or other. In that company, through July and August, I first began to be ashamed of my evil ways, and no amount of smug scorn for the bookworms could disguise the fact.

"Vous trouverez ici sans doute que Hugo a beaucoup emprunté à Chateaubriand; n'est-ce pas, Mademoiselle?" the professor would inquire innocently, smiling across his desk at an eager spinster from Indiana. And then off she would go, talking about Hugo and Chateaubriand in a French accent that would have been incomprehensible to either of those gentlemen—but talking, just the same, with information and intelligence. The professor would argue with her; others would join in; and it appalled me that I could not even follow their battle from afar. I had never read a word of Chateaubriand; my interest in Christianity was almost nonexistent; I had no real idea why it had ever seemed intellectually important to Victor Hugo or to anybody else. And I looked at the summer students in amazement. Their excitement over such subjects actually brought colour to their wan faces; they could smile, make jokes, go through all the movements of living organisms when their attention was aroused.

My salvation was that the instructor was a Frenchman. If he had been an American or an Englishman he would have seen at once that my glibness in French was a sheer accident, and that I actually understood nothing of the turmoil through which Victor Hugo had lived and written. But, being French, the professor had a natural prejudice in favour of hearing his language pronounced correctly. In spite of all their knowledge and interest, most of the students in this course had abominable accents; it seemed to be a rule among American school teachers. I had learned French so young that all the laziness in the world could never rob me of a fairly good pronunciation. Consequently, when I had occasion to read some of Victor Hugo's detested verses aloud, the professor would lean back in his chair with satisfaction. This, combined with a prudent silence when the discussions were out of my depth, gave the good man the idea that I really knew something of the subject, and I finished the course with an unjustifiably handsome record.

But something important happened to me during the summer of 1919, thanks chiefly to the Hugo poems. I had been realizing with increasing clarity, week after week, the superficial character of my own mind. I was nineteen, and I knew nothing. The fact that I could speak a sort of French had nothing to do with me; what credit there might be for that should have gone to the devout and kindly Irish priest who had tutored me in it for years. Of the actual meaning of French literature I knew far less than the scrubbiest high-school teacher from Iowa. The struggles of the men's minds—whether of contemporary minds or of those like Chateaubriand's and Hugo's, long gone to dust—meant nothing to me at all. I had existed without realizing that it seriously mattered to anybody what men believed, or under what form of government, in what structure of society, they lived. The summer's study gave me no love for the poetry of Victor Hugo: on the contrary, the mere thought of *La Légende des Siècles* made me feel slightly uneasy for years to come. But I did derive from it some idea of what the process of literature could be— some hint of the stormy sincerity in which minds like Hugo's sought for the truth. The suggestion, however dim, was sufficient reward for the boredom of reading what then seemed to me an intolerable quantity of pompous, overstuffed verse.

My ideas of what I might get out of the University thereafter submitted to rearrangement. Words could no longer suffice: I understood Hugo's words well enough, the upholstery of his mind, but it was the mind itself that escaped me. If a mind of Hugo's quality was incomprehensible, how could I expect to know anything about the rarer minds that did (even then) seem to me most worth the effort of comprehension: Molière, Racine, Shakespeare? And, even in a world I found tiresome beyond my powers of resistance, the world of the "Victorian Prose Writers," what could I hope to understand by words alone? It was clear, after the Hugo experience, that literature involved something at once more complex and more ordinary, more closely related to the whole life of mankind, than the science of stringing words together in desirable sequences, however fascinating the contemplation of such patterns might seem to a bookish and word-conscious nature.

Nothing could be learned about literature by studying literature: that was what it came to. Courses in literature seldom took on the vitality of that special Hugo course with its special participants. In general, they were either arranged to suit the average students with no interest in the subject, or specialists with an interest so minute that it was (in my view) equivalent to no interest at all. I had no desire to count the feminine endings in the lines of the Canterbury Tales. What I wanted to know—in so far as I really wanted to know anything about them—was why the Canterbury Tales were written; what mysterious springs existed in the mind and heart of a man named Geoffrey Chaucer to bring forth such a particular stream of articulated language; what the world was like for which he wrote, in which he lived, and what was his particular struggle with it. Professors did sometimes try to convey this sort of information; but it was obvious that they had obtained it elsewhere and were passing it on in capsule form. Where had they obtained it?

History, perhaps, was the answer; philosophy might be part of it.

That autumn, when the regular academic year began, I switched from the faculties of English literature and Romance languages to those of history and philosophy. And perhaps if this had been the arrangement two years before I might not have wasted quite so much time.

I am not suggesting that I became a model of industry and scholarship promptly at nine o'clock on the morning of registration day in October, 1919. I still frittered away a good three-quarters or four-fifths of my time, still registered for an occasional course of lectures that could be treated cavalierly as a "snap" (History of Venetian Art, for instance). But at least I was not behaving altogether as if the University were a country club. Both in history and in philosophy I learned something—not much, but something. There was a course in Plato that conveyed the meaning to me; another, on the German idealists, I found as exciting as a romantic novel. But perhaps the most interesting of all—the one to be recalled most often in subsequent life—was a term of lectures and reading on the Decline of the Ottoman Empire.

This—an "advanced," and therefore a rather small, class—was in charge of an inspired teacher. I never knew what made the difference between a good and a bad teacher, but I did know that Ferdinand Schevill was a superlatively good one. He was a German, short and rather formidable in appearance, with eyeglasses and a neatly trimmed Vandyke beard. His university was Heidelberg or Bonn, I believe, and yet he had none of that pedantry which is supposed to be the vice of German scholarship. When he led us through the immense and complicated story of the decay that fell upon Suleiman's empire after the seventeenth century he did not try to treat it microscopically as an isolated phenomenon. He talked about the Arabs, the Turks, the Balkan peoples, as if they were alive; and they soon began to come to life for me. Schevill's system was to allow his students to read at will through the whole literature of the subject, and therefrom to choose, halfway through the course, a particular aspect for further reading and a final paper. I began to read everything I could find about the Asiatic empire of the Turks. Almost from the first day that side of the Bosphorus seemed to me of greater interest than this. I extended my researches to the files of newspapers and magazines, and when it came time to choose, I took for my term paper the history of the Wahabite movement.

An odder choice for a nineteen-year-old undergraduate at the University of Chicago would he hard to imagine. Ibn es-Sa'ud was then almost unknown to the Western world, and the literature on the Wahabi was scarce indeed. I read everything I could find in English, French, or German, and performed the best piece of honest work I had ever done. For a few weeks, while I was reading in the library, I nearly persuaded myself that I was living in Arabia, and sometimes the vast cloaks and camel turbans of the Bedawin seemed more real than the swishing skirts of the co-eds going by. Later on I obtained permission to go down into the stacks of that huge library—steel stacks with glass floors running among them, layer upon layer. The world's knowledge lay there like a sunken continent swimming in subaqueous light, and through its fields I ranged more or less at will. My interest in Islam, such as it was, began that year, and what I learned in Schevill's course was never wholly forgotten. If other teachers had been like him, other subjects as vivid to me as the disintegration of Turkey became, I might have learned more in my long sojourn under the sham-Gothic towers.

For questions and exercises, see p. 28, p. 427, p. 470, and p. 531.

# Research Paper

## SPANISH HORSES AMONG THE PLAINS TRIBES

### D. E. WORCESTER

Much has been written on the changes wrought in the lives of the Plains tribes by the advent of horses to the Plains region. Hunting buffalo became a sport rather than a duty; the range of the nomadic tribes was increased many times; and horse stealing became the chief occupation of the young men. But it was in warfare that the greatest changes occurred. Whereas formerly battles fought on the Plains ended with few or no casualties, mounted warfare was of a more deadly nature. No longer were there two lines of men lying behind their shields at a respectable distance from one another. Instead, skilled horsemen dashed at their enemies, armed with clubs, lances, and bows and arrows. Tribes without horses were forced to take refuge in the wooded areas bordering the Plains. The full story of the northward spread of horses from the Spanish settlements to beyond the Canadian border has not been told. The purpose of this article is to relate briefly the earliest accounts of horses among the Plains and Northwestern tribes.

By the middle of the seventeenth century, the use of horses had reached some of the southern Plains tribes. In the third quarter of the century, natives as far north as the confluence of the Mississippi and Missouri rivers are known to have used horses in hunting and

SPANISH HORSES AMONG THE PLAINS TRIBES: From *The Pacific Historical Review*, Vol. XIV, 1945. Copyright, 1945, by the Pacific Branch, American Historical Association.

in warfare. A contemporary map made to illustrate Marquette's discoveries in 1673, described the Indians of the region south of the Missouri and west of the Mississippi as "Nations which possess horses. . . ." [1] Nearly a decade later, Henri de Tonty visited the same region, and wrote:

It is called Emissourita, and is well peopled. There are even villages of Savages which use horses to go to war and to carry away the carcasses of the cattle which they kill. [2]

Spanish horses reached the Plains Indians through trading and through stealing. In 1717, Derbanne spoke of the ease by which the Illinois region could be reached by way of the Caddos, for that tribe frequently took herds of horses to the Illinois. [3] A few years later, Du Tisné traveled through the Arkansas River territory and found the Toucara (Wichita) mounted on very fine horses, and using saddles and bridles similar to those of the Spaniards. [4] The Osage Indians possessed horses that were acquired by theft from the Pawnees, and which they were quite willing to sell. The two Pawnee villages seen by Du Tisné had about three hundred horses. These animals were so prized that it was difficult to buy even one. In warfare, the Pawnee horses were protected by leather armor, after the Spanish manner. [5]

In 1724, when Bourgmont led an expedition through the territory of the Kansas, Pawnee, and Comanche Indians, he saw evidence of a well-established horse trade. When he offered the Kansas Indians two measures of powder and other trade items as the price for a horse, the Kansas replied that Frenchmen and Indians from the Illinois region gave them double that amount of merchandise. [6] The Comanches told Bourgmont that they traded buffalo robes to the Spaniards for horses, knives, and axes. Three robes were given

[1] Louise P. Kellogg, ed., *Early Narratives of the Northwest, 1638-1699* (New York, 1906), p. 288.

[2] P. Margry, ed., *Memoires et documents pour servir a l'histoire des origenes françaises des pays d'outre mer* (6 vols.; Paris, 1879), I, 595.

[3] *Ibid.*, VI, 211.

[4] *Ibid.*, VI, 288.

[5] *Ibid.*, VI, 311-312.

[6] *Ibid.*, VI, 405-406.

for one horse.[7] The Comanches also were found to shield their horses with leather armor.[8]

During the 1730's and 1740's, the Sieur de la Vérendrye made a number of expeditions to the Missouri region. He reported that some of the tribes, especially the Mandans, used horses in their hunting.[9] The *Gens du Chevaux*, or Arickara, had horses and mules, as did several other tribes.[10] Not all of them had horses enough to carry all of their baggage when they moved; the use of women and dogs for this purpose was still common. The Arickara declared that they carried on a large trade with the Spaniards, giving buffalo robes in exchange for horses and merchandise.[11]

The Blackfoot tribes (Piegans, Bloods, and Blackfeet proper) probably were among the first of the northern tribes to have horses. The Blackfeet acquired their first horses from the Snake (Shoshoni) Indians. One of the earliest accounts of the use of horses in Plains warfare was given to the explorer David Thompson by an old Piegan chief, who told of combats with the Snake Indians about 1730:

By this time . . . we had more guns and iron-headed arrows than before; but our enemies the Snake Indians and their allies had *Missitutin* (Big Dogs, that is Horses) on which they rode, swift as the Deer, on which they dashed at the Peeagans, and with their stone *Pukamoggan* knocked them on the head. . . . This news we did not well comprehend and it alarmed us, for we had no idea of Horses and could not make out what they were. . . .[12]

We were anxious to see a horse of which we had heard so much. At last . . . we heard that one was killed by an arrow shot into his belly. . . . Numbers of us went to see him, and we all admired him. . . . But he was a slave to Man, like the dog, which carried our things; he was named the Big Dog.[13]

[7] *Ibid.*, VI, 440.

[8] *Ibid.*, VI, 446.

[9] L. J. Burpee, ed., *Journals and Letters of Pierre Gaultier de Varennes de la Vérendrye and His Sons* . . . (Toronto, 1927), p. 156.

[10] Margry, *op. cit.*, VI, 602.

[11] *Ibid.*, VI, 608.

[12] J. B. Tyrrell, ed., *David Thompson's Narrative of His Explorations in Western America, 1784-1812* (Toronto, 1916), p. 330.

[13] *Ibid.*, p. 334.

The chief told of the Piegans finding a camp of Snakes where nearly all the occupants were dead or dying of smallpox. The Snake horses, which were wandering about loose, were taken by the Piegans.[14] In 1757, Anthony Hendry visited the Blackfeet in Canada, and saw them using horses to hunt buffalo. Hendry's report to the Hudson's Bay Company officials at York Factory was the first notice they had received of mounted warriors on the Canadian plains.[15] The horses of the Blackfeet were carefully guarded against theft by other tribes. They were fine, lively animals, fourteen hands high,[16] apparently about the same size as the horses of the Spanish ranches of New Mexico and Texas.

About 1787, a large war party of Piegans traveled far to the south in search of Snakes. The scouts discovered a file of horses and mules led by Black Men (Spaniards). The Piegans attacked the train, and drove off most of the horses and mules. Said Thompson:

I never could learn the number of the animals[;] those that came to the camp at which I resided were about thirty horses and a dozen mules, with a few saddles and bridles. The Horses were about fourteen hands high finely shaped, and though very tired yet lively, mostly of a dark brown color, head neat and small, ears short and erect, eyes fine and clear.[17]

Alexander Mackenzie, who explored the Northwest during the years 1789 to 1793, mentioned that the Blackfoot tribes had many horses which were acquired in raids to the south.[18] The Blackfeet were found by Alexander Henry to possess vast numbers of horses, some men owning as many as forty or fifty. The Piegans had by far the greater number; one man owned three hundred. These horse herds were constantly replenished by raids against the Snakes, Flatheads, and other tribes which did not possess firearms, and who were, therefore, easy victims for the Blackfeet.[19]

[14] *Ibid.*, p. 337.

[15] L. J. Burpee, ed., *The Search for the Western Sea* (New York, 1908), p. 123.

[16] *Ibid.*, p. 130.

[17] Thompson, *op. cit.*, p. 371.

[18] A. Mackenzie, *Voyages from Montreal . . .* (London, 1801), p. 76.

[19] E. Coues, ed., *New Light on the Early History of the Greater Northwest. The Manuscript Journals of Alexander Henry . . .* (3 vols.; New York, 1897), II, 526-527.

Horses had already entered the mythology of the Blackfeet by the end of the eighteenth century. When a man died, his spirit was believed to go instantly to a great hill between the Red Deer River and the south branch of the Saskatchewan, in sight of the Rocky Mountains. Here the spirit rose into the air and proceeded southward to a delightful country which was well stocked with horses, buffalo, and women.[20]

Horse stealing was the main occupation of the young Blackfoot warriors. As one party returned from a raid, another would be setting out.[21] Warfare was the Piegan's chief delight, and horses were the main plunder won from their enemies.[22]

The Siouan tribes, Hidatsa or Gros Ventres, Mandans, Tetons, Assiniboines, Yanktons, and Crows composed one of the most powerful groups in the Northwest. These tribes frequently were at war with one another; in fact, the Assiniboines were more closely associated with the Crees, and the Mandans with the Pawnees, than with other Sioux. The Sioux probably obtained horses about the same time as the Blackfeet; the Mandans may have acquired them earlier.

The Yankton Sioux were observed in 1774 to be using large numbers of horses and dogs to carry their belongings, though many of the horses were saved mainly for hunting.[23] In 1880, Alexander Henry was in the region of present-day Polk County, Minnesota, where he came upon the camp of an Indian who took his party to be Sioux, for he knew of no other people who had horses in that part of the country.[24]

The Mandans and Pawnees at one time lived in the same village, and it is likely that the Mandans acquired their first horses from the Pawnees. As has been stated previously, the Mandans were using horses at the time of la Vérendrye's expeditions. In 1797, when they were visited by David Thompson, the Mandans customarily locked their horses in stalls within their own dwellings at night, to prevent theft by the Assiniboines. Each morning the

[20] *Ibid.*, II, 528.

[21] *Ibid.*, II, 666.

[22] *Ibid.*, p. 726.

[23] H. A. Innis, *Peter Pond, Fur Trader and Adventurer* (Toronto, 1930), p. 58.

[24] Henry, *op. cit.*, I, 130.

young men took the animals out to graze, and watched them carefully till evening. At nightfall, the horses were brought again to the huts, fed a portion of maize, and secured for the night. The Mandans actually had not enough horses to serve their needs, although they required fewer than the nomadic tribes.[25]

The Lewis and Clark expedition spent the winter of 1804-1805 with the Mandans. Chroniclers of the party also described the Mandans' method of keeping their horses. They mentioned that the animals were fed upon cottonwood branches,[26] probably because of a shortage of maize.

Alexander Henry also commented upon the Mandans' singular custom of guarding their horses, remarking chiefly on the offensive smell which permeated their dwellings as a result of keeping the horses under the same roof with themselves.[27] The buffalo-hunting methods of the Mandans differed from those of other tribes. They always hunted in large parties, because of the constant danger from their enemies whenever they left their villages. Another reason was that, not being nomads, they could not follow the herds from place to place. To prevent the buffalo from being driven away from the hunting grounds, they surrounded one herd at a time, and killed every animal. This method gave poor horsemen an equal chance with the best to share in the hunt. Bows and arrows were the only weapons used for hunting buffalo.[28]

In 1806, Henry accompanied a band of Mandans and Gros Ventres to the Cheyenne village for a peace council. The men, dressed in their finest buckskins and mounted on their best horses, rode in parties of from ten to thirty abreast, making a very spectacular sight. Many had scalps dangling from the bits of their Spanish bridles, or attached to spears or other weapons.[29] The Mandans proceeded ahead of the Gros Ventres, and the chief of the latter tribe wished both parties to stop:

He caught up his spear, threw his robe upon his horse, and without either saddle or bridle, rode off after them. . . . He returned in the

[25] Thompson, *op. cit.*, p. 230.

[26] P. Gass, *Gass's Journal of the Lewis and Clark Expedition* (Chicago, 1904), p. 64.

[27] Henry, *op. cit.*, I, 325-328.

[28] *Ibid.*, I, 336-337.

[29] *Ibid.*, I, 368.

same manner, at full speed, up the hill, among the rocks. . . . But to my surprise, the horse never once stumbled, nor appeared to strain himself. . . . He was a bright sorrel gelding with a yellowish mane, seven years old, and fourteen hands high. . . .[30]

The Crow Indians had many horses and were excellent horsemen. Larocque, a fur trader, described them as being skillful horse traders as well. The Crows possessed such a vast number of horses that their women carried no loads when moving camp—an unusual circumstance among the Northwest Indians. The Crows obtained their horses in trade from the Flatheads at small cost, and sold them to the Gros Ventres and Mandans at great profit. Every year a great trade meeting was held on the Missouri. A Crow who had only ten horses before the meeting was considered a poor man; many had thirty or forty. The women rode astride in high saddles, and children that were too small to keep their seats were tied to their saddles. Some of the men were so skillful that in time of battle they could ride with one leg over the horse's back and their arms clasped about its neck, thus presenting a poor target for their enemies. The Crows took excellent care of their horses, since they placed utmost confidence and reliance in them, both for attack and for flight.[31]

The Gros Ventres were extravagantly fond of horses, and many men owned twenty or thirty. Common pack horses they sold for a high price; their best horses they would not part with for anything except a white buffalo hide.[32]

While Henry was at the Gros Ventre village, he learned at first hand the practice of the natives which became known as "Indian giving." He purchased an excellent horse for many articles worth altogether two hundred beaver skins. A short time later, the Indian returned all of the merchandise, led away his horse, and refused to listen to further offers. This was considered proper conduct on the Indian's part, since all of the articles were returned intact.[33]

A Chippewayan chief told David Thompson of the difficulty his tribe had in resisting the Sioux:

[30] *Ibid.,* I, 372.
[31] L. J. Burpee, ed., *Journal of Larocque from the Assiniboine to the Yellowstone, 1805* (Ottawa, 1910), pp. 58, 64, 65.
[32] Henry, *op. cit.,* I, 352-353.
[33] *Ibid.,* I, 355.

While they keep to the Plains with their Horses we are not a match for them; for we being foot men, they could get to windward of us, and set fire to the grass; when we marched for the Woods, they would be there before us, dismount and under cover fire on us. Until we have Horses like them, we must keep to the Woods, and leave the Plains to them.[34]

The Crees and Assiniboines were generally closely associated, although not of the same linguistic stocks. The Crees were known to have horses and saddles for sale in 1753.[35] The Assiniboines were the most renowned horse thieves in the Northwest, where horse stealing was often a tribal occupation. Many of their horses were taken in raids far to the south near the Spanish settlements, and bore Spanish brands. Pack horses could be bought from these Indians for a gun worth only twenty-one shillings in Great Britain. The hunters and war horses scarcely could be bought for any amount. Very little care was taken of the horses; summer or winter, they were turned loose to forage for themselves.[36]

In 1801, Alexander Henry camped on the Assiniboine River, where one of his men traded a mare for a young Indian girl, it being customary in the Northwest to give a horse for a woman.[37] Five years later, Henry was again in that area with a band of Saulteurs who were on their way to the Missouri to purchase horses. The shortest trail would have led them through the hunting grounds of the Crees and Assiniboines. A different route was chosen, as they knew that the Assiniboines often followed people for many days, awaiting a favorable opportunity to run off with their horses.[38] Henry described the Crees, in 1808:

Those who inhabit the plains are a useless set of lazy fellows . . . much addicted to horse-stealing. They are idle throughout the year. Buffalo is their only object. . . . If they procure a gun, it is instantly exchanged with an Assiniboine for a horse.[39]

[34] Thompson, *op. cit.,* p. 264.

[35] Margry, *op. cit.,* VI, 650-651.

[36] Mackenzie, *op. cit.,* pp. 77-78.

[37] Henry, *op. cit.,* I, 228.

[38] *Ibid.,* I, 314.

[39] *Ibid.,* II, 512-513. It must be remembered that Henry was a fur trader, and prejudiced against Indians who had few beaver skins.

A Cree camp, Henry admitted, made a very picturesque sight—tents pitched regularly on a level plain, and many bands of horses seen grazing in all directions.[40] The Assiniboines were excellent riders as well as horse thieves. Transportation of their belongings was still performed by dogs, for their horses generally were kept for hunting and for warfare.[41]

When Henry went to the Cheyenne village for the peace council previously mentioned, he learned that the Indians there had the best horses in that region. On the way to the council, he and his party wanted to travel ahead of the Gros Ventres and Mandans, but the chiefs would not permit it. They knew of some famous horses at the Cheyenne village, and were afraid that Henry's men would bargain for the animals.[42] The Cheyennes did not stable their horses within their dwellings as did the Mandans, but housed them in small enclosures adjoining their huts. Some of the families had twenty or thirty horses.[43]

The chief of the Cheyennes, dressed in a blue Spanish coat and mounted on a splendid black stallion, rode forth to greet the cavalcade of Mandans and Gros Ventres. The peace council failed and nearly ended in hostilities, which proved a disappointment to those who had hoped to obtain some of the Cheyennes' fine horses.

The Snake Indians were among the first Plains tribes to possess horses, although the southern Shoshoni, the Comanches, were in contact with the Spaniards or with horse-using Indians from the seventeenth century. The Snakes traveled great distances to trade with the Spaniards. In 1805, Larocque met a Snake Indian on the Big Horn River who had just returned from the Spanish settlements, and who brought back some of the prized blue glass beads obtained from the Spaniards at the price of one horse for one hundred beads.[44] In the same year, the Lewis and Clark expedition crossed the Rockies and stopped for a time at the Snake villages near the Columbia River. Gass wrote:

They have many fine horses, and nothing more; and on account of these they are much harassed by other nations. . . . They told us that they were sometimes reduced to such want as to be obliged to eat their

40 *Ibid.*, II, 514.
41 *Ibid.*, II, 518.
42 *Ibid.*, I, 373.
43 *Ibid.*, I, 377.
44 Larocque, *op. cit.*, p. 45.

horses. . . . They . . . catch goats and some other animals by running them down with horses.[45]

At the time of this visit, an event occurred which may illustrate how the use of horses spread northward among the Shoshoni. Ordway's journal tells of the arrival of two southern Shoshoni men (Comanches?) who came from near the Spanish settlements. The chiefs assembled a council to hear the news.[46] By such travelers as these, it is very likely that horses and horsemanship were carried to the tribes in areas remote from the Southwest.

The Shoshonis declared that they could not sell any more horses to Lewis and Clark unless they received arms and ammunition in exchange, so that they could defend themselves from their enemies.[47]

The Salish Indians also lived west of the Rockies, and crossed them each summer to hunt buffalo in the Missouri region. Because of their many horses, as well as their lack of firearms, they were much harassed by the Piegans. However, in 1809, David Thompson supplied them with guns, and they crossed the mountains and defeated the Piegans on their own hunting grounds.[48]

The Salishan tribes, Flatheads, Pend d'Oreilles, and Nez Percés, were all very well provided with horses, for their country was open and permitted the raising of vast herds.[49] They were passionately fond of horse races, and often lost all they possessed in betting. A Salishan horseman used a cord of horsehair tied around the animal's lower jaw for a bridle, and guided his mount simply by laying a hand on either side of its neck. The saddles were of two types— leather covered pads, and regular wooden tree saddles similar to those of the Spaniards. As one eyewitness wrote:

They procure their horses from the herds of these animals which are found in a wild state in the country extending between the northern latitudes and the gulf of Mexico, and which sometimes count a thousand or fifteen hundred in a troop. These horses come from New Mexico, and are of Spanish race. We even saw some which had been marked with a

[45] Gass, *op. cit.*, pp. 127-131.
[46] M. M. Quaife, ed., *The Journals of Captain Meriwether Lewis and Sergeant John Ordway* . . . (Madison, 1916), p. 276.
[47] *Ibid.*, p. 277.
[48] Thompson, *op. cit.*, p. 424.
[49] Henry, *op. cit.*, II, 711-712.

hot iron by Spaniards. . . . The form of the saddles used by the females, proves that they have taken their pattern from the Spanish ones. . . .[50]

David Thompson remarked on the trouble one of his expeditions experienced from horses going lame, especially the ones with white hoofs.

As the Horses of this country have no shoes, the colour of the hoof is much regarded; the yellow hoof with white hair is a brittle hoof and soon wears away; for this reason, as much as possible, the natives take only black hoofed Horses on their War expeditions.[51]

Thompson left an account of wild horses in the Northwest. These animals, descended from strays from Indian camps, apparently became very numerous around the last decade of the eighteenth century. Thompson hunted them for two summers, and caught several by running them down. When tamed and broken to saddle, they could be used for running down other wild horses.[52]

In 1803, Alexander Henry deplored the coming of horses to the Northwest, for he believed they made the natives too indolent, insolent, and independent (from the fur trader's point of view).[53] On another occasion, Henry praised the qualities of the horses of the Northwest, and described some of the extraordinary rides he had made and seen. He also told how wild horses were caught by running them down with relays of fresh horses, or by driving them into some narrow mountain pass. Some of the wild horses were excellent animals and made fine saddle horses, but such was not the general rule.[54]

Duncan McGillivray traded with the tribes along the Saskatchewan River in the 1790's, and wrote of the horses he saw:

Most of these horses are trained from their youth to the exercise of hunting. . . . The Horse of this country though not large is bold and intrepid; he delights in the pleasures of the chase, and is so animated at sight of a Band of animals that he can scarcely be restrained from pursuing them. The operation of gelding is seldom performed by the Indians

[50] R. G. Thwaites, ed., *Early Western Travels, 1748-1846* . . . (32 vols.; Cleveland, 1904-1907), VI, 340-341.

[51] Thompson, *op. cit.*, p. 214.

[52] *Ibid.*, pp. 377-378 (footnote).

[53] Henry, *op. cit.*, I, 225-226.

[54] *Ibid.*, II. 707.

as it generally diminishes the strength and vigour of the Horse[;] he is therefore full of fire and can with ease outrun most of the large animals on which we depend for subsistence.[55]

Although not many of the tribesmen of the Northwest came in contact with Spaniards, their horsemanship and riding gear were, however, styled after those of the Spanish. The best horses that many tribes possessed came from the Spanish ranches of New Mexico or Texas. It is apparent that the northward spread of the use of horses was from tribe to tribe and man to man. It is possible that wild horses may have entered some sections of the Plains in advance of the knowledge of horsemanship, but there is no evidence of any tribe learning to use horses except from horsemen of other nations. The Plains Indians, in fact all Indians, apparently became horsemen very readily. Horses and horsemanship were introduced into the Plains area by the Apache, Comanche, Pawnee, and Osage Indians. The natives in the region west of the Rockies, in what is now the state of Washington, had many horses before the advent of the Spaniards to California. The Sioux and Blackfeet were induced by the acquisition of horses to forsake the forest regions of the Northwest, and to move on to the Plains. Tribes which possessed horses found more time for warfare, because buffalo hunting came to be merely an exercise in horsemanship. The stealing of horses from one's enemies was, as in the Southwest, the crucible test of manhood for young warriors.

[55] D. McGillivray, *Journal of Duncan McGillivray of the North West Company at Fort George on the Saskatchewan, 1794-1795* (Toronto, 1939), pp. 28-29. In regard to the practice of gelding horses by the Indians, the Lewis and Clark expedition continually had trouble with their young stud horses. One of the natives west of the Rockies performed the operation on ten of these animals. Gass, *op. cit.*, pp. 232-238. There were many other instances cited.

---

Making use of Worcester's footnotes, construct a bibliography for his research paper (see Appendix 3, p. 924). Since Worcester's footnotes do not give the name of the publisher, consult your instructor as to whether you are to look up the publishers of each book in your library, or whether you are to submit a bibliography with publishers' names omitted. Note the first paragraph in his paper and the last paragraph. What special functions do these paragraphs perform? The quoted material is obviously used to document Worcester's statements. Can it be said that some of this quoted material also serves to make an otherwise dry account vivid and interesting? Illustrate. For a further exercise, see p. 333.

# Appendixes

# APPENDIX
# 1

# Causal Analysis

THERE are four methods which are helpful in investigating a situation to determine a cause. They are called the methods of AGREEMENT, of DIFFERENCE, of AGREEMENT AND DIFFERENCE, and of VARIATION. After examining them the student may feel that he has always been acquainted with them, for they merely describe how his mind *does* work when it is working straight on problems of this kind. But studying the methods may sharpen his awareness of the processes of his own reasoning.

1. AGREEMENT. If we have two or more situations from which we get the effect X, and find that these situations have only one constant factor, E, then that constant factor may be taken as the cause of X. Let us set this up as a chart:

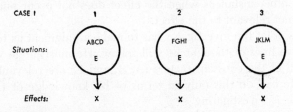

Here E is the cause of X.

The method here stated is sound in theory but in some cases is difficult to apply. Even in the laboratory, where the experimenter can create his situation with a degree of control, it is hard to be sure that only one factor E is constant. But it is especially difficult to apply this method to a complicated event outside of the laboratory. The investigator rarely finds a set of situations in which *only* one factor is constant. Ordinarily he will encounter a set of situations such as may be indicated by the following chart:

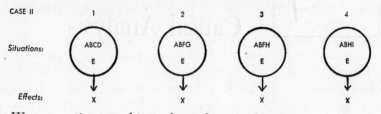

CASE II

Situations:

| 1 | 2 | 3 | 4 |
| ABCD E | ABFG E | ABFH E | ABHI E |

Effects: X      X      X      X

We can notice two things about this set of situations.

First, several factors occur in more than one situation. For instance, factor F occurs in situations 2 and 3; factor H occurs in situations 3 and 4.

Second, three factors (A, B, and E) occur in all situations.

When the investigator sees that certain factors are repeated, as is true of F and H, he must inquire whether they are repeated in *all* situations. If they are not repeated in all situations he can discard them. So F and H can be discarded. When the investigator sees that two or more factors, as is true of A, B, and E, are repeated in all situations, there are two lines of thought open to him.

First, he may explore the possibility that A, B, and E are to be taken as components of the cause—that no one by itself would be sufficient to bring about the effect.

Second, he may explore the possibility that one or two of the factors which are present in all of his available instances might not occur in other instances when the effect does not occur and therefore are not relevant to the effect.

At this point the investigator has to make a judgment as to which of the two lines of thought he will follow. He must judge whether or not all of the constant factors (A, B, and E) are relevant to the effect. He can do this only in terms of his knowledge of the field which he is investigating.

Let us take an example. Suppose we wish to learn why a certain school lost most of its football games over a period of years. We find certain things true every year. Most of the players every year are Catholic, for it is a Catholic school. Let us call this constant factor A. The same coach had been employed for a number of years (factor B). The school has very high academic standards and no one is permitted to participate in any athletic event who does not have an average grade of "fair" (factor E). The question is: Do we have a complex of factors here (A, B, and E) which are all necessary components of the cause?

Common sense and our experience with athletics at once make us rule out factor A—for we know that Catholicism bears no relation to the matter of football losses. But we cannot so readily rule out factors B and E, the matter of the coach and the matter of the high academic average required. At this point we have to make further investigation. We have to look into the coach's previous record, we have to pass a judgment on the type of instruction he gives now, and so forth. Or we must try to learn how many good players have been disqualified by the rule requiring a certain scholastic average, and so forth. We may satisfy ourselves that both of these factors (B and E) contribute to the defeats. Or we may decide that only one is the cause.

In any event, this is not a foolproof formula. Knowledge and experience are required to apply it. Even when it is applied we cannot be absolutely sure that we have determined the cause of X. We have merely indicated a certain degree of probability.

2. DIFFERENCE. If we have two situations, identical save that one involves the factor E and the effect X, and the other does not involve the factor E and the effect X, then E may be taken as the cause of X or an indispensable factor in the cause. Let us put it as a chart:

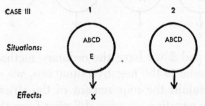

If we can be quite sure that the first situation resembles the second in all significant factors except E and X, then we may take E as the cause of X or an indispensable factor in the cause. But it is often difficult to find such clear-cut instances, and we have to draw on our judgment and experience to decide what factors are relevant. For instance, we might get the following case:

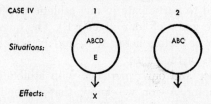

CASE IV

Situations:    1    2

Effects:    x

Here D as well as E is missing from the second situation. The following possibilities suggest themselves. First, D may be irrelevant, and E is the cause. Second, D may be relevant and in conjunction with E constitutes the cause. If we can control the situation, we may test the second possibility by setting up the factors ABCE. If we still get X, then we know that D is irrelevant. But if we cannot control the situation, we must consult our judgment and experience in deciding about the relevance of D.

3. AGREEMENT AND DIFFERENCE. This is, of course, a combination of the two previous methods. Therefore the method involves both *positive* and *negative* instances. In the positive instances we apply the method of agreement, and then check the negative instances against the positive instances by the method of difference.

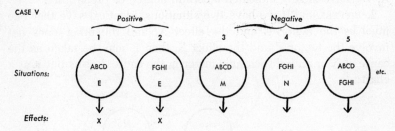

CASE V

Positive    Negative

Situations:    1    2    3    4    5

Effects:    x    x

In situations 1 and 2 we have the ordinary method of agreement. But when we come to the negative situations, we notice that there is none which fulfills the requirement of the strict method of difference; i.e., the negative situation differing from the positive situation only in that it does not have the factor which appears to be the cause. But here, though situation 3 has all the factors of situation 1 except E, the factor of cause, it does have a new factor, M. And so on with the other cases: they would always involve, in differing combinations and sometimes with new factors, the various factors, except E, which were present when X took place.

We can set up a simple example of the method. Let us assume

that in a family of five people three suffer from an attack of food poisoning. The problem is to determine what item of the restaurant meal was the cause. John, Mary, and Sue are ill.

John ate beans, potatoes, beef, and ice cream.

Mary ate a salad, a soup, and ice cream.

Sue ate sweet potatoes, broccoli, ham, and ice cream.

So much for the positive cases. Since ice cream is the only item common to the meals eaten by the victims there is a strong probability that it is the cause. But we can check this against the negative cases, i.e., cases of persons who were *not* ill.

Mildred ate beans, potatoes, beef, and lemon pie.

Thomas ate a salad, sweet potatoes, and ham, with no dessert.

These negative cases include most of the dishes eaten by the victims—with the exception of ice cream. So the argument for ice cream becomes even stronger. Few situations, however, are as simple as the one given above, and in making our analysis we are often called upon to rule out many common factors which we judge to be unrelated to the effect (for instance, we might rule out the color of the plates used in all the above meals).

4. VARIATION. If one factor in a situation varies whenever a certain other factor varies, there is a causal connection between the factors.

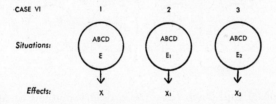

For instance, as the temperature rises mercury expands, as the supply of a commodity increases, its price goes down, or as the amount of advertising of a product increases, its sale increases. These are illustrations of the principle, but in them are great differences in the degree of complication. In the first instance, the relation between the variation of temperature and the variation in the mercury is regular and constant. We depend on the fact, and our thermometers operate on that principle. But an economist cannot depend on the relation between supply and price with the same certainty, nor can a sales manager be sure that an increase in his advertising appropriation will pay off in the market. Here too many unpredictable factors may be involved in the situation.

In applying the method of variation, we must remember that it does not matter whether the variation is direct or inverse. For instance, we have direct variation with temperatures and mercury: as the temperature increases the mercury increases in volume. And we have inverse variation with supply and price: as the supply increases the price decreases.

## APPLICATIONS

I. Which of the methods discussed above do you find illustrated in the experiments described in "The Colors Animals See," by H. Munro Fox (p. 547)?

II. Make up incidents to illustrate two of the methods in operation.

# The Syllogism:
# Distribution of Terms

IN STUDYING the syllogism we are led to what is called the DISTRIBUTION OF TERMS. A term is said to be distributed when it refers to every member of the class which it names. Let us return to our first syllogism (p. 178):

> All men are mortal.  (major premise)
> Socrates was a man.  (minor premise)
> ∴ Socrates was mortal.  (conclusion)

The premise, "All men are mortal," contains two terms. The first, *men,* is obviously distributed, as the word *all* indicates, but the second term, *mortal,* is not distributed; that is, it is not used, in that premise, to refer to every member of the class which it names, only to those (mortals) who are also men. It does not exhaust the class *mortal creatures.* The premise really says: "All men are some of the class of mortal creatures," or, "The class *men* is included in, but does not exhaust, the class *mortal creatures.*"

We may ask about the term Socrates. Is it distributed or undistributed? It is distributed, for there is only one member, Socrates himself, of the class Socrates. This comes clear if we substitute some such term as "Frenchmen" in a similar statement: "Frenchmen are men." We would mean, of course, "*All* Frenchmen are men."

To determine whether a term is distributed we must look at the meaning of the proposition in which it appears. If we take the proposition, "Graduates of Hawkins School are honest," we see that the real meaning is, "*All* graduates of Hawkins School are *some* of the class of honest people."

There are four basic types of propositions in which we must inspect the question of distribution of terms. Here the underscoring of a letter in a proposition indicates distribution, and the shading of an area in the accompanying chart indicates distribution.

1. All x̲ is y

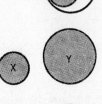

All x̲ is referred to here but only some of y, the part overlapped by x̲: i.e., all x̲ is (some) y.

2. No x̲ is y̲

All x̲ is referred to here, and all y̲, for there is no overlap; i.e., no (part of all) x̲ is any part of (all) y̲.

3. Some x is y

Here some of x overlaps some of y; i.e., some x is (some) y.

4. Some x is not y̲

All y lies outside some of x: i.e., some x is not (any part of all) y̲.

To distinguish distributed from undistributed terms is very important, for the distribution of terms may affect the validity of a syllogism. But before discussing that topic we must glance at what is meant by validity in this connection. It does not mean the same thing as the truth of the conclusion. We may have a valid conclusion which is not true. For instance:

All legless creatures that crawl are snakes.
Worms are legless creatures that crawl.
∴ Worms are snakes.

This syllogism is valid. That is, given the premises we must grant the conclusion. But the validity of the conclusion does not mean that it is true. In fact, we know it to be untrue. But it is untrue, not because the reasoning is wrong (the syllogism is valid), but because one of the premises is not true. So when we use the word *valid* we are referring to the correctness of the reasoning from the given set of premises, whatever they are, true or untrue.

As we have said, the distribution of terms may affect the validity of a syllogism. We can set up two rules for distribution which must be observed if a syllogism is to be valid:

I. The middle term must be distributed at least once.

II. No term can be distributed in the conclusion if it is undistributed in its premise.

Let us examine some cases which violate the first rule.

CASE I

All sergeants are soldiers.
Some soldiers are corporals.
∴ All sergeants are corporals.

This is obviously untrue in fact, as we know from our information about military organization. But, above and beyond that, the syllogism is not valid, as we can see if we set it up. (The middle term is represented by M, the major term by A, and the minor term by B. Numbers in parentheses indicate the type of proposition.)

All B̲ is M.   (1)
Some M is A.   (3)
∴ All B is A.

Here the middle term is not distributed as we can readily tell by looking at our table of the types of propositions. This means that the major term (A) and the minor term (B) do not, for certain, have any members in common. All we can be certain of is that both A and B fall within M.

The following syllogism with a changed content still illustrates the same formal defect:

CASE II

All Marines are soldiers.          All B̲ is M.   (1)
Some soldiers are corporals.       Some M is A.   (3)
∴ All Marines are corporals.       ∴ All B is A.

The fact that *some* Marines are corporals, that a partial truth may be involved in the conclusion, does not alter the case, for the proposition to be proved concerns *all* Marines.

If we shift the positions of the terms in the major premise of Case I, the syllogism remains invalid.

CASE III

| All corporals are soldiers. | All A is M. (1) |
| All sergeants are soldiers. | All B is M. (1) |
| ∴ All sergeants are corporals. | ∴ All B is A. |

Again the middle term is undistributed, as we can see from consulting the table of types of propositions. If we drew a chart of this we would have a figure identical to that of Case I.

There are other possible combinations which violate the first rule about the distribution of terms, but the cases given are the most common. In all cases, it is only necessary to inspect the premises carefully to determine the situation.

The second rule about the distribution of terms declares that no term can be distributed in the conclusion if it is not distributed in its premise. That is, you cannot argue necessarily from a "some" to an "all." Since there are two terms in a conclusion, the major and the minor, two possibilities of error are open here. We may have ILLICIT distribution in the major term or in the minor term. The following syllogism illustrates illicit distribution in the major:

| All banks are financial institutions. | All M is A. (1) |
| Some building and loan organizations are not banks. | Some B is not M. (4) |
| ∴ Some building and loan organizations are not financial institutions. | ∴ Some B is not A. (4) |

Here the major term ("financial institutions"—A) is not distributed in the premise, but it is distributed in the conclusion. The error results from assuming that the major term is distributed in the major premise—that is, from assuming that it says, "All banks are *all* financial institutions," and therefore that whatever is true of banks will be true of all financial institutions. Actually, the major premise says, "All banks are some financial institutions," and therefore what may be true of those financial institutions which are banks may not be true of those which are not banks.

The same principle applies in the case of the illicit minor:

| No member of the Jones family is a drunkard. | No A is M. (2) |
| All drunkards are irresponsible people. | All M is B. (1) |

∴ No irresponsible person is a member      ∴ No <u>B</u> is <u>A</u>.  (2)
of the Jones family.

Here the minor term ("irresponsible people"—B) is not distributed in the premise, but is distributed in the conclusion. Therefore the conclusion is not valid.

To the two rules concerning distribution of terms we may add two rules concerning negative premises or conclusion.

III. From two negative premises nothing can be inferred.

IV. If one premise is negative the conclusion must be negative.

Here is a syllogism with both premises negative:

No royalist is a democrat.                  No M is A.  (2)
No true American is a royalist.            No $\overline{\text{B}}$ is $\overline{\text{M}}$.  (2)
∴ No true American is a democrat.      ∴ No <u>B</u> is <u>A</u>.  (2)

The trouble here is that no necessary common ground is established for the major and the minor premise.

Here is a violation of rule IV:

No true American is a royalist.            No M is A.  (2)
Our children are true Americans.        All $\overline{\text{B}}$ is M.  (1)
∴ Our children are royalists.              ∴ All B is A.  (1)

When we pause to think that the major premise says that all members of class M lie outside of class A, and that the minor premise says that all members of class B lie within class M, we see immediately the absurdity of affirming that members of class B lie necessarily within class M. But occasionally such an argument can be so buried that the absurdity does not appear without some analysis.

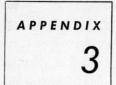

# The Outline, Summary, and Précis; Notes; Research Paper; and Book Report

## THE OUTLINE[1]

THE OUTLINE has two uses. It can help the writer to organize his own thoughts and lay a plan for his work before he begins the actual composition. It can help the reader define the basic meaning and structure of what he reads. The two uses have much in common, for both mean that the maker of the outline is dealing with the structure of a discourse. In fact, once an outline is completed, an observer might not be able to tell whether it was designed by a writer or a reader.

There are several common types of outlines: (1) the suggestive outline, (2) the topic outline, (3) the sentence outline, and (4) the paragraph outline. Variations may be worked out for special purposes.

### 1. THE SCRATCH OUTLINE

The scratch outline is a set of notes and jottings which may come in handy either for writing or for understanding and remembering what one has read. It is probably not highly organized. For instance, the writer, in making a preliminary survey of his subject, may simply put down the various topics and ideas that come to him in the order in which they come. As some line of thought begins to emerge he may indicate this, too. But

---

[1] The form of outline called the brief is discussed in the chapter on argument (p. 194).

his primary purpose is not to define the form and order from the beginning. It is to assemble suggestive material. Some of it he may not use because, in the end, it may seem superfluous or irrelevant. The scratch outline embodies the early exploration of a subject, and may be meaningless to everybody except the maker of the outline. When such an outline is made by a reader, there is naturally some indication of the order of topics in the thing read; but even here the outline does not undertake to record the details of relations among the parts. It is merely a jog to the reader's mind, a record of the first acquaintance with the thing read.

## 2. THE TOPIC OUTLINE

The topic outline does indicate the order of treatment of individual topics and does indicate in a systematic fashion, by heads and subheads, the relation among the parts in degree of importance. But as the name indicates, it proceeds, not by sentences, but by listing topics. There is, however, one exception: the outline is to be introduced by a statement of the theme of the composition in the form of a fully rounded sentence. Let us set up a topic outline of the first section of "The Threat of Science," by Christian Gauss (p. 659):

*Statement:* This essay is a discussion of the pretensions and limitations of science as a means to social, moral, esthetic, or religious truth.

  I. Question whether science can make men healthy, wealthy, and wise.
    A. Increase of health and wealth by science.
    B. Wisdom not a matter of mastery over nature but over human nature.
  II. Nature of wisdom.
    A. Academic notion of wisdom.
      1. Understanding of Bohr atom or Einstein theory.
      2. Intelligence, not wisdom.
    B. True wisdom a sane course of action in life.
  III. Science not concerned with general values.
    A. Scientific goodness in a thing the fulfillment of its nature.
      1. TNT good when it explodes.
      2. Lion good when it kills antelope.
    B. Science pure as divorced from any consideration of useful or profitable applications.

  1. Example explosive discovered by pure science but used later
     for destructive purposes.
  2. Beauty, holiness, goodness impurities in science as such.
C. Truth of pure science a mutilated truth.

When you check this outline by the essay, you will see that headings I and II correspond to single paragraphs in the text, but that III corresponds to four paragraphs. That is, the outline is not an outline of paragraphs but by topics. The last four paragraphs of the section are really concerned with one topic, the limitations of science in regard to certain human values—beauty, holiness, goodness. This notion is developed, (A) by reference to what science means by goodness, (B) by what it means by purity, and (C) by a statement of the kind of truth which science can give—a mutilated truth, incomplete in regard to social, moral, and esthetic values. Here even the subheads, A, B, and C, do not correspond to paragraphs in the text. Topic III, A really involves two paragraphs, and topic III, B involves the better part of one paragraph, the last. Topic III, C involves only the last part of the last paragraph. Not infrequently we find that a topic which looms very important in the outline will correspond to only part of a paragraph in the text. The outline indicates the relative importance of a topic and not the amount of space devoted to it. Sometimes, however, after we have finished an outline we may feel that the author has failed to use proper proportion or emphasis. And in this instance we may feel that the author would have been well advised to develop such an important point as III, C in a separate paragraph. But that is his problem, not ours. We have to face such a problem only when we are writing from our own preliminary outline.

### 3. THE SENTENCE OUTLINE

The sentence outline is the most complete and formal type. Here every entry is in the form of a complete sentence. As with the topic outline, the entries in the sentence outline should correspond to the content and the order of arrangement in the text. The sentence outline differs from the topic outline in indicating more fully the content of each item and the relation among the items. To fulfill these requirements, the sentences should be very precise and to the point. Vague statements defeat the very purpose of the sentence outline and make such an outline look like merely an inflated topic outline. For the sentence outline should really take us deeper into the subject, defining the items more closely and indicating the structure more fully. By and large, the topic outline will serve for fairly simple material, the sentence outline for more complicated material.

Here is an example of the sentence outline as applied to the first two paragraphs of Mill's essay, "On Liberty" (p. 697).

*Statement:* This essay is a discussion of the nature of civil liberty, and of the development of effective checks upon the power which the state may exercise over the individual.

I. The nature of the power exerted by society over the individual is and has been a very important question.
  A. This question influences the present age by its *latent* presence.
    1. The question is seldom stated.
    2. It is rarely discussed in general terms.
  B. This question, however, is likely to be regarded as the vital question of the future.
  C. It has in the past divided mankind.
    1. The struggle between liberty and authority is the salient feature in the history of Greece.
    2. The struggle between liberty and authority is the salient feature in the history of Rome.
    3. The struggle between liberty and authority is the salient feature in the history of England.

II. In the past the contest between liberty and authority was a contest between subjects and their rulers.
  A. Rulers were regarded as necessarily antagonistic to the governed.
    1. The rulers did not hold their power at the pleasure of the governed.
    2. Subjects did not venture to contest their supremacy.
  B. The rulers' power was regarded as necessary but also as dangerous.
    1. Their power might be used against external enemies.
    2. Their power, however, might be used against their subjects.

III. It was highly important, therefore, to set limits to the power which the ruler might exercise over the subject.
  A. This limitation of the ruler's power took two forms.
    1. The subjects tried to obtain a recognition of certain immunities, infringement of which justified
      a. specific resistance, or
      b. general rebellion.
    2. The subjects attempted to set up constitutional checks.

B. The first mode of limitation was successfully secured in most European countries.

C. The second mode of limitation has proved much more difficult to secure.

## 4. THE PARAGRAPH OUTLINE

In the paragraph outline each sentence corresponds to a paragraph in the text. In dealing with a very obviously organized piece of writing, the paragraph outline may be practically composed of the topic sentences, or adaptations of the topic sentences, of the paragraphs. (It is possible, of course, to make a paragraph outline of entries which are not complete sentences, but such a paragraph outline would have little utility. It would consist of little more than suggestive notes for paragraphs.) In dealing with other kinds of writing, however, it is necessary to summarize for each paragraph the content and intention. The paragraph outline has a very limited utility. On the one hand, in dealing with work composed by someone else, the paragraph outline often misses the real logical organization; for, as we have seen, paragraphs do not necessarily represent logical stages. On the other hand, in dealing in a preliminary way with material which one himself intends to write about, not only may the outline fail to indicate the logical organization desired, but it may be arbitrary and misleading. It is very hard to predict the paragraph-by-paragraph development of any relatively extensive or complicated piece of work. To try to do so sometimes cramps and confuses the writer in the actual process of composition. The paragraph outline is chiefly valuable as a check on your own writing. Before you attempt to make a paragraph outline of one of your own compositions, you must first decide whether each of your paragraphs has a real center and function.

Here is a sample of a paragraph outline designed to schematize the first three paragraphs of "Should the Scientists Strike?" (p. 200 ff.).

I. Though the scientists have done much to bring plenty to our modern world, some of the scientists themselves must be aghast to realize the tremendous destructive power of the atomic bomb which they have created.

II. Certainly the scientists themselves, as well as laymen, have testified to the destructive power of the atomic bomb.

III. Efforts are being made to curb the use of atomic energy for war.

Each of these three sentences sketches out the matter to be developed in the corresponding paragraph of the essay. These headings might be developed somewhat more elaborately; but for the purpose of laying out the order of the paragraphs and suggesting what is to be covered in each paragraph, they probably are developed as far as is useful.

The student ought to compare this fragment of a paragraph outline with the corresponding part of the brief on page 200 ff. He will notice that the paragraph outline does not correspond with the brief at all points. II, A becomes paragraph one. All the material under subheadings 1 and 2 become the second paragraph; and II, B, with its subheadings 1 and 2, becomes the third paragraph. The paragraph outline, in short, is a way of outlining what sections of the sentence outline (in this case a sentence outline which is also a brief) are to be grouped together in particular paragraphs.

## SUMMARY AND PRÉCIS

A SUMMARY summarizes. It gives in compact form the main points of a longer discourse. If it misses any fundamental points or introduces material not found in the text summarized (no matter how relevant or interesting) or gives a false notion of how the points are related to each other, it fails as a summary.

A summary is a digest or reduction of a longer discourse, but it is a discourse itself. It is composed of complete sentences, and observes the principles of unity, coherence, emphasis, and proportion. This means that the connection among sentences must be obvious in itself or indicated by suitable transitions. If the summary is composed of more than one paragraph the connection between paragraphs must be clear.

Any such reduced and complete statement is a summary. The general organization of a summary is a matter to be decided by reference to the purpose for which it is intended. For instance, a summary may follow the order of the original text and thereby give some notion of the approach used by its author. Or a summary may, on the other hand, be organized by a new method. Suppose, for example, an article agitating for the reform of the public school system in a certain city begins with an illustrative anecdote, then moves forward by analyzing certain particular situations, and ends by an appeal for reorganization. The summary might change this method. It might very well begin with a statement of the appeal for reform, and then proceed to give the analysis of particular situations as reasons for reform. The summary might read as follows:

Summary of "DO WE GIVE OUR CHILDREN A BREAK?"
   by William Becker

The conditions in our public schools are deplorable on several accounts. It is well known that the record in college of graduates of our high schools falls below the average for graduates of schools in cities of comparable size. Local businessmen, industrialists, and editors are not satisfied with the general or vocational training of job-holders from our schools. And the schools are not doing their part in maintaining the moral health of the young, as is witnessed by the alarming and disproportionate increase in juvenile delinquency. It is time to have a general overhauling of our system.

Before we can remedy the situation, however, we must diagnose the causes. First, the school system has become a political football: members of the school board are chiefly concerned with building their political fences, and many appointments to supervisory and teaching positions are not made on merit. Second, parents have been uninterested in the schools, and many with influence have been more concerned to get special favors for their children than to raise the educational level. Third, local salaries are deplorably low, below the national average, and far below those paid in neighboring cities. No one of these causes can be taken in isolation, and any serious attempt to improve our schools must attempt to deal with all of them.

The organization of the original article might have provided more interesting reading and have been better adapted to catch the attention of a general audience, but the method used here is more systematic and states the logic of the case in a clearer form. Organize a summary in the way that will serve your own purpose best. At times you will wish to follow the author's organization; at other times the author's organization will be irrelevant to your purposes and your own organization will be more appropriate.

The question of the scale of a summary, like the question of organization, is to be determined by the purpose the summary is intended to serve. What do you need to have at your disposal in this capsule form? Occasionally a summary of one brief paragraph would give an adequate digest of a whole book. Or, the summary of an essay might require a number of paragraphs. In general, the important thing to remember is that a summary means a very drastic reduction.

The form of summary known as the PRÉCIS (pronounced *pray-see*) is more standardized than the general kind of summary we have been discussing. It undertakes to retain the basic order of the original text, the same proportions of part to part, and the same tone. Like any summary, however, it is committed to presenting the fundamental points of the original and indicating the relation among them. This closer relation to the original text does not mean a dependence on quotation and paraphrase. Material should be restated for economy and emphasis. The scale of the précis, like that of any outline, may vary according to the purpose it is to serve, but since it is committed to maintain the relative proportions of an original, it can never be as drastic in its reduction as a general summary may be.

Here is a précis of the first section of "The Threat of Science," by Christian Gauss, of which we have already given a topic outline.

There is a widespread belief that science may make us healthy, wealthy, and wise. It may make us healthy and wealthy by increasing our mastery over nature, but the question is whether it can make us wise by increasing our mastery over human nature. The academic notion of wisdom is that of understanding things like the Bohr atom, but such an understanding means intelligence, not wisdom, for wisdom implies a sane course of action in life. The scientist's use of words like *good* and *pure* should not trick us into believing that he is dealing with the values we ordinarily indicate by such words. For him the good thing is simply the thing that fulfills its essential nature, as TNT does when it explodes or the lion does when it kills an antelope. And by pure science he means science divorced from any useful or profitable application. The pure scientist may, for instance, discover an explosive later used for the most immoral purposes. Therefore, the truths of science are not necessarily of a higher sort than those arrived at by other means. Considerations of the beautiful, the holy, or the good are impurities for science, that is, are irrelevant to its special business. But they remain considerations for man in his total living, and the truth or science is really truth mutilated.

Here the original passage runs about 1,200 words, and the précis a little over 200. The précis itself might be reduced a little more if that seemed desirable.

# NOTES

Notes may be taken on any subject, from any source, for any purpose, and by many methods.

Some people take casual notes on all sorts of things, experiences and observations, conversations and thoughts, as well as books they have read. The casual note-taker records anything that strikes him as interesting. He is merely providing a jog to his memory and a sort of record for himself. But notes on a wide range of subjects and from a wide range of sources may be drawn by a person who has a special interest. The novelist may keep notes on little turns of phrase he hears, gestures or facial expressions he observes, little episodes he witnesses, his own experiences, or ideas he has. At the moment he takes the note he may see no specific use for it, but he knows that in the future it may, in some form, be usable. The anthropologist living with an Indian tribe will probably keep very careful notes on customs, rituals, language, games, and so forth. At the time he takes the note he may not see the importance of the particular item, but he knows that this is the sort of material which he must analyze and try to fit into a comprehensible pattern.

Either casual note-taking or note-taking in terms of some general interest, like the novelist's or anthropologist's, is a good habit. It sharpens the powers of observation and reflection, and can sometimes give a keener pleasure to experience. But most of your note-taking, as a student, will be of another sort. You will take notes on lectures, on textbooks and other books connected with your courses, notes on special books for book reports, and notes in preparation of research papers or critical studies.

We have said that there are many methods of note-taking, but fundamentally the method is dictated by the purpose for which the notes are taken. The main thing is to have some method, to be systematic, and to keep in mind your purpose. Good lecture notes are difficult to take. For one thing, many lectures are not carefully organized and may be conversational and informal in tone. But as you become acquainted with the general subject of a course you will see the relevance of information or ideas and will have some notion of what is important. A good lecturer will, of course, help you to establish this relevance, but no lecturer will do all of your thinking for you. It is your responsibility to assess the importance of everything said. If you are studying with a professor who organizes his lectures carefully, you may do well to try to follow his line of organization, to set up, as it were, a sort of outline of what he says, indicating degrees of importance. If the lecturer is more casual, you should review your notes while the lecture is still fresh in your mind and try to create some outline and indicate the relation of the content to what you already know. Your own queries, objections, and expansions may well form a part of such notes—a sort of marginal or parenthetic commentary. In any case, your notes should not be random jottings and isolated remarks. They should be systematic enough to carry meaning to you after the particular occasion is dim in your memory.

When you are listening to a lecture, you should try to understand the basic line of the lecturer's thought rather than try to put down everything he says. Good notes may be very brief. Sometimes it may be a good procedure to jot down during the lecture only the main topics or ideas, and afterwards, while the lecturer's development of them is still fresh, to go back and fill in from memory. Experiment to find out what will work best for you with a particular lecturer.

Here is a sample of notes that might be taken on a lecture on "The Differences between British and American Pronunciation."

Many American pronunciations represent earlier forms of British pronunciation.

So-called broad a became standard in late 18th cent. in England. Gives other examples. See G. P. Krapp's English Lang. in America.

Some American pronunciations represent local dialects of Great Britain.

Standard in England not rigidly fixed at time of settlement of America. (Sir Walter Raleigh spoke "broad Devon" to his dying day—Aubrey.)

Southern half of Great Britain prominent in early colonization.

Eastern New England and east Anglican counties.

South Atlantic states and counties of southwestern England—Devon, Dorset, etc.

Examples: from early New England town records "evidence of spelling."

This fragment would represent "fresh notes"—not yet carefully organized. But, even so, the student has been able to suggest an organization by means of underscoring, parentheses, the notation "Examples," and so on.

When you are dealing with textbooks or collateral reading various methods may be useful, the sentence outline, the general summary, or the précis. The whole point is to get the main ideas or pieces of information on record and to establish the relation among them. There are three basic questions to ask:

1. What important information does your author give?
2. What use or interpretation does he make?
3. How does he justify his interpretation?

The outline, summary, or précis will help you to answer these questions. But there are other questions which you must ask yourself:

4. How does this author's information relate to other information on the subject which I already have from other sources?
5. How do his uses or interpretations compare with uses or interpretations of such material by other writers?
6. How do I assess his work? Is he logical? Does he present adequate evidence? Is his organization clear? And so on?

And so with these questions you depart from the outline or summary. You may do so by following the presentation of your author's material by answers to these questions or by marginal or parenthetic commentary, putting in your own queries, comparisons, and judgments at the appropriate points.

When you take notes for a book report or a research or critical paper, you are working for a special purpose, and the nature of the purpose determines the kind of notes you will take. So we shall discuss note-taking for these in the course of discussing their purposes and forms.


## THE RESEARCH PAPER

The research paper draws its material from many sources. Its aim is to assemble facts and ideas and by studying them to draw new conclusions as to fact or interpretation, or to present the material in the light of a new interest. For instance, a military historian who wanted to understand why General Lee lost the Battle of Gettysburg would study the written records of orders and events, the correspondence and memoirs of witnesses, the actual terrain, and the interpretations of other historians. In the light of that evidence, he would try to frame an explanation. Or a literary critic who wanted to understand why a certain novelist often used certain themes would study the facts of the novelist's life as found in whatever sources (letters, memoirs, public records, biographies), the kind of education he received, the kind of ideas current in his particular place and time, and so forth. Such material would be his evidence. The researcher might discover new facts, and new facts can easily upset old theories. But he might have to depend on facts which were already available but available in scattered sources. Then his task would be to collect those facts into a new pattern of interpretation.

The difference between the book written by the professional historian or literary critic and the term paper written by a student may appear so great that they seem to have no relation. But the basic method should be the same: to collect the facts and interpret them. The term paper can be intelligent, well informed, interesting, and original in its conclusions, and the student should try to make it so. But first of all he should try to make his work systematic. If it is not systematic it will probably not have the other qualities.

The first step toward making his paper systematic is to learn how to investigate his subject. The historian going to the order book of a general, the documents of a politician, the terrain of a battlefield; the anthropologist observing the Indian tribe; or the literary scholar studying the manuscripts or letters of an author is using what are called primary sources. He goes to original source of information for his facts. But the college student must usually use secondary sources. He reads the report of the anthropologist or he studies an edition of a poet prepared by a scholar. But even here there are degrees. He should try to use material which is as close as possible to the original source of information. He should not depend on digests or commentaries of the anthropologist's report, but should go to the report itself. He should not merely read what has been said about a novelist, but should read the novelist's actual work. He should not rely on interpretations of the Declaration of Independence, but should study the actual text. Get as close to the facts as possible. No matter how good your reasoning is, it is useless if the facts on which it works are not dependable.

The research paper, we have said, draws its material from many sources. It is not a digest of one book or article. But how do you get at the useful sources?

Special reference books give a good starting point, standard encyclopedias and dictionaries, and such compilations as the *American Yearbook*, the *Statesman's Yearbook*, and the *World Almanac*. In addition to such general reference works, there are those devoted to special fields, for example, the *Dictionary of National Biography* (limited to the British), the *Dictionary of American Biography, Living Authors, Who's Who* (British), *Who's Who in America*, the *Encyclopedia of the Social Sciences*, the *Catholic Encyclopedia*, the *Cambridge History of English Literature*, the *Cambridge History of American Literature*, the *Oxford Companion to English Literature*, the *Oxford Companion to American Literature*, Bartlett's *Familiar Quotations*, and the *Reader's Guide to Periodical Literature*. Reference books are so numerous and sometimes so specialized that it is often helpful to consult the *Guide to Reference Books*, by I. G. Mudge, to know where to go in the first place.

The reference book will give an introduction to a subject and certain basic facts. Best of all for the student, it will usually offer a list of other works, books or articles less limited in scope than the treatment in the reference book itself. With this as a starting point the student can make up his own *working bibliography* for his subject. As he reads into his subject he will encounter references to other works, and can gradually extend the range of his working bibliography. The subject catalogue of the library will also provide new items.

The working bibliography should be kept on convenient cards of uniform size, with only one entry to a card. This allows the student to arrange them in alphabetical, or other order (by topics, for example), according to his need. The entry on the card should contain all the basic information about a book or article; the author's name with the last name first, the title of the work, the volume number if any, the place of publication, the publisher, the date of publication. If the work appears in a periodical or collection, that fact should be indicated with volume number, the date, and the pages occupied by the work.

This form is to be retained in making up the final bibliography to be attached to your finished paper. There the order will be alphabetical by authors. Your final bibliography may be shorter than your working bibliography, for the final bibliography should contain no entry from which you have not taken material for the actual paper, whereas certain items in your working bibliography will be dropped as more valuable items come to light.

```
Strachey, Lytton, Elizabeth and Essex, London,
    Chatto and Windus, 1928.
```

*Entry for a book*

```
Barrington, Margaret, "The Censorship in Eire,"
    Commonweal, XLVI, August 15, 1947, 429-432.
```

*Entry for an article*

The professional scholar may want to work through all the material on his subject, but the student preparing a term paper scarcely has the time for such a program. And many items in the bibliographies he encounters are antiquated or trivial. So to save his time and energy, he should try to select the items which will best repay his attention. There is no rule for this. Selected bibliographies sometimes appear in textbooks and other works. Sometimes an author will refer with special respect to another work on his subject. But the student can always take his working bibliography to an instructor and ask for comment.

Unless you take notes on your reading you will probably not be able to remember much of the relevant material and will certainly not be able to organize it well when you come to write your paper.

If you have taken your notes carefully, you will be able to lay out before you the whole subject and put it in order. The paper will almost write itself. But if the notes are to give you the most help, they must have a convenient mechanical form.

Notes can be put on note cards (usually 3″ by 5″), on small or half sheets, or on full sheets. What you use does not much matter, so long as the size is manageable and uniform. As already mentioned, not more than one note, however brief, should be on a single card or sheet. This rule should be strictly adhered to, even when the notes are on the same topic; for when you take the notes, you cannot be sure in what order you will eventually use them. Only if each note is independent can you arrange them in the order desired when you come to write your paper. Each note should carry at the top, at left or toward the center, some indication of the precise content, not the general subject of your investigation, but some subtopic. And at the top right, or at the bottom, the note should carry an adequate reference to the source from which it is drawn. Presumably the full bibliographical information about that source is already in your working bibliography, and so some skeleton notation will be adequate here. (When you are taking notes not related to a working bibliography, say when you are doing general reading, you should record full bibliographical information with the note.) Below is a specimen card or sheet:

American success worship    Chesterton, What I Saw
                                    in America, pp. 107-10.

American worship of success not materialistic.  Fact
of worship means a mystic rather than a materialist.
Frenchman who saves money to retire and enjoy his
omelet more of a materialist.  American does not work
for the enjoyment of things, but for some ideal vision
of success.  He does not want the dollar for what it
will buy but as a symbol.  Phrase "making good" illustrates the fact; carries a moral connotation by
a "sort of ethical echo in the word" good (p. 108).
Not necessarily an admirable morality, but a morality
implied, and idealism of a kind.

When we look at the actual note on the card we see that several other phrases might have been used to indicate the topic discussed. For instance, "American business mysticism," or "American materialism." All that is needed is a word or phrase which will remind the note-taker of the content. We notice, too, that after the direct quotation there is a parenthesis with the page number. The note-taker apparently feels that this is a telling phrase worth remembering and perhaps using. If he quotes it, he will want the exact page reference.

As for the bibliographical indication at the upper right, he might have reduced it simply to "Chesterton" if there was no Chesterton other than G. K. Chesterton on his bibliography and no other book by that author. This, like the topic indication, is for his own convenience and need tell no more than he himself has to know to identify the source.

So much for the mechanics of note-taking. As for the process, you should make your notes relevant, accurate, and clear. To make them relevant you must keep constantly in mind the main purpose of your investigation. You are studying a particular subject with particular limits. You are not concerned with anything only casually associated with the subject. If, for instance, when your subject is the economic backgrounds of the American Revolution, you are reading a general history of the period, you should not be distracted by military strategy of the French and Indian Wars or an analysis of Puritan theology. Your job is to follow your main purpose through a body of various materials, and often what is major for you will be minor in the work you are investigating.

It is possible to take notes prematurely. Therefore, it is always best to become acquainted with a work before you take notes from it. In your first reading you may indicate material for possible notes, and pass on. When you have finished the work, or those parts relevant to your interest, you can then better assess the material for possible notes. In this way you will get from any particular work only the most pertinent notes, and you will avoid duplication.

The note itself may be direct quotation or summary. If direct quotation is used, it is sometimes valuable to record the context of the quotation. What leads the author to make his statement? What point does he try to establish by it? You do not want to misinterpret your author by implication. For instance, suppose a critic should write:

Although Herman Melville has created in Captain Ahab of *Moby Dick* a character of intense interest and monumental proportions, he has in general little sense of the shadings of personality and motive. Most of his creations are schematic, mere outlines without flesh. He lacks that basic gift of the novelist, a sense of character.

If you, assembling material for a paper on Melville as a novelist, should merely quote, "Herman Melville has created in Captain Ahab of *Moby Dick* a character of intense interest and monumental proportions," you would have a misleading note. An accurate note would run something like this:

Even though William —— believes that Melville in general lacks a sense of character, he admits that Captain Ahab is a "character of intense interest and monumental proportions."

But this principle of context holds good for the note by summary as well as the note by quotation.

When you are taking notes by summary, the kind of summary to be used depends on the special case. In one case, the author's method of reasoning may be very important, and then the summary should be of a form to indicate the logical structure of the original text. In another case, where mere facts or scattered opinions are involved, the summary need record merely these facts and opinions. As for the scale of the summary, there is no guiding principle except the note-taker's need. Try to forecast what you will need when you actually come to write your paper, not merely what you will want to incorporate in the paper but what you will need to understand your subject fully.

Once your notes are taken, how do you use them? This again depends on the kind of subject you are dealing with. Some subjects suggest a chronological order, others a logical order. For instance, if you are doing a paper on Keats's development as a poet you might first arrange your notes chronologically—notes on early poems, notes on middle poems, notes on late poems. But if your subject is an analysis of the themes of Keats's poems, you might try to arrange your notes by themes, running various classifications until you had one that seemed to make sense. Or you might find, sometimes, that two levels of organization were necessary. For instance, certain themes of Keats's poems might be characteristic of certain periods. Then having established one type of classification (by theme) you might run another type (by chronology). Notes are flexible. You can use them as a device to help your thinking, or to help you organize your material.

Notes record questions and issues. The different authors you have consulted have had individual approaches to the general subject, different interests, different conclusions. As you work over your cards you can locate these differences and try to see what they mean to you in your special project. Ask yourself if there is any pattern of disagreement among the authors you have consulted. List the disagreements. Are they disagreements of fact or of interpretation? Compare the evidence and reasoning offered by the authors who are in disagreement. Can you think of any new evidence or new line of reasoning on disputed points? Can you think of any significant points not discussed by your authors? What bearing would such points have on their conclusions? Again, use your notes as a device to help your thinking.

By working over your notes and thinking about ideas suggested in them you will probably strike on some vague general plan for your paper. But do not commit yourself to the first plan that comes into your head. Consider various possibilities. Then when you have struck on the most promising, try to work up an outline on that basis. You will undoubtedly start with a sort of rough suggestive outline, the barest shadow of the paper you want to write. By checking back on your material you can begin to fill in the outline and determine the relation among the facts and ideas you wish to present. So you will arrive at a more fully organized outline. Perhaps a topic outline will serve your purpose, but at some stage a sentence outline will probably be helpful, for to make it you will have to state clearly exactly what you mean.

Once you have an outline prepared you can begin the actual composition. Use your outline as a guide, but do not consider yourself bound by it. As you write, new ideas will probably come to you, and if they are good ideas you should revise your outline to accommodate them. The outline is not sacred. Like your notes, it is simply a device to help you think. And remember that your paper should be a fully rounded composition, unified and coherent, emphasizing matters according to the scale of their importance. The outline is only a start toward creating a balanced, fluent, well-proportioned discussion.

Your paper should be more than a tissue of facts and quotations from your notes. It should represent your handling of a subject and not a mere report on what other writers have said. Naturally, a large part of your material will be derived from other writers, but you should always ask yourself just what a fact or idea means in terms of your own purpose. It should find a place in your pattern, and if there is no proper place for it, it should be excluded. In the end, you will always find that some of your notes are not usable. A writer who has studied his subject always has more material than he can well use.

Full credit should be given for the source of every fact or idea derived from another writer. In your own text you will want to acknowledge any important item as a matter of help to your reader. It is easy to introduce a statement or a quotation by a clear explanatory phrase or sentence. We are all accustomed to such introductory remarks as these:

> Charles A. Beard has proved that . . .
> James Truslow Adams maintains that . . .
> An excellent statement of this view is given by James Truslow Adams in his *Epic of America:* . . .
> As Sinclair Lewis shows in *Main Street,* the culture of the American town is . . .
> On the other hand, such a liberal as Henry A. Wallace holds that . . .
> As Thomas Wolfe observed . . .

Some facts or ideas can simply be stated in your text if the fact or idea is not specially to be associated with the particular writer from whom you derived it. But in all cases, authority should be given in a footnote.

Exactly what demands a footnote? First, every direct quotation is identified in a footnote. Second, every statement of fact is referred to its source in a footnote. Third, every opinion or interpretation drawn from another writer should be referred to its source in a footnote, *even if the opinion or interpretation is one which you have independently come upon in your own thinking.* In cases where a group of facts or opinions treated together in one paragraph are drawn from the same source, one note at the end of the paragraph will serve for all the material. In cases where more than one source is involved for a single item in the text, one note will serve to acknowledge the several sources.

Variation in certain details is permissible in the form of foot-notes—*e.g.*, note the forms used in Worcester's paper (pp. 877-88)—*but not* in the same paper. Learn one of the standard forms and use it consistently in all your work. Here are a few general principles:

1. The author's name appears in direct form, not with the last name first, as in the bibliography.

2. The title of a book or periodical is underlined in typescript or writing. This corresponds to italics in print. Even a relatively short piece of writing which has independent publication is considered a book. Sometimes a piece of writing, a poem for instance, first appears independently as a little book and is later included in a collection of the author's work. Practice varies in treating such items, but it is permissible to treat it as a book. Thus, we would underscore the title of T. S. Eliot's Four Quartets, but we might quote "Burnt Norton" (which is one of the four poems included) or we might underscore it, thus: Burnt Norton.

3. The title of an item in a periodical appears in quotation marks.

4. When an item is first mentioned in a footnote full bibliographical information is given. Later references use a brief identifying form, to be described later.

Here are examples of various types of footnotes. Observe carefully the form of punctuation, the nature of the material included, and the order of the items presented.

FOOTNOTES FOR BOOKS:

*One author:*

(1)  ¹ Gerald G. Walsh, *Dante Alighieri: Citizen of Christendom,* Milwaukee, Bruce Publishing Company, 1946, p. 17.
     [But the punctuation might be handled in this fashion: Gerald G. Walsh, *Dante Alighieri: Citizen of Christendom* (Milwaukee: Bruce Publishing Company, 1946), p. 17.]

*More than one author:*

(2)  ¹ William Buell Meldrum and Frank Thomson Gucker, Jr., *Introduction to Theoretical Chemistry,* New York, American Book Company, 1936, p. 133.

*Translation:*

(3)  ¹ Anton Chekhov, *The Party and Other Stories,* tr. Constance Garnett, London, Chatto and Windus, 1919.

FOOTNOTES FOR ITEMS FROM COLLECTIONS:

(4) [1] Wendell L. Willkie, "Freedom and the Liberal Arts," in *The Humanities after the War,* Norman Foerster, ed., Princeton, Princeton University Press, 1944, p. 5.

[Here the abbreviation *ed.* is for editor: Norman Foerster is the editor of the collection.]

FOOTNOTES FOR ITEMS FROM PERIODICALS:

(5) [1] Henry Albert Phillips, "The Pith of Peru," *National Geographic,* LXXXII, August 1942,[2] 169.

[Here the Roman numerals give the volume number of the periodical. The last number, 169, is the page reference. Notice that the abbreviation *p.* is omitted for periodicals after the volume number.]

(6) [1] Arthur Mizener, "The Desires of the Mind," *Sewanee Review,* LX, Summer 1947, 462.

[For a quarterly magazine, as in this case, the season instead of the month is given, if that is the practice of the magazine itself.]

(7) [1] Peter F. Drucker, "The Industrial Revolution Hits the Farmer," *Harper's,* No. 1074, November 1939, 593.

[When, as here, the magazine carries an issue number and not a volume number, the issue number appears: "No. 1074."]

FOOTNOTES FOR ITEMS FROM THE BIBLE:

(8) [1] Psalms 23:6-8.
[Here the first number is for chapter, the others for verses, inclusive.]
(9) [1] II Cor. 6:9.
[Here the abbreviation *Cor.* is for Corinthians. Certain books of the Bible have such standard abbreviations. The Roman numeral indicates Second Corinthians.]

All the forms given above indicate the first reference to a work. For subsequent references, three forms may be used. When the source in a footnote is the same as that indicated in the footnote immediately preceding, the abbreviation *ibid.* (for *ibidem:* in the same place) is used, with a new page reference, if that is needed. For example:

(10) [1] Arthur Mizener, "The Desires of the Mind," *Sewanee Review,* LX, Summer 1947, 462.
[2] *Ibid.* 464.

When the reference repeated does not immediately precede, either of two basic forms may be used. If the author has only one

[2] Although some authorities still prefer a comma between month and year, the trend in current usage is toward omission of the comma.

work referred to in the footnotes, his last name may be used, followed by the page reference, or his last name with the abbreviation *op. cit.* (for *opere citato:* in the work cited), with the page reference. The first practice is simpler, and is becoming more common than the other. For example:

(11)  ¹ Arthur Mizener, "The Desires of the Mind," *Sewanee Review,* LX, Summer 1947, 462.
² Wendell L. Willkie, "Freedom and the Liberal Arts," in *The Humanities after the War,* Norman Foerster, ed., Princeton, Princeton University Press, 1944, p. 5.
³ Mizener, 464.

If the author has more than one work referred to in the footnotes, then his last name will not be enough, and an abbreviated title will be necessary.

(12)  ¹ Mizener, "Desires," 464.    *Or:*    ¹ Walsh, *Dante,* p. 19.
[Notice that the abbreviation *p.* is omitted in the Mizener reference, for the reference is to a periodical, while it is used in the Walsh reference, which is to a book. In other words, the short form follows the practice of the long form in this respect.]

When material is not drawn directly from its original source but from some intermediary source, acknowledgment should be made to both sources. For instance, the following note indicates that the writer has used a quotation from Stephen Spender which appeared in a book by Moody E. Prior:

(13)  ¹ Stephen Spender, *The Destructive Element,* Boston, Houghton Mifflin Company, p. 11, quoted Moody E. Prior, *The Language of Tragedy,* New York, Columbia University Press, 1947, p. 343.

We have already referred to the abbreviations *ibid.* and *op. cit.* But there are a number of other abbreviations found in notes and bibliographical forms. You will not find a use for all of them in your own writing, but you will sooner or later encounter them in works which you read. Some of the Latin abbreviations are now commonly replaced by English forms or may be omitted altogether (as with *op. cit.*). In using such abbreviations, the main thing is to be consistent. For instance, do not use *vide* (for *see*) in one place and *ff.* (for *seq.*) in another.

*c. (circa)*  About a certain date (to be used to indicate an approximate date, when the real date cannot be determined).

*cf. (confer)*   Compare (English form: see).

ch. or chaps.   Chapter(s).

col. or cols.   Column(s).

ed.   Edited by, or edition.

*et al. (et alii)*   And others (when a book has several authors, the first, with *et al.*, may replace the full list).

f. or ff.   One or more pages following the page indicated.

*ibid. (ibidem)*   In the same work (referring to a work cited in a note immediately preceding).

*infra*   Below (indicating a later discussion).

l. or ll.   Line(s).

*loc. cit. (loco citato)*   In the place cited (when there is an earlier reference to the source).

MS.   Manuscript.

n.d.   No date (when publication date cannot be determined).

no.   Number (as when listing the number of the issue of a periodical or series).

n.p.   No place (when place of publication cannot be determined).

*op. cit. (opere citato)*   In the work cited (used with author's name to indicate source already referred to).

p. or pp.   Page(s).

*passim*   In various places (when the topic referred to appears at more than one place in a work cited).

*q.v. (quod vide)*   Which see (English form: see).

see   Used to suggest that the reader consult a certain work referred to.

*seq. (sequentes)*   Following (English form: F. or ff.).

*supra*   Above (when the topic referred to has already been discussed).

tr.   Translated by.

*vide*   See (English form: see).

vol. or vols.   Volume(s) (but vol. and p. are not used if figures for both are given, as in listing a periodical reference; in such cases, use Roman numerals for volume and Arabic for page: II, 391).

After you have prepared a draft of your paper and established all your footnotes, you are ready to set up your final bibliography. This may differ from your working bibliography, in that it contains only items which are actually referred to in your paper, not items which have been consulted but not used.

The form for such a bibliography permits certain minor variations. For instance, the place without the publisher is sometimes given; and there may be differences in punctuation. For example, the following entry can be punctuated in two ways:

Barnes, Harry Elmer, *The Genesis of the World War,* New York, Alfred A. Knopf, 1926.

*Or:*

Barnes, Harry Elmer. *The Genesis of the World War.* New York: Alfred A. Knopf, 1926.

But in all forms the author's name comes first, with the last name first, followed by the full title of the work, the periodical or series if any, the place of publication, the publisher (if this form is used), and the date of publication. The items may be arranged in either of two ways. First, in a straight alphabetical order, according to the last name of the author or, if there is no author, by the main word of the title. Second, alphabetically within certain groups determined by the material dealt with: "Books," "Periodicals," "Documents," and so forth. Here are some examples of entries as they might appear in the bibliography of a paper on Woodrow Wilson:

(Periodical)    Baker, Ray Stannard, "Our Next President and Some Others," *American Magazine,* LXXIV, June 1912, 131-143.

(Book)    Barnes, Harry Elmer, *The Genesis of the World War,* New York, Alfred A. Knopf, 1926.

(Document)    *Congressional Record,* XLIX-LI, Washington, 1913-1914.

(Document)    *Legislative Manual, State of New Jersey,* 1912, Trenton, 1912.

(Book)    McAdoo, Eleanor R. W., *The Woodrow Wilsons,* New York, Macmillan Company, 1937.

(Book)    Wilson, Woodrow, *The Public Papers of Woodrow Wilson,* Baker, Ray Stannard, and Dodd, William Edward, eds., New York, Harper and Bros., 1925-1927.

(Periodical)    Wilson, Woodrow, "Democracy and Efficiency," *Atlantic Monthly,* LXXXVII, March 1901, 289-299.

(Collection)    Wilson, Woodrow, "Leaderless Government," in *Report of the Ninth Annual Meeting of the Virginia State Bar Association,* Richmond, 1897.

Notice that an over-all alphabetical order is given, by author when an author is specified, and by leading word when there is no author ("Congressional" and "Legislative"). In this short bibliography all types of sources are grouped together—books, collections, periodicals, and documents. In a long bibliography such types might be set up as separate, each group in alphabetical order.

At this stage you should have an outline and a draft of your paper, with all quotations properly inserted, all acknowledgments for facts and opinions (either quoted or summarized) indicated in footnotes, and a final bibliography attached for all works actually referred to in your footnotes. Now is the time to check carefully to see if there is any need for revision. Try to answer the following questions to see if all is in order.

1. Does my paper have a guiding purpose? That is, is there a subject properly fixed and limited? Have I stated it clearly?

2. Is my paper really a discussion of the subject and not a mere tissue of quotations and summaries? Does it really go somewhere? What is my own contribution to the discussion of the subject? Have I offered evidence and arguments for my point of view? Have I indicated how my point of view differs from the points of view held by other writers? If my paper is primarily exposition and not argument, have I added new facts to the discussion, or have I made the pattern of facts clearer than before?

3. Is my paper well organized and proportioned? Is there a clear introduction? Does the discussion really constitute the main body of the paper? Is my conclusion an accurate statement of what I have accomplished? Is it brief and pointed? Are my transitions clear? Have I introduced irrelevant material?

4. Is my style clear and grammatical? Are my paragraphs well organized? Is my punctuation correct?

5. Is my outline a satisfactory one for my paper as it now stands?

6. Am I sure that all my quotations and summaries are accurate?

7. Am I sure that my footnote references are accurate?

8. Is my final bibliography accurate?

9. Are my footnotes and bibliography in the proper form? Is the form I have used consistent?

If your paper is deficient on any of these counts, revise it. In checking on the paper or in making revisions, it is wise not to try to do everything at once. Take one question and follow it through the whole paper, say the matter of organization, or the matter of punctuation. You cannot do everything at once, and you will get your best results by concentrating on one consideration at a time.

# THE BOOK REPORT

The book report is to be sharply distinguished on one hand from the research paper and on the other hand from the book review or the critical essay. It is to be distinguished from the research paper primarily because it deals with one book in its entirety, and from the review or critical essay because it merely reports on a book, presents that book, and does not compare it with other books or attempt to make judgments as to its value. But the book report may include a certain amount of background material about the author himself, his other work and his reputation, or the circumstances of the composition of the book being reported on. Such material is to be used as a means of presenting the book in question. It is not to become an end in itself, and in proportion it should be subordinated to the actual presentation of the book. Some book reports do not require this background material at all. The nature of the assignment determines its inclusion.

To write a good book report you need to answer the following questions:

1. Who is the author? (What is his nationality and origins? What is his period?)
2. What other work has he done?
3. What is his reputation?
4. Are there any important or enlightening circumstances connected with the composition of this book?
5. What kind of book is this? (Is it fiction, history, literary criticism, biography, poetry, drama, or what?)
6. What is the subject of this book?
7. What material does it treat?
8. What is the theme of the book—the author's basic interpretation of the material?
9. What method of organization does he employ?
10. What is the tone and style of the book?

You will notice that the first four questions involve background information. If your report is to present such information, you do not need to make a full-dress research paper on that part of the assignment. You can merely consult a few standard reference works to get the basic facts, or look into one or two good biographies or historical or critical works. In doing this, however, it is wise to take your notes as if for a research paper so that your material will be conveniently available and can be put into order.

The kind of book you are dealing with determines to a considerable extent the kind of treatment you can appropriately give it. For instance, if you are dealing with a biography, you should identify the character who is the subject of the work, summarize his career as given by the author (including the basic pieces of evidence which he employs to support his interpretation of the character), give some idea of his method of organization, and comment on his tone and style. This last consideration may involve such questions as these: Is he writing a scholarly treatise or a popular biography? Is his work adapted to the audience he has in mind? Does he give interesting anecdotes and colorful personal touches, or does he devote himself to facts and historical or psychological analysis? If you are dealing with a book on public policy—say on the reconstruction of Germany or international relations—the important considerations would be somewhat different. You would primarily be concerned to present the author's picture of the situation provoking the discussion, state the policy which he recommends, and offer the arguments for that policy. You might even be led to present the philosophical or political assumptions on which he bases his policy. The kind of audience he has in mind would still be important, and you should define it; but in general in this type of book, questions of tone and style, except in so far as mere clarity is concerned, would not be important. Or if you are dealing with a novel, the emphasis in your report would again be different. It would now be important to define the kind of world your author is interested in. Does he write of drawing rooms or village parlors, or farms or battlefields? What kind of characters and issues interest him? What is the outline of his plot? How do the motivations of his characters fit the plot? What is the theme of his book? And here questions of tone and style might become very important. But in all cases, remember that the book report *presents* a book, primarily in its own terms. It does not compare, criticize, or evaluate.

# AUTHOR-TITLE INDEX

# SUBJECT INDEX